1990 Supplement for
Pacific Crest Trail, Volume 1: California
appears on the last two pages
of this edition

Dedicated to James Charles Jenkins

1952–1979

Coauthor of the first three editions of this book

THE
PACIFIC CREST

Volume 1: California

TRAIL

Jeffrey P. Schaffer
Ben Schifrin
Thomas Winnett
Ruby Jenkins

Acknowledgments

Each author was responsible for a particular length of trail, and hence each wishes to acknowledge different people.

Schifrin (Sections A–E): Various help, including continued updates on trail construction, plans and priorities, from Phil Horning and John "Skip" Noble of Cleveland National Forest; Bob Snyder, Pam Elliott, Don Banks and Steven Nelson of the Bureau of Land Management; Karen Fortus, Karen Snigowski, Kim Vandehar and Ed Medina of Angeles National Forest; and Thomas Horner, Joe Astleford and Bob Ota of San Bernardino National Forest.

Jenkins (Sections F and G): A man in failing health due to his age was responsible for a freeway accident that took the life of J. C. Jenkins, the former author of these sections. Jenkins' mother, Ruby, assisted by his father, Bill, assumed the field work and update of his work to honor his memory.

Winnett (Section H, Mt. Whitney to Devils Postpile): Jason Winnett rehiked parts of the John Muir Trail section of the Pacific Crest Trail. Kathy Morey did the same.

Schaffer (from Devils Postpile, in Section H, through Section R): In addition to the people I've acknowledged in previous editions, I would like to mention those who have written us with comments since the last edition. Foremost, Thomas Zurr offered dozens of suggestions or corrections for the California PCT, particularly for my long stretch. I've rechecked most of the points Zurr raised, and found his information very accurate. Jeff Stone, Bob Ellinwood, John Olley, Scott Anderson, Steve Queen, and Bruce and Sharon Gilbert also offered useful information, which I've tried as much as possible to double check.

Photo credits

Bureau of Land Management   191
Haber, Lyn   177, 205
Jenkins, J.C.   196, 209
Jenkins, Ruby Johnson   181, 190, 200, 201, 211
Robinson, John W.   176
Schaffer, Jeffrey P.   title page, 23 left & right, 41, 216, 242, 245 bottom through 469
Schifrin, Ben   23 center, 42 through 162
Winnett, Thomas   220, 225, 231, 233, 237, 240, 241, 243, 245 top

Title page: Backpackers on the PCT just north of Mt. Etna

First edition June 1973
Revised second printing August 1975
Second edition September 1977
Second printing July 1979
Third edition June 1982
Second printing April 1985
FOURTH EDITION January 1989
Second printing April 1990

Copyright © 1973, 1977, 1982, 1989 by Wilderness Press
Cover photo: Mt. Ritter and Banner Peak above Ediza Lake © 1989 by Ed Cooper
Cover design by Larry Van Dyke
Maps revised by Jeffrey P. Schaffer, Noëlle Liebrenz and Hugh Dodd
Design by Thomas Winnett
Library of Congress Card Catalog Number 85-041030
International Standard Book Number 0-89997-089-3
Manufactured in the United States of America
Published by Wilderness Press

2440 Bancroft Way   Write for free catalog
Berkeley, CA 94704   or phone (415) 843-8080

Library of Congress Cataloging-in-Publication Data

Pacific Crest Trail.

    Bibliography: p.
    Includes index.
    Contents: v. 1. California. - v. 2. Oregon & Washington.
    1. Hiking--Pacific Crest Trail--Guide-books.
2. Pacific Crest Trail--Description and travel--Guide-
books. 3. Hiking--California--Guide-books. 4. California
--Description and travel--1981-   --Guide-books.
I. Schaffer, Jeffrey P.
GV199.42.P3P3 1986   917.9'043   85-41030
ISBN 0-89997-089-3 (v.1)
ISBN 0-89997-060-5 (v.2)

Contents

Introductory Chapters

Trail Chapters

The
PACIFIC CREST TRAIL
in
CALIFORNIA

0   50   100 miles

Letters A–R on this map refer to
trail chapters A–R

Chapter 1: History of the PCT

The first proposal for the creation of a Pacific Crest Trail that we have been able to discover is contained in the book *Pacific Crest Trails,* by Joseph T. Hazard (Superior Publishing Co.). He says that in 1926 he was just ending a business interview with a Miss Catherine Montgomery at the Western Washington College of Education in Bellingham when she said,

"Do you know what I've been thinking about, Mr. Hazard, for the last twenty minutes?

"Just what have you in mind, Miss Montgomery?

"A high trail winding down the heights of our western mountains with mile markers and shelter huts–like those pictures I'll show you of the 'Long Trail of the Appalachians'–from the Canadian Border to the Mexican Boundary Line!"

To go back six years in time, the Forest Service had by 1920 routed and posted a trail from Mt. Hood to Crater Lake in Oregon, named the Oregon Skyline Trail, and with hindsight we can say that it was the first link in the PCT.

Hazard says that on that very night, he conveyed Miss Montgomery's suggestion to the Mt. Baker Club of Bellingham, which was enthusiastic about it. He says that soon a number of other mountain clubs and outdoor organizations in the Pacific Northwest adopted the idea and set about promoting it. Then, in 1928, Fred W. Cleator became Supervisor of Recreation for Region 6 (Oregon and Washington) of the U.S. Forest Service. Cleator proclaimed and began to develop the Cascade Crest Trail, a route down the spine of Washington from Canada to the Columbia River. Later he extended the Oregon Skyline Trail at both ends so that it too traversed a whole state. In 1937 Region 6 of the Forest Service developed a design for PCT trail markers and posted them from the Canadian border to the California border.

But the Forest Service's Region 5 (California) did not follow this lead, and it remained for a private person to provide the real spark not only for a California segment of the PCT but indeed for the PCT itself. In the early Thirties the idea of a Pacific Crest Trail entered the mind of Clinton C. Clarke of Pasadena, California, who was then chairman of the Executive Committee of the Mountain League of Los

1

Angeles County. "In March 1932," wrote Clarke in *The Pacific Crest Trailway,* he "proposed to the United States Forest and National Park Services the project of a continuous wilderness trail across the United States from Canada to Mexico. . . . The plan was to build a trail along the summit divides of the mountain ranges of these states, traversing the best scenic areas and maintaining an absolute wilderness character."

The proposal included formation of additional Mountain Leagues in Seattle, Portland and San Francisco by representatives of youth organizations and hiking and mountaineering clubs similar to the one in Los Angeles. These Mountain Leagues would then take the lead in promoting the extension of the John Muir Trail northward and southward to complete a pathway from border to border. When it became evident that more than Mountain Leagues were needed for such a major undertaking, Clarke took the lead in forming the Pacific Crest Trail System Conference, with representatives from the three Pacific Coast states. He served as its President for 25 years.

As early as January 1935 Clarke published a handbook-guide to the PCT giving the route in rather sketchy terms ("the Trail goes east of Heart Lake, then south across granite fields to the junction of Piute and Evolution Creeks"–this covers about 9 miles).

In the summer of 1935–and again the next 3 summers–groups of boys under the sponsorship of the YMCA explored the PCT route in relays, proceeding from Mexico on June 15, 1935, to Canada on August 12, 1938. This exploration was under the guidance of a YMCA secretary, Warren L. Rogers, who served as Executive Secretary of the Pacific Crest Trail System Conference (1932-1957) and who continues his interest in the PCT by currently serving on the Advisory Committee appointed by the Secretary of Agriculture.

Nevertheless, for California, nothing beyond Clarke's rough description and generalized maps, published in hardback in 1945, appeared until the late 1960s. Anyone who wanted to walk or ride the PCT from Mexico to Oregon–or vice versa–was pretty much on his own for large portions of the existing 1600-mile distance. Clarke died in 1957, at age 84, confident that his dream would one day be fulfilled.

In 1965 the Bureau of Outdoor Recreation, a Federal agency, appointed a commission to make a nationwide trails study. The commission, noting that walking for pleasure was second only to driving for pleasure as the most popular recreation in America, recommended establishing a national system of trails, of 2 kinds–long National Scenic Trails in the hinterlands and shorter National Recreation Trails in and near metropolitan areas. The commission recommended that Congress establish 4 Scenic Trails–the already existing Appalachian Trail, the partly existing Pacific Crest Trail, a Potomac Heritage Trail and a Continental Divide Trail. Congress responded by passing, in 1968, the National Trails System Act, which set the framework for a system of trails and specifically made the Appalachian and the Pacific Crest trails the first 2 National Scenic Trails.

Meanwhile, in California, the Forest Service in 1965 had held a series of meetings about a route for the PCT in the state. These meetings involved people from the Forest Service, the Park Service, the State Division of Parks and Beaches, and other government bodies charged with responsibility over areas where the trail might go. These people decided that so much time had elapsed since Clarke had drawn his route that they should essentially start all over. Of course, it was pretty obvious that segments like the John Muir Trail would not be overlooked in choosing a new route through California. By the end of 1965 a proposed route had been drawn onto maps. (We don't say "mapped," for that would imply that someone actually had covered the route in the field.)

When Congress, in the 1968 law, created a citizens Advisory Council for the PCT, it was the route devised in 1965 which the Forest Service presented to the council as a "first draft" of a final PCT route. This body of citizens was to decide all the details of the final route; the Forest Service said it would adopt whatever the citizens wanted. The Advisory Council was also to concern itself with standards for the physical nature of the trail, markers to be erected along the trail, and the administration of the trail and its use.

In 1972 the Advisory Council agreed upon a route, and the Forest Service put it onto maps for internal use. Since much of the agreed-upon route was cross-country, these maps were sent to the various national forests along the route, for them to mark a temporary route in the places where no trail existed along the final PCT route. This they did—but not always after field work. The result was that the maps made available to the public in June 1972 showing the final proposed route and the temporary detours did not correspond to what was on the ground in many places. A common flaw was that the Forest Service showed a temporary or permanent PCT segment following a trail taken off a pre-existing Forest Service map when in fact there *was no trail* where it was shown on that map in the first place.

Perfect or not, the final proposed route was sent to Washington for publication in the Federal Register, the next step toward its becoming official. A verbal description of the route was also published in the Federal Register on January 30, 1973. But the material in the register did not give a precise route which could be unambiguously followed; it was only a *general* route, and the details in many places remained to be settled.

As construction on PCT trail segments began, many were optimistic that the entire trail could be completed within a decade. Perhaps it could have were it not for private property located along the proposed route. While some owners readily allowed rights-of-way, many others did not, at least not initially, and years of negotiations passed before some rights were finally secured. While negotiations were in progress, the Forest Service sometimes built new trail segments on both sides of a parcel of private land, expecting to extend a trail segment through it soon after. At times this approach backfired, such as in the northern Sierra Nevada in the Gibralter environs (Map M3). The owners of the Cowell Mine never gave up a right-of-way, and so a new stretch of trail on Gibralter's south slopes had to be abandoned for a snowier, costlier stretch on its north slopes, completed in fall 1985. But at least the stretch was built, which was not true for a short stretch northwest of Sierra Buttes (Map 1, Section 7), where the PCT route is a road.

The major obstacle to the trail's completion has been the mammoth Tejon Ranch, which began in Civil War days as a sheep ranch, then later became a cattle ranch, and in 1936 became a public corporation that diversified its land use and increased its acreage. This "ranch," about the size of Sequoia National Park, straddles most of the Tehachapi Mountains, and since the powerful corporation's directors have steadfastly refused to permit a trail across their land, a crest route along the Tehachapis (most of Section E) appears very remote. Perhaps indefinitely, the PCT route in this part of the state will remain as miles of roads along the west side of desertlike Antelope Valley. A stretch of trail is planned to climb from the desert floor to the north end of the Tehachapis, but whether this will be built remains to be seen.

Finally, there is another stretch in northern California (the end of Section Q and the start of Section R), where a trail will not replace existing roads. Private property was part of the problem, but also building a horse bridge across the Klamath River proved economically unfeasible. Consequently, one still treads 7.3 miles along roads, which is a blessing in disguise, for if the trail and bridge had been built, you would have bypassed Seiad Valley, a very important resupply point.

Some who walked

No doubt hikers did parts of the Pacific Crest Trail in the 19th Century—though that name for it didn't exist. It may be that someone walked along the crest from Mexico to Canada or vice versa many years ago. But the first person to claim he did the whole route in one continuous journey—in 1970—was Eric Ryback, in *The High Adventure of Eric Ryback*. In the first edition of this book, the authors said there were strong reasons for doubting Ryback's claim. In response Ryback and his publisher each sued the authors for $3,000,000 damages. The suit was never tried. After Ryback, his publisher and their lawyers saw copies of the evidence the authors had, including letters from people who said they had given rides to Ryback, they dropped the suit. The authors did not have to make any promises or compromises; the suit was just plain dropped.

Ryback's book, however, focused attention on the Pacific Crest Trail, and other people began to plan end-to-end treks. The year after his book came out, 1972, was a big year on the trail. The first person to hike the entire PCT in one continuous trek finished it on September 1. His name was Richard Watson. Barely behind him, finishing four days later, were Wayne Martin, Dave Odell, Toby Heaton, Bill Goddard and Butch Ferrand. Very soon after them, Henry Wilds went from Mexico to Canada solo. In 1972 Jeff Smukler did the PCT with Mary Carstens, who became the first woman to make it. The next year, Gregg Eames and Ben Schifrin set out to follow the official route as closely as possible, no matter whether trail or cross country. Schifrin had to drop out with a broken foot at Odell Lake, Oregon (he finished the route the next year), but Eames got to Canada, and is probably the first person to have walked the official route almost without deviation. They even managed to go through the Tejon Ranch, though shot at.

In 1975, at least 27 people completed the PCT, according to Chuck Long, who was one of them and who put together a book of various trekkers' experiences. Perhaps as much as 200–300 hikers started the trail that year, intending to do it all. In 1976, one who made it all the way was Teddy Boston, the first woman to solo the trail, so far as we know. Teddy, then a 49-year mother of four, made the trek the hard way, north to south.

Fascination with the trail steadily dropped, so that by the late 1980s, perhaps only a dozen or so people per year hiked the entire trail. When the trail, including its road segments, is declared completed, perhaps in the early 1990s, there will likely be renewed interest, for a while, in walking its entire length. The trail's main users will remain day hikers, and backpackers on relatively short (two weeks or less) trips. Interestingly, we know of no one who has ridden the entire route on horseback, although an appreciable number of equestrians have done sizable chunks of it. If you know of an equestrian who has done the entire route, let us know. And if you walk all of it or a significant part of it, we at Wilderness Press would like to hear of your adventure.

Chapter 2: Planning Your PCT Hike

Miles and Days

Some readers of this book will take only day hikes along the PCT, and will enjoy them very much. Slightly more ambitious walkers will go on short backpacking trips along parts of the Pacific Crest Trail, and experienced backpackers may plan trips of several hundred miles. Altogether, about 99.9% of the people who walk on the PCT do not go from one end to the other. Every year, a few "do" the entire PCT. That takes more than 5 months. (Those who walk the whole trail or a large part of it end up averaging something like 17 miles a day.) If you do it all the same year, you have to start by early May. The California part takes more than 3 months. You should try to do the hottest part, south of the Tehachapi mountains, before June. Not far from there you enter the High Sierra, which is best in August in most years, but you will travel it in June if you started in early May. In the northern Sierra, from Yosemite to Lassen, July is best, and north of Lassen June is best. North of Castle Crags and Interstate 5 there is not much of a drought problem or a snow problem, so you can do this part any time in the summer, though perhaps after mid-July is best. Clearly if you travel the trail end to end, you cannot be in each area at its best time.

We do not recommend hiking all three states in one continuous 5–6 month trek. First, if you commit yourself to averaging 15–20 miles a day, you may become resentful, for lack of time, over not being able to take interesting side trips and not being able to linger in a scenic area. Second, July and August are optimal for hiking, but before and after these months you can run into lots of bad weather and/or snow-covered ground. Such weather is not pleasant; indeed, just to survive could require a lot of mountaineering sense. Finally, and most important, if you're not in top shape, you risk developing serious bone and ligament problems in your feet and legs.

If you are not thinking of hiking the entire PCT, then first decide how long you can spend on it. Then decide which part of the PCT you would like see. In this book the California PCT is divided into 18 sections, each a suitable backpack trip. Of course, you don't have to begin or end at the start of a section; you can choose a hike that suits your own goals. Now, match up your days available with the overall mileage of that part of the PCT you plan to hike, using an estimate of:

- 20 miles a day if you are in top shape and have extraordinary discipline
- 16 miles a day if you are in good shape and don't want to take any layover days
- 12 miles a day if you are in good shape and want to lay over every fourth day
- 12 miles a day if you are in only fair shape and want to suffer
- 6 miles a day if you are in fair shape and want to enjoy yourself.

In your planning, you should allow for some miles walked in error which you will have to retrace. PCT trekkers report missing junctions, especially when these are under snow, and going some distance out of their way before discovering their error. The figure above of 17 miles a day refers to 17 miles of PCT route covered. It does *not* include additional miles walked in error or in taking side trips to lakes, campsites, towns or other places. So, in reality, you may have to hike 19+ miles per day to complete the entire three-state PCT in 5+ months.

After you decide how much of the PCT you want to cover, next comes the question of transportation. Greyhound and Trailways buses travel the major highways, and so offer access to a number of spots along or near the PCT. From south to north, such spots are Palm Springs, Cabazon, Newhall, Acton junction, Palmdale, Tehachapi, Mojave, Lone Pine, Independence, Bishop, Mammoth Lakes junction, Lee Vining, Yosemite Valley (local bus to Tuolumne Meadows), Little Norway, South Lake Tahoe, Truckee, Quincy, Belden, Dunsmuir, Mt. Shasta City and Ashland. Schedules change, of course, so check in advance.

By using city and county transit lines, you can go from San Diego to Campo, which is near the south end of the PCT. Also, Southern California's counties have rapid transit districts that provide service between all the cities and major towns, and such service may get you to within a day's hike of a specific trailhead. But rather than walk for a day, you'll probably hitchhike. We've provided four hitchhiking signs (north, south, east and west) at the end of the book, and we've been told that they provide faster results than just using your thumb. Out-of-state trekkers should be aware that it's illegal to hitchhike along a freeway, though one can do so at the start of a freeway onramp.

In contrast to tri-state hikers, most short-distance hikers use their own vehicles. If you don't want to hike a stretch and then retrace it, the best solution is to hike with friends, leaving one vehicle at the starting point and another at the ending point. Leaving a vehicle for several weeks may invite a break-in, so try to find out, perhaps at a local ranger station, if there has been a problem in the area. Expensive cars, cars with fancy audio systems, and cars with gear in plain view are the most likely targets. Schaffer, driving a rather ordinary station wagon, hasn't had a break-in during his 20+ summers in the mountains, and you probably won't either.

If you are going by yourself, you may have to rely on hitchhiking and/or buses, or perhaps you can hide a bike near your end point, if your trek is not too long, and then pedal back to the start—along roads of course. Mountain bikes are banned on most of California's trails.

Logistics

How can a book describe the psychological factors a person must prepare for . . . the despair, the alienation, the anxiety and especially the pain, both physical and mental, which slices to the very heart of the hiker's volition, which are the real things that must be planned for? No words can transmit those factors, which are more a part of planning than the elementary rituals of food, money and equipment, and how to get them.

—Jim Podlesney, in *Pacific Crest Trail*
Hike Planning guide, edited by Chuck Long
(Signpost Publications)

The authors agree with that quotation. Furthermore, they do not believe a trail guide is the place for an extensive explanation of basic backpacking techniques, and in any event the PCT end-to-end is no trip for novices. However, the peculiar problems of an expeditionary trek do warrant a few pages.

If you are going to be on the trail for more than a couple of weeks, you will want to have supplies waiting for you at one or more places along the route. For this you can mail packages to yourself. Alternatively, you can drive to a place and leave a package with someone, if you are sure that person will be responsible for it. You can also hide caches in the wilderness, if you are willing to carry the heavy load in from the nearest road and carry all the packaging out—and if you trust the wildlife. There are a few towns near the PCT which will perhaps have adequate supplies and equipment—Idyllwild, Big Bear City, Mojave, South Lake Tahoe, Burney, Dunsmuir. However, even those towns may not have an adequate selection of lightweight backpacking food. It is best to depend on post offices. A list of post offices on or near the trail appears at the end of this chapter.

SUPPLIES

This discussion of supplies attempts to tell you what you will need, and how best to get it. The discussion relies heavily on co-author Schifrin's experiences during his hike of the entire PCT.

The first thing to know about supplies along the PCT is that they are scarce. Too many young people try to do the PCT without pre-planning their food and other supplies. So at Agua Dulce they find that there is no white gas in town, and the store is so limited that they will have to eat the same macaroni and cheese for the next five days. If one wants to go light, the *only* choice is to pre-plan your menus and the rest of your needs, and mail things ahead to yourself.

Food

The main thing to have waiting your arrival at a post office is food. When hiking the PCT, food is the main concern. It causes more daydreaming and more bickering than anything else, even sex. As for the bickering, most people hike in groups, and much of the friction in a group is due to different eating habits. Some hikers don't eat breakfast; others won't hike an inch until they've had their steak and eggs. Some people eat every hour; others take the traditional 3 meal breaks. Many of these problems can be cured if each hiker carries his own food, and suits his own prejudices. This arrangement also allows flexibility in pace and in hiking partners.

As for the daydreaming, it comes to focus on delicious food, and lots of it. Schifrin's first rule is that it won't hurt to take too much, because it will turn out to be too little anyway. He and his 2 companions ate over 6000 calories a day out of their packs, and still lost weight. The mental stresses, as well as the obvious physical ones, use up energy. So food serves 2 purposes: to provide fuel, and to bolster morale. Take the things you crave. Most goodies—Hershey bars, beer, double fudgies, fresh cheese, mint cakes—are great energy sources, as well as providing variety and what Schifrin calls a "body con": At the bottom of some horrible ascent, you say to yourself, "You get a double helping of Hershey bar when you get to the top." It's something to sweat for.

Then there's the usual egregious gluttony upon reaching a town—steaks, quarts of ice cream, gallons of chocolate milk, giant shrimp salads. Besides being good for morale and filling you up, these binges can give you a good idea of what's been missing from your diet, namely, whatever you craved and stuffed yourself on. For the next trail segment, correct the deficiency, insofar as you can. And for the whole trek, take a supply of multi-vitamin pills, just in case your diet is deficient in important vitamins.

The only time people told Schifrin they had brought too much food was when they thought they had brought too much of a *certain item*. One attractive young lady carried only soybeans and powdered milk. She made it—but only after she'd stopped at each ranger station along the route for a few days, and made it with the ranger in exchange for palatable food. Two men, carrying soybeans and something else unpalatably organic, got so sick of this menu that they ripped off the Rae Lakes Ranger Station. (They didn't finish the trail; the ranger caught them 2 days later, and they went to jail.)

Other hikers seem to think that wild foods are theirs for the taking. They might remember that the Indians spent their entire lives searching out foodstuffs that even they admitted were unpalatable. A PCT hiker doesn't have the time to search, and it's against the law and immoral, anyway. Similarly with trout: don't plan to rely on trout—they may not be biting during the time you have to devote to fishing.

At home, or in towns along the way, supermarkets are the best sources of your pack food. Sporting-goods stores and some specialty shops offer freeze-dried food, but for many hikers the cost is prohibitive. You can compromise by buying freeze-dried meats and vegetables at such stores and the rest of your food at supermarkets. If you plan to buy a lot of freeze-dried food, you might contact **Trail Foods Company** (P.O. Box 9303, North Hollywood, CA 91609-1309; phone 818-897-4370), which carries several brands of freeze-dried food. Ask for a catalog of their complete product line. They offer long-distance hikers at 35% discount if they buy foods by the case (usually a dozen items) and if their minimum order is at least $100 (before discount). Furthermore, the company will ship the food to the destinations you desire, and they will do so for the dates you specify.

Hikers will most likely want a balance between cold and hot foods. Cold foods are of course more appropriate for lunch, though we meet hikers who go 100 miles without cooking. Some people refuse to face the dawn without hot drinks, but hot drinks are a little out of place in the Mojave Desert, even at dawn. Those who dispense with hot foods to save weight and time may suffer mentally on a freezing evening in the North Cascades. Variety is the key. No matter how much time you spend planning your food, however, you are sure to be dissatisfied, somewhere down the trail, with what you brought or with how much of it you brought. You may find that eventually all freeze-dried dinners taste the same to you. You may find that you can never get a full feeling. You may lose 30 pounds. Or you may find that you brought too much. Just be prepared for such things to happen. Fortunately, you are not totally locked into your planned menus. You can mail back—or abandon—what you can't stand, and buy something else in towns and resorts along the way—although it will not be cheap in such places. You can even ask your contact at home to buy some new food items and mail them to you.

In planning menus, remember that at 5000' elevation, cooking time is double what it is at sea level, and at 10,000' it is quadruple. So don't bring foods that take very long to cook at sea level.

Wood won't always be available, and if you are hiking 15+ miles a day, you'll find a stove is far more convenient than a wood fire. You should know the rate at which your stove consumes fuel, for you will need lots of it if you do the whole PCT. Cartridge stoves, such as the Bleuet, do not burn as hot as white-gas stoves, particularly when the cartridge is low on fuel, but they do have several advantages: they are very easy to start, and virtually foolproof, and you can mail propane cartridges whereas you can't mail white gas. (But most unleaded gasoline from gas stations works fine in gasoline stoves.)

Clothing

In planning what clothes to take, realize that rain or snow is possible at any time at any point along the PCT—assuming you start at Mexico roughly in late April. Therefore have good protection against wet and cold, whatever it costs. Remember that cotton clothing is useless when wet. Assume there will be a snowstorm on Mt. San Jacinto when you are there that deposits 4 feet of new snow, and plan accordingly. It could happen. It has happened, and ended the Mexico-to-Canada adventures of several trekkers before they fairly got started.

Boots are the most important piece of clothing. They must be broken in before the trip. Otherwise, they may turn out not to fit, and they will surely give you a crop of blisters. For the entire PCT, it's best to have two pairs of boots in the same size and same style. Mail one pair ahead. Schifrin broke his foot because his two pair were of two different styles, and one pair didn't give his feet the support the other pair had accustomed them to. You might go all the way on just one pair, after 1 or 2 resolings, but if you try to make it through the North Cascades with the boots you started with, you will be sticking your neck out—and maybe your toes. Treat the boots with Snoseal or another effective compound often, to keep them waterproof and to prevent cracking from heat.

It may not occur to you in advance how tough walking will be on your socks too. One PCT trekker said he wore out one pair every 125 miles on the average, though we think that's a little extreme. Still, you will need replacements. You might start out with a 3-day supply of socks—3 pairs of heavy wool socks and 3 (or 6, if you wear double inners) pairs of inner socks. Schaffer has gone 1000+ miles with this combination. If you hope to equal that, you must change socks daily and wash them daily.

Besides boot soles and socks, you are going to wear out some underwear, shirts and, probably, pants. The less often you wash them, the faster they will wear out, due to rotting. In choosing your clothes to start with, remember that as you hike your waist will get smaller and your legs bigger.

Light footwear is very nice to have for fording streams and for comfort in camp. It's damn near heaven to take off those 5-pound boots after a 20-mile day. Tennis shoes are traditional, but gymnastic slippers work almost as well around camp (not in streams), and they weight only a few ounces. A recent invention may be the best of the three: SCUBA diving booties weigh only 6 ounces, wear well, can be worn in bed, don't absorb water, have great traction, are warmer than down booties, can be worn inside your boots, and can even keep your socks dry in stream fords.

Equipment

Spare no expense. Mistakes and shortcuts in equipment mean lost time, lost money, lost sleep and lost health.

Besides your usual summer backpacking equipment, you may need a tent, skis or snowshoes, an ice ax and a rope. You will need a guidebook with maps—this one. And even if you don't normally carry a camera, PCT trekkers say you'll be sorry if you don't take one on the BIG hike.

Almost all PCT hikers carry a *tent,* and are glad they did. A tent is important for warmth in the snowy parts, and for dryness in all the parts except the desert. In Oregon, a tent allows you to sleep by keeping the mosquitoes off you. We recommend a quality 2-man mountain tent—on the large side, or you and your companions may become less than friends.

The question of *skis* versus *snowshoes* for early season in the high mountains remains under debate, and some PCT hikers say they'd rather take their chances without either, considering the cost and the weight. The main advantage of skis, of course, is that you can cover a lot of ground downhill in a hurry—if you know how to ski with a pack. We suspect many of the trekkers who chose snowshoes would have used skis if they had been better cross-country-with-pack skiers. The main disadvantage of skis is that you can't mail them; you have to ship them by Greyhound or some other way.

Many PCT through hikers say an *ice ax* is definitely a necessity, and others say it is at least worth its weight for the many different things it will do. We recommend one for any segment where you expect to be in snow.

You should take a *rope* for belaying on steep snow or on ice, and for difficult fords at the height of the snowmelt. (The Introduction to each trail section that may have fording problems tells you what you may face in that section.)

A *camera* is a necessity for most long-distance hikers. Schaffer recommends a 35mm compact camera or a 35mm single-lens reflex (SLR). Compact cameras are smaller, lighter and cheaper, and virtually all have a motor drive to advance the film, which unfortunately "eats up" batteries—not desirable. Sadly, most SLRs also have energy-hungry motor drives. Buy an "old-fashioned" SLR with a manual advance. The battery operating the light meter and the electronic shutter will easily last the duration of your trip. The advantage of SLRs is their lens interchangeability. Buy an SLR *body* and *one* zoom lens. A popular lens is a 28-70mm zoom, which goes from wide angle to short tele-photo. A 28-105mm zoom is better, but a 28-200mm zoom is too bulky. Instead carry a 2x teleconverter to double the lens length, though this magnifies your lens's flaws by 2x.

You should take slides rather than prints, since you can always make prints from slides, but not vice versa. Films come in different speeds (ASAs), and Schaffer recommends an ASA of 64, 100 or 200. While ASA 64 film is the sharpest, it can be too slow for dim-light or action shots. On the other hand, ASA 200 film is a bit too grainy for sharp 8 x 10 or 11 x 14 prints.

The cost

You can expect to spend several thousand dollars for the whole PCT unless you already have almost all the equipment you will need. Take plenty of money in traveler's checks. You won't be able to resist the food when you are in civilization, and you will find yourself with unforeseen needs for equipment. In addition, you will want to be able to correct some original decisions that you have later found unwise or unworkable, and to do so usually takes money.

MAILING TIPS

You can mail yourself almost any food, clothing or equipment. Before you leave home, you won't know whether you are going to run out of, say, molefoam, but you will have a good idea of your rate of consumption of food, clothing, and fuel for your stove. You can arrange for mailings of quantities of these things, purchased at home, where they are probably cheaper than in the towns along the way.

Address your package to

> Yourself
> General Delivery
> P.O., state ZIP
> HOLD UNTIL (date)

Don't mail perishables. Make your packages strong, sturdy and tight. You are *really* depending on their contents. Have your home contact mail packages at least 24 days before you expect to get them, and even then, pay for the postal service called "Special Handling." Do not seal the packages when you pack them, because you are likely to have second thoughts. You can then write your mail contact and ask him to add certain things to (or take certain things out of) the box that goes to X place, or wherever. Before you leave home, phone the post offices you will be sending mail to, to make sure they will hold your mail for your arrival. They are legally required to hold it only 10 days. Also find out what hours they are open.

Remember that if you change your plan, you can pick up a package at a post office and mail some or all of its contents to yourself farther along the route—or you can mail it home.

WATER

There are two concerns about water: its availability and its purity. Hikers who are used to the High Sierra or the Cascades may be out of the habit of worrying about water, since it is seldom far away, even in late summer. But dehydration can be a problem along parts of the PCT. The trail description mentions every place where you will have to hike more than 5 miles between water sources, and the Introduction to Section E discusses water needs when hiking in the desert. Of course, some years are drier than others, and so you should be prepared—some usually reliable springs and creeks may go dry. Also be aware that campgrounds and picnic areas with tap water often have their water turned off in the cold months to prevent water freezing in the system's pipes.

Water purity is an equally serious concern. A *very small* percentage of streams, springs and lakes may contain cystic forms of *Giardia lamblia* microorganisms, which can give you a case of giardiasis (jee-ar-dye-a-sis). Although this disease can be incapacitating, it is not usually life-threatening, and so you may not feel it is worth your effort to take precautions. Symptoms, which can develop a week or two after infection, usually include diarrhea, gas, loss of appetite, abdominal cramps and bloating. Weight loss may occur from nausea and loss of appetite. These discomforts may last up to six weeks. If not treated, the symptoms may disappear on their own, only to recur intermittently over a period of many months. Other diseases can have similar symptoms, but if you drank untreated water, you should suspect giardiasis and so inform your doctor. If properly diagnosed, the disease is curable with medication prescribed by a physician.

To play it safe, you can avoid risking giardiasis by several ways. The traditional, most effective way to make the water safe is to boil it for 3 minutes (for 5 minutes at the highest elevations, where water boils at lower temperatures). You can avoid the wait if you carry two water bottles, so you can drink from one while you're boiling water to fill the other.

Chemical disinfectants, such as iodine and chlorine, are not as reliable as boiling unless you use them for a long time—say, an hour. But if you carry two water bottles, then while you're drinking from one, the second can be sitting in your pack, with the disinfectant working in it. The recommended dosages, *per quart,* for these substances are: 5 tablets of chlorine or 4 drops of household bleach or 2 tablets of iodine or 10 drops of 2% tincture of iodine.

Another option, which became readily available in the mid-'80s, is to carry a water filtration system. These cost about $40 and up, and most weigh under 2 pounds. It takes about 2 minutes to purify a quart of water. The filter in the unit eventually clogs up, but with luck, you should be able to do all the California without buying a replacement filter.

Hypothermia

Every year you can read accounts of hikers freezing to death in the mountains. They die of hypothermia, the #1 killer of outdoor recreationists. You too may be exposed to it, particularly if you start hiking the PCT in April in order to do all 3 states. Because it is so easy to die from hypothermia, we are including the following information, which is endorsed by the Forest Service and by mountain-rescue groups. Read it. It may save your life.

Hypothermia is subnormal body temperature, which is caused outdoors by exposure to cold, usually aggravated by wetness, wind and exhaustion. The moment your body begins to lose heat faster than it produces it, your body makes involuntary adjustments to preserve the normal temperature in its vital organs. Uncontrolled shivering is one way your body attempts to maintain its vital temperature. *If you've begun uncontrolled shivering, you must consider yourself a prime candidate for hypothermia and act accordingly.* Shivering will eventually consume your energy reserves until they are exhausted. When this happens, cold reaches your brain, depriving you of judgment and reasoning power. You will not realize this is happening. You will lose control of your hands. Your internal body temperature is sliding downward. Without treatment, this slide leads to stupor, collapse and death. Learn the four lines of defense against hypothermia.

Your first line of defense: avoid exposure.

1. *Stay dry.* When clothes get wet, they lose much of their insulating value. Cotton is the worst when wet, wool is intermediate, and synthetics generally the best in this respect.

2. *Beware of wind.* A slight breeze carries heat away from bare skin much faster than still air does. Wind drives cold air under and through clothing. Wind refrigerates wet clothes by evaporating moisture from the surface.

3. *Understand cold.* Most hypothermia cases develop in air temperatures between 30 and 50 degrees. Most outdoorsmen simply can't believe such temperatures can be dangerous. They fatally underestimate the danger of being wet at such temperatures. But just jump in a cold lakelet and you'll agree that 50° water is unbearably cold. The cold that kills is cold water running down neck and legs, cold water held against the body by sopping clothes, cold water flushing body heat from the surface of the clothes.

Your second line of defense: terminate exposure.

If you cannot stay dry and warm under existing weather conditions, using the clothes you have with you, *terminate exposure.*

1. *Be brave enough* to give up reaching your destination or whatever you had in mind. That one extra mile might be your last.

2. *Get out of the wind and rain.* Build a fire. Concentrate on making your camp or bivouac as secure and comfortable as possible.

3. *Never ignore shivering.* Persistent or violent shivering is clear warning that you are on the verge of hypothermia. *Make camp.*

4. *Forestall exhaustion.* Make camp while you still have a reserve of energy. Allow for the fact that exposure greatly reduces your normal endurance. You may think you are doing fine when the fact that you are exercising is the only thing preventing your going into hypothermia. If exhaustion forces you to stop, however briefly, your rate of body heat production instantly drops by 50% or more; violent, incapacitating shivering may begin immediately; you may slip into hypothermia *in a matter of minutes.*

5. *Appoint a foul-weather leader.* Make the best-protected member of your party responsible for calling a halt before the least-protected member becomes exhausted or goes into violent shivering.

Your third line of defense: detect hypothermia.

If your party is exposed to wind, cold and wetness, *think hypothermia.* Watch yourself and others for hypothermia's symptoms:

1. Uncontrollable fits of shivering.
2. Vague, slow, slurred speech.
3. Memory lapses; incoherence.
4. Immobile, fumbling hands.
5. Frequent stumbling; lurching gait.
6. Drowsiness—to sleep is to die.
7. Apparent exhaustion, such as inability to get up after a rest.

Your fourth and last line of defense: treatment.

The victim may deny he's in trouble. Believe the symptoms, *not* the patient. Even mild symptoms demand immediate, drastic treatment.

1. Get the victim out of the wind and rain.
2. Strip off *all* wet clothes.
3. If the patient is only mildly impaired:
   a. Give him warm drinks.
   b. Get him into dry clothes and a warm sleeping bag. Well-wrapped, warm (not hot) rocks or canteens will hasten recovery.
4. If the patient is semiconscious or worse:
   a. Don't give him hot drinks unless he is capable of holding a cup and drinking from it. Forcing drinks on a semiconscious person could cause him to gag and *drown* (this unfortunately is quite common with inexperienced would-be rescuers)!
   b. Leave him stripped. Put him in a sleeping bag with another person (also stripped). If you have a double bag or can zip two together, put the victim between two warmth donors. *Skin to skin contact* is the most effective treatment. Never leave the victim as long as he is alive. To do so is to kill him—it's just that simple!
5. Build a fire to warm the camp.

Other notes on avoiding hypothermia.
1. Choose rainclothes that are effective against *wind-driven* rain and cover head, neck, body and legs. Gore-Tex and other PTFE laminates are best, but won't last as long as some other materials.
2. Take clothing that retains its insulation even when wet, such as polypropylene, capilene or dacron fabrics. These hold even less water than the traditional wet-weather favorite, wool, and so make it easier for your body to keep warm. Always carry a two-piece underwear set, and a heavier pair of pants, plus a sweater or pullover (the new "fleece" and "pile" designs are rugged and perform well). Never forget a knit wool or fleece headpiece that can protect the neck and chin. Cotton underwear and down-filled parkas are worse than useless when wet, as are cotton shirts and pants. As native Americans long ago discovered, one stays warmer in a cold rain when he is stark naked than when he is bundled up in wet clothes.
3. Carry a stormproof tent with a good rain fly and set it up *before* you need it.
4. Carry trail food rich in calories, such as nuts, jerky and candy, and keep nibbling during hypothermia weather.
5. Take a gas stove or a plumber's candle, flammable paste or other reliable fire starter.
6. Never abandon survival gear under any circumstances. If you didn't bring along the above items, stay put and make the best of it. An all-too-common fatal mistake is for victims to abandon everything so that, unburdened, they can run for help.
7. "It never happens to me. I'm Joe athlete." Don't you believe it.

Outdoor Courtesy

Traveling a wild trail, away from centers of civilization, is a unique experience. It brings intimate association with nature—communion with the earth, the forest, the chaparral, the wildlife, the clear sky. A great responsibility accompanies this experience—the obligation to keep the wilderness as you found it. Being considerate of the wilderness rights of others will make the mountain adventures of those who follow equally rewarding.

As a wilderness visitor, you should become familiar with the rules of wilderness courtesy outlined below.

Trails

Never cut switchbacks. This practice breaks down trails and hastens erosion. Take care not to dislodge rocks that might fall on hikers below you. Improve and preserve trails, as by clearing away loose rocks (carefully) and removing branches. Report any trail damage and broken or misplaced signs to a ranger.

Off trail

Restrain the impulse to blaze trees or to build ducks where not essential. Let the next fellow find his way as you did.

Campgrounds

Spread your gear in an already-cleared area, and build your fire in a campground stove. Don't disarrange the camp by making hard-to-eradicate ramparts of rock for fireplaces or windbreaks. Rig tents and tarps with line tied to rocks or trees; never put nails in trees. For your campfire, use fallen wood only; do not cut standing trees nor break off branches. Use the campground latrine. Place litter in the litter can or carry it out. Leave the campground cleaner than you found it.

Fire

Fire is a great danger in the mountains, especially in southern California; act accordingly. Smoke only in cleared areas along the trail where a sign authorizes it. Report a mountain fire immediately.

Litter

Along the trail, place candy wrappers, raisin boxes, orange peels, etc. in your pocket or pack for later disposal; throw nothing on the trail. Pick up litter you find along the trail or in camp. More than almost anything else, litter detracts from the wilderness scene. Remember, you can take it with you.

Noise

Boisterous conduct is out of harmony in a wilderness experience. Be a considerate hiker and camper. Don't ruin another's enjoyment of the wilderness.

Good Samaritanship

Human life and well-being take precedence over everything else—in the wilderness as elsewhere. If a hiker or camper is in trouble, help in any way you can. Indifference is a moral crime. Give comfort or first aid; then hurry to a ranger station for help.

Land-use Regulations

The California portion of the PCT passes through national parks, national forests, state parks, land administered by the Bureau of Land Management and private land. All these areas have their own regulations, which you ignore only at your risk—risk of physical difficulty as well as possibility of being cited for violations.

On private land, of course, the regulations are what the owner says they are. The same is true on Indian lands. In particular, don't build a fire on private land without the owner's written permission.

Regulations on U.S. Bureau of Land Management land are not of major consequence for users of this book, since the route passes through only about 40 miles of it, mostly in the Tehachapis and southeast of San Gorgonio Wilderness.

The Forest Service and the Park Service, for good reason, have more regulations. These are not uniform throughout the state, or as between the two services. We list below the Forest Service and Park Service regulations that *are* uniform along the trail, plus some that are peculiar to the Park Service. Special regulations in particular places are mentioned in the trail description when it "arrives" at the place.

1. *Wilderness permits,* which also serve as fire permits, are required to enter a few of the wildernesses, for overnight stays in other wildernesses, and for the backcountry of the national parks. In the less-used wildernesses, wilderness permits usually aren't required. Where one is required, this information will be mentioned in the introductory

material in the book's appropriate trail section. Addresses and phone numbers for agencies that dispense permits and information are given at the end of this chapter.

If you are hiking through several national-forest and/or national-park wildernesses along the PCT, you do not need a separate permit for each. Write only to the one you will begin in. Hikers planning to walk all of California southbound should get a permit from Klamath National Forest headquarters. Those hiking California northbound should get a permit from Cleveland National Forest headquarters. State that you are going to hike along the PCT beginning in Place A on X date and ending in Place B on (roughly) Y date, and you want a Joint-Use Permit. Such a permit is good only for one continuous trip along the PCT—but we don't think it would be revoked if, say, you went out to Bishop to resupply.

2. If you are not hiking in wildernesses that require a wilderness permit, you will still need a *campfire permit*. In northern California these are issued for the entire year. They may be obtained free at offices or stations of the U.S. Forest Service, U.S. Bureau of Land Management and California Division of Forestry.

In southern California within the Cleveland, San Bernardino and Angeles National Forests, a special campfire permit is necessary for each visit. Obtain this permit free from an office or station in the National Forest you are visiting.

Campfire permits require each party to carry a shovel. If you don't build any fires but use only gas stoves, then you can leave the shovel behind but you'll still need the permit. A stove is particularly recommended—and sometimes required—for the high country, where dead and down wood is scarce. Rotting wood should be preserved, since it enriches the soil and hosts organisms which larger animals feed on.

3. A California *fishing license* is required for all persons 16 years old or older who fish. The limit is 10 trout per day, with some exceptions, given in the state Department of Fish and Game regulations.

4. *Destruction,* injury, defacement, removal or disturbance in any manner of any natural feature or public property is prohibited. This includes:

    a. Molesting any animal, picking flowers or other plants;

    b. Cutting, blazing, marking, driving nails in, or otherwise damaging growing trees or standing snags;

    c. Writing, carving or painting of name or other inscription anywhere;

    d. Destruction, defacement or moving of signs.

5. *Collecting specimens* of minerals, plants, animals or historical objects is prohibited without written authorization, obtained in advance, from the Park Service or Forest Service. Permits are not issued for personal collections.

6. *Smoking* is not permitted while traveling through vegetated areas. You may stop and smoke in a safe place.

7. Pack and saddle *animals* have the right-of-way on trails. Hikers should get completely off the trail, on the downhill side if possible, and remain quiet until the stock has passed.

8. *Cutting switchbacks* is prohibited, since it can lead to the trail's erosion and possibly to dangerous footing.

9. Use *existing campsites* if there are any. If not, camp away from the trail and at least 100 feet from lakes and streams, on mineral soil or unvegetated forest floor—never in meadows or other soft, vegetated spots.

10. *Construction* of improvements such as rock walls, large fireplaces, bough beds, tables, and rock-and-log stream crossings is prohibited.

11. *Soap* and other pollutants should be kept out of lakes and streams. Use of detergents is not recommended, since they affect the water detrimentally.

12. *Toilets* should be in soft soil away from camps and water. Dig a shallow hole and bury all.

13. You are required to *clean up* your camp before you leave. Tin cans, foil, glass, worn-out or useless gear, and other unburnables must be carried out.

14. *National Parks but not Forests* prohibit dogs and cats on the trail and prohibit carrying or using firearms.

Post Offices Along or Near the Route
South to North

* = recommended for use

Some stations are seasonal. The best pickup time is weekdays 1-4 p.m. Hours of most are 9-12 and 1-5 or longer. Some are open Saturday mornings.

*Campo 92006
*Mount Laguna 92048
 Julian 92036
*Warner Springs 92086
*Terwilliger:
   The Valley Store
   Star Rte. 1, Box 243
   Anza, CA 92306
   Phone (714) 763-4411
 Anza 92306
*Idyllwild 92349
 Cabazon 92230
 Palm Springs 92263
*Big Bear City 92314
*Fawnskin 92333
 Lake Arrowhead 92352
 Crestline 92325
*Wrightwood 92397
 Acton 93510
 Saugus 91350
*Agua Dulce 91350
 Green Valley 91350
*Lake Hughes 93532
*Mojave 93501

*Cantil 93519
 Onyx 93255
 Kernville 93238
*Kennedy Mdws. Gen. Store
   P.O. Box 367
   Inyokern, CA 93527
 Lone Pine 93545
 Independence 93526
 Big Pine 93513
*Bishop 93514
 Mono Hot Springs 93642
*Lake Edison
   Vermilion Valley Resort
   c/o Rancheria Garage
   Huntington Lake Road
   Lakeshore, CA 93634
*Mammoth Lakes 93546
 June Lake 93529
*Tuolumne Meadows 95389
 Lee Vining 93541
 Bridgeport 93517
 Markleeville 96120
*Little Norway 95721
*Echo Lake 95721

 South Lake Tahoe 95706
 Tahoma 95733
 Olympic ("Squaw") Valley
   95730
 Soda Springs 95728
*Norden 95724
 Truckee 95734
*Sierra City 96125
 La Porte 95981
 Meadow Valley 95956
 Quincy 95971
*Belden 95915
 Chester 96020
*Old Station 96071
 Hat Creek 96040
*Cassel 96016
 Burney 96013
*Castella 96017
 Dunsmuir 96025
 Sawyers Bar 96027
 Callahan 96014
 Etna 96027
*Seiad Valley 96086
*Ashland, OR 97520

Federal Government Agencies
South to North

Bureau of Land Management
333 S. Waterman Avenue
El Centro, CA 92243
(619) 352-5842

Cleveland National Forest
880 Front Street
San Diego, CA 92188
(619) 557-5050

Bureau of Land Management
1695 Spruce Street
Riverside, CA 92507
(714) 351-6394

San Bernardino Nat. For.
1824 S. Commercenter Cir.
San Bernardino, CA 92408
(714) 383-5588

San Jacinto Wilderness
contact:
Idyllwild Ranger Station
P.O. Box 518
Idyllwild, CA 92349
(714) 659-2117

Angeles National Forest
701 N. Santa Anita Avenue
Arcadia, CA 91006
(818) 574-5200

Sheep Mountain Wilderness
contact Angeles Nat. For.

Bureau of Land Management
800 Truxtun Ave. #311
Bakersfield, CA 93301
(805) 861-4191

Sequoia National Forest
900 West Grand Avenue
Porterville, CA 93257
(209) 784-1500

South Sierra and Golden
Trout Wildernesses
contact Sequoia Nat. For.

Sequoia and Kings Canyon
National Parks
Backcountry Permits
Three Rivers, CA 93271
(209) 565-3341

Inyo National Forest
873 N. Main Street
Bishop, CA 93514
(619) 873-5841

John Muir Wilderness
contact Inyo Nat. For.

Sierra National Forest
Federal Building
1130 "O" Street
Fresno, CA 93721
(209) 487-5155

Ansel Adams Wilderness
contact:
Mammoth Ranger District
P.O. Box 148
Mammoth Lakes, CA 93546
(619) 934-2505

Yosemite National Park
Wilderness Office
P.O. Box 577
Yosemite, CA 95389
(209) 372-0310

Toiyabe National Forest
1200 Franklin Way
Sparks, NV 89431
(702) 355-5300

Stanislaus National Forest
19777 Greenley Road
Sonora, CA 95370
(209) 532-3671

Emigrant Wilderness
contact:
Summit Ranger District
Star Route 1295
Sonora, CA 95370
(209) 965-3434

Carson-Iceberg Wilderness,
Sonora Pass trailhead
contact Summit Ranger
District

Carson-Iceberg Wilderness,
Ebbetts Pass trailhead
contact:
Carson Ranger District
1536 South Carson Street
Carson City, NV 89701
(702) 882-2766

Mokelumne Wilderness
contact Carson Ranger
District

Eldorado National Forest
Information Center
3070 Camino Heights Drive
Camino, CA 95709
(916) 644-6048

Desolation Wilderness
L. Tahoe Basin Mgmt.
P.O. Box 731002
S. Lake Tahoe, CA 95731
(916) 573-2600

Tahoe National Forest
Hwy 49 and Coyote St.
Nevada City, CA 95959
(916) 265-4531

Granite Chief Wilderness
contact Tahoe Nat. For.

Plumas National Forest
P.O. Box 11500
Quincy, CA 95971
(916) 283-2050

Bucks Lake Wilderness
contact Plumas Nat. For.

Lassen National Forest
55 South Sacramento Street
Susanville, CA 96130
(916) 257-2151

Lassen Volcanic Nat. Park
P.O. Box 100
Mineral, CA 96063
(916) 595-4444

Shasta-Trinity National Forest
2400 Washington Avenue
Redding, CA 96001
(916) 246-5222

Castle Crags and Trinity
Alps Wildernesses
contact Shasta-Trinity N. F.

Klamath National Forest
1312 Fairlane Road
Yreka, CA 96097
(916) 842-6131

Russian and Marble Mountain
Wildernesses
contact Klamath Nat. For.

Rogue River National Forest
Federal Bldg., P.O. Box 520
Medford, OR 97501
(503) 776-3600

Red Buttes Wilderness
contact Rogue River N. F.

Chapter 3: PCT Natural History

Geology

It is very likely that the California section of the Pacific Crest Trail is unequaled in its diversity of geology. Many mountain trails cross glacial and subglacial landscapes, but which ones also cross arid and semi-arid landscapes? Some parts of your trail will have perennial snow; others are always dry. Precipitation may be more than 80" per year in places, less than 5 in others. In each of the 3 major rock classes— igneous, sedimentary and metamorphic–you'll encounter dozens of rock types. Because the PCT provides such a good introduction to a wide spectrum of geology, we have added a liberal dose of geologic description to the basic text. You start among granitic rocks at the Mexican border, and then we inform you of almost every new major rock outcrop you'll encounter along your trek northward. We hope that by the end of your journey you'll have developed a keen eye for rocks and that you'll understand the relations between the different rock types. Since we assume that many hikers will have only a minimal background in geology and its terminology, we'll try to cover this broad subject for them in the next few pages. Those wishing to pursue the subject further should consult the list of references at the end of this book.

ROCKS

First, you should get acquainted with the 3 major rock classes: igneous, sedimentary and metamorphic.

Igneous rocks

Igneous rocks came into being when the liquid (molten) rock material (*magma*) solidified. If the material solidified beneath the earth's surface, the rock is called *intrusive*, or plutonic, and a body of it is a *pluton*. If the material reached the surface, and erupted as *lava,* the rock is called *extrusive*, or volcanic.

Intrusive rocks. The classification of an igneous rock is based on its texture, what minerals are in it, and the relative amounts of each mineral present. Since intrusive rocks cool more slowly than extrusive rocks, their crystals have a longer time to grow. If, in a rock, you can see an abundance of individual crystals, odds are that it is an intrusive rock. These rocks may be classified by crystal size: fine, medium or coarse-grained, to correspond to average diameters of less than 1 millimeter, 1-5, and greater than 5.

Some igneous rocks are composed of large crystals (*phenocrysts*) in a matrix of small crystals (*groundmass*). Such a rock is said to have a *porphyritic* texture. The Cathedral Peak pluton, which is well exposed on Lembert Dome at the east end of Tuolumne Meadows in Yosemite National Park, has some feldspar phenocrysts over 4 inches long. High up on the dome these phenocrysts protrude from the less resistant groundmass and provide rock climbers with the holds necessary to ascend the dome.

The common minerals in igneous rocks are quartz, feldspar, biotite, hornblende, pyroxene and olivine. The first 2 are light-colored minerals; the rest are dark. Not all are likely to be present in a piece of rock; indeed, quartz and olivine are never found together. Intrusive rocks are grouped according to the percentages of minerals in them. The 3 common igneous groups are *granite, diorite* and *gabbro*. Granite is rich in quartz and potassium feldspar and usually has only small amounts of biotite. Diorite is poor in quartz and rich in sodium feldspar, and may have 3 dark minerals. Gabbro, a *mafic* rock (rich in magnesium and iron), lacks quartz, but is rich in calcium feldspar and pyroxene, and may have hornblende and olivine. You can subdivide the granite-diorite continuum into granite, quartz monzonite, granodiorite, quartz diorite and diorite. These rocks, which are usually called "granitic rocks" or just plain "granite," are common in the Sierra Nevada and in most of the other ranges to the south. If you start your hike at the Mexican border, you'll begin among granitic rock known as Bonsall tonalite. *Bonsall* refers to the location where this rock is well exposed. *Tonalite* is the name given to diorite with quartz, or quartz diorite. In trail section D you'll encounter another intrusive rock with an unusual name: anorthosite. This rock, usually found with gabbro, is overwhelmingly composed of calcium-rich feldspar crystals.

Since it is unlikely that you'll be carrying a polarizing microscope in your backpack, let alone a great deal of mineralogical expertise in your head, your best chance of identifying these granitic rocks lies in making educated guesses based upon the following table.

rock	color	% dark minerals
granite	creamy white	5
quartz monzonite	very light gray	10
granodiorite	light gray	20
quartz diorite	medium gray	30
diorite	dark gray	40
gabbro	black	60

At first you'll probably estimate too high a percentage of dark minerals, partly because they are more eye-catching and partly because they show through the glassy light minerals. If the intrusive rock is composed entirely of dark minerals (no quartz or feldspar), then it is an ultramafic rock. This rock type, which can be subdivided further, is common along the trail from Interstate 5 at Castle Crags State Park northwest to the Oregon border.

Extrusive rocks. Extrusive, or volcanic rocks are composed of about the same minerals as intrusive rocks. *Rhyolite, andesite* and *basalt* have approximately the same chemical compositions as granite, diorite and gabbro, respectively. As with the intrusive rocks, these 3 volcanics can be subdivided into many groups so it is possible to find ordinary rocks with intimidating names like "quartz latite porphyry"– which is just a volcanic rock with quartz phenocrysts and a composition in between rhyolite and andesite.

Texture is the key feature distinguishing volcanic from plutonic rocks. Whereas you can see the individual crystals in a plutonic rock, you'll have a hard time finding them in a volcanic one. They may be entirely lacking, or so small, weathered and scarce that they'll just frustrate your attempts to identify them. If you can't recognize the crystals, then how can you identify the type of volcanic rock? Color is a poor indicator at best, for although rhyolites tend to be light gray, andesites dark gray, and basalts black, there is so much variation that each can be found in any shade of red, brown or gray.

One aid to identifying volcanic rock types is the landforms composed of them. For example, the high silica (SiO_2) content of rhyolite makes it very viscous, and hence the hot gases in rhyolite magma cause violent explosions when the magma nears the surface, forming *explosion pits* and associated rings of erupted material (*ejecta*). For the same reason a rhyolite lava flow (degassed magma) is thick, short, and steep-sided and may not even flow down a moderately steep slope. The Mono and Inyo craters, north of Devils Postpile National Monument, are perhaps the best examples of this volcanic rock in California. You will find very little of it along the trail.

You'll become very familiar with andesite, such as the flow that makes up the Devils Postpile. Most of the six-sided columnar flows you'll be encountering north of it will also be andesite. The landform characteristically associated with andesite is the *composite cone,* or volcano. Mt. Shasta and some of the peaks in the Lassen area, including Brokeoff Mountain, are examples. These mountains are built up by alternating flows and ejecta. In time *parasitic vents* may develop, such as the cone called Shastina on Mt. Shasta, and the composition of the volcano may shift to more silica-rich *dacite* rock, an intermediate between rhyolite and andesite, which gives rise to tremendous eruptions, like several at Lassen Peak.

The least siliceous and also the least explosive of volcanic rocks is basalt. A basaltic eruption typically produces a cinder cone, rarely over 2000' high, and a very fluid, thin flow. When in Lassen Volcanic National Park, take the alternate route up to the rim of the Cinder Cone. From this vantage point you can see what an extensive, relatively flat area its thin flows covered. Contrast this with Lassen Peak, to the west, with its steep-sided massive bulk armed with protruding dacite domes.

Sedimentary rocks

We often think of rocks as being eternal—indeed, they do last a long time. But even the most resistant polished granite eventually succumbs to the effects of physical and chemical weathering. Next time you're in an old stone granite building, take a look at the steps, even the inside ones. Chances are you'll notice some wear. Constant traffic may account for some of it, but even more may be attributed to their use on rainy days and to repeated cleanings with solutions. In most environments, chemical wear is greater than physical wear. Granite rocks solidified under high pressures and rather high temperatures within the earth. At the surface, pressure and temperature are lower and the rock's chemical environment is different, and in this environment it is unstable. The rocks weather and are gradually transported to a place of deposition. This place may be a lake in the High Sierra, a closed basin with no outlet such as the Mono Lake basin, an open structure such as the great Central Valley, or even the continental shelf of the Pacific Ocean. The rocks formed of the sediment that collects in these basins are called sedimentary rocks.

Most sedimentary rocks are classified by the size of their particles: clay that has been compacted and cemented forms *shale*; silt forms *siltstone*, and sand forms *sandstone*. Sandstone derived from granitic rock superficially resembles its parent rock, but if you look closely you'll notice that the grains are somewhat rounded and that the spaces between the grains are usually filled with a cement, usually calcite. Pebbles, cobbles and boulders may be cemented in a sand or gravel matrix to form a *conglomerate*. If these particles are deposited on an *alluvial fan* and then gradually cemented together to form a hard rock, collectively they become *fanglomerate*. Alluvial fans are usually formed when a stream debouches from the mouth of a canyon and drops its sedimentary load, or alluvium, over a fan-shaped area. Alluvial fans are seen along the south edge of the Mojave Desert, where it abuts the north base of the San Bernardino and the San Gabriel mountains. If the larger particles in a conglomerate or fanglomerate are angular rather than rounded, the sedimentary rock is called a *breccia*.

Limestone, another type of sedimentary rock, is formed in some marine environments as a chemical precipitate of dissolved calcium carbonate or from fragments of shells, corals and foraminifers. The individual grains are usually microscopic. If the calcium in limestone is partly replaced, the result is *dolomite*.

Since the PCT attempts to follow a crest, you'll usually find yourself in an area being eroded, rather than in a basin of deposition, so you'll find very ephemeral sediments or very old ones. The young ones may be in the form of alluvium, talus slopes, glacial moraines or lake sediments. The old ones are usually resistant sediments that the intruding granitic plutons bent (*folded*), broke (*faulted*) and changed (*metamorphosed*).

Feldspar phenocrysts   **Gneiss**   **Marble cave**

Metamorphic rocks

A volcanic or sedimentary rock which undergoes enough alteration (metamorphism) due to heat and pressure that it loses its original characteristics becomes a *metavolcanic* or *metasedimentary* rock. Metamorphism may be slight or it may be complete. A shale undergoing progressive metamorphism becomes first a *slate,* second a *phyllite,* then a *schist.* The slate resembles the shale but is noticeably harder. The schist bears little resemblance and is well-foliated with flaky minerals such as biotite or other micas clearly visible.

Hornfels is a hard, massive rock, common in parts of the High Sierra, formed by contact of an ascending pluton with the overlying sediments. It can take on a variety of forms. You might find one that looks and feels like a slate, but it differs in that it breaks across the sediment layers rather than between them.

Gneiss is a coarse-grained metamorphic rock with the appearance of a layered granitic rock. *Quartzite* is a metamorphosed sandstone and resembles the parent rock. The spaces between the grains have become filled with silica, so that now if the rock is broken, the fracture passes through the quartz grains rather than between them as in sandstone. Metamorphism of limestone yields *marble*, which is just a crystalline form of the parent rock. Check out Marble Mountain, in northern California, when you reach it.

Geologic Time

You cannot develop a feeling for geology unless you appreciate the great span of time that geologic processes have had to operate within. A few million years' duration is little more than an instant on the vast geologic time scale (see Geologic Time Table). Within this duration a volcano may be born, die and erode away. Several major "ice ages" may come and go.

A mountain range takes longer to form. Granitic plutons of the Sierra Nevada first made their appearance in the late Jurassic, and intrusion of them continued through most of the Cretaceous, a span of 60 million years. Usually there is a considerable gap in the geologic record between the granitic rocks and the sediments and volcanics that they intrude–often better than 100 million years.

GEOLOGIC TIME TABLE				
Era	**Period**	**Epoch**	**Began** (years ago)	**Duration** (years)
	Quaternary	Holocene	10,000	10,000
		Pleistocene	1,600,000	1,590,000
Cenozoic		Pliocene	5,300,000	3,700,000
		Miocene	23,700,000	18,400,000
	Tertiary	Oligocene	36,600,000	12,900,000
		Eocene	57,800,000	21,200,000
		Paleocene	66,400,000	8,600,000
Mesozoic	Cretaceous	*Numerous*	144,000,000	77,600,000
	Jurassic	*epochs*	208,000,000	64,000,000
	Tertiary	*recognized*	245,000,000	37,000,000
Paleozoic	Permian		286,000,000	41,000,000
	Carboniferous	*Numerous*	360,000,000	74,000,000
	Devonian		408,000,000	48,000,000
	Silurian	*epochs*	438,000,000	30,000,000
	Ordovician		505,000,000	67,000,000
	Cambrian	*recognized*	570,000,000	65,000,000
Precambrian	No defined periods or epochs; oldest known rocks about 3.8 billion years old; Earth's crust solidified about 4.6 billion years ago.			

Source: Simplified version of the Geological Society of America's 1983 Geologic Time Scale, compiled by Dr. Allison R. Palmer

GEOLOGIC HISTORY

With the aid of a geologic section, like the one on the next page, we can reconstruct the geologic history of an area. Our example represents an idealized slice across the Sierra Nevada to reveal the rocks and their relations.

Through dating methods that use radioactive materials, geologists can obtain the absolute ages of the 2 granitic plutons, the andesite flow and the basalt flow, which would likely be Cretaceous, Pliocene and Holocene. The overlying, folded sediments intruded by the plutons would have to be pre-Cretaceous. The metabasalt could be dated, but the age arrived at may be for the time of its metamorphism rather than for its formation. A paleontologist examining fossils from the marble and slate might conclude that these rocks are from the Paleozoic era.

Before metamorphism the Paleozoic slate, quartzite, metabasalt and marble would have been shale, sandstone, basalt and limestone. The shale-sandstone sequence might indicate marine sediments being deposited on a continental shelf, then on a coastal plain. Lack of transitional rocks between the shale and the sandstone leads us to conclude that they were eroded away, creating a gap in the geologic record. We then have an *unconformity* between the 2 *strata* (layers), the upper resting on the *erosional surface* of the lower. The basalt, shale and limestone sequence indicate first localized volcanism followed by a marine then a shallow-water environment.

These Paleozoic rocks remained buried and protected from erosion for eons of time until the intrusion of granitic plutons, associated with regional uplift. Radiometric dating would show that the quartz-monzonite pluton was emplaced before the granodiorite pluton. Field observations would verify this sequence because the latter intrudes the former as well as the overlying sediments. During this period of mountain building, the Paleozoic rocks became folded, metamorphosed and often faulted.

As the range continued to grow, erosion removed much of the Paleozoic rocks, cut into the granodiorite and rounded the topography. Then in the Pliocene volcanic eruptions to the east spewed andesite flows westward down the gentle valleys. In our geologic section, a remnant of a flow, resting on the bottom of a granitic valley, is preserved today as a high ridge.

Uplift quickly followed this volcanism as faults developed along the east side of the range, and it tipped westward. This tipping caused the andesite flow to have a steeper apparent gradient than it had when it solidified. These faults were mostly more or less vertical, unlike the horizontal direction of the right-lateral San Andreas Fault (during an earthquake, objects on the opposite side of the fault appear to shift to the right). Most faults exhibit a combination of vertical and horizontal movement. Since the fault in this section does not offset the lateral *moraine*, it must have stopped its activity before the Pleistocene. (Note that this is not a true section, since it has a dimension of width: the lateral moraine alongside the canyon floor, included for illustrative purposes, is really beneath the plane of the paper.)

During the Pleistocene epoch, glaciers carved and scoured the canyon east of the high peak, and they deposited massive boulders and other debris along their sides and end. Today we see this preserved evidence of glaciation as lateral and terminal moraines. The steep-walled *cirque* and its bedrock lake (*tarn*) together with a moraine-dammed lake, are further signs of glaciation.

After this Ice Age a cinder cone erupted and partly overlapped the terminal moraine, thereby indicating that it is younger. A radiometric date would verify its youth. Erosion is attacking the range today, as it did in the past, ever seeking to reduce the landscape to sea level.

When you encounter a contact between 2 rocks along the trail, you might ask yourself: Which rock is younger? Which older? Has faulting, folding or metamorphism occurred? Is there a gap in the geologic record? When you can begin to answer these questions, you'll feel a great satisfaction as you slowly solve this great geologic jigsaw puzzle.

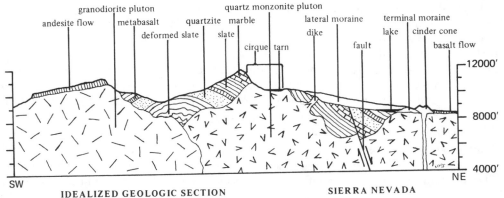

IDEALIZED GEOLOGIC SECTION   SIERRA NEVADA

Biology

One's first guess about the Pacific Crest Trail–a high adventure rich in magnificent alpine scenery and sweeping panoramas–turns out to be incorrect along some parts of the trail. The real-life trail hike will sometimes seem to consist of enduring many repetitious miles of hot, dusty roads, battling hordes of mosquitoes, or slogging up seemingly endless switchbacks. If you find yourself bogged down in such unpleasant impressions, it may be because you haven't developed an appreciation of the natural history of this remarkable route. As there is a great variety of minerals, rocks, landscapes and climates along the PCT, so also is there a great variety of plants and animals.

Even if you don't know much about basic ecology, you can't help noticing that the natural scene along the Pacific Crest Trail changes with elevation. The most obvious changes are in the trees, just because trees are the most obvious–the largest–organisms. Furthermore, they don't move around, hide, or migrate in their lifetime, as do animals. When you pay close attention, you notice that not only the trees but the shrubs, flowers and grasses also change with elevation. Then you begin to find altitudinal differences in the animal populations. In other words, there are different *life zones*.

Life zones. In 1894 C. Hart Merriam divided North America into 7 broad ecosystems, which he called "life zones." These zones were originally based primarily on temperature, though today they are based on the distribution of plants and animals. The zones correspond roughly with latitude, from the Tropical Zone, which stretches from Florida across Mexico, to the Arctic Zone, which includes the polar regions. Between these 2 are found, south to north, the Lower Sonoran, Upper Sonoran, Transition, Canadian and Hudsonian zones. All but the Tropical Zone are encountered along the California PCT.

Just as temperature decreases as you move toward the earth's poles, so too does it decrease as you climb upward–between 3° and 5.5°F for every 1000' elevation gain. Thus, if you were to climb from broad San Gorgonio Pass 10,000' up to the summit of San Gorgonio Mountain, you would pass through all the same zones that you would if you walked from southern California north all the way to Alaska. It turns out that 1000' of elevation are about equivalent to 170 miles of latitude. Although the California PCT is about 1600 miles long, the net northward gain in latitude is *only* about 650 miles–you have to hike 2.5 route miles to get one mile north. This 650-mile change in latitude should bring about the same temperature change as climbing 3800' up a mountain. On the PCT you enter Oregon at 6000' elevation, finding yourself in a dense, Canadian Zone pine-and-fir forest. Doing your arithmetic, you would expect to find an equally dense fir forest at the Mexican border at 3800' higher–at 9800' elevation. Unfortunately, no such elevations exist along the border to test this prediction. However, if we head 85 miles north from the border to the Mt. San Jacinto environs, and subtract 500' elevation to compensate for this new latitude, what do we find at the 9300' elevation? You guessed it, a Canadian Zone pine-and-fir forest. Ah, but nature is not quite that simple.

Plant geography. Every plant (and every animal) has its own *range, habitat* and *niche*. Some species have a very restricted range; others, a very widespread one. The Sequoia, for example, occurs only in about 70 small groves at mid-elevations in the western Sierra Nevada. It flourishes in a habitat of tall conifers growing on shaded, gentle, well-drained slopes. Its niche–its role in the community–consists in its complex interaction with its environment and every other species in its environment. Dozens of insects utilize the Sequoia's needles and cones, and additional organisms thrive in its surrounding soil. The woolly sunflower, on the other hand, has a tremendous range: from California north to British Columbia and east to the Rocky Mountains. It can be found in brushy habitats from near sea level up to 10,000 feet.

Some species, evidently, can adapt to environments and competitors better than others. Nevertheless, each is restricted by a complex interplay of *climatic, physiographic* (topography), *edaphic* (soil) and *biotic* influences.

Climatic influences. Of all influences, temperature and precipitation are probably the most important. Although the mean temperature tends to increase toward the equator, this pattern is camouflaged in California by the dominating effect of the state's highly varied topography. As mentioned earlier, temperature decreases between 3° and 5.5° F for every 1000' gain in elevation, and vegetational changes reflect this cooling trend. For example, the vegetation along San Gorgonio Pass in southern California is adapted to its desert environment. Annuals are very ephemeral; they quickly grow, blossom and die after heavy rains. Perennials are succulent or woody, have deep roots, and have small, hard or waxy leaves–or no leaves at all. Only the lush cottonwoods and other associated species along the dry streambeds hint at a source of water.

As you climb north up the slopes of San Gorgonio Mountain, not only does the temperature drop, but the annual precipitation increases. On the gravelly desert floor below, only a sparse, drought-adapted vegetation survives the searing summer temperatures and the miserly 10'' precipitation. A doubled precipitation on the mountainside allows growth of chaparral, here a thick stand of ocean spray, birchleaf mountain mahogany, Gregg's ceanothus and great-berried manzanita. By 7000' the precipitation has increased to 40'', and the moisture-loving conifers–first Jeffrey pine, then lodgepole pine and white fir–predominate. As the temperature steadily decreases with elevation, evaporation of soil water and transpiration of moisture from plant needles and leaves are both reduced. Furthermore, up here the precipitation may be in the form of snow, which is preserved for months by the shade of the forest, and even when it melts is retained by the highly absorbent humus (decayed organic matter) of the forest soil. Consequently, an inch of precipitation on the higher slopes is far more effective than an inch on the exposed, gravelly desert floor. Similar vegetation changes can be found wherever you make dramatic ascents or descents. In northern California significant elevation and vegetation changes occur as you descend to and then ascend from Highway 70 at Belden, Interstate 5 at Castle Crags State Park and Highway 96 at Seiad Valley.

Physiographic influences. As we have seen, the elevation largely governs the regime of temperature and precipitation. For a *given* elevation, the mean maximum temperature in northern California is about 10° F less than that of the San Bernardino area. Annual precipitation, however, is considerably more; it ranges from about 20'' in the Sacramento Valley to 80'' along the higher slopes, where the snowpack may last well into summer. When you climb out of a canyon in the Feather River country, you start among live oak, poison oak and California laurel, and ascend through successive stands of Douglas-fir and black oak, incense-cedar and ponderosa pine, white fir and sugar pine, then finally red fir, lodgepole and silver pine.

The country near the Oregon border is one of lower elevations and greater precipitation which produces a wetter-but-milder climate that is reflected in the distribution of plant species. Seiad Valley is hemmed in with forests of Douglas-fir, tan oak, madrone and canyon live oak. At higher elevations, mountain chaparral and knobcone pine cover your route. When you reach Cook and Green Pass (4750') you reach a forest of white fir and noble fir. To the east, at higher elevations, you encounter weeping spruce.

A low minimum temperature, like a high maximum one, can determine where a plant species lives, since freezing temperatures can kill poorly adapted plants by causing ice crystals to form in their cells. At high elevations, the gnarled, grotesque trunks of the whitebark, limber and foxtail pines give stark testimony to their battle against the elements. The wind-cropped, short-needled foliage is sparse at best, for the growing season lasts but 2 months, and a killing frost is possible in every month. Samples of this subalpine forest are found on the upper slopes of the higher peaks in the San Jacinto, San Bernardino and San Gabriel mountains and along much of the John Muir Trail. Along or near the High Sierra crest and on the highest Southern California summits, all vestiges of forest surrender to rocky, barren slopes pioneered only by the most stalwart perennials, such as alpine willow and alpine buttercup.

Other physiographic influences are the *location, steepness, orientation* and *shape* of slopes. North-facing slopes are cooler and tend to be wetter than south-facing slopes. Hence, on north-facing slopes, you'll encounter red-fir forests which at the ridgeline abruptly give way to a dense cover of manzanita and ceanothus on south-facing slopes. Extremely steep slopes may never develop a deep soil or support a coniferous forest, and of course cliffs will be devoid of vegetation other than crustose lichens, secluded mosses, scattered annuals and perhaps a tenacious weather-beaten Sierra juniper.

Edaphic influences. Along the northern part of your trek, at the headwaters of the Trinity River and just below Seiad Valley, you'll encounter outcrops of serpentine, California's official state rock. This rock weathers to form a soil poor in some vital plant nutrients but rich in certain undesirable heavy metals. Nevertheless, there are numerous species, such as leather oak, that are specifically or generally associated with serpentine-derived soil. There is a species of streptanthus (mustard family) found only in this soil, even though it can grow better on other soils. However, experiments demonstrate that it cannot withstand the competition of other plants growing on these soils. It therefore struggles, yet propagates, within its protected environment. Another example is at Marble Mountain, also in northern California, which has a local assemblage of plants that have adapted to the mountain's limey soil.

A soil can change over time and with it, the vegetation. If a forest on a slope is burned, the organic layer on the forest floor is destroyed, leaving only charred stumps as tombstones. With no protective cover, the rest of the soil is soon attacked by the forces of erosion. This mute landscape may still receive as much precipitation as a neighboring slope, but its effective precipitation is much less; it will take years to make a recovery. Herbs and shrubs will have to pioneer the slope and slowly build up a humus-rich soil again.

Biotic influences. In an arid environment, plants competing for water may evolve special mechanisms besides their water-retaining mechanisms. The creosote bush, for example, in an effort to preserve its limited supply of water, secretes toxins which prevent nearby seeds from germinating. The result is an economical spacing of bushes along the desert floor.

Competition is manifold everywhere. On a descending trek past a string of alpine lakes, you might see several stages of plant succession. The highest lake may be pristine, bordered only by tufts of grass between the lichen-crusted rocks. A lower lake may exhibit an invasion of grasses, sedges and pondweeds thriving on the sediments deposited at its inlet. Corn lilies and lemmon willows border its edge. Farther down, a wet meadow may be the remnant of a past lake. Water birch and lodgepole pine then make their debut. Finally, you reach the last lake bed, recognized only by the flatness of the forest floor and a few boulders of a recessional moraine (glacial deposit) that dammed the lake. In this location, a thick stand of white fir has overshadowed and eliminated much of the underlying lodgepole.

When a species becomes too extensive, it invites attack. The large, pure stand of lodgepole pine near Tuolumne Meadows has for years been under an unrelenting attack by a moth known as the lodgepole needle-miner. One of the hazards of a pure stand of one species is the inherent instability of the system. Within well-mixed forests, lodgepoles are scattered and the needle miner is not much of a problem. But species need not always compete. Sometimes 2 species cooperate for the mutual benefit, if not the actual existence, of both. That is true of the Joshua tree and its associated yucca moth, which are discussed in the Antelope Valley section of Trail Chapter E.

Unquestionably, the greatest biotic agent is man. For example, he has supplanted native species with introduced species. Most of California's native bunchgrass is gone, together with the animals that grazed upon it, replaced by thousands of acres of one-crop fields and by suburban sprawl. Forests near some mining towns have been virtually eliminated. Others have been subjected to ravenous scars inflicted by man-made fires and by clear-cutting logging practices. The Los Angeles basin's smog production has already begun to take its toll of mountain conifers, and Sierra forests may soon experience a similar fate. Wide-scale use of pesticides has not eliminated the pests, but it has greatly reduced the pests' natural predators. Through forestry, agriculture and urban practices, man has attempted to simplify nature, and by upsetting its checks and balances has made it unstable. Along the Pacific Crest Trail, you'll see areas virtually unaffected by man as well as areas greatly affected by man. When you notice the difference, you'll have something to ponder as you stride along the quiet trail.

The role of fire. Fires were once thought to be detrimental to the overall well-being of the ecosystem, and early foresters attempted to prevent or subdue all fires. This policy led to the accumulation of thick litter, dense brush and overmature trees–all of them prime fuel for a holocaust when a fire inevitably sparked to life. Man-made fires can be prevented, but how does one prevent a lightning fire, so common in the Sierra?

The answer is that fires should not be prevented, but only regulated. Natural fires, if left unchecked, burn stands of mixed conifers about once every 10 years. At this frequency, brush and litter do not accumulate sufficiently to result in a damaging forest fire; only the ground cover is burned over, while the trees remain intact. Hence, through small burns, the forest is protected from flaming catastrophes.

Some pines are adapted to fire. The lodgepole pine, for example, releases its seeds after a fire, as do numbers of shrubs and wildflowers. Particularly adapted to fires, if not dependent on them, are plants of Southern California's chaparral community, which is discussed in the introductory section of Trail Chapter B. But in the Sierra and other high ranges, fire is important too. For example, seeds of the genus *Ceanothus* are quick to germinate in burned-over ground, and some plants of this genus are among the primary foods of deer. Hence, periodic burns will keep a deer population at its maximum. With too few burns, shrubs become too woody and unproductive for a deer herd. In like manner, gooseberries and other berry plants sprout after fires and help support several different bird populations.

Without fires, a plant community evolves toward a *climax*, or end stage of plant succession. Red fir is the main species in the climax vegetation characteristic of higher forests in California's mountains. A pure stand of any species, as mentioned earlier, invites epidemic attacks and is therefore unstable. Fire promotes stability by giving the nonclimax vegetation a chance to get rooted.

Fire also unlocks nutrients that are stored up in living matter, topsoil and rocks. Vital compounds are released in the form of ash when a fire burns plants and forest litter. Fires also can heat granitic rocks enough to cause them to break up and release their minerals. In one study of a coniferous forest, it was concluded that the weathering of granitic rock in that area was primarily due to periodic fires. This may be true even in the high desert. For example, in Anza-Borrego Desert State Park a large fire ravaged many of its granitic slopes, and a post-fire inspection revealed that the fire was intense enough to cause thin sheets of granite to exfoliate, or sheet off, from granitic boulders.

Natural, periodic fires, then, can be very beneficial for a forest ecosystem, and they should be thought of as an integral process in the plant community. They have, after all, been around as long as terrestrial life has, and for millions of years have been a common process in the California plant communities.

Plant communities and their animal associates. As you can see, plant communities are quite complex and the general Life Zone system fails to take into account California's diverse climates and landscapes. Consequently, we'll elaborate on the biological scenario by looking at California's plant communities. Phillip Munz, California's leading native-plant authority, uses the term *plant community* "for each regional element of the vegetation that is characterized by the presence of certain dominant species." Using this criterion, we devised our own list of California plant communities, which differs somewhat from the list proposed by Munz. We found that for the PCT, the division between Red Fir Forest and Lodgepole Pine Forest was an artificial one. True, you can find large, pure stands of either tree, but very often they are found together and each has extremely similar associated plant and animal species. For the same reason we grouped Douglas-Fir Forest with Mixed Evergreen Forest. Finally, we've added 2 new communities that are not recognized by Munz, though they are recognized by other biologists: Mountain Chaparral and Mountain Meadow, each being significantly different from its lowland counterpart. Certainly, there is overlapping of species between adjacent communities, and any classification system can be quite arbitrary. Regardless of how you devise a California plant community table, you'll discover that along the PCT you'll encounter over half of the state's total number of communities–only the coast ranges and eastern desert communities are not seen.

As mentioned earlier, each species has its own range, which can be very restricted or very widespread. Birds typically have a wide–usually seasonal–range, and therefore may be found in many plant communities. In the following table we've listed only the plants and animals that have restricted ranges, that is, they generally occur in only one-to-several communities. Of the thousands of plant species we reviewed for this table, we found most of them failed to serve as indicator species since they either inhabited too many plant communities or they grew in too small a geographic area. Terrestrial vertebrates pose a similar classification problem. For example, in the majority of the PCT plant communities you can find the Oregon junco, robin, raven, mule deer, coyote, badger and Pacific treefrog, so we didn't include them in the table.

The following table of plant communities will be useless if you can't recognize the plants and animals you see along the trail. Our trail description suggests plant communities, such as "you hike through a ponderosa-pine forest." This would clue you into plant community #11, and by referring to it, you could get an idea of what plants and animals you'll see in it. But then, you'll need a guidebook or two to identify the various plants and animals. We have a few suggestions. If you can spare the luxury of carrying 12 extra ounces in your pack, then obtain a copy of Storer's *Sierra Nevada Natural History*, which identifies over 270 plants and 480 animals. Although it is dated and overdue for revision, it is the only general book on the subject. Not only does it provide identifying characteristics of plant and animal species, but it also describes their habits and gives other interesting facts. Its title is misleading, for it is generally applicable to about three-fourths of the California PCT route: Mt. Laguna, the San Jacinto, San Bernardino and San Gabriel mountains, and from the Sierra Nevada north almost continuously to the Oregon border. To better appreciate Southern California, read Jaeger's much smaller book, *Introduction to the Natural History of Southern California*. Covering the same geographic range as Storer's book, and taking only 12 ounces is Weeden's *A Sierra Nevada Flora*. Essentially a condensation of Munz's 4½-pound *A California Flora and Supplement,* this excellent volume easily surpasses all other current Sierra-wildflower books in comprehensiveness. Furthermore, it includes ferns, shrubs, trees and also plant uses. For a 4-ounce pocket book, take Keator's *Sierra Flower Finder*. Finally, if you're doing all three states, bring Niehaus and Ripper's *Pacific States Wildflowers,* which has almost 1500 species.

Plant Communities of California's Pacific Crest Trail

1. Creosote Bush Scrub
Shrubs: creosote bush, bladderpod, brittle bush, burroweed, catclaw, indigo bush, mesquite
Cacti: Bigelow's cholla, silver cholla, Calico cactus, beaver tail cactus, Banning prickly pear, desert barrel cactus

Wildflowers: desert mariposa, prickly poppy, peppergrass, desert primrose, spotted langloisia, desert aster, Mojave buckwheat

Mammals: kit fox, black-tailed jack rabbit, antelope ground squirrel, Mojave ground squirrel, desert kangaroo rat, Merriam's kangaroo rat, cactus mouse, little pocket mouse

Birds: roadrunner, Gambel's quail, LeConte's thrasher, cactus wren, phainopepla, Say's phoebe, black-throated sparrow, Costa's hummingbird

Reptiles: spotted leaf-nosed snake, coachwhip, western blind snake, Mojave rattlesnake, western diamondback rattlesnake, chuckwalla, desert iguana, collared lizard, zebra-tailed lizard, long-tailed brush lizard, desert tortoise

Amphibian: red spotted toad

Where seen along PCT: base of Granite Mountains, southern San Felipe Valley, San Gorgonio Pass, lower Whitewater Canyon, Cajon Canyon, L.A. Aqueduct in Antelope Valley, Butter-bredt Canyon

2. Shadescale Scrub

Shrubs: shadescale, blackbush, hop sage, winter fat, bud sagebrush, spiny menodora, cheese bush

Mammals: kit fox, black-tailed jack rabbit, antelope ground squirrel, desert wood rat, desert kangaroo rat, Merriam's kangaroo rat

Bird: black-throated sparrow

Reptiles: gopher snake, Mojave rattlesnake, zebra-tailed lizard

Where seen along PCT: western Mojave desert north of Mojave, lower Jawbone Canyon

3. Sagebrush Scrub

Shrubs: basin sagebrush, blackbush, rabbit brush, antelope brush (bitter brush), purple sage, Mojave yucca

Mammals: kit fox, white-tailed hare, pigmy rabbit, least chipmunk, Merriam's kangaroo rat, Great Basin pocket mouse

Birds: green-tailed towhee, black-chinned sparrow, sage sparrow, Brewer's sparrow

Reptiles: side-blotched lizard, desert horned lizard, leopard lizard

Where seen along PCT: Doble Road, Soledad Canyon, southern Antelope Valley, terrain near Pinyon Mountain

4. Valley Grassland

Grasses, native: bunch grass, needle grass, three-awn grass

Grasses, introduced: brome grass, fescue, wild oats, fox tail

Wildflowers: California poppy, common muilla, California golden violet, Douglas meadow foam, Douglas locoweed, whitewhorl lupine, Kellogg's tarweed, redstem storksbill (filaree), roundleaf storksbill

Mammals: kit fox, Heermann's kangaroo rat, California meadow mouse

Birds: horned lark, western meadowlark, burrowing owl, Brewer's blackbird, savannah sparrow

Reptile: racer

Amphibians: western spadefoot toad, tiger salamander

Where seen along PCT: Buena Vista Creek area, Big Tree Trail near Sierra Pelona Ridge, Dowd Canyon, Seiad Valley (manmade grassland)

5. Chaparral

Trees: big-cone spruce, digger pine, interior live oak

Shrubs: chamise, scrub oak, birch-leaved mountain mahogany, chaparral whitethorn, Gregg's ceanothus, bigpod ceanothus, hoaryleaf ceanothus, bigberry manzanita, eastwood manzanita, Mexican manzanita, Parry's manzanita, pink-bracted manzanita, toyon, ocean spray, holly-leaf cherry, California coffee berry, redberry, coyote brush (chaparral broom)

Wildflowers: California poppy, fire poppy, Parish's tauschia, charming centaury, Cleveland's monkey flower, Fremont's monkey flower, scarlet bugler, Martin's paintbrush, foothill pen-stemon, Coulter's lupine, buckwheat spp.

Mammals: gray fox, brush rabbit, Merriam's chipmunk, dusky-footed wood rat, nimble kangaroo rat, California mouse, California pocket mouse

Birds: turkey vulture, California quail, scrub jay, California thrasher, green-tailed towhee, brown towhee, rufous-sided towhee, orange-crowned warbler, Lazuli bunting, blue-gray gnatcatcher, wrentit, bushtit

Reptiles: striped racer, western rattlesnake, western fence lizard, southern alligator lizard, coast horned lizard

Where seen along PCT: Mexican border, Hauser Mountain, Fred Canyon, Monument Peak, Chariot Canyon, Agua Caliente Creek, Combs Peak, Table Mountain, upper Penrod Canyon, middle Whitewater Canyon, Crab Flats Road, west slopes above Silverwood Lake, west of Pinyon Flats, Fountainhead Spring, North Fork Saddle, Soledad Canyon, Leona Divide, Spunky Canyon, Sawmill and Liebre mountains, Lamont Canyon to north of Kennedy Meadows

6. Joshua Tree Woodland

Trees: Joshua tree (tree-like stature, but really a yucca), California juniper, single-leaved pinyon pine

Shrubs: Mojave yucca, Utah juniper, box thorn, bladder sage, saltbush

Wildflowers: wild buckwheat, rock echeveria, rock five-finger, heart-leaved jewel flower, coiled locoweed, pigmy-leaved lupine, Parish's monkey flower, mouse-tail, Mojave pennyroyal, two-colored phacelia, tetradymia

Mammals: kit fox, antelope ground squirrel, desert wood rat, Merriam's kangaroo rat, white-eared pocket mouse

Birds: pinyon jay, loggerhead shrike, Scott's oriole, Bendire's thrasher

Reptiles: Mojave rattlesnake, California Lyre snake, desert night lizard, desert spiny lizard, desert tortoise

Amphibian: red-spotted toad

Where seen along PCT: middle Whitewater Canyon, Nelson Ridge, Antelope Valley, western Mojave Desert, Jawbone Canyon, Walker Pass

7. Pinyon-Juniper Woodland

Trees: single-leaved pinyon pine, California juniper

Shrubs: Utah juniper, scrub oak, Mojave yucca, basin sagebrush, blackbush, box thorn, curl-leaved mountain mahogany, antelope brush, ephedra

Wildflowers: rock buckwheat, Wright's buckwheat, golden forget-me-not, adonis lupine, yellow paintbrush, Hall's phacelia

Mammals: black-tailed jack rabbit, California ground squirrel, Merriam's chipmunk, southern pocket gopher, pinyon mouse

Birds: pinyon jay, rock wren, poor-will, California thrasher, gray vireo, black-throated gray warbler, ladder-backed woodpecker

Reptiles: speckled rattlesnake, Mojave rattlesnake, leopard lizard, sagebrush lizard, western fence lizard, desert spiny lizard, coast horned lizard, Gilbert's skink

Amphibian: red-spotted toad

Where seen along PCT: just south of Burnt Rancheria Campground, Onyx Summit, Camp Oakes, Van Dusen Canyon, West Fork Mojave River, Pinyon Mountain to west of Kennedy Meadows

8. Northern Juniper Woodland

Trees: western juniper, single-leaved pinyon pine, Jeffrey pine

Shrubs: basin sagebrush, antelope brush, rabbit brush, curl-leaved mountain mahogany

Wildflowers: sagebrush buttercup, ballhead ipomopsis, three-leaved locoweed, Humboldt's milk-weed, western puccoon, sagebrush Mariposa tulip

Mammals: least chipmunk, Great Basin kangaroo rat, sagebrush vole

Birds: sage grouse, pinyon jay, sage thrasher, northern shrike, gray flycatcher, sage sparrow

Reptiles: striped whipsnake, sagebrush lizard, short-horned lizard

Amphibian: Great Basin spadefoot toad

Where seen along PCT: Kennedy Meadows, Little Pete and Big Pete meadows, upper Noble Canyon, much of the volcanic landscape between Highways 108 and 50, Hat Creek Rim, Buckhorn Mountain

9. Southern Oak Woodland

Trees: coast live oak, Englemann oak, interior live oak, California juniper, Coulter pine, digger pine, big-cone spruce, California black walnut

Shrubs: sugar bush, lemonade-berry, gooseberry, bigberry manzanita, fremontia, squaw bush

Wildflowers: elegant clarkia, slender eriogonum, wild oats, California Indian pink, golden stars, wild mountain sunflower, Kellogg's tarweed, Douglas locoweed, Douglas violet

Mammals: gray fox, raccoon, western gray squirrel, dusky-footed wood rat, brush mouse, California mouse

Birds: California quail, acorn woodpecker, scrub jay, mourning dove, Lawrence's goldfinch, common bushtit, black-headed grosbeak, plain titmouse, Nuttall's woodpecker, western wood peewee, band-tailed pigeon, red-shouldered hawk

Reptiles: California mountain kingsnake, Gilbert's skink, western fence lizard, southern alligator lizard

Amphibians: California newt, California slender salamander, arboreal salamander

Where seen along PCT: Lake Morena County Park, Cottonwood Valley, Flathead Flats, Barrel Spring, Cañada Verde, Warner Springs, Tunnel Spring, Vincent Gap, Three Points, upper Tie Canyon, Mt. Gleason, Big Oak Spring, San Francisquito Canyon

10. Douglas-Fir/Mixed Evergreen Forest

Trees: Douglas-fir, tanbark-oak, madrone, bay tree, big-leaf maple, canyon oak, black oak, yew, golden chinquapin

Shrubs: Pacific blackberry, California coffee berry, Oregon grape, poison oak, wood rose, salal, Fremont's silk-tassel

Wildflowers: California pitcher plant, Indian pipe, striped coralroot, American pine sap, sugar stick, giant trillium, long-tailed ginger, one-sided wintergreen, wedge-leaved violet, California skullcap, grand hounds-tongue, Bolander's hawkweed

Mammals: black bear, porcupine, long-eared chipmunk, Townsend's chipmunk, red tree mouse

Birds: winter wren, hermit thrush, golden-crowned kinglet, purple finch, brown creeper, chestnut-backed chickadee

Reptiles: rubber boa, northern alligator lizard, western pond turtle

Amphibians: northwestern salamander, rough-skinned newt

Where seen along PCT: Middle Fork Feather River canyon, North Fork Feather River canyon, Pit River canyon, Sacramento River canyon, lower Grider Creek canyon, lower slopes around Seiad Valley, Cook and Green Pass, Mt. Ashland Road 20

11. Ponderosa Pine Forest

Trees: ponderosa pine, sugar pine, Jeffrey pine, incense-cedar, white fir, Douglas-fir, black oak, mountain dogwood, grand fir

Shrubs: deer brush, greenleaf manzanita, Mariposa manzanita, mountain misery, western azalea, Scouler's willow, spice bush

Wildflowers: elegant brodiaea, spotted coralroot, draperia, rigid hedge nettle, Indian hemp, slender iris, leopard lily, grand lotus, dwarf lousewort, Sierra onion, Yosemite rock cress, shy Mariposa tulip

Mammals: black bear, mountain lion, mountain beaver, porcupine, western gray squirrel, golden-mantled ground squirrel, yellow-pine chipmunk, mountain pocket gopher

Birds: Steller's jay, hairy woodpecker, white-headed woodpecker, western tanager, band-tailed pigeon, pigmy nuthatch, western bluebird, flammulated owl

Reptiles: rubber boa, California mountain kingsnake, western rattlesnake, western fence lizard

Amphibians: foothill yellow-legged frog, ensatina

Where seen along PCT: Laguna Mountains, upper West Fork Palm Canyon, Apache Spring, upper Whitewater Canyon, much of the Big Bear Lake area, most of the San Gabriel Mountains, Piute Mountain, Haypress Creek, Chimney Rock, Burney Falls, lower Rock Creek, Castle Crags, lower slopes of Lower Devils Peak

12. Mountain Chaparral

Trees: Jeffrey pine, sugar pine, western juniper

Shrubs: huckleberry oak, snow bush, tobacco brush, greenleaf manzanita, bush chinquapin

Wildflowers: showy penstemon, dwarf monkeyflower, hounds-tongue hawkweed, pussy paws, mountain jewel flower, golden brodiaea

Mammals: bushy-tailed wood rat, brush mouse

Birds: mountain quail, dusky flycatcher, fox sparrow, green-tailed towhee

Reptiles: western rattlesnake, sagebrush lizard

Where seen along PCT: near Tahquitz Peak, near Strawberry Cienaga, in small areas from north of Walker Pass to Cow Canyon, above Blaney Hot Springs, slopes north of Benson Lake, upper North Fork American River canyon, Sierra Buttes, Bucks Summit, slopes west of Three Lakes, lower Emigrant Trail, upper Hat Creek Valley, Pigeon Hill, above Seven Lakes Basin, slopes south of Kangaroo Lake, South Russian Creek canyon, upper Right Hand Fork canyon, south slopes of Lower Devils Peak and Middle Devils Peak, between Lily Pad Lake and Cook and Green Pass, Mt. Ashland Road 20

13. Mountain Meadow

Shrubs: arroyo willow, yellow willow, mountain alder

Wildflowers: California corn lily, wandering daisy, elephant's head, tufted gentian, Douglas knotweed, monkshood, swamp onion, Lemmon's paintbrush, meadow arnica, mountain carpet clover, California cone flower, Gray's lovage, Kellogg's lupine, meadow monkey flower, tall phacelia, Jeffrey's shooting star, Bigelow's sneezeweed

Mammals: Belding's ground squirrel, California meadow mouse, long-tailed meadow mouse, deer mouse, ornate shrew

Birds: marsh hawk, Lincoln's sparrow, white-crowned sparrow, Brewer's blackbird

Amphibians: mountain yellow-legged frog, Yosemite toad

Where seen along PCT: Little Tahquitz Valley, Vidette Meadow, Grouse Meadows, Evolution Valley, Tully Hole, Tuolumne Meadows, Grace Meadow, upper Truckee River canyon, Benwood Meadow, Haypress Meadows, Corral Meadow, Badger Flat, Shelly Meadows, Donomore Meadows, Sheep Camp Spring area, Grouse Gap

14. Red Fir/Lodgepole Pine Forest

Trees: red fir, Shasta red fir, noble fir, lodgepole pine, silver pine (western white pine), Jeffrey pine, aspen, mountain hemlock, weeping spruce

Shrubs: pinemat manzanita, bush chinquapin, snow bush, red heather, Labrador tea, mountain spiraea, caudate willow, MacKenzie's willow, Scouler's willow, black elderberry, thimbleberry

Wildflowers: snow plant, pine drops, nodding microseris, broadleaf lupine, western spring beauty

Mammals: black bear, red fox, mountain beaver, porcupine, yellow-bellied marmot, golden-mantled ground squirrel, lodgepole chipmunk, mountain pocket gopher

Birds: blue grouse, great gray owl, mountain chickadee, red-breasted nuthatch, dusky flycatcher, olive-sided flycatcher, Williamson's sapsucker, black-backed three-toed woodpecker, ruby crowned kinglet, Cassin's finch

Where seen along PCT: upper Little Tahquitz Valley, upper San Bernardino Mountains, Mt. Baden-Powell, Kern Plateau, lower portions of John Muir Trail, much of northern Yosemite, most of the stretch from Yosemite to central Lassen Volcanic National Park, Bartle Gap, Grizzly Peak, most of the trail from Seven Lakes Basin to Mt. Ashland

15. Subalpine forest

Trees: whitebark pine, foxtail pine, limber pine, lodgepole pine, mountain hemlock

Shrubs: Sierra willow, Eastwood's willow, white heather, bush cinquefoil

Wildflowers: Eschscholtz's buttercup, Coville's columbine, mountain monkey flower, Suksdorf's monkey flower, Sierra penstemon, Sierra primrose, mountain sorrel, cut-leaved daisy, silky raillardella, rock fringe

Mammals: red fox, yellow-bellied marmot, pika, Douglas squirrel (chickaree), alpine chipmunk, heather vole, water shrew
Birds: Clark's nutcracker, mountain bluebird, mountain chickadee, Williamson's sapsucker
Amphibian: Mt. Lyell salamander
Where seen along PCT: Mt. Baden-Powell summit, much of the Sierra Nevada (above 10,000' in the southern part, above 8,000' in the northern part), higher elevations in Marble Mountain Wilderness

16. Alpine Fell-Fields
Shrubs: alpine willow, snow willow
Wildflowers: alpine gold, Sierra pilot, alpine paintbrush, alpine sandwort, ruby sandwort, dwarf lewisia, dwarf ivesia, Muir's ivesia, Brewer's draba, feeble saxifrage, Sierra primrose
Mammals: pika, alpine chipmunk
Birds: gray-crowned rosy finch, mountain bluebird, rock wren
Where seen along PCT: at and just below the following passes: Forester Pass, Glen Pass, Pinchot Pass, Mather Pass, Selden Pass, Silver Pass, Donohue Pass

A final word. Plant communities aren't the final word in plant-animal classification, since each community could be further subdivided. For example, Edmund Jaeger divides the desert environment into even more compartments than Munz does, including Desert San Dunes, Desert Wash, Salt Water Lake (Salton Sea), Desert Canal, Colorado River Bottom, Desert Urban and Desert Rural. Farther north, in a glaciated basin near Yosemite's Tioga Pass, Lionel Klikoff has identified 8 vegetational patterns within the Subalpine Forest plant community, each distribution pattern the result of a different set of microenvironmental influences. Once you start looking and thinking about organisms and their environments, you'll begin to see that all is not a group of random species. There is continual interaction between similar organisms, between different organisms and between organisms and their environment. They are there because they fit into the dynamic ecosystem; they are adapted to it; they belong.

Chapter 4: Using This Guide

Our Route Description

The bulk of this guide is composed of route description and accompanying topographic maps of the Pacific Crest Trail. In 18 section chapters this guide covers the California PCT from the Mexican border north to Interstate 5 in southern Oregon. We have divided the route description into sections because the vast majority of PCT hikers will be hiking only a part of the trail, not all of it. Each section starts at or near a highway and/or supply center (town, resort, park) and ends at another similar point. The one exception is the end of Section G and start of Section H, which occurs where the Pacific Crest Trail joins the John Muir Trail near Crabtree Meadows. From this point most PCT hikers will go east to climb Mt. Whitney and perhaps descend to Lone Pine to resupply. We also chose this break point because many hikers skip southern California and start their PCT hiking on the John Muir Trail–this guide's Section H. This section is the only one that is too long for *most* hikers to do without resupplying. All of the other sections are short enough to make comfortable backpack trips ranging from 3 to 10 days. Nevertheless, most of these have resupply points along or close to the actual route, thereby allowing you to carry a little less food.

At the beginning of each section is an introduction that mentions: 1) the attractions and natural features of that section, 2) the declination setting for your compass, 3) a mileage table between points within that section, 4) supply points on or near the route, and 5) special problems. Attractions and natural features will help you decide what part of the trail you'll want to hike–very few do all of California. The declination setting for your compass is important if you have to get a true reading. The declinations vary from 14½°E near the Mexican border to 20°E in southern Oregon. If your compass does not correct for declination, you'll have to add the appropriate declinations vary from 13°E near the Mexican border to 17°E in southern Oregon. If your compass does not correct for declination, you'll have to add the appropriate declination of 15°E, then you should add 15°, getting 90° (due east) as the true bearing of that hill. If you can identify that *hill* on a map, then you can find where *you* are on the PCT by adding 180°, getting 270° (due west) in this example. By drawing a line due west from the hill to the PCT route, you'll determine your position. *No one* should attempt a *major* section of the PCT without a thorough understanding of his compass and of map interpretation.

Each mileage table lists distances between major points found within its PCT section. Both distances between points and cumulative mileages at points are given. We list cumulative mileages south to north *and* north to south so that no matter which direction you are hiking the PCT, you can easily determine the mileages you plan to hike. Many of the points listed in the tables are at or near good campsites. If you typically average 17 miles a day–the on-route rate you'll need to do to complete the tri-state PCT in 5+ months–then you can determine where you should camp to maintain this rate, and you can estimate when you should arrive at certain supply points. Of course, in reality your time schedule may turn out to be quite different from your planned schedule, due to unforeseen circumstances.

At the end of this short chapter we've included a mileage table for the entire California PCT. Any 2 adjacent points represent the start and end of one of this books 18 section chapters. By scanning this table's *distance between points,* you can easily see how long each section is. Then you can pick one or more of appropriate length, turn to that section's introduction, and see if it sounds appealing. Of course, you need not start at the beginning of any section, since a number of roads cross the PCT in most sections. (Sections H and I are exceptions, having only a few access points.)

Supply points on or near the route are mentioned, as well as what you might expect to find at each. You will realize, for example, that you can't get new clothes at Old Station, but can at Burney, the next major settlement. Many supply points are just a post office and/or small store with minimal food supplies. By "minimal" we mean a few odds and ends that typically cater to passing motorists, e.g., beer and potato chips.

Finally, the introduction mentions special problems you might encounter in each section, such as desert thirst, snow avalanches and early-season fords. If you are hiking all of the California PCT, you will be going through some of its sections at very inopportune times and will face many of these problems. Backpackers hiking a short stretch can pick the best time to hike it, and thereby minimize their problems.

When you start reading the text of a PCT section, you will notice that a pair of numbers follows the more important trail points. For example, at Highway 120 in Tuolumne Meadows, this pair is (8595-0.8), which means that you cross this highway at an elevation of 8595 *feet* and at a distance of 0.8 *miles* from your last given point, which in this example is at a junction with a parking-lot spur road. By studying these figures along the section you are hiking, you can easily determine the distance you'll have to hike from point A to point B, and you can get a good idea of how much elevation change is involved. Along this guide's *alternate* routes, which are set aside by asterisks, there are occasional second mileage figures, which represent the distance along the alternate route to that point.

In the trail description, numbers below the columns indicate what maps to refer to. This description of the route also tells something about the country you are walking through—the geology, the biology (plants and animals), the geography, and sometimes a bit of history. After all, you're not hiking the Pacific Crest Trail just to rack up the miles/make your pedometer click/prove your man(woman) (child)hood.

Following the Trail

The "Pacific Crest Trail" is usually trail, sometimes road and rarely cross country. Quite naturally, you want to stay on the route. For that purpose, we recommend relying on the route description and maps in this book. To be sure, there are various markers along the route—PCT emblems and signs (blue and white), California Riding and Hiking Trail posts (brown and yellow) and signs (orange and blue on tree trunks), metal in the shape of diamonds and discs nailed to tree trunks, plastic ribbons tied to branches, and blazes and ducks. (A blaze is a place on a tree trunk where bark has been removed. Typically a blaze is about 4-6 inches in its dimensions. A duck is a small rock placed on a very large boulder or a pile of several small rocks whose placement is obviously unnatural.)

Our route descriptions depend on these markers as little as possible because they are so ephemeral. They get destroyed by loggers, packers, motorbikers, hikers, wilderness purists, bears and other agents. Furthermore, the blazes or ducks you follow, not having any words or numbers, may or not mark the trail you want to be on.

One way to find a junction is to count mileage from the previous junction. If you know the length of your stride, that will help. We have used yards for short horizontal distances because one yard approximates the length of one long stride. Alternatively, you can develop a sense of your ground speed. Then, if it is 1½ miles to the next junction and your speed is 2¼ miles an hour, you should be there in ⅔ hour, or 40 minutes. Be suspicious if you reach an unmarked junction sooner or later than you had expected. We go to great lengths to describe the terrain so that you can be alerted to upcoming junctions. For example, along Lake Aloha in Section K, we mention a pond found 150 yards before a trail junction. Without this visual clue you could easily miss the junction in early season, when snow still obscures many parts of the trail.

The Maps

Each section contains all the topographic maps you'll need to hike that part of the California PCT. All but two of these maps are at a scale of 1:50,000, or about 0.8 mile per inch. The two exceptions are Maps E19 and F6, which show the partly completed PCT route through the Tehachapi Mountains. On the maps the PCT route appears as a solid black line where it exists as a trail and as a dashed black line where it exists along roads. Any alternate route that is set apart in the text by asterisks is also shown on the maps, and it is indicated by an alternating dot-dash black line. Proposed PCT segments and PCT segments under construction are shown as dotted lines. The following legend lists most of the symbols you'll see on this guide's topographic maps.

LEGEND

Heavy-duty road		PCT route along trails
Medium-duty road		PCT route along roads
Improved light-duty road		Authors' alternate route
Unimproved dirt road		Proposed PCT
Jeep road or trail		
Railroad: single track		Year-round streams
Railroad: multiple track		Seasonal streams
Scale of maps, 1:50,000		O I MILE

California PCT Mileage Table

Mileages:	South to North	Distances between Points	North to South
Mexican border near Campo........................	0.0		1706.4
Section A		111.1	
Highway 79 southwest of Warner Springs............	111.1		1595.3
Section B		103.5	
near Interstate 10 in San Gorgonio Pass..............	214.6		1491.8
Section C		132.8	
Interstate 15 near Cajon Pass	347.4		1359.0
Section D		110.2	
Agua Dulce near Antelope Valley Freeway	457.6		1248.8
Section E		99.7	
Highway 58 near Mojave...........................	557.3		1149.1
Section F		69.7	
Highway 178 at Walker Pass........................	627.0		1079.4
Section G		113.5	
John Muir Trail junction...........................	740.5		965.9
Section H		177.2	
Highway 120 in Tuolumne Meadows.................	917.7		788.7
Section I		76.4	
Highway 108 at Sonora Pass........................	994.1		712.3
Section J		75.2	
Echo Lake Resort near Highway 50	1069.3		637.1
Section K		63.7	
trailhead-parking lateral near Interstate 80...........	1133.0		573.4
Section L		38.4	
Highway 49 near Sierra City.......................	1171.4		535.0
Section M		96.2	
Highway 70 at Belden Town bridge	1267.6		438.8
Section N		136.0	
Burney Falls in Burney Falls State Park	1403.6		302.8
Section O		82.4	
Interstate 5 near Castle Crags State Park	1486.0		220.4
Section P		99.8	
Somes Bar-Etna Road at Etna Summit	1585.8		120.6
Section Q		56.1	
Highway 96 at Seiad Valley........................	1641.9		64.5
Section R		64.5	
Interstate 5 near Mt. Ashland Road 20..............	1706.4		0.0

18 Trail Chapters

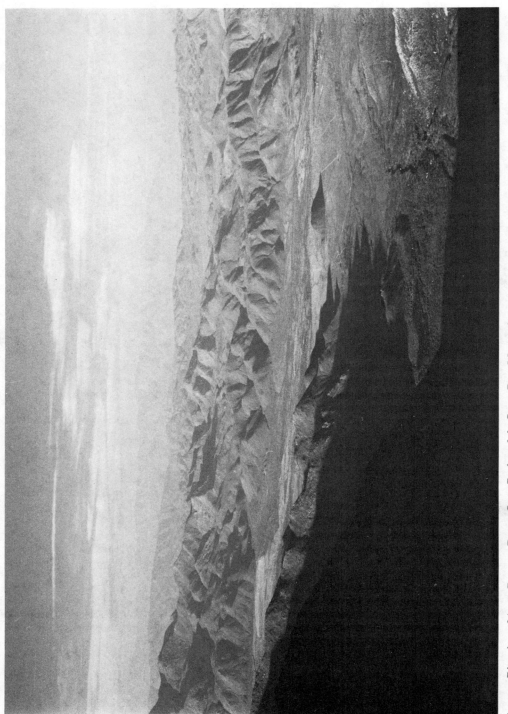

Laguna Rim view of Anza-Borrego Desert State Park and the Santa Rosa Mountains

Section A: Mexican Border to Warner Springs

Introduction: Belying later grandeur, the Pacific Crest Trail begins in scraggly, rather unimpressive chaparral that ill fits most Americans' mental images of our southwest borderlands. Although cacti and sand are encountered often, and late-spring and summer temperatures frequently rise above 100°, the PCT in this section does not traverse true desert, but rather keeps just west of the searing Colorado Desert—which we often glimpse—passing through an area influenced by moist Pacific Ocean air. In fact, at the time when most long-distance hikers will be traversing the southernmost part of the PCT, in April and May, they are quite likely to encounter late-season snowstorms while climbing into the Laguna Mountains. In the Lagunas, which are a fault-block range of granitic rock closely related to the Sierra Nevada geologically, walkers might forget sun and thirst while walking beneath shady oaks and pines also similar to those found in the Sierra. But the next day, as they swoop down to San Felipe Valley, the stifling heat returns as the route enters Anza-Borrego Desert State Park and the Colorado Desert. The furnace breath of this arid land above the Salton Sea follows us as we traverse the San Felipe Hills to Warner Springs.

Declination: 13°E

Mileages:

	South to North	Distance between Points	North to South
Mexican border	0.0		111.1
Campo, near Border Patrol station	1.2	1.2	109.9
Lake Morena County Park	20.1	18.9	91.0
Boulder Oaks Campground	26.0	5.9	85.1
Fred Canyon Road 16S08	32.7	6.7	78.4
Long Canyon	36.9	4.2	74.2
Burnt Rancheria Campground	41.5	4.6	69.6
Stephenson Peak Road to Mt. Laguna	42.8	1.3	68.3
Sunrise Highway near Laguna Campground	47.6	4.8	63.5
Pioneer Mail Picnic Area	52.9	5.3	58.2
jeep track to Cuyamaca Reservoir	62.0	9.1	49.1
detour to water in upper Chariot Canyon	64.4	2.4	46.7
leave Highway 78 in San Felipe Valley	78.6	14.2	32.5
Barrel Spring	102.4	23.8	8.7
Highway 79 southwest of Warner Springs	111.1	8.7	0.0

Supplies: Last-minute supplies may be bought in Campo, 1.2 miles along the walk, but sophisticated camping items still needed must be bought in San Diego before starting out. You can reach Campo via public transit by first taking a city bus from San Diego to El Cajon, then taking a Southeastern Rural Bus, which runs daily, to Campo. Morena Village, with a small store and cafe, lies 0.3 mile off route at Lake Morena County Park, 20 miles into the journey. Mount Laguna, a tiny mountain community with a store, post office, restaurants and motels, is the next opportunity, about 43 miles into the hike. Walkers should carry lots of water from Mount Laguna, for it is a long, blistering 23.4 miles (including a 1.8-mile detour) to springs in Chariot Canyon. And carry a big water container, since from these springs to Barrel Spring is a mind-broiling 39.8 miles! The tourist-oriented, apple-growing ex-mining town of Julian, with stores, restaurants, lodging and post office, lies 12.5 miles west of the PCT where it strikes Highway 78 in San Felipe Valley. Julian is a welcome respite for the PCTer sporting a first set of desert-induced blisters. Warner Springs, at the end of this section, is the next supply point. This little resort community, clustered around a rejuvenating hot spring on the Aguanga Fault, has a post office and private spa but no supplies.

Permits: Wilderness permits are usually required for both day and overnight visits to Hauser Wilderness, through which you briefly pass early in this section. PCT trekkers, however, are exempt. Still, if you'll be heading into future wildernesses on your north-ward trek, then you should get a permit at the Cleveland National Forest's office—see Chapter 1's "wilderness permits" and "Federal Government Agencies."

Rattlesnakes: Few animals are more unjustly maligned in legend and in life than the western rattlesnake, and no other animal, with the possible exception of black bears (see Section I), causes more concern among walkers and riders along the California PCT.

Frequenting warmer climes generally below the red-fir belt (although they have been seen much higher), rattlers will most often be encountered basking on a warm rock, trail or pavement, resting from their task of keeping the rodent population in check. Like other reptiles, rattlesnakes are unable to control their internal body temperature (they are "cold blooded"), and therefore can venture from their underground burrows only when conditions are suitable. Just as rattlers won't usually be seen in freezing weather, it is also no surprise that they are rarely seen in the heat of day, when ground temperatures may easily exceed 150°—enough to cook a snake (or blister human feet, as many will learn). One usually will see rattlers toward evening, when the air is cool but the earth still holds enough heat to stir them from their lethargy for a night of hunting. They naturally frequent those areas where rodents feed—under brush, in rock piles, and at streamsides.

It is their nocturnal hunting equipment that has inspired most of the legends and fears concerning rattlesnakes. Rattlers have heat-sensitive pits, resembling nostrils, in their wedge-shaped heads that can sense nearby changes in temperature as subtle as 1°F. Rattlers use these pits to locate prey at night, since they do not have well-developed night vision. More important perhaps is their sensitivity to vibrations, which can alert a rattler to footfalls over 50' away. With such acute organs to sense a meal or danger, a rattler will usually begin to hurry away long before a hiker spots it. Furthermore, if you do catch one of these reptiles unawares, these gentlemen among poisonous snakes will usually warn you away with buzzing tail rattles if you get too close for comfort.

Like many of man's pest-control projects, his efforts to quell rattlesnake populations has been to his detriment—rattlers are invaluable controllers of agricultural pests, and fewer people are hurt each year by rattlers than by household pets. One unsuccessful program carried out in the 1960s eliminated the conspicuous, noisy rattlers and left the silent ones to breed. A population developed in which the snakes would strike without buzzing. Luckily, most rattlers encountered along your PCT way will gladly move aside without incident.

State Highway 94 leads 50 miles east from San Diego to Campo, where one turns south on Forest Gate Road, which in one block passes a U.S. Border Patrol station, where hikers should check in. The pavement ends beyond Rancho del Campo, and you continue south up the graded road. It jogs east at Castle Rock Ranch, turns south at a **T** junction with a poorer road, then climbs moderately along a telephone line. After passing under a 500 KV powerline, you reach the Mexican border (2895'), marked by a fence and a wide, defoliated swath, this spot lying 1.5 miles south of Highway 94. The steep southern flanks of the Laguna Mountains form the northern horizon, while the low green dome of Hauser Mountain stands in the northwest. The prominent orange buttresses of Morena Butte overlook its northern shoulder.

Walk up and somewhat left for 100 yards to the shoulder of a low knoll. Here at the border fence is a unique wooden monument erected at the southern terminus of the Pacific Crest Trail (2905). Poke a fist through the fence for a feel of *tierra mexicana;* then turn north and start your adventure.

Obvious trail tread, constructed in Fall 1988 by volunteers, leads easily down hill, quickly crossing a graded dirt road that parallels the border. Leaving the clearcut strip, you enter a low, arid chaparral of chamise, sagebrush and ribbonwood, which is punctuated with protruding boulders of bonsall tonalite—a light gray granitic rock. Quickly cross the road we took up to the border (2835-0.1), then parallel it to cross a second time (2805-0.2), just before passing under the San Diego Gas & Electric powerline. Further descent, essentially due north, leads to the southern edge of dry Campo Valley, where we step across an east-west dirt road (2705-0.2). Now the path swings west, passing the northern perimeter of sleepy Castle Rock Ranch to quickly bend back north and cross to the west side of Forest Gate Road (2690-0.2). Walk north easily along the foot of a hillside staying just above the now-paved road, past ranchos del Campo and del Reyo—cavalry camps in World War I and Japanese-American concentration camps in World War II, but now San Diego County boys' camps.

Across from the latter camp's entrance, just up Forest Gate Road from the Border Patrol station, the PCT tread veers northwest, away from the roadside (2600-0.5). Here we are just 75 yards north of a cluster of green bungalows with white trim that stand across Forest Gate Road from the honor ranchos. Before heading off on the PCT, be sure you are adequately provisioned, since the next certain water is at Lake Morena County Park, 18.0 miles away. A post office lies only 2 blocks north, in sleepy, agricultural Campo. A good store lies 0.3 mile north, at the junction of Forest Gate Road and Highway 94. The next supply point is in Mount Laguna, about 41 miles away.

Now turning our attention to the trail, we climb gently from the road, pass a lone live-oak tree, momentarily reach a terrace and then cut obliquely across a road serving the bungalows. Beyond, the sandy path climbs minimally across a brushy slope, then swings southwest at an overlook of Highway 94 and Campo Valley. Paralleling the highway, the PCT undulates over a string of low ridges, comes close to a descending jeep road, then descends easily to a PCT-posted crossing (2475-1.0) of two-lane Highway 94. North of it, the PCT leads counterclockwise around a low hill, then descends into a grove of cottonwoods alongside Campo Creek. Just before crossing that attractive, but seasonal, stream on rickety logs, we ignore a jeep road climbing south. Instead, we follow PCT posts to the northwest bank, then traverse southwest on an alluvial terrace for a few minutes. Presently the route veers uphill, soon to find the abandoned San Diego & Arizona Eastern Railroad's tracks (2475-0.6). We have a gentle ascent as we continue over the tracks and wind westward over the nose of a low ridge. Now in a maze of small gullies and waist-high chamise chaparral, the tread descends gently to a larger ravine, which is just north of the tracks. Here the cool shade of willows and cottonwoods, with an understory of mint and cattails, makes a picturesque lunch spot. Alas, the creeklet here flows only in winter and early spring.

After momentarily coming close to the tracks again, we undertake a longer but still easy

A1, A2

see MAP A3

climb northwest to a low gap. A minute's walk beyond it, we strike a poor jeep road (2550-2.2), which descends in a south-trending valley. Now climbing more in earnest, we swing southwest on Hauser Mountain's broad, sunny slopes, then switchback to find a north-ascending line. The well-built, alternately sandy and rocky path soon rises high enough to afford fine, clear vistas southeast back to the border, and east over a lovely ranch, named Hacienda del Florasol, which lies below Hauser Mountain's eastern escarpment. Pleasant walking leads northwest, more or less level, then the trail abruptly switchbacks up to the south to gain a canyon rim. Here the steep slopes yield to the chaparral-covered summit dome of Hauser Mountain. The path continues south, ascending gently and then passing through a pipe gate to a little-used road (3350-3.7). Beyond it we climb only minutes more before striking a second jeep road (3400-0.2). Next we undertake a contour north, and we can see our trail snaking ahead for over a mile. Umpteen hillside ravines later, we step across an east-descending jeep road (3345-2.0) before winding up to a viewful point (3400-0.5) low on the northeast ridge of Hauser Mountain. To the north and west, an impressive panorama of Hauser Canyon unfolds. On the northern canyon wall stand orange granitic pillars of Morena Butte. This area now lies in one of California's smallest wilderness areas, Hauser Wilderness, created in 1984.

The trail now descends in a northwestern direction along the north face of Hauser Mountain, making a long traverse down-canyon. Presently, we note a road below us, and continue out onto the nose of a low ridge to meet it—South Boundary Road 17S08 (2910-2.7). The permanent PCT route heads southeast on this little-traveled road, first climbing gently and then descending likewise to a junction (2910-0.8) with a 1988-vintage trail segment. This branches left, east, dropping rapidly from the road where it begins to bend north on a rocky hillside. To stay on public lands, but to avoid unnecessary elevation loss, the trail makes a willy-nilly, rocky descent northwestward across the canyon wall, via five switchbacks. Finally, the grade moderates to reach a pleasant glade of live oaks and sycamores. In it, the PCT crosses Hauser Creek (2320-0.7), which is usually flowing in winter and early spring. A small flat just downstream could offer the best first night's camp north of the Mexican

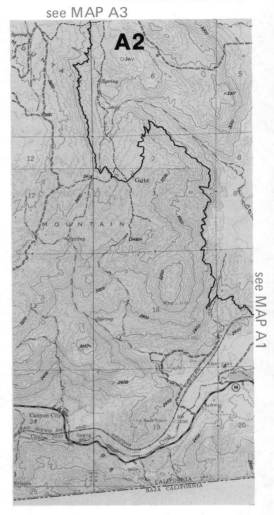

see MAP A1

border for those who are disinclined to make the 1,000' climb to reach Lake Morena County Park. However, beware of cattle pollution of the stream and of plentiful poison oak.

Just across Hauser Creek we find Hauser Creek Road, then cross it to begin an earnest, sweaty ascent of the southern slopes of Morena Butte. The first leg of this climb lies in the southeastern corner of Hauser Wilderness, and it consists of a moderate-to-steep grade through straggly chaparral. As the climb progresses, vistas unfold down-canyon to meadows and to sky-blue Barrett Lake, which is framed by the bluffs of nearby Morena Butte. Switchbacks long and short eventually bring us to a saddle

A2, A3

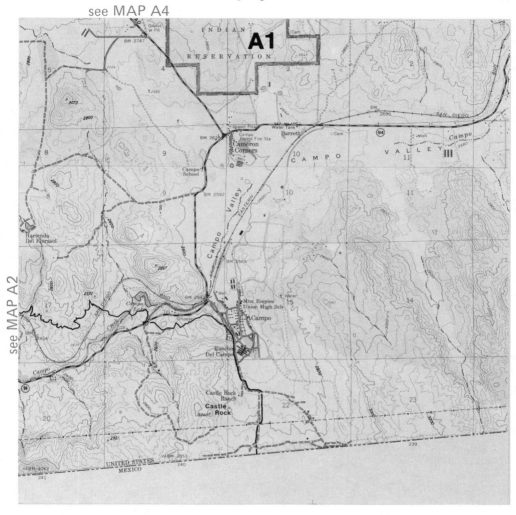

(3210-1.3) on the granitic southeastern spur of Morena Butte. Now the PCT undertakes a traversing descent north, shortly joining and then leaving a jeep trail (3150-0.2), which climbs more directly up from Hauser Canyon. Beyond it, we wind for a minute or two along a dry creek bed, then step across its sandy wash to climb moderately north, then east, through lush mixed chaparral. In spring, the heavy perfume of startling lilac-blue ceanothus shrubs hangs heavy in the air, while a number of red-and-yellow-flowered globe mallows line the trailside. After reaching a low ridgecrest, we climb southeast a bit to a fair viewpoint (3495-1.0), which gives panoramas north over the southern Laguna Mountains.

Now we drop gently east to find a good jeep road in a saddle (3390-0.3). Walk right, east, on the jeep road for 50 yards, then leave it to angle first northeast and then north along a viewful, outcrop-strewn ridge. Eventually the route veers northwest down a chaparral-cloaked nose, then leaves the heights for a descending traverse east to an oak grove and a gate in a barbed-wire fence at the corner of Lake Morena Road and Lakeshore Drive (3065-1.7). Just north is the entrance to Lake Morena County Park. This large facility offers, for a fee, 90 campsites with showers, water, picnic areas, and angling for bass, bluegill and catfish in

A3

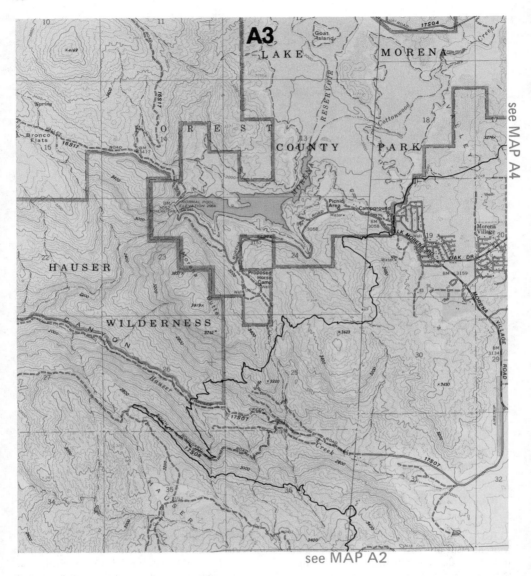

see MAP A4

see MAP A2

Morena Reservoir. A trailhead parking area and a lateral trail ½ mile west to primitive camping are planned for the future. Just 0.3 mile southeast on Lake Morena Road is a malt shop and grocery store.

The PCT continues from the corner of the two paved roads, following Lakeshore Drive north 80 yards to where one steps through a fence to follow a dirt road that traces the campground's perimeter. Beyond the camp area the route becomes trail and continues north to an oak-shaded overlook of Morena Reservoir and its chaparral-cloaked basin. Only 0.1 mile from the campground the path turns east through a gated barbed-wire fence, then curves northward around the upper limits of the fluctuating reservoir. The route next crosses many jeep tracks in the open chamise chaparral as it turns east, then northeast, climbing gently to a low ridgetop (3220-1.5). Now the way drops northeast into a nearby secluded, oak-shaded canyon, hops its seasonal creek, and climbs mod-

see MAP A5

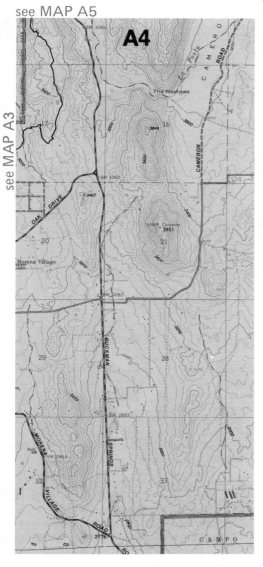

see MAP A3

Creek (3065-2.6). The PCT's ford of the seasonally swollen creek may be too deep. If so, use the road's bridge (BM 3079 on the map) and drop off its west end to find the PCT—an abandoned road. You can camp here, although grazing cattle may have contaminated the creek.

Continuing north, PCT trail tread soon diverges from the roadbed to wind through a pleasant mile of oak stands and dry meadows, always within earshot of Buckman Springs Road. Abruptly the route then veers east and descends to the 0.1-mile wide, sandy-gravelly bed of Cottonwood Creek (3105-1.4). Dry most of the year, the creek in winter and spring may be flowing and may be a couple of yards wide. Across it the trail heads east up a ravine, then joins a steadily improving and climbing jeep road that leads through a gate and over a low ridge to reach the equestrian section of Boulder Oaks Campground (3170-0.4). This pleasant and little-used facility offers picnic tables, piped water, toilets and horse corrals among boulders and shady live oaks. Marked by posts the PCT winds east across the campground, then momentarily goes north to reach paved, 2-lane Boulder Oaks Road (3165-0.1) just south of the campground's entrance. Now walk north along the road's west shoulder to small Boulder Oaks Store (3150-0.3), which offers snack items and limited supplies.

The PCT resumes opposite the store, beginning as a dirt road leading east. Soon becoming trail, the route leads north and then east under two concrete spans of Interstate Highway 8. Just beyond the second bridge, switchbacks climb south to an ascending traverse that heads to a brushy gap. Here the route turns northeast for a long, traversing climb on open, sometimes rocky slopes, eventually finding a position some 100' above the cool, pooling early-season flow of Kitchen Creek. Arcing north around Peak 4382, we then switchback up, east, to find paved Kitchen Creek Road (3990-3.8) on a viewful pass.

The northbound PCT from atop the pass is found beyond a firebreak east of the pavement. Panoramas expand back to the Mexican border and to Cameron Valley as one ascends gently-to-moderately along slopes composed of foliated, red-stained gneiss, colored in season with blossoms of white forget-me-nots. After leveling off momentarily on a 4310' saddle, the trail drops, flanked by nodding, brown-flowered peonies and mixed chaparral, to a glade of oaks

erately east, then southeast, to gain a 3375' ridge with expansive vistas west over the reservoir, Morena Butte and Hauser Mountain. The Laguna Mountains are seen on the northern skyline. You romp easily north on the spine of the ridge in mixed chaparral. After a mile the route makes a traversing descent along the ridge's west flank to a switchback, then to a gate on the ridge's northern nose. You quickly reach Buckman Springs Road S1, which you parallel briefly to its bridge over Cottonwood

A3, A4, A5, A6

see MAP A6

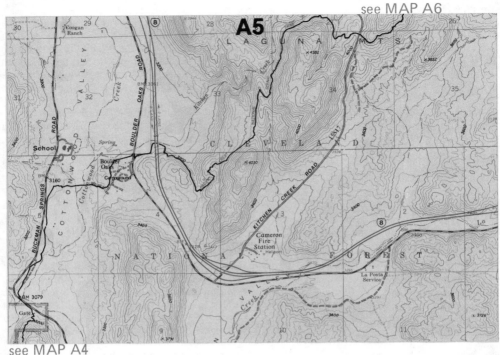

see MAP A4

beside the usually dry creek of Fred Canyon (4205-1.9). Now on the west side of the canyon, the trail ascends to Fred Canyon Road 16S08 (4410-0.6), which descends 0.8 mile northwest to Cibbets Flat Campground with toilets, tables and water.

Now the path climbs moderately in heavy ceanothus/ocean spray/chamise cover, switchbacking once around a nose and then climbing to a traverse past Peak 5036 over to the dry headwaters of Fred Canyon. Next the PCT gains 500', passes a jeep trail east to Fred Canyon Road, and then makes an undulating traverse and a gentle descent into Long Canyon (5230-4.2), where a camp could be made beside a seasonally trickling creek near wild roses. A gentle ascent in this pretty, meadowed canyon, dotted with black oaks, finds a ford (5435-0.8) of Long Canyon creek, followed by switchbacks and two crossings of a jeep road from Horse Meadow. At the second crossing (5900-1.1) you could follow the jeep road northwest 0.3 mile to pretty Lower Morris Meadow, which has a horse-trough spring and a cozy cluster of Jeffrey pines—the best camp so far. The USFS plans an equestrian/backpacker trail camp here in the future.

Climbing still into the relatively cool Laguna Mountains proper, we alternate between mountain mahogany and Jeffrey-pine/black-oak forest to cross a saddle, then descend slightly to a crossing of Morris Ranch Road (6005-1.2). Now routed along duff the PCT descends gently north to cross a dirt road beside shaded La Posta Creek (5825-0.7). Here you'll see outstanding examples of acorn-woodpecker food caches—custom-built niches for individual black-oak and interior-live-oak acorns in Jeffrey pine bark. When tasty insect larvae hatch in the stored acorns, the birds return to feast! Leaving La Posta Creek, the route contours above a pumphouse that in the future may become the site of a backpacker camp. Trekkers should be aware that in the Laguna Mountain Recreation Area camping is restricted to designated sites. The recreation area stretches from near this site north 10.4 miles to Pioneer Mail Picnic Area.

Our trail ascends into the recreation area, passing abandoned wood-rat nests and the first pinyon pines of the trail before reaching the south boundary of Burnt Rancheria Campground (5950-0.8). This has toilets, water and tables. Cattlemen invaded the Laguna Mountains in the later 1800s, fattening their herds to the displeasure of the natives, called "Die-

A6, A7

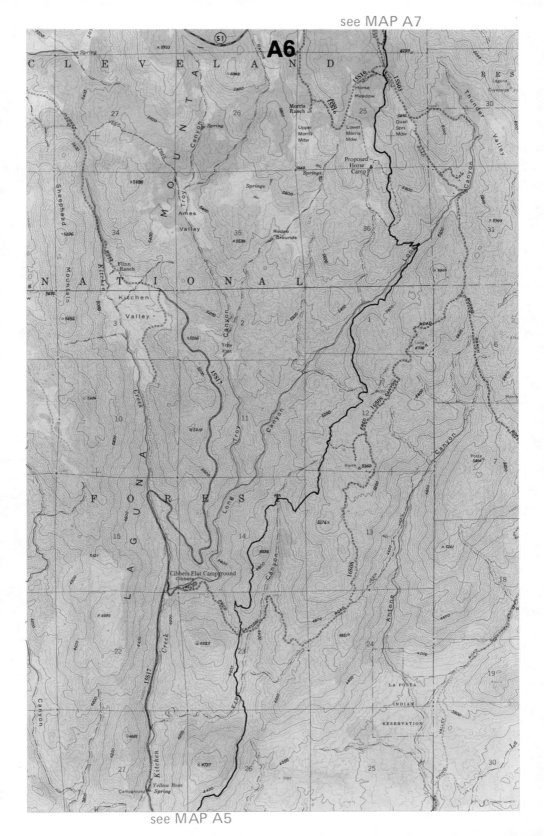

see MAP A7

A6

see MAP A5

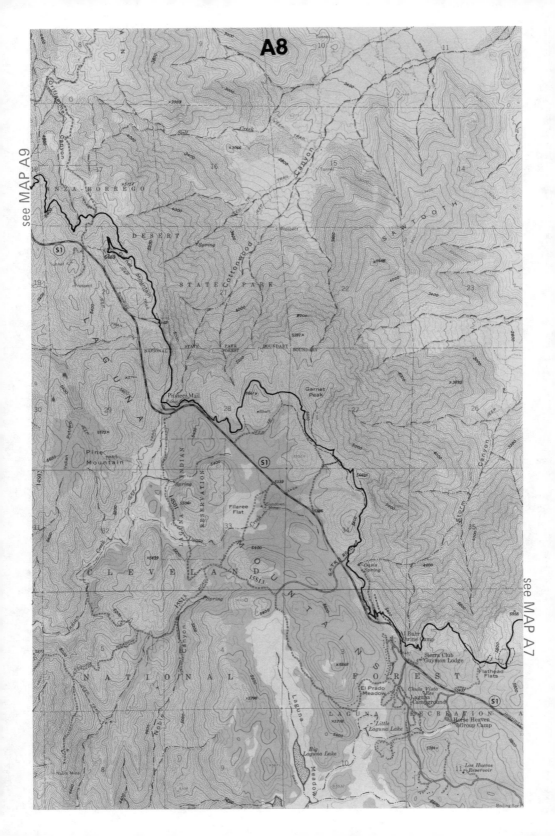

see MAP A9

see MAP A7

gueños" by the Spanish padres. The Indians attested to their dislike of the white man's invasion by burning down a seasonal ranch house— whence the name "Burnt Rancheria." Northbound hikers should know that unless wells have been dug at Pioneer Mail Picnic Area, the next water lies in Chariot Canyon, a 1.8-mile detour from the PCT after a long, usually too warm, 22.7-mile trek.

Climbing away from the campground, the PCT does double-duty as the Desert View Nature Trail, passing live-forever, pearly everlasting, thistle, yerba santa and beavertail cacti, all of them xeric (drought-tolerant) plants that reflect our proximity to the searing Colorado Desert to the east. Bending north and passing numerous, poorer side trails, our now nearly level path leads back into restful forest, joins Desert View Road, passes a dirt-road spur

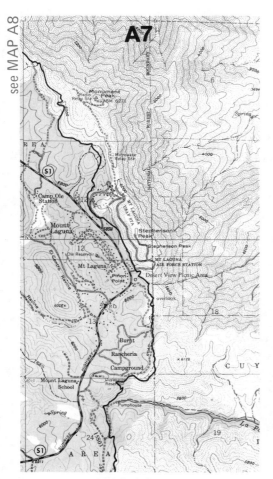

leading southwest to Burnt Rancheria Campground, and strikes a junction (5970-0.6) where the Desert View Road swings westnorthwest.

From here the PCT climbs north along the Desert View Nature Trail, reaching a spectacular overlook of arid Anza-Borrego Desert State Park, its floor—Vallecito Valley—lying 4400' below us in the rain shadow of the Laguna Mountains. The rocks we stand on are now-familiar banded Mesozoic intrusive rocks: just to the east, a contact separates these from well-foliated pre-Cretaceous metasediments blotched with yellow lichens—a cliff on the east face of Stephenson Peak, to the north, is a good example. To our east Vallecito Valley is bedded in Pleistocene sediments, and beyond it the Tierra Blanca Mountains are composed of intrusive tonalite and the Vallecito Mountains of several-million-year-old nonmarine sediments.

Leaving this overlook, the PCT descends into cooler black-oak forest, passes below tables of the Desert View Picnic Area, and then switchbacks up to a paved road (5980-0.7), which leads to Stephenson Peak and the abandoned Mount Laguna USAF Western Air Defense Network Station. Hikers in need of supplies can turn left on the road and walk 70 yards west to Sunrise Highway S1, and thence south 0.4 mile to Mount Laguna Post Office, a store, phones, restaurants and motels, and a Forest Service station. The next supply point along the PCT is Warner Springs, 68.4 miles away.

Continuing on the PCT, we have an easy traverse through high scrub and forest that lie below the golf-ball radar domes on Stephenson Peak. The traverse then ends at a second paved road (5895-0.6) climbing to the summit. Iris, snowberry, yellow violets and baby blue eyes lend springtime color to the forest floor as the route skirts north around the Air Force station's boundary. Then it crosses a succession of jeep roads, and rises moderately in huckleberry-oak, manzanita and ocean-spray chaparral below Monument Peak before dropping easily to a saddle (5900-2.0) where some jeep roads terminate.

A startling contrast of vegetation is presented when the PCT tops the next small ridge. To the east nothing but drought-tolerant, clumped shrubbery survives, while on the Laguna Mountains' summits to the west, a nearly uniform Jeffrey-pine and black-oak forest stretches from North, Cuyamaca and

Stonewall peaks, in Cuyamaca Rancho State Park, over to hazy mountains above San Diego. A disparity of rainfall maintains these two different life zones, caused by the Laguna Mountains' geography. Warm, moisture-laden air sweeping inland from the Pacific Ocean cools as it rises over the obstructing Lagunas. This cooling causes moisture in the air to condense, bringing rain to nurture pine forests, and leaving parched, water-absorbing air to blast down desert slopes in the mountains' lee.

Leaving this instructional vista, the PCT descends, perhaps vaguely, through a small burn, crosses bulldozer tracks that encircle it, and then turns west, descending easily into oak-shaded Flathead Flats (5175-0.9). Here an obvious patchwork of poor roads leads west for 75 yards at the head of Storm Canyon. If the tread has been vague, it will become obvious here, as the trail ascends just under a north-west-trending road, crossing that road in a moment to emerge from shade onto a chap-arral-covered nose. Merging with the road, our thoroughfare narrows as it descends viewfully northwest past rock and chaparral, then turns south to switchback down to a ravine and resume a gently undulating traverse below the Sunrise Highway. In just a moment we reach a

dirt spur (5440-1.3) descending from the high-way. To get water, head west up the road to the highway and take it south 0.2 mile to Laguna Campground. This is the last source close to our route until Cuyamaca Reservoir, 14.4 miles farther along the PCT and then 1.7 miles along a lateral.

Back on route, a few minutes' walk leads to a lone switchback that raises us to a ridgetop pole-line road, which we cross westward to descend to a quiet draw and a better dirt road (5430-0.5) that descends north to Oasis Spring. After we leave this road, live and black oaks, scattered pines and mountain mahogany line the viewful way around the spectacular fur-nace-breathed head of Storm Canyon to reach G.A.T.R. Road (5440-0.9), on cooler, for-ested land. For many years a trailhead parking area, with water, has been planned to go here.

North across the road, the PCT soon veers east, recrossing the road to climb easily under the Lagunas' steep eastern scarp to a saddle with the end of a jeep road (5540-0.5). From it the route undulates northwest on scrub-bound slopes while keeping just above the rough jeep track. Our path crosses jeep spurs to the sum-mits of Peak 5663 and Garnet Peak and then strikes another spur at a saddle (5495-1.6) west of Garnet Peak. The PCT next traverses

A8

Vallecito Valley and Mountains, from south of Oasis Spring

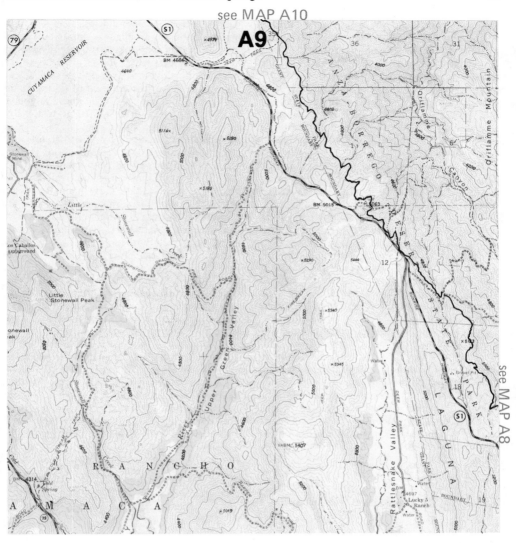

see MAP A10

A9

see MAP A8

around Peak 5661, passing through hoary-leaved ceanothus brush and providing excellent vistas of Oriflamme Mountain to the north. Beyond, the route drops first south and then west to a sandy saddle with a grass-floored pine forest. The route then heads northwest before winding west to waterless but shaded Pioneer Mail Picnic Area (5260-1.8), which lies at the end of a parking spur coming from Sunrise Highway. Here the PCT is signed as Laguna Rim Trail 5E08. For years the USFS has planned to drill a well here and establish a

hikers' camp a short distance down Cottonwood Canyon below the picnic area.

The PCT's continuation north from the picnic area follows the old, unpaved alignment of Sunrise Highway gently up across a cliff at the head of Cottonwood Canyon to meet the end of paved Kwaaymii Point Road (5450-0.7). Northbound tread recommences a few yards up this road, only 40 yards south of a defunct jeep road climbing Garnet Mountain. Now we contour on the mountain's eastern declivity and enter Cuyamaca Rancho State Park. At the mountain's north end, an unnecessary climb to a gap and the defunct jeep road results in wasting one's time dropping north around that peak to a jeep road (5250-1.9) that descends into Oriflamme Canyon. The next leg meanders northwestward along steep hillsides of light-colored granodiorite—weathered to futuristic knobs—and affords excellent panoramas of seemingly sterile Vallecito Valley. But these views hardly compensate for the shadeless, monotonous trail.

Vallecito Valley was once the site of a Butterfield Overland Mail Stage station. Following an old Spanish trail from Fort Yuma, stages ran from St. Louis to California from 1858 to 1861. The first Europeans to traverse this part of the Colorado Desert, however, were Spanish forces led by Lieutenant Pedro Fages from the San Diego Presidio, who marched through in search of deserters in 1772. Two years later Captain Juan Bautista de Anza, for whom the park is named, scouted this area for a life-line trail from Mexico to impoverished Alta California settlements.

Presently the route descends to meet a second road to Oriflamme Canyon (4875-2.8). Across it we climb through brush on a trail that soon closely parallels Sunrise Highway. The rocks lining our route from here to Chariot Canyon are Julian schist—metasediments of Paleozoic age. This particular schist (a rock, once a shale, that now breaks along paper-thin parallel planes) shows abundant flecks of re-

flective, glassy mica, and it weathers to a rusty brown containing frequent mineral-stain bandings. Presently we cross a ridgetop jeep road, and then another (5025-1.3).

To the north we see greenly forested Volcan Mountain and arid San Felipe Valley as the PCT undulates above Oriflamme Canyon to reach a faint jeep track (4770-2.4) at a low gap.

Here thirsty hikers may opt to follow that track west for 1.0 mile through a verdant meadow to Sunrise Highway. From there, follow California Riding and Hiking Trail (CRHT) posts 0.7 mile west to Cuyamaca Reservoir, where long-overdue draughts of water are available. Los Caballos Campground, in Cuyamaca Rancho State Park, is 1.6 miles farther along the well-marked CRHT. Cuyamaca Rancho State Park (from the Indian "Ah-ha-kwe-ah-mac", meaning "the place where it rains") is a recommended layover spot, having cool forests, seasonally chortling streams, and campgrounds with showers. An excellent Indian cultural exhibit and the old Stonewall Mine could round out the visit.

Returning to our trek, we follow the PCT as it winds north along chaparral-clothed summits to the Mason Valley Truck Trail (4690-1.1), just east of a locked gate. Northbound travelers here turn right and curve 100 yards east to a junction with Chariot Canyon Road. The temporary PCT leads north down this little-used, rocky track, on a bone-jarring de-

Oriflamme Mountain, from west of Garnet Peak

Cameron Valley, view south from Peak 4737

scent, which ends at a lupine flat holding the canyon's seasonal creek. Fair but waterless camping may be found here, by a road junction (3860-1.3).

If you are low on water, you should consider continuing north down Chariot Canyon Road, past stands of cottonwoods and live oaks, to two stream fords that mark permanent springs—a 1.8-mile detour (and a 370' drop) from the PCT. Barrel Spring, 38.0 blistering hot miles ahead from the junction, has the next water for the northbound. The next near-trail water for the southbound is at Laguna Campground, 16.8 miles away.

From the road junction in upper Chariot Canyon we conclude the temporary PCT segment by climbing steeply east up the Mason Valley cutoff road to a resumption of PCT trail tread (4075-0.3). This branches left, northeast, the junction perhaps marked with a brown and white state park sign. Now, a well-built tread snakes gently uphill around the western and northern slopes of rounded Chariot Mountain. Eventually the path skirts briefly northwest along a crest saddle, veers left, and then soon veers northeast across a gap (4240-2.6). Just beyond it we get vistas southeast, down desertlike Rodriguez Canyon and into the mirage-wavering, incandescent heart of Anza-Borrego Desert State Park. Thankfully, our way continues north and skirts the hottest regions. A businesslike descent now leads down to the head of Rodriguez Canyon, where we cross Rodriguez Spur Truck Trail (3650-

2.0). Immediately beyond this good dirt road we pass through a pipe gate and angle across an east-curving jeep track, then we too swing east. A graded but persistent descent next leads northward on the steep, rocky, barren slopes of Granite Mountain, offering impressive panoramas north over arid San Felipe Valley. Look carefully for the next leg of the PCT, which traverses along the San Felipe Hills, low on the northern horizon. In the far distance, green San Jacinto Peak and glistening, bald San Gorgonio Mountain rear above 2-mile heights. Closer by, the rusty headframes of a few old gold mines—part of the once rich Julian mining complex which caused excitement in 1869–70—lie in ravines below us.

After winding down a succession of dry slopes, the PCT turns more east and almost levels just above the gentle, brushy alluvial fans at the foot of Granite Mountain. Unfortunately, a logical, direct PCT route from here—northeast to the southern San Felipe Hills—was blocked by uncooperative landowners, who denied right-of-way to trail construction. Hence our route now makes a frustrating, hot, time-consuming detour east to remain on public lands.

First we ascend to a rocky gap (3390-3.2) on Granite Mountain's north ridge. Next we descend to cross a succession of bouldery washes, then undulate east some more to a second gap (3130-1.9) behind a prominent light-colored granitic knob. A final descent is begun on four small switchbacks, followed by a descending

A10, A11

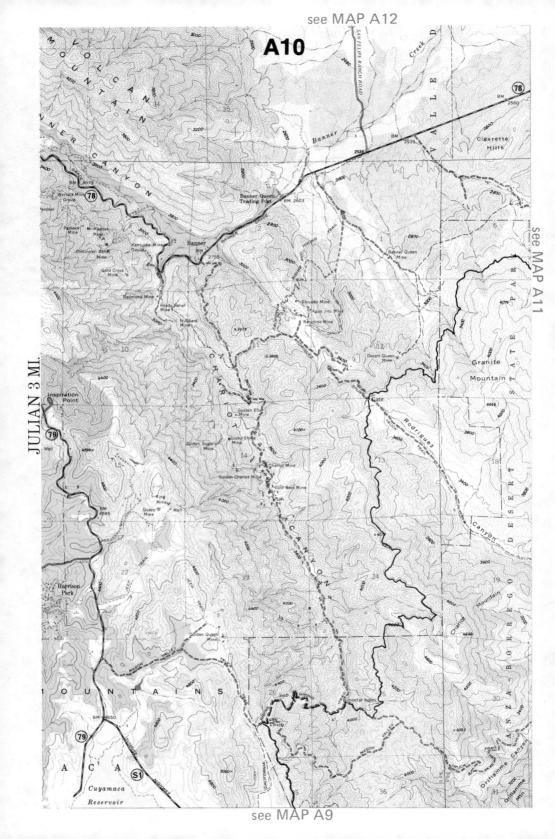

A10

see MAP A11

JULIAN 3 MI.

Pacific Crest Trail, Volume 1

1991 Supplement

p. 3, next-to-last paragraph, last line "7" should be "M".

p. 8, par. 3, line 6 It's Box 9309.

p. 8, par. 4, last sentence They drop ship for foreigners only.

p. 11 Water. With winter 1991 we have entered the 5th year of California's drought. A seasonal creek near Schaffer's home in the S.F. Bay Area hasn't flowed since 1986. That creek's frog pond is now bone-dry, its cattails replaced with coyote brush. What this bodes for PCT hikers is a lack of water at usually dependable sources in Sections A–G. Permanent sources now may be seasonal, and seasonal ones may be bone-dry. Even if California gets an average amount of precipitation, dry springs and creeks may not flow until the groundwater is first recharged, which could take 2 or more years of average or above average precipitation.

p. 18. The following are new addresses and/or phone numbers of federal agencies:

Cleveland National Forest
10845 Rancho Bernardo Rd.
San Diego, CA 92128

Bureau of Land Management
(same address)
new phone: (714) 276-6394

Sierra National Forest
1600 Tollhouse Rd.
Clovis, CA 93612
(same phone)

Emigrant Wilderness *and* Carson-Iceberg Wilderness, Sonora Pass trailhead
Summit Ranger District
#1 Pinecrest Lane Rd.
Pinecrest, CA 95364
(same phone)

Desolation Wilderness
Lake Tahoe Basin Mgmt.
870 Emerald Bay Rd., Suite 1
S. Lake Tahoe, CA 95731
(same phone)

p. 37, par. 2, lines 9–10 Delete these lines and substitute: declination to get the true bearing. For example, if your compass indicates that a prominent hill lies along a bearing of 75°, and if the section you're hiking in has a

Page, 43, Mileages As the California drought worsens, the southern PCT's meager accompaniment of streams and springs is inexorably disappearing. Especially in May and June, hikers should not count on *any water away from civilization*. In Section A, this will certainly require some waterless camps and, probably, some long detours for water. Carry at least one gallon of water per person for each day! In Section A, expect to find water *only* in Campo, Lake Morena County Park, Boulder Oaks Campground, Burnt Rancheria Campground, Laguna Campground and Warner Springs. *Expect Hauser Creek, Cottonwood Creek, Long Canyon Creek, Chariot Canyon, San Felipe Creek and Barrel Spring to be dry!*

Page 46, col 1, line 4th from bottom Hauser Creek: Probably dry by April in drought years.

Page 48, col 2, last line Seasonal creek: Probably dry by April of drought years.

Page 49, col 1, last line Cottonwood Creek: Probably dry by April of drought years.

Page 56, col 1, first line Unnecessary climb: The PCT has been rerouted here, eliminating the intersection of the jeep road and the unnecessary climb and huge switchback seen on Map A8, A9, A10. It also shortens the route by about one-half mile.

Page 57, col 1, par 2, line 4 Permanent Springs in Chariot Canyon. Probably dry by April of drought years, condemning the through traveler to *a hellacious trek of about 63.5 miles without nearby water,* from Laguna Campground to Warner Springs! (Better to detour to Banner for resupply!)

Page 60, col 1, par 1, 3rd from last line Highway S2. The PCT has been rerouted here, staying farther south of the Highway, but continues west-northwest on the same tack to cross under the road at San Felipe Creek. The author doubts the presence of potable water here after April of drought years.

Page 63, col 1, par 3, line 18 Barrel Spring. Now in disrepair. Probably dry, especially by April of drought years.

Page 66, Mileages. The drought has been no kinder to Section B. Except high in the San Jacinto Wilderness, do not expect to find water away from civilization. In particular, be prepared for dry camping north of the usually flowing lower reaches of Agua Caliente Creek to beyond Tunnel Spring. Expect no water after April 1 at Tule Spring or Tunnel Spring.

Page 69, col 2, last line This entire stretch, built 10 years ago, is now becoming painfully overgrown with chaparral—get used to this condition, for it prevails in much of the ensuing 200 miles!

Page 70, col 2, par 3, line 2 Tule Spring. May be dry after April of drought years. The concrete water tank has been reported to be cracked, but a seeping spring may be found uphill from the tank, in high grass.

Page 74, col 1, par 3, line 5 Tunnel Spring. Probably dry after April of drought years.

Page 80, col 1, 5th line from bottom Marion Ridge Trail. Strawberry Junction Campground is now found just yards downhill. It is *waterless.*

Page 80, col 2, par 2, line 2 Deer Springs Campground. Now closed to prevent further ecological damage. The stream here is reliable.

Page 82, col 2, par 2, line 17 Snow Canyon Road. Actual mileage should be *4.2* miles.

Page 82, col 2, par 3, line 4 Western branch of Snow Creek. Probably dry by April of drought years. The closest water is available from homes in Snow Creek Village, but there is no camping thereabouts.

Page 90, col 2, par 2, line 4 Whitewater River. Usually has water into June, but may be dry by early May of drought years.

Page 92, col 1, par 2, line 5 East Fork Mission Creek. Probably not flowing in late May of drought years.

Page 93, col 2, line 2 Mission Creek Trail Camp. In drought years, water will likely be found at least ¼ mile back down-canyon.

Page 100, col 2, par 3, line 12 Sweeping vistas. Just beyond these vistas, a junction is reached with the Cougar Crest Trail, which descends about 2 miles south to Highway 38 on the north shore of Big Bear Lake.

Page 104, col 1, par 2, line 7 Deep Creek Road. The PCT is now rerouted to avoid the congruence with Deep Creek Road. Instead, it stays below it and descends to a sturdy bridge that now crosses Deep Creek.

Page 107, col 2, par 2, line 4 Nearby saddle. This area is now overgrown with brush, and the road crossing is not obvious. Be vigilant.

Page 114, Mileages With the current 5-year drought, the San Gabriel Mountains also pose a challenge to the PCT walker. Don't count on water at Guffy Campground or west of North Fork Saddle Ranger Station, except at man-made facilities.

Page 114, Supplies, line 3rd from bottom: Wrightwood: It no longer has a laundromat. The PCT register is at the pharmacy. Check with the Methodist Church camp—they sometimes offer bunks, showers and laundry facilities.

Page 115, col 2, par 2, line 1 Southern Pacific Railroad Tracks. There are now two sets. Look carefully for the resumption of trail west of the second tracks.

Page 119, col 2, line 5 Guffy Campground. Trekkers have always complained that water here, the first logical campsite west of Interstate 15, was hard to find. It is—especially now that the drought has endured. However, some water should still be found throughout April, even in drought years. A better option, however, would be to detour to the logical resupply point of Wrightwood and avoid the uncertainty.

Page 120, col 1, line 7 Blue Ridge. The PCT has now been rerouted south around the ridgetop, and similarly around the outskirts of Holiday Hill Ski Area.

Page 123, col 1, first line Mount Hawkins. Also pass two southward-branching signed spurs to Mount Hawkins summit and South Mount Hawkins.

Page 128, col 1, par 1, 4th line from bottom Seeping spring. Probably dry by early May of drought years.

Page 128, col 1, par 2, line 4 Fountainhead Spring. May be waterless by early May of drought years.

Page 129, col 1, par 1, 6th line from bottom Mount Gleason Young Adult Center. Waterless Buck Trail Camp has been constructed in this vicinity. Be aware that the trail from here to North Fork Saddle has become very overgrown with thigh-shredding brush. Since the construction of the PCT is now nearly completed, the USFS has plans to commit more money to trail-maintenance efforts such as re-brushing much of the Southern California PCT. But with national priorities elsewhere, don't hold your breath.

Page 138, Mileages Water is again a critical issue in Section E, especially so in these drought years. After about April 1, don't count on water at sites away from human improvement. In particular, don't rely on Big Oak Spring, which is, in any event, bypassed by a new trail alignment.

Page 141, col 1, par 3, line 10 Sierra Pelona Ridge Road. A new trail segment (Map E3) now bypasses Big Oak Spring. Walk right, east, up the road to a jeep trail and a resumption of PCT tread, which arcs northeast down across the head of Martindale Canyon. It eventually strikes an old ridgetop firebreak overlooking Bouquet Canyon. Turn left, west, down this to intersect the old PCT route. Here take the right-branching path northeast down in heavily over-

We begin our trek at the south end of Cameron Overpass (3800-0.0), crossing busy State Highway 58 to the trail on the north side of the highway. The PCT parallels the highway east-northeast along a fenced corridor and through a gate (3780-1.2) opposite a *Cameron Road exit 1 mile* sign. The trail dips through a large wash soon after and turns northeast to ascend to the right of a flood-control berm by the wash. Leaving the berm we progress east-northeast, passing groves of juniper trees interspersed with yuccas and a mishmash of granitics and metamorphics (mafic and ultra-mafic plutonic rocks and associated amphibolite, gneiss, and granulite) exposed in canyons as we cross over the northeast-southwest Garlock fault zone, the second largest fault zone in California. Movement along this fault is approximately 7–8 millimeters per year. To the north the fault is locked, and that is where scientists expect a major earthquake. Climbing north via switchbacks and curves, we arrive on a broad slope 3.0 miles into our trip, ideal for a first night's camp if one started in the afternoon.

Moving on, we climb a long, tight series of switchbacks that on the map resemble an earthquake recorded on a seismograph. At length our trail reaches gentler slopes with camping possibilities, and we climb along the ridge. Views of the Mojave Desert to the east reveal a grid of roads with California City at the hub.

The PCT descends to straddle a narrow ridge between steep canyons and shortly crosses from east-facing to west-facing slopes and enters the pinyon-pine plant zone.

Now our trail seeks the crest on ascending slopes, then descends. To the west, views of colorful Waterfall Canyon attract our attention. We cross a jeep road that leads to a prospect, then its spur, and then climb a ridge via a few switchbacks, passing a chalky white hill of tuff protruding from an east-facing canyon. Soon we parallel the jeep road, cross it, and curve around the head of Waterfall Canyon and beyond. Abruptly, our trail segment ends and we join the jeep road (6120-7.1) we crossed previously.

On the seldom-used jeep road usurped by the PCT, our course heads generally north, then descends east, then again north. At the bottom of the descent, 2.0 miles along the road, we curve around a huge digger-pine tree on a flat offering several sites for camping. Pine Tree Canyon falls away to the east. Then once again we climb a ridge, still on the road, perhaps serenaded by a mountain chickadee's clear three-note "How-are you"—the quarter notes "are you" at a lower pitch. Ahead we see the first of many towers perched on peaks and ridges as our route descends into a swale. In this depression we cross a dirt road, pass an obscure road, and fork right where the sign on the gated road to the left declares *Sky River Ranch* and shouts *No Trespassing*. In 0.2 mile from the gated road our route branches right, leaves the jeep road (6000-4.3) before it descends abruptly, and curves west.

The PCT, a trail now, zigzags, crosses a tower road, turns sharply left, and crosses the road we were on. Here we see our first view of Olancha Peak far to the north over waves of ridges, with 14,000-foot Mounts Langley and Whitney barely reaching above the waves. The first view of pointed Owens Peak, with Mount Jenkins next to it, is southeast of Olancha Peak. The PCT eventually passes near all of these features, and hikers are given many vignettes of this scene as they progress.

Our path now makes its long traverse around the east side of Sweet Ridge, cut on very steep slopes, then around the flanks of Cache Peak, the highest peak in the southernmost Sierra. The trail crosses a jeep road and arrives at a stone-and-cement trough catching a piped-in, year-round trickle from Golden Oaks Spring (5480-3.5).

Now satiated within with water and burdened with full water containers to last 16.2 miles to a private spring, or 19.0 miles to a seasonal spring, or 21.8 miles to the most reliable source of water, we progress along our route heading generally northwest. More roads to wind testing towers are passed, and we make our way by traversing steep slopes and then rounding prominent point 5683. A pair of switchbacks leads us on a descending route below a jeep road to gradually declining slopes with the first camping potential other than on dirt roads since the spring, 3.7 miles back. The trail then crosses a ravine, climbs up its north side, and arcs around the west drainage of Indian Creek. Then we reach an east-west ridge, which we cross via a cattle fence's green gate (5102-6.5).

Beyond the gate our route heads generally west, then curves north, following the crest, a hydrographic divide between Caliente Creek to the west and Jawbone Canyon to the east. Our trail undulates near or on the crest, then descends a north-facing ridge to a blue-oak savannah with camping potential, crossed by an east-west road (5010-3.0). This extensive road connects with others to afford access to the trail from Highway 14 in the east and Highway 58 in the west, but it is a private gated and locked road.

Traveling north, we ascend easily up a ridge, curve around a minor east extension and then hike along a narrow saddle. The trail ahead looks ominous, and it is a steep climb by PCT standards. The curious upslope swath cut through scrub oak followed the original trail design. Grateful we're not panting up that route, we ascend north through a scrub-oak aisle. Upon turning northwest, we leave the chaparral oak for the domain of lofty Jeffrey pines and spreading black oaks. A shaded flat by the trail at the northern limits of the forest offers campsites. The trail descends just beyond the flat to traverse below Hamp Williams Pass (5530-3.3).

Once again we are faced with a steep climb by PCT standards, lined with scrub oak, relieved slightly by four switchbacks. Then a traverse, a zig and a zag, and we cross over a saddle to west-facing slopes, again among welcome Jeffrey pines. Just where the Piute Mountains begin in the south is uncertain, but we are surely on the Piutes now. Our trail declines on a traverse around two peaks and part way around Weldon Peak before the descent increases down a west-facing ridge, then decreases as the trail turns northeast to enter a cluster of privately owned small parcels. No camping allowed. Much of the land we crossed to here was privately owned large blocks of land and BLM-governed land. Our path ends on a curve of a private dirt road (5620-3.2).

A parcel owner has offered to hikers the use of his spring ¼ mile west on this road. This is a wonderful gift; the next water is a seasonal spring 3.0 miles ahead. The route now proceeds up the private road permitted for PCT use: left at the first fork at 0.1 mile, along the main road past several spurs, past a triangle left fork at 0.8 mile, then on to the PCT path, which resumes on the left side of the road (6160-1.2). The road continues to Jawbone Canyon Road 0.2 mile beyond.

We walk north on the path below and parallel to Jawbone Canyon Road, enter Forest Service land in 0.2 mile, pass a campsite with a fire ring on the left, pass a use trail to the right, and angle across a dirt road coming from the road above after 1.0 mile along our path. The trail then climbs up to unpaved Jawbone Canyon Road (6620-1.3). Here we find the place reached at the end of paragraph 3, column 2, and continue on our way.

pp. 163–213 Most springs and their effluents are not dependable water sources during a prolonged drought in the Southern Sierra.

p. 187 Delete all of **Other Problems**

p. 189, line 3 Change to read: Next water is at year-round Joshua Tree Spring, 11.5 miles ahead on the PCT, plus ¼ mile down-canyon.

p. 189, par. 3 Trailside campsite. Correct elevation is 6190.

p. 191, col 1, paragraph 2, line 5 Delete: "In this drainage—develop for hikers."

p. 191, col 1, par 2, line 10 Insert: Beyond the road, we reach a ¼ mile-long spur trail (5410-0.4) to year-round Joshua Tree Spring. At the spring, boughs of golden oak, not arthritic arms of Joshua trees, arch over possible campsites near an elongated cattle trough. A pipe brings clear water from a spring box. Volunteers from the American Hiking Society helped BLM develop the trail and lay the spring box. The next seasonal water is 4.4 miles ahead at Spanish Needle Creek, the next nonseasonal water 17.0 miles ahead at Chimney Creek.

p. 191, col 1, paragraph 2, line 13 Change 1.5 to 1.1.

p. 196 Caption. It should read: Canebrake Road below Lamont Peak.

p. 198, col. 2, par. 3 Year-round creek in Rockhouse Basin. Dry in late summer.

p. 198, col. 2, par. 5 Willow-lined all-year creek. Dry in late summer.

p. 218, Supplies No store at Onion Valley. Some hikers have found Independence to be very friendly. It has several convenience stores, a gas station, a grocery store, a laundromat, two cafes, a post office and a campground.

p. 218, last par. Shuttle-bus fees are $5.00, round trip. However, backpackers heading out toward Mammoth Lakes *might* be able to ride for free. Ask at the Devils Postpile visitor center or ask a bus driver.

p. 219, 1st line Devils Postpile visitor center. It has a phone.

p. 220, col. 1 High Sierra trail junction (10,890-1.6). Elevation should be 10,390.

p. 221, Map H1 The trail now stays north of Whitney Creek in the vicinity of Crabtree Ranger Station.

p. 232–233 Muir Pass to Piute Pass. The Kings Canyon National Park signs indicate this stretch is 18.8 miles long, 2.0 miles longer than the mileage we measured.

p. 237, col. 2 Mono Creek (7750-4.6). Elevation should be 7850.

p. 250, col. 2, lines 2–4 Tantalizing trail. The PCT here was reconstructed in 1990, and hopefully the true route will be more obvious and attractive.

p. 265, col. 2, par. 2, end of line 9 Comma should be a period.

p. 266, col. 1, last line The closed road is open, typically by mid-July.

p. 271, mileage table Delete "River" from East Carson River trail.

p. 275, col. 1, last line Small flat by junction with the East Carson trail. Add (8100-5.2). The mileage table on p. 271 is correct (5.2).

p. 277, col. 1, par. 2, lines 11–20 Replace the prose, due to trail reconstruction and rerouting between saddle (9080-1.4) and the east fork of Wolf Creek. The distance between points, formerly 1.5, is now 2.0, so correct the mileage table on p. 271 (6.5 becomes 7.0).

From the saddle you descend 80 yards to a junction in a gully, from which Trail 015 starts north, bound for the Murray Canyon Trail. Staying northwest, we pass a conspicuous spring in 0.4 mile, and then soon turn north and descend a ridge to a small flat. We head west across it, then traverse southwest, having fine views of Arnot Peak and the Wolf Creek drainage. We then enter forest, switchback twice, and wind down to the slightly cloudy east fork of Wolf Creek (8320-2.0), with a small camp above the west bank, just below the trail.

p. 277, col. 1 Poorly defined ridge (8000-1.6). The elevation should be 8800.

p. 277, col. 2, 1st par. Replace this paragraph with the following paragraph.

The PCT at first parallels this trail, but then diverges from it while climbing north to a shallow gully (8480-0.3). From here a trail climbs north steeply up the gully to the southwest end of Asa Lake, 0.1 mile distant. The PCT winds northeast at a much easier grade up to Asa Lake's outlet creek (8520-0.2), a former cross-country route to the lake. This 2-acre lake, like its creek, is spring-fed, and hence too cold for comfortable swimming. During some years, beavers reside at the lake.

p. 285, col. 1 Blue Lakes Road (8900-2.7). Elevation should be 8090.

p. 287, col. 1, 2nd par. Replace this paragraph with the following paragraph. The distance between the TYT reunion and Carson Pass, formerly 0.8, is now 1.2, so correct the mileage table on p. 272.

Now reunited with the Tahoe-Yosemite trail, which we left below Bond Pass in northern Yosemite National Park, we quickly reach a junction (8870-0.1) immediately south of Frog Lake. An older PCT route used to continue north past the lake and then steeply down to a closed stretch of the *old* Highway 88. We veer north for a snaking traverse to the south end (8580-1.1) of a long parking lot at Carson Pass. From the lot's north end . . .

p. 302, col. 1, par. 4 (7965-0.9). The mileage should be 1.9, not 0.9. However, the mileage table on p. 294 is correct.

p. 305, top of col. 1 First four lines of the 1st par. are missing. The chapter's mileage table on p. 294 is correct despite the omission in the text of 1.9 miles as given in the following missing prose:

Our trail continues its traverse through viewless forest, crossing Bear Lake's reliable outlet creek about ⅓ mile before slanting across Bear Lake road (7120-1.9). For almost ½ mile the

p. 309, col. 2 Remove diagonal blue line.

p. 309 Map reference letter-numbers should be K6, K7.

p. 310 Map reference letter-numbers should be K7, K8.

p. 313, Map L1 "see MAP K9" should be "see MAP K8".

p. 321, col. 2, par. 4 We cross Milton Creek. Now we bridge the creek.

p. 334, col. 1 Last four lines of the 1st par. are missing: We won't pass any more sizable volcanoes, active or extinct, until the Lassen Park area. We finally gain the Sierra crest and cross a jeep road at the south end of Bunker Hill Ridge (6750-3.0).

p. 334, col. 1, par. 2 Small, unnamed lake on a bench just below and west of the trail. Elevation-mileage point here, above the lake, is (6810-1.5). The next mileage point (2.2), near the end of the paragraph, now becomes 0.7. The mileage table on p. 323 is unchanged.

p. 376 Hat Creek Rim PCT. This has been rebuilt.

p. 386 PCT's condition in Section O. This stretch has been brushed out, so the trail should be in good condition for the next several years.

p. 402, Map O11 Incomplete label at bottom right edge of map should read "see MAP O10".

p. 403, col. 2, line 6 to end of par. Schaffer prefers taking Old County Road to Castella. Though it winds, dips and climbs, it is shady and only lightly driven. More importantly, it provides access to the Sacramento River. After about a 1.4-mile hike along it, you reach a short trail down along the lower end of a cascading creek that originates in the southeast corner of Section 23. You'll find a wonderful Sacramento River swimming hole just upriver from

Declination: 13¾°E Mileages:	South to North	Distances between Points	North to South
Cameron Overpass at Highway 58	0.0		84.4
Golden Oak Spring.................................	16.1	16.1	68.3
Jawbone Canyon Road in Piute Mountains	34.6	18.5	49.8
Cottonwood Creek..................................	36.4	1.8	48.0
Piute Mountain Road, first crossing..................	40.2	3.8	44.2
Piute Mountain Road, second crossing................	43.6	3.4	40.8
Kelso Valley Road.................................	48.4	4.8	36.0
Butterbredt Canyon Road	50.5	2.1	33.9
Bird Spring Pass	63.8	13.3	20.6
road toward Yellow Jacket Spring	69.8	6.0	14.6
road to McIvers Spring.............................	76.5	6.7	7.9
Walker Pass Campground spur trail..................	83.8	7.3	0.6
Highway 178 at Walker Pass	84.4	0.6	0.0

inhabiting species, and the green-tinged Mojave green rattlesnake, a desert dweller, has been seen on the eastern slopes of the Sierra crest. Envenomation by any of the species affects the circulatory system, but that of the Mojave green also affects the nervous system and is therefore the most dangerous.

A snake never chases you, it strikes (⅓ of its body length) only when it feels threatened, and not always does it inject venom. Swelling at the bite site and numbness and tingling around the mouth are symptoms of venom injection. According to the latest medical advice, one should remain calm, rest the affected part and get to the hospital—immediately if you suspect it to be a Mojave green. The hospital in Ridgecrest has Mojave green antivenin. Do not cut skin at the fang marks or apply a tourniquet. Most envenomations are not fatal to adults.

Rattlesnakes are seen most often in spring when they emerge from their dens and mate, then seldom the rest of the hiking season. But always be careful. Watch where you step and place your hands, and wear boots and long pants. The snake is alerted to you by your body heat, your odor, and ground vibrations as you hike. Their searching tongue helps their sense of smell. They cannot hear. Not one hiker envenomation in the Southern Sierra has been reported. For more information see page 44 in this book.

Ticks This insect climbs to the tips of grass or low brush such as sagebrush, then transfers to an animal or to your pant leg, should you pass by. It then climbs up to exposed skin and it attaches itself for a meal. Until 1976 people associated only Rocky Mountain Spotted Fever with ticks. In that year inflammatory Lyme disease was added. Early signs of this disease are a rash at the bite site and flu-like symptoms. If not treated with antibiotics, the disease can progress to arthritis and other involvements. So far no cases of Lyme disease have been attributed to ticks in the Southern Sierra. Still it is wise to wear long pants and tuck them into your sock tops, wear long-sleeved shirts, buttoned up and tucked in, and check your clothes frequently when brushing by low vegetation. Ticks seem to be most abundant in late winter, in early spring and after a rain.

To remove a tick, grasp the insect with tweezers as close to your skin as possible, trying not to squeeze it, and gently pull it out.

Storms: Storms are infrequent, but when they do come, cloudbursts and flash floods can occur: avoid camping in washes or in narrow canyons at such times.

Off-highway Vehicles: Be forewarned that the seemingly unlimited open space along some stretches in this section attracts weekend OHVs, but very few during the week. They are prohibited on the PCT.

Plans are for the BLM to establish a trailhead campground for PCT hikers on the south side of Cameron Overpass where facilities, including much needed water, will be available. The next water source is Golden Oak Spring 16.1 miles ahead. Hydrate yourself well before starting this section as this sunny, windy country takes its toll on body fluids. The trail passes through a crazy quilt of private and BLM lands. Because of private lands, users are asked not to stray from the trail in pursuit of such activities as peakbagging.

grown brush to intersect Bouquet Canyon Road 6405.

Page 147, col 2, line 11 Bear Campground. Long segments of trail in this vicinity are sorely in need of brush clearing.

Page 150, col 2, par 1, last line West Oakdale Canyon Road. Final PCT routing north of here to join the Los Angeles Aqueduct is still many years away, due to pending right-of-way litigation.

Page 151, line 8 Three Points. The store's ownership has changed. There is no longer a gas station.

Page 156, par 2, line 7 Concrete bridge. Northbound PCT tread has been constructed hereabouts, heading gradually uphill toward the Tehachapi Mountains. *Don't take it!*—it is still incomplete, and will likely be for many years to come. The unfortunate intransigence of owners of the Tejon Ranch to allow right-of-way for a small segment of PCT tread in the Tehachapi foothills has forestalled the use of the entire remaining stretch of PCT up to Tehachapi Pass.

To get to Tehachapi Pass, follow the temporary route to Highway 58, and go 5.4 miles west on the highway to the Cameron Road exit.

The following replaces p. 163 to p. 173.

Section F: Highway 58 to Highway 178

Introduction: Geographers differ on where the mighty Sierra Nevada begins in the south. Some include the Tehachapi range, calling it the "Sierran Tail" or the "Sierran Hook." The Sierra would then be bordered on the west by the San Andreas fault zone and on the southeast by the Garlock fault zone. Others suggest that the Sierra begins with the mountains north of the Tehachapi range.

On these mountains to the north of the Tehachapi range, the PCT immediately climbs onto the Sierra crest, where it remains for most of this section, traversing the granitic Sierra Nevada batholith, which is exposed so widely. It quickly climbs from a Joshua/juniper woodland to a pinyon-pine/oak woodland, with five species of oaks along the route. A cool Jeffrey-pine forest in the Piute Mountains offers a refreshing mid-section change for the hiker before he drops to a desert community of plants, then progresses again to a pinyon-pine woodland. However, the charm of this section lies not only in the diversity of flora, but also in the unobstructed views of rows of sharp ridges and deep valleys, of sprawling desert and distant peak silhouettes, of evidence of man's quest for riches and of faraway pockets of populated, sometimes historic enclaves.

Supplies: You have your choice between the rapidly growing town of Tehachapi, 9.6 miles west, or the desert town of Mojave, 9.6 miles east on Highway 58. Of the two, Mojave is probably your better choice. It caters to the needs of travelers by offering motels (Motel 6 built in the 1980s), numerous fast-food franchises and large markets. Its post office is 10.8 miles from Cameron Overpass, off Highway 58 on Belshaw Street. Until BLM builds a campground at Cameron Overpass, you'll have to pick up your supply of water in either town too. Your first water on the trail is 16.1 miles in.

At the end of this section, Onyx Post Office, groceries and limited supplies are 17.6 miles west of Walker Pass on Highway 178. A KOA Campground is 7.0 miles west of Onyx P.O. on Highway 178. Kernville, 37 miles west of Walker Pass, has a post office, supplies, motels, etc., and for your rest and relaxation days, kayak rentals and one-hour to multiday raft trips on the tumultuous Kern River, during adequate water flow.

Permits: A fire permit is required for this section, but only if you do not already have a wilderness permit. It can be obtained from the Bureau of Land Management or Sequoia National Forest.

Special Problems:

Water Available year-round springs are sparse in this section. One stretch is 27 miles between water sources if a seasonal spring is dry. And although there is usually a breeze, days can be hot, with low humidity. During periods of extended drought even usually reliable springs dry up. It's advisable to hydrate yourself well before you start and at every water source, and to carry a *minimum* of two quarts per 10 miles. Most springs are impounded for cattle use, but boiling or filtering should render the water suitable for humans.

Rattlesnakes All rattlesnakes are potentially poisonous, even recently killed snakes. Nonvenomous gopher snakes are often mistaken for rattlesnakes, but they do not have the triangular-shaped head and thin neck of a rattler, nor its rattles. Both snakes are important to the environment where they live—you are the visitor. Of the many types of rattlesnakes, three species can be found along the PCT corridor in the Southern Sierra. The biggest—up to 5 feet—is the western rattlesnake, the speckled rattlesnake is a rock-the trail's end. About ⅓ mile farther along Old County Road is the state park's riverside picnic area, which is also worth a visit.

If you don't take this alternate route, then from the end of the PCT tread (at point 2200-3.7), head northwest down Old County Road to nearby Soda Creek Road (2150-0.1). On it you stroll a few minutes over to the wide Sacramento River, then to the nearby Southern Pacific railroad tracks. Unfortunately, no road connects your road to Dunsmuir—a town that has just about everything, including boot repair. So if you need services there, you may have to hike north along these patrolled tracks. After about 1.2 miles, you can branch onto a spur road and then take 3 miles of roads to central Dunsmuir.

Just past the railroad tracks you curve over to Frontage Road (2125-0.4), then cross under adjacent Interstate 5, where Section O ends at a locked gate, the eastern boundary of the west half of Castle Crags State Park (2130-0.1).

p. 407, col. 1, par. 1 Start of route. Instead of following a service road ½ mile, you now take a trail that begins near the entrance station and ends part way up that road. This trail was built to bypass employee residences located along the lower part of the road.

p. 407, col. 2, 2nd paragraph From the start of this section's PCT, you go almost 0.4 mile south up to a fair viewpoint, then angle west for a 160-yard stroll to a junction. From here, a winding, though fairly level route—composed of segments of trails and roads—starts southeast, eventually winding about 1¼ miles west over to the park's paved road that climbs north toward Kettlebelly Ridge. On it you can wind first 0.3 mile southward and then 0.3 mile westward over to the park's PCT campsite (no. 25).

p. 417, col. 1, line 16 The Parks Creek Road ends just before Interstate 5, at Stewart Springs Road, which reaches the interstate about 3 miles west of Weed.

p. 421, col. 1, par. 1, last 2 lines Replace these with: trail starts a traverse northeast toward Peak 6434.

p. 444, Map Q6 Blue on map is out of registration.

p. 445, par. 2 Paradise Lake. A safer source of water is the spring just south of the lake, located among bushes on the west side of the PCT's junction with the Rye Patch Trail.

p. 451, line 3 "Burney falls" should be "Burney Falls".

p. 451, Mileages "Lowdens Cabin site" should be "Lowdens Cabin site spur trail".

p. 456, Map R3 Beardog Spring is 0.2″ east (right) of the Lowdens Cabin site junction. It is immediately below the PCT.

p. 458, col. 1, last 3 lines. Lowdens Cabin site. Distance is 230 yards, not 130.

p. 459, Map R5 The road east-northeast from Wards Fork Gap is now signed 40S01, not 4135.

p. 460, col. 1, line 2 Beardog Spring. See note for p. 456 for spring's true location. The mislocation of the spring was due to incorrect information supplied by a well-intentioned PCT hiker, as Schaffer later found out when he rehiked this stretch.

p. 460, col. 1, line 8 Seep near the hollow's west edge. This is seasonal. It was dry when Schaffer visited it in late summer.

p. 460, col. 2, lines 7–8 Reeves Ranch Springs. The northernmost spring is seasonal, but the two others appear to be perennial. Dense groves of alders give away their location but also make reaching them an effort.

p. 461, col. 2 Mud Springs. The campsites near the springs are small and sloping. You may prefer to camp up by the PCT near the start of the spur road down to the springs.

p. 463, col. 2, 1st par. Wrangle Campground's water. If the piped-in water hasn't been reinstated when you arrive here, get water from a nearby spring. It is at the upper end of a small bowl. To reach this spring from the shelter, head 210° for 150 yards.

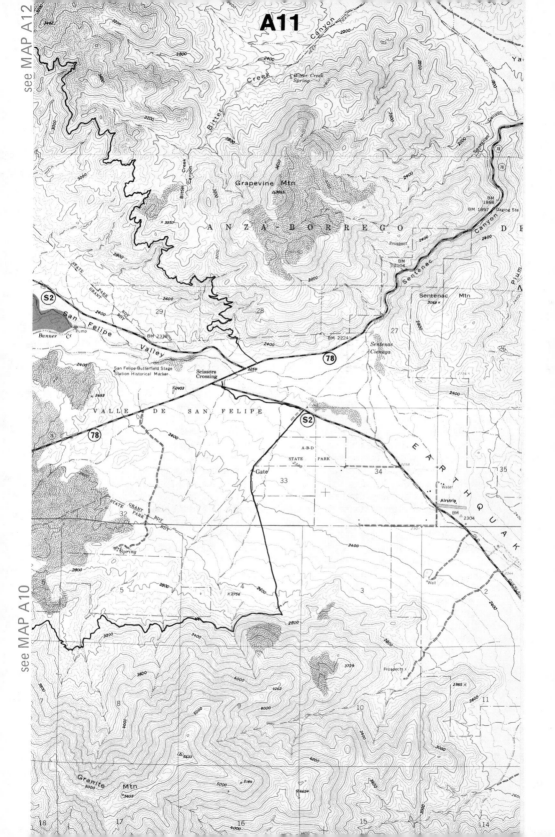

see MAP A12

see MAP A10

traverse eastward. Abruptly, near the base of a cluster of pinnacles below Granite Mountain's northeast ridge, we veer north, debouching onto a sandy alluvial plain. After quickly crossing a jeep track, we proceed almost arrow-straight across northern Earthquake Valley, imperceptibly descending through an open desert association of low buckwheat, rabbitbrush and teddy-bear cholla shrubs, these sprinkled with larger junipers and graceful agave. We eventually pass through a gate in a barbed-wire fence, then swing northeast, tracing an old jeep road that is immediately west of the fenceline. This stretch ends at busy, 2-lane Highway S2 (2245-2.9) at a spot just west of a white, wooden cattle guard.

Now we locate a trail that turns left, west, near the south shoulder of Highway S2. This path winds fairly level past low shrubs, many of them equipped with murderously efficient, thigh-slashing, clothes-grabbing spines. Nearing a junction with Highway 78, the path finally peters out, leaving us to trace Highway 52's shoulder, safe from attack by menacing vegetables, but now exposed to a considerable traffic of desert-bound vacationers. Soon we strike 2-lane Highway 78 (2285-0.9) in San Felipe Valley, where the southbound PCT route along the highway is signed GREAT SOUTH 1849. Here too is a commemorative marker describing the Butterfield Stage Line, which carried mail across the western U.S., passing this way in the 1850s.

We continue straight ahead, northeast on Highway 78, and quickly find the sandy wash of San Felipe Creek running under our highway bridge. Water will be found here often in spring, but should not be counted on. Even when present, it is usually heavily contaminated by cattle. Just a minute beyond San Felipe Creek, we meet northbound San Felipe Road S2 (2254-0.3), branching left, northwest. We stay on Highway 78, heading northeast momentarily to find PCT tread (2252-0.1) branching left, northwest, up from the highway at a junction that may be marked with a CHAINS REQUIRED road sign. Northbound hikers should be reminded that Barrel Spring, the next possible (but not certain) waterhole, is still 23.8 potentially scorching miles away. If your water reserves are low, consider walking one mile northeast on Highway 78 to Sentenac Cienaga, a marsh along San Felipe Creek. Water is usually found here all spring. Better yet, hitchhike 5 miles southwest to Banner to

refill. Southbound hikers will find water in Banner too, or in Chariot Canyon, still 16.3 miles distant.

Commencing a long, exposed traverse of the San Felipe Hills, the PCT ascends briefly across a cobbly alluvial fan to the southern foot of Grapevine Mountain. Here we cross into Anza-Borrego Desert State Park and, now on rotten granite footing, begin to climb Grapevine Mountain's truly desertlike southwestern flanks. Even in springtime PCT hikers would do well to attack this ascent in the very early morning, since temperatures over 100° are commonplace, and most of the next 24 miles are virtually shadeless. Hikers trying to walk the length of the San Felipe Hills in one hot day will be either gratified or frustrated by the extraordinarily gentle grade of the route, which adds many extra switchbacks and a few unnecessary miles to the task. Early on the walk, however, the easy grade allows one to marvel at the "forest" of bizarre ocotillo shrubs. Standing 10–15′ tall and resembling nothing more than a bundle of giant, green pipe cleaners, ocotillos are perfectly adapted to their searing desert environment. Much of the year, ocotillos' branches look like spiny, lifeless stalks. But within just 2–3 days after a rainstorm, the branches sprout vibrant green clusters of delicate leaves along their entire length, allowing renewed growth. Almost as quickly, the leaves wither and die as groundwater becomes scarce. In this manner ocotillos may leaf out 6–8 times a year.

The PCT continues to climb imperceptibly in and out of innumerable small canyons and gullies, none of which holds running water except during a rainsquall. Still in a very desertlike association of agave, barrel cactus and teddy-bear cholla, we eventually reach the crest of the San Felipe Hills, and cross to their northeastern slopes at a pipe gate (3360-8.5). Now the path descends gently into a small, sandy valley where a sparse cover of scrub oak and juniper would make for adequate but waterless camping. Our trail tread becomes indistinct for a moment as we cross a dry, sandy wash (3210-0.6) which drains the valley, but we can see the trail's switchbacks on the slopes ahead, so navigation is easy.

An ascent of those switchbacks leads gently back to the ridgecrest (3600-1.6). The next leg of our journey stays high on the San Felipe Hills' steep southwestern slopes on an undulating course ranging between 3400′ and 3600′.

A11, A12

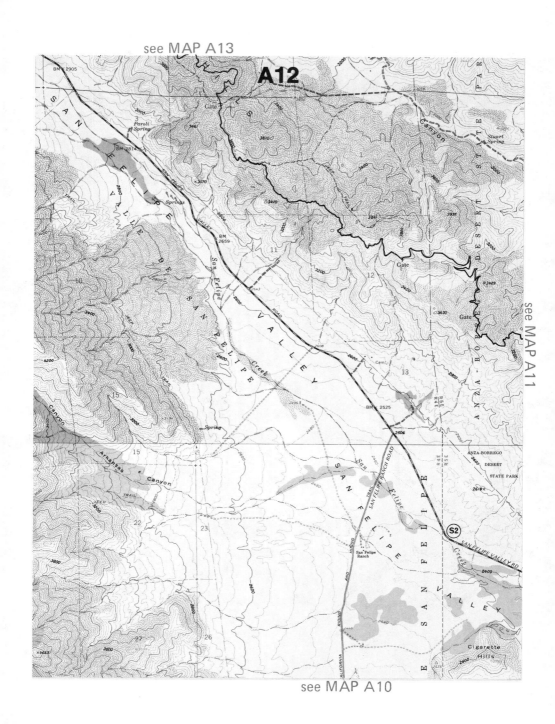

see MAP A13

A12

see MAP A11

see MAP A10

see MAP A14

A13

see MAP A12

Just below a ridge saddle we pass a junction (3485-2.1) with an east-branching jeep road, and then our path crosses the next saddle to the north, bisecting another, poorer jeep road (3550-0.8) just beyond a pipe gate. Either of these roads may be followed east, down into Grapevine Canyon. There, approximately 2½ miles from the PCT, travelers who are desperately short of water will find a ranch at permanent Grapevine Spring.

Pressing on, we begin a long ascent, again on the eastern slopes of the San Felipe Hills, climbing now past dense chamise. An excruciatingly gentle, time-consuming switchback finally brings us back to the ridgetop and a cattle gate (4155-2.7). A more interesting trail then traverses the headwalls of two treacherously steep canyons, these plummeting 1200' to linear San Felipe Valley. Across that valley the Volcan Mountains rise in pine-green splendor, an enviable cool contrast to our scorched environs. The San Felipe Hills are dry and brown for the same reason that the Volcan Mountains are lush and green: a rain-shadow situation causes moisture-laden Pacific storms to dump their rain on the higher Volcan Mountains, leaving little for the San Felipe Hills.

Presently we veer northeast through a gap (4395-1.9), back into dense chaparral on the east side of the San Felipe Hills. Beginning a long, gentle downgrade, the route winds infuriatingly around minor ridges and into nooks, crannies and (it seems) every gully in sight. After a few miles of such mistreatment, most hikers will yearn for a more direct, if steeper, route. But slowly the PCT loses elevation as it circumnavigates a branch of Hoover Canyon, and we gain vistas northeast over sparsely populated Montezuma Valley to San Ysidro Mountain. After only a short eternity we pass through three gates in quick succession, then just a few minutes later, descend under live-oak cover to join a poor road. Now, perhaps marked by a PCT post, our route goes left, west, just a few yards on the road to find Barrel Spring (3475-5.6). Here, after the first major spring rains, cool water is piped into a concrete trough. Adjacent litter notwithstanding, this good waterhole and a pleasant, shady stand of canyon live oaks make a hospitable campsite, which the Forest Service may improve. Northbound hikers can be assured of reliable water in 8.7 miles at Warner Springs Fire Station. Southbound hikers have a longer walk to water—39.8 miles to off-route springs in Char-

iot Canyon. If no water is available at Barrel Spring, hitchhike 4.5 miles east on Montezuma Valley Road S22 to Ranchita, which is a small village with a gas station/minimarket.

Resuming our northward trek, we follow the dirt road from Barrel Spring, down through a gate to a dirt-road pullout just south of paved Montezuma Valley Road S22 (3445-0.1). Just across the highway is a poor dirt road, on which we head north just 50 yards to a barbed-wire cattle gate. Just beyond it PCT posts indicate a treadless route leading left, northwest, which quickly crosses the sandy wash of usually dry Buena Vista Creek. The poorly defined way continues northwest across a sagebrush flat to the southern foot of a ridge. As the trail turns west at the ridge's base, the tread becomes well-defined, soon contouring north into a small canyon. Then the trail begins to climb easily, and we are treated to pleasant views west as we ascend to a 3550' ridgetop. The trail next drops easily west along its northern slope and, nearing the southern margin of a narrow, grassy, west-trending valley, the tread abruptly ends. But looking north across the pasture, you'll hopefully spot a PCT post marking the crossing of a jeep road (3285-2.1). You'll then note tread immediately to the north, ascending north along the next low ridge. Climb it, then drop northeast to its base on the edge of another, much larger rolling grassland where, again, tread simply ceases. This time, however, far too few PCT posts show the way, so, with compass in hand, follow a bearing of 355° quite level for almost 0.2 mile to a PCT post, then a bearing of 5° for another 0.2 mile to the crest of a gentle ridge northeast of hill 3406. Here, ignore a much-better-defined cattle trail descending northwest, and instead proceed along an average bearing of 350°, traversing through a sloping pasture. Hikers have complained that they have become lost on this stretch, so find your route carefully.

Passing a few PCT posts and crossing some jeep trails en route, walk almost level for about 0.6 mile until you come within view of the sandy wash of San Ysidro Creek, which emerges from a narrow canyon to the north. Here, actual PCT trail tread resumes among scrub oaks at the edge of the eastern hillside. This path contours north along the canyon's east slopes, but soon drops to cross San Ysidro Creek (3355-1.7), which usually flows in spring. Like other key points on this frustrating, poorly constructed trail segment, this

A12, A13

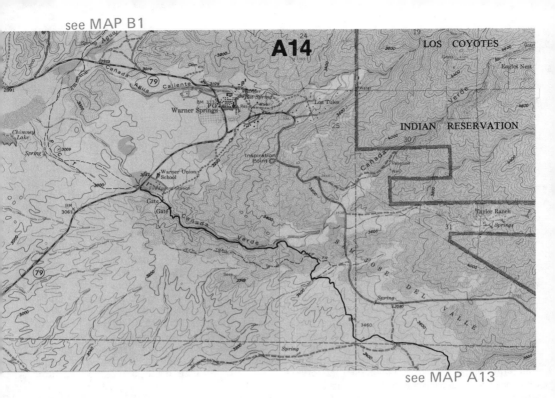

see MAP A13

crossing is inadequately marked and is confused by a jeep track just north of the creek. Anticipate the crossing where San Ysidro Creek first bends northeast, up-canyon, under the first white-barked sycamore tree to shade our path. A fair camp could be made here.

Across San Ysidro Creek, head straight uphill for 20 yards to find the path, which continues up-canyon for only a moment before switchbacking west moderately up out of the shade onto an open hillside. Ineptly built and poorly maintained, the tread ascends from San Ysidro Creek, soon turning north to attain the canyon's rim. Here you have views west over Warner Valley to Lake Henshaw, a sag pond along the Elsinore Fault, and to famous Mount Palomar Observatory, on the horizon. After a brief course north the trail turns west and re-enters grassland. This time, however, tread is visible. It leads gently up, then down, to cross a good dirt road (3495-1.2), then soon it adopts a more northern course as it rolls across a corrugation of ridgelets and dry washes. After crossing a poor jeep trail in one such ravine, the trail climbs through low chaparral and soon crosses a ridgetop jeep road (3510-1.6), which served as part of the temporary PCT route for many years.

From the ridge we descend gently past shady canyon live oaks and cottonwoods which line the pretty valley called Cañada Verde (Spanish for "Green Ravine"). Soon the PCT closely parallels the southern banks of a small stream that flows until late spring of most years. A fine camp can be made almost anywhere along the next mile of creek, in grassy flats adorned with pink wild roses. The Forest Service may develop a formal camping area here. We follow the canyon bottom for almost a mile, and then, near Cañada Verde's mouth, pass through two pipe gates, the second one at a jeep road. Across the jeep road we continue northwest just south of Cañada Verde's banks, and in ¼ mile find the concrete bridge of two-lane Highway 79 (3040-2.0), just west of Warner Springs Fire Station. Although the PCT actually heads under the highway, the bridge clearance is too low for horses, so a pipe gate allows access to the highway. Warner Springs Post Office lies 1.2 miles northeast along the highway. Water is available at the fire station. The next water for northbound hikers lies in Agua Caliente Creek, in 5.3 miles, while for the southbound, water is next obtained at Barrel Spring, 8.7 miles away.

A13, A14

Section B: Warner Springs to San Gorgonio Pass

Introduction: The San Jacinto Mountains are the high point—and the highlight—of the Pacific Crest Trail's excursion through the northern Peninsular Ranges, and they afford the first true high-mountain air and scenery of our journey. But this section of trail also includes many miles of walking under shady live oaks and through the shadeless chaparral community (see below). On the Desert Divide, where we have our first taste of the San Jacinto Mountains, we find an interesting combination of pine forest, chaparral and desert species. Leaving the San Jacintos, the PCT plunges almost 8000' down to arid San Gorgonio Pass, and in so doing passes through every life zone in California save for the alpine zone.

The Peninsular Ranges stretch from the southern tip of Baja California, paralleling the coastline, some 900 miles north to San Gorgonio Pass, which truncates the range along the Banning Fault and lesser faults. The ranges' core, forming the Laguna Mountains, the Anza Upland and the San Jacinto Mountains, where the PCT winds, is made of crystalline rocks—granite and its relatives—which were first intruded in a liquid state several miles beneath the surface and then later solidified. These rocks are similar in age and kind to the granitic rocks of the Sierra Nevada.

Our walk from Warner Springs to San Gorgonio Pass treads mostly upon these rocks, which are usually fine-grained, gray-to-creamy in color, and strongly resistant to weathering, as demonstrated by obdurate monoliths around Indian Flats and Bucksnort Mountain, by outcrops jutting from the alluvium of Terwilliger and Anza valleys, and by the jagged, saurian spine of the San Jacinto Mountains, as on Fuller Ridge. The remainder of the terrain we tread is across either sand and gravel weathered from the granite, found in basins, or metamorphic rocks. These rocks are seen in Agua Caliente Creek's canyon and along much of the Desert Divide.

Section B ends at San Gorgonio Pass, a broad, cactus-dotted trough running east-west, flanked by the San Bernardino and San Jacinto mountains to the north and south respectively. Once a major corridor of Indian traders, San Gorgonio Pass is bounded by faults on either side. It lies some 9000' below the summits of San Jacinto and San Gorgonio, each standing just a few air miles to one side.

Proof that awesome geologic processes are at work today can be seen right at the start of this section, at Warner Springs. Now a tourist spa, but used for centuries past by neighboring Cahuilla and Cupeño Indian tribes, the hot springs here bubble up from deep within the earth's crust and escape along the Aguanga Fault, which cuts just yards behind this small resort community. Warner's hot spring also served Kit Carson in 1846, and was an overnight stop on the Butterfield Stage Line from 1858 to 1861.

Declination: 13°E

Mileages:	South to North	Distances between Points	North to South
Highway 79 southwest of Warner Springs............	0.0	1.8	103.5
Highway 79 west of Warner Springs	1.8	3.5	101.7
Agua Caliente Creek ford in Section 13..............	5.3	3.6	98.2
Lost Valley Road to Indian Flats Campground	8.9	10.8	94.6
east shoulder of Combs Peak	19.7	8.1	83.8
Tule Canyon Road to Tule Spring...................	27.8	6.5	75.7
jeep road to Terwilliger...........................	34.3	8.9	69.2
Pines-to-Palms Highway 74 to Anza	43.2	6.6	60.3
Tunnel Spring Trail	49.8	4.1	53.7
Cedar Spring Trail.................................	53.9	3.5	49.6
Fobes Ranch Trail.................................	57.4	10.4	46.1
Tahquitz Valley Trail..............................	67.8	1.9	35.7
Saddle Junction and trail to Idyllwild...............	69.7	6.2	33.8
Deer Springs Campground.........................	75.9	5.8	27.6
Fuller Ridge Trailhead Remote Campsite	81.7	18.2	21.8
Snow Canyon Road................................	99.9	3.6	3.6
near Interstate 10 in San Gorgonio Pass.............	103.5		0.0

Supplies: The Warner Springs spa and facilities are now a private club, and public access is not allowed. Camping food may be mailed to Warner Springs Post Office, located 1.2 miles northeast of the start of this section on Highway 79. The next possibility for resupply is in the mobile-home community of Terwilliger, a 4.4-mile detour from the PCT, 34.3 miles along this section's stretch. There, the Valley Store, open 7 days from 8:30 a.m. to 6:00 p.m., has limited supplies, precious water, a PCT register and a telephone. They will cash money orders and hold food parcels, but request two weeks prenotification of any package. The larger town of Anza, a 6.0-mile detour from the route 43 miles beyond the section's start, boasts a post office, stores and restaurants. At Saddle Junction, high in the San Jacinto Wilderness and 69.7 miles from the start, one may chose to descend the historic Devils Slide Trail to Idyllwild, which is a restful mountain-resort community with a complete range of facilities, including a mountaineering-supply shop. Get showers at the state park, only yards from the center of town.

Ending this section in West Palm Springs Village, a tiny community without any supplies, you have a choice of supply stations. Here, about 103 miles from the start, you can hitchhike east 12.5 miles via Interstate 10 and Highway 111 to revel in the fleshpots of Palm Springs, that famous movie-star and golf-course-studded desert oasis. It offers complete facilities, including a not-to-be-missed tour for PCTers fresh from their conquest of the first major mountain range on the Trail: an aerial-tram ride from Palm Springs up 6000' to the subalpine shoulder of San Jacinto Peak, for a lavish dinner at the viewful summit tram station!

Alternatively, hikers may elect to hitchhike west on Highway 10 from West Palm Springs Village. From the Verbenia Avenue exit you go 4.5 miles on Highway 10 to the Main Street exit of Cabazon, a small town with a post office and store. It also boasts The

Wheel Inn, a good restaurant complete with life-size concrete models of a brontosaurus and a tyrannosaurus. Hadley's, a backpacker's dream market, lies 2 miles farther west on Highway 10 (Apache Trail exit), and it sells an astounding variety of dried fruits and nuts.

Permits: The San Jacinto Wilderness consists of two units—the national-forest wilderness and the state-park wilderness. If you are camping in only one of these, you need a permit only for it; if you are camping in both, you need two permits. Obtain the national-forest permit by writing Idyllwild Ranger Station, Box 518, Idyllwild, CA 92349. You can also pick one up at the station, at 25925 Village Center Drive in Idyllwild, which is open between 8 a.m. and 4:30 p.m. Monday through Friday until about June 1, and then 7 days a week through summer. Obtain the state-park permit by writing Mt. San Jacinto Wilderness State Park, Box 398, Idyllwild, CA 92349, or by going to the station at the north edge of Idyllwild on the highway to Banning between 8 and 5 o'clock 7 days a week.

The Chaparral: Hikers along the California PCT cannot help but become familiar with the chaparral, that community of typically chest-high, tough, wiry, calf-slashing shrubs and small trees that we meet first by the Mexican border. Draped like a green velvet blanket over most of that part of Southern California reached by ocean air, and extending from close beside the sea up to about 5000', where it mingles with conifers and oaks, chaparral lines most of the PCT south of the Sierra. Chaparral surrounds Warner Springs, at the beginning of this section.

Named by early Spanish Californians, who were reminded of their "chaparro," or live-oak scrub from Mediterranean climes, the California chaparral is a unique assemblage of plants—mostly shrubs—that find this region's long, rainless summers and cooler, wet winters ideal for growth. Chamise, also known as "greasewood" because of its texture and its almost explosive flammability, is the most widespread species, but several species of ceanothus (mountain lilac, buckbrush, tobacco brush and coffee brush), plus ribbonwood, ocean spray, sumac, sagebrush, mountain mahogany, holly-leaf cherry and yerba santa also rank as major members of chaparral, depending on topographic and soil conditions.

All true chaparral plants have small, evergreen, thick, stiff leaves and many have leaves with waxy outer surfaces. The plants' roots are long, to reach deep into rocky subsoil for scarce water. Chaparral plants are suited to survive not only the protracted rainless, hot months, but also a low annual rainfall and a rapid runoff from the thin, poorly developed soils. The plants' main defense against loss of precious water is near-dormancy during the hot, dry summer spells. Almost all photosynthetic activity ceases during this time, but the stiff evergreen leaves are ready to resume photosynthesis within minutes of a rainfall, unlike those plants which lose their leaves or wilt in the face of heat. The small size of the leaves themselves, with the addition of a waxy coat or a hairy insulating cover, plus the presence of relatively few evaporative stomata, greatly reduces water losses.

Not only can chaparral plants vie successfully for, and conserve, scant water resources, but they also win out by thriving in the face of fire. All of the most widespread species are adapted to reproduce well in the aftermath of fast-moving range fires that are a hallmark of Southern California wildlands. In fact, fires actually benefit these species, and most of them contain highly flammable volatile oils, which promote fires. Before the advent of white man, wildfires burned the Southern California chaparral every 5 to 8 years! Not only does fire exterminate encroaching species, but it returns valuable nitrogen to the soil, thus promoting growth. Some of the species, like scrub oak and ceanothus, need fire to weaken their seeds' coatings to allow germination. Most of the other chaparral plants circumvent the ravages of fire by resprouting—in as little as 10 days—from tough root crowns or by putting out so many seeds that at least some will survive any fire. Chaparral is also unusual in that it succeeds itself right after a fire, unlike other plant communities, such as pine forests, which after a major fire pass through one or more vegetational stages before returning to the final, climax stage.

Before leaving Warner Springs, northbound hikers must be sure to stock up on water. The next certain source along the route, barring the seasonal flow of Agua Caliente Creek (reached in 5.3 miles), is Tule Spring, a long, usually hot, 27.8-mile trek away.

Pedestrians can start north on Section B's PCT by simply ducking under Highway 79 via Cañada Verde's streambed, but equestrians must climb through the gate onto the highway shoulder. Then they should follow the highway northeast 200 yards to the entrance to Warner Union School. Across the street from this entrance, a short dirt road along a fence heads left, northwest, 100 yards to a short spur trail that turns south back to Cañada Verde's wash and to the PCT. Our trail departs west away from the wash, quickly crosses a jeep road, and curves gently down into spring-wildflower meadows. Well marked by posts and having a refreshingly well-defined tread, the PCT soon recrosses the jeep road (2960-0.7).

Next our trail skirts the flanks of low knob 3009, then turns north across sandy flats speckled with mature canyon live oaks to cross the usually dry bed of Agua Caliente Creek (2910-0.6). In just a minute or two, our deep-sand trail recrosses the creek to its east bank and then climbs east a few yards into a cozy oak grove and to a privately operated campground (2925-0.2), which is closed to public use. Here the PCT momentarily joins the dirt road that gives access to the campground's sites, and then it turns northward before branching left to cross another usually dry streambed in Cañada Agua Caliente. Moments later, the PCT passes under Highway 79 (2930-0.3) via a concrete bridge, while simultaneously crossing Agua Caliente Creek, which

Opuntia **cactus in bloom**

often flows lazily here. Warner Springs Post Office and sure water can be found 1.3 miles east along Highway 79.

North of the highway the PCT leaves the western margin of Agua Caliente Creek's sandy bed just beyond a sandbag-reinforced slope. The trail clambers up to an alluvial terrace, which is then followed northeast, up-canyon, staying some 30' above Agua Caliente Creek, which usually flows in this vicinity, if only as a

B1

see MAP B2

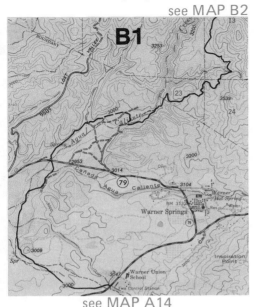

see MAP A14

trickle. The PCT dips momentarily to cross a jeep road in a north-trending wash, then shortly merges with a rough dirt road (2960-0.6) that continues eastward, up-canyon, well marked by PCT posts. A few minutes' walk brings us to a junction (2965-0.2) with another dirt road that merges from the southwest. Just beyond this junction the trail, indicated by PCT posts, branches right, east. Ignoring a trail that continues directly up-canyon, PCT hikers should curve south to strike another trail (2965-0.1), which leads up-canyon. For a moment, however, the PCT turns right, southwest, down-canyon to cross Agua Caliente Creek to its south bank. Marked by a PCT post, the way now turns east, up-canyon, along Agua Caliente Creek, leaving behind a short trail that goes down-canyon to strike a dirt road. We soon pass through a small, waterless, private campground, closed to the public, at the mouth of a narrow ravine, which is eroding along the trace of the Aguanga Fault. Moments later we rejoin a trail coming in from the left (2985-0.3), then begin to climb north and east away from Agua Caliente Creek.

Chia, white forget-me-not and beavertail cacti line the moderate ascent across the Cleveland National Forest border to a terrace, along which the sandy path winds north through ribbonwood chaparral. Then we soon descend to cross Agua Caliente Creek (3195-2.3),

where tall grasses, squaw brush, brodiaea and forget-me-nots grow below screening oaks, sycamores and willows in the narrow, usually watered canyon—a refuge for mourning doves and horned lizards. Particularly in winter and spring, ticks also inhabit the grasses and shrubs, and travelers should check their legs often. We cross Agua Caliente Creek four more times in the next mile, alternating shady, cool creekside walking with hot, yucca-dotted Paleozoic Julian schist hillsides. Camping possibilities are frequent. A final, shaded traverse north of the seasonal stream leads to a switchback (3520-1.5) in a side canyon, after which the moderately ascending route winds northwest in chaparral laced with deer brush and white sage. Soon the grade eases to contour west, then north, below Peak 4844 and above Lost Valley Road. Here the trail affords good views southwest across Warner Valley to Lake Henshaw, a large sag pond on the Elsinore Fault, and northwest to weathered tonalite outcrops near Indian Flats. Upon striking Lost Valley Road (4170-2.1), trekkers may opt to detour left (west) to Indian Flats Campground for oak-shaded camping and fresh water. This is reached by first walking south 0.5 mile down the dirt road—now closed to vehicles—to oiled Puerta La Cruz Road, both part of Road 9S05. Turn right on the latter and go 2.6 miles to Indian Flats Campground, which is nestled among oaks and boulders on the site of an old Cahuilla Indian camp.

Continuing north, the PCT turns right onto poor Lost Valley Road and ascends it to reach a spur road (4450-1.1). From here Lost Valley Road descends north 0.2 mile to reach vandalized, often dry Lost Valley Spring, while the PCT climbs northeast along a 0.3-mile spur—an overgrown jeep track—to reach a continuation of trail tread where the spur ends in a ravine. We ascend briskly to the south to find excellent views back over boulder-dotted Indian Flats and south over Valle de San Jose (San Dose del Valle). Soon the way swings eastward on a gentle, sandy ascent through chaparral and past scattered Coulter pines. After climbing over three low, fire-scarred ridges, we drop moderately east to a saddle (4945-3.2) that lies along the northwest-trending Hot Springs Fault. To the southeast, Hot Springs Mountain's lookout tower rises above tree-lined Agua Caliente Creek.

The PCT ascends east a bit, then turns north to undulate through dry brushland—often spar-

B1, B2

ingly shaded by oaks and Coulter pines—to the east of a boulder-castellated ridge. After about 2 miles from the saddle we pass unheralded into Anza-Borrego Desert State Park, then cross a gap to the sunnier west slopes of the ridgeline. With vistas west over Chihuahua Valley, we contour generally north to yet another gap, then descend quickly east, cross a ravine, and traverse northwest to strike nearby Lost Valley Road (5050-4.6), which drops west into Chihuahua Valley. Directly across the dirt road the PCT starts a sustained, moderate ascent along Bucksnort Mountain's east slopes. The climb ends at the east shoulder of Combs Peak (5595-1.9), where a grove of Coulter pines, outstanding vistas, and the first level spot for miles combine to make a nice, if water-less, campsite.

The 180° panorama here encompasses a sizable chunk of Southern California real estate. To the north, distant, seasonally snow-capped San Gorgonio Mountain peers over the west shoulder of nearer, sometimes snowy San Jacinto Peak. Closer in the north, Thomas Mountain stands behind sprawling Anza and Terwilliger valleys. The rocky spine descending right (southeast) from San Jacinto Peak is the PCT-traversed Desert Divide. To the east-northeast, the dry summits of the Santa Rosa Mountains loom above desert-floored Coyote Canyon, while we spy to the east the vast Salton Sea beyond Anza-Borrego Desert State Park. The park and the town of Anza to the north both commemorate Captain Juan Bautista de Anza, who in 1774 rejoiced upon entering the valley now bearing his name. He had struggled through the Borrego Desert and Coyote Canyon with a couple dozen men—mostly soldiers—while scouting a route from Sonora, Mexico, to San Francisco. He returned a year later, leading more than 200 settlers and many cattle.

Continuing on, the northbound PCT contours across the steep east face of Bucksnort Mountain, then begins to descend in earnest, on rocky, sandy tread in low chaparral. We eventually cross a usually dry creekbed at the head of Tule Canyon (4710-2.4), just south of where some level spots offer waterless camping. From here our way becomes less steep and rolls northward into a tall brushland dominated by ribbonwood and chamise. The PCT rounds the canyon's eastern slopes, drops easily to a broad saddle, then climbs gently north to gain the west end of a low ridge. A few minutes' gentle downhill walk leads to a trail junction (4675-0.9). The north-descending old, temporary-PCT route heads left for 0.3 mile before deadending.

We take the newer, 1987-vintage tread, which first contours east and then drops moderately across the nearby Riverside County line on a northward tack. After traversing east-facing slopes, the PCT descends across to the west side of a small saddle, next descends southwest, and then soon levels to momentarily strike a fair dirt road (4110-2.3) at the Anza-Borrego Desert State Park boundary. Northwest across it the path resumes, making an easy but shadeless descent through Section 30. After an unnecessary switchback the way bends north, still descending. Some hikers may wonder about the logic of the PCT's route between the county line and the Pines-to-Palms Highway. In order to avoid conflicts with local landowners, the PCT is forced to traverse a checkerboard of public-land parcels. Hence the PCT crosses each section near one of its corners to essentially avoid treading on private property. Ponder this situation as you continue north, past a white-pipe post marking a section's corner. You then drop for a moment to a shallow, hop-across ford of Tule Canyon Creek (3590-2.1). Water usually flows here, sometimes merely at a trickle, for most of the year. It is more reliable downstream at Tule Spring. Due to land-ownership constraints the PCT is forced to climb very steeply up the sandy hillside north of Tule Canyon Creek. Afterward it side-hills gently northeast, down-canyon, soon to cross good Tule Canyon Road (3640-0.4).

Just ¼ mile southeast down this dirt road is year-round Tule Spring, the only reliable water-hole on the PCT for miles. It emerges from a dry, brushy hillside to feed a stand of large cottonwoods that in turn shade a sandy, grassy creekside terrace—a fine campsite. In the morning quiet, one may see desert bighorn sheep watering here, having escaped the scorching heat of the Borrego Sink. If the spring itself is not running well, check the 12' diameter concrete water tank, which has a large hole in its top that gives access to water within. Everyone should fill water bottles here. North-bound hikers have 22.8 usually hot miles until the short detour to Tunnel Spring, on the Desert Divide, while southbound hikers have an even hotter 22.4 miles to Agua Caliente Creek in Section 13.

B2, B3, B4

see MAP B3

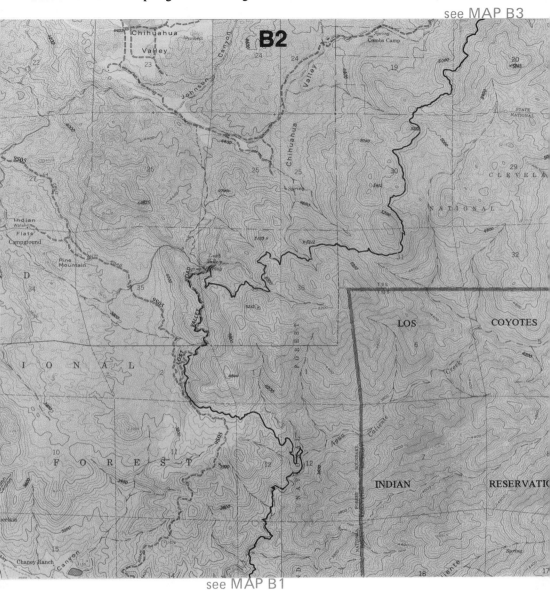

see MAP B1

After refreshing yourself, return to the PCT's northward continuation. It starts a sandy, hillside traverse, undulating through rocky ravines, first overlooking the environs of Tule Spring, then bending northeast. After dipping to a broad valley, the easy trail climbs slightly to a small pass with an interesting self-replenishing wildfowl "guzzler" water tank, then drops on sandy, indistinct tread to nearby Coyote Can-

yon Road (3500-2.9). Across it you continue down a ravine to a single switchback leading to the pleasant grassy floor of Nance Canyon. Step across its seasonal creeklet (3350-0.5) to find some small flat spots that offer potential dry camping. Beyond, a moderate grind leads up around a low knob, then across a rugged bluff where the trail was unnecessarily routed, at the expense of much dynamite and at least

B4

see MAP B4

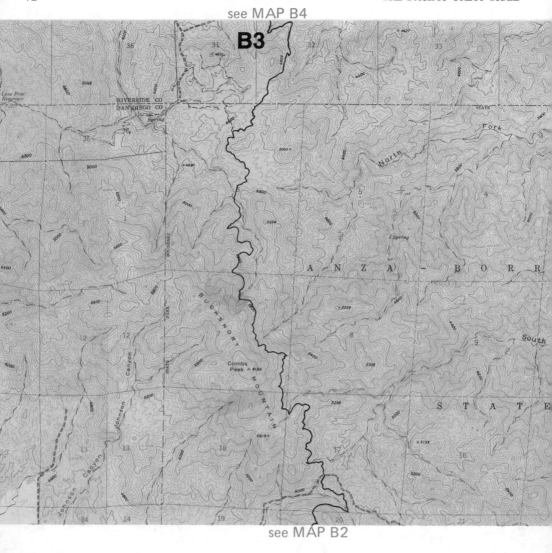

see MAP B2

one badly injured trail-crew worker. This route does, however, offer panoramas south and east over Anza-Borrego Desert State Park's wild, northern canyons, which are visible through a haze of heat waves and salt particles from the Salton Sea. After pausing momentarily, you continue the ascent, which eventually makes two small switchbacks to reach a chamise-covered gap (4185-2.4) on the southern end of Table Mountain. Now you wind north and descend gently to a narrow, very sandy jeep road (4075-0.7), which comes down from a saddle to the east. This hard-to-spot junction occurs where the road is obscured in a broad white-sand wash draining a far eastern part of Terwilliger Valley. Look for this junction a few yards south of a prominent 10′ tall plastic post.

B4

*   *   *   *

The reason this jeep road is so important is that it leads out to the community of Terwilliger and on to Anza—both logical resupply sites for long-distance PCT travelers. To reach Terwilliger, turn left, west, and gently descend the road, which rapidly becomes more distinct. After 1.1 miles it ends with a slight ascent to a good dirt road, signed HIGH COUNTRY TRAIL. Turn right onto it, and walk north ¼ mile easily up to a broad road, Sunset Sage Trail, which branches left, west. Take this dirt road ¾ mile easily down past numerous north-branching dirt roads and past a few homes to its end at Yucca Valley Road (3925-2.1). Turn left and follow this dirt road south for just a minute to a four-way junction, from where larger Coyote Canyon Road heads both south and west. Follow this road right, west, across the arid, level grassland, finally making a small dogleg before ending at paved Terwilliger Road (3870-1.8).

Terwilliger Road may be followed south just 0.3 mile, to paved Bailey Road. Just 250 yards west on it is the Valley Store, with water and a warm welcome for PCT hikers. From Coyote Canyon Road's junction with Terwilliger Road, hikers can walk north to Kamp Anza Kampground (3990-1.3), with phones, a surprisingly good grocery selection, laundry, hot showers and campsites available at a very reasonable cost. Hikers who are intent on an Anza resupply can continue north past the trailer park to Wellman Road (4245-1.5). Take it west to Kirby Road (3935-1.0), then take that road north to Cahuilla Road (Highway 371) (3970-1.0-8.7). Now turn left, west, and head over to the small town of Anza (3920-1.6-10.3), which has a post office, well-stocked grocery stores, restaurants and a laundromat.

If you don't want to backtrack from Anza to the PCT at the far eastern part of Terwilliger Valley, walk east back along Cahuilla Road, passing Kirby Road and later crossing a 4855' summit just before reaching a junction with Pines-to-Palms Highway 74 (4790-6.0). Then go southeast on this highway, which starts southeast and then climbs gently through a grassy valley to reach the PCT just short of a paved parking turnout (4919-1.0-17.3).

*   *   *   *

From the obscure jeep-road junction at the far eastern part of Terwilliger Valley, the PCT ascends indistinctly northwest for a moment before good tread resumes. It leads moderately and persistently uphill, in an ascending traverse along the granitic, boulder-strewn southwestern flanks of Table Mountain. Soon we gain excellent vistas over Terwilliger Valley and south to our PCT's route along Bucksnort Mountain. On a breezy day this stretch is quite enjoyable, particularly in spring when it's likely to be flanked by clusters of California poppy, purple chia, baby-blue-eyes, and feathery green ribbonwood shrubs among white boulders. At one point we must hop across a barbed-wire fence, where a trail leads a few yards south to a dirt road serving some hillside homes. Beyond, our climb continues, eventually rising to top Table Mountain's shoulder and cross a dirt road (4910-3.9) at a point just northeast of the long mountain's highest point.

Now the route drops and leads us into a narrow ravine, switchbacks once to cross it, then descends to the bottom of the dry head of Alkali Wash (4540-1.2). A steep, rocky and sometimes hot quintet of switchbacks accomplish the ensuing ascent of the far slope. They lead to atop a chaparral ridge, where our trail merges with a jeep road (4840-0.6). This we follow east, easily over a low saddle and down to where PCT trail tread resumes (4820-0.2) as the road fades into a dry grassy flat. Now the path winds north, right along the raw, precipitous lip of Horse Canyon. Uplifting of the area with each passing earthquake is making the course of Horse Canyon's stream steeper, and it is responding by aggressively eroding into the red and white strata of the surrounding uplands. This has resulted in a badland of tortuous ravines and ridgelets, which we see stretching east to Vandeventer Flat, at the foot of Toro Peak. Eventually this erosive process will result in a drainage rearrangement in Burnt Valley, to our northwest, as Horse Canyon's stream advances headward into that valley.

We walk along a narrow divide, enjoy instructional views, then push on, moderately up across the flanks of Lookout Mountain. Eventually the trail finds a low pass (5070-2.5) on the peak's northwestern shoulder, and we have a delightful panorama north over the entire length of the San Jacinto Mountains. In the leftmost distance the rounded form of lofty San Jacinto Peak reigns, usually with a regal coat of snow in spring. Leaving the gap we descend into San Bernardino National Forest. The trail levels and then turns north across a sandy,

B4, B5

sagebrush-matted valley to quickly strike 2-lane Pines-to-Palms Highway 74 (4919-0.5) at a point just west of Santa Rosa Summit. Water may be obtained by detouring left, northwest, for 1.0 mile to a restaurant at the junction of Highway 74 and Cahuilla Road (Highway 371). For supplies, one could walk 6.0 miles farther west on Highway 371 to Anza.

Once across Highway 74 we ascend gently north to a ridgetop, then switchback once on its north side. We are soon engaged in a sandy, fitful ascent into and out of numerous small ravines and around picturesque blocky cliffs of crumbling granite. We pass close along the western face of a low ridge, then descend short switchbacks to hop across the usually dry creek (5040-3.7) that drains Penrod Canyon. Here, a comfortable waterless camp could be made under Coulter pines and live oaks. The track winds up-canyon, crossing the stream bed twice more before climbing to sunnier chamise and oak chaparral for a contour of the canyon's eastern slopes. The PCT eventually strikes Road 6S01A (5700-2.0), ascending from the west to reach an open-pit limestone quarry just above our trail. Our way proceeds directly across the road to resume the ascent, now steeper, along Penrod Canyon's east wall. Excellent vistas west over the shoulder of Thomas Mountain and south to Bucksnort Mountain are obtained on this stretch, just before we swing east around a nose to abruptly encounter marble bedrock. The first leg of the PCT's climb into the San Jacinto Mountains ends soon, as we first go through a stock gate, then pass southeast-traversing Trail 3E15 to Bull Canyon, and in 50 yards top out at a saddle on the Desert Divide (5950-0.9). Here is a junction with the Tunnel Spring Trail.

Travelers low on water might choose to drop very steeply southwest 0.3 mile down the rough trail to a point where the path joins a stream bed, then follow the stream bed 100 yards north to Tunnel Spring, its cattle-trough shaded by box-elders. It makes a poor campsite. Alternatively, one could descend east from the saddle one mile on better graded Live Oak Trail 4E03 to Live Oak Spring, also with poor camping. The Forest Service may develop this campsite in future years.

Resuming our northbound trek, we turn north along the east face of the Desert Divide. Shady interior live oaks and Coulter pines alternate with xeric chaparral areas (look for shaggy Mojave yuccas) as the trail ascends gently

across Julian schist to the east slopes of Lion Peak. We get sporadic vistas down Oak Canyon to subdivided upper Palm Canyon, then a rough switchback leads to the ridgetop north of Lion Peak. For the next 2 miles the route remains on or near the divide, traversing gneiss, schist, quartzite and marble bedrock and skirting past low chaparral laced with rabbitbrush and cacti. Little Desert Peak (6883') offers panoramas east and north to the Coachella Valley and Palm Springs, and west to coniferous Thomas Mountain and pastoral Garner Valley. Moments later, a short descent ends at a saddle where we cross the Cedar Spring Trail 4E17 (6780-4.1), which descends southwest to Morris Ranch and north a short mile to Cedar Spring Camp (6330')—the best camp and the only permanent water along the southern Desert Divide.

Our route, however, steeply ascends the ridgecrest, then it briefly descends to another saddle with a junction (6945-0.6). A very rough trail, which descends steeply south to Morris Ranch, passes a polluted cattle trough at Eagle Spring, while a similar trail, which descends north ¾ mile to Cedar Spring Camp, passes often-dry Lion Spring.

Continuing northwest, we soon pass Trail 4E04 (7080-0.5), which starts east from near Palm View Peak, then drops north toward Garnet Ridge. Then, past a 7123' summit, we descend, often steeply, on a rocky, nebulous tread back into a cooler environment of white firs growing at the head of the spectacular West Fork Palm Canyon. Presently the route emerges on brushy Fobes Saddle and meets Fobes Ranch Trail 4E02 (5990-2.4), which descends west. Thirsty hikers may choose to go west down this overgrown trail to reach a spring in ½ mile (poor camping), but must respect private property and descend no farther.

The PCT north from this saddle ascends steeply to the upper slopes of Spitler Peak, where one encounters a charred forest of black oak, white fir, incense-cedar and Jeffrey pine, gloomy mementos of a massive 1980 blaze that blackened almost the entire upper West Fork Palm Canyon and Murray and Andreas canyons. One will find evidence of it all the way to Red Tahquitz. Along our climb we enter San Jacinto Wilderness and then beyond some very steep pitches the PCT levels to wind around to the north of Spitler Peak. It then descends just east of the rocky spine that forms the ridge between Spitler and Apache peaks. Gaining

B5, B6, B7

see MAP B5   see MAP B5

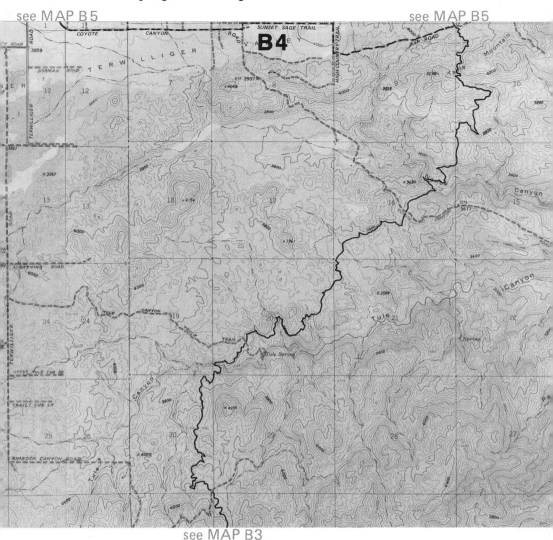

see MAP B3

this knife-edge col, where the PCT was widened by fire fighters to form a fuelbreak, the trail wastes no time in attacking the next objective: Apache Peak. Steep rocky-sandy tread leads up its southern slopes to emerge on a black, burned summit plateau. Here we find a sign marking the Apache Spring Trail (7430-2.6), which descends steeply east ½ mile to poor camps at burned-over, usually flowing Apache Spring. From our junction too, a short use trail ascends northwest to the viewful, if ugly, summit of Apache Peak.

The PCT now begins to descend gently along the eastern flanks of Apache Peak, passing through a ghost forest of immense, burned manzanitas. After a useless 0.2-mile-long switchback we reach a fine overlook of the northern Coachella Valley and of Joshua Tree National Monument, which lies well beyond the valley in the Little San Bernardino Mountains. A well-constructed stretch next leads west along a cliff face to a gap, where one can dry-camp, at the head of Apple Canyon. To circumvent the granitic ramparts of Antsell

B7, B8

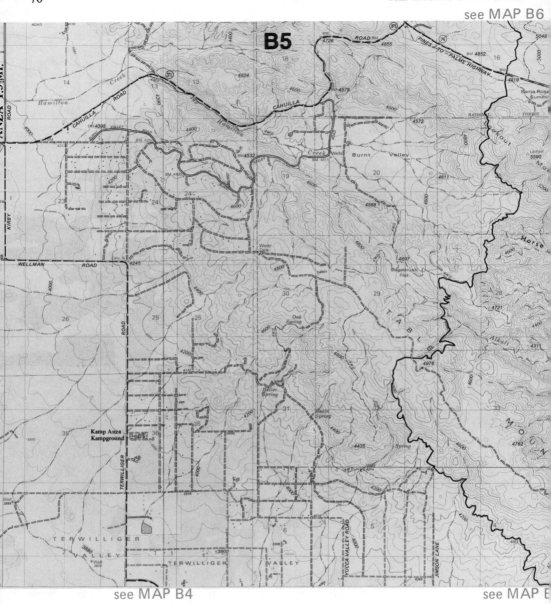

see MAP B4

see MAP B

Rock, the PCT's next leg follows a dynamited path under its sweeping northeast slopes, which are thankfully shaded by conifers spared from the 1980 fire. Once north of Antsell Rock's major buttresses, we take switchbacks for a 400′ elevation gain to reach the San Jacinto's crest at a pleasantly montane gap (7200-2.9). Big-cone spruce, a close relative of Douglas-fir,

plus white fir and mountain mahogany provide pleasant cover as the often-dynamited path ascends another 400′, first on the east and then on the southwest slopes of Southwell Peak. Notice Lake Hemet, lying just east of the active Thomas Mountain Fault, at the head of Garner Valley, to your southwest.

North of Southwell Peak the rocky PCT is

B8

dynamited to traverse under precipitous, granitic gendarmes, and the ascending hiker can gaze northwest to Tahquitz Peak and north to Red Tahquitz, or east down rugged Murray Canyon. The ascent ends (8380-3.4) above Andreas Canyon's deep gorge, where our route turns west to descend gently on duff and sand

and eventually to cross South Fork Tahquitz Creek in a forest, and then join, moments later, the Tahquitz Valley Trail (8075-1.5). This trail descends north ⅓ mile to good camps and water in Little Tahquitz Valley, and then traverses to Tahquitz and Skunk Cabbage meadows.

B8, B9

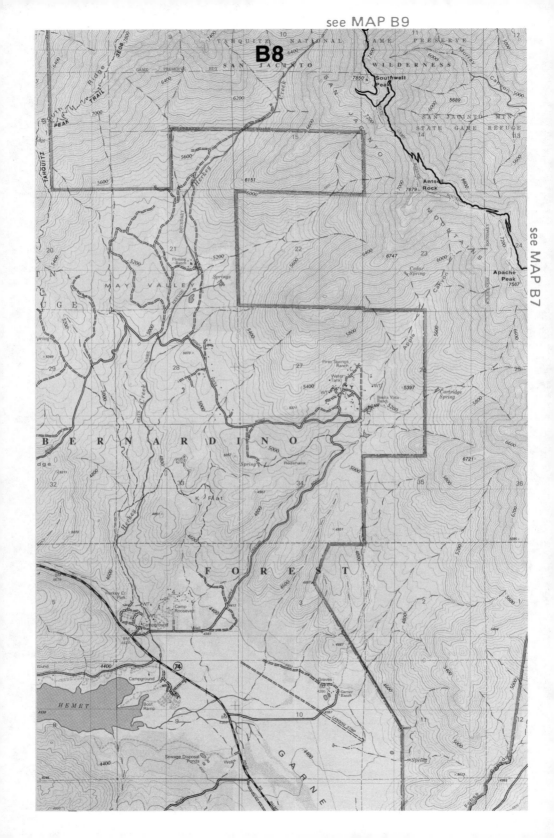

see MAP B7

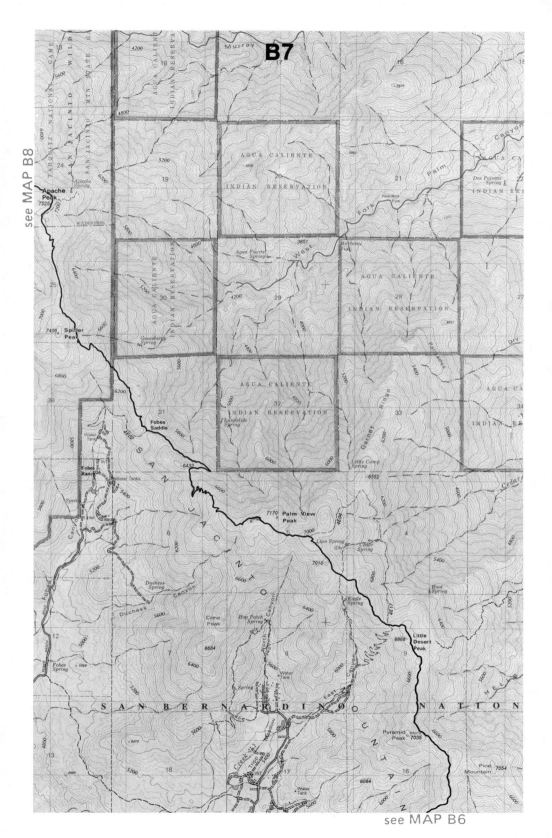

see MAP B8

see MAP B6

From our junction the PCT climbs southwest through dense groves of lodgepole pines to manzanitas and western white pines, which grow on gravelly slopes of decomposed granite. Presently we come to a junction with the Tahquitz Peak Trail 3E08 (8570-0.6), which offers a side trip ½ mile up to the peak's airy summit lookout. This trip is well worthwhile, for from the 8846' summit you can get an idea of how steep canyons, such as Strawberry Valley below, are eroding back into the high, rolling landscape that lies between Red Tahquitz and San Jacinto Peak. Tahquitz Peak commemorates a legendary Cahuilla Indian demon who lived hereabouts, dining on unsuspecting Indian maidens and, when displeased, giving the weather a turn for the worse.

Those who need to press on will turn north and ease down the PCT to Saddle Junction (8100-1.3), the crossroads for an array of trails into the San Jacinto Wilderness. From the saddle Devils Slide Trail 3E05 descends 2.5 miles west past three springs to Fern Valley Road 5S22. The mountain-resort community of Idyllwild—a good place to resupply and take a layover day—lies 2 miles down this road. Also leaving the saddle are two more trails, one branching northeast to Long Valley, and another one southeast to Tahquitz Valley.

The PCT continues north, soon switchbacking out of the forest to slopes that offer excellent over-the-shoulder vistas toward Tahquitz (Lily) Rock, a magnet for Southern California rock climbers. Almost 1000' higher than Saddle Junction, the PCT levels to turn left from a junction with the Wellmans Cienaga Trail (9030-1.8), just within the confines of Mount San Jacinto Wilderness State Park. This trail arcs about 2 miles northeast to Round Valley Trail Camp and beyond to 10,804' San Jacinto Peak, a recommended side trip.

From the junction the PCT immediately leaves the state park and descends on a generally westward bearing above Strawberry Valley's steep headwall to Strawberry Cienaga (8560-0.9), a trickling sphagnum-softened freshet and a viewful lunch stop. "Cienaga" is a Spanish word, often seen in Southern California, meaning "swamp" or "marsh." Further descent leads to a forested junction with Marion Ridge Trail 3E17 (8070-1.4), which reaches Idyllwild after a southward, 3.8-mile descent. Now out of the Federal wilderness and back in Mount San Jacinto State Park, the PCT turns north to ascend Marion Mountain's

pleasant mixed-conifer slopes, and eventually passes two closely spaced trail junctions. The first, the Marion Mountain Trail, descends west-southwest to the environs of Marion Mountain and Fern Basin campgrounds. The second, the Seven Pines Trail, descends generally northwest, then west to a saddle, from which Road 4S02 switchbacks almost 2 miles down to Dark Canyon Campground.

Soon after the second lateral our trail heads along a marshy, dank creek and reaches Deer Springs Campground (8830-2.1), a grossly overused site with water, toilets and fire rings. (Overuse may be due in part to a state-park restriction that prohibits camping along the park's PCT stretch except at Deer Springs Campground.) Before leaving, hikers should restock their water bottles, since the next water along the route is from Snow Creek, at the northern base of the San Jacinto Mountains, a punishing 25-mile descent away.

A minute beyond Deer Springs Campground, after a momentary traverse that leads across the infant San Jacinto River, we climb to a nearby junction with the San Jacinto Peak Trail, which is the return route of the recommended side trip to the peak's summit. From the junction we switchback down to Fuller Ridge (8725-1.9), a rocky, white-fir-covered spine separating the San Jacinto and San Gorgonio river drainages. Here the northbound trekker gets his first view of the San Bernardino Mountains' 11,499' San Gorgonio Mountain, to the north, which is Southern California's highest point. Separating that range from ours is San Gorgonio Pass, 7000' below us, lying between the Banning Fault and other branches of the great San Andreas Fault (also known as the San Andreas Rift Zone).

The PCT's route along Fuller Ridge is a tortuous one, composed for the most part of miniature switchbacks, alternately descending and climbing, which wind under small gendarmes and around wind-beaten conifers. In a little over 2 miles, though, the route takes to north-facing slopes, and, exchanging state wilderness for a brief stint in the Federal wilderness, it gently descends to a small dirt-road parking circle at Fuller Ridge Trailhead Remote Campsite (7750-3.9). Pleasant but waterless, the sites lie in open stands of ponderosa pine and white fir. The PCT, marked by a post, resumes on the west side of the road loop, heading due north past a site. It rounds northwest above, then drops to cross, well-used

B9, B10

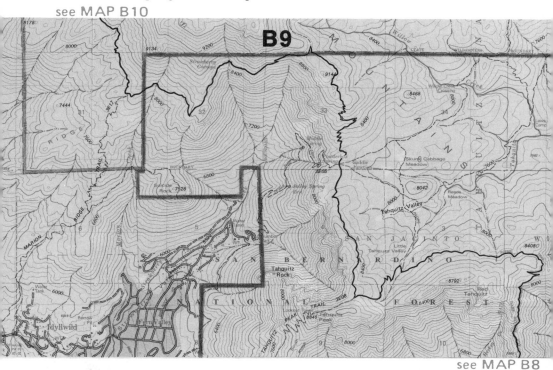

see MAP B10

see MAP B8

Tahquitz Peak and Tahquitz Rock, from near Wellman Divide trail

Black Mountain Road 4S01 (7670-0.2). Those low on water may opt to follow this road left, descending 1.3 miles to Black Mountain Group Campground.

Our trail leaves the road on a gentle-to-moderate descent north along a ridge clothed in an open stand of mixed conifers. We switch-back down three times across the nose of the ridge separating Snow Creek from chaparral-decked Brown Creek. More-open conditions on the west side of the ridge allow for sweeping vistas: hulking San Gorgonio Mountain looms to the north, above the desert pass that bears its name, while, stretching to the northwest, the San Bernardino and San Gabriel valleys, flanked by the lofty summits of the San Gabriel Mountains, extend toward the Los Angeles basin. On a clear day in winter or spring, snow-flecked Mount San Antonio (Mount Baldy) and Mount Wilson are both visible in that range.

We re-enter San Jacinto Wilderness and presently our sandy, lupine- and penstemon-lined path meets a switchback in a dirt road (6860-1.9), which winds eastward into a shallow basin. Marked by large ducks the trail leaves the northwest side of the open gap containing the road, but soon our route turns south to descend alongside and just below that road. After a bit our course veers from the road and winds east down dry washes and under the shade of low scrub oaks to a narrow gap (6390-1.3) in a sawblade ridge of granodiorite needles. Four long switchbacks descend the east face of this prominent ridge, depositing us in notice-ably more xeric environs. Initially, Coulter pines replace other montane conifers, and then, as the way arcs north in continual descent, we enter a true chaparral: yerba santa, buckwheat, holly-leaf cherry, scrub oak, manzanita and yucca supply the sparse ground cover, while scarlet gilia and yellow blazing star add spring color. Unlike chaparral communities moistened by maritime air, the desert-facing slopes here force these species to contend with much more extreme drought conditions. As a result, many more of the plants growing here are annuals, which avoid drought by lying dormant as seed, while others, such as yerba santa, wilt and drop their soft leaves to prevent water loss during sustained dry periods.

A continued moderate downgrade and another set of long switchbacks soon allow us to inspect the awesome, avalanche-raw, 9600′ north es-carpment of San Jacinto Peak, which rises above the cascades of Snow Creek. To our northeast the confused alluvial terrain beyond San Gorgonio Pass attests to recent activity along the San Andreas Fault. Beyond, sub-urban Desert Hot Springs shimmers in the Coachella Valley heat, backdropped by the Little San Bernardino Mountains.

Inexorably, our descent continues at a mod-erate grade, presently switchbacking in broad sweeps across a dry ravine on slopes north of West Fork Snow Creek. After striking a small saddle (3200-8.6) just west of knob 3252, the trail, now taking an overly gentle grade, swings north, then northwest down a boulder-studded hillside. We note the small village of Snow Creek lying below us at the mountain's base before our way makes three small switchbacks and then heads back southeast toward Snow Canyon. After winding our way through a veritable forest of 20–30′ high orange, granitic boulders, we negotiate a final set of switch-backs before dropping to cross a dry creekbed on the western edge of Snow Canyon. Soon after, we strike narrow, paved Snow Canyon Road (1725-6.2). Here a sign points northeast, across the road, indicating a mile-long deadend segment of PCT tread that has been aban-doned in favor of an eventual alignment west of Snow Canyon Road. Snow Canyon is both a game refuge and a water supply for Palm Springs, so camping here is not allowed. Addi-tionally, most of Snow Creek's water is carried east in a pipeline, and no water is available here, so continue a bit farther to reach water.

Doing this, we make a moderate descent along narrow Snow Canyon Road, which winds north down Snow Canyon's rubbly alluvial fan, often near a small, usually flowing western branch of Snow Creek. Eventually the road simultaneously leaves San Bernardino National Forest and its San Jacinto Wilderness at a Desert Water Agency gate, and then it veers northwest to hop across the western branch. Just beyond, our route joins paved Falls Creek Road (1225-1.0) at the outskirts of the small village of Snow Creek. Southbound hikers should note that this community is their last certain water source until Deer Springs Camp-ground, a grueling 24 miles and a 7600′ climb away high in the San Jacintos.

Now we briefly follow Falls Creek Road northwest to a junction with Snow Creek Road 3S01 (1230-0.2). From here the permanent PCT route starts a contour northwest. Con-structed by Sierra Club volunteers and the Bureau of Land Management, the next 2 miles

B10, B11

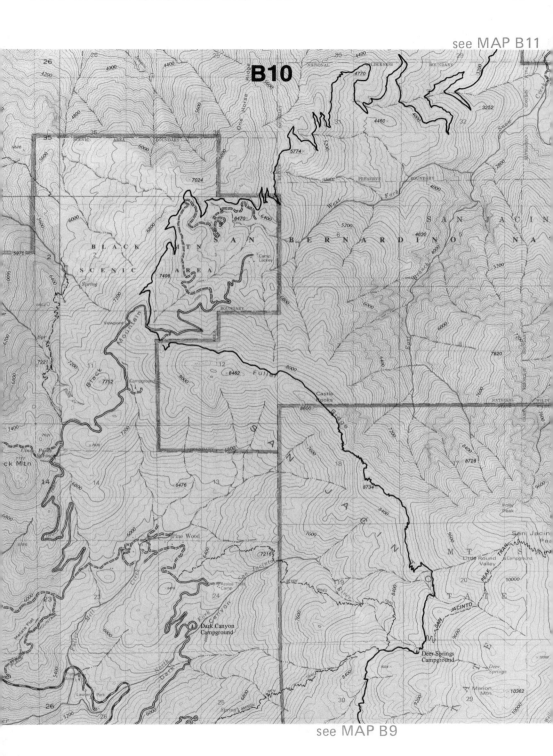

see MAP B11

see MAP B9

of PCT are not really trail at all. Because of shifting sands and the possibility that off-road-vehicle enthusiasts might abuse an actual trail, they decided not to build an actual trail across broad San Gorgonio Pass. Instead, the PCT route is indicated by a row of 5' tall 4 x 4 posts, some metal, some redwood, each emblazoned with the triangular PCT shield and with white directional arrows. Standing beside one post, you can usually see the next one without much difficulty. The first metal post stands a few yards northwest of Snow Creek Road, in a field of foxtails. It indicates the way (330° bearing) to the first of a long line of redwood posts that march due north along a section boundary.

Our actual route is somewhat more tor-turous, winding through well-spaced head-high yellow-flowered creosote bushes on a very gentle descent. A few minutes' walk leads across a sandy wash, which at about 1188' elevation is the PCT's lowest point south of the Columbia Gorge on the Oregon-Washington border. Another few minutes finds our not-a-trail intersecting a pair of crossing jeep roads (1195-0.7) under a high-tension powerline. Beyond, the wooden posts continue north, now across a more cobbly desert floor with mixed shrubbery. We cross a good gravel road (1210-0.2), then proceed across numerous sandy washes that constitute the ephemeral San

B11

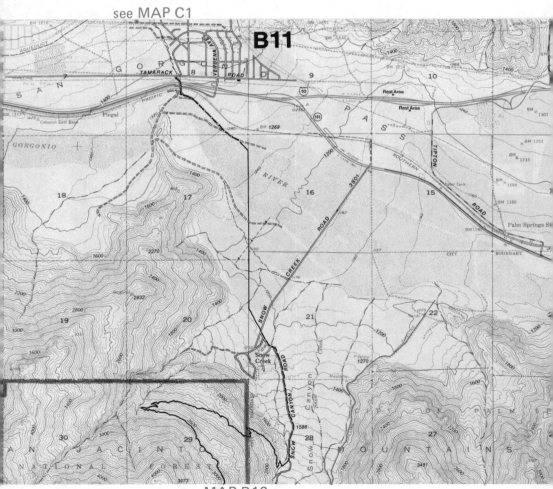

see MAP C1

see MAP B10

Gorgonio River. Usually no water at all is to be found, but often there is a strong westerly wind, which throws stinging sand in our faces. Also it sets hundreds of power-generating wind turbines flapping like alarmed sea gulls, these standing to the north, across Interstate 10. In the rainy season, look for purple-flower clusters of sand verbena hereabouts.

Eventually, metal posts indicate a bend northwest in the route to soon join a good dirt road (1265-0.7). This we trace left, northwest, keeping just south of a 20' high alluvial bank upon which runs the busy Southern Pacific Railroad. We soon diverge from the good road to a poorer one, well-marked by posts, which leads obviously to a tangle of roads at the mouth of Stubbe Canyon Creek (1320-0.7). Here the route emerges from three concrete bridges, one of Southern Pacific Railroad and two of Interstate 10. Now we follow a dirt road that goes north under the bridges, then clamber up a road bank to paved Tamarack Road (1360-0.1). A slowly dying suburb, West Palm Springs Village, is centered ⅓ mile east along Tamarack Road, at Interstate 10's Verbena Avenue offramp. Although water might be obtained in an emergency from a few homes there, the village has no other resources for PCT travelers. To resupply, hitchhike, as recommended under "Supplies," 12.5 miles east to Palm Springs or 4.5 miles west to Cabazon.

B11

Mt. San Jacinto, from slopes above West Fork Snow Creek

San Gorgonio Mountain and Big Bear Lake, from Delamar Mountain

Section C: San Gorgonio Pass to Interstate 15 near Cajon Pass

Introduction: Running the entire length of the San Bernardino Mountains, this long trail section samples most of the diverse ecosystems found there. Beginning in San Gorgonio Pass in the sweltering heat of a typical Colorado Desert (Lower Sonoran Zone) ecosystem, the Pacific Crest Trail crosses the San Andreas Fault and then climbs through a sparse, drab chaparral of bayonet-sharp cacti and thorny scrub along the Whitewater River and Mission Creek. Though sprung from subalpine snowbanks high in the San Gorgonio Wilderness, these streams almost all evaporate or sink beneath desert gravels before reaching the foothills.

As you climb higher, small drought-tolerant pinyon pines, favored food source of Indians and various animals, soon border the trail, heralding our passage through the Upper Sonoran Zone. These trees gradually mingle with Jeffrey pines and incense-cedars until, at about 7000', we find ourselves in the crisp air and enveloping forests of the Transition Zone. Just north of Coon Creek, at the 8750' apex of the PCT in the San Bernardino Mountains, the route touches the Canadian Zone, where isolated snow patches might linger into early summer. Hikers traversing the high San Bernardinos in April or May should expect possible hail or snow and nightly subfreezing temperatures. Bring warm clothing and carry a tent. From the high point, one can turn southwest to scan the San Gorgonio Wilderness' high summits, where hardy subalpine conifers huddle below gale-screening ridges. The PCT was routed around the wilderness because its backpacker population was already excessive.

Nearing dammed Big Bear Lake, a popular resort area, the PCT alternates between Jeffrey-pine and pinyon forest. In this northern rainshadow of the San Bernardinos, plant and animal life is much more influenced by proximity to the high Mojave Desert, stretching northward, than by the terrain's elevation, which would normally foster a uniform montane Jeffrey-pine-and-fir forest. Instead, Joshua trees, cacti, mountain mahogany and sagebrush share the rolling hillsides with dry pinyon-pine groves, and drive Jeffrey pines, incense-cedars and white firs away to higher summits or to the cold-air microclimates of stream beds.

North of Big Bear Lake the PCT begins to trend west, following the main axis of the San Bernardino Mountains. A part of the Transverse Range Province, which includes the San Gabriel Mountains and other mountain chains stretching west to the Channel Islands, the San Bernardinos cut conspicuously across the lay of other California physiographic features, which trend northwest-southeast. Long before being intruded by molten rock that solidified to form granitic plutons, the region now straddled by the San Bernardinos had been alternately low land and shallow sea floor. Evidence of this lies in two rock types we will encounter often: the Furnace marble—derived from marine carbonates that became limestone—and the Saragossa quartzite—derived from sand that became sandstone. The limestone and sandstone were then altered under heat and pressure, perhaps several times, to reach their present metamorphic states.

Near Lake Arrowhead, another reservoir originally constructed to store water to irrigate foothill orange groves, the PCT again veers north, now down Deep Creek, a permanent stream feeding the ephemeral Mojave River. The floral composition of the Mojave Desert, seen here and also later as the PCT skirts Summit Valley, differs strikingly from the lower Colorado Desert flora seen farther south. Bitter-cold, windy winters here account for many of the differences.

Section C ends unremarkably under 6-lane Interstate 15 in Cajon Canyon, overshadowed by massive workings of humanity—the freeway, the powerlines from the Colorado River, and the multiple railroad tracks. These in turn are dwarfed by an awesome artifact of nature—the cleft of the San Andreas Fault, which slashes through Cajon Canyon and bends east to demarcate the southern base of the San Bernardino Mountains.

Declination: 13°E

Mileages:	South to North	Distances between Points	North to South
near Interstate 10 in San Gorgonio Pass	0.0		132.8
water fountain at Mesa Wind Station.	3.9	3.9	128.9
camps by Whitewater River ford	10.7	6.8	122.1
East Fork Mission Creek Road.	15.9	5.2	116.9
Forks Springs.	22.3	6.4	110.5
Road 1N93 and Mission Creek Trail Camp	29.5	7.2	103.3
Coon Creek Jumpoff Group Camp.	36.1	6.6	96.7
dirt road just east of Onyx Summit	41.8	5.7	91.0
Arrastre Trail Camp at Deer Spring.	45.9	4.1	86.9
Highway 18 near dry Baldwin Lake.	55.4	9.5	77.4
Doble Trail Camp	57.9	2.5	74.9
Van Dusen Canyon Road to Big Bear City	64.3	6.4	68.5
Holcomb Valley Road to Fawnskin	67.8	3.5	65.0
Little Bear Springs Trail Camp	75.0	7.2	57.8
Crab Flats Road	81.8	6.8	51.0
Holcomb Crossing Trail Camp	83.7	1.9	49.1
Roads 3N34 and 3N15 to Lake Arrowhead	87.8	4.1	45.0
Deep Creek Hot Spring	97.2	9.4	35.6
Mojave River Forks Reservoir Dam.	102.2	5.0	30.6
Highway 173 above Mojave River Forks Reservoir. . . .	103.7	1.5	29.1
Road 2N33 near Cedar Springs Dam	113.2	9.5	19.6
Silverwood Lake Area's entrance road	119.2	6.0	13.6
Little Horsethief Canyon's dry creek bed	126.3	7.1	6.5
Interstate 15 near Cajon Pass	132.8	6.5	0.0

Supplies: West Palm Springs Village, at the beginning of Section C, has nothing for hikers. Supplies may be purchased 4.5 miles west on Interstate 10, in Cabazon, which has limited services, or 10 miles west on that freeway, in Banning, which has all services. Better still, though possibly more expensive, is Palm Springs, lying 12.5 miles east via Interstate 10 and Highway 111. It has a dazzling array of markets, hotels and fine eateries. Be sure to carry ample water north from West Palm Springs, since the White-water River and the lower reaches of Mission Creek that the PCT traverses are usually dry by June, making the most certain water source Fork Springs, a mind-broiling 22.3 miles into the journey.

Big Bear City, 3 miles south down Van Dusen Canyon Road from the 64.3-mile point on the PCT, is the next convenient provisioning stop. It boasts a post office, stores, restaurants, motels and laundromats beside shallow, picturesque Big Bear Lake. Fawnskin, another resort community, is located on the northwest shore of Big Bear Lake, and it is 3.7 miles off-route along Holcomb Valley Road, 67.8 miles from the start. It has a post office, stores, restaurants and motels. The next chance for supplies lies in Lake Arrowhead, 3½ miles from the PCT's crossing of Deep Creek, 87.8 miles from the start. Here you'll find post office, stores, restaurants and motels. Crestline, a similar mountain village, also offers similar accommodations for hikers who hitchhike south 10 miles on Highway 138 from the 119.2-mile point of the PCT, at Silverwood Lake State Recreation Area. Travelers with less extensive needs may avail themselves of a small store and cafe a short distance off the trail in the recreation area.

Section C terminates at a roadend just shy of Interstate 15 in Cajon Canyon. This paved spur road leads 0.6 mile northwest to meet Highway 138 about 200 yards east of its overpass of Interstate 15 at Cajon Junction. Gas stations and a fine 24-hour restaurant lie near this cloverleaf, from where Highway 138 continues northwest 8½ miles to Highway 2, which goes 5½ miles to Wrightwood. This pleasant mountain community has a post office, stores, restaurants, motels and a laundromat. Those who don't mind a return to true civilization—smog, congestion, street lights and concrete—may go south 17 miles on Interstate 15 to San Bernardino, which has all the dubious advantages of a hectic metropolis.

Reach the southern terminus of Section C via Interstate 10's Verbenia Avenue exit. Head briefly north to Tamarack Road, which parallels the freeway, and follow it ⅓ mile west to the posted PCT, just west of Fremontia Road.

Easy-to-follow PCT trail tread climbs gently north from Tamarack Road, first just west of the dry bed of Stubbe Canyon Creek, then on a low levee to its east. We wind past numerous roads of a failed subdivision and then pass under a powerline and its attendant road. Across a second such road (1475-0.5) the tread may be vague, but it is easily traced in the sandy wash, since it is marked by 4 x 4 PCT posts and it runs just west of a green-wire fence. Beyond it, we wind up to a dirt road over the buried Colorado River Aqueduct (1580-0.4). A minute later, we cross a better road, then veer northeast and ascend to better views south of the incredible north wall of San Jacinto Peak.

Keeping to a low bench with knee-high scrub, we traverse across a succession of jeep roads, then cross better Cottonwood Road (1690-0.6). Now the expediently routed PCT turns left, north, uphill alongside Cottonwood Road, keeping always within 10 yards of it, in a delightful, thigh-high garden of silver-flannel-leaved, yellow-flowered brittlebush, a drought-tolerant shrub of the sunflower family. Nearing the mouth of Cottonwood Canyon, the trail crosses two side-by-side roads (1850-0.6) then makes a slightly indistinct ford of the almost always dry stream that drains Cottonwood Canyon. Across it, the way merges with a jeep track to strike east to the mouth of Gold Canyon, whose unusual east-west orientation is due to erosion along the Bonnie Bell fault, a splinter of the great San Andreas rift.

Entering Gold Canyon, our jeep track strikes Gold Canyon Road (1845-0.2), then we wind just south of it on trail constructed by the Sierra

C1

Club. In the next long mile, our pleasant way recrosses the road, passes through a stock fence at a corral, then crosses the road twice more, all in desert vegetation of Mojave yucca, rabbitbrush, creosote bush and multiple species of cacti. Presently, numerous windmills of the Mesa Wind Farm come into view, and the canyon bends north. Here, just off the trail, is the Mesa Wind Farm's electric transformer station. At a road junction just above it is a water fountain (2310-1.6), which usually has a trickling flow throughout springtime. Camping—in the company of range cattle—could be done anywhere nearby.

Sometimes vague, our path now leads more moderately up a small parallel ravine west of the road. Later, we come back alongside the main ravine and momentarily join a rough jeep road (2470-0.5). Now inside a BLM study area for possible inclusion in the San Gorgonio Wilderness, the way leads easily up-canyon, keeping just west of its dry wash and braiding with a network of cattle paths. After passing through a stock drift fence, the path steepens to climb the head of Gold Canyon. Mostly, the way is unrelentingly shadeless, but occasional, small laurel sumac trees do offer respite. During the wet season, a profusion of wildflowers may sprinkle the route, including many members of the sunflower family, and also white, blue and lavender phacelias, chia and popcorn flower. Lizards too numerous to count also scurry from underfoot. Finally, four small switchbacks help us gain a narrow pass (3225-1.3) between Gold and Teutang canyons. The most impressive vistas are southeast, contrasting the granite and seasonal snow of the San Jacinto massif with the Colorado desert sands of Coachella Valley.

Starting north, we descend moderately to a ridge nose, down which small, tight switchbacks descend. These bring the PCT to a dry crossing of the stream bed in Teutang Canyon (2815-0.7), just upstream of a chasm of gray granite. Next we round an intervening promontory to step across another canyon tributary, then proceed fairly level down-canyon. When we gain a narrow ridgetop, our path doubles back on itself to climb northwest, perhaps indistinctly, up an open grassy slope, before resuming a traversing line high above the canyon's floor. This stretch does afford interesting panoramas east over the cleft of Whitewater Canyon to the sun-browned Little San Bernardino Mountains.

Eventually we descend, first directly along a ridgelet, then in a sweeping arc that leads to the lip of Hatchery Canyon. Now on switchbacks that are susceptible to erosion, we drop quickly to the floor of Hatchery Canyon, where we step across its dry stream bed. The trail now heads sandily downstream, soon passing through a stock gate, and then striking an old jeep road (2285-2.7) at the canyon's mouth in Whitewater Canyon, just beneath an impressive conglomerate scarp. Here we turn left, north, on sandy alluvium of the west bank of the Whitewater River, which is a raging torrent true to its name in early season, but more often is a noisesome brook. Our route—essentially a jeep road—winds across sandy washes where the flanking scrub is alive with phainopeplas, which are crested silky flycatchers closely related to waxwings.

Just past red basalt outcrops of Miocene age that mark two good camps (2605-1.6), large ducks and a sign lead us northeast across the Whitewater River's bouldery granite and marble bed to a narrow canyon peppered with boulders of basalt and gneiss, among junipers, catclaws and bladderpods patrolled by collared lizards. Here the best jeep track jogs northwest, paralleling the river bed for a moment, to find a resumption of trail at an old California Riding and Hiking Trail (CRHT) sign post. From the post our path ascends moderately northeast in a terrain not unlike Death Valley, soon switchbacking to gain a ridgetop (3075-1.3) in deeply incised gneiss and fanglomerate. Ignore a short deadend trail climbing south along the ridge from here. Fiddleneck and foxtail brush against one's legs on the descent northeast from this saddle, and one soon reaches and turns north beside West Fork Mission Creek Road (2918-0.6). Just minutes later the PCT veers north away from this dirt road (3010-0.2) in a dry, sandy wash. Look for CRHT posts and follow them east to start a switchbacking ascent of an east-trending nose eroded from Quaternary and Tertiary sediments. Atop this ridge, views are panoramic and startling. The southern horizon is dominated by 10,804' San Jacinto Peak, often frosted in winter and spring with snow and contrasting markedly with the red, yellow and gray hues of the desert's alluvial landscape, in the foreground. To the west, gneissic rocks support Kitching Peak, while the Whitewater River Canyon ascends as a rocky scar northwest to the Jumpoffs below barren San Gorgonio

C1, C2

C1

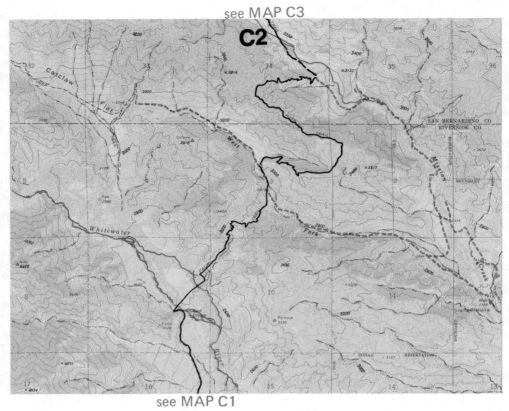

see MAP C3

C2

see MAP C1

Mountain. The gully just north of the ridge that we ascended, plus West Fork Mission Creek, Catclaw Flat, and Middle Fork Whitewater River are all aligned with the north branch of the San Andreas Fault, which is partly responsible for this region's varied geology.

The PCT continues to wind northwest up the ridgetop dividing the East and West forks of Mission Creek, then the ascent gives way to a moderate descent east down a chaparralled nose, bringing us to East Fork Mission Creek Road (3060-3.1). Here we turn northwest up-canyon to cross usually flowing East Fork Mission Creek in about ½ mile, then continue along its shadeless north bank to the end of the dirt road (3360-1.4). From this point our hike up Mission Creek is often difficult, despite reconstruction efforts by C.C.C. trail crews. Mission Creek's narrow gorge, incised in tortured granite gneisses, leaves little room for a trail, so washouts are frequent and the path is often vague through alluvial boulder fields and jungles of baccharis (false willow), alder, wil-

low and cottonwood. Rattlesnakes inhabit the grassy stream margins, as do garter snakes, racers, horned lizards, antelope ground squirrels, summer tanagers and bobcats—so keep an eye open while making any of the 20+ fords of Mission Creek lying south of Forks Springs. Note too where prominent faults cross the canyon—at 3400', at 3900' and at 4080', where the Pinto Mountain Fault further tortures the banded gneisses. Chia, yerba santa, catclaw, baccharis and bladderpod are the most frequent plants, but you also see notable specimens of Joshua tree, yucca and cactus.

Just below the confluence of the South and North forks of Mission Creek we pass nice campsites, then cross this major creek (4830-5.0), which is fed just up-canyon by Forks Springs. Water is generally available here year-round, but may not be elsewhere in Mission Creek due to the porous sediments of its bed. North of Forks Springs, the now discernible PCT keeps usually to northeastern banks in an ocean-spray chaparral. Near 5200' the path

C2, C3

crosses granitic bedrock emplaced at the same time as Sierran granites, and later, at 5600', the tread turns to sugar-white and yellowish Saragossa quartzite. Near 5900' the PCT veers away from Mission Creek into a side canyon and quickly reaches a pleasant creekside camp (6110-3.1) shaded by alders, incense-cedars, Jeffrey pines and interior live oaks. Eight switchbacks lead west from this spot, elevating us to atop a phyllite-and-quartzite promontory. The friability and instability of the quartzite bedrock are demonstrated both by vegetational scarcity and by a massive landslide cutting across our path as we contour a steep slope shortly after gaining this ridge. Just past this slide, we leave BLM jurisdiction for San Bernardino National Forest.

White firs and Jeffrey pines soon shade the PCT as it resumes its ascent close beside Mission Creek, which usually has flowing water near its headwaters. Tank up here, for there might not be water at Mission Creek Trail Camp. A rough jeep road, built to log the forested flats south of Mission Creek, is met at a junction (7490-3.0) which may still be marked by yellow paint-daubs on nearby trees. Follow its overgrown tracks west up along willowy creekside meadows to meet gravel

Road 1N93 (7965-1.1) at a PCT marker. A sign here pretentiously announces MISSION CREEK TRAIL CAMP, which is merely a pleasant flat spot with fire rings, located south of North Fork Mission Creek. Fill your water bottles here, since the next water on route is at Arrastre (Deer Springs) Trail Camp, in 16.4 miles.

PCT trail tread resumes here, starting north up from Road 1N93 on a well-graded trail in an open stand of pines. The route rounds northeast, with some fine backward glimpses of subalpine Ten Thousand Foot Ridge in San Gorgonio Wilderness. Soon we reach a sandy gap and cross Road 1N05 (8240-0.6). Now we have some fine views northwest to rounded Sugarloaf Mountain and its smaller western sibling, Sugarlump. Next on our agenda is a pleasant, level traverse, first northward, then southeastward, in cool forest on the north side of the divide, which here separates the Santa Ana River and the Whitewater River drainages. Eventually the trail dips easily to a post-marked crossing of Road 1N05 (8115-0.8) at a saddle. Now, the easy route leads east under a forested summit, and we have panoramas northwest to Sugarloaf Mountain. Later, dropping rockily, the PCT finds a junction (7980-

C3, C4

Terrain in East Fork Mission Creek canyon

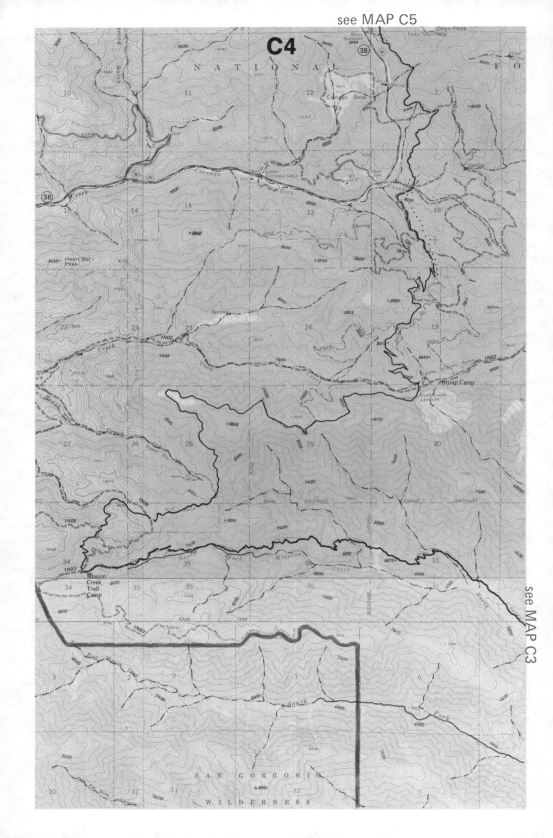

C4

see MAP C3

0.8) with a CRHT-marked trail that descends northwest from just below a forested saddle. Travelers low on water may trace this trail about ½ mile down to usually flowing Heart Bar Creek.

The PCT proceeds north from this junction, contouring at first, then making a sustained moderate ascent through a woodland of mountain mahogany, manzanita, pinyon and Jeffrey pines and scraggly white fir. Vistas gradually

C4

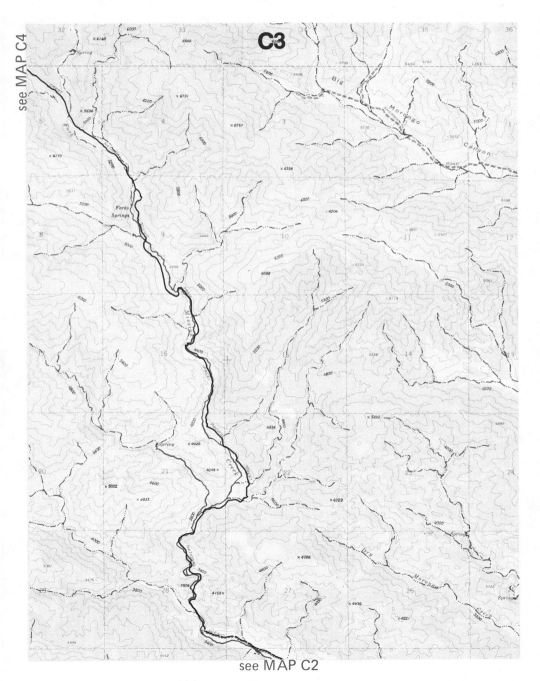

see MAP C4

see MAP C2

unfold southwest over to San Gorgonio Mountain and Ten Thousand Foot Ridge and west down Heart Bar Creek to lush Big Meadows and the popular Barton Flats camp area. Bending northwest, the path soon levels out atop the long west ridge of Peak 8828, and then it swings east into shady mixed-conifer forest lying north of that summit. For a few minutes the PCT skirts across white, granular Furnace marble, and the surrounding vegetation also changes markedly: edaphic effects (see Chapter 3's "Biology") allow only hardy whitebark pines and junipers, the former normally found in higher, colder climes, to muster a scattered occupation of the crumbly slopes. Rounding to the east of Peak 8828, we descend gently to a ridgetop and join Road 1N96 (8510-2.5), where good views southeast over North Fork Mission Creek to the San Jacinto Mountains and the Coachella Valley help to make a pleasant, but waterless, camp surrounded by lupine and purple sage.

We continue east down the poor dirt road to a road junction (8340-0.6) located on the ridge east of Peak 8588. From here the PCT continues east along the ridgeline as Road 1N96, while a better dirt road, 1N95, branches northwest, downhill. The route soon crosses onto north slopes, becomes a trail, and drops gently around Peak 8751 to Coon Creek Jumpoff—a spectacular, steep, granitic defile at the head of a tributary of North Fork Mission Creek. The raw scarp here points to rapid erosion east of the Jumpoff and illustrates the process of stream capture. The small stream draining the Tayles Hidden Acres basin and part of adjacent Section 20, to our northeast, used to connect with Coon Creek, to the west, but accelerated headward erosion of Mission Creek at the Jumpoff has intercepted that stream. Its waters now flow southeast, eventually to the Salton Sea, rather than west to the Santa Ana River and the Pacific Ocean.

From this thought-provoking overlook, the trail climbs gently for a moment to Coon Creek Road 1N02 (8090-1.3). Coon Creek Jumpoff Group Camp, with toilets but no water, is just to the east. Until midsummer, water may be obtained by walking as much as 1.5 miles west down the dirt road.

Our way now attacks, via moderate switchbacks through scattered pines, firs and montane chaparral, the south slopes of the ridge dividing Coon and Cienaga Seca creeks. Extensive views compensate for the climb. Seasonally

Mt. San Jacinto, from ridge north of Coon Creek Jumpoff

snowy Grinnell and San Gorgonio mountains loom in the southwest, Mounts Baldy and Baden-Powell mark our upcoming travels west, and glimpses of the Santa Rosa Mountains and Palm Springs shimmer in the southeast. Rounding north of a conifered hillock alive with mountain bluebirds, Clark's nutcrackers, white-headed woodpeckers and dark-eyed juncos, we strike a trail (8610-1.3) which cuts perpendicularly across our route and meets a jeep road immediately east of our trail. The PCT continues ascending for ⅓ mile, passing under small, granitic cliffs before reaching a viewless, forested ridgetop. This 8750' point is the highest spot our trail reaches in the San Bernardino Mountains.

Now the way drops sandily on a gentle gradient to cross a dirt road (8635-0.7), then it switchbacks down into a canyon, the path flanked by tall mountain-mahogany shrubs. At the mouth of a gully in the canyon bottom, we cross a jeep road (8390-0.6), and then the PCT momentarily parallels its northward course before routing itself onto this road. Private land in Section 18 prevents the Forest Service from constructing permanent PCT trail tread at this time, so we continue north on the jeep road/ CRHT right-of-way. Soon the jeep road yields to a better dirt road (8260-0.4), which you trace north down-canyon to a five-way junction—four roads and a trail—(8100-0.6) located beside often dry Cienaga Seca Creek. The PCT rises north from this junction out of

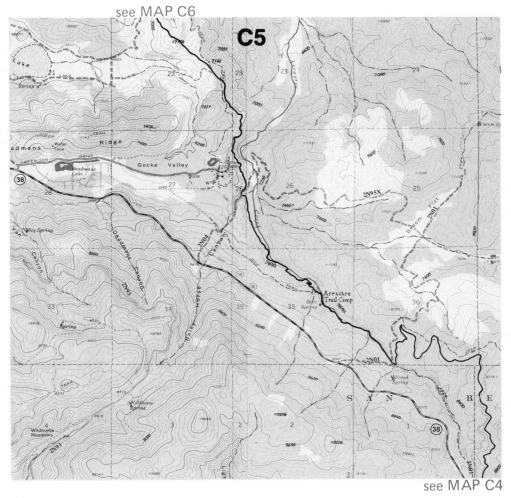

see MAP C6

C5

see MAP C4

Baldwin Lake, Bertha Peak and Gold Mountain, from Nelson Ridge

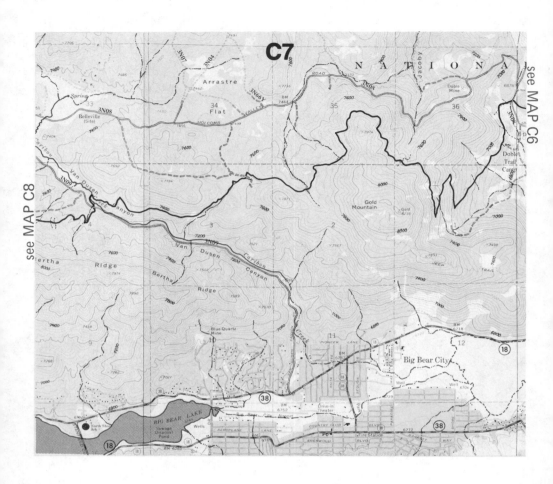

lodgepole pine into stands of juniper and mountain mahogany, then descends west along a dirt road for 130 yards to a junction (8440-1.0). Here the trail picks up again to contour the west slope of Onyx Peak over to a dirt road (8510-1.1) that is just east of Highway 38 and Onyx Summit.

The PCT crosses the road and climbs gently-to-moderately above Road 1N01, gaining increasingly good views of Baldwin Lake and Gold Mountain, in the northwest. Presently the path levels and crosses Road 1N01 (8635-1.0), then descends, first north, then west below a ridge. Lower, the well-marked route crosses a jeep road twice in quick succession before a switchback drops the trail to Broom Flat Road 2N01 (7885-2.2), a good dirt road running alongside shaded Arrastre Creek. Now we

enter fragrant white-fir groves to descend easily northwest along the seasonal creek, and soon find Arrastre Trail Camp at Deer Spring (7605-0.9). This has a fire pit, toilet, hitching posts, benches, and the last water until Doble Trail Camp, 12 miles away.

Two minutes onward, we turn north at a junction with a jeep road that leads to Balky Horse Canyon. Our route continues down Arrastre Canyon to Balky Horse Canyon and crosses Road 2N04 (7155-1.5). One can appreciate the subtle changes in vegetation that have occurred on the descent into this region, which are influenced more by the Mojave Desert's parching winds than by moisture-laden ocean breezes. Minutes later, we reach wooden berms that lead under Camp Oakes' rifle range, and then we climb gently across Saragossa quartz-

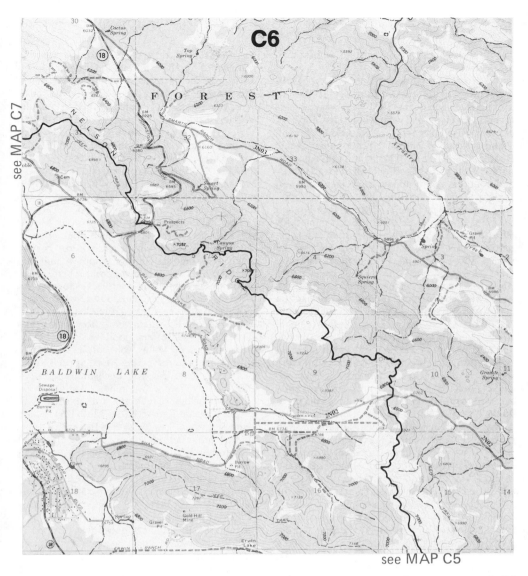

see MAP C7

see MAP C5

ite in a true high-desert plant community: pinyon pines, buckwheat, ephedra, and a shiny yellow-green shrub with wiry stems called Mormon Tea—after its use by Mormon pioneers. Atop a 7240′ shoulder, we gaze eastward and see gold mines near Tip Top Mountain's summit and also see a high-desert woodland of Joshua trees and pinyon pines.

Now paralleling an expansive, desertlike ridge, the PCT crosses two jeep roads and first gives us views west over seasonal Erwin Lake and east to the Mojave, then later views west to large, shallow, sometimes completely dry Baldwin Lake. Eventually the sandy path descends to cross Arrastre Creek Road 2N02 (6775-3.8) amid pinyon pines, Joshua trees and sagebrush. From that road the PCT climbs north, then contours northwest for alternating vistas of desert and mountain as it wanders among pinyon pines and crosses the Doble Fault just northeast of Peak 7057. Here the rock underfoot abruptly changes from banded Precambrian gneiss to whitish Paleozoic quartzite. The Helendale Fault, stretching from north of Victorville southeast to Tip Top Mountain, runs parallel to Nelson Ridge, lying below us to the northeast. Presently, with fleeting glimpses of Baldwin Lake we descend to meet Highway

18 (6829-4.2) just yards west of some interesting mining prospects.

North of the highway, the trail is not well-marked. Veer left into a small forest just west of a bulldozed slope. The PCT next switchbacks to cross a jeep road, then contours north of Nelson Ridge before angling west down through a dense stand of pinyon pines to meet Doble Road 3N08 (6855-2.0) just south of the county dump. West across Doble Road the trail curves and contours south across three jeep tracks in sagebrush and rabbitbrush, affording good views of Baldwin Lake's playa surface beyond the ruins of Doble. Baldwin Lake is named for Elias J. "Lucky" Baldwin, owner of the prosperous Doble Gold Mine, located high on the slopes above us. The PCT contours low on Gold Mountain, and soon reaches a short spur (6880-0.5) down to signed Doble Trail Camp, which has a corral and a pipe spring. The spring may dry up by early summer in drought years.

Continuing on, we make a gentle ascent in scrubby vegetation, crossing two jeep roads and making three switchbacks to gain a saddle on the northeast ridge of Gold Mountain. Here we leave pinyon pines behind for incense-cedars, Jeffrey pines and junipers. A gentle traverse around Gold Mountain's northern flanks bisects a jeep road and offers vistas over Arrastre and Union flats, scenes of the fevered Holcomb Valley mining excitement in the 1860s. This gold rush began when William F. Holcomb discovered flecks of placer gold at the head of Van Dusen Canyon, one mile west of Arrastre Flat. Hired by other prospectors for his ability with a rifle, Holcomb and a companion trailed a wounded grizzly bear north from Poligue Canyon. His experience prospecting in the mines of the Sierra Nevada's Mother Lode paid off when his bear-tracking led to the alluvial flats on Caribou Creek. Soon the sagebrush-and-pine-dotted basin swarmed with prospectors, and a camp, named Belleville, was erected.

History records that this settlement was one of the least law-abiding of the California gold camps—over 40 men died by hanging or gun battles. Causes for argument included not only the usual charges of claim-jumping and theft, but also political affiliations in the Civil War. Southern sympathizers were particularly numerous, as they had been forcibly ejected from many pro-Northern mining camps in the Mother Lode. Although the site of fevered and hectic activity for almost a decade, Holcomb Valley was relieved of most of its readily accessible placer gold by 1870, and its inhabitants moved on to greener pastures. Belleville was soon a ghost town. Interest in the region revived, however, when hard-rock mines opened to seek the Mother Lode—the source of the Holcomb Valley placer gold. Soon shafts and their adjunct tailings dotted the land. Lucky Baldwin's Doble Mine was one of these, but, like the other hard-rock mines, it failed to locate the Mother Lode, and it is doubtful that Baldwin recouped his $6 million purchase price for the mine.

The PCT veers south along Gold Mountain's flanks to strike one jeep road, then a second (7630-3.9), which leads north ⅔ mile down to Saragossa Spring. About ¼ mile beyond the next small rise we cross a better road (7560-0.7), then turn southwest down to a tributary of Caribou Creek, dotted with mining ruins. A mile-long contour then leads to Caribou Creek itself, which rarely flows later than early June, but offers good camping before then. The next water for northbound PCT hikers is not until Little Bear Springs Trail Camp, 10.8 miles; for the southbound, at Doble Trail Camp, 6.3 miles. Just 0.1 mile beyond Caribou Creek the trail bisects Van Dusen Canyon Road 3N09 (7260-1.8), which leads southeast 3 miles to Big Bear City.

More mountain mahogany, Jeffrey pines and junipers shade the PCT as we leave Van Dusen Canyon, crossing numerous jeep tracks as we make a gentle ascent west under Bertha Ridge. Finally, a switchback leads to a saddle north of Bertha Peak, where we cross a jeep road (7720-1.6), then another (7735-0.7), leading to the summit, in excellent exposures of marble. West of the second road, sweeping vistas open up to the south across dammed Big Bear Lake to Moonridge and to the high summits of the San Gorgonio Wilderness. The PCT recrosses the last jeep road midway down to wide Holcomb Valley Road 2N09 (7550-1.2). From here travelers can head 3.7 miles to Fawnskin for supplies by first walking south along the dirt road, which descends Poligue Canyon to reach Highway 38 beside Big Bear Lake, then walking west along the highway.

From Holcomb Valley Road the PCT continues its traverse of the San Bernardino Mountains' spine by continuing west, easily up along the south side of Delamar Mountain's east ridge. This pleasant and viewful walk under open conifers and oaks ends after a long mile

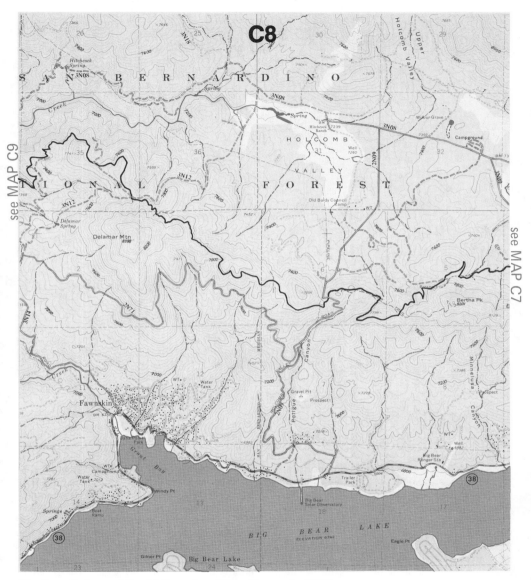

Big Bear Lake and the high peaks of San Gorgonio Wilderness

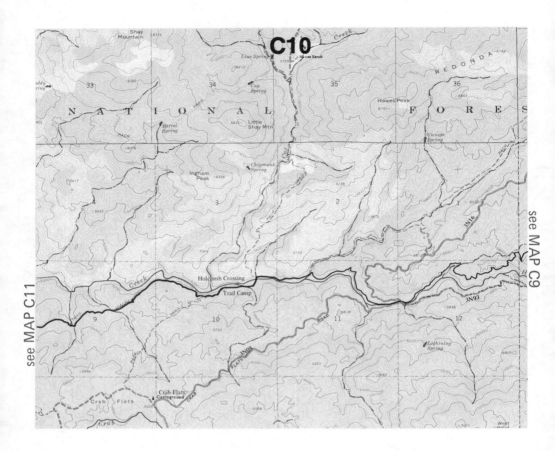

when the route crosses to the shadier north side of the ridge to traverse past an east-ascending jeep track, then descends to Road 3N12 (7755-2.8), atop a saddle. Delamar Spring, with poor camping nearby, lies 0.9 mile west down this dirt road.

The PCT contours north from Road 3N12, then arcs west around a nose covered with mountain mahogany before crossing another good dirt road (7610-0.8). Dropping gently, the trail rounds north on a steep hillside with vistas east over Holcomb Valley, but soon turns southwest and eventually strikes a jeep road (7305-1.1), which we follow downhill for 35 yards before resuming trail tread. Next, continued descent for 0.3 mile leads into a small canyon, then northwest along its south wall, then into another, similar canyon, now just below a dirt road. Later, near the bottom of Holcomb Creek's wide canyon, the route

switchbacks, crosses one poor dirt road, then another, and immediately reaches Little Bear Springs Trail Camp (6600-2.5), with corral, toilets, benches and piped water. Southbound PCTers should tank up here, since the next seasonal water is 10.8 miles away, at Caribou Creek in Van Dusen Canyon. Most wilderness lovers will likely not spend the night at this poorly sited campground, which is a haven for buzzing motocross enthusiasts, but rather will sack out farther down Holcomb Creek.

From the trail camp the PCT turns northwest down a creek's mouth to quickly reach the willow-lined, sagebrush-dotted banks of year-round Holcomb Creek. The trail follows its south bank, crossing a jeep road leading to the trail camp, then parallels the lower shoulder of Coxey Road 3N14 as it descends west a few yards to Holcomb Creek (6510-0.3). Here, at a concrete pad across the creek bed, you'll have

C8, C9

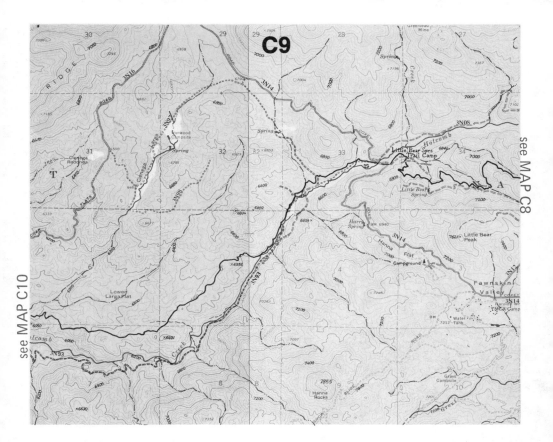

see MAP C10

see MAP C8

an 8-yard-wide wade in early spring.

The PCT resumes above Holcomb Creek's north bank, 35 yards up Coxey Road, and proceeds gently down-canyon in an open ponderosa-pine forest, staying just above canyon-bottom dirt Road 3N93, which is repeatedly drowned under beaver-dammed pools. The trail passes two dirt roads and a jeep track, and then about ½ mile later it turns west up a side canyon, climbing moderately to a saddle (6485-2.1). From it a gentle descent southwest in warm groves of conifers and black oaks leads across a dirt road (6350-0.9), beyond which the route follows a sunny, rock-dotted divide north of Holcomb Creek. Drier conditions prevail as the easy descent continues, eventually leading to a rock-hop crossing of the Cienega Larga fork of Holcomb Creek. From it the trail parallels some 50′ above shaded, bouldery Holcomb Creek, soon passing some nice campsites and dropping to cross it via boulders. Moments later the streamside canopy of willows and cottonwoods opens where wide Crab Flats Road 3N16 (5465-3.5) has a junction with rough Road 3N93.

The PCT now continues on Holcomb Creek's south bank, via very rocky tread under white alders. We soon enter a sandy flat with adequate camps and again cross Holcomb Creek (5430-0.2). The trail now winds northwest above it in a dry chaparral of mountain mahogany, buckwheat, and yellow, fleshy-petalled flannelbush. Turning more westward, the way drops once again alongside Holcomb Creek, traverses the perimeter of a bouldery sand flat with a good camp, and then crosses the permanent Cienega Redonda fork of Holcomb Creek to find the north-branching Cienega Redonda Trail (5325-1.0). Many horned lizards might be seen as the trail continues its gentle descent west on rotting granitic rock along Holcomb Creek and soon enters a grassy flat to reach a junction with the Hawes Ranch Trail (5230-0.4), just shy of the PCT's bouldery fourth ford of Holcomb Creek. Minutes later, one finds Holcomb Crossing Trail Camp (5190-0.3), with firepits and a toilet under large Jeffrey pines. No camping is allowed at present along the creek between here and below the dam of Mojave River Forks

Holcomb Creek near PCT junction with Hawes Ranch trail

Reservoir, 19 miles ahead, so get a good night's sleep here! The Forest Service plans to construct at least one trail camp along the PCT route beside Deep Creek in the future.

Just 300 yards after Holcomb Camp, the Crab Flats Trail climbs southwest, but the PCT stays near Holcomb Creek's alder- and cedar-shaded banks a while longer before gently ascending, alternately in forest and in high chaparral. In a mile the trail begins to descend, and eventually it reaches Deep Creek Road 3N34 (4875-3.7) in a small canyon where this dirt road turns south to Crab Flats. You head west along this road for a minute, then regain trail tread just north of the shoulder. This tread heads northwest, dropping via four oak-shaded switchbacks to a wide, sometimes deep ford of Deep Creek (4580-0.4), which flows among granitic boulders. Just beyond the ford a poor

trail strikes left back upstream to cross diminutive Bear Creek and end beside a small house at the end of Road 3N34. This road leads west up-canyon 0.5 mile to Hooks Creek Road 3N15, this dirt road continuing 3½ miles past numerous cabins to Lake Arrowhead.

After crossing Deep Creek the PCT briefly climbs northeast, then contours under live oaks and near crumbling granitic parapets. After ½ mile the path descends gently, matching the gradient of Deep Creek, which is flanked by spruces and pines 140' below. The way presently becomes hot and exposed near ocean spray and holly-leaf cherry, and many will wonder why the trail wasn't routed lower, along the cool streamside. Soon we get our answer, in the form of steep, friable bluffs, above which the PCT must skirt. Later, the route bends west and strikes Bacon Flats Road 3N20 (4255-2.6), which offers the last chance to head out to Lake Arrowhead to resupply.

Across Bacon Flats Road the PCT winds along the canyon walls, well above quietly flowing Deep Creek and its streamside willows, cottonwoods and alders. Though sometimes shaded by steep, granitic bluffs, our route soon becomes more exposed to sun and seasonally stifling heat. Our proximity to the Mojave Desert is reflected in both the shimmering heat and in the flora and fauna. Coarse chamise chaparral, harboring flitting phainopeplas and somnolent horned lizards, lines our way, while scurrying insects and pursuant roadrunners share our sandy path. Rattlesnakes are also seen, although not in the heat of day—their cold-blooded metabolism cannot stand extreme ground temperatures, but they love to bask when shadows are long.

Soon after passing a streamside terrace where the Forest Service plans an equestrian camp, our undulating descent alters its northwestward course to a more westward one. Shortly thereafter, it passes a jeep road that rolls ½ mile east to Warm Spring, and then it drops ¼ south to Deep Creek Hot Spring (3535-6.8), which is situated on a prominent northeast-southwest fault. The hot spring, with its bubbling water, high-diving rocks, warm sunbathing, and green grass, is a surprisingly popular and crowded spot at almost any time of the year. Trail-dusty would-be swimmers should heed this caution, however: a very rare, microscopic ameba living in the hot water has caused deadly amebic meningoencephalitis by

C10, C11, C12

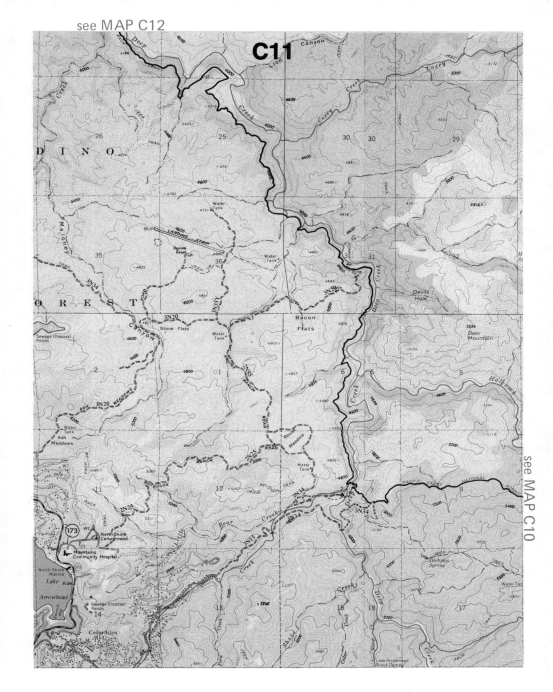

invading a few swimmers' bodies through their noses. Swimming or drinking the water without prior boiling may cut your hike short! Also, camping here is illegal, and a small burned area nearby is mute testimony to the environs' flammability.

Taking leave of the skinny-dippers, we eventually cross Deep Creek via an arched bridge (3315-2.0), and then start a traverse west along the almost barren north wall of Deep Creek canyon. This walk ends at the spillway of the Mojave River Forks Reservoir dam (3131-3.0).

C12, C13

This mammoth flood-control dam, over a mile long, is an example of overkill, since West Fork Mojave River and Deep Creek don't have that much flow. Fair camping exists below the dam's spillway, our first legal campsite since Holcomb Crossing Trail Camp.

The next morning, rejoin the PCT atop the dam and drop south from its spillway along a route marked by 4 x 4 posts, which connect the myriad jeep roads leading to its base. Walk more or less levelly west along the dam's base on a well-used jeep road, staying north of shallow, pooling Deep Creek. Shaded flats hereabouts make for potentially pleasant camping, but pick your site with care since 2-, 3- and 4-wheeled off-road vehicles can be everywhere. Just west of a small canyon's mouth on the opposite bank, our posted PCT route makes a shallow but wide and rocky ford (2990-0.5) to the south side of Deep Creek. For a few minutes we trace another jeep track west above a fringe of baccharis and willows before dropping again to the creekside. Here, Deep Creek is sucked north through the dam, down a massive, iron-gated outlet tunnel.

From here, you're back on a trail, which winds west in a thicket of willows and cottonwoods that show evidence of beaver cuttings. These trees are just south of another sandy arroyo, this one draining ephemeral West Fork Mojave River. Presently we cross the base of a narrow ravine, where our trail begins to trace the grade of an abandoned, torn-up paved road (3010-0.6). This is followed moderately uphill, southwest, giving us a fair overlook of the "reservoir." Soon we level out on a terrace to strike a wide turnout on a curve of Highway 173 (3190-0.4).

To relocate PCT trail tread, first head 160 yards west down Highway 173 to a jeep road. Follow the PCT/jeep road gently up, first southwest then southeast, staying left at all diverging tracks, to find a resumption of trail (3205-0.5), which climbs briefly south into a small canyon. The path ascends around several ridges on a southward, winding course, soon leveling in the process to undulate at about 3500'. Just after heading around a north-dropping ridge, we reach a small canyon that spawns a trailside spring (3470-1.7). This flows through late spring of most years, but has no nearby camping. Turning more westward, the route traverses hillsides clothed in an open, desert-dry low chaparral of chamise, buckwheat and flannelbush, with panoramas north-

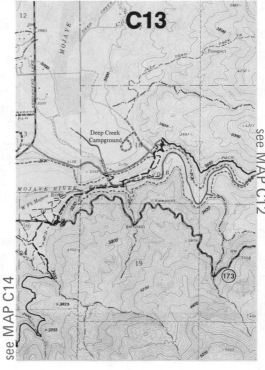

west over the broad expanse of Summit Valley to the aberrant alluvial scarp forming its northern limit. This long, steep-faced ridge is actually the upslope edge of an early Pleistocene alluvial fan, whose sediments originally came from canyons of the San Gabriel Mountains, seen far to the west. However, subsequent right-lateral movement along the San Andreas Fault displaced the range northwest, thereby cutting off the fan's source of sediments. Continuing lateral and vertical movement along the San Andreas Fault and associated parallel faults not only altered the landscape but also brought about drastic changes in the stream-drainage pattern.

The PCT drops slightly as it winds south into a broad valley, then climbs to a ridgetop saddle where it joins a jeep road (3430-1.5) serving a powerline. We follow this road south down to an easy ford of Grass Valley Creek (3330-0.3), which flows most summers. Unfortunately, private lands prohibit camping here. The trail resumes just across the stream, on the jeep road's east side, and momentarily it crosses a second, poor jeep track before climbing north-

C13, C14

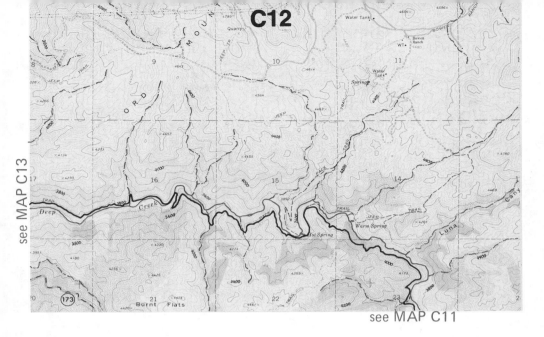

see MAP C13

see MAP C11

west. Around a nose, the trail hairpins south across another steep jeep road (3480-0.7), then undulates interminably west in and out of gullies and ravines in shadeless chaparral. Eventually the way strikes Road 2N33 (3400-4.8), a paved road ascending west to the nearby east end of Cedar Springs Dam. Walking a few minutes up to that end will give you vistas over giant Silverwood Lake, which is part of the California Aqueduct system. From Road 2N33 the PCT descends steeply, then turns south around a sharp ridge and joins a west-branching dirt road close under the base of 249' high, rockfill Cedar Springs Dam. PCT travelers lacking a fast mode of transportation might be less than enthused to learn that the active Cleghorn Mountain Fault lies not far south of the damsite: the reservoir's northern east-west arms lie along the fault.

Now, possibly with a brisker stride, we turn west down the dirt road for a few yards to the end of a paved road (3170-0.4) that bridges the canyon bottom and continues northwest to some dam-maintenance facilities. Rather than following it, the PCT route here turns north along a faint jeep track, soon striking Highway 173 (3160-0.1). Until permanent trail is constructed, walk west along the paved highway, crossing a bridge straddling the concrete spillway flume of Cedar Springs Dam. Just past dirt Las Flores Ranch Road (3185-0.3), walk cross-country southwest along the State of California barbed-wire fence. This route leads

across a paved, gated road to a southwest-climbing dirt road (3200-0.4), where the PCT's trail tread resumes, climbing parallel to the dirt road, which is immediately above it.

Entering Silverwood Lake State Recreation Area, the PCT continues below the road for a bit, then crosses it and switchbacks southeast to a nearby saddle (3460-0.6), on which it crosses a similar road. Here northbound hikers gain their first vistas over windy Silverwood Lake. The warm water will likely prove irresistible to most, as the PCT route traverses near the reservoir's western shoreline. Twice we follow jeep roads for 60 yards as the route winds through sparse chaparral, crossing many gullies. North of the westernmost arm of northern Silverwood Lake, a meager spring wets the trail, then the path meanders south before climbing moderately east above the Chamise Boat-in Picnic Area, which lacks running water. Now 200' above the reservoir, the trail bends south to an unsigned spur trail (3580-2.5) that drops south to another trail and to Garces Overlook—an octagonal hilltop gazebo—which makes a fine, albeit waterless, picnic spot.

Back on the PCT, we descend easily west across a jeep road (3455-0.8) and eventually come to within 10' of a paved, two-lane bike path next to a paved road leading east to Cleghorn Picnic Area, which has water, tables, bathrooms and telephones. Then, near three sycamore trees, the PCT peters out, so we step

C14, C15

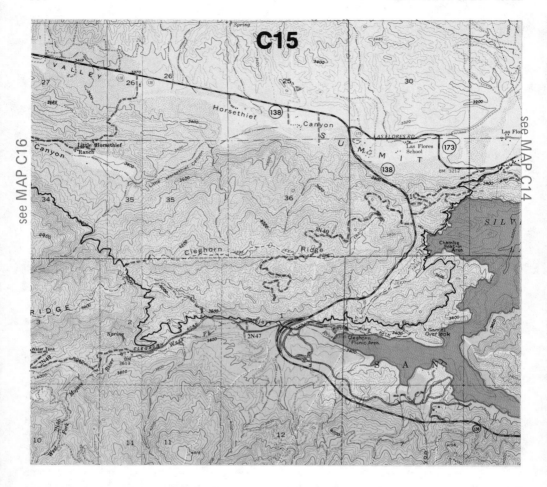

south onto the bike path, walk southwest 150 yards across West Fork Mojave River's usually dry wash, and find a signed junction (3370-0.8) with another paved bike path that leads west, toward the group-camp complex. Follow the path up to the paved Silverwood Lake State Recreation Area's entrance road (3390-0.1). This road may be traced south to the entrance station and then 1.7 miles east beyond it for camping, water, showers, telephones and a small store and cafe at the reservoir's marina. Northbound hikers must note that the next certain water lies in lower Crowder Canyon, 13.2 miles west of the SRA, while, except for the reservoir, the next water for those southbound flows in Grass Valley Creek, 11.5 miles east.

Continuing on the PCT route from the SRA entrance, you first walk west under the High-way 138 overpass to its offramp (3395-0.1). From here one may hitchhike southeast to Crestline for supplies at its post office and stores. Here too, the trail resumes 80 yards northwest of the offramp's junction with the SRA's entrance road, against the northern hillside behind five clustered sycamores. The PCT leads gently up-canyon, then dips into West Fork Mojave River's sandy wash for a moment before crossing a dirt road that serves a small picnic area (3440-0.4). From it the route continues up along the base of a canyon wall cloaked in chamise, buckwheat and pungent yerba santa. The trail's tread is interrupted as we follow the paved group-camp access road for 25 yards, then it resumes to strike a narrow paved road (3530-0.4) that climbs steeply to a water tank. Three lavish group camps lie just

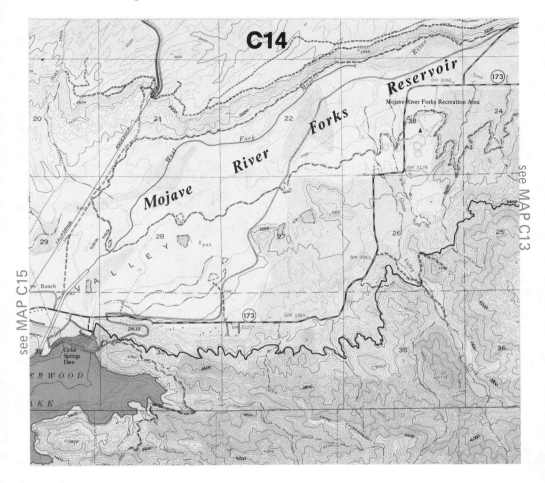

down this road, in Silverwood Lake State Recreation Area.

Now we leave the SRA and begin climbing in earnest, winding southwest up numerous dry gulches, then around an east-jutting nose, and finally turning north up to join a jeep road (4040-2.2) at a small promontory. Here the PCT turns west, following the track which climbs moderately to its junction with a road (4160-0.3) atop viewful Cleghorn Ridge. Eastward gazes take in the Lake Arrowhead region, Miller Canyon, Silverwood Lake and West Fork Mojave River, the last three aligned along the east-west Cleghorn Fault, which separates Mesozoic granitic rocks, found here, north of the fault, from older Precambrian metamorphic rocks south of the fault.

Resuming our trek, we follow the ridge road

north 100 yards down to where the trail's tread resumes. The way descends moderately northwest across hillside gullies, presently reaching a deeper canyon with a small stream (3830-0.9), which usually flows through late spring. No camping is possible, however. The next leg winds northwest across numerous similar ravines while it contours above ranches in Little Horsethief Canyon. This canyon and Horsethief Canyon to its north commemorate Captain Gabriel Moraga's pursuit of an Indian band suspected of horsethievery in 1819. The first known crossing of nearby Cajon Pass occurred in 1772, and this key pass was heavily used by the Mormon Battalion and Death Valley borax teams. Eventually the route drops into the canyon's head, where PCT posts show the way through a grassy flat. The Forest

C15, C16

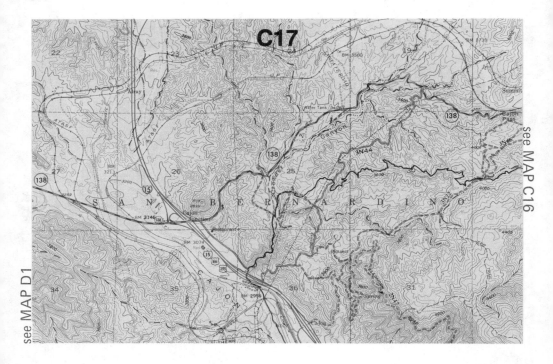

Silverwood Lake, from Garces Overlook

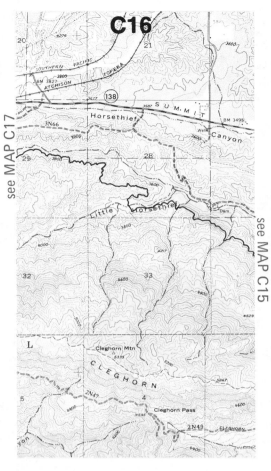

see MAP C17

see MAP C15

road, then west along a spur beneath a mammoth power pylon. Trail tread continues west from here, vaguely at first along a gravelly wash, then more obviously as it climbs to an overlook of spectacularly eroded badlands above Cajon Canyon. The Pliocene sediments here were eroded from the infant San Gabriel Mountains, then shifted east, relatively speaking, along the San Andreas Fault, which now cuts through Cajon Canyon, below. Because these sediments have been removed from their source of rejuvenating alluvium, stream flow has easily incised their once gently sloping surfaces into a dramatic series of razorback ridges.

Our path climbs to top the most spectacular of these ridges, then winds tortuously down, west, along it, giving us superb vistas of the San Gabriel Mountains' crown, Mount San Antonio, and of Lytle Creek Ridge, which we will climb on the PCT one day hence. Presently we cross Road 3N44 (3355-2.4) and minutes later our route becomes an old jeep track leading southwest down from a saddle. The way quickly crosses another road (3300-0.4), from which trail tread resumes to lead west, momentarily passing under power-transmission pylon #63 to the junction (3265-0.2) of two descending dirt roads. We follow the right-hand road, which drops steeply west into quiet Crowder Canyon, dotted with baccharis and willows. Here our road joins with stream-bottom jeep tracks and crosses the sandy intermittent creek. On the west side of the canyon the PCT route joins a gas-pipeline access road and climbs northwest along it for 40 yards to a resumption of trail (3165-0.3), branching south.

This pleasant path winds along the narrow, shady gorge of lower Crowder Canyon, where pools and trickles of water (3045-0.3) afford the last on-route water until Guffy Campground, a long 23 miles away. The trail ends abruptly at six-lane Interstate 15 (3000-0.4) in Cajon Canyon, just south of a roadend memorial to Santa Fe Trail pioneers. No facilities are available here (save for a weighing station on the freeway if your backpack loads are "over gross"), but they are found in Wrightwood and San Bernardino, as described in the introduction to this section. Just 0.6 mile northwest up the access road to the trail's terminus, just before the Route 138 cloverleaf, is a fine 24-hour restaurant. If no palatable water is available in lower Crowder Canyon, this restaurant is a recommended detour.

Service plans to build a trail camp with well water here.

Our trail turns north across Little Horsethief Canyon's dry creek bed (3570-2.8), then climbs again, up to a narrow ridgecrest, which we traverse in low, bedraggled chamise chaparral—an impoverished indicator of our proximity to the Mojave Desert. The PCT then proceeds west up into another draw, and near its head strikes a road (3840-2.5) under a huge power-transmission line. We walk across the

C16, C17

Mt. San Antonio, from Throop Peak

Section D: Interstate 15 near Cajon Pass to Agua Dulce

Introduction: True to its name, the Pacific Crest Trail through the San Gabriel Mountains remains on or close to the watershed dividing streams that flow into the Pacific Ocean from those that run north, losing themselves in the sand or evaporating from muddy playas in the Mojave Desert. The PCT climbs quickly from smoggy, arid Cajon Canyon to the subalpine reaches of the San Gabriel Mountains, and soon ascends its Southern California apex—wind-torn, 9399' Mount Baden-Powell. Most of the PCT's winding route lies between these two extremes, treaded in pine-needle duff under groves of shading, hospitable Transition Zone forest trees: Jeffrey pine, incense-cedar, black oak, sugar pine, white fir and water-loving white alder.

Except for frequent roads and resorts that the PCT skirts, much of the trail route traverses country unchanged, at first glance, by the encroachment of modern man. But on closer inspection, the San Gabriels are seen to be no longer the wild and remote range that moved legendary mountaineer John Muir to call them "more rigidly inaccessible than any other I ever attempted to penetrate." Man has tamed the San Gabriels' clawing chaparral and steep-walled gorges with miles of highway, and has prevented once-devastating floods with dams and catchment basins. Bear and bighorn sheep, which once roamed the range, have been driven by thousands of hikers, skiers, picnickers, hunters and loggers into the most remote and forbidding canyons. The forests, however, show the most insidious and far-reaching effects of California's burgeoning population. Smog, that yellow pall that has made Los Angeles infamous, now rises well into the surrounding mountains, and the pollutants are severely damaging timber—yellowed needles on thousands of acres of dying pines and firs are mute testimony.

A part of the Transverse Ranges geologic province, the San Gabriels are thought to be rather young, at least in their present stature. Despite their relative youth, geologists state that some of California's oldest rocks lie in the San Gabriels. Precambrian anorthosite (a light-colored, plutonic rock composed almost entirely of plagioclase feldspar and high in aluminum content) and gabbro estimated to be 1.22 billion years old both line the PCT route in the vicinity of Mount Gleason. These rocks are much older than most of the rocks along the San Gabriel Mountains segment of the PCT. Most of the trail tread lies in familiar granitic rocks of Mesozoic age; these were intruded at the same time as similar rocks in the Sierra, San Bernardino and San Jacinto mountains, and in Baja California. Other rocks, like the Pelona schist, which we first encounter on Upper Lytle Creek Ridge as we enter the San Gabriels, are metamorphic rocks, once volcanic and ocean-bottom sediments, which may have been altered by the intruding granites.

The present-day San Gabriels are a complex range, cut by and rising along numerous faults that occur along their every side. The major San Andreas Fault is the most famous, and it bounds the San Gabriels on their northern and eastern margins. This great fault stretches from near Cape Mendocino southeast about 1000 miles into the Gulf of California. Geologists now know that hundreds of miles of horizontal shift along the fault (with the western side moving north) have occurred in the last 30 million years, since about the time the fault first formed. Where the San Andreas Fault slashes through Cajon Canyon, at the start of this section, one can see an example of long-term motion along the fault: the bizarre Mormon Rocks and Rock Candy Mountains, all sedimentary rocks, lie northeast of the fault about 25 miles east of related rocks at the Devils Punchbowl, on the fault's southwest side. The Punchbowl and the trace of the San Andreas Fault can be seen easily from atop Mount Williamson, a short side hike from the PCT.

Declination: 13½°E

Mileages:	South to North	Distances between Points	North to South
Interstate 15 near Cajon Pass	0.0		110.2
		5.5	
Lone Pine Canyon Road	5.5		104.7
		3.7	
Sheep Creek Truck Road	9.2		101.0
		12.0	
Acorn Canyon Trail to Wrightwood	21.2		89.0
		0.9	
Guffy Campground	22.1		88.1
		4.8	
Angeles Crest Highway near Inspiration Point........	26.9		83.3
		2.3	
Jackson Flat Campground	29.2		81.0
		4.0	
Lamel Spring Trail.............................	33.2		77.0
		5.7	
Lily Spring Trail	38.9		71.3
		2.0	
Little Jimmy Campground	40.9		69.3
		7.2	
Rattlesnake Trail	48.1		62.1
		4.1	
Cooper Canyon Trail Campground..................	52.2		58.0
		6.4	
Three Points..................................	58.6		51.6
		3.3	
Sulphur Springs Campground	61.9		48.3
		12.3	
Mill Creek Summit Picnic Area	74.2		36.0
		11.8	
Messenger Flats Campground	86.0		24.2
		5.5	
North Fork Saddle Ranger Station	91.5		18.7
		8.7	
Soledad Canyon Road	100.2		10.0
		7.3	
Antelope Valley Freeway at Escondido Canyon.......	107.5		2.7
		1.9	
Vasquez Rocks County Park entrance	109.4		0.8
		0.8	
Agua Dulce	110.2		0.0

Supplies: No supplies are available at the start of Section D. A complete selection of needed items may be purchased in San Bernardino, 17 miles south on Interstate 15. Be sure to restock on water before leaving Cajon Canyon, since the next water won't be found until Guffy Campground, high in the San Gabriels, about 22 miles away. Wrightwood, a ski-resort community with a post office, stores, restaurants, motels, laundromat and PCT register, is the next possible supply point. It is a 4.4-mile detour down from the PCT via the Acorn Canyon Trail, 21 miles from Interstate 15.

Cajon pass area near Sullivans Curve

Acton, a small town with a post office, grocery stores and motel, lies 5.8 miles east off the PCT route in Soledad Canyon, about 100 miles from Interstate 15. Saugus, a larger town with complete amenities, lies west of the PCT some 12½ miles from the same point in Soledad Canyon. Agua Dulce, at the end of Section D, is the most logical resupply point, and still a long carry from Wrightwood. Not more than a village in a ranching community, Agua Dulce offers a post office, a small grocery store and a restaurant.

The beginning of Section D is reached by taking Interstate 15 north 17 miles from San Bernardino to Cajon Junction, where Highway 138 passes over the freeway. Leave the freeway here, turn right and head 120 yards east along Highway 138 to a paved road branching south. Paralleling Interstate 15, you take this road 0.6 mile to its end, beside a stone monument to Santa Fe Trail pioneers, this spot being just short of narrow Crowder Canyon. Just south of the memorial plaque, the Pacific Crest Trail curves south under the freeway via a boxed culvert, emerging on the other side in a verdant thicket. Moments later, you pass under the Atchison, Topeka and Santa Fe Railroad tracks, turn right, and follow them west on a gradually improving trail. Pass north of a private orchard, then swing south over a sandy ridge to a dirt road that heads west to Sullivans Curve. One crosses this road to a culvert under

another AT&SF RR track, walks right (southwest) along a dirt road for a few yards, and finds the PCT climbing south once again.

Soon the trail crosses the newer Southern Pacific Railroad tracks (3020-1.2), and then bends southwest to wind among the hills and sandstone-conglomerate outcrops of the Mormon Rocks, a badland of Miocene alluvium. At one point, we amble south along a jeep road for 100 yards. The Mormon Rocks commemorate Mormon pioneers who were among the first Caucasians to utilize Cajon Pass, and who settled San Bernardino Valley. Pedro Fages, who on one trip discovered the Colorado Desert and the San Jacinto Mountains, crossed the mountains in this vicinity when he tired of leading a contingent to capture Army deserters, and an urge to explore captured him. The De Anza-Garces forces passed near here 4 years after Fages, in 1776, on their way north

D1

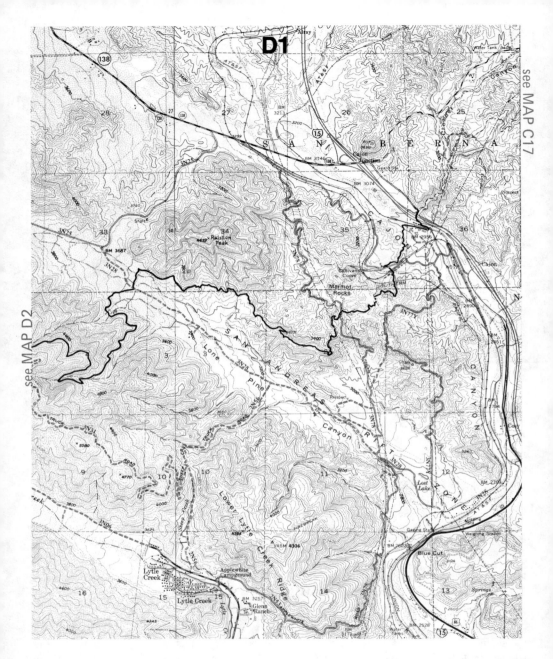

from Sonora, Mexico. By 1813 the Cajon Pass route, part of the Santa Fe Trail, was seeing frequent use by American trapper-trader Ewing Young and others. The Mormon Battalion used this route both coming from and going to the Great Salt Lake, and borax teams from Death Valley and the Santa Fe Railroad also crossed here.

Pushing on, we cross first one powerline road, Road 3N78, and then in ¼ mile cross another (3360-1.2) amid bush sunflower, chamise and scattered cacti. Next the PCT ascends to a sandy ridge dominating lower Lone Pine Canyon, eroded along the San Andreas Fault. The path traverses this ridge, which presents some striking blue clays, then cuts across sandy washes under the south face of Ralston Peak to Lone Pine Canyon Road 3N28 (3560-3.1). The PCT route strikes invisibly west from the road, marked by 4 x 4 posts in the cobbly alluvium, then turns south across a bouldery wash to a jeep road (3700-0.5). Two concrete tubs at Bike Springs are found just yards north, but their polluted nature relegates them to emergency use only. A horse camp is planned here for later years.

Attacking the chaparral-clothed eastern flanks of Upper Lytle Creek Ridge, our trail swings into a canyon, then switchbacks north across three canyons and finally arrives at Sheep Creek Truck Road 3N31 (4920-3.2), atop the ridge. From this shadeless ridge, cooling vistas are had of the Mount San Antonio massif and the rugged Cucamonga Wilderness to the west and southwest, in the San Gabriel Mountains proper. Now the PCT traverses, ascending gently all the while, first on Upper Lytle Creek Ridge's south side and then on its north side, alternately overlooking North Fork Lytle Creek and arid Lone Pine Canyon from a slightly cooler vantage point. In the 1890s Lytle Creek was the setting for a spirited but short-lived gold rush.

After crossing Sheep Creek Truck Road a third time (6300-4.9) where the road turns

north into Lone Pine Canyon, our chia-lined path winds south around a prominence to a roadend (6480-1.1) just east of Gobblers Knob. Above this point the way becomes more shaded, with frequent groves of big-cone spruce, mountain mahogany and some juniper. As the route swings under Blue Ridge, both the Devils Backbone and Dawson Peak dominate the southern horizon, thrusting ridges of platy brown Pelona schist above timberline. These points mark the eastern boundary of Angeles National Forest's new Sheep Mountain Wilderness, a 43,600-acre preserve which protects the rugged San Gabriel River drainage, just west of Mount San Antonio.

Look for black-granular phyllite and outcrops of white quartz and fibrous green, shiny actinolite, a close relative of asbestos, in the schist before the PCT switchbacks east up to a jeep road (8115-4.3) atop Blue Ridge. This road climbs northwest up to a posted trailhead (8176-0.1) just north of the jeep road's intersection with Road 3N06. The PCT contours south around Jeffrey-pine-forested Wright Mountain, staying just above dirt Road 3N06. Soon Prairie Fork San Gabriel River comes into view, incised along the San Jacinto Fault. Mount Baden-Powell dominates the western horizon, while San Gabriel Valley smog is

D1, D2, D3

Over millions of years the San Andreas Fault moved these Mormon Rocks tens of miles away from those of the Devils Punchbowl, with which they were formed

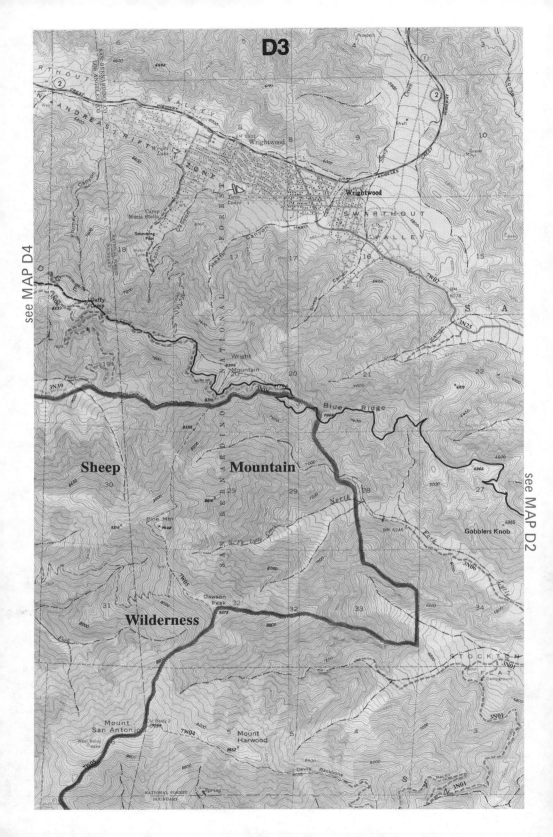

partly screened by the Pine Mountain Ridge to the south. West of Wright Mountain we meet the Acorn Canyon Trail (8250-1.6), which descends 2 miles north to a road that drops 1½ miles to the western edge of Wrightwood. The next possibility for reprovisioning on the route

lies in Agua Dulce, about 91 miles ahead.

The PCT continues west up Blue Ridge, sometimes on Road 3N06, but often to its north on short trail segments, then it enters Angeles National Forest and arrives at Guffy Campground (8225-0.9), which has water at a good

D3

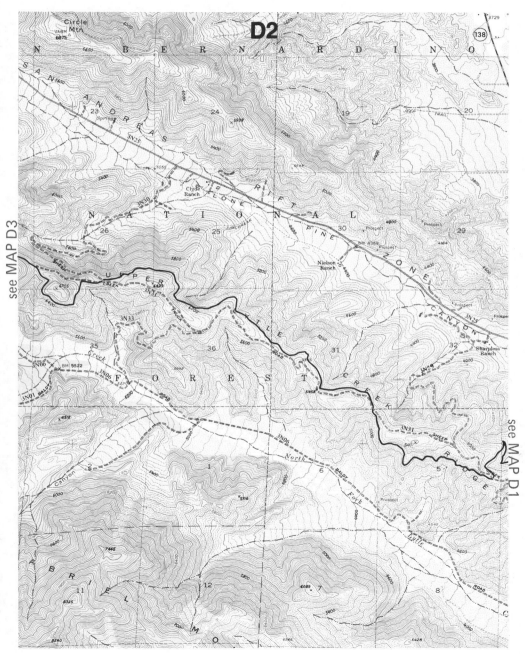

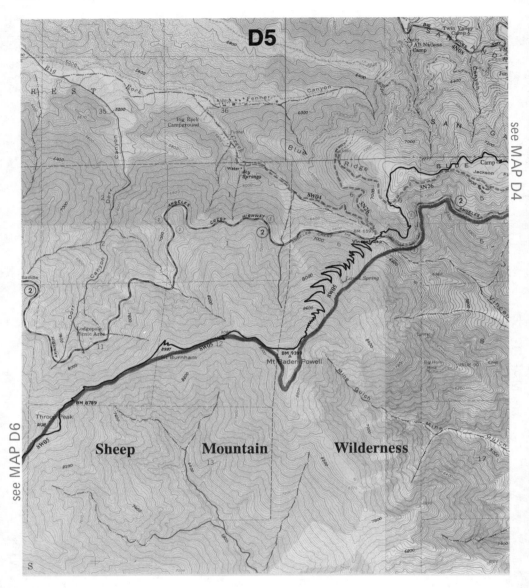

spring reached by a side trail 270 yards down Flume Canyon to the north. The trail-and-road route that continues near the crest of Blue Ridge offers vistas mostly to the north, over Swarthout Valley and the San Andreas Fault to pinyon-cloaked ridges abutting the Mojave Desert. Our high point on Blue Ridge (8480-1.7) is "forested" with microwave arrays, white firs and Jeffrey pines. Holiday Hill Ski

Area, a beautiful log cabin, and then waterless Blue Ridge Campground (7910-0.9) are next passed in succession via a patchwork of trail and jeep tracks well-marked by CRHT (California Riding and Hiking Trail) and PCT posts. Beyond the campground, Road 3N06 is paved, and we parallel the boundary of Sheep Mountain Wilderness, to our southwest. Black oaks and white firs join the ecosystem as we near

D3, D4

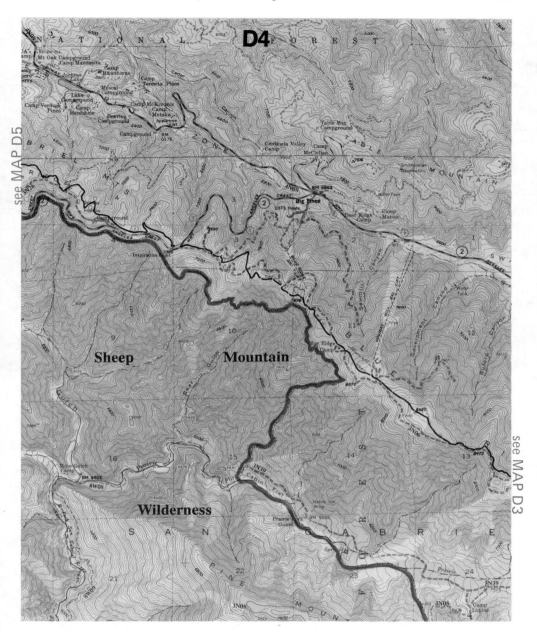

Angeles Crest Highway 2 (7386-2.2), just east of Inspiration Point, a sweeping overlook of the East Fork San Gabriel River basin.

North of the highway parking area, you turn west through flats of whitethorn and bitter cherry to reach forested Grassy Hollow Camp-ground (7300-1.0), with water. About ½ mile northwest of the campground the PCT route goes along Jackson Flat Road 3N26 for 100 yards before returning to trail tread on the north side of Blue Ridge. Next on the itinerary is a short spur (7480-1.3) to walk-in Jackson

D4, D5

Pine Mountain, from Wright Mountain

Flat Campground, in shading pines and firs. After passing north of Jackson Flat and turning Blue Ridge, the PCT drops south across Road 3N26 (7220-1.5), then switchbacks moderately down past interior live oaks and ocean spray to Angeles Crest Highway 2 at Vincent Gap (6585-0.8).

South of the highway, beside a parking area and a trail east to the interesting Bighorn Mine, is Mount Baden-Powell Trail 8W05—a popular pilgrimage for Southern California Boy Scouts. We take this trail, which starts southwest before switchbacking gently-to-moderately up in Jeffrey-pine/white-fir groves on crunchy Pelona schist tread. After a number of switchbacks we reach a side trail (7765-1.7) that contours 100 yards south to Lamel Spring. This marks a good rest stop, and one might choose to camp at either of two level spots a minute farther along the main trail.

Above, the switchbacks become tighter, the air grows crisper, and firs give way to lodgepole pines, which yield in turn, above 8800′, to sweeping-branched, wind-loving limber pines.

These hunched, gnarled conifers, believed by some botanists to be 2000 years old, are the only obvious living things at the Mount Baden-Powell Spur Trail (9245-2.1). Take this side hike to the 9399′ summit for superlative views north across desert to the southern Sierra, west to Mount Gleason, south down Iron Fork San Gabriel River (in Sheep Mountain Wilderness) to the Santa Ana Mountains, and east to Mounts San Antonio, San Gorgonio and San Jacinto. A concrete monument here is a tribute to Lord Baden-Powell, founder of the Boy Scout movement, and this summit marks the terminus of the Silver Moccasin Trail, Scouting's 53-mile challenge through the San Gabriel Mountains, which is congruent with the PCT until Three Points, about 23 miles away.

Back on the PCT, our route bears west, descending generally under Mount Burnham, Throop Peak and Mount Hawkins in open pine-fir forest with an understory of manzanita, whitethorn and sagebrush. Where we cross south of the ridgeline, we momentarily enter Sheep Mountain Wilderness. On the sparsely

D5, D6

conifered ridge just west of Mount Hawkins we pass a lateral (8540-3.6) that drops ⅓ mile north to Lily Spring, then later come to aptly named Windy Gap (7588-1.6), from where a trail drops south to campgrounds in the Crystal Lake Recreation Area. From here the PCT descends north off the ridge to Little Jimmy Spring (7460-0.2), lying just below the trail. This is the last water until Little Rock Creek, in 7.7 miles. Little Jimmy Campground (7450-0.2) is just a couple of minutes farther, with toilets, tables and firepits.

Beyond the campground we curve west on a trail that soon passes above Windy Spring. Now our route parallels dirt Road 9W03, keeping some distance below it. Presently, the road hairpins across the trail (7360-1.2), and here you should find a sign identifying the PCT route. The trail heads west moderately down to Angeles Crest Highway 2 (6670-1.0), reaching it just east of its Islip Saddle intersection with now-closed Highway 39. Just west of the parking area and restrooms on Islip Saddle, turn right on Mount Williamson Trail 9W02 and ascend moderately northwest past white firs and whitethorn ceanothus to the Mount Williamson Summit Trail (7900-1.6), which climbs 0.4 mile north to good views of fault-churned Devils Punchbowl. While you switch-

back west down from your ridgetop, you can look south down deep ravines in the friable tonalite to the San Gabriel Wilderness, which is a Southern California refuge of mountain big-horn sheep. Ending the descent, the route merges with a jeep road for 200 yards, and then crosses Angeles Crest Highway 2 (6700-1.3).

Trail resumes about 50 yards west to ascend Kratka Ridge in a heterogeneous forest of white fir, sugar and ponderosa pines, interior live oak and mountain mahogany. Soon back on the Angeles Crest Highway, you walk 180 yards to waterless Eagles Roost Picnic Area (6650-0.9). At its entrance just west of the highway, turn west down a rocky, unsigned dirt road and descend to its end at Rattlesnake Trail 10W03 (6165-1.2), in a shady gully. This little-used path drops north under the stone gaze of Eagles Roost, leaves behind an older, poor path that climbs south, and crosses melodious Little Rock Creek (6080-0.3) in cedar-lined Rattle-snake canyon. A cozy camp can be made here by the stream, but no more campsites are available as the PCT continues, contouring to Rattlesnake Spring and another spring a mile later. Past the second spring, a pleasant descent leads to several delightful camps beside Little Rock Creek, where the PCT merges with Burk-hart Trail 10W02 (5640-2.3) and turns south

Mt. San Antonio, from Inspiration Point

D6, D7

Near the summit of Mt. Baden-Powell

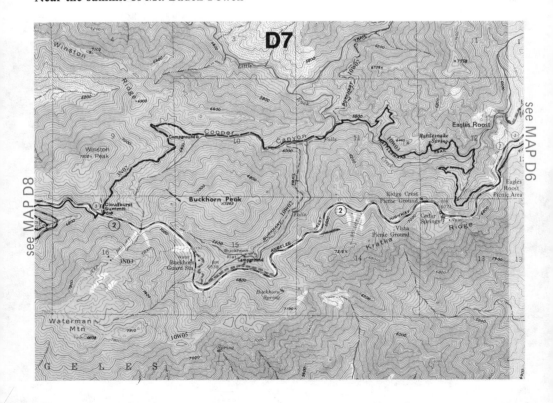

across the stream to ascend southwest into Cooper Canyon. Past a pristine waterfall and the south-branching Burkhart Trail (5730-0.3), which climbs to Buckhorn Flat Campground, the PCT route becomes an often steep jeep road, Road 3N02. It passes Cooper Canyon Trail Campground (6240-1.2), with reliable water, as it climbs to Cloudburst Summit (7018-1.7), where we cross the Angeles Crest Highway again.

On the west side of this forested gap, our path drops to contour just south of the highway in open forest, then crosses the highway again below a hairpin turn, now following another jeep road, Road 10W15, to Camp Pajarito (6545-1.5), situated in Cloudburst Canyon. Camp Glenwood is next, and in ¼ mile our jeep road climbs to the highway once again (6320-1.3). At a saddle 100 yards west of our junction, the route crosses to the south and again traces a dwindling dirt road, still Road 10W15, this time above the highway, to emerge from big-cone spruce as it descends to Three Points (5885-1.9), on the Angeles Crest Highway.

The Chilao Flat/Waterman Mountain Trail here continues southwest, but the PCT goes

north across the highway. In a moment it reaches Horse Flat Road 3N17 and a trailhead parking area with restrooms and seasonal water. This is just beyond the left-branching Silver Moccasin Trail, which continues west to Bandido Campground and Chilao Flat. Across gravel Horse Flat Road, the PCT, indicated by a 4 x 4 post, continues north, climbing slightly onto a granite-sand hillside shaded by interior live oaks. A northward contour on this slope soon ends as the PCT swings west through a gap, then drops gently west under big-cone spruces to an unused dirt road (5760-1.5). Turn left along this track, descending to reach, in 200 yards, a continuation of the trail, which branches right from the track. This short leg drops to another dirt road (5655-0.2) which, like the one before it, leads left to populous Pasadena Camp. The PCT here follows the gently descending dirt road north just 130 yards down to a resumption of trail where the road ends. Winding in and out of small, sandy ravines, the trail descends easily out onto a chaparralled ridge on a more-or-less north-ward tack. This descent ends at a usually dry stream bed, where the trail climbs for a

D7, D8

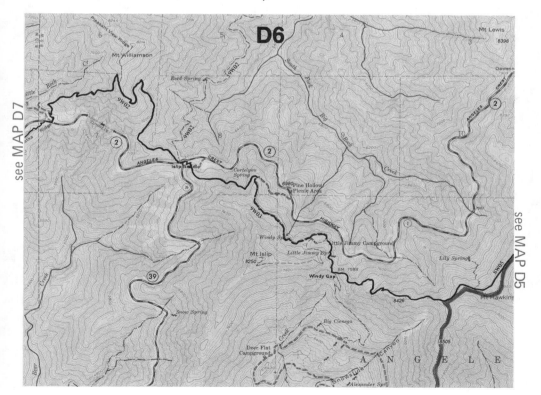

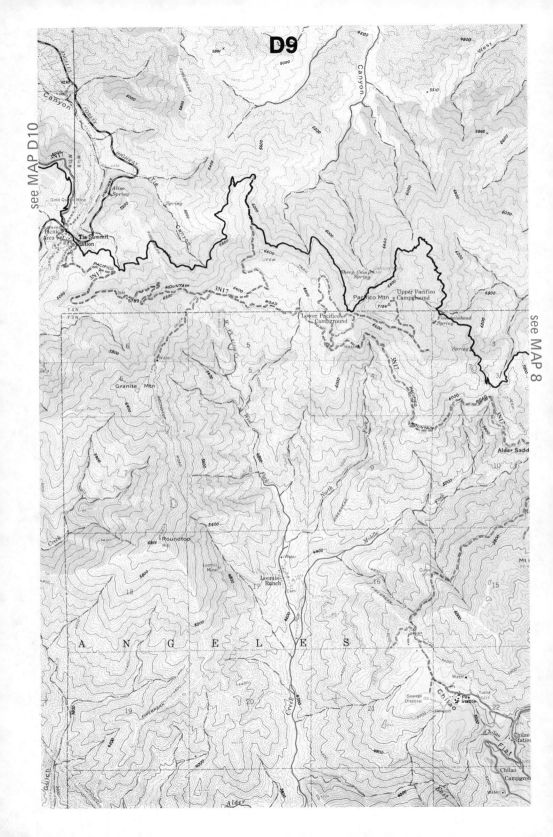

moment to terminate at another jeep road. Turn right and walk ¼ mile down this track to a dirt roadend and metal corrals marking the equestrian-camp part of Sulphur Springs Campground (5200-1.6). Good water, lasting until summer, and adequate campsites are available in the main campground, 0.2 mile east down the oiled access road.

Continuing on the PCT, you go left upcanyon along the access road just 120 yards to locate the trail on the road's north shoulder. This segment parallels the road, keeping 40'

D8

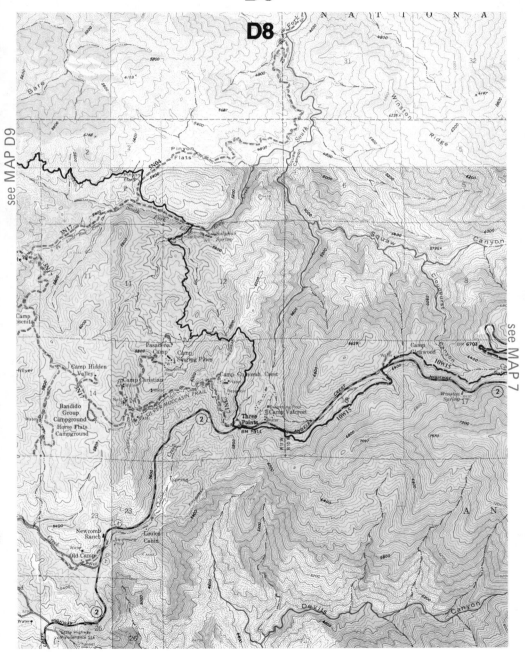

above it, through sagebrush on a gullied hillside. Soon the path turns north into a small canyon and comes to oiled Little Rock Creek Road 5N04 in tree-dotted Pinyon Flats (5395-0.8). This shallow valley's name is a misnomer, since only incense-cedar and Jeffrey pine grow here, in a Forest Service tree plantation. The trail resumes across Road 5N04, just 5 yards north of a jeep road that climbs northwest. The PCT first climbs north, then turns west, crossing the jeep road and then gently ascending across the rotting granite slope. Soon our path starts to zigzag in and out of numerous small ravines, sometimes shaded in their bottoms by interior live oaks, but usually a sunny mixture of ocean spray, hoary-leaved ceanothus, yellow-blossomed flannelbush, and pungent yerba santa. Eventually the PCT winds through a gap (5830-2.1) and turns southwest at the head of Bare Mountain Canyon, but not before we notice how easily the orange-rust-stained, rotting granite is quickly eroded by torrential rains into a badland of sharp-crested, barren ravines. Just below the level of a saddle at the head of Bare Mountain Canyon, the route turns northwest, then switchbacks briefly south, and ascends easily northwest to a grassy flat just shy of a shaded, seeping spring (6240-1.1) that emerges from the side of Pacifico Mountain. The Forest Service plans a trail camp hereabouts.

Leaving the spring, our path climbs north to a notched ridge, then swings west to a chaparral-and-boulder-choked canyon dampened by Fountainhead Spring, 140' above us. Next our trail leads in to and out of many small gulches clothed in 10' high green-bark ceanothus, but these are soon left behind for a gentle amble up in an open forest of Jeffrey pine floored with rabbitbrush. After gaining Pacifico Mountain's north ridge, the trail swings southwest to a bare ridgetop vista point (6760-1.9), giving panoramas north down Santiago Canyon to Little Rock Reservoir, Soledad Pass, and the environs of Lancaster and Palmdale in the Antelope Valley.

From here the PCT begins a gentle descent southwest on steep, sparsely shaded slopes, passing above Sheep Camp Spring, where a planned side trail and camping area will eventually serve PCT users. Where the trail turns north in a shady gap (6645-0.8), trekkers may leave the PCT and walk south a few yards to a dirt road that can be ascended east to Pacifico Mountain Campground (no water) for out-

Eagles Roost

standing sunrise views, or one may descend south on the road and then east on Road 3N17 to a water fountain 0.9 mile from the PCT.

Returning to the PCT, we descend gently northwest, then west under shading interior live oaks and big-cone spruces to a jeep road (6380-1.7), which is followed north down to its end and a resumption of trail (6210-0.5). Now our path gently descends the head of spruce-mottled Tie Canyon, then swings west through a Forest Service tree nursery, passing buildings of the Forest Service's Mill Creek Summit Ranger Station before dropping to Angeles Forest Highway at Mill Creek Summit (4910-3.4). Mill Creek Summit Picnic Area, with piped water, lies just south of the highway. Tank up here since the next absolutely certain water on the PCT route is at North Fork Saddle, 17.3 miles away. Cut by the Mill Creek Fault, which is the cause of this saddle, the Mill Creek/Big Tujunga Wash area was the scene of a considerable mining rush in the 1880s, with men searching for the legendary Los Padres gold mines.

D8, D9

North across Angeles Forest Highway, the PCT begins to climb close alongside paved Mount Gleason Road 3N17, then leaves yerba-santa scrub as it turns west, just north of the ridgetop, in shading interior-live-oak stands. Frequent glimpses north include the shimmering Antelope Valley and the barren Sierra Pelona (Spanish for "a bald range—or ridge—devoid of trees"). The PCT dips to cross Mount Gleason Road (5590-2.6), then keeps north of and below that road. An undulating traverse at about 5600' soon turns south to more-open slopes and switchbacks down to a narrow dirt road in a small northeast-trending canyon. Our route follows this track 0.1 mile southwest gently down to dirt Road 4N24 (5500-3.7). Across the road, trail resumes and interior live oaks, ponderosa and Coulter pines, brodiaea and lush grasses line the cooler parts of the way north of the Mount Gleason Young Adult Conservation Corps Center—once an Army Nike missile base. Later, the PCT switchbacks up to black oaks and Jeffrey pines surrounding a junction with a south-branching trail (6360-4.6).

Ignoring a north-branching trail, which was part of an earlier, now defunct PCT route down to Acton, we start along the south trail, which climbs for a moment to top Mount Gleason's north ridge and cross a narrow dirt road (6410-0.1). One could ascend southeast about 300 yards along this road to Mount Gleason's viewful 6502' summit. The PCT, however, crosses the road and abruptly turns downhill into the head of Paloma Canyon, sadly burned in a fall 1985 fire. Soon we are switchbacking down on poorly maintained, heavily eroded tread in a charred woodland of oak and manzanita. The trail then quickly makes a traverse just above Santa Clara Divide Road, but after a short while we leave the burned brush behind and, at the entrance to Messenger Flats Campground (5870-0.8), come to within a few feet of that road. This delightful area, nestled in a stand of ponderosa pines, has 10 campsites plus tables, toilets and a horse corral. Piped water is usually available during the spring and summer hiking seasons. The next water is at North Fork Saddle Ranger Station in 5.5 miles.

Leaving the campground, the PCT descends northwest momentarily, staying on the road's northern shoulder. This gentle descent soon becomes moderate-to-steep, however, as the trail veers from the roadside to traverse under the north rim of the Santa Clara Divide. This 1980s trail segment is narrower and more tortuous than we have become used to. It was built by Forest Service crews, local Boy Scouts and service clubs after it had become apparent that the original PCT route, northward through Acton, had to be abandoned due to private-property considerations.

Initially we are shaded by the now familiar trio of big-cone spruce, live oak and ponderosa pine, but as the route drops, a low, chamise chaparral supervenes. The otherwise monotonous scrub does, however, allow us excellent, if smog-shrouded, vistas north over Soledad Canyon and Acton, and northwest to ranks of low, seasonally green mountains, over which the PCT will pass on its way to the High Sierra. Soon we dip into a small ravine to strike Moody Canyon Road (5320-1.4). Hikers desperately low on supplies could follow it north down to Acton, 11.6 miles away.

The PCT crosses west below Moody Canyon Road, and adopts a fairly level route, once again under open oak-and-spruce shade. This course eventually leads us to intersect a ridge-line gap and its Santa Clara Divide Road (5425-1.3). Here the PCT and the road coincide, descending gently west for just a moment to the next gap on the ridge, where PCT tread resumes (5395-0.1). Climbing west, initially beside a poor jeep road, the trail now keeps on the sunnier south side of the divide, in low, dry chaparral. Beware of the multitudes of ticks residing on the brush hereabouts, and check your legs for them often. Presently, an easy ascent yields to a gentle descent, and we pass the scattered wreckage of an airplane—its pilot missed clearing the ridge by only a few feet. Soon after, the PCT reaches a firebreak atop the main divide, and descends from its steeply west-descending jeep track (5395-0.7). Just a minute down the jeep track is a small flat, shaded by a single Coulter pine, which is the only nice, though waterless, campsite between Messenger Flats and North Fork Saddle.

After an initial descent northeast, the PCT turns northwest to descend moderately across the forested head of Mill Canyon. A few short switchbacks lead to a more earnest descent on often rocky tread. We get frequent glimpses down into Soledad Canyon, and later, as the tree cover thins, we can look northwest to the fantastic, red Vasquez Rocks, this assemblage being the next major point of interest on our northward agenda. Another set of small switch-

D9, D10, D11, D12

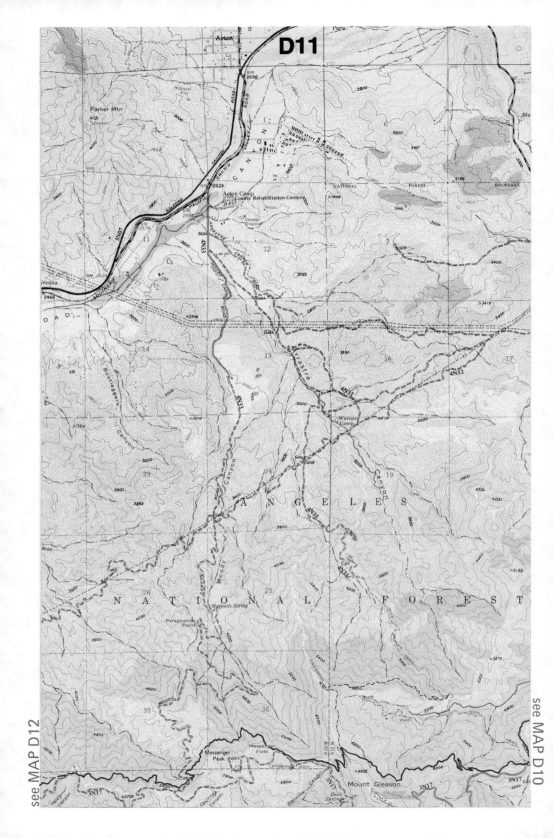

D11

see MAP D12

see MAP D10

backs and further bone-jarring presently deposit us at North Fork Saddle, where we find BPL Road 4N32 (4210-2.0), under a crackling high-tension powerline. On the north side of the saddle is the Forest Service's North Fork Saddle Ranger Station, which has year-round water and a picnic area with tables and toilets. No camping is allowed here, but hikers may camp anywhere along the nearby PCT. Northbound trekkers will find their next certain water in Soledad Canyon, 8.7 miles away, while southbound trekkers must carry water at least up to Messenger Flats Campground, 5.5 miles away, or possibly all the way to Mill Creek Summit, a long 17.3 miles away.

Bound for Soledad Canyon, the PCT descends northward from the BPL road, initially just under Santa Clara Divide Road, but soon far below it, on a diagonaling descent on steep, rocky hillsides above Mill Canyon. Soon we are clambering steeply up and down across narrow ravines, on poorly constructed tread that is destined to quickly erode. In one spot, it already has, for a landslide has swept away a 50′ stretch of trail. Later, the PCT drops at a gentler angle, but as it rounds the east side of point 4173, the path virtually plummets northward, into the head of Mattox Canyon. For the most part, our "economy model" PCT stretch steeply traces a ridgetop firebreak, but in one place, switchbacks do relieve the strain of our aching thigh muscles. When we can afford not to watch our footing, views east reveal a tree plantation in Mill Canyon. Beside the trail in springtime, yerba santa bears fragrant blue blossoms, and chia and fiddleneck show small purple and white flowers, respectively. Eventually, we encounter a second set of switchbacks, which deposit us at a step-across ford of Mattox Canyon creek (2685-4.3). This small stream usually flows into May, but should not be relied on for water. However, some small

D12

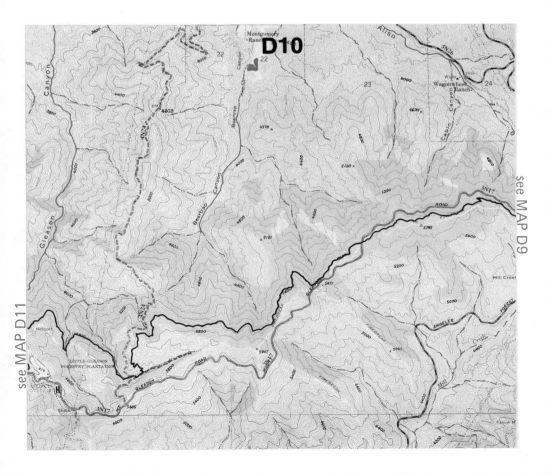

flats next to the trail—and a pretty line of sycamores—make this the nicest camping area between North Fork Saddle and Soledad Canyon.

Pushing on, we ascend moderately west and north through dry chaparral to gain a 3000' ridgecrest. A short drop from its north end leads to a contouring traverse above Fryer Canyon. From here, we can identify the PCT route, under some large pink cliffs, climbing the north slopes of Soledad Canyon. About one mile later, our path starts a swoop down to a nearby saddle, just feet above Indian Canyon Road. This pass is formed by the Magic Mountain Fault, one of a series of southwest-northeast trending faults that transect the PCT in the next few miles. Notice how the Precambrian feldspar-rich granitic rocks have here been crushed to a fine white powder by the fault's action. Now the PCT makes a steep initial climb, paralleling Indian Canyon Road 4N37 and staying just above it. In a few minutes we reach a pass and dip to cross this dirt road (2640-3.3), which switchbacks steeply north down into Soledad Canyon. The PCT instead continues west, traversing gently down above the mouth of Indian Canyon before rounding back east to terminate on Indian Canyon Road at a point just 35 yards above that road's signed junction with 2-lane, paved Soledad Canyon Road (2237-1.1).

Congratulations are in order at this time, for you have now finished walking the length of the San Gabriel Mountains! Acton, with a post office, market, restaurants and a PCT register, lies 5.8 miles east up Soledad Canyon Road. Saugus, a larger town with complete facilities, is 12.5 miles west down the road. A number of RV parks are found in nearby Soledad Canyon. They all have water, and some offer hikers and equestrians use of their campground, showers, laundromats and small stores. Northbound, the next certain water is in Agua Dulce, 12.0 miles ahead. Southbound trekkers will next get water up at North Fork Saddle, a usually hot 8.7-mile ascent into the San Gabriel Mountains.

Following the chaotic route of the northbound PCT across the Santa Clara River on the floor of Soledad Canyon can be very difficult if it is not properly signed. To achieve success, simply keep in mind that you want to attain the railroad tracks running along the north side of the canyon, and respect private property as you go.

From Indian Canyon Road 4N37, northbound PCT travelers amble east along the shoulder of Soledad Canyon Road for about 50 yards to a short, poor dirt-road spur that drops left, down-canyon, toward the riverside. In spring 1988, the Santa Clara River's bed and banks hereabouts were being extensively bulldozed, obscuring your way over the loose, sandy soil to a hop-across ford of the Santa Clara River (2198-0.2) amid patchy false-willows and large, ankle-high patches of watercress. In the quiet of morning, one might disturb nesting mallards or a great blue heron, fishing in the clear shallow stream for a strange-looking fish, the endangered finger-long three-spine stickleback. This fish is now restricted in range primarily to Soledad and San Francisquito canyons.

Now work east along the river's north bank, over a jumble of broken concrete, just below a long, 8' high retaining wall constructed of rust-brown metal railroad-car walls. Just upstream of the wall's end, we enter the west side of Cypress Park Resort, a subscription-only RV campground. Here we find and follow a poor dirt road (2205-0.1), marked by plastic PCT posts, which snakes left northward from the riverside up onto a low, cottonwood-shaded bench. The route crosses a slightly better road that goes east along a line of picnic tables and water spigots to the main camp area of Cypress Park Resort. This road also goes west into The Robin's Nest RV park, which may accommodate hikers and equestrians. Just a few yards north, our road ends at a better service road that runs along the south side of the Southern Pacific Railroad tracks (2240-0.1). This junction is located just east of a fence and two prominent railroad signals. Now walk right, east, on the service road to a resumption of actual PCT trail tread. This begins as an unmarked, indistinct trail (2243-0.1) ascending north from the railroad bed on the west side of a small valley that drains slopes north of us. The trail starts beside a low, square concrete culvert and a 6' high metal box labeled "431.7."

Leaving the shady canyon bottom to climb briskly back onto a brushy hillside, the trail quickly gains a saddle (2485-0.4), but hardly pauses before continuing upward. Soon we pass beneath strange, pinkish cliffs—our first encounter with the Vasquez Formation, which is a conglomerate of igneous and metamorphic

D12, D13

see MAP D13

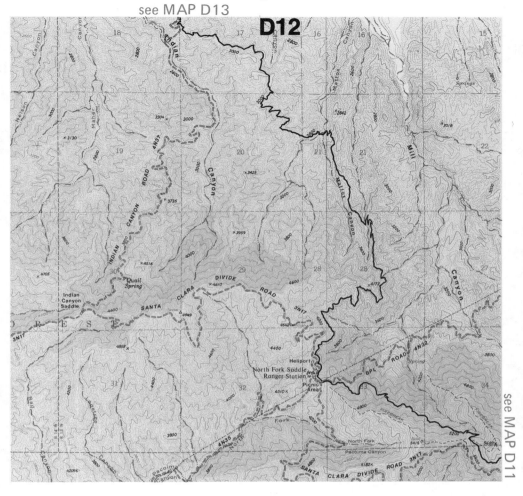

see MAP D11

cobbles set in a fine-grained pink siltstone. Our sometimes steep ascent finally abates as the trail rounds the east side of a summit to cross Young Canyon Road (2960-1.5), which serves a trio of parallel, humming, high-voltage transmission lines. Across the good dirt road our way swings northwest, descending gently-to-moderately below the road, soon to cross a gap (2980-0.7) near the head of Bobcat Canyon. Around here we see, to the southwest, a spectacular formation of rock-candy pink Vasquez outcrops. Next the PCT climbs a bit, then drops into Bobcat Canyon's dry wash before climbing in earnest to cross a jeep road (3160-1.6) on the divide separating Soledad and Agua Dulce canyons.

Vistas south, and east to Mount Gleason, and north to the Sierra Pelona are obtained as we catch our breath, then we descend west, quickly recrossing the jeep road once, and then again at a saddle (2960-0.5), from where the trail leaves the ridgetop. In an unusual economy of PCT construction, the trail north from this saddle wastes no time—nor does it spare our knees—in a willy-nilly, steep descent north to a narrow branch of Escondido Canyon. After a bone-jarring half mile, the incline abates as the route hops to the ravine's west side, then levels out to turn west along a terrace above Escondido Canyon's seasonal creek. White-trunked sycamores in the canyon bottom contrast starkly with the surrounding

D13

see MAP E2

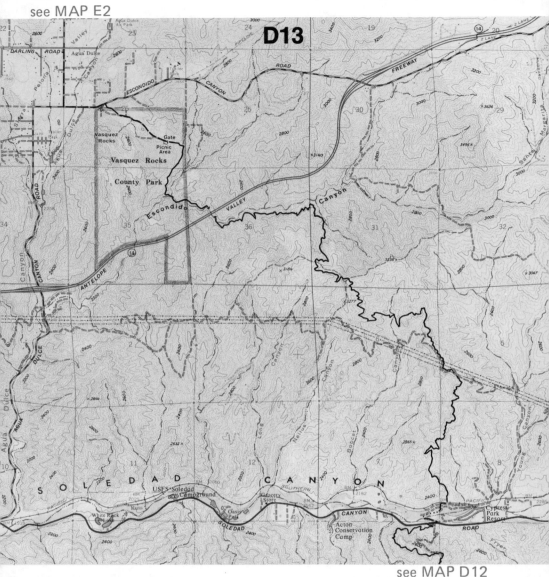

see MAP D12

red, rocky bluffs, dappled by yellow lichens, while yerba santa and white-flowered buckwheat dot the ruddy hillside. Across the canyon to our north is an even greater contrast—four-lane Antelope Valley Freeway 14 climbing toward Palmdale.

A gradual descent carries us down to the level of the stream bed at a side canyon and a use trail from the south (2400-2.0). Here a sunny, if often waterless and noisy, camp could be made. Now Escondido Canyon's trickling springtime stream, lined with watercress, bends more northward, and the PCT follows it, to abruptly enter a lengthy, 10' high tunnel under Antelope Valley Freeway 14 (2370-0.1).

Emerging from the north end of the 500' passage, we find an abrupt change of scenery. Here the creekside is lined by thickets of willows and baccharis shrubs, while lush groves of squaw bush, flannelbush and poison

D13

oak stand just back from the creek's edge. The air is noticeably cooler, and myriad birds call from the underbrush. Our route proceeds directly down the shallow, sandy stream bed for a few yards, then picks up a well-traveled path near the creek's north edge. We continue downcanyon and enter Vasquez Rocks County Park. Please be aware that camping in the park is allowed only in designated areas and only with the permission of the ranger; contact him at the northwest entrance ranger station.

In the park, note how the canyon's south wall begins to steepen into pink and red cliffs of sandstone and conglomerate. These rocks are layered sediments of Oligocene and Miocene age, having a nonmarine origin. Our path soon crosses to the canyon's south side, and then ascends slightly under a fantastic precipice of multilayered overhangs. Rounding north of this cliff, the route then drops to cross once again to the north bank (2335-0.6).

Here, at a major side canyon from the north, the southern cliff bulges into a huge, cobbled overhang. Just downstream, the northern canyon wall is also overhung by cliffs. Now, look north for a rudimentary path leading steeply up an easy slope on the far hillside. Any safe route that gets us onto the north rim of Escondido Canyon will do, and there are many of them to choose from. Once on the canyon's rim, we find a different world, an almost flat upland dotted with low buckwheat, sagebrush shrubs and head-high junipers. Lying in the northwest are the spectacular Vasquez Rocks, the 1850s hideout of famed badman Tiburcio Vasquez. If you lose your path, simply head for the rock that resembles a tilted Matterhorn, since our route eventually takes a dirt road that lies along its north base. With a bit of luck we find a little-used dirt road, hopefully still marked with a brown plastic PCT post.

On it, we start a very gentle ascent northeast as we parallel the western rim of the major tributary of Escondido Canyon, ignoring a north-branching track. Soon, across the canyon from some ridgetop homes, the route strikes a junction (2535-0.5) with another poor dirt road, descending west. This junction is marked by a yellow pipe post, and on the road, we follow a succession of similar posts west down past a cluster of picnic tables and across a large grassland to a gate (2485-0.1) at a large parking area. Amble northwest along a good dirt road, climbing gently between the two most spectacular rock outcrops. A number of tables and fire rings are scattered about, in secluded nooks, but this park is currently designated for day use only. Now the road curves west and drops gently to a short segment of PCT trail tread (2310-0.5), perhaps signed by a lone brown plastic PCT post standing on the low rise just north of our road. This PCT segment winds northwest, around a half-dozen clifflets, to strike Escondido Canyon Road (2510-0.2) at the signed entrance to Vasquez Rocks County Park. The ranger station, where information concerning camping and water may be obtained, is just a minute's walk south down the entrance road.

Here we turn left, west, onto a temporary PCT segment, along Escondido Canyon Road, soon coming to a stop sign at larger Agua Dulce Canyon Road (2470-0.3). Turn right, north, onto it, and head into the village of Agua Dulce. Passing a cafe, we soon reach "downtown" Agua Dulce at Darling Road (2530-0.5). Here is Agua Dulce Post Office (combined with "Hall 'n' Oats" Feed Store, open 7 days a week, and offering complete supplies for horsemen). There is also a small, but surprisingly complete, grocery store next door.

D13

The long desert march through Antelope Valley

Section E: Agua Dulce to Highway 58 near Mojave

Introduction: The Mojave Desert is the arid setting for this short, least characteristic segment of the Pacific Crest Trail. Much of the route is not even really trail, but rather it follows dusty dirt roads along the Los Angeles Aqueduct. The Forest Service's proposed route, which will climb into the eastern reaches of the Tehachapi Mountains via Cottonwood Canyon, probably will not be passable until after 1990. The major snag in the government's plan to construct a true mountain-crest route is the refusal of the owners of the mammoth Tejon Ranch, which lies astride the Tehachapi Mountains, to allow right-of-way for the PCT. This refusal, backed up by gun-toting guards and numerous gates, prevents construction of a mountain path north from Liebre Mountain.

So for the time being, the PCT drops north from Liebre Mountain, abandoning any pretense of being a crest route, and strikes north across the heart of the Antelope Valley, which is the western arm of the immense Mojave Desert. The pronghorn antelopes seen by John C. Fre'mont when in 1844 he forced passage through Tejon Pass via this valley are gone, exterminated by hunters and later by encroaching alfalfa fields, but Antelope Valley's desert flavor remains.

Even in early spring, temperatures can soar over 100°F, and swirling dust devils can send unwary hikers sprawling or ducking for cover behind a grotesque Joshua tree. The temporary route strikes due north across the shrub-dotted desert, and then, at the alluvial stoop of the Tehachapi Mountains—a southern extension of the Sierra Nevada—we turn east beside the underground Los Angeles Aqueduct.

Beginning in the Owens Valley, on the east side of the Sierra, the Los Angeles Aqueduct was the brain child of William Mulholland, a former L.A. County Water Superintendent. It was constructed in 1913 and later extended northward to the Mono Lake basin. Bitter disputes, court battles, and even shooting wars raged when Owens Valley farmers realized that the water needs of a growing Los Angeles would turn their well-watered agricultural region into a dust bowl. Litigation continues today, as does resentment. But Mulholland is a hero to some Angelenos, for millions of Southern Californians drink Owens Valley water, and without this project Los Angeles might have remained a sleepy patchwork of orange groves.

Declination: 13¾°E

Mileages:	South to North	Distances between Points	North to South
Agua Dulce	0.0		99.7
		1.8	
Old Sierra Highway	1.8		97.9
		6.4	
Big Oak Spring Trail	8.2		91.5
		1.9	
Bouquet Canyon Road	10.1		89.6
		6.1	
Road 6N09 in Spunky Canyon	16.2		83.5
		6.3	
San Francisquito Canyon Road to Green Valley	22.5		77.2
		7.6	
Elizabeth Lake Canyon Road to Lake Hughes........	30.1		69.6
		7.0	
Upper Shake Campground Trail	37.1		62.6
		6.0	
Atmore Meadows Spur Road.......................	43.1		56.6
		4.3	
Bear Campground	47.4		52.3
		9.5	
Three Points....................................	56.9		42.8
		3.1	
Los Angeles Aqueduct	60.0		39.7
		0.8	
California Aqueduct	60.8		38.9
		5.3	
Waterhole 1953+00	66.1		33.6
		10.5	
Cottonwood Creek bridge........................	76.6		23.1
		5.0	
140th Street West	81.6		18.1
		5.8	
Tehachapi-Willow Springs Road...................	87.4		12.3
		6.2	
Oak Creek Road	93.6		6.1
		6.1	
Highway 58 near Mojave.........................	99.7		0.0

Supplies: Agua Dulce, at the start of Section E, has only a post office and limited supplies at a small grocery store. Many hikers reaching this point choose to hitchhike southwest 14 miles on Highway 14 to Saugus, a large town with complete accommodations. Later, the settlement of Green Valley is a short detour from the PCT where it drops into San Francisquito Canyon, 22.5 miles from Agua Dulce. It is reached by walking southwest 1.7 miles down San Francisquito Canyon Road to Spunky Canyon Road in quiet Green Valley, then heading southeast 0.9 mile to the combined post office, grocery store and restaurant. A 2.2-mile detour to Lake Hughes, 30.1 miles into your journey, is the last chance to reprovision before facing the Mojave Desert. This small village has a post office, restaurants, stores, motels and a private campground with showers. Mojave lies 3½ miles off the PCT route at the end of this section. Most hikers will make the detour, if only to tank up on cold drinks. A fairly large community, Mojave has stores, restaurants, motels and laundromats as well as a post office.

The Mojave Desert and Desert Survival: The Mojave Desert was a formidable barrier to early travelers, causing much hardship and greatly slowing Southern California's growth. That part of the Mojave traversed by the PCT is now tamed by criss-crossing roads and dotted with homes and ranches, eliminating any dangers—as imagined by the uninformed—of dying like French Legionnaires, with parched throats and watery dreams. Still, the Mojave Desert stretch of the PCT can broil your mind, blister your feet, and turn your mouth to dust—in all, an unpleasant experience—if you are not adequately prepared. With a little forethought, enough water, and the right equipment this hike can be an enjoyable variation from the PCT's usual crestline surroundings.

Water is the key to all life, and enough of it will make yours more enjoyable. While planning your nightly stops or possible side hikes to water sources, you might consider the following government figures, arrived at by subjects operating under optimal experimental conditions. (They weren't carrying heavy packs!) Without water you can survive only 2 days at 120°F if you stay in one spot, 5 days at 100°F, and 9 days at 80°F. If you walk during the day, you will survive only one third as long. If you rest during the day and hike at night, then these figures become 1, 3 and 7 days, with 12, 33 and 110 miles being covered. At 100°F, the mid-figure, you'll be able to hike 20 or more miles for every gallon of water you carry, though Schaffer's actual field experience is that he consumed 2–3 gallons a day under these conditions.

The best way to conserve water is to hike at night, and night-hiking has added bonuses in the Mojave Desert: astounding star-filled skies, fewer passing cars, and the chance to observe some little-seen desert wildlife—inquisitive kit foxes sometimes play tag with hikers. Yucca night-lizards, which spend their days under fallen Joshua trees, also scurry about at night. But use a flashlight, even on moonlit nights, because rattlesnakes like to lie on the warm roads.

If you prefer to hike in daylight, start early, before sunrise, say at 5 in the morning during spring. Hike about 4 hours, perhaps getting in 12 miles, rest until evening, and then hike about another 2 hours. Doing so, you should get across the desert in 3 days. By day, walkers should ignore their desire to shed sweaty shirts or pants, since clothing prevents excessive moisture loss and overheating, and it also forestalls an excruciating high-desert sunburn. While drinking, be sure also to replace salts and electrolytes lost by sweating—their depletion would disable you long before you were affected by the loss of body water.

San Gabriel Mountains above L.A. smog, from the Sierra Pelona crest

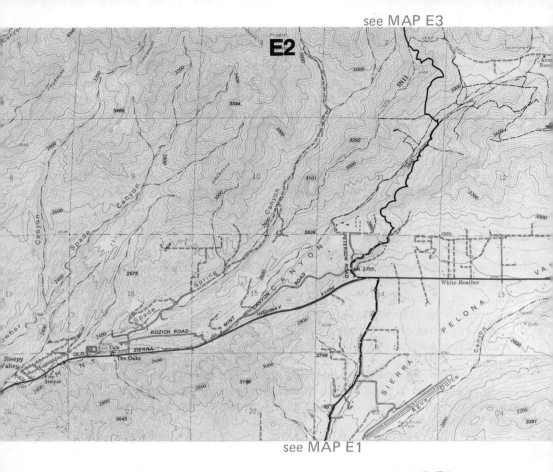

E2

see MAP E1

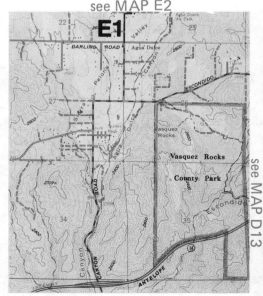

E1

Agua Dulce is reached via Highway 14, 18 miles east of its junction with Interstate 5 in Sylmar or 21 miles south of Palmdale. Take Highway 14's Agua Dulce Canyon Road exit, then head north 2.5 miles up that road to east-west Darling Road, in Agua Dulce. Your first reliable source of water north of this town, discounting homes, is at Big Oak Spring, about 8½ miles away.

Leave Agua Dulce by walking northward on temporary PCT, following Agua Dulce Canyon Road very gently up grassy Sierra Pelona Valley. You pass numerous homes and side roads, a few businesses, an airfield, and finally a church before your road ends at wide, paved Old Sierra Highway (2725-1.8). Turn left and go west along its north shoulder for just a bit to paved Mint Canyon Road (2730-0.1). Follow that road up and right, west, shortly to a low gap where paved Petersen Road (2755-0.1) branches north. Turn right on Petersen Road and descend gently to the southern edge of a

E1, E2

ranch-dotted bench in Mint Canyon. Here a dirt road (2750-0.1) servicing a line of high-tension electric wires, branches right.

The permanent PCT route begins by climbing momentarily northeast up this road, then down, and then ascends moderately again. Quickly, the road gains exposed slopes of withered chamise on the eastern flank of Mint Canyon. Just back inside the Angeles National Forest boundary, trail tread resumes (2905-0.4), marked, hopefully, by a large PCT emblem. Follow the tread left, northward, as it contours around a nose, then makes a long, easily descending traverse to the shadeless southeast banks of Mint Canyon's infrequently flowing stream. At a step-across ford of the creek (2865-1.3) we pass a horse trail that continues up-canyon. The PCT, however, clambers west up onto a low bench with an equestrian trail register. Beyond, we walk straight uphill on an old jeep road, passing another that runs down-canyon. We now see evidence of a brush fire that burned here in 1985. Where a jeep road climbs left along an old barbed-wire fence, we follow the obvious PCT right, ascending north. A promontory overlooking large Annan Ranch is soon reached, after which the path climbs moderately northwest to survey more blackened chaparral on the headwall of Mint Canyon. By walking a few minutes more, we reach Big Tree Trail 14W02 (3330-1.1) astride a saddle.

The PCT is routed along this old path, which ascends steeply north on cobbly schist tread much abused by dirtbikers. The climb moderates near the top, presenting excellent vistas south to the bizarre Vasquez Rocks, purported refuge of bandit Tiburcio Vasquez, and more eastward to Mounts Gleason, Williamson and Baden-Powell. Atop Sierra Pelona ridge, where gusts of wind have been measured at 100 miles per hour, we turn west on Sierra Pelona Ridge Road 6N07 (4500-2.2) and walk ¼ mile to Big Tree Trail 14W02, which branches northwest from a short parking spur. A delightful descent follows: vistas stretch to Owens Peak in the southern Sierra, and in spring the grassy slopes underfoot are graced with wallflowers, yellow mariposa lily, farewell-to-spring and lupine. Soon we enter a small stand of live oaks that hides nodding orange mallows, and here we find a side trail (4005-1.1) to Big Oak Spring. A secluded camp at the spring, ¼ mile west of the PCT, once nurtured the world's largest known canyon live oak, now dead from a fire.

You'll see elderberry, western virgin's bower, poison oak, and a fair number of birds. The small spring lies almost right under the dead oak, guarded by a patch of fierce nettles. These 3' tall, serrate-leaved herbs have minute hairs that inject formic acid, and will cause hours of stinging discomfort if brushed accidentally.

Back on the PCT, we quickly pass the old, straight-down-the-hill trail, then cross fault-aligned Martindale Canyon, and ascend briefly to a ridgetop jeep road. A graded descent thereafter leads northeast to paved Bouquet Canyon Road 6N05 (3340-1.9). Merging under Bouquet Reservoir, 2¼ miles to the west, the San Francisquito and Clearwater faults run Bouquet Canyon's length and separate southern Pelona schists from granites on the canyon's north wall. The PCT drops across the dry wash draining Bouquet Canyon, then arcs easily up, northwest, to cross a jeep road near a water tank in a small canyon. Now the trail ascends moderately on coarse granitic sand to just north of a powerline, where the PCT branches northwest from the old CRHT (California Riding and Hiking Trail) (3985-2.7), which continues north up to Leona Divide Truck Road 6N04.

The PCT climbs along the steep south-facing slope through sickly, low chamise, crosses a descending firebreak, and then veers more northward, just under the Leona Divide Road, to gain a pass (4300-1.4) with another firebreak, which tops a ridge dividing Spunky and Bouquet canyons. A gentle switchback in now-denser chaparral and occasional shading oaks drops us to the head of Spunky Canyon, where we turn west down-canyon, then climb slightly to strike Road 6N09 (3725-2.0). If you're thirsty, seeking a campsite, or needing supplies, then first walk west 1.7 miles down this dirt road to paved Spunky Canyon Road 6N11. On it, wind northwest 1.1 miles to Spunky Campground or 0.8 mile farther to Green Valley, with a post office, grocery store and restaurant.

The PCT climbs gently away from Road 6N09, winding in and out of small ravines on a westward bearing. Eventually the path tops a small ridge, again with a firebreak (3815-2.1), and then the trail angles northeast, through a gap and down into the upper end of Dowd Canyon. Seen from here, Jupiter Mountain looms impressively across the valley. We reach a low point of 3475' in Dowd Canyon, in a gully where native bunchgrasses grow, then we amble first north-northwest before heading southwest around Peak 4087 over to a ridgetop

E2, E3, E5

separating Dowd and San Francisquito canyons. From here a final northeastward swoop under shady interior live oaks brings the PCT to paved San Francisquito Canyon Road (3385-4.2). San Francisquito Ranger Station, with water, is 250 yards southwest, just beyond tiny San Francisquito Picnic Area. San Francisquito Campground, with tables scattered amid sagebrush and under canyon live oaks, is 1.0 mile southwest down-canyon. Green Valley, which has a combined post office, grocery store and restaurant, can be reached by continuing 0.7 mile farther down to Spunky Canyon Road.

Across San Francisquito Canyon Road the PCT begins its climb of Grass Mountain by ascending northwest into a nearby side canyon, above which it strikes a dirt road (3520-0.3) serving two powerlines. The trail follows the road north momentarily, then switchbacks west and progresses unremittingly up chaparralled slopes to Grass Mountain Road (4275-1.3), striking this dirt road just above its junction with Leona Divide Truck Trail. Panoramas unfold northward over Elizabeth Lake—a sag pond on the San Andreas Fault—to distant Antelope Valley and the Tehachapi Mountains, and if one is enjoying a smogless spring day, Owens Peak in the southern Sierra Nevada may be seen. We enjoy this scenery as the path contours, then descends the north slopes of Brass Mountain to a saddle (3900-1.3), where four dirt roads converge at the head of South Portal and Munz canyons.

Keeping on a steep hillside south of the ridge, the PCT contours from this gap over to another saddle, where it crosses dirt Tule Canyon Road 7N01 (3900-1.2) by its junction with Lake Hughes Truck Trail. Onward our route rolls across dry ravines in dense chaparral, switchbacks once to pass through a gap, and then descends unhesitatingly toward misnamed Elizabeth Lake Canyon by crossing an interminable array of narrow, rocky gulches. At the bottom of this unpleasant segment, our path bursts from brush cover to traverse the broad, sandy wash of Elizabeth Lake Canyon. Southbound trekkers may lose their way here in a welter of game trails; they should head straight for the ridge's shoulder, where it strikes the canyon's bottom. Northbound hikers head for nearby, paved Elizabeth Lake Canyon Road 7N09 (3050-3.5).

The next permanent on-route water hole along the PCT is a distant 26.8 miles north-

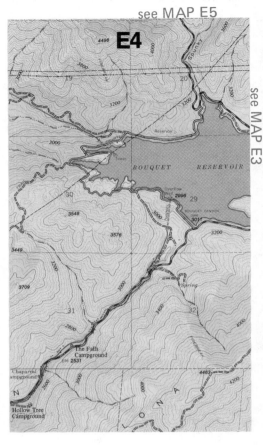

see MAP E5

see MAP E3

west, at the village of Three Points, so be sure you have at least two gallons. The next usually reliable water source near the northbound PCT is at Upper Shake Campground, a 0.6-mile detour that leaves the PCT in 7.0 miles. If you need water or supplies, you should detour north, 1.5 miles up-canyon along Elizabeth Lake Canyon Road to Newvale Drive, which is on the west side of the small resort community of Lake Hughes. At this junction are a cafe, a phone, and the best store in town. Lake Hughes Post Office, stores, cafe and the entrance to a private campground and picnic area are on the west shore of small Hughes Lake (great for your blistered feet!). These are reached by following Newvale Drive east 0.3 mile to Elizabeth Lake-Pine Canyon Road, then walking 0.4 mile farther east to the center of town—a 2.2-mile detour, one-way, from the PCT. The next chance to resupply on the northbound

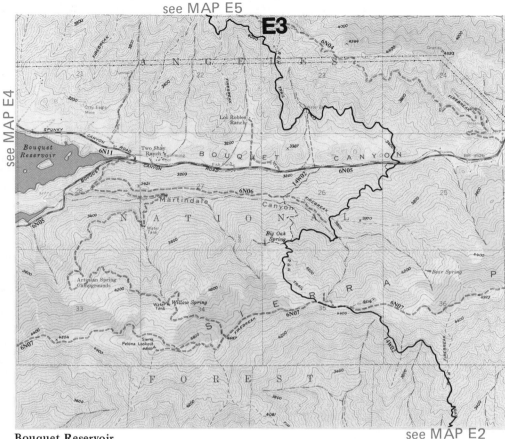

see MAP E5

see MAP E4

E3

see MAP E2

Bouquet Reservoir

PCT is at Mojave, which lies east of the PCT near the end of Section D.

Across Elizabeth Lake Canyon Road 7N09, the PCT attacks Sawmill Mountain's east flank. The trail climbs quickly northwest into a small valley, which has a sycamore-shaded flat that could serve as an adequate, though waterless, campsite. Soon the route, now back in chamise-and-oak chaparral, passes the mouth of an old graphite mine tunnel, then switchbacks to climb more steeply southwest past two more tunnels. After reaching a ridge, the trail again swings northwest to ascend moderately through yerba santa and chamise back into the canyon. Here

E6

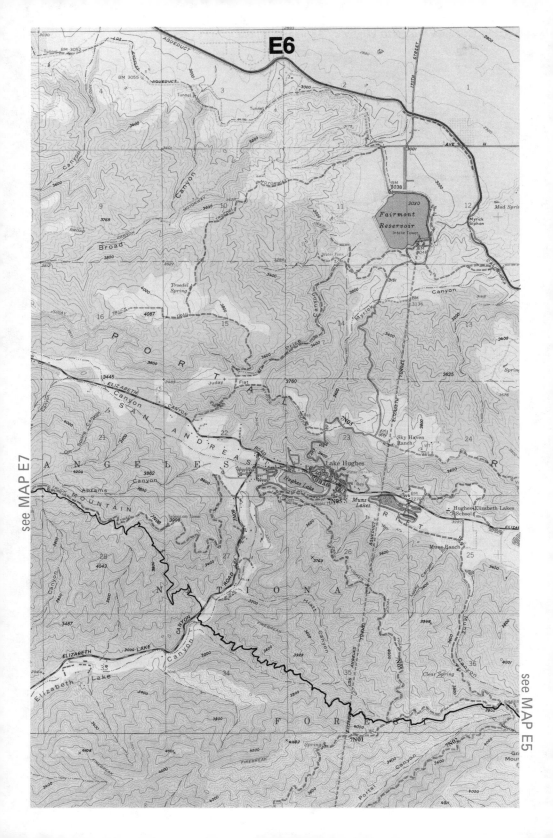

E6

see MAP E7

see MAP E5

we find some shade in the form of interior live oaks and a cluster of disheveled big-cone spruces surrounding a trailside wet-season spring (3710-1.2). No camping is possible on the steep slope here. Continuing on, the path leads up the now-narrow ravine, then veers southwest at its head to reach a viewful intersection with the Sawmill-Liebre Firebreak

(4190-0.6), just above a wide dirt road, Maxwell Truck Trail 7N08.

Now-familiar vistas north over the western part of Antelope Valley to the Tehachapi Mountains are presented here and accompany us as the PCT adopts a leisurely, traversing ascent of Sawmill Mountain's spine, always keeping just a stone's throw south of Maxwell Truck Trail.

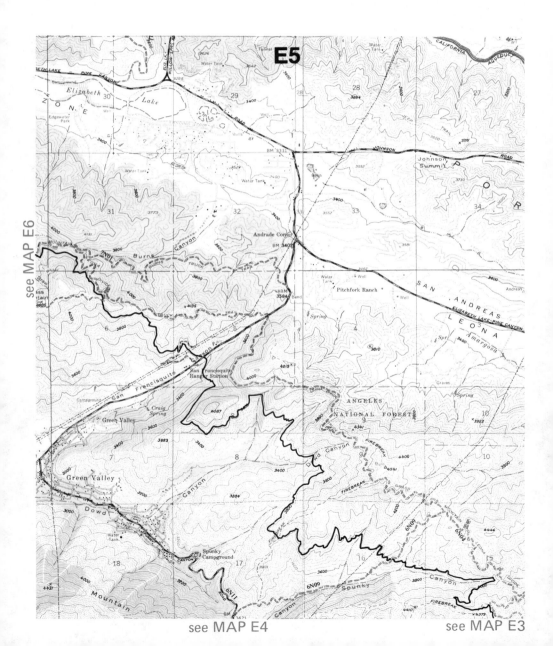

Repeated crossings of the ridge and its fire-break in a mix of chaparral eventually lead us to Maxwell Truck Trail 7N08 (4505-1.9) in an open glade of black oaks. We walk 35 yards northwest along this road to where the trail's tread resumes, near the start of a poorer road. The PCT drops slightly, then assumes an undulating traverse in and out of gullies on the north slope of Sawmill Mountain. After a short while the PCT becomes situated just below moderately ascending Maxwell Truck Trail and maintains that arrangement through chaparral sprinkled with Coulter pines. Eventually the PCT turns south into a larger ravine to cross two dirt roads (4680-2.9) in quick succession. These rough access roads mark the site of a small plantation of trees, whose young Coulter pines and incense-cedars offer a potentially pleasant though waterless campsite.

Pushing on, we ascend a shadier hillside and soon reach a trail intersection (4805-0.4). The poorer branch climbs steeply southeast to strike Maxwell Truck Trail, while a good branch, descending northwest, drops via switchbacks 0.6 mile to Upper Shake Campground, which has tables, fire rings, toilets and seasonal piped water. If the campground water supply is

turned off in early or late season, a small, usually flowing stream can be found in Shake Canyon, just north of the campground. Note that this is the only campsite close to the PCT with reliable water until Three Points, still a dry 19.8 miles away.

The northbound PCT heads southwest gently up from the Upper Shake Campground trail junction, traversing the hillside first under shady oaks and big-cone spruces as it ducks into and then heads out of a small canyon. This pleasant segment crosses an abandoned jeep road dropping into the head of Shake Canyon, then continues to a ridgetop road junction (5245-2.6). From here Maxwell Truck Trail 7N08 starts south on a generally eastward traverse, Burnt Peak Road 7N23A traverses west, and Sawmill Mountain Truck Trail 7N23 traverses northwest and also descends northeast to Elizabeth Lake-Pine Canyon Road.

The PCT descends gently north under the upper branch of Sawmill Mountain Truck Trail, now in even shadier mixed forest and chaparral. Next a long, descending traverse leads across a broad black-oak-clothed ridge nose to a junction (5015-1.8). From here a spur trail ascends southeast 0.2 mile to small Sawmill

E7, E8

Panorama of the Sierra Pelona highlands and the distant Tehachapi Mountains

Campground, which is pretty but waterless.

We first contour and then switchback twice to resume a position just north of and below Sawmill Mountain Truck Trail. Presently, we cross that road (4790-1.1) at a large turnout. Across the road, our trail drops indistinctly southwest, through a corridor of Coulter pines, then winds west around the head of wild, rugged North Fork Fish Canyon. Soon we reach a saddle junction of Sawmill Mountain Truck Trail and Atmore Meadows Spur Road 7N19 (4705-0.5). The PCT follows the latter road southwest for 80 yards to a resumption of trail tread in a steep ravine. Before continuing, however, hikers may wish to detour 1.7 miles farther along Atmore Meadows Spur Road to a fair spring, or another 1.0 mile beyond it down to a series of shaded glens, the site of Atmore Meadows Campground, which has water, tables and toilets.

Next on the PCT's agenda of chaparral-cloaked summits is Liebre Mountain, and the steep, seasonally hot trail that climbs from Atmore Meadows Spur Road quickly dispels any thoughts of a sedate ascent. After an effort we are high on brushy slopes, panting toward a grassy saddle (5655-2.1), which marks an end

to the unpleasant grind. Now descending easily, zigzags lead northwest first close to Liebre Mountain Truck Trail, then into and out of interminable dry washes that alternate with brushy ridgelets. Sometimes we have good views south to the wildlands of deep Cienega Canyon. Eventually the undulating descent ceases and the grade becomes a moderate ascent. Moments later, we encounter a junction with a spur trail (5370-2.2) that climbs north a few yards to waterless Bear Campground. An additional three minutes' climb along the PCT leads to a crossing of Liebre Mountain Truck Trail 7N23 (5545-0.2).

Now on the cooler north slopes of Liebre Mountain, our way becomes much nicer, winding almost level along hillsides shaded by open groves of black oaks. In spring the grassy turf underfoot is a green sea dotted with brodiaea, baby blue-eyes and miner's lettuce. Soon we cross a north-descending dirt road (5580-0.9) on a ridge nose as the PCT winds west close to the gentle summit of Liebre Mountain, and eventually we find a trail junction (5745-1.2) beside a large, multi-trunked interior live oak. Here the newer PCT branches right, northwest, to descend gently away from the older,

E8, E9

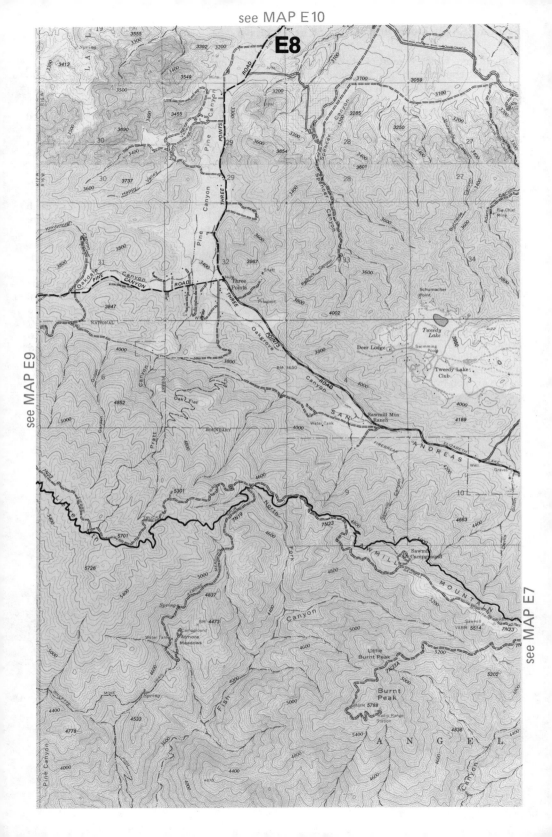

see MAP E10

E8

see MAP E9

see MAP E7

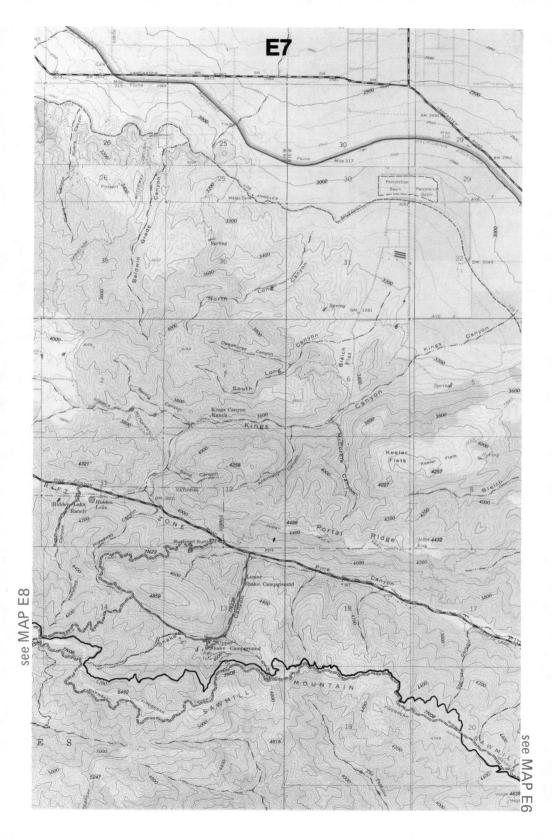

see MAP E8

see MAP E6

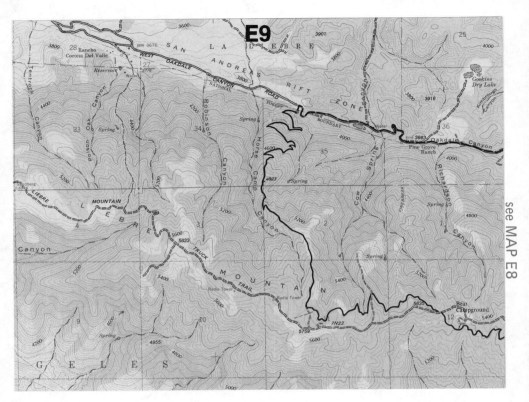

abandoned PCT alignment which continued along the summit ridge of Liebre Mountain and then down to Quail Lake. Either trail, however, continues only a minute before striking a fair dirt road (5720-0.1).

The newer PCT heads north, downhill, on this closed ridgetop road, passing through a plantation of young black oaks and their older in-laws. Soon the downgrade steepens and sagebrush replaces much of the understory. Windswept panoramas over the westernmost corner of Antelope Valley remind us that we have now ended a sweeping 300-mile skirting of the southwestern border of the Mojave Desert, which has led us west from Whitewater along the summits of the San Bernardinos, the San Gabriels, and Sawmill and Liebre mountains—a job well done!

Continuing our descent, we lose these views as we re-enter big-cone spruce, pine and oak cover below 5200' elevation. Soon thereafter, the road, which has diminished to a rough jeep track, ends (5140-1.0). Switchbacks lower us gently from just beyond this point into a

saddle—a good but dry camp—just short of a conifer-clad 4923' knob. Beyond, the enjoyable trail enters thick chaparral, descends moderately via switchbacks, and presently levels out at a dirt road spur (3995-2.5) atop a minor pass just south of paved West Oakdale Canyon Road.

Keeping to the safer south shoulder, the temporary PCT route turns right, east, down along the narrow road, which soon reduces its grade in an open stand of pines and black oaks. Here is a small, seasonal sag pond which, like our road, lies on the San Andreas Fault (labeled on the map as the San Andreas Rift Zone). Liebre Mountain and the hillside to our south are creeping slowly northwest along the fault. After passing the pond, our route begins to ascend, crosses seasonal Cow Spring Canyon Creek, and then climbs moderately, via a switchback, to a narrow saddle (3983-1.4). Here we encounter the first of an increasing number of mini-ranches and homes that the road will pass on its long, gentle descent into Oakdale Canyon. Initially the way is shaded by

E9, E8

151

see MAP E11

black oaks and Coulter pines, but soon enough manzanita, other brush and digger pines line the now-shadeless route. After a mile the canyon floor broadens, making room for small vineyards and horse corrals. A bit more walking leads to a junction with paved Three Points Road (3424-2.2), in the village of Three Points. At this junction is Felix's 3 Points Store, which has a limited selection of picnic and snack foods, a small cafe, and telephones. Here also is a small private campground, with restrooms and picnic tables.

The northbound temporary PCT now turns left, northwest, along Three Points Road. Walk gently down through broad, sandy Pine Canyon as your road first traces the foot of low hills that border the flat valley floor, which is home to a succession of apricot and grape orchards. Later, as the canyon widens at its mouth to debouch an alluvial fan into westernmost Antelope Valley, Three Points Road descends easily to gain wind-blown panoramas of sunburned high desert. Eventually we come to a junction with busy, two-lane Lancaster Road (3050-2.9). We are now in the BLM's massive California Desert Conservation Area.

We turn right and walk east along the shoulder of Lancaster Road—or better, on a poor dirt road paralleling it just a few feet to its north—to the Los Angeles Aqueduct (3046-0.2). The aqueduct, which we will now follow (on the temporary route) for about 60 miles, is here a length of huge, buried pipe, glimpsed here and there under a mantle of sand and rabbitbrush. To its west is an open concrete ditch, while a fair dirt road traces its eastern side, initially marked by a row of low, gray-green cypress trees. We turn left, north, along this road, and follow the historic aqueduct— life-blood of Los Angeles—arrow-straight across Antelope Valley. Soon our way is blocked by an even more formidable product of southern California's efforts to build a paradise from desert sands—the immense California Aqueduct (2965-0.8).

Here, the California Aqueduct takes the form of a veritable concrete-lined river, and engineers were faced with the rather bizarre problem of routing the larger California aqueduct under the smaller Los Angeles Aqueduct. For the northbound, the next water lies in the Los Angeles Aqueduct at a point 5.3 miles ahead. If you're heading south on the temporary PCT, the next water is in Three Points, in 3.9 miles.

E8, E10

Our temporary route skirts west to find a bridge at a siphon, then returns the same distance east to resume trekking north alongside the Los Angeles Aqueduct. We pass a few habitations, all built in the peculiarly eccentric style of California desert residents. Later we descend to our lowest Antelope Valley point, 2865', to cross the sandy wash of a seasonal creek bed. Here the shade of a wooden trestle supporting the massive, black-tarred, 8' diameter aqueduct pipe offers a rest spot amid another quintessentially California desert feature, an ad-hoc garbage dump of cans, household appliances and auto carcasses, all riddled with bullet holes.

Now the route north leads into a low, scraggly "woodland" of Joshua trees, the hallmarks of the Mojave Desert. At one time Joshua trees, or tree yuccas, were more widely distributed, as evidenced by fossils of the extinct giant yucca-feeding ground sloth, found in southern Nevada, where Joshua trees are no longer living. These giant members of the lily family, with their unusually branched, sometimes human forms, were likened by Mormon pioneers to the figure of Joshua, pointing the route to the Great Salt Lake—whence the

Joshua trees

E10

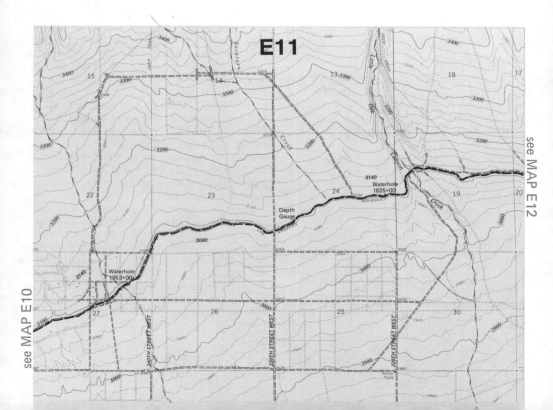

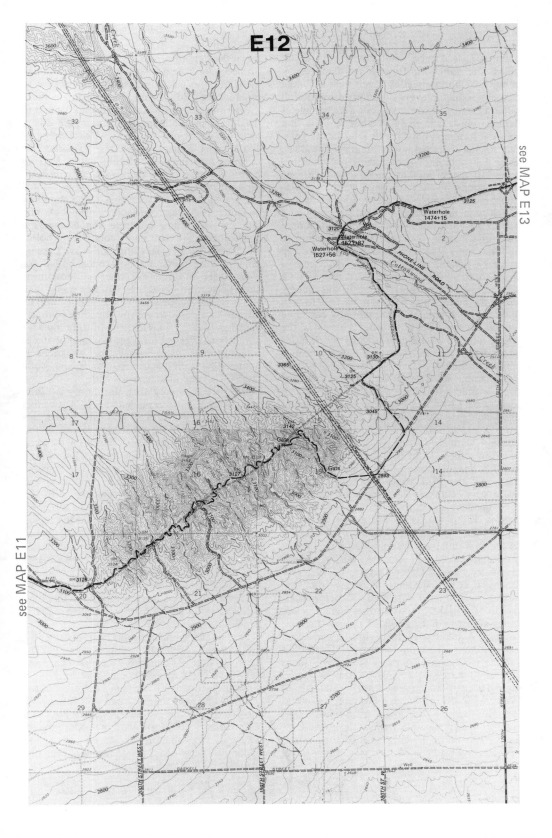

E12

see MAP E13

see MAP E11

name. These "trees" will not branch at all unless the trunk's tip flowers are damaged by wind or by boring beetles. Each time a Joshua tree blossoms, an event determined by rainfall or temperature, it sprouts a foot-long panicle of densely clustered, greenish-white blooms that become football-shaped fruit later in the year. But Joshua trees cannot pollinate themselves. Like that of other yuccas, their pollen is too heavy to reach another plant, even in strong desert winds, so they rely on a symbiotic relationship with female Joshua tree yucca moths, which have mouthparts adapted for carrying a ball of pollen. Unlike other insects, which may unwittingly carry pollen from one plant to another, the yucca moth makes a separate trip to carry pollen, which it stuffs deep into a Joshua tree's blossom, and then it drills a hole in the base of the flower, where it lays an egg. When the moth grub hatches, it has fruit to feed upon. Another animal that apparently can't live without Joshua trees or other yuccas is the small, mottled desert night lizard, which hides under fallen Joshua trees, feeding on termites, spiders and ants.

We amble into Kern County, and then just over a mile later, our straight-north course turns east (3090-3.2) as the L.A. aqueduct itself bends east, transforming at the same time from a black-tarred pipe to an underground channel with a broad, flat, concrete roof. (Contrary to a U.S.G.S. topo, the aqueduct actually lies just north of the main dirt access-road that the PCT route follows.) Our way leads east, climbing imperceptibly alongside the aqueduct as it traces a scalloped, contouring route across a succession of broad alluvial fans footing the Tehachapi Mountains. In the first mile, we pass through a nice grove of Joshua trees—a possible, but waterless, place to camp. Unfortunately, barbed-wire fences make it difficult to stray from the aqueduct. The next mile leads us below scattered, windswept homes to the first of many water-access points (3095-2.1) on the Los Angeles Aqueduct, each so vital to our desert journey. Here, the monotonously flat aqueduct surface is broken by a padlocked, 2½' square iron hatch marked "1953+00." Next to it, a 6" diameter cast-iron pipe cover reads "L.A. Water." Lift off this small lid to smell, hear and feel the pristine goodness of Sierran high-country water. Unfortunately, it's about 2–3' away—too far to reach! But ingenious hikers may lower a water bottle tied to a strong string

down the cast-iron pipe, thereby tapping some of the underground river one has been walking along for the last 2 miles. Please be sure to replace the lid. Learn to recognize these "waterholes," for they are your only access to the life-giving underground stream. *Be aware that on occasions the L.A. Department of Water and Power drains the aqueduct for maintenance purposes. Then, you'll have to hightail it east to Highway 14 and head north along it past Rosamond to Mojave.*

Forging ahead, we soon find a long stretch of aqueduct that was resurfaced in 1986. A mile later, a tall, yellow concrete hopper marks a construction site with our second "waterhole," 1825+00 (3105-1.3) along our way. Passing innumerable branching dirt roads bound for everywhere and nowhere, the route now turns across Sacatara Creek's broad, dry wash, then winds monotonously across a gentle alluvial hillside to a point where the aqueduct abruptly vanishes (3105-2.1). Here the hillside likewise abruptly changes to a rugged badland of steep-sided ravines and ridges. The aqueduct is tunneled beneath this tortured landscape, while the PCT's road clambers over it.

We ascend steeply, then drop, only to climb and drop again, repeatedly, on a twisting course. Although difficult and usually hot, this stretch of road is the most picturesque of our entire aqueduct route. Flash floods have carved the firm red and yellow sediments here into a complex of narrow gullies, which has a sparse flora of low juniper trees and rabbitbrush that give color contrast. Unfortunately, dirt-bike riders take pleasure in these canyons too, their loud insect-buzz echoing throughout the region on weekends, when riders challenge themselves on the steep slopes. Our road trends upward, almost reaching 3200', then crosses two more ridges before crossing a creek that may flow through late spring (3127-2.5). This ford is marked by a large patch of tall bamboo. A fair camp could be made here when water is available.

Beyond, we climb once again, pass through a locked gate, and descend southeast in a narrow canyon. After passing through another gate and out of the badlands, we come to a trio of high-tension electric lines marching uphill from the southeast. Ignore the dirt road that runs along their route and instead turn left, northeast, at a Y junction (2893-2.0) with a better-graded, wide dirt road that has traversed around the badlands. Very soon we strike a poorer dirt

<h1 style="text-align:center">E10, E11, E12</h1>

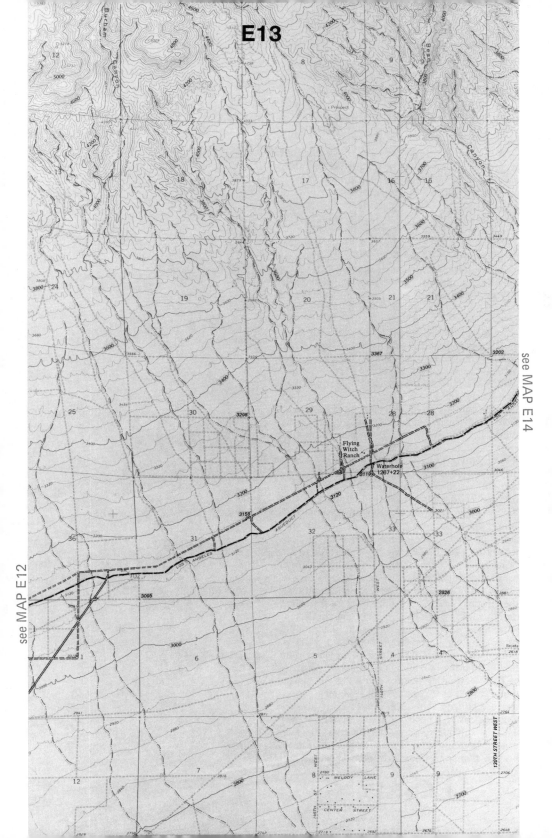

E13

see MAP E14

see MAP E12

Flying Witch Ranch

Waterhole 1267+22

LOS ANGELES AQUEDUCT

130TH STREET WEST

MELODY LANE

CENTER STREET

156

road, our first left turn, at a triangular junction (2915-0.4). It takes us gently but directly up-slope, soon coming along the southwest side of a small, shallow canyon. Quickly we once again rejoin the Los Angeles Aqueduct (3105-0.6), here underground, and turn right, northeast, along its road.

We climb over a low rise, then descend momentarily to resume a nearly level amble, curving north and then northwest into the massive, broad valley of Cottonwood Creek. There are no cottonwoods in evidence along the usually dry creek bed, but there is a nice stand of Joshua trees. A concrete bridge (3120-1.6) carries us across the main wash, and a "waterhole" on either end of the bridge and a nice quiet flat just north of the wash make this spot a pleasant campsite. Hopefully in the early 1990s, a trail will be constructed northwest up this creek's canyon and into the Tehachapi Mountains.

Keeping to the temporary route, we now ignore a plethora of roads, including a good one with a phone line that heads up-canyon, and instead keep to the aqueduct's road, which leads back into the frying-pan shadeless desert. Waterhole 1474+15 (3115-1.0) soon breaks the emptiness, then later the ocean of sand casts up an incongruous 35′ wooden boat hulk, lying north of our route. It heralds a junction with wide, dirt 170th Street West (3120-0.7). In this vicinity note how evenly spaced the green, glossy-leaved creosote shrubs are. They secrete a toxin, washed to the ground by rains, that poisons nearby plant growth, thereby allowing them enough root space to gather the water supply they need. Observant walkers may note some of the creosote bushes growing in clustered rings, the bushes up to a few yards apart. Botanists have discovered that root-crown branching by these bushes results in a ring of plants, each one a genetically identical clone of the original colonizing plant. By radiocarbon dating and growth-rate measurements, scientists have found some creosote-bush clonal rings growing in the Mojave Desert with an estimated age of 11,000 years—far older than the well-known longevous bristlecone pine!

The temporary route continues northeast along two subterranean Los Angeles Aqueducts, and you can take any of their accompanying roads. These climb imperceptibly over washes and alluvium while innumerable jeep roads, bound for nowhere and everywhere, branch from the obvious route. The alluvium

see MAP E13

E12, E13

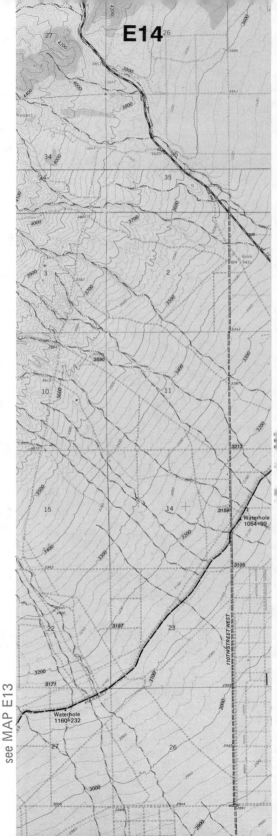

E15

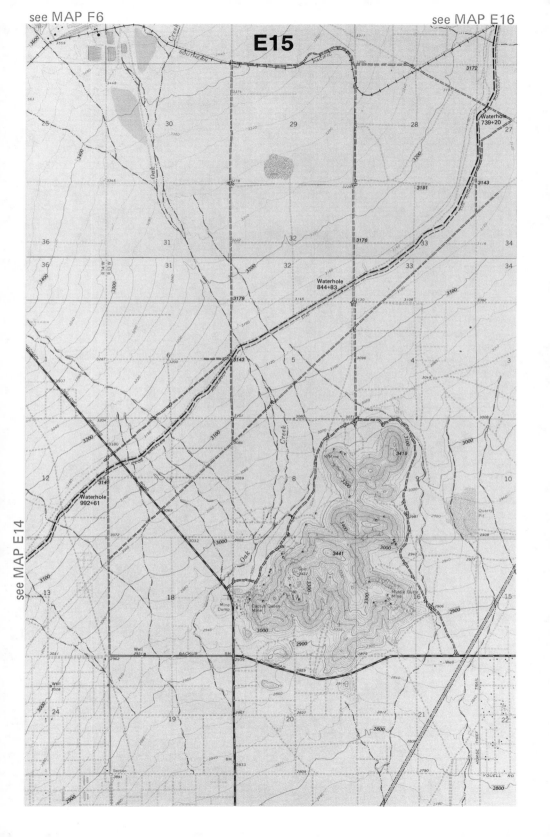

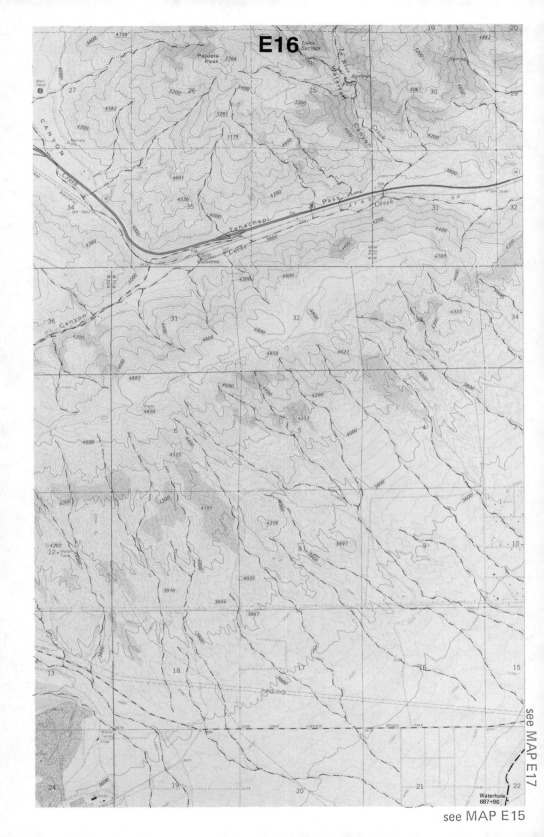

see MAP E17

see MAP E15

Western Antelope Valley, from Sawmill Mountain

Rattlesnakes may be found almost anywhere along Section E

underfoot, spewed south from the Tehachapi Mountains, has formed a bajada—a geomorphic term for several alluvial fans that have coalesced to form a somewhat regular, gently graded surface.

At dirt 140th Street West (3140-3.3), we find waterhole 1267+22 along the older, slightly lower aqueduct just east of the road junction. Beyond, we continue to amble northeast, past waterhole 1160+232 (3130-1.9) to 110th Street West (3135-2.1), marked by a prominent line of wooden powerline poles. Waterhole 1054+99 lies two minutes farther northeast. Next on the otherwise monotonous schedule is waterhole 992+61 (3140-1.4), then a pole line and paved Tehachapi-Willow Springs Road (3142-0.4). The rugged summits of Middle Buttes, rising directly from the alluvium southeast of this point, as well as Soledad Mountain and Elephant Butte to the east, are plugs of rhyolite that in Miocene times intruded older, granitic rocks. When they did, mineralization along superheated contact zones resulted in sometimes fabulously rich deposits of gold, silver and uranium.

Continuing northeast, we strike waterhole 844+83 (3145-2.4), and then our route eventually bends more northward, passing waterhole 739+20 (3150-2.1). We then pass a railroad line (3155-0.8), which goes west to a mammoth cement plant, and just beyond the tracks lies waterhole 687+96. Minutes later, the temporary PCT intersects paved Oak Creek Road (3158-0.9), on which hikers may trudge 4.3 miles east to Mojave.

Past the paved road we meet waterhole 640+01 in 0.2 mile and later encounter a road, with a pole line, just before we reach waterhole 583+19 (3158-1.3). Beyond the waterhole the previously flat-topped aqueduct becomes topped with arched ribs. Four more waterholes lie spaced about one mile apart along the next segment, before we reach a pair of railroad tracks, a dirt road, and a huge Los Angeles County Department of Water and Power maintenance garage beside Highway 58 (3165-4.8). Mojave, with water, post office, restaurants, stores and laundromats, lies about 3½ miles south along the highway.

E13, E14, E15, E16, E17, E18, E19

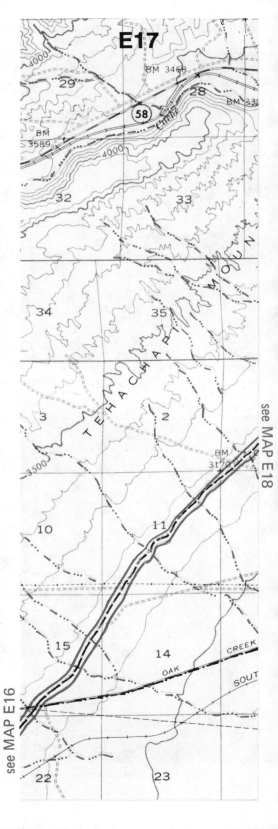

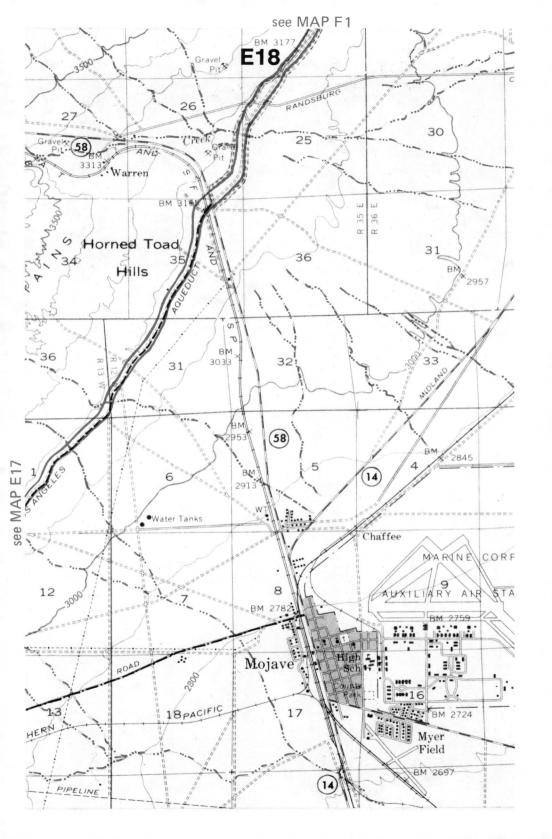

E18

BM 3177

Gravel Pit

RANDSBURG

27

26

25

30

Gravel Pit

(58)

BM 3313

Creek

Gravel Pit

Warren

R 35 E

R 36 E

BM 3166

AND S F

Horned Toad

34

35

36

31

Hills

AND

BM X 2957

S P

36

R 13 W

R 12 W

AQUEDUCT

31

BM X 3033

32

33

3000

MIDLAND

BM X 2953

(58)

BM X 2845

see MAP E17

LOS ANGELES

1

6

BM X 2913

5

(14)

4

WT

Water Tanks

Chaffee

MARINE CORP

9

AUXILIARY AIR STA

12

8

3000

7

BM 2782

BM 2759

T

ROAD

High Sch

16

Mojave

County Park

2800

BM 2724

13

18 PACIFIC

17

HERN

Myer Field

BM 2697

PIPELINE

(14)

see MAP F6

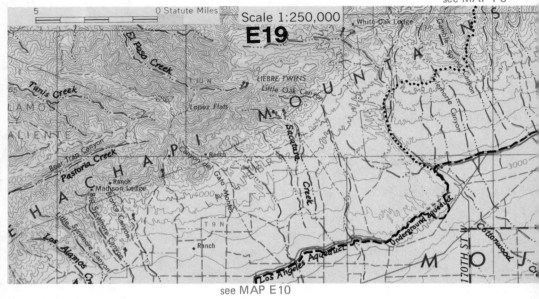

see MAP E10

Section F: Highway 58 to Highway 178

Introduction: Geographers differ on the subject, but many suggest that the mighty Sierra Nevada begins with the low mountains north of the Tehachapi range. Easy walking prevails first along the desert edge of these low mountains, then along the semiarid Sierra crest. Here metamorphic and volcanic rocks that crop up en route wanly echo the vivid colors of locally abundant spring wildflowers. A spring-fed, reed-lined pond in a cottonwood-grove oasis, designated a bird and wildlife sanctuary, makes a pleasing midway reward between the creosote-bush, Joshua-tree desert and the pinyon-pine-clad Sierra crest.

Declination: 13¾°E throughout this section.

Mileages:

	South to North	Distances between Points	North to South
Hwy 58 near Mojave (old aqueduct)	0.0		69.7
		14.8	
Cinco..	14.8		54.9
		2.9	
Cantil...	17.7		52.0
		3.2	
Aqueduct caretakers' houses	20.9		48.8
		1.8	
Mouth of Alphie Canyon	22.7		47.0
		5.7	
Butterbredt Spring (along alternate route)	28.4		41.3
		7.6	
reach PCT	36.0		33.7
		13.1	
Bird Spring Pass	49.1		20.6
		6.0	
road toward Yellow Jacket Spring..................	55.1		14.6
		6.7	
road to McIvers Spring...........................	61.8		7.9
		7.3	
Walker Pass Campground spur trail.................	69.1		0.6
		0.6	
Highway 178 at Walker Pass......................	69.7		0.0

Supplies and Permits: Mojave, 2.8 miles south of the temporary route that begins this section, has all the amenities to serve the recreation-bound traveler. Its post office is 4 miles from the aqueduct on Belshaw Street. Cinco, 15.1 miles northeast along the temporary route, has a restaurant and gas station; the Cantil Post Office, a small store and a gas station are 2.9 miles farther. At the end of this section, Onyx Post Office, groceries and limited supplies are 17.6 miles west of Walker Pass on Highway 178. A KOA Campground is 7.0 miles west of Onyx P.O. on Highway 178. Kernville, 37 miles west of Walker Pass has a post office, supplies, motels, etc., and for your rest and relaxation days, kayak rentals and one-hour to multiday raft trips on the tumultuous Kern River, during adequate water flow. (The beauty of the Kern River was recognized by the U.S. Congress and by President Reagan when in 1987 they added the river's north and south forks to the National Wild and Scenic Rivers System.)

A fire permit is required for this section, but only if you do not already have a wilderness permit. It can be obtained from the Bureau of Land Management or Sequoia National Forest.

Special Problems: Continue to protect your skin and eyes from the intense sun and hot wind; avoid dehydration. Because many of the springs have been impounded for cattle use, and to prevent debilitating intestinal illness caused by *Giardia lamblia,* which is now endemic in the Sierra, boil all except faucet water for 3–10 minutes—the higher the elevation, the longer the boiling time.

Be ever alert lest you disturb the extremely venomous Mojave green rattlesnake, which resides in the desert and along the eastern flanks and valleys of the Sierra. This greenish tinged snake, like all rattlesnakes, is not aggressive and will not attack unless it feels threatened. The hospital in Ridgecrest, northeast of this section off Highway 14, has special antivenin to treat victims of this snake, and if bitten, one should get there posthaste.

Storms are infrequent, but when they do come, cloudbursts and flash floods can occur; avoid camping in washes or in canyons at such times.

Be forewarned that the seemingly unlimited open space hereabouts attracts weekend off-highway vehicles, but very few during the week.

The PCT route north of Highway 58's Cameron overpass, through Bureau of Land Management (BLM) land, to the established trail in Sequoia National Forest is not yet constucted. However, problems causing its delay have been resolved and construction should begin in 1989. Until its completion, hikers are asked to take the following long temporary route.

PCT trekkers will approach the old aqueduct, the temporary route, from three directions. Hikers from the PCT in the Cameron Creek area: cross Highway 58 on the overpass, make your way east 5.1 miles along the busy highway to paved Randsburg Cutoff, then continue 1.2 miles along the cutoff to the bisecting aqueduct. Those who detoured to Mojave: walk north 2.8 miles along Highway 58 from its northern junction with Highway 14. Other hikers coming from the southwest aqueduct road: cross the highway as best you can. Mileage totals for Section F begin at the junction of the old aqueduct and Highway 58.

Northeast of Highway 58 are two unpaved roads parallel to the aqueduct, one on each side (3165'). Commence on either road, for you will be on route as long as you can keep an eye on the aqueduct roof. Water bottles can still be filled from the water test holes along the old pipe (unsanctioned by the water company) but

not when the route branches off to the second aqueduct, so keep them full. The next water source, other than water taken from old pipe test holes, is at the restaurant, when open, in Cinco, 14.8 miles.

The original aqueduct, built between 1908 and 1913, tapped water from Owens River, which is fed by eastern Sierra snowfields. It was later extended to Mono Lake, 340 miles in all, and a second aqueduct was added. This water delivered to Los Angeles is directly responsible for the city's growth explosion: a blessing some say, a curse say others. A foul act, say the citizens of Owens Valley, who claim the water, no matter how "legally" derived, was stolen from them.

During the first several miles our road follows ribs, roughly 30 inches apart and 6 inches high, which protrude from the old aqueduct. The washes it dips across vary in size. After a length of 1.1 miles, it crosses paved Randsburg Cutoff at an unsigned junction. Then along our route numerous unpaved roads head for the hills to the northwest, but not one road forks right until we reach an unsigned scissors junction (3175-5.7), where we veer east onto a service road for the second Los Angeles aqueduct. This length of big pipe was laid and then buried during the early 1970s. En route, the temporary PCT passes capped standpipes protruding from

F1, F2

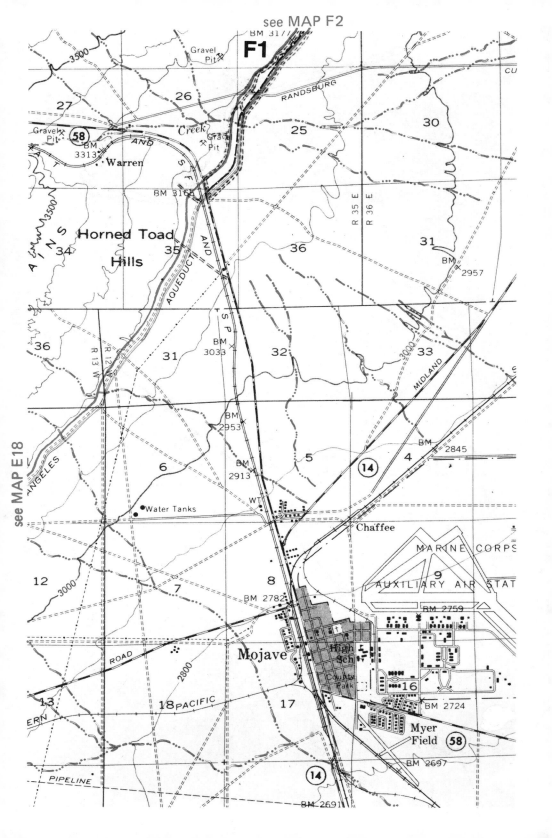

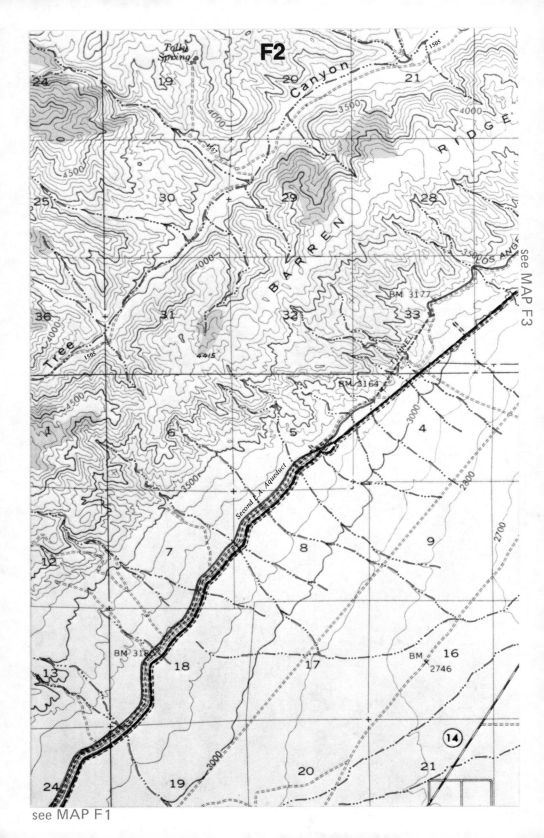

F2

see MAP F3

see MAP F1

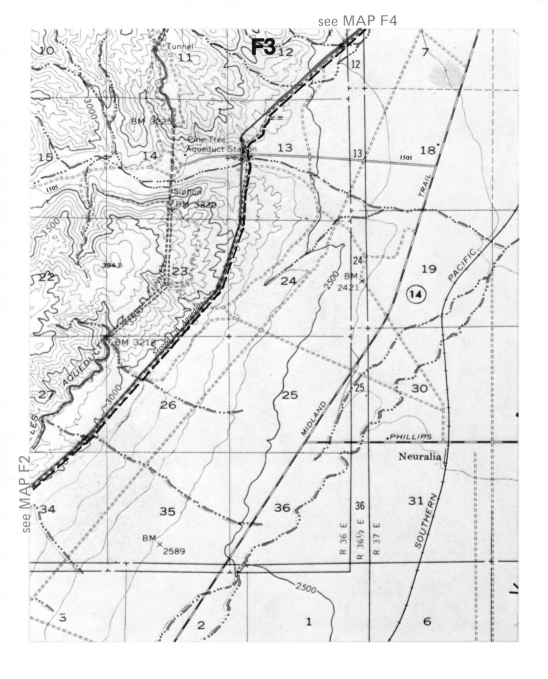

the buried pipeline and cisterns with locked-on manhole covers. It crosses three-way and four-way intersections with other dirt roads, some well-traveled. The best campsites found along this route are generally northwest of it, near the mouths of canyons along the Garlock Fault.

As you stride along its western edge, the vast Mojave Desert may seem boring to you, but this desert, in fact, has varied features. To the east, a large preserve has been set aside by the BLM, maintained by volunteers, for the protection of the lumbering, benign desert tortoise.

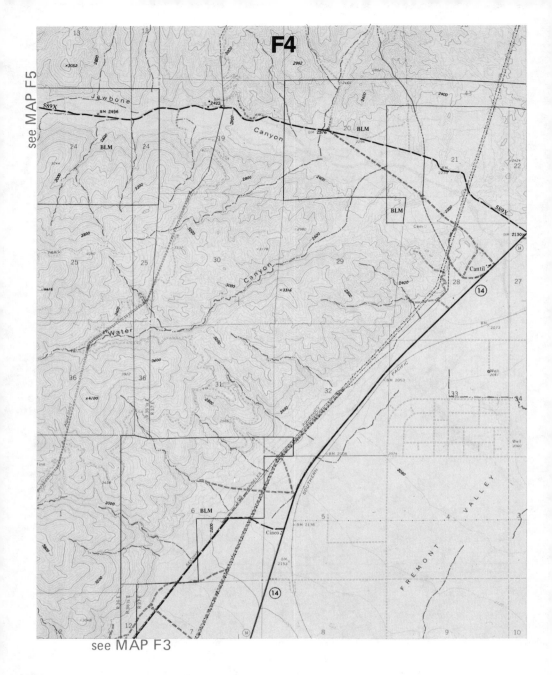

see MAP F5

see MAP F3

Sometimes curled in an old tortoise burrow, another reptile, the extremely venomous, non-aggressive Mojave green rattlesnake is found throughout this spacious land. Scurrying about on their sturdy legs are the comical road-runners, birds who forgot they have wings. Using their wings in silent flight are the bur-rowing owls, whose castings you may find around posts and other perches. Castings are the regurgitations of bone, hair, fur and feathers that are not digested by the bird.

In contrast to these native creatures, this section of desert is where thousands of people have gathered to observe the space shuttles, creatures of man, glide on swept-back wings from supersonic space travel to landings on the dry lakebed at Edwards Air Force Base. The base is the home of the X-1 aircraft that in 1947 broke the sound barrier, and the X-15 that explored the edge of space. In 1986 PCT hikers observed the tiny Voyager, a "flying fuel tank" developed in Mojave, on test flights before it flew around the world from here without refueling—a first.

This desert has beauty too. If you arrive during early spring, it is awash with blooming bushes and wildflowers. The ubiquitous creosote bushes sport their windmill-vanelike flowers of yellow; the cheese bush, with leaves that smell like cheese when crushed, presents its waxy, cupped, creamy blooms. And if you stroll by in a favorable year, you'll see fragile desert primroses clustered along roadsides and sandy flats. The showy, heart-shaped petals of their white flowers wilt to a pink in the heat of day.

Contemplating these things, we travel ahead as our course rolls over a few steep hills where the Sierra Nevada Fault Zone forks off from the Garlock Fault, then passes by the white aqueduct that emerges briefly to run above the wash and alluvium of Lone Tree Canyon. Next, our course passes some distance downslope from a habitation surrounded by the hulks of junked cars. Although the buildings of Tokiwas Restaurant and Gas Station are seen from a considerable distance signaling a trail change, we should not leave the road until these buildings are east-southeast of us. Then we turn east (right) on a lesser dirt road (2190-8.6), which soon passes beneath powerlines at a powerline-service road. An easy traverse leads us past a private home and directly to Tokiwas, all there is to the town of Cinco (2135-0.5).

Upon leaving Cinco we slog northeast, braving the fumes along the shoulder of busy Highway 14, and note ahead the cultivated green fields in Fremont Valley, which contrast startlingly with chalky, magenta-orange sediments to our left, by the mouth of Jawbone Canyon. These sediments were laid down several million years ago, later elevated by movements along the Sierra Nevada and Garlock faults, and then weathered to the form of foothills.

Just beyond the hills, to the left of Highway 14, on the alluvial fan of Jawbone Canyon, stand Cantil Post Office (PCT register) and Jawbone Canyon Store (2125-2.9) with its modest supply of food staples and lots of cold drinks and ice cream. Leaving this possible resupply point beside Highway 14, now a divided four-lane highway, we cross Jawbone Canyon wash and then turn left (2135-0.4) along a new course west on paved Jawbone Canyon Road. Our route follows this hot, undulating road, crossing a boundary into BLM's Jawbone-Butterbredt Area of Critical Environmental Concern.

In 1982, BLM concluded a lengthy study of this area and confirmed what is apparent: off-highway vehicles (OHV) have caused extensive damage to the terrain, including some Native American sites, and cattle overgrazing has greatly damaged the flora. Since then, BLM has restricted OHV use to specific "Open" areas and roads and is reducing cattle grazing. Abuse is still apparent, but the area shows signs of recovery.

A 1976 BLM report stated, "Habitat in the area supports approximately 343 species of animals: 2 species of amphibians, 46 species of reptiles, 89 species of mammals and 206 species of birds." Eager to observe some of the abundant life in this stark area, we travel on.

Our road leads us over the second Los Angeles aqueduct, then across the Sierra Nevada Fault Zone. We then cross the original Los Angeles aqueduct (2420-2.8) just downslope from the tree-shaded aqueduct caretakers' houses, where there are a PCT register and a friendly invitation from the Waring family (upper house) to relax under their trees and make camp for the night. You're also invited to help yourselves to their water. The water obtained here will have to last until Butterbredt Springs, 7.5 miles ahead on the alternate route, or for 20.5 miles to Cottonwood Creek on the temporary route to a truncated segment of PCT trail.

Beyond the houses, the road soon dips through the main wash, then parallels it to the south. The blue-green hue of Blue Point to the west stands in contrast to the browns of the surrounding country, and as a sentinel it alerts PCT hikers to a change in direction where they leave Jawbone Canyon Road and turn into the yawning mouth of Alphie Canyon (2562-1.8). However, there is a choice of routes here. If one is hiking all sections of PCT that are open, then continue west on the temporary route along Jawbone Canyon Road. That route is described later. The recommended alternate route through Butterbredt Canyon to a PCT trail junction is 24.6 miles shorter than the

F2, F3, F4, F5

route to the same junction. That route travels 22.0 miles along hot, treeless Jawbone Canyon Road and then follows a 15.9-mile piece of PCT.

Turning right onto the 13.3-mile long alternate route, we follow a dirt road north, up-canyon, through wide, sandy plains. Blue Point, to our left, is a remnant of basalt flow and volcanic ejecta deposited 8–12 million years ago. Today this remnant drifts on a sea of granite, convoyed by a swarm of little faults. Several OHV roads intertwine along the way, and the canyon's configuration changes somewhat after each heavy rain. It can be confusing. Continuing to hike north, our route passes Hoffman Well Road (2680-1.0), signed SC 251, which ascends northwest out of the canyon. Soon another wash comes in from the northeast, but we seek the narrowing passage ahead. A large solitary rock formation to our right in this brief narrow section stands as another needed sentinel. Once again our canyon spreads to broad plains.

Our route next shifts from the wide wash into Butterbredt Canyon. To find its entrance, continue up the wash on a dirt road until you near a hill ahead with a wide, diagonal stripe, which is a cantaloupe-colored dike of intrusive ryolite. This diked foothill fronts higher hills and stands between narrow, twisting Butterbredt Canyon climbing northwest and wide Alphie Canyon continuing north-northeast. Yet another canyon is to the right of Alphie as you identify this important junction.

The road continues up Alphie Canyon, but you leave it before you reach the diked hill and fork left onto a cyclepath (2940-1.7). Once in the canyon one negotiates cascade sites, which may have a trickle of water, on flash-flood-smoothed granite. After 0.2 mile a large, blocky headwall with a seasonal waterfall is bypassed to the left on a shelf above—a remnant of an old mining road. OHVs, if not turned back by the shelf, can go no farther as a 10-foot waterfall also nearly dry, soon blocks the canyon. It requires an easy Class 3 climb of us, and then we skirt a broken 20-foot fall near its south side on another section of sloughing old roadbed where OHV tracks reappear. Following the cyclepath, our route begins to climb out of the narrow canyon, first heading northwest to the shade of willows and cottonwoods by the loading ramp of an abandoned prospect, then near a row of smoke trees by a roofless, eroded adobe-and-stone hut. Now on the dirt road, we

see MAP F7

see MAP F6

see MAP F4

F5

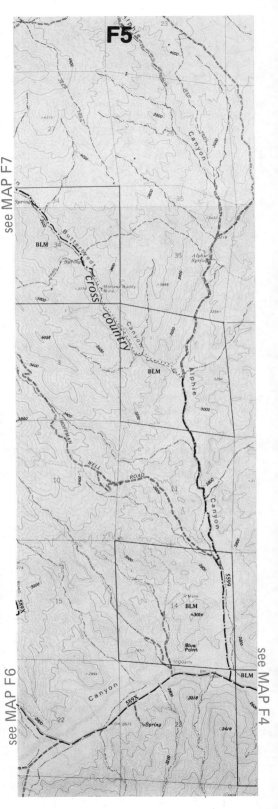

Impounded water at Butterbredt Spring

continue past a discontinuous procession of willows and cottonwoods. Ignoring junctions with a jeep road that branches southwest up a gulch and a second that forks north up a small ridge, we soon approach the cottonwood thicket and impounded water of Butterbredt Spring (3800-3.0). Once a haven for cattle, this fenced area is now a wildlife sanctuary administered by the Audubon Society and Onyx Ranch with the approval of BLM. They ask that you not camp here for you may disturb the wildlife; however, by opening the wide gate, which is cumbersome, or by rolling under the barbed wires, you can get to the pond to get water. The next spring water is 8.7 miles ahead.

The reed-lined pond is a favorite habitat of red-winged black birds. Occasionally, yellow-billed cuckoos nest in riparian areas just north, so they may be seen here, too. This brown-coated, white-bellied, dove-sized bird with large white spots on its tail is listed as rare by the State Department of Fish and Game. Its famous German cousins are captured in caricature in quaint cuckoo clocks.

We exit to the north by squeezing between the locked gate and a rubber flange. Large people will have to find another way. Our route, Butterbredt Canyon Road, continues to ascend northwest up a gentle grade past a southwest road (3805-0.1) to Jawbone Canyon Road. The slopes are dotted with Joshua trees, plus a few beavertail and cholla cacti. In spring, numerous, showy Parry's linanthus flowers hug the granitic sand, and desert senna, bushes which are nothing but greenish twigs most of the year, burst forth with stocks of yellow sunflowers. Former canyon cyclepaths are signed prohibiting OHVs, but some still show their tracks. Numerous jackrabbits and a variety of their rodent friends keep us company as they dart across our route. They need to hurry as this is golden-eagle country as well as home for other predatory birds and animals.

The trek now takes us near the ruins of an old mine and stone hut and then past a jeep road (3892-0.3) forking northeast, bound for Alphie Canyon. Butterbredt Peak, at 5997', is the culmination of a ridge separating the watershed of Butterbredt Canyon from that of Kelso

F5, F7

Scale 1:250,000

0 Statute Miles

Valley to the west, and it warrants attention while we slowly put it behind us.

The windmill has been removed at Butter-bredt Well (4400-2.3) and our road diverted around a barbed-wire enclosure designed to regulate cattle in the treeless pond area now designated WATER FOR WILDLIFE. The well water is now obtained by a submersible generator. If the water is palatable and you're in need, the critters may share it with you, but do not tarry or camp within 100 yards. Next water is 5.9 miles at a roadside spring, 1.0 mile off route, down-canyon.

Alert to an impending crossing of the Sierra crest, we trudge along, passing another small fenced area straddling a closed road to Gold Peak, and, in time, we reach the pass (5220-2.7). To our left, the buckled granite of Peak 6274 has proved more resistant to erosion than its neighboring rocks. Gradually our road descends, veers west, becomes ensconced in the wash of a little canyon and passes an "open" road to Gold Peak. Then, at last, there is the 40-yard offset junction of the PCT trail (4540-2.2) and the end of this alternate route.

*   *   *   *

Construction of approximately 40 miles of PCT from Highway 58 to the Piute Mountains will soon begin. When it is complete, it will meet the south end of a segment of trail whose northern reaches connect with the rest of the PCT. The following temporary route, which consists of that segment and the access to it, is not recommended for Mexico-to-Canada travelers at this time, but others may wish to experience it.

From the junction of Jawbone Canyon Road and Alphie Canyon wash at Blue Point, 4.6 miles west of Highway 14, the temporary route makes a wide loop west and returns to cross Butterbredt Canyon Road (the alternate route previously described) to the north. This segment is 37.9 miles for the trekker, of which 22.0 miles are hiked on dry, shadeless Jawbone Canyon Road to get to the trail. The alternate route through Butterbredt Canyon totals 13.3 miles to the same point, considerably less distance.

We leave those hikers taking the alternate route at Blue Point. Going west on Jawbone Canyon Road, the temporary route, we walk along a wide washboard dirt surface. The road dips, twists and climbs while passing several lesser closed roads and cyclepaths as it gains elevation to pass a spur road (4000-7.2) that leads north through a gap to Butterbredt Canyon. Beyond here our route reaches a saddle (4850-3.3) where climbs to Butterbredt Peak begin, and then descends on Pleistocene sediments to meet Kelso Valley Road (3949-3.4), which bisects Kelso Valley. In an emergency one may be able to obtain water here at Skyline Ranch.

Soon our road curves sharply south, passes a cattle guard in ½ mile and another one a mile later. Next it ascends gently west into thickening forest and then dips to cross Cottonwood Creek (4705-4.8), which usually flows till late summer. This will be a welcome sight, but purify the water.

Next the Geringer Grade section of the road acquaints you with digger, pinyon and Jeffrey pines, mountain juniper, blue oak and white fir as you toil up short, steep, deeply rutted hairpin curves into the Piute Mountains, topping out at the southern boundary of Sequoia National Forest (6250-2.2). Still on Jawbone Canyon Road, our route passes a waterless campsite in ½ mile; this is probably the flattest area near the trailhead. One now has an easy hike northwest to a saddle, which is the start of the completed PCT (6650-1.1).

Finally leaving the extended temporary route, we descend north on the PCT among scattered Jeffrey pines and black and live oaks decked with mistletoe. On it we hike down a few switchbacks and wind along east-facing slopes. Tiny namas, phacelias, gilias and dainty spreading phlox perk up the early-season wayside scenery. Soon a glance south over our shoulders (on a clear day) reveals vignettes of the Piute Mountains' peaks against silhouettes of the distant San Gabriel and San Bernardino mountains. In ½ mile the trail passes above a spring whose protecting willows hide it from our view. The path gently undulates now as it dips through several snowmelt streamlets, then sees gravel added to the dirt tread as boulders surrounded by manzanitas make an appearance.

In a short time trekkers cross a willow-lined branch of Cottonwood Creek that should be a good source of water until late summer. This water comes from Mace and Grouse meadows, above, and since the Piute Mountains are a multi-use area, this may be water that cattle have enjoyed as well. Campsites can be found in this area. Quickly the hiker briefly parallels another willow-hemmed branch of that creek,

F7, F5, F6, F7, F8, F6

see MAP F9

F8

see MAP F7

see MAP F6

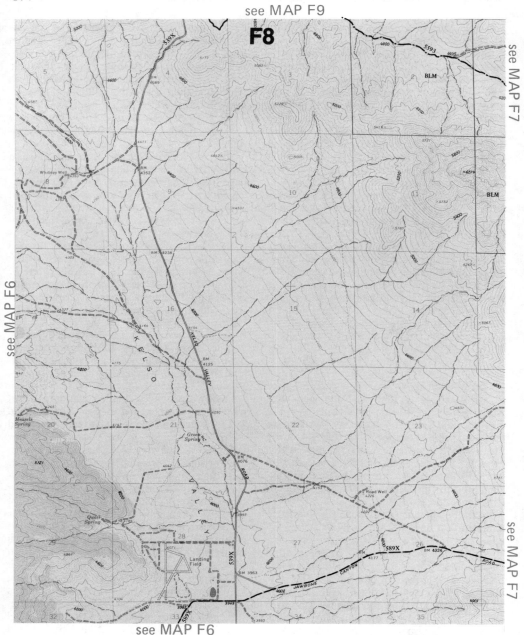

see MAP F7

see MAP F6

crosses it on a log footbridge (6480-1.8) and proceeds above it.

The well-defined path continues to wind and dip, generally heading north. To the west below us is a strip of Jawbone Canyon Road, and soon we ascend to cross one of its branches, a logging road (6720-1.0). Within ½ mile, there is a spring above the trail, whose water is caught by a crude structure. Below us is an old, roofless log cabin with smaller ancillary huts. This area, with its mine shaft, is worth investigating.

F6

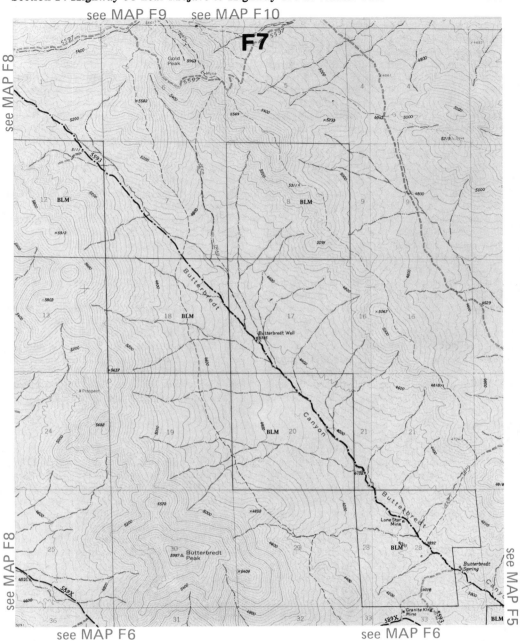

see MAP F9   see MAP F10

Back on the trail, we saunter above the head-waters of Landers Creek, which descends through a pocket meadow that has potential campsites, and then we pass another miner's shack with a dilapidated trailer nearby. There were many active mines in these mountains, but now tree harvesting and cattle grazing predominate.

You next make a stroll alongside Landers Creek, cross it (6300-1.9), then immediately cross back to the east side again. Shortly after crossing back you'll see a dirt road along the

F6

creek's west bank. This road quickly leads to creekside Waterhole Trail Camp, and you can easily make your way there. There you'll find a table and piped-in spring water, although a sign indicates it should be treated. This is one of three "fire-safe areas" in the Piutes where campfires are allowed during dry summers. The road continues on to another old structure, the Waterhole mine shack, a relic of a golden yesteryear.

On the trail you remain in your little canyon until it opens near Landers Meadow, to the east. First you step across the meadow's outlet stream and then cross Piute Mountain Road (6220-0.9), aided by footbridges over the trenches flanking the road. Once again the PCT skirts along the east side of Landers Creek, then leaves it to begin an arc to the east, first above and then on a short piece of road, then back on trail to cross an older dirt road.

In a short while we reach a wide road (6300-1.1). A 0.3-mile walk north down the road leads to another "fire-safe area" among Jeffrey pines. This was once a campground where a summer ranger resided, and it still is a nice place to camp. All that remains of the amenities now are a concrete fireplace and the protruding pipes once used for trailer hookups. The spring above the road is captured in a tank and piped to a cattle trough, the last water for 10.5 miles. A curious stone hut sits near the spring.

Returning to the trail, we note that wallflowers brighten our way and lupines add a dash of contrasting color as we approach the drier climes of pinyon pines and golden oaks. Dramatic, lichen-splashed granitic boulders begin to add extra interest to our walk, and a few yuccas appear, their blossoms exploding in spring. Once again we cross Piute Mountain Road (6620-2.3), this time above Harris Grade, Piute Mountains' best access road, and locate the trail where it descends beyond the crossing. In 0.1 mile, as we begin our trek along the north and then east slopes of St. John Ridge, we see far off to the north majestic Olancha Peak, reigning over the Kern Plateau. To the northeast, pointed Owens Peak and dome-shaped Mount Jenkins divide the desert from the mountains, and all three delineate the Sierra crest. This panoramic view presents itself several times while we hike along, gradually losing elevation, sometimes by switchbacking and being careful not to veer off onto the OHV trails. (If you find yourself to the right of a

chimney-like outcrop, you are on the wrong trail. The PCT is down slope from the outcrop, but you can continue along the cyclepath, since it meets the PCT at the paved road below.

In time we spot a post just below the path near a large fremontia bush, which makes the boundary of a mining claim. Soon in the east the serpentine sliver of paved Kelso Valley Road appears, ascending from Weldon Valley, and our trail descends through a colony of blackbush to meet it at a pass (4950-4.8).

After crossing the road where it loses its pavement, our path initially winds generally east on a crenulated course across gullied north-facing slopes. Pepper-colored debris excavated from several claims collectively known as the St. John Mine is visible downslope in a gully crossed 170 yards from the road. Beginning in 1867 miners extracted gold here for over 70 years. Most of them lived in the now vanished settlement of Sageland, just a few miles north of the road.

Shortly we descend north-northeast amid the sagebrush, blackbush, buckwheat and Mormon tea that mantle a prominent ridge. Then the path loops across a ravine, rounds another north-facing ridge, passes beavertail and cholla cacti and wolfberry shrubs, and eventually meets Butterbredt Canyon Road, where we join the shorter alternate route at the mouth of a ravine (4540-2.1-13.3).

*   *   *   *

All hikers are now on completed PCT, but before continuing beyond the Butterbredt Canyon Road/PCT junction, check your water. The next year-round water is at McIvers Spring, 26.1 miles from this junction, or seasonal Yellow Jacket Spring, 20.5 miles ahead. There is also water at Willow Spring, 5.9 miles ahead, down-canyon, of which 1.8 miles is off-trail.

To refill your supply, descend 0.7 mile along Butterbredt Canyon Road, turn right, and descend 0.3 mile on paved Kelso Valley Road to where a grove of large willows and cottonwoods flourishes left of the road. A spring in this private property issues from under the road near the first tree. Its water is sometimes dammed, forming a pool, sometimes channeled into cow troughs and sometimes free flowing. Try to fill your water bottles at its source.

Our route ahead is often hot, windy and shadeless; therefore, drink up and carry as much water as you can manage, and ration it to

F6, F9

last until the next sure source. Satiated and supplied now, we retrace the mile back to the 40-yard offset junction (4540') with the established PCT.

East of Butterbredt Canyon Road the PCT climbs to a switchback, then eases to a gentle-to-moderate grade, remaining just south of a gulch draining a valley southeast of Mayan Peak. The slopes of this gulch—and of its neighbors—presently flatten as we trace the valley's elongated curve to the east. Hiking along the trail we notice that while the temple of 6108' Mayan Peak rules out northwestward views of the Piute Mountains, it cannot block out the face that 7704' Sorrell Peak turns on Kelso Valley. Nor can it hide the ribbon of Kelso Valley Road draped on a shoulder of the Sierra crest.

A few six-petaled, many-stamened cream cups and other blooms of spring are scattered amid the scraggly bushes that mat trailside slopes, punctuated by scattered junipers and Joshua trees. The path winds around the heads of two canyons, undulating gently and then contouring past many lesser ravines cut in the north slope of 6182' Pinyon Mountain. The moderately dense stand of pinyon pines that cloaks the north slopes is the only forest for miles around.

As we proceed east across north-facing slopes, the ranks of the forest dwindle and we regretfully leave the pinyons behind. Some sagebrush, bitterbrush, rabbitbrush and buck-wheat fill in the wayside now. Glistening like a distant mirage below us are the impounded waters of Willow Spring. Still on the slopes of Pinyon Mountain, parallel to a crude access road, our path reaches a multi-road and cycle-path junction on a Sierra-crest saddle (5283-4.1).

Should you need more water, take the road leading 1.8 miles northwest down canyon to Willow Spring, where there are no willows but plenty of cows. Southwest from the saddle a cyclepath gains 900' in 0.6 mile, reaching the shady, view-commanding summit of Pinyon Mountain. The most-used road from the saddle finds Dove Spring 3.3 miles to the east, while another dirt road follows the crest north. Many cyclepaths and jeep roads cut errosively across the PCT, and sometimes it is hard to distin-guish our path from their tracks.

With the next source of year-round water at McIvers Spring 22 miles ahead or the seasonal water of Yellowjacket Spring 16.4 miles, we leave the saddle to wind north around gullied, east-facing slopes, climbing a little at first and then contouring. Along the way the El Paso

F9, F10

Lower Rock Creek, Mitre Basin rim

F9

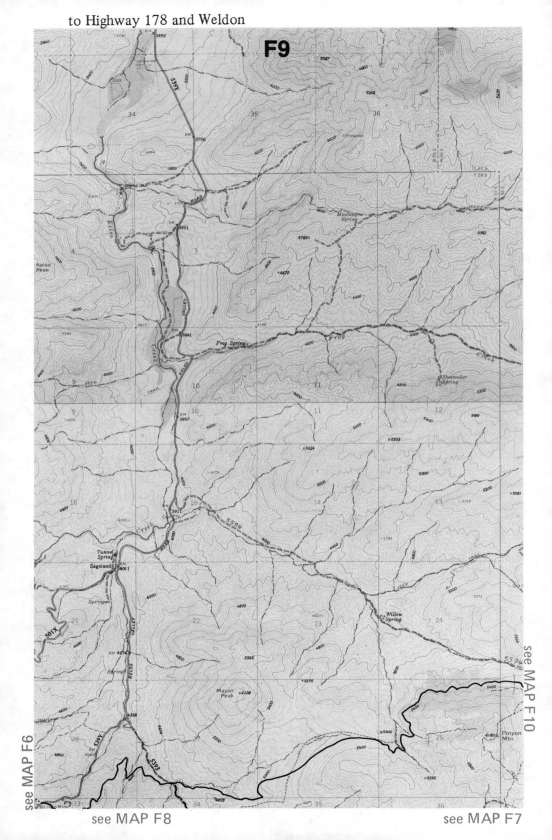

see MAP F6

see MAP F10

see MAP F8

see MAP F7

F10

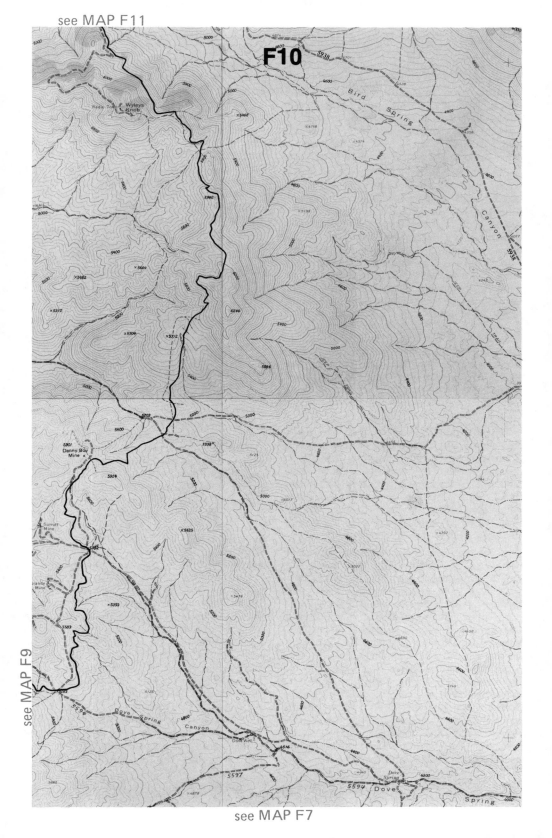

see MAP F9

Mountains, Fremont Valley and Indian Wells Valley intercept our gaze in a sweep of the eastern horizon. In the first big gully we cross, we encounter blocks which, rounded by weathering, stand precariously stacked. Presently we arrive at a saddle junction (5382-1.6) with six jeep roads. One leads west past the Sunset Mine Road to connect with the Willow Spring Road just below the spring.

Our path diagonals northwest across the junction saddle, then winds gently upward, staying west of the crest. Glancing back, we see rubble from the Ora Grande Mine scarring a west-projecting ridge, while closer at hand in downslope corners old timbers, rust-spattered auto husks and a shack stand in disarray around Sunset Mine. Slightly removed are more structures and signs of activity. One north-to-south hiker reported getting emergency water here. From it a deep ravine with a floor occupied by a linear grove of Joshua trees rises northeast to meet us. Once again we take to the slopes, climbing beside and then crossing a road before eventually topping out on a ridge (5700-1.1). To the left, churned ground and parallel concrete slabs slash across the slope, the result of renewed activity in Danny Boy Gold Mine.

Wyleys Knob, the 6465' microwave-tower-crowned summit to the north, stands as a gauge of our progress, one we will refer to often on the trail ahead. Now our wide path makes a moderate-to-steep descent via two switchbacks to meet three jeep roads on a crestline saddle at a junction (5300-0.8) where roads diverge for Frog Spring (northwest), Dove Spring (southeast) and endless sloping plains (east).

Ahead our austere journey takes us generally north over a low hill to another crestline saddle, crosses Frog Canyon Road and tops a low east-west ridge with good campsites among the boulders. Next it dips to a brushy gap, climbs north at a moderate grade, paralleling a gully, and then curves around a ridge. Trailside buckwheat and Mormon tea tend to hide lucia, horsebrush and a blue-petaled variety of gilia. Soon our gradient eases and we first wind around spur ridges emanating from the Sierra crest then cross a gap in the crest itself. The Scodie Mountains and, of course, the granitic outcrop of Wyleys Knob loom to the north. We ramble along, now traversing parallel to the crest just east above us. The route soon runs past three rounded crestline boulders that form a balanced stack. A switchback, erosively cut by cyclists, leads us down to skirt a hill on the crest and reach a junction (5740-3.0) with cyclepaths leading northwest and southeast along the ridge and down canyons to the northeast and the southwest.

Now our trek takes us north diagonally across the junction, curves west, and rounds a bevelled spur ridge. The path soon dips from a granite bluff, then around a ridge that drops off to the northeast. A gentle-to-moderate downgrade ensues, at first among pinyon pines but later across the sunnier, northeast-facing slopes of Wyleys Knob. Presently we find ourselves strolling just downslope from the chuckholed Wyleys Knob Road, and then we clamber down to a junction (5355-2.5) at Bird Spring Pass.

A possible but windy campsite, Bird Spring Pass was first crossed by Caucasians when in March 1854, John Charles Fremont, on his fifth expedition, finding Walker Pass blocked by snow, led his party through this passage. It is now used by OHVs and for access to the PCT and to Wyleys Knob tower from Kelso Valley Road (west) and Highway 14 (east).

Ahead we have a moderate, sometimes steep (by PCT standards) climb to Skinner Peak. Ascending northeast into a side canyon along a sandy trail ornamented with nosegays of blue penstemons, we pass a trail-register box and a spur road. Ahead, we climb south from the canyon's wash. The curious fenced-in square seen below is a "quail guzzler," constructed there by the Forest Service to catch rain water for the local fauna. (At this point we could use a "PCT guzzler!") An occasional Joshua tree and then some straggly pinyon pines dot the slopes that abruptly slant away to the vast alluvium of Bird Spring Canyon spreading below.

Glancing southwest across the pass, you see the radio tower, its road and the path you just left all slowly recede as you first climb up long-legged switchbacks and then cross over a ridge with a western orientation (6460-2.5). If needed, you can find small flats to sleep on here. A long ascending traverse and several short, steep switchbacks take you over a ridge above the Horse Canyon watershed, which has more spots for possible waterless camping. To the north, the High Sierra rises above the waves of east-west Scodie Mountain ridges, while around you manzanita and canyon live oak (golden oak) join the scattered pinyon pines and numerous spring wildflowers.

F10, F11

Foxtail pines and craggy outcrops line the PCT

Yellow-gold, in many forms, accents our hike along these semi-arid mountain slopes. Much of this land is composed of metamorphic rock whose quartz veins attracted gold miners of yore, as attested to by the numerous prospects. Golds more visible to us are in the canyon live oaks, whose fine, yellow-powder leaf undercoating and numerous catkins give the tree a golden hue, and the showy fremontia (flannelbush) when clothed in spring frocks of large, waxlike yellow flowers. And at out feet is more gold in bold clusters of wallflowers, large, wavy-leafed balsamroot flowers, and several varieties of butter-colored dandelions.

For an easy climb up Skinner Peak leave the trail between its summit and the first descending switchbacks and climb south-southwest to the summit boulders (treeless), where there are good views and a register can.

Soon beyond the trail summit (6980-1.1), near Skinner Peak summit (7120′), we descend northwest, staying close to the ridgecrest above the headwaters of Cane Canyon. Along this stretch we have views of Heald and Nicolls peaks on the northern extension of the Piute mountains bordering Kelso Valley. Two quick switchbacks ensue, and then we turn east across north-facing slopes, getting glimpses of the eastern reaches of Lake Isabella. Lower down we see a mining scar on slopes opposite us, and see Continental Telephone's microwave relay station serving Ridgecrest, Kernville and the Lake Isabella area perched on a peak to the northeast. Our descent east ends at a saddle from which we traverse ⅓ mile across the steep, grassy slopes of minor Peak 6455, above wide, sprawling Horse Canyon. In a few minutes we cut across a road (6260-2.4), that reaches the mine we just saw, and seconds later cross another road, both branching from Horse Canyon Road, which serves the tower and continues north in rutted fashion to McIvers Spring. We will be walking on a section of that road later.

There are camping possibilities here and seasonal water 0.7 mile down the second road to a stream from Yellow Jacket Spring, which crosses the jeep road. To reach the spring itself, hike up the drainage 0.6 mile, fork up the hill another 0.1 mile to a trough with piped-in water, missigned WILLOW SPRING. The next water is at McIvers Spring, 7.0 miles farther.

F11

see MAP F12

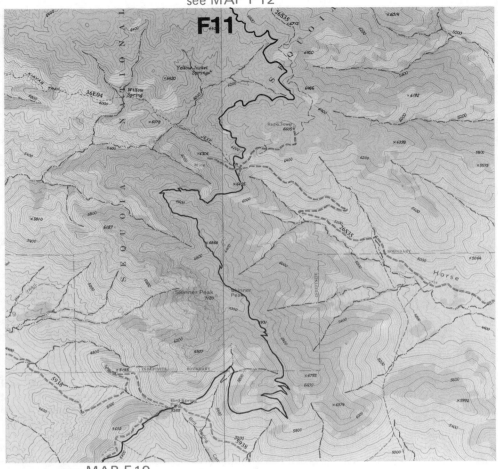

F11

see MAP F10

Slopes are less steep now as the path curves among sagebrush and pinyon pines below the tower. As you lope around ensuing scalloped slopes, gradually gaining altitude, you might amuse yourself by looking for a football-sized rock dissimilar to other rocks scattered about. In April 1983 a meteor streaked across the sky above Los Angeles. It was estimated that, if it did not burn up completely, it could have landed somewhere very near or on the Scodie Mountains. With this tidbit occupying your thoughts, you quickly reach and join the road (6670-4.5) that served the relay tower and now threads along the crest.

Here an "Ichabod Crane" forest surrounds you as you walk northeast along the road. The naturally denuded lower branches of pinyon pines, gnarled and twisted, reach in contorted figurations to set one's imagination soaring;

and all about you are broken branches, up-rooted trees and a tangled forest in great disarray. This disheveled scene was caused by the heavy, wet snows of the unusually severe winter of 1982–83, which greatly burdened the pinyons, unused to more than a dusting, and by strong winds that toppled these trees then rooted in soft, soggy soil.

Abruptly, the forest flanking our route gives way to a sagebrush-buckbrush meadow. A jeep road with forked access peels off to the northwest, then one leads northeast, and after we re-enter the woods, a roadlike wash forks to the right and then a bit later another road takes off to the left. We begin to cross rills that have early-season water and later-season puddles of lavender-flowered, inch-high "belly" plants, and 0.3 mile before the road to McIvers Spring we cross a brooklet, also with seasonal water.

F11, F12

Once again the route resumes as trail (6680-2.2), now heading northeast, but you stay on the road for 0.3 mile to reach McIvers Spring. Next water is 7.4 miles ahead at Walker Pass Camp. Snuggled among picturesque slabs at the springs is a small batten-board hut with porch and outhouse once owned by McIvers and Weldon. They equipped it with the bare necessities of a 1938 rustic retreat and thus, although run down, it remains today. Hunters, cyclists and 4WDers have used it over the years, as the litter and graffiti attest. It is probable, barring a drought, that some water issues from these springs year-round, and good campsites abound here in this bright green oasis among the gray-green pinyons.

Back at the junction, now a trail, we hike northeast on an ascending, undulating path past a jeep-road crossing. Manzanita reappears, as do a few stands of Jeffrey pines and black oaks. The declivitous slopes of Boulder Canyon fall away to the southeast from a shallow saddle, and vistas of the Mojave Desert and the distant San Gabriel-San Bernardino mountains appear through the haze. Soon our path rounds some 3-story boulders, dashed with rust and chartreuse lichen, sporting a determined pinyon pine tenaciously growing from a slight crack. Then, leaving our gentle tableland, we begin a descent out of the Scodie Mountains on north-facing slopes, with views of the Mount Whitney group in the distant north and, in the northeast, the top of Olancha Peak, whose summit one later approaches on the PCT. Our trail curves around a steep canyon, briefly reaches over the ridgetop at a switchback where one is offered a fleeting glimpse of Owens Peak, with Mount Jenkins at its south shoulder. Then it continues a long descent on west-facing slopes high above Jacks Creek canyon. In time we pass an entrance to an overgrown use trail angling down the slope, cross a slight ridgeline saddle and descend on northeast-facing slopes of the same mountain that we have semicircumambulated.

Striding ahead buoyantly, we switchback down the mountainside. After the second switchback, our trail takes us just below a ridgetop where, obscured from our view, the Forest Service has placed another guzzler for small animals. Soon, while skirting around the lower slopes of Peak 6018, the hairpin curve of Highway 178 attracts our attention, with Walker Pass Campground and signed WALKER PASS TRAILHEAD at the south end of that curve. Far to the north Canebrake Road cuts across slopes of the Kern Plateau, and to the northeast the PCT rises above Walker Pass.

The twiggy, jointed Mormon tea shrub has made frequent appearances on our hike through the Scodies, and here the narrowleaf goldenbush, with irregular-petaled yellow flowers, flourishes alongside our path. An occasional tissue-paper-thin, large, white-flowered prickly poppy (startlingly resembling a fried egg, sunny side up) is here, too. Quite soon we cross fledgling Canebrake Creek, where it may be wise to get water in case the camp's faucets are not turned on. Shortly, we leave the trail (5100-7.3) on a path leading down 0.1 mile to the comfortable campground built especially for PCT trekkers. If the faucets are not in use, spring water flows from a pipe into a 9′ square cement-enclosed cattail garden, 0.1 mile down Highway 178. The trail continues northeast from the campground access path to Walker Pass (5246-0.6).

F12, F13

see MAP F13

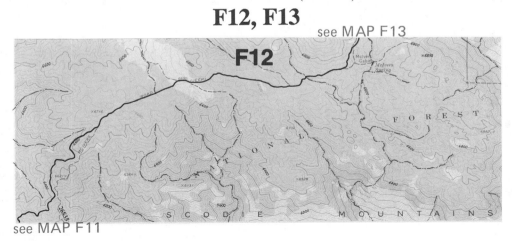

see MAP F11

F13

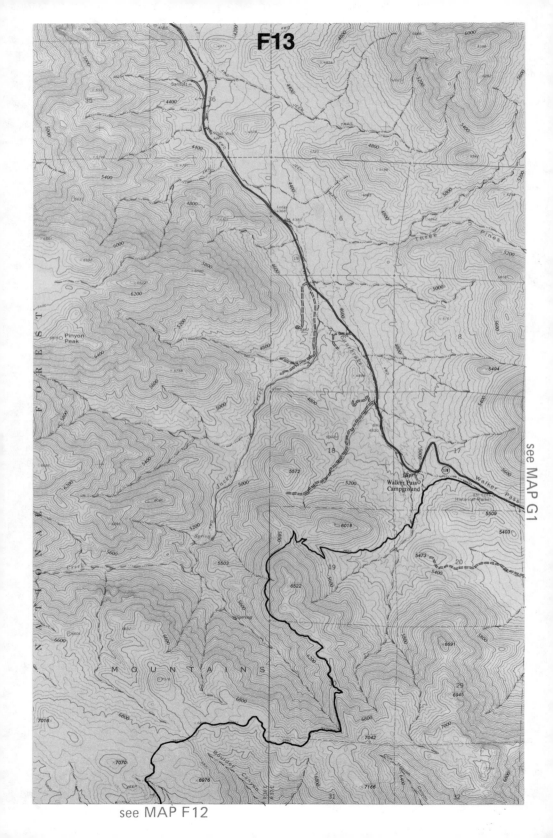

see MAP G1

see MAP F12

Section G: Highway 178 to Mount Whitney

Introduction: A sinuous river, included in the National Wild and Scenic Rivers System; a vast meadow, the largest in the Sierra; a hardy, high-elevation tree, new to the PCT—these features among others elicit admiration for the Southern Sierra. Through this section's many meadows and unglaciated mountains, the trekker journeys north to the High Sierra, the climax of the Sierra Nevada with its Mount Whitney, the highest peak in the contiguous United States.

In this section the PCT is almost completely within federally designated wilderness. Beginning north of Walker Pass, the proposed Owens Peak Wilderness will almost certainly be approved. The route continues in wilderness country through the newly extended Dome Land and the newly created South Sierra, then enters the huge Golden Trout, in which it stays until it enters Sequoia National Park. All these wildernesses assure the hiker an undisturbed adventure in nearly pristine country—nearly, because cattle are still allowed to graze there.

As always, the PCT seeks the high crest, and therefore it remains on the semiarid eastern edge of the Sierra Nevada. In doing so it offers a panoply of expansive, panoramic views.

Declination: 14¼°E throughout this section.

Mileages:

	South to North	Distances between points	North to South
Walker Pass at Highway 178	0.0		113.5
		8.5	
Mount Jenkins/Owens Peak saddle	8.5		105.0
		7.6	
Spanish Needle Creek	16.1		97.4
Canebrake Road near Chimney Creek		12.4	
Campground	28.5		85.0
		7.9	
Long Valley Loop Road	36.4		77.1
Sherman Pass/Kennedy Meadows Road		13.0	
near general store	49.4		64.1
		2.2	
Kennedy Meadows Campground	51.6		61.9
South Fork Kern River bridge		11.7	
in Monache Meadows	63.3		50.2
		3.8	
Monache Meadows/Olancha Pass trail	67.1		46.4
		4.0	
saddle west of Olancha Peak	71.1		42.4
		6.1	
Death Canyon creek	77.2		36.3
		13.2	
Mulkey Stock Driveway at Mulkey Pass	90.4		23.1
		0.8	
Trail Pass Trail at Trail Pass	91.2		22.3
		4.8	
Cottonwood Pass Trail at Cottonwood Pass	96.0		17.5
		0.6	
Chicken Spring Lake's outlet stream	96.6		16.9
		10.1	
Rock Creek crossing	106.7		6.8
		6.0	
Mount Whitney lateral/Crabtree Meadows	112.7		0.8
		0.8	
John Muir Trail junction	113.5		0.0

Supplies and Permits: The closest P.O. and groceries to Walker Pass are in Onyx, 17.6 miles west off Highway 178. At Kennedy Meadows General Store, 50.1 miles north of Walker Pass, there are groceries, gas and usually a Saturday night movie. The owner will drive down the mountain to pick up your packages at Inyokern P.O. for a small fee. (Confirm this service, enclose SASE. Refer to "Post Offices" section for address.)

For major resupplying at the north end of the Kern Plateau, descend 2.2 miles north from Trail Pass to the parking lot at the end of Horseshoe Meadow Road, and hitchhike 23 miles down it and the Whitney Portal Road to Lone Pine.

Short-trip hikers will need a permit for Golden Trout Wilderness and Sequoia National Park. Only a fire permit, good for one year, is needed for Dome Land and South Sierra wildernesses and for non-wilderness areas.

Bears: Before the 1960s, a backpacker in the Sierra Nevada rarely had to worry about a black bear stealing his food. But somewhere along the line, black bears learned that people carry delicious food in their packs. As backpackers increased in numbers, their food became an ever more desirable resource for hungry bears. By the start of the 1970s, the backcountry of Yosemite National Park had a serious problem with marauding bears. Backpackers were urged to hang their food on a tree limb, then later to hang it on steel cables that rangers installed between trees. Bears, being very intelligent animals, learned how to get most food, regardless what measures were taken, and mothers passed this knowledge on to cubs, some of whom, once on their own, migrated to other parts of the Sierra with their new-found acquisition skills. By the late 1980s these knowledgeable bears had spread as far south as the Kern Plateau and as far north as Desolation Wilderness.

Man's latest counter to the bear threat is a supposedly bear-proof metal box, and you may see one or more of these along your trek through Sequoia and Kings Canyon National Parks (north part of Section G, south half of Section H). These have been placed at campsites that have been popular with bears.

However, there may be many sites on your trek through the Sierra Nevada where there are no boxes, and then you'll have to bearbag your food. This involves suspending your food either from a tree limb or from a steel cable between two trees. The procedure is the same for both. First, put your food in two sacks. Then tie a short, lightweight rope ("parachute cord") to a rock and throw the rock over a high branch. Ideally, the branch should be at least 16 feet up, and the rope should be at least 8 feet out from the trunk. Now tie your heavier food sack to the rope and haul it all the way up to the branch. Next, tie on the lighter food sack as high up as you can, and stuff any excess rope into it. Now push the lighter sack upward with a stick until both sacks are at the same level. To retrieve the food, simply push up on either sack, and the other will descend.

In Yosemite National Park, the rangers recommend that your food be *at least 15 feet above the ground.* So you'll need a stick at least 10 feet long. Good luck finding one, especially up at the high elevations the PCT traverses, where most trees are stunted. The rangers also recommend that the spot on the branch from which the cord hangs should be at least 10 feet from the main trunk. Furthermore, they recommend that the food be *at least 5 feet below the branch or cable.* In other words, you have to select a branch at least 20 feet above the ground—but no subalpine tree is like that. In reality, you'll likely have to settle for your food being much closer to the ground, and perhaps within reach of bears.

There are three easier methods Schaffer has tried with success. One is to stuff your sack far enough into a crack in a rock that bears can't get it. Push the sack in a bit with a stick, but be sure you can retrieve it. Another method is to climb 15 or so feet off the ground on a nearly vertical cliff and put the sack on a ledge. Using either of these methods, you'll have to rodent-proof your sacks. Try spraying them with insecticide or some other foul-smelling chemical to deter the rodents.

The last method—to sleep atop your food or very close to it—may be very risky. This has worked for Schaffer and for a high-ranking Park Service backcountry employee— whom we can't mention, since this procedure violates park policy. Generally, a bear won't attack you just to get your food, but you have no guarantee of that. So if you try this method, remember you have been forewarned. If you are not comfortable dealing with bears in the middle of the night, don't even consider trying it.

There are two more points to consider about marauding bears. First, burn or pack out all garbage. Do not bury it, since that would only provide a bear with a free meal and encourage it to visit more campsites. Second, do not attempt to retrieve food taken by a bear; it is incredibly stronger than you, and it will regard the food it took as its own.

Other Problems: PCT trekkers attempting the entire tri-state route usually reach the southern Sierra just before or during the period of maximum snowmelt. Then South Fork Kern River swells and grows swift in its sand-bottomed channel where the PCT fords it twice. A 60′ safety rope may be called for at each of these fords to belay waders across. On the northern Kern Plateau, a snowpack's presence is likely. The route is mostly on south-facing slopes, where afternoon melt fosters sun cups and a slushy, too-soft surface which freezes at night. Then the best times to travel are early mornings and other cold times. An ice ax, crampons, protection against severe wind chill, and an informed respect for avalanches are essential for safe travel here.

Hikers unskilled in winter survival may prefer to design their own alternate route by way of Owens Valley. Such a route has some tremendous advantages. The Sierra's spectacular eastern escarpment, invisible from the PCT, remains always in sight for Owens Valley travelers, who also get the benefit of warm spring weather, abundant wildflowers, plentiful water and numerous food depots. One can readily gauge when it is safe to return to the PCT while making considerable progress toward the Canadian border. Some hikers take the bus through Owens Valley to bypass the mountain snow, then return to do the high country at the end of the trip before the next winter's storms set in. Leave the snowbound PCT to winter mountaineers!

Snow. Deep snow can be troublesome for end-to-end hikers. The greatest success is had by those who use crampons and ice axes and who do most of their hiking early in the day and late in the afternoon when the snow is relatively firm. Proper clothes, knowledge of hypothermia and avalanches, and skill with compass are essential. Some hikers take the bus through Owens Valley to bypass the Sierra snow, then return to do the high country at the end of the season before the next winter's storms set in. One alternative is to experience the snow until Trail Pass, and there decide whether or not to exit. If exiting, hitchhike to Lone Pine and catch the bus there. This plan also helps avoid crossing streams when they are swift and swollen with snowmelt, and avoids emerging swarms of mosquitoes too. Anticlimatic? Maybe, but think of finishing your PCT odyssey in the High Sierra during its most accommodating season. Still, at any time of the year, be prepared for unexpected snow storms in the high country.

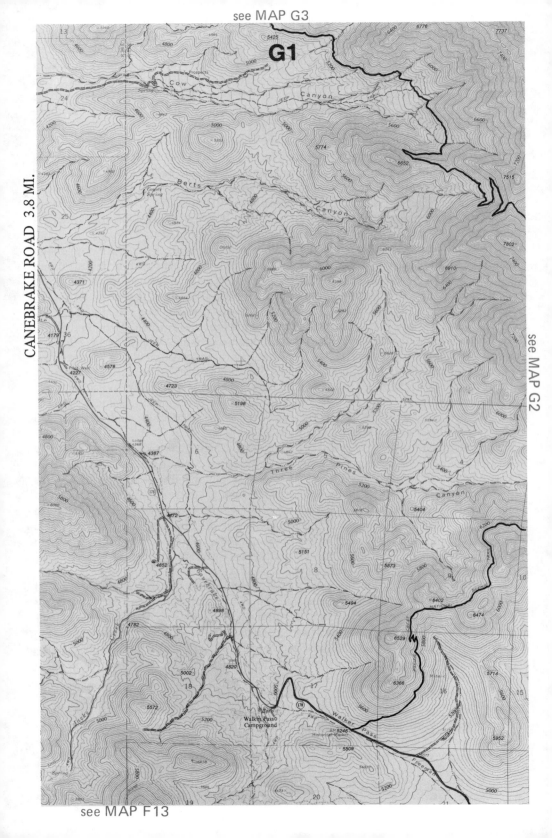

see MAP G3

G1

CANEBRAKE ROAD 3.8 MI.

see MAP G2

see MAP F13

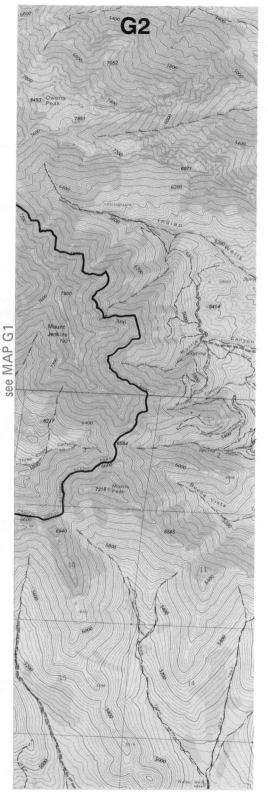

The PCT resumes across Highway 178 opposite the Walker Pass historical monument (5246'). Next water is at Spanish Needle Creek; 16.1 miles ahead. It may not be present during late summer or unusually dry years, so plan carefully. Our trail ascends moderately northeast, making a highly visible line across steep, sandy slopes, and then the grade becomes gentle as it winds above a canyon. A look back spies pinyon-pine-clad Scodie Mountain, which we just left. Below us our gaze is nudged east by Highway 178 to the distant El Paso Mountains. In early spring the slopes hereabouts are carpeted with blue chia, a sage that has two and sometimes three pom-poms ringing one stem. Native Americans roasted its seeds for food and Spaniards used the seeds of this wildflower for medicinal purposes. Lupines and tiny white forget-me-nots perfume the air. In the fall the scattered rabbitbrush displays profuse yellow disc flowers.

The path veers gradually north, upslope from a mine shack and its associated rubble, and then we negotiate six switchbacks in the welcome shade of pinyon-pine trees. In a short time we cross the crest at a saddle eroded along the Pinyon Peak Fault, one in a series of minor faults perpendicular to the trend of the major Sierra Nevada Fault Zone. Northwest views from here appear to foreshorten the Southern Sierra, putting Dome Land Wilderness in immediate contrast with the distant High Sierra.

The trail, an easy grade now near the crestline, crosses a south-facing slope, then regains the crest amid forest near a trailside campsite (6390-2.1). A long traverse ensues across northwest-facing slopes, a crestline gap, and then west- and north-facing slopes to a saddle southwest of Morris Peak and another campsite (6585-1.7), the launching site for climbers of this peak. After rounding Morris Peak we attain the Morris Peak/Mount Jenkins saddle (6500-0.9), where another campsite sits to the south of the small hill on the crest.

After passing the campsite and striding past the small hill on the saddle, you cross the crest to the east side of Mount Jenkins. The trail ascends slightly to a commemorative plaque cemented to a granite boulder, which has a natural bench where one may rest, reflect and view. Indian Wells canyon spreads to the desert below where the towns of Inyokern and, farther out, Ridgecrest shimmer in the desert sun. Vast China Lake Naval Weapons Center, where many sophisticated weapons are conceived and

G1, G2

Mt. Jenkins, named for former co-author of this book

developed, blankets the land north of Ridge-crest.

In December 1984 the United States Board on Geographic Names officially named the mountain we are hiking around "Mount Jenkins." This sprawling, serrated 7921′ mountain on the Sierra crest commemorates James (Jim) Charles Jenkins, who as a teenager hiked across its steep slopes while helping scout a route for this trail. As a budding author and naturalist and as an accomplished hiker, he was assigned to write the section of the PCT from the town of Mojave to Mount Whitney for this guidebook.

Jim soon expanded his interest to include the whole Southern Sierra, approximately 5,000 square miles. While doing field work and research, he developed a deep appreciation for these mountains, and his two-volume book, *Self-Propelled in the Southern Sierra,* published by Wilderness Press, reflects this feeling.

He also became greatly involved in promoting conservation and protection for the Southern Sierra. For his contribution to this area he was honored by the Board, a culmination of a five-year, grassroots effort by his many friends. The official record in the archives of the United States Department of Interior reads, "—named for James Charles Jenkins (1952-1979), noted authority on the flora, fauna and history of the southern Sierra Nevada who wrote guidebooks on the area."

When moving on, look for spring blooming Charlotte's phacelia, a vivid deep-blue member of the Hydrophyllaceae family. This exquisite flower, found beside the plaque when the mountain was dedicated, is rare and should be treated with respect and left to propagate. In contrast to the less-than-foot-high velvety phacelia is the huge *Nolina parryi,* indigenous to this small area, and rarely found elsewhere. One may mistake them for yuccas, for they are of the same lily family, but nolinas are greater in size and their lingering dry blossoms, resembling creamy parchment paper, distinguish this remarkable plant.

Our path, weaving around the extensions and recesses of Mount Jenkins, undulates slightly, passes a prominent ridge where camping is possible, curves deeply into the mountain and then rounds another ridge. At this point, by the ducks, climbers of Mount Jenkins turn west to scramble up the ridge and follow the ducks over the sky-scraping, nontechnical Class 3 summit rocks to the highest point, 7921′, where another, similar commemorative plaque rests. The views are spectacular and the register pad put in a can by Sierra Club members is fun to read and sign. Registers are found on most named peaks above 5000′ in the Southern Sierra.

G2

Striding along, the hiker sometimes clanks over chunks of metamorphic rocks, negotiates rock slides, observes the uncommon appearance of Jeffrey pines, sugar pines and white firs in this high-desert environment and ambles around another ridge. He then gradually descends while traveling back to the depths of the mountain creases. One of these creases, 2.9 miles from the trail plaque, conceals scattered pieces of a Navy C-45 twin engine Beechcraft. The 1948 crash took the lives of 5 scientists and 2 pilots from China Lake Naval Weapons Center who were on their way to a classified symposium on the Manhattan project in Oakland. Moving on, we soon reach the Mount Jenkins/Owens Peak saddle (7020-3.8). A small campsite is tucked under the trees at this jumping-off point for 8453' Owens Peak, the highest peak in Kern County.

The PCT descends west from the saddle by switchbacks, then contours northwest, skirts a minor knob and reaches a saddle (6300-1.5) east of Peak 6652. Again it zigzags down to curve around the watershed of Cow Canyon. In this drainage there is a seasonal spring, which BLM hopes to develop for hikers. Next our path crosses a jeep road (5680-1.3) from Highway 178, which was used by work crews for access to the trail. The PCT continues to lose elevation as it tracks a northwest route around a major ridge from Owens Peak. After crossing this ridge at a saddle (5225-1.5), we climb northeast up a draw before again resuming a northwest direction to still another saddle (5860-1.1) and perhaps a moment to consider some local history.

The pinyon forests through which we hike, were favored by Tubatulabal Native Americans for nut gathering, and probably by prehistoric tribes before them. The area is rich in archeological sites; for instance, some bedrock mortars are within easy access of the trail. A reminder, however, since Congress passed the antiquities legislation: it is illegal to remove or disturb anything pertaining to our Native Americans' culture: even so much as pocketing an obsidian chip or two is unlawful. But respect alone would dictate our nondisturbance of another's historic past.

The fall gathering season of protein-rich pinyon nuts was one of reverence and fellowship for Indian families. After a solemn ritual, the men shook the trees or loosened the cones with hooks fashioned on willow poles. Children gathered the cones in woven willow baskets for the women to roast. Some nuts were eaten whole, but most were ground into flour, creating the many grinding holes (mortars) in boulders scattered about this country. These nuts are still gathered by Tubatulabul descendants today as part of their diet, continuing to bind them to this important aspect of their past.

We continue to hike in the pinyon forest and its associated understory brush. The wide, smooth trail loses elevation by a series of short switchbacks, while below and off to the west the prominent slash of Canebrake Road gains elevation via an elongated switchback. A summit block of Lamont Peak looms directly north of us, hiding its sheer, jagged north ridge. The trail nearly levels beyond its switchbacks before again descending east along the steep slopes. Within our view below, a private, gated road hugs the path of Spanish Needle Creek, while our path bends north after crossing a canyon with early-season runoff. The gradient again eases, and ½ mile later it crosses, on a neatly laid path of flat rocks, the main branch

Co-author Ruby Jenkins with husband Bill on Mt. Jenkins dedication hike

G2, G1, G3

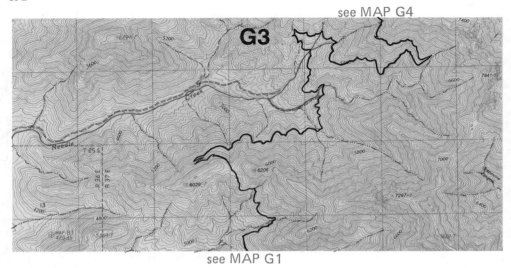

see MAP G4

see MAP G1

of Spanish Needle Creek, which we saw below (5160-2.2).

Even in a dry year some water trickles along this drainage, which is sprinkled with willows and cottonwood trees. A shelf just off the trail before the creek crossing makes an ideal campsite for weary PCTers.

Leaving the trees momentarily, our trail climbs out of the watered canyon around sunny slopes and again enters a forest, here with a few alders added, well-watered by a spring-fed finger of Spanish Needle Creek (5300-0.7). Because water is so scarce along the crest trail, the PCT was especially routed to take advantage of this series of springs, but in so doing it had to add a drop into the canyon and create several extra miles of trail.

Ample camping is 0.1 mile farther ahead under pinyon pines as we reach and hike along a minor ridge, perhaps scattering coveys of picturesque mountain quail, seemingly abundant in these mountains. A sharp turn in a side canyon directs us now generally east to cross a spring-fed streamlet, this one frocked with wild roses (5560-0.6). We then clamber briefly along a blasted area, cross a seep and again enter a shady canyon blessed with occasional bracken ferns. Here we cross the spring-fed finger of Spanish Needle Creek (5620-0.2). This is the last of the Spanish Needle springs; the next reliable water is 10.9 miles away at Chimney Creek.

After a brief stretch south, the trail climbs east across the south-facing slopes of Spanish Needle Creek canyon, then contours around another ridge. Here blasting of a white marblized vein was needed to carve the path. On this stretch we are treated to open views of jagged peaks on either side of Spanish Needle, which is like a rounded, protruding thumb on a clenched fist. The trail again turns southeast, climbs a switchback, abruptly turns north, then west, then northwest and climbs out of the canyon above the section of trail we just hiked. A pair of short switchbacks, spaced 0.3 mile apart, help us gain elevation to reach the ridge between the Spanish Needle group of pinnacles and Lamont Peak (6800-3.0). Campsites were developed here along the divide to accommodate trail crews and are useful now to PCTers, and also to those climbing Lamont Peak.

Once again our trail curves above a canyon, but this eastward leg takes us through another break from pinyons and scrub/live oaks to north-facing slopes of Jeffrey and sugar pines, white firs and black oaks—a mix of trees found in abundance on the west side of the Kern Plateau. Gaining some elevation, our trail then curves north along the Sierra crest, opening expansive eastern views for us of Sand Canyon below, Boulder Peak on its north wall, and the desert beyond. A large pinyon protects a campsite from the usual ridgetop winds (7000-1.3). Here climbers traverse the peak to the south to gain the summit of Spanish Needle, the second peak southeast.

Ahead, the PCT cuts a nearly straight swath northwest, just below ridgeline, taking us once

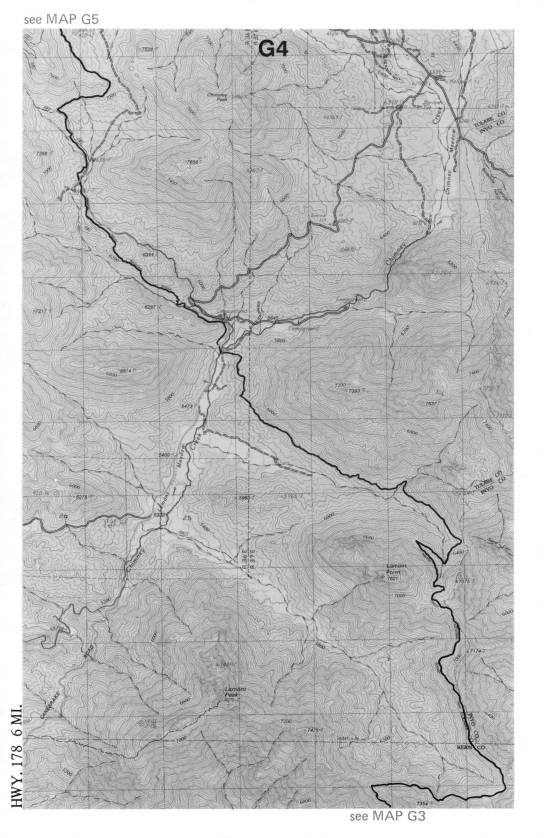

G4

G6

DOME

Creek

Creek

Creek

Creek

34

35

36

31

Water

VABM
Canyon 7315

Rockhouse

Kern

Basin

Mile
40

LAND

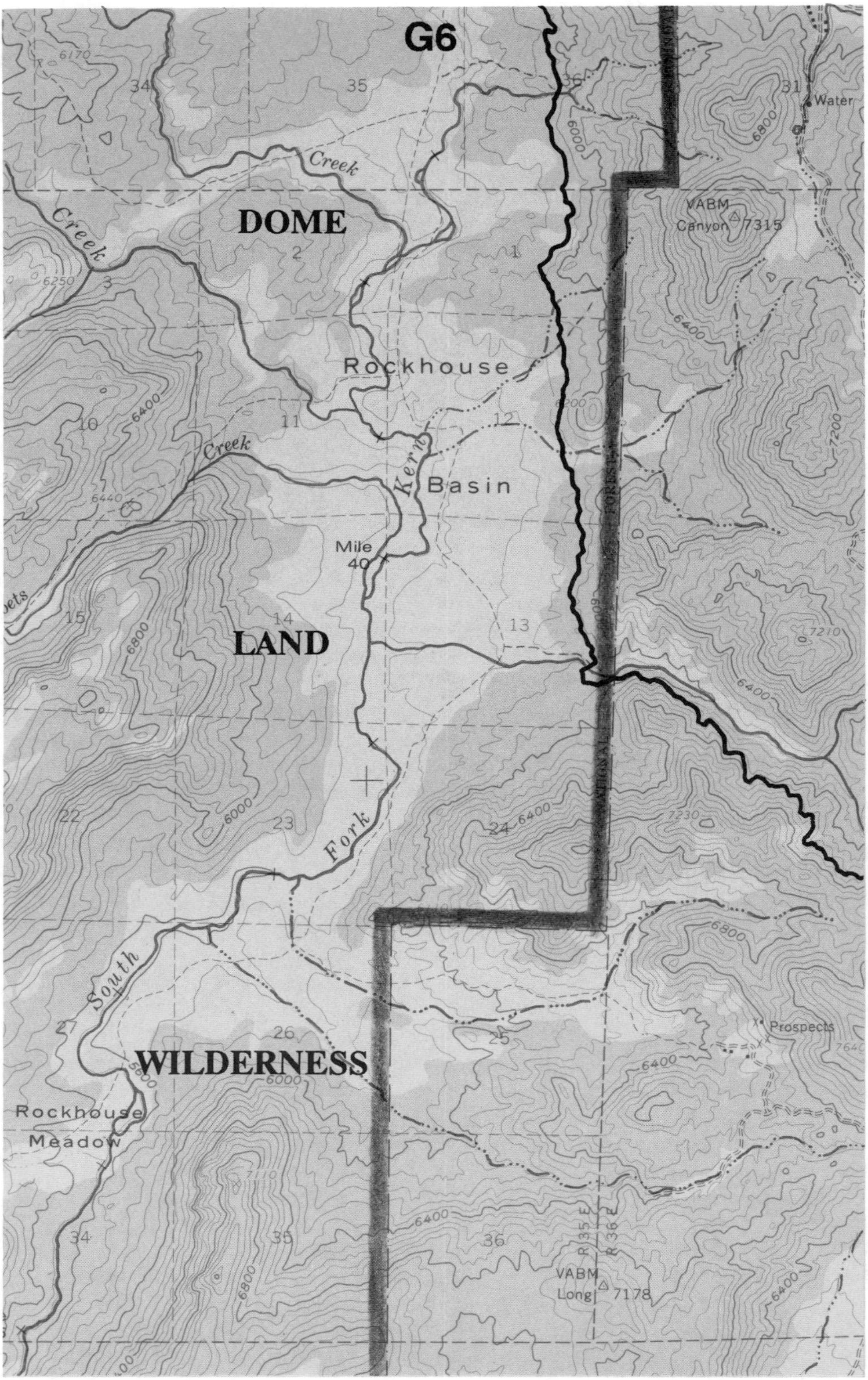

FOREST

Long Canyon

Prospects

7210

7230

VABM
Long 7178

South

Fork

WILDERNESS

Rockhouse
Meadow

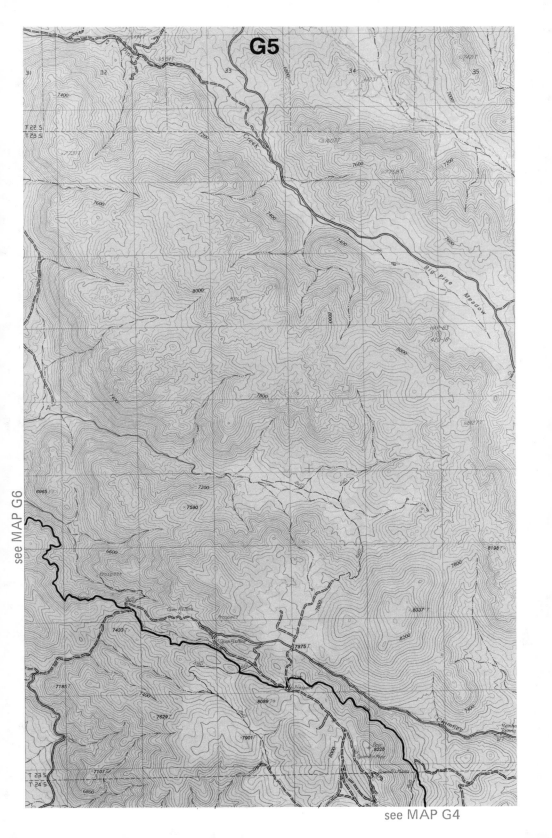

see MAP G6

see MAP G4

again through pinyons, oaks and brush in sunny, dry country, then swings briefly east into a canyon where again a small stand of Jeffrey pines and firs flourishes. These few patches of pine and fir occur occasionally on north slopes where moisture lingers longer in this dry climate. Now we traverse to a narrow saddle and then climb a bit to a broader one (6900-2.0), just beyond which, at the climbers' trailhead to Lamont Point, are areas for camping among the pinyons.

Now an extended descent to Chimney Creek Campground begins. A short switchback leads us northwest to a ½-mile-long leg along Lamont Point slopes. Then, rounding boulders, we head back nearly as far before turning north onto another Sierra-crest saddle (6260-1.4) with limited views, the starting point for hikes to Sawtooth Peak to the north. Heading in a general northwest direction again, the PCT slowly loses elevation, occasionally making small rises as it heads along lower slopes of the north side of the canyon between Lamont Point and Sawtooth Peak. Digger pines add to the forest along with more low shrubs; the gravelly path continues, now with sandy stretches from rotting granite.

A seasonal creek whose water tumbles down multicolored, sheer-sided canyons of sedimentary rocks above, crosses our path (5950-0.8), accompanied by its water-loving willows. Here and there along the path, in the most tenuous spots, solitary rust-brown, shreddy-barked junipers thrive. Soon Lamont Meadow and a pri-

vate inholding in this BLM-administered public land come into view, then Canebrake Road. Finally we drop, cross a north-south dirt road, and then cross adjacent Chimney Creek, the first nonseasonal water since the Spanish Needle springs. But wait to wet your cottonmouth with water from the faucets at Chimney Creek Campground. Finally you are ushered through a corridor of late-summer-blooming rabbitbrush to Canebrake Road (5540-2.4). The campground, 0.2 mile up the road, provides 37 shaded sites with tables, grills, pit toilets and—from May through October—faucet water. The creek, however, flows year-round.

Back on the trail, our route leaves the rabbitbrush and sagebrush behind for a short while to climb above and parallel the road and campground amid a flurry of spring blooms. The path, less sandy now, dips a tad to cross a creek and then proceeds up the south-facing slopes of the creek's canyon. It soon tops out of that canyon and enters another above a stream whose chortle echoes off the precipitous granodiorite slopes as the canyon walls close in.

The curious trekker will find a scattering of debris to poke through where the collapsed multilevel ruins of a barite mill appear to the left of our route. This mineral, used in drilling muds, was mined hereabouts until the early 1950s. Gold and tungsten were also mined in the area. This clutter overlooks a sagebrush-and willow-choked meadow where the stream mentioned previously provides the last water

G4
The PCT traverses beneath the Spanish Needles and Owens Peak

G7

Ball Mountain
VABM 925

SOUTH SIERRA

36

Kennedy Meadows
Camp

Fork

WILDERNESS

Creek

6

5

4

Kennedy

Windy Springs

12

8

9

OME LAND

Meadows

13

18

17

16

24

19

20

21

ILDERNESS

Kennedy   Meadows

19

20

21

Mile
46

24

Mile
45

Kennedy Peak
7495

25

30

29

28

River

for 10.2 miles, in Rockhouse Basin, except for a seasonal stream 5.7 miles ahead, by Long Valley Loop Road. Immediately we cross a dirt road (6580-2.2) coming from above the mill site and a flat camping area.

The trail continues to wend its way along slopes, passing an eroded dirt track. The gray-greens of the pinyon forest enhance the red-browns of the soil, and an occasional juniper adds to the pleasing palette. Several sagebrush meadows diminish below, while Chimney Peak seems just a stone's throw across the canyon to the northeast. Don't scan the peak for a chimney—it was named for one still standing in Chimney Meadow.

Soon we cross another dirt road (6900-0.7), round a nose about ½ mile to the northeast, then tramp through sagebrush and cross another road (7540-1.4). Now we begin a northwest trek involving a series of seemingly endless curves around steep ridges and retreats across dry furrows, continuing to slowly ascend over metamorphic soils and chunks of rock. To the east, beyond the meadows below and the dirt roads that snake through them, stand the peaks that anchor the eastern Sierra. Attaining the trail summit (8020-1.5) at last, on a minor ridge just south and above a fairly large flat, which is suitable for camping.

The PCT begins a descent now, bearing west and crossing a road (7980-0.2) then immediately crosses another, both leading to a large excavation sliced into the earthy-red slate. Several of these gouges catch our attention as we progress down the trail. Also, raising our sights as we progress, the northwest tapestry of Rockhouse Basin appears, with the stark granites of Dome Land Wilderness weighting the basin's southwest border. The deep forest-greens of Sirretta and other Kern Plateau peaks delineate the northwest curve of the basin where the muted sage-greens of Woodpecker Meadow are barely visible. On the northern horizon is the jagged High Sierra: the Great Western Divide and the Mount Whitney group. A bit nearer we again glimpse aloof and solitary "Miss" Olancha, called thus by local residents.

Our trail, curving northwest, quickly crosses a road and then descends along a canyon where a sun-dappled seasonal creek glitters in the recesses, and a weathered hut squats by its banks. We are soon at a bend in this canyon, arching over an artfully constructed culvert containing the seasonal stream mentioned earlier. There is camping potential in this area. In 100 yards we cross Long Valley Loop Road (7220-1.9), hike over a slight saddle, and descend along the southwest side of a deeper canyon.

There are better views now of Woodpecker Meadow, an area burned in the Woodpecker Fire of 1947. The trees, unable to re-establish themselves, were replaced by sagebrush and buckbrush. Stegosaurus Fin, Dome Land's resident dinosaur, which sits prominently in the wilderness' interior, peeks above the intervening ridge. The South Fork Kern River, weaving through the basin below, remains hidden. A dry flat on a small northeast spur ridge (6600-2.7) offers us one last place to camp before the broader lands of Rockhouse Basin. We continue to descend, sometimes clinking over loose, rocky slopes, then slowly plodding through sandy soils near the foot of the descent.

Now in Rockhouse Basin, the path turns north and crosses first a year-round creek (5845-1.8), then immediately crosses a closed road. Once again we are in national forest and are entering Dome Land Wilderness, near a large campsite. Domes, spires and obelisks make up the semi-arid 94,686 acres of wilderness. Rock climbers find it an excellent place to practice their skills. But surprisingly, there are grassy meadows, forests and sizable fishing creeks too, along with the serpentine flow of the South Fork Kern River.

Our path roughly follows the South Fork Kern River, but, alas, the river is around a mile away for the next several miles. However, we do catch vignettes of it occasionally as we tromp north along the sandy trail, still through a pinyon-pine forest. Being a sandy trail, it is subject to erosion—if eroded, just follow the corridor through the trees scarred from sawed-off branches.

Hikers soon dip through the sagebrush-lined wash of a waterless basin (5010-1.2), and then pad across a northeast-southwest-trending closed road descending along a gully (5895-0.6). In a bit over a mile you cross a willow-lined, all-year creek (5870-1.4). A large campsite is to the north of the creek below the path at the end of a closed jeep road. Contouring slightly northwest now, one approaches a gateway of resistant metamorphic bedrock, and through this gateway flows the South Fork Kern River (5760-1.0).

Beginning on the slopes of Trail Peak near Cottonwood Pass, a place you will visit as you travel north on the PCT, the South Fork Kern

G4, G5, G6, G7

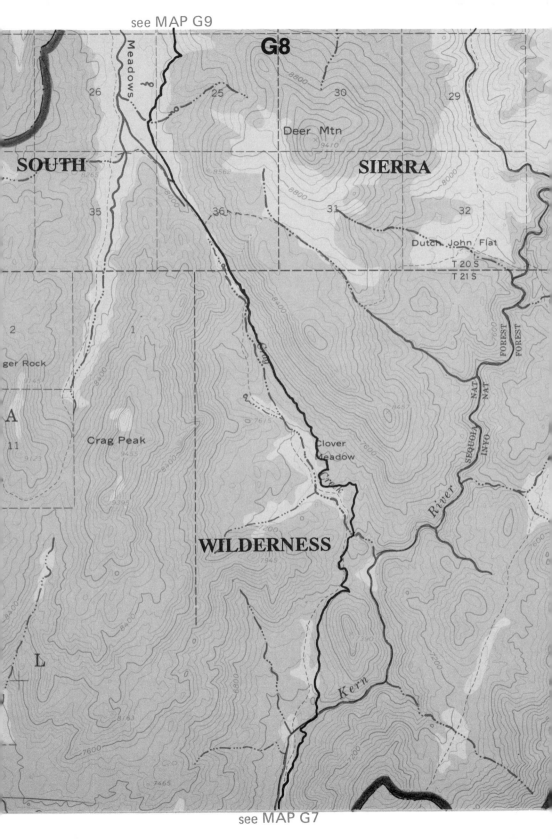

see MAP G9

G8

SOUTH   SIERRA

WILDERNESS

see MAP G7

South Fork Kern River at bedrock gateway

River flows south, wandering across the Kern Plateau, gathering much of the eastern plateau's drainage and eventually flowing into Lake Isabella, a reservoir. Most of the year it resembles a placid creek with good fishing holes and refreshing bathing pools, but during snowmelt the river becomes tumultuous, charging wildly through its containing banks. Then it is dangerous to cross. But during snowmelt this river, unspoiled by man, displays its most scenic value, and illustrates why in 1987 it was included with the North Fork Kern River in the protective custody of the prestigious National Wild and Scenic Rivers System.

Turning north again, our path treads the first of two passages between the willow-wild rose tangles that edge the river and the boulders composing the cliffs. Sprinklings of flowers add an artist's touch to the captivating scenery around us, and vanilla-scented Jeffrey pines line the water's edge. The trail soon climbs and dips, generally following the watercourse but allowing the river to loop away now and again.

Shortly we cross spring-fed Pine Creek, and then about ½ mile later we join a road (5940-1.3) where 4WDers have left tracks leading to campsites and river views. In time we leave the road at a junction (5950-0.6) where it curves west toward the river; our path continues straight ahead, north, following the fence on our right. Soon we pass west of a whimsical hut (now sporting a new addition) with a stovepipe chimney just before crossing a stream garnished with sedges and watercress (5916-0.1), with a 4WD road next to it. A vast outlier of sagebrushy Kennedy Meadows stretches before us, and we begin hiking through it.

Just ¼ mile later the PCT approaches a fence corner, then leaves the fence and angles off to the northeast, away from the river. In minutes amid the sagebrush, we pass a treeless, grassy area with a fire ring. And in the midst of this meadow romp the path crosses a 4WD road (5980-0.6) that connects a paved Forest Service highway—about a mile to the east—with other river roads. Not far north of the meadow, you climb the lower west slope of a hill and catch your first sight of the highway, a few buildings along it, and the general store where trekkers may have a package pickup. Hiking beside the river toward the highway, you pass through three cattle gates (please close). Between the first two gates, the trail rounds west of the outcrops and is often washed out by high

G7

water. The path then nears a large campsite spread under a juniper tree, and 0.4 mile later winds its way up to the Kennedy Meadows/Sherman Pass Road just east of the bridge (6020-1.7).

At this point, if you need supplies or refreshments, have a package pickup, or just wish to sign the PCT register and chat and maybe catch the Saturday night movie, continue 0.7 mile, generally southeast, along the highway to tree-shaded Kennedy Meadows General Store. When it is time to move along, return to the trail to start a hike north to Kennedy Meadows Campground. You'd walk the same distance if you took the northbound road just beyond the store to reach the campground.

In 1984 a new California wilderness bill became law. It added 32,000 acres to Dome Land Wilderness; you have been hiking within its expanded boundaries since you entered Sequoia National Forest at the east edge of Rockhouse Basin. Also added, sandwiched between the enlarged Dome Land Wilderness and vast, relatively new (1978) Golden Trout Wilderness, and north of the highway corridor, is the new 63,000-acre South Sierra Wilderness, which you soon enter. So, as you see, Section G's PCT odyssey takes place on land that will be left in or returned to a nearly natural state, although cattle grazing is still allowed.

Continuing on sandy turf among high-desert flora such as orange, silvery-leaved apricot mallows, shiny, yellow blazing stars and very tiny sand mats, we undulate through washes and cross dirt roads that head west to riverside campsites, fishing and swimming holes. Occa-sional junipers offer dots of shade as we pass fences first on our right and then on our left, then we go through one gate and soon through another. Enticing murmurs of the river increase as the path reaches and then rounds above the musical South Fork. Slowly it leaves the vast sagebrush meadow embraced by the gentle peaks of the semi-arid side of the Kern Plateau, and heads toward a distant fire-scarred mountain, seen through the river canyon to the north.

Soon the trail is tightly confined between the river and the campground road, and we're forced to cross the road (6080-1.8) and proceed along higher ground. Here we hike for a short time around boulders among pinyon pines and brush. Then the path crosses the road (6120-0.4) once again to bisect Kennedy Meadows Campground.

The PCT leaves the campground (6150-0.2) at its north end, following the old Clover Meadow Trail, shaded by pinyons with increasing numbers of Jeffrey pines. Promptly it dips into a side canyon, goes through a stock-fence gate, enters South Sierra Wilderness, approaches the river and winds to a forked junction (6240-1.1). The abandoned, riverside Clover Meadow Trail continues ½ mile north to its river crossing, which can be extremely dangerous during snowmelt. Because most long-distance PCT hikers are here during this usually wild period in the river's yearly cycle, the Forest Service carved another path leading to a sturdy, yet scenic, steel-girdered wooden bridge built in 1984 for their safe crossing; therefore, take the upper trail at the junction and hike to the bridge (6300-0.8).

Bridge north of Kennedy Meadows   ## G7, G8

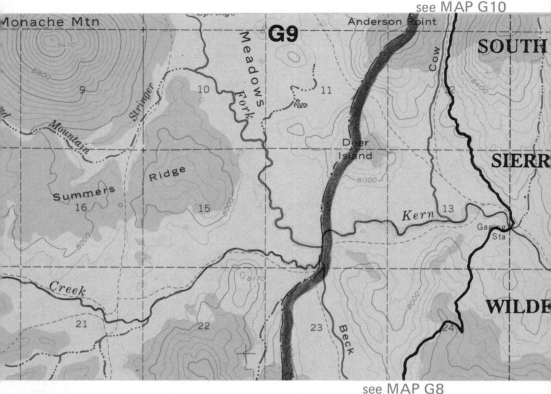

see MAP G10

see MAP G8

Beyond the bridge, the trail climbs north past a knoll over gravelly terrain to where it branches away from a closed connecting piece of trail to the old, deeply rutted route. Abandoned sections of the Clover Meadow Trail return occasionally to cross or coincide with the present trail. Soon our path gains the slopes of a craggy 7412′ mountain whose soils nurture an occasional prickly-pear cactus. The prominent yellow-orange blossoms of this spiny plant turn pink-to-rose as they mature. The path switchbacks once to reach a saddle, then we make a weaving traverse above the rumble of the South Fork Kern River, heard but not seen in its canyon to the east, before our trail dips to cross Crag Creek (6810-2.0). Yellow monkey flowers, gaping with two-lobed upper lips and three-lobed lower lips, luxuriate near the banks of this creek, along with an occasional yellow cinquefoil, whose green sepals reach above the flower's petals. There are places to camp here and upstream along the old trail, all of which, however, are within 100′ of the water—easily damaged areas the Forest Service wishes to protect.

After a short hike beyond the crossing, you abruptly confront the skeletal remains of burned trees, destroyed in the 1980 Clover Meadow blaze. Started by a PCT hiker's campfire that was too close to tree branches and not correctly extinguished, the wind-whipped fire engulfed 5,000 acres before it was contained. Very few if any pine seedlings have sprouted in this now shadeless burn site; only buckbrush ceanothus and associated xeric plants have appeared among the standing dead and down tree remains. The stark grays and blacks of the burn contrast sharply with the creek's riparian expanse and the plush greens of Clover Meadow seen in the canyon as you continue along the way.

The PCT passes an unburned pocket of trees that has campsites, and after 1.8 miles into the burn reaches the welcome shade of live Jeffrey pines, junipers and woody mountain mahogany shrubs, with their small leaves that cluster near the branch tips. This shrub is a silvery bush when dressed with its corkscrew, feathered plumes. Crag Creek is dry when we again meet it, but as the path climbs up the narrowing, boulder-strewn slot, its flow reappears. A heavy growth of willow and wild rose along its banks indicates water is probably present most of the year. An interesting campsite 0.1 mile below the water source along the dry bed, was established, according to a concrete slab, in 1936. A rusted length of pipe seems to indicate a flow of water at that time. The old trail was probably built by CCC crews during the Depression. The grade abates amid yellow-flowered bitterbrush, and ends at a pass with campsites and a **T** junction (8060-3.6) with a trail that follows an ancient Indian path east to the river and on through Haiwee Pass to Owens Valley—a route once considered for the eastern leg of a trans-Sierra highway.

Beyond the pass, the trail drops gently to Beck Meadows, a sagebrush-dusted finger of Monache Meadows. A spacious view of this largest meadow in the Sierra includes distant Mount Whitney peering over plateau peaks. The PCT veers north from the northwest-leading Beck Meadows trail (7953-0.4), then from grooves of an old jeep road. Jeeps first penetrated into Monache Meadows in 1949, but long before that horse-drawn buckboards left their parallel treads. Among the seasonal flowers, the yellow evening primrose with its heart-shaped petals makes a dramatic appearance.

In 0.6 mile we leave the old PCT path, left to revert to nature, and turn north-northeast to directly face Olancha Peak, beyond the lower northern slopes of nearby Deer Mountain. After crossing a seep, the path climbs above Beck Meadows and through a wash whose trickle is gathered in a cow trough below, then passes through another stock-fence gate. To the north, Mount Langley, framed by Brown and Olancha mountains, comes into view. Its rounded backside resembles Mount Whitney's, and it is often confused with our highest mountain in the Lower 48. In 0.7 mile from the gate we top out on Deer Mountain's northern ridge (8390-2.2), and then briefly head southeast to a switchback. Next we head north to drop out of the forest, and then cross a retired jeep road that skirts a low, broad ridge (7940-1.0). We head northeast along the ridge to its end and then drop to an arched 1986 vintage bridge over South Fork Kern River (7820-0.4), at an unused gauging station. Interestingly, the steel in this bridge was treated to resemble an old rusted structure. Our presence here may disturb a flock of barn swallows that have found this bridge to their liking. We appreciate it, too, during high snowmelt. The rest of the time it arches over very shallow water, which is refreshing to wade. Here we leave Sequoia National Forest and enter Inyo National Forest, but still remain in South Sierra Wilderness.

Resuming its path, here briefly overlapping a jeep road, the PCT passes the southeast-heading Wildrose Trail (7840-0.1), a cyclepath that vibrated with motorcycles before the wilderness was established, and pass a once heavily used jeep road, which heads north. Our path leaves the roadbed and easily climbs northwest above the meadow while jogging laterally across washes and around ridgelets, a feat the PCT does so well and so often in order to stay within its required 15% or less grade. (One can usually identify sections of PCT that follow old trails, as there it usually drops into washes and climbs over ridgelets instead of traversing them.) In time we mount a low ridge (8050-1.2) and head north, leaving open slopes sparsely dotted with chartreuse lichen-painted boulders and entering forested Cow Canyon. Midway up this canyon we're back on old trail, and we immediately cross Cow Creek (8260-1.3) near a cluster of campsites. (Future plans for the PCT include realigning the trail to remain on the east side of Cow Creek.)

The trail soon crosses the creek again but quickly returns and ascends a canyon where Kern Plateau ceanothus debuts. This bush has hollylike leaves and blue-to-purple pom-pom flowers. And as the name implies, it is a denizen of the plateau, occurring only occasionally in other areas, such as along the Little Kern River. Briefly, the trail merges with a stock driveway, crosses over the creek and back, and rejoins the multiple twining path of the driveway for a short stint. Almost one mile later, where the creek turns east, we continue north and quickly reach a trickle from a spring just above, and after a brief, winding ascent we join the Monache Meadows/Olancha Pass trail (8920-1.2). Vegetation coils about the spring immediately south of our junction.

Our route on the conjoined trail runs eastward, now on a gentle ascent around the head of Cow Canyon. Along the way it passes disturbed terrain on the canyon side created by stock drives, and then crosses Cow Creek again. Only 250 yards beyond we bear east at a junction (9090-0.5), leaving the trail we briefly joined. This goes southeast to the nearby northwest end of long, level, linear Summit Mead-

G8, G9, G10

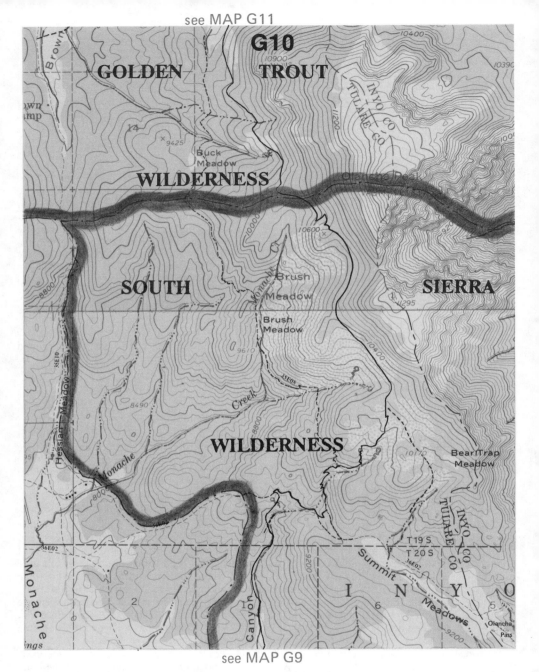

see MAP G9

ows, which stretch 1¼ miles southeast to Olancha Pass.

The ascending path switchbacks, arcs northeast up a rounded ridgelet, and then turns north where a lateral (9160-0.1) branches off to the trail we just left. The PCT runs across slopes of chinquapin and manzanita, fords Cow Creek ¼

mile upstream from the last crossing, and zigzags many times amid currant (a favorite berry of black bears), other brush and pines to a junction (9500-0.6) with an unmaintained trail to private Bell Camp Meadow.

Now leaving the forest, we continue to parallel the creek, which flows amid groups of corn

G10

lilies, aptly named plants resembling corn-stalks. The open tread is sandy and often very dusty, but it still supports the colorful scarlet gilia. The gradient presently steepens, and the trail zigzags sporadically as it climbs a side canyon. Then we ford a perennial brook, which originates in the meadow springs above, where cattle and horses sometimes frolic. After 75 yards along the brook, the trail switchbacks near a large campsite among boulders by a foxtail pine. Here one is treated to an encom-passing view of Monache Meadows, cone-shaped Monache Mountain and the sandy flood plain of South Fork Kern River.

Minutes beyond this bouldery campsite, a short path climbs off our trail to a small plateau where a verdant, watered meadow sports numerous mountain bluebells. Several camp-sites and a corral ring the meadow. Mosquitoes here, as in all meadows, may make camping in spring or early summer a bit unpleasant. As you move into the shade of lodgepole and occa-sional foxtail pines, the grade diminishes. Ahead, you'll see large groves of impressive foxtail pines, which grow in gravelly soil just below timberline along with very few under-story plants. This tree's short, five-clustered needles surround the branches, which resemble a fox's tail. They thrive in the extreme weather of the high country.

Atop a ridge we proceed past a junction (10,100-1.1), obscured by a large fallen tree, with a faint cow trail that descends near Bear Trap Meadow to the Monache Meadows/ Olancha Pass trail. North of the fallen tree our path assumes a gentle-to-moderate ascent, curves northwest and crosses another open slope with a seasonal streamlet. The farther north we hike on this slope, the more we can see of the Southern Sierra. Even the San Gabriel Mountains, which stand above the Los Angeles basin, show faintly through the distant haze. In almost one mile the trail crosses a flat, forested ridge, where considerable potential for camping exists, although it is a long way from reliable water. Provocative vignettes of Olancha Peak, Mount Langley, the Kaweah Peaks Ridge and Kern Peak may be seen between the trees.

Continuing to climb, the path curves around a headwaters bowl of Monache Creek and then levels off to a saddle (10,575-1.7) on a ridge that juts out from the west-facing slope of Olancha Peak. Since this is the highest point the trail reaches on the side of Olancha Peak, it is a good departure point for a nontechnical

Foxtail pine

climb to the top, about 1550' above us. To reach the peak of this climb, aim for the slope north of the summit where the rounded and gentler terrain makes for an easy final ascent after one has pulled up over scores of large boulders. Surprisingly, these boulders are inter-spersed with remarkably lush plants of yellow columbine. A much easier climb, just south-west of the saddle, and the PCT, would put one atop Point 10,600. The view from its summit is amply rewarding, and it abounds in dry-camp-ing potential.

From our saddle the PCT begins dropping to Gomez Meadow on a gentle-to-moderate grade. It zigzags five times and then curves around the headwaters bowl of Monache Creek. Soon we cross a watershed divide, where we leave South Sierra Wilderness and enter Golden Trout Wilderness. As we saunter along this nearly effortless, northern descent, we may contem-plate some events that involve this area.

Before the late 1940s the only way one could reach the gentle Kern Plateau was on foot, on animal or by a breathtaking flight in a small aircraft. Then logging began in the southern part, and it slowly pushed northward. The loggers' roads opened the land to jeeps and their cousins, motorcycles. All these intrusions resulted in slope erosion, damaged meadows

G10

and silted streams. Environmentalists became alarmed, and campaigned to protect the remaining land. They were successful. In 1978 President Carter signed into law 306,000-acre Golden Trout Wilderness, named for the colorful trout—our state fish—that evolved in this area. The northern third of the Kern Plateau is part of this wilderness.

As we ponder this recent history, we pass above a seasonal spring while hiking across sunny slopes with views of brown-tipped Kern Peak across the Kern Plateau. This 11,510′ peak counterbalances Olancha Peak, and the two constitute the highest points on the plateau.

Now the PCT meanders northwest, dropping into a forest of lodgepole pines. Soon a picturesque "rabbit ears" outcrop appears up the slope northeast of us, just before we cross a seasonal seep. Hiking 0.7 mile beyond this view, we leave the forest for a westward, downslope look at Long Stringer. Our path crosses a sagebrush slope and a pine patch and then crosses a seasonal creek. Beyond, it crosses a spur ridge, encounters mountain mahogany, and returns into forest. The trail gradually curves to meander northeast, then bends southeast to a nearby ford of a spring-fed, year-round creek (9000-3.7). Considerable camping potential exists near its banks. A common Sierra plant that graces many such wet areas as this is the tall, flat-topped, yellow-flowered arrowleaf senecio.

From the creek we saunter along the path north and then east on a slightly rolling course. The path then bends sharply north-northwest and crosses a meadowside trail at a causeway abutment (8960-0.7). This is just west of very level Gomez Meadow.

The causeway's 35-yard length separates us from the sodden stringer beneath. Shooting stars seem almost airborne across the meadow. This is another flower whose common name is well-chosen, because its swept-back petals suggest flight. Our path resumes at the north abutment and immediately crosses another meadowside path. The PCT then curves northeast, into a dense lodgepole-pine forest, touching the inconspicuous Sierra crest. The trail then curves gradually northwest and soon skirts Big Dry Meadow. A path to the meadow leaves our trail opposite a tree-posted sign. Reminiscent of Indian lore, it says "May the Great Spirit shine on your day in rainbow colors."

Now we pass creekside campsites, then ford the step-across stream (8910-1.7) at the mouth of Death Canyon. A path immediately beyond the creek crossing takes PCT equestrians to another in a series of corrals and camping areas built for the PCT trail crews of Inyo National Forest. None are maintained, some are usable. Beyond the path we labor up 26 broadly spaced switchbacks on the blocky, spired ridge west of the canyon. The PCT crosses the crest of this ridge for the last time at a saddle near the Sierra crest. Foxtail pines now shade our way and red mountain-pride penstemons decorate our path as it descends gently to a crestline saddle (10,390-3.7) from which the eastern slope drops precipitously to Owens Lake. This is a usually dry alkali flat because Los Angeles diverted its inflow. Climbing again, the path makes seven switchbacks, and then attains a long, 10,700′ crestline prominence, which offers more views of Owens Lake and the Inyo and Coso mountains east of it. Kern and Olancha peaks dominate the southern half of the horizon. Our path at length leaves the ridgetop in a descending traverse of west-facing slopes. You then curve west, and just before leveling out near a saddle, you meet a junction (10,425-1.5). From it a faint, ½-mile-long lateral descends north to campsites and a corral. There is usually water from nearby springs. Just below the junction, the PCT skirts west across a saddle, then it meanders more or less northwest, crossing two more crest saddles. Just east of the second saddle (10,260-1.6) is another corral, campsite and spring. About ½ mile later the PCT crosses yet another saddle.

Now we leave one cattle allotment and enter another. In fact, the whole plateau is a patchwork of these parcels, and wilderness classification does not ban grazing. Most of the cattle people involved have been summering their animals in these allotments for several generations.

The path curves north where Sharknose Ridge juts off to the west, then skirts the west edge of wide Ash Meadow, traversing along a nearly level stretch of Sierra crest. We leave the crest and travel briefly north on an easy descent of west-facing slopes before passing a path (10,000-1.8) to another corral down in a ravine above Mulkey Meadows. Mount Langley, the southernmost 14,000′ peak in the Sierra Nevada, sinks behind the shoulder of Trail Peak, and views of Mulkey Meadows improve as we drop along the dusty trail. Our path bends east around a spur ridge, and then we stroll almost a mile on nearly level trail to

G10, G11, G12

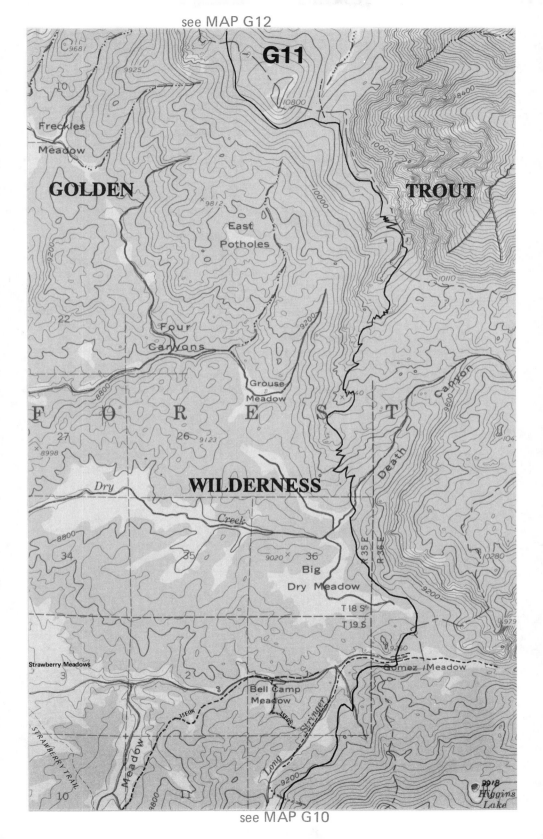

G11

Freckles
Meadow

GOLDEN

TROUT

East
Potholes

Four
Canyons

Grouse
Meadow

Canyon

F O R E S T

Death

WILDERNESS

Dry

Creek

Big
Dry Meadow

T 18 S

T 19 S

R 35 E
R 36 E

Strawberry Meadows

Gomez Meadow

Bell Camp
Meadow

35E08

35E08

STRAWBERRY TRAIL

Meadow

Long Stringer

Higgins
Lake

regain the Sierra crest. Here at a low saddle between the watersheds of Diaz Creek and Mulkey Creek the path turns north (9670-1.8).

The PCT now climbs the crest in a gentle-to-moderate grade and curves gradually northwest. After a mile it switchbacks on the crest, then leaves it for a short climb north to top a broad ridge south of Dutch Meadow. Unless you need water or are ready to camp, you should bear northwest at a junction (9960-1.3) with a 0.2-mile lateral to the Dutch Meadow campsites and corral. You can usually find water here, although at least one PCT hiker complained about its bad quality and the overabundance of cow dung.

Past the junction our trail switchbacks twice, climbs west to the Sierra crest, attains a nearby spur ridge, bends from north to west around a canyon, and then contours over to cross Mulkey Stock Driveway at Mulkey Pass (10,380-1.5). Beyond the driveway, the PCT traverses around the south side of a crestline-straddling hill to reach Trail Pass and a junction with the Trail Pass Trail (10,500-0.8). If you're short on supplies, you can descend 2.2 miles north on it to Horseshoe Meadow Road,

then hitchhike to Lone Pine. The lower ⅔ of this trail was realigned to exit through the Kern Plateau hikers' overnight campground and paved parking lot. This along with the adjoining equestrian and Cottonwood Lakes campgrounds makes this a popular place, and hikers have no trouble finding rides down the mountain. From the pass the PCT ascends gently amid foxtail pines and talus, switchbacks twice and then rounds a spur ridge emanating from 11,623′ Trail Peak. Portals in the forest frame exhilarating views of Mount Langley and some precipitous ridges associated with it, then frame nearer views of Poison Meadow below us. Our trail continues west to a path (10,710-1.3), which descends to a corral, and soon we cross cold, refreshing Corpsmen Creek.

In about ⅓ mile the PCT crosses the crest at a saddle (10,780-0.6). It next traverses southwest across slopes that offer views of Mulkey Meadows, then crosses southwest-facing slopes, passing small meadows whose seeps and springs combine to become the headwaters of South Fork Kern River. This is the river PCT hikers first met in Dome Land Wilderness. Foxtail-pine boughs overhead continue to shade us as we go, but part occasionally to

Olancha Peak seen between trailside pinnacles near Trail Pass

G12, G13

Big Whitney Meadow, from the PCT above Chicken Spring Lake

enhance views of the Great Western Divide. In time our path crosses a west-facing meadow. No longer in South Fork watershed, this meadow's drainage eventually feeds into Golden Trout Creek, which travels west to tumble off the Kern Plateau into the Kern River. Soon we pass over a spur-ridge saddle, then turn north-northeast and traverse about ½ mile to Cottonwood Pass. Just a few yards west of the pass we cross the Cottonwood Pass Trail (11,160-2.9). This, too, reaches Horseshoe Meadow Road to the east.

North of the junction, the PCT climbs imperceptibly, turning west upon entering forest. The path now meanders over to a hummocky dell below Chicken Spring Lake, then crosses the lake's sometimes dry outlet stream (11,225-0.6). The thought of catching shoreline views of the lake in its granite cirque prompts us to leave the trail before the stream and stroll northwest to the shore. The lake is the last reliable water source before a brook that leads into Rock Creek, 9.2 miles ahead. Campsites abound at the lake, and on weekends so do people using them. On any summer day, though, you'll not be alone since Clark's nutcrackers will hop to your pad and caw at you for handouts.

Back on the PCT, we switchback beyond the outlet, over a spur ridge overlooking the lake. The path then makes a seemingly endless timberline traverse of southwest-facing slopes below 12,900' Cirque Peak. Through the fox-

tail-pine forest, Big Whitney Meadow appears intermittently to the southwest. Our trail becomes annoyingly sandy as it describes a horseshoe around a small cirque. Contrary to old maps, there is no lake in the little basin below us, only a meadow with several potential campsites. Near a seasonal trailside spring, which often flows through summer, a no-stock-grazing sign is posted on a foxtail pine.

Climbing a little, the trail soon swings around a flat-topped ridge, and then begins a descent that doesn't end until it reaches the Rock Creek ford. The path bends around a little ridge at an entrance to Sequoia National Park (11,275-3.1), leaving Golden Trout Wilderness. Pets, firearms, grazing cattle and logging activities within the park are illegal.

On this descent, excellent views of the Great Western Divide appear across Siberian Outpost in the west. Our downgrade first steepens somewhat, then becomes gentle as we skirt the northeasternmost prong of Siberian Outpost. Though named for its desolate aspect, the Outpost is surrounded by weathered foxtail-pine snags whose reddish-brown hues lend the place an impression of warmth and mellowness. Now the PCT wanders westward, turning left at a Rock Creek cutoff, and then crossing the Rock Creek/Siberian trail (10,980-0.9).

We next head toward the broad, gently rolling ridgetop separating the watershed of Rock Creek to the north from that of stagnant

G13, G14

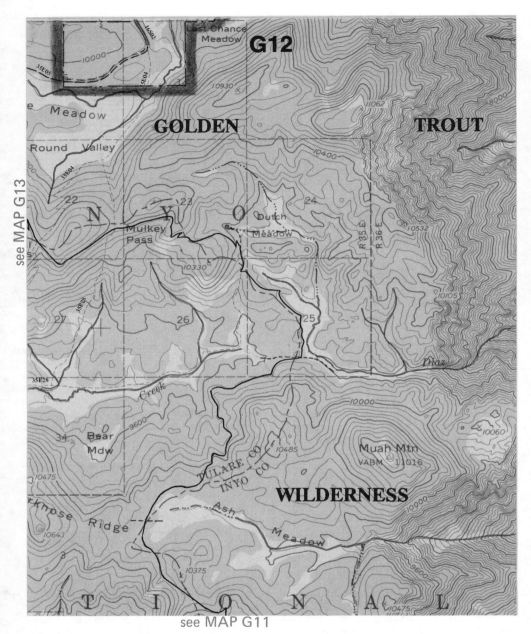

GOLDEN   TROUT

see MAP G13

WILDERNESS

see MAP G11

Siberian Pass Creek to the south. Sky-piercing crags have been visible all about us from occasional clearings along the path, and now the massive Miter Basin Peaks north of Rock Creek canyon attract our attention. Soon the gravelly route gently rolls, continuing west and staying just south of the ridgecrest. After an hour's walk into the national park, we start to descend and then switchback. The PCT here describes an **S** we can only visualize on the map. It then levels out and crosses a sand flat. Lodgepole pines, at first only scattered among foxtail pines, come to dominate the forest as we stroll northwest along a ridgetop, then descend moderately via nine switchbacks northward, pass a seasonal spring, and hike down to a junction (9880-4.9) with the Rock Creek Trail.

Now our wanderings turn westward and zig-

G14, G15, G14, G15

zag several times more before crossing a brook (9740-0.3), the first reliable water since Chicken Spring Lake, 9.2 miles back. Pausing to drink, we can easily identify the wild aromatic onions with their pinkish-purple blooms gracing the banks upstream. The path beyond follows the south edge of a meadow for a while, then crosses it diagonally. Back in forest, we drop to large campsites overlooking Rock Creek, but alas, a favorite site by a waterfall is now closed for restoration. Better bearproof your food here and throughout the park. One can be cited for noncompliance. Heavy metal, rectangular food lockers have been placed at popular campsites to facilitate this task. You are asked to share the lockers, keep them clean, close the doors and always secure the latches.

A meadow with snow-survey signs lies directly east of the camps. The Rock Creek Snow Survey cabin and summer ranger station is 0.2 mile east of the snow-survey meadow. This post is manned only when funds are available. At other times the backcountry ranger at Crabtree Meadow includes Rock Creek in his territory. To reach the cabin, leave the PCT at the campsites, follow Rock Creek east through the snow-survey meadow, through the forest, across a feeder brook and then up a rounded little ridge. You'll soon find the cabin.

On the westbound PCT, hikers approach Rock Creek, cross a rivulet while swerving away from the creek a bit, and then finally cross it on steppingstones (9480-0.9). Just downstream is a log for high-water crossings.

Our path ahead switchbacks, first north and then west-northwest as it begins to climb a moderate-to-steep grade through stands of lodgepole pine and juniper. After trekkers pass several cold, thirst-quenching brooks just below their springs, Sawtooth Peak, monarch of Mineral King, becomes briefly visible astride the Great Western Divide in the west. Then we switchback northward, out of glacier-carved Rock Creek canyon, the first such canyon we pass through on the PCT. Clumps of chinquapin sporadically dot trailside slopes as the grade abates.

Our path, engineered to meet PCT specifications, sometimes runs near, sometimes coincides with the disappearing former trail. Guyot Creek (10,350-1.5), the last source of water until Whitney Creek 4.5 miles ahead, is easily crossed. Then we hike through a wreckage of mature trees, snapped and broken into pieces by a 1986 avalanche. The young resilient trees on Guyot's slope survived. Beyond, we labor up and over an unnamed pass (10,920-1.0) northeast of 12,300' Mt. Guyot, then we zigzag down, level out and stroll through the forest east of Guyot Flat, a deep, grit-filled depression. In foxtail-pine forest the path rolls along and gradually veers north. Beyond another sand flat, we ascend to a broad, flat-topped ridge and then drop down a series of switchbacks successively farther northeast.

If the highest point in the contiguous United States, 14,494' Mount Whitney, makes us stiff-necked from gazing northeast at its rounded

G15

Smithsonian hut atop Mt. Whitney

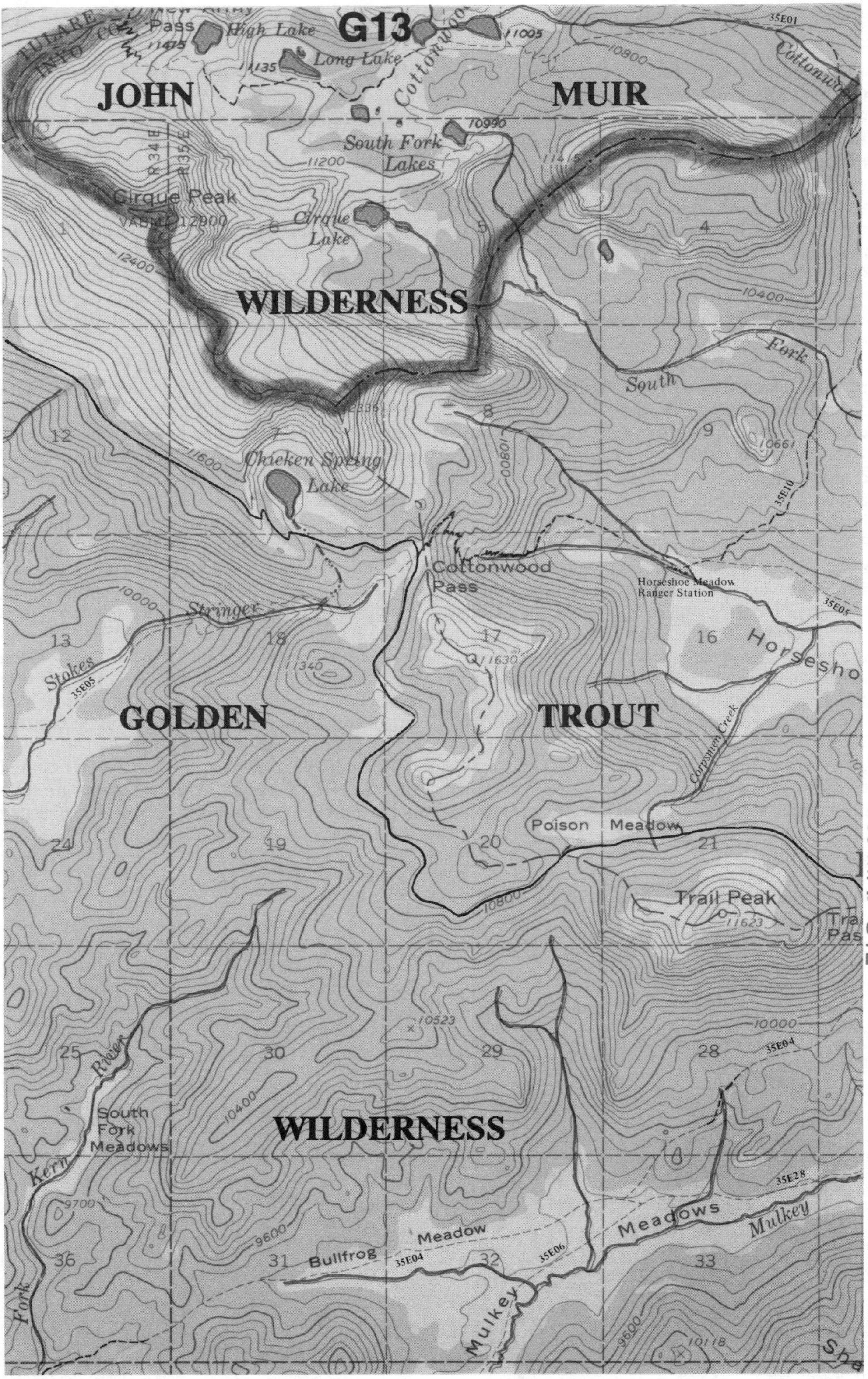

see MAP G14

see MAP G12

backside along this descent, that's understandable. Our path passes through a wooden-gated fence, levels out, curves north and then passes a westbound use trail to Whitney Creek. The PCT proceeds north to ford Whitney Creek near a cluster of large campsites, and immediately meets a lateral (10,329-3.5) to Mt. Whitney. If you didn't plan to climb up Mount Whitney, proceed along the winding path north-northwest to a signed junction (10,870-0.8) with the John Muir Trail, the start of Section H.

$$* \qquad * \qquad * \qquad *$$

But if you're heady with the thought of climbing this famous mountain, turn northeast to ramble along the lateral, favored on the way with painterly views of Mount Whitney. On this path you skirt Crabtree Meadow, ascend a little canyon beside Whitney Creek, cross the creek, and then quickly end the lateral at a junction with the John Muir Trail (10,640-1.1), to which you'll return later. Now, continue northeast on the John Muir Trail.

Shortly, at a bulletin board, you meet a lateral (10,675-0.1) to the Crabtree Ranger Station and numerous campsites. You are reminded, among other things, that a ranger station is not a trash receptacle, but that emergency services are available during summer months.

With knowledge that the summit can be bitterly cold, and assessing the time and weather so as not to be caught on the open slopes in an afternoon lightning storm, we proceed northeast, passing north of a seasonal lake. Our path soon runs over a minor north-south ridge, probably a recessional moraine. Large campsites abound on both sides of the stream, both on the moraine and north of it.

After we boulder-hop Whitney Creek, the path climbs moderately and arcs away through forest but returns to the creek before reaching Timberline Lake. Once overused as a base camp for climbing Whitney, these shores are now closed to all camping and stock grazing. Above the lake our trail passes the last of the forest on a moderate grade away from Whitney Creek up a draw. Glacial polish is much in evidence on the granite here. After topping a broad, rounded ridge, the path winds around boulders down to the inlet of Guitar Lake. Our path undulates east-southeast not far from the shore, then climbs on a rerouted path to another meadowy lake. Here, amid frugal

displays of fragile alpine wildflowers, we get water at this last reliable source. Enjoying a brief level stretch beside the lake, we catch our breath preparing for the high-altitude climb ahead and then wind up a rocky grade to a spur ridge. After following ducks through a rocky-sandy stretch, we climb on steps beautifully constructed and carefully carpeted with sand.

The Hitchcock Lakes come into view; they were hidden until now in a deep cirque at the foot of 13,184' Mt. Hitchcock. The appearance of many other glacier-carved peaks punctuates our climbing efforts. Nine switchbacks, linked by long, straight stretches of trail, plus two short switchbacks, lead us to a signed junction (13,560-5.1) with the eastbound Mount Whitney trail, which in 8.7 miles meets a road at Whitney Portal.

We turn north at the junction, laboring breathlessly on a long traverse beside a row of gendarmes. In between gendarmes, we can look through crestline notches down to indigo lakes nestled in polished cirques straight down, far below, and yet well above the pale Owens Valley. More reassuring to us are the blue clusters of sky pilot that grow in nooks along the path, evoking admiration for the hardy flowers that flourish in such harsh elements. Our path makes a final few switchbacks up Mount Whitney's back, then approaches a stone cabin with its register and at last attains the summit of Mount Whitney (14,494-1.8-8.1).

Strictly enforced quotas on the number of hikers allowed to leave Whitney Portal per day have reduced the population problem up here, but it's still possible to find a crowd when you arrive, and a line at the chemical toilet. Encompassing views from the summit include the dim, pointed Owens Peak and rounded Mount Jenkins tandem silhouette in the southeast, showing the distance you have hiked since Walker Pass.

From the summit, you backtrack just beyond the Crabtree Ranger Station to a ford of Whitney Creek (10,640-6.9) at the trail junction mentioned earlier. Then you progress across a sandy flat from lodgepole pines to foxtail pines. A few zigzags and a long westward traverse with lingering views of Whitney lead to a signed junction (10,870-0.9-15.9) where you turn north on the Pacific Crest Trail, which joins the John Muir Trail to begin Section H.

G15, H1

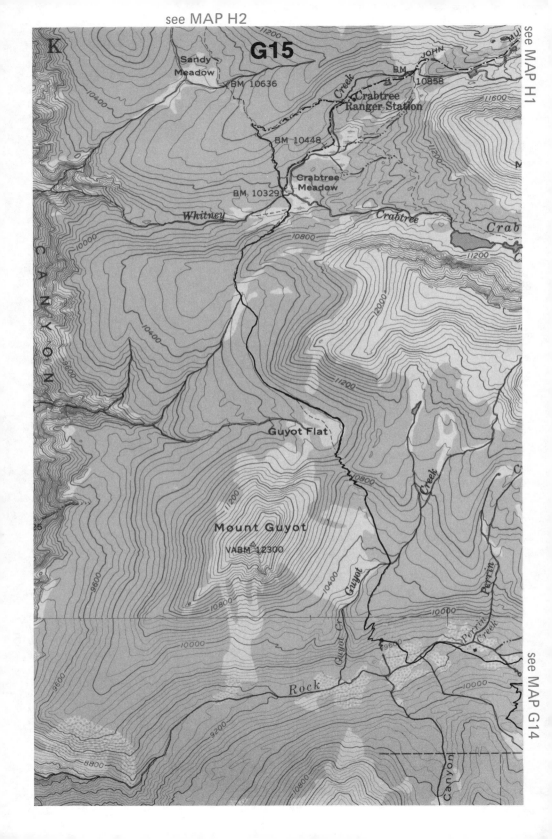

see MAP G14

K

G15

Sandy
Meadow

BM 10636

JOHN

BM
10858

Crabtree
Ranger Station

Creek

BM 10448

Crabtree
Meadow

BM 10329

Crabtree

Crab

Whitney

10800

11200

10000

CANYON

10400

12000

9600

11200

Guyot Flat

10800

Creek

11200

Mount Guyot

VABM 12300

Guyot

10400

Perrin

9600

10800

Guyot Cr

10000

Perrin
Creek

10000

Rock

10000

9200

Canyon

9600

8800

10800

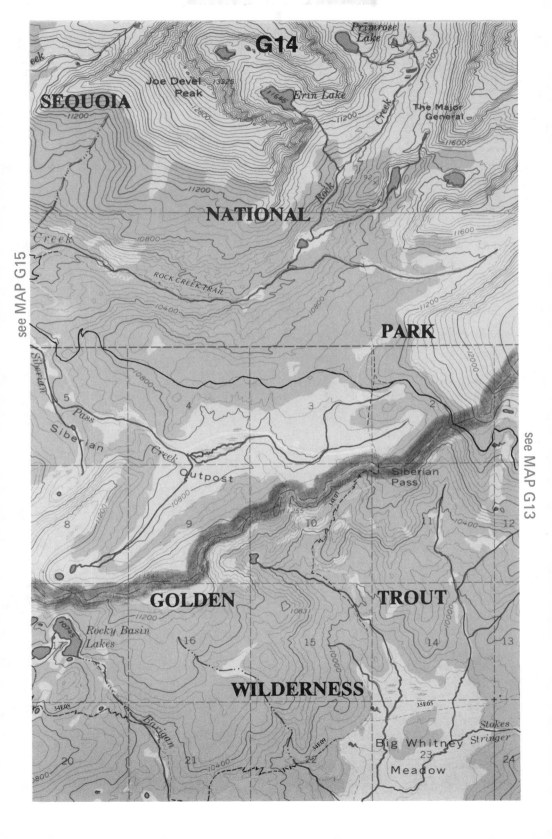

Banner Peak towers over Thousand Island Lake

Section H: Mt. Whitney to Tuolumne Meadows

Introduction: The Pacific Crest trail from the Mt. Whitney trail junction to Tuolumne Meadows passes through what many backpackers agree is the finest mountain scenery in the United States. Some hikers may give first prize to some other place, but none will deny the great attractiveness of the High Sierra.

This is a land of 13,000' and 14,000' peaks, of soaring granite cliffs, of lakes literally by the thousands, of canyons 5000' deep. It is a land where man's trails touch only a tiny portion of the total area, so that by leaving the trail you can find utter solitude. It is land uncrossed by road for 150 airline miles from just north of Walker Pass to Tuolumne Meadows. And perhaps best of all, it is a land blessed with the mildest, sunniest climate of any major mountain range in the world. Though rain does fall in the summer—and much snow in the winter—the rain seldom lasts more than an hour or two, and the sun is out and shining most of the hours that it is above the horizon.

Given these attractions, you might expect that quite a few people would want to enjoy them. And it is true that some hikers joke about traffic signs being needed on the John Muir trail—which the PCT follows for most of this section. But the land is so vast that if you do want to camp by yourself, you can. While following the trail in the summer, you can't avoid passing quite a few people, but you can stop to talk or not, as you choose.

Declination: 14+°E

Mileages:

	South to North	Distance between Points	North to South
John Muir trail above Crabtree Meadows	0.0		177.2
		3.3	
Wallace Creek	3.3		173.9
		5.3	
Lake South America trail	8.6		168.6
		4.3	
Forester Pass	12.9		164.3
		8.0	
Bubbs Creek trail	20.9		156.3
		2.2	
Kearsarge Pass trail	23.1		154.1
		2.3	
Glen Pass	25.4		151.8
		8.3	
Woods Creek	33.7		143.5
		7.1	
Pinchot Pass	40.8		136.4
		4.3	
South Fork Kings River	45.1		132.1
		5.2	
Mather Pass	50.3		126.9
		10.2	
Middle Fork Kings River	60.5		116.7
		3.3	
Bishop Pass trail	63.8		113.4

Muir Pass	70.8	7.0	106.4
Evolution Lake Inlet	75.4	4.6	101.8
Evolution Creek in Evolution Meadow	82.5	7.1	94.7
Piute Pass trail	87.6	5.1	89.6
Florence Lake trail	89.4	1.8	87.8
Selden Pass	97.0	7.6	80.2
Mono Creek	111.7	14.7	65.5
Silver Pass	118.7	7.0	58.5
Tully Hole	123.5	4.8	53.7
Duck Lake outlet	129.8	6.3	47.4
Reds Meadow	141.3	11.5	35.9
Agnew Meadows Trailhead	149.1	7.8	28.1
Thousand Island Lake outlet	156.9	7.8	20.3
Rush Creek Forks	160.1	3.2	17.1
Donohue Pass	163.5	3.4	13.7
Lyell Base Camp	167.5	4.0	9.7
Highway 120 in Tuolumne Meadows	177.2	9.7	0.0

Supplies: This section does not allow easy resupply. To reach any kind of civilization you must—except at Reds Meadow—walk at least 18 miles round trip. Even then, if you have major needs, you will have to hitchhike many miles farther. At the beginning of this section, you can take the Mt. Whitney trail 15½ miles to Whitney Portal, where there is a very small store, or hitchhike from the portal 13 miles to Lone Pine, which has almost everything you might want. Twenty-one miles into Section H, at the Bubbs Creek trail, you can hike 14 miles west to Cedar Grove, with another very small store and a modest cafe plus post office. To hitchhike from there to Fresno would be a major project. About 2 miles farther, at the Kearsarge Pass trail, you can hike 9 miles east to Onion Valley, with yet another store, or hitchhike from there 15 miles out of the mountains to Independence, which has just one store, albeit a rather large one for such a small town. About 41 miles farther, at the Bishop Pass trail, you can hike northeast 12 miles to South Lake, which has nothing, and hitchhike 19 miles to Bishop, which has everything. Then, 24 miles farther, at the Piute Pass trail, you can hike northeast 18 miles to North Lake, which has nothing, and hitchhike 18 miles to Bishop. About 2 miles farther, you can hike north 11 miles along the Florence Lake Trail to the roadend, where there is a tiny store. Then 22 miles farther, from where you bridge Mono Creek, you can walk 6 miles west, mostly beside Lake Edison, to Vermilion Resort, again with a small store plus meals, showers, and a package-holding service. (Write ahead to confirm this service; the address is in Chapter 2, under "Post Offices Along or Near the Route." Enclose an SASE.) Seven miles west by road from there is Mono Hot Springs, with meals, supplies and a post office.

About 29 miles farther, you are at Reds Meadow, with a somewhat-more-than-minimal store and a cafe. Just down the paved road is Reds Meadow Campground, which has a nearby, free public bathhouse fed by a hot spring. If you need more than a few supplies, take a shuttle bus out of Reds Meadow to the Mammoth ski area. During the summer, the buses operate from about 8 a.m. to 6 p.m., and one leaves about every 15 minutes. In 1988 the trip out to the ski area was free, while the ride back in was $3.50. You can catch these buses at Reds Meadow Resort and at Rainbow Falls trailhead, Reds

Meadow Campground, Devils Postpile visitor center, the entrance to Upper Soda Springs Campground and the start of the Agnew Meadows road. All these stops are near the PCT route. Note that the shuttle service goes only to the Mammoth Ski Area, not to downtown Mammoth Lakes, which is reached by a 5-mile walk or hitchhike from the ski area.

Finally, in the Tuolumne Meadows area, at the end of this section, you can get hot meals and showers at Tuolumne Meadows Lodge, a mile east of the principal meadow, or you can stop at a good store, with a cafe and post office, just southwest of the entrance to Tuolumne Meadows Campground.

Special Problems: *Snow.* For hikers trying to do the whole PCT in one year, the biggest problem in the High Sierra is snow. If you leave Mexico in early April, you will reach the Sierra before the end of May. In most years there will be a lot of snow in the High Sierra in May and June. A few people use snowshoes or skis to travel over the snow, but as the sun cups get deeper, these devices become useless. What you will need for the snowy sections is crampons and an ice ax, and the knowledge of how to use them. You need a tent. You need plenty of warm clothing, including mitts. And you need a basic understanding of avalanches—where they tend to occur, why they tend to occur, what to do if caught in one. *The ABCs of Avalanche Safety,* published by The Mountaineers, is a good primer. Finally, where the trail is hidden by snow, you need some skills with map and compass to follow the route.

Cold. Even in midsummer it may freeze on any given night, so you need appropriate warmth.

Fords. Before you finish the John Muir trail, the snowmelt will have become heavy. That means problems fording streams. You need a rope, and the skill to use it safely in fording. You need patience, sometimes, to wait for morning, when the stream will be much lower.

Bears. In most of this section and adjacent lands, you are in bear territory. The introduction to Section G tells how to save your food from these hungry animals.

Lack of signs. Some hikers are glad to see signs disappear. Others are glad to have signs confirm their notion of where they are. In Sequoia and Kings Canyon National Parks virtually all place signs (for example, "Lake Marjorie") have been removed, and there appears to be a trend toward removing or at least not replacing signs at trail junctions too.

To help you cope with some of the difficulties mentioned above, a number of summer rangers are stationed along or near the trail in Sequoia and Kings Canyon National Parks from about July 4th to Labor Day. The trail description below tells where they are. Two points deserve special mention. First, if you go to a summer ranger station to report a friend in trouble and find the ranger out, please realize he might be gone for several days, and so leave a note for him and walk out for help yourself. Second, remember that the ranger has to buy his own food and camping gear, so he, not the government, is the loser if it is taken.

Permits: If you are northbound, you can get a permit for this entire section by writing to Sequoia and Kings Canyon National Parks. If you are southbound, write Yosemite National Park. If you are southbound (or northbound) and are starting in the Mammoth Lakes-Devils Postpile area, write Mammoth Ranger District. (Refer to page 18 for addresses.)

In this trail section you will be on the Muir trail almost all the way to Tuolumne Meadows, 178 miles ahead. Northbound on the combined PCT/John Muir trail, you skirt what the map calls Sandy Meadow and ascend to a high saddle (10,964-1.7). Beyond it the trail winds among the huge boulders of a glacial moraine on the west shoulder of Mt. Young and brings you to excellent viewpoints for scanning the main peaks of the Kings-Kern Divide and of the Sierra crest from Mt. Barnard (13,990') north to Junction Peak (13,888'). Soon you descend moderately, making several easy fords, and then switchback down to Wallace Creek and a junction (10,890-1.6) where the High Sierra trail goes west toward a roadend near Giant Forest and a lateral trail goes east to Wallace Lake. The Wallace Creek ford, just north of the popular campsites, is difficult in early season.

Now your sandy trail climbs up to a forested flat, crosses it, and reaches the good campsite at the ford of Wright Creek (10,790-1.1), also difficult in early season. You then trace a bouldery path across the ground moraines left by the Wright Creek glacier and rise in several stages to Bighorn Plateau. Views from here are indeed panoramic. An unnamed, grass-fringed lake atop the gravelly, lupine-streaked plateau makes for great morning photographs westward over it. Now the PCT descends the talus-clad west slope of Tawny Point past many extraordinarily dramatic foxtail pines. At an

unnamed lake beside the trail there are fair campsites and warmish swimming, but hardly any wood. At the foot of this rocky slope a trail departs southwest for the Kern River, and 200 yards past the junction you come to the unsigned Shepherd Pass trail (10,930-3.5) going northeast. Immediately beyond is a formidable ford of Tyndall Creek. On the west side of the creek are many highly used campsites—a good place not to camp.

From these gathering places your trail makes a short climb to the junction with the Lake South America trail (11,160-0.7), passes some fair campsites, and rises above timberline. As you tackle the ascent to the highest point on the PCT, you wind among the barren basins of high, rockbound—but fishy—lakes to the foot of a great granite wall, then labor up numerous switchbacks, some of which are literally cut into the rock wall, to Forester Pass (13,180-4.3), on the border between Sequoia and Kings Canyon National Parks. Wearing your wind garment, you will enjoy the well-earned, sweeping views from this pass before you start the (net) descent of 9000 feet to Canada. Down the switchbacks you go, unless they are buried under snow, and then stroll high above the west shore of Lake 12248. The trail soon doubles back to ford splashing Bubbs Creek just below that lake, then fords it twice more within a mile. Soon you reach timber, ford Center Basin creek (high in early season), pass the Center Basin trail (10,500-4.5) and then ford more tribu-

H2, H3

The Great Western Divide rises beyond Bighorn Plateau

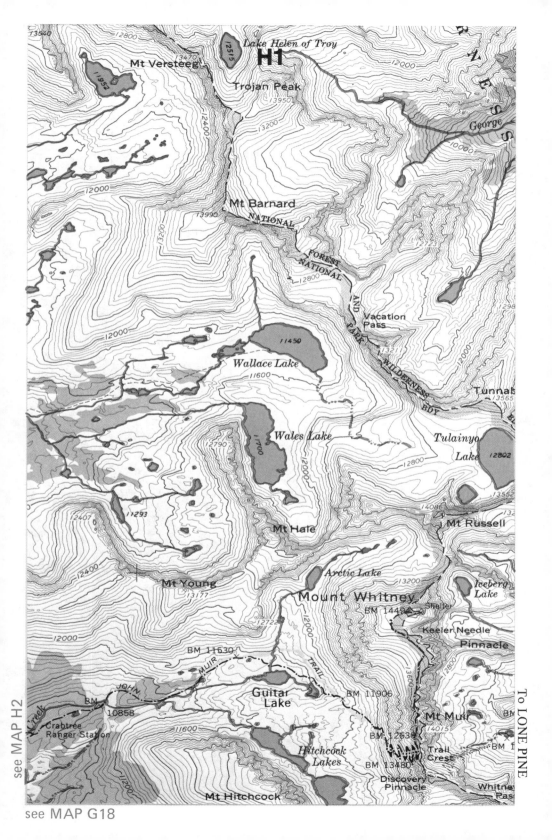

see MAP H2

see MAP G18

To LONE PINE

H1

Lake Helen of Troy

Mt Versteeg

11952

13540

12800

12515

Trojan Peak
13950

13470

12400

13200

George

10000

12000

Mt Barnard
13990

NATIONAL

12000

3200

FOREST

NATIONAL

12723

12800

Vacation
Pass

1298

AND

PARK

1321

11450

Wallace Lake
11600

WILDERNESS

BDY

Tunnab
13565

12790

Wales Lake
11700

12000

12800

Tulainyo
Lake
12802

13552

12407

11293

14086

132

Mt Hale

Mt Russell

12400

Arctic Lake
13200

Iceberg
Lake

Mt Young
13177

Mount Whitney
BM 14494

Shelter

Keeler Needle

Pinnacle

12722

12000

BM 11630

12800

MUIR

TRAIL

13600

BM 11906

Guitar
Lake

Mt Muir
14015

JOHN

BM

10858

Creek

Crabtree
Ranger Station

11600

BM 12638

Hitchcock
Lakes

BM 13480

Trail
Crest

BM f

12000

Discovery
Pinnacle

Whitney
Pass

Mt Hitchcock

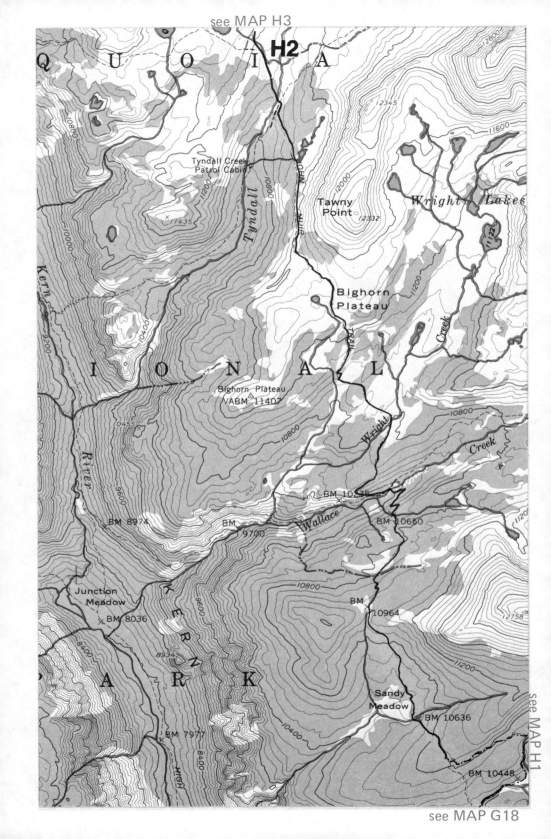

Q U O I A

12800

12345

11600

10800

Tyndall Creek
Patrol Cabin

Tawny
Point
12332

Wright Lakes

11200

10800

Tyndall

12000

x 11435

10000

Bighorn
Plateau

Creek

11200

Kern

10400

I O N A L

Bighorn Plateau
△VABM 11407

Wright

10800

10455

River

9600

Creek

11200

BM 10.?8
x

Wallace

BM 10650

BM 8974

BM
9700

10800

12758

Junction
Meadow

K E R N

BM
x 10964

x BM 8036

9600

8934

A R K

11200

Sandy
Meadow

10400

BM 10636

8400

BM 7977
x

8400

HIGH

BM 10448

see MAP H1

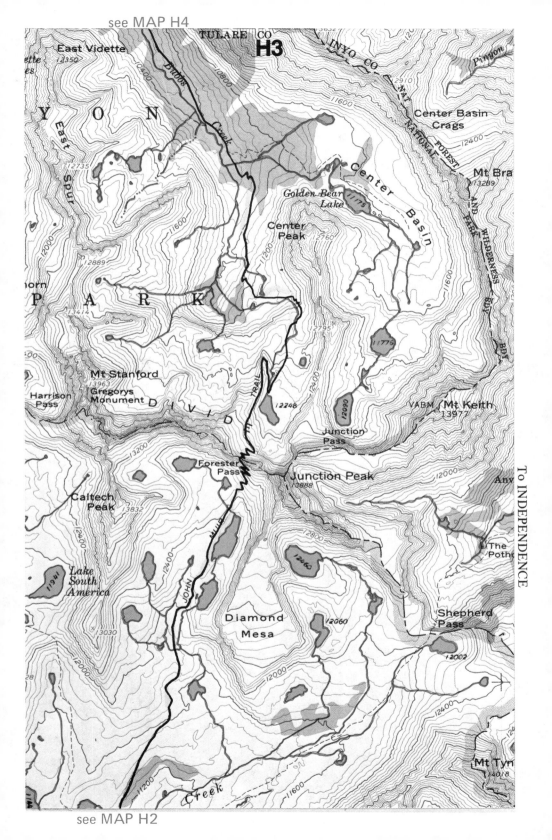

see MAP H4

TULARE CO

INYO CO

H3

East Vidette
12350

YON

East Spur
12735

12889

PARK

horn

13414

DIVID

Mt Stanford
13963
Gregorys
Monument

Harrison
Pass

Caltech
Peak
13832

Lake
South
America
11941

× *13030*

JOHN MUIR TRAIL

Forester
Pass

Diamond
Mesa

Golden Bear
Lake

Center
Peak
12760

Center Basin
Crags

Mt Bra
13289

Center Basin

INYO NATIONAL FOREST AND KINGS CANYON NATIONAL PARK WILDERNESS BDY

12795

11776

12090

12248

Junction
Pass

VABM Mt Keith
13977

Junction Peak
13888

Any

The
Poth

Shepherd
Pass

12460

12060

12002

Mt Tyn
140/8

Creek

To INDEPENDENCE

see MAP H2

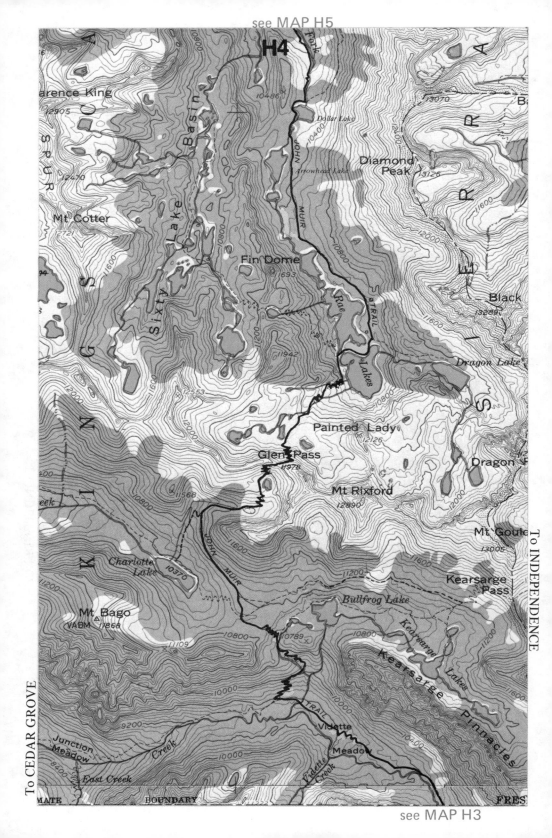

H4

To CEDAR GROVE

To INDEPENDENCE

taries of Bubbs Creek. Many good campsites are located near some of these fords and along the main creek, but wood is scarce, as it is almost everywhere along the Muir trail.

Continuing down the east side of dashing Bubbs Creek, you reach Vidette Meadow (9600-2.8), long a favorite camping spot in these headwaters of South Fork Kings River. High use has made the place less attractive, but its intrinsic beauty has not been lost, and the mighty Kearsarge Pinnacles to the northeast have lost only a few inches of height since Sierra Club founders like Joseph Le Conte camped here at the turn of the century. Camping is limited to one night in one place from here to Woods Creek. A summer ranger may be in Vidette Meadow east of the trail to assist traffic flow. Beyond the meadow, a trail goes west to Cedar Grove and the PCT turns north (9550-0.7) to fiercely attack the wall of Bubbs Creek canyon. You pause for breath at the Bullfrog Lake junction (10,530-1.5) and then finish off the tough climb at a broad, sandy saddle that contains the junction of the Charlotte Lake and Kearsarge Pass trails (10,710-0.7). There is a summer ranger on the east

H3, H4

Painted Lady above Rae Lake

shore of Charlotte Lake. In ¼ mile you pass a shortcut (for southbound hikers) to the Kearsarge Pass trail, and then you traverse high above emerald Charlotte Lake. As the route veers eastward, it passes another trail to Charlotte Lake, then climbs past a talus-choked pothole and ascends gently to the foot of the wall that is notched by Glen Pass. It is hard to see where a trail could go up that precipitous blank wall, but one does, and after very steep switchbacks you are suddenly at Glen Pass (11,978-2.3). The view north presents a barren, rocky, brown world with precious little green of tree or meadow visible. Yet you know by now that not far down the trail ahead there will be plenty of willows, sedges, wildflowers and, eventually, groves of whitebark, lodgepole and foxtail pines. To be sure you get there, take special care on your descent from Glen Pass as you switchback down to a small lake basin, ford the lakes' outlet and switchback down again.

When you are about 400 vertical feet above Rae Lakes, you will see why Dragon Peak (12,995'), in the southeast, has that name. Where the 60 Lakes trail turns off to the west (10,550-2.0) your route turns east, then crosses the isthmus between two of the Rae Lakes and skirts the east shore of the middle lake, passing the Dragon Lake trail and a summer ranger station. As of this writing, wood fires are not allowed between Glen Pass and the Baxter Pass trail. Beyond Rae Lakes your gently descending trail passes above an unnamed lake and drops to the northeast corner of aptly name Arrowhead Lake. Then it fords gurgling South Fork Woods Creek on boulders and reaches scenic, heavily used Dollar Lake. The unsigned Baxter Pass trail heads northeast from below the outlet of this lake (10,230-2.6). The lower slopes just east of Dollar Lake are composed of Paleozoic sediments that were later metamorphosed to biotite schist. Granitic rock separates these metasediments from a higher, north-south band of Triassic-Jurassic lava flows that have been changed into metavolcanic rocks. The metamorphism of all these rock types probably occurred during the Cretaceous period, when bodies of molten granite rising up into them deformed and altered them. As we progress north to Yosemite, we'll see many more examples of similar metamorphosed rocks.

From the Baxter Pass trail junction you descend gently down open, lightly forested slopes, crossing several good-sized though

H4, H5

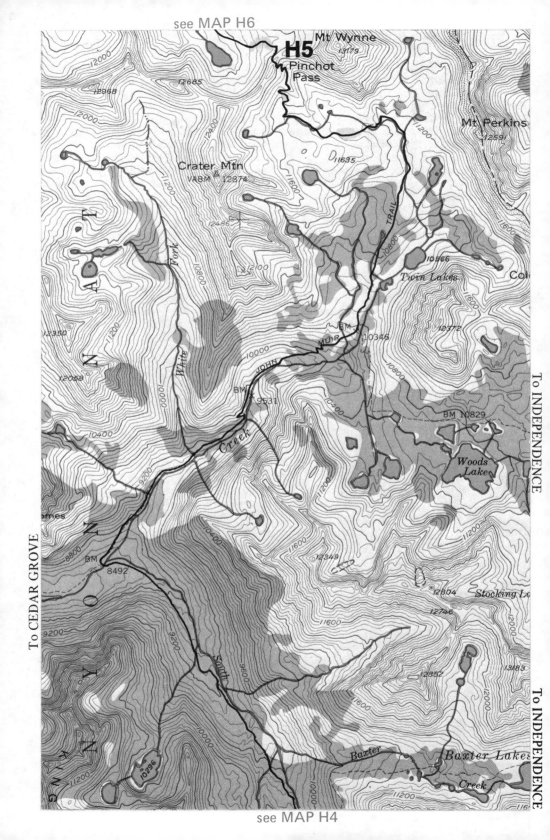

H5

Pinchot
Pass

Mt Wynne
13179

Mt Perkins
12591

12968

12685

12000

11635

Crater Mtn
VABM Δ 12874

12486

12400

12100

Fork

White

12350

12058

10800

10000

10400

9200

Creek

JOHN

MUIR

BM
10346

BM
9531

Twin Lakes

10566

12372

TRAIL

10800

10800

10400

BM 10829

Woods
Lake

11200

To INDEPENDENCE

To INDEPENDENCE

8800
BM
8492

To CEDAR GROVE

9200

9300

South

9600

10000

10296

11200

11600

12349

12804

Stocking Lo

12746

11600

12952

13185

12000

Baxter

Baxter Lakes

Creek

11200

10000

11600

unnamed streams, including the bridged creek from Lake 10296. The reward for all this descent is a chance to start climbing again at Woods Creek (8492-3.7), crossed on a wood bridge, where the campsites are good but much used. Immediately beyond the bridge a trail to Cedar Grove goes south down the creek. As you perspire north from the crossing up the valley of Woods Creek, there is no drinking-water problem, what with the main stream near at hand and many tributaries, some of good size, to jump or boulder-hop. After the junction of the Sawmill Pass trail (10,370-3.4), the grade abates and the traveler reaches the alpine vale where this branch of the Kings River has

its headwaters, bounded by glorious peaks on 3½ sides. With one last, long spurt you finally top Pinchot Pass (12,130-3.7), one of those "passes" that are regrettably not at the low point of the divide.

From this pass the PCT swoops down into the lake-laden valley below, runs along the east shore of at-timberline Lake Marjorie, touches its outlet (11,160-1.7), and then passes 4 lakelets, fording several small streams along the way. A summer ranger station is sometimes located beyond the fourth lakelet, just south of the Bench Lake trail junction. Bench Lake, on a true bench high above South Fork Kings River's canyon, has good campsites that

H5, H6

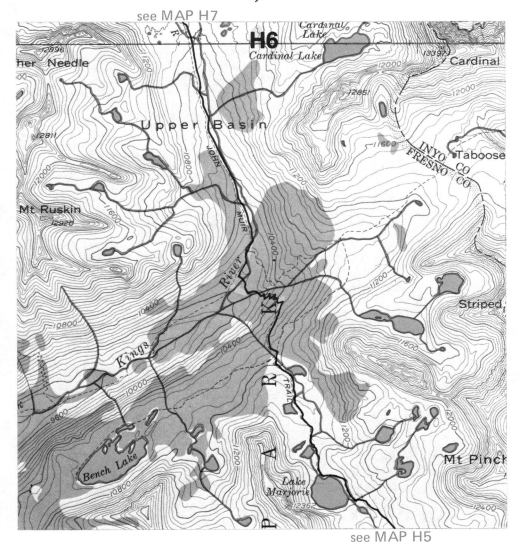

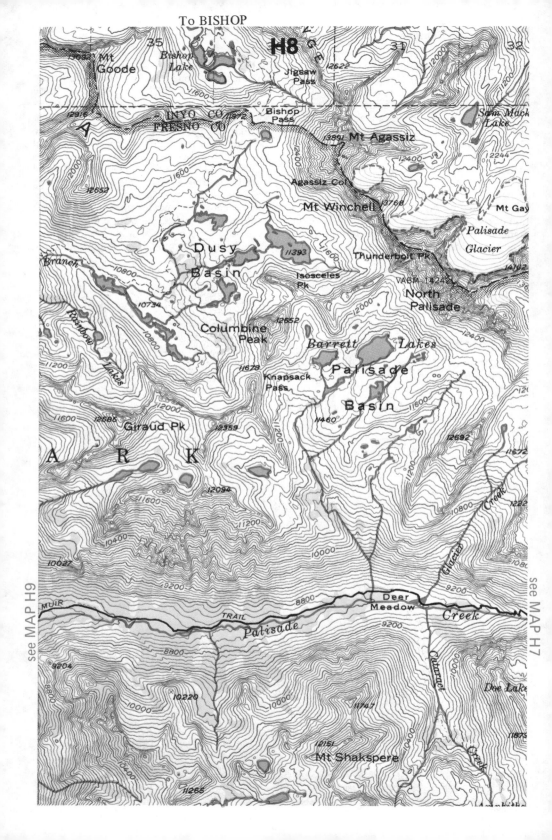

H8

Mt
Goode

Bishop
Lake

Jigsaw
Pass

INYO CO.
FRESNO CO.

Bishop
Pass

Sam Mack
Lake

Mt Agassiz

Agassiz Col

Mt Winchell

Mt Gay

Palisade
Glacier

Dusy

Basin

Isosceles
Pk

Thunderbolt Pk

VABM 14242

North
Palisade

Rainbow
Lakes

Branch

Columbine
Peak

Barrett   Lakes

Knapsack
Pass

Palisade

Basin

Giraud Pk

A   R   K

MUIR

TRAIL

Palisade

Deer
Meadow

Creek

Glacier

Cataract

Creek

Doe Lake

Mt Shakspere

see MAP H9

see MAP H7

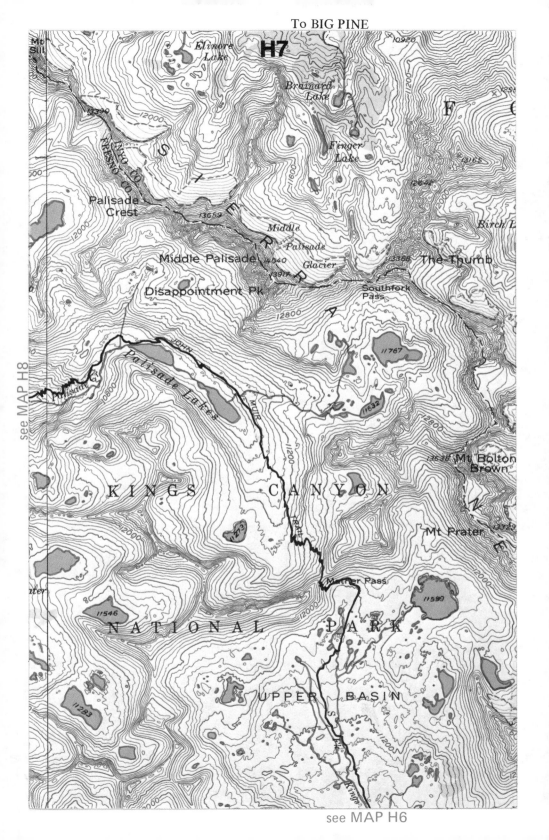

H7

Mt
Sill

Elinore
Lake

Brainard
Lake

Finger
Lake

F

13390

12000

S

13155

2842

Fresno Co.

Inyo Co.

I

Palisade
Crest

13659

E

Birch L

Middle

R

Middle Palisade

Palisade

14040

Glacier

3359

The Thumb

13517

R

Disappointment Pk

Southfork
Pass

12800

A

11767

see MAP H8

JOHN

11767

Palisade Lakes

10800

7632

12800

MUIR

11200

13638 Mt Bolton
Brown

K I N G S   C A N Y O N

TRAIL

13329

Mt Prater

11283

Mather Pass

11599

N A T I O N A L   P A R K

11546

12000

U P P E R   B A S I N

11283

11200

see MAP H6

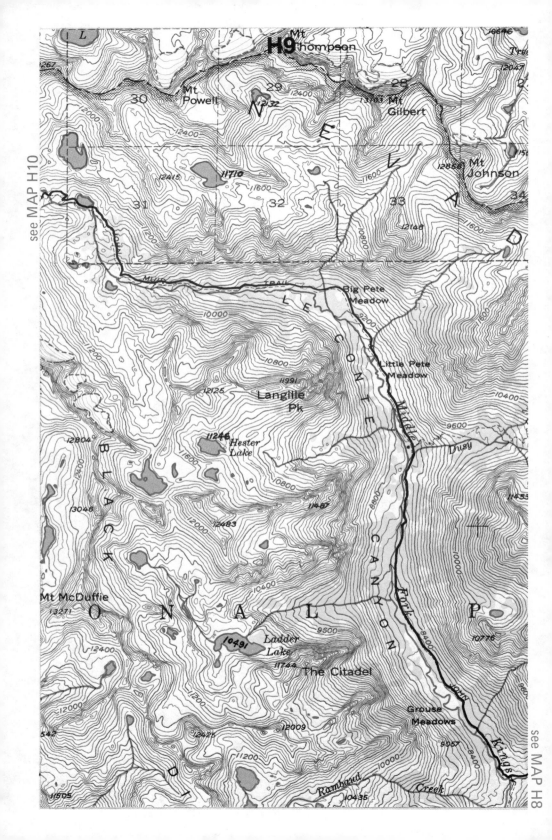

Mt Thompson

9646

12047

30
Mt Powell

29
12400

28
13103 Mt Gilbert

2

N 32

L

E

12000

12400

12415

11710

1600

11600

12858 Mt Johnson

15

31

32

10800

33
12148

11600

34

L

A

D

see MAP H10

Mud

TRAIL

Big Pete Meadow

9200

10000

L

E

C

O

N

T

E

Little Pete Meadow

10400

10800

9600

10800

11991

12125

Langille Pk

Middle

Dusy

11453

12804

11246
Hester Lake

11600

9600

13046

10800

11487

8500

8600

C

A

N

Y

O

N

10000

Mt McDuffie
13271

12000

12483

10400

Fork

P

O

N

A

L

9500

10776

12400

10491
Ladder Lake

11744
The Citadel

8400

JOHN

11505

12000

12425

12009

1200

Grouse Meadows

9957

8400

96

Kings

11200

10000

Rambaud

Creek

10435

Mt. Clarence King, from Woods Creek headwaters

are off the beaten track. Just beyond this junction we ford the outlet of Lake Marjorie and in 200 yards meet the Taboose Pass trail (10,750-1.3) at the upper edge of a lodgepole forest. Another downhill segment of forested switchbacks brings you to the South Fork, which is best crossed a few yards upstream from the trail. On the far bank the South Fork trail (10,050-1.3) leads downstream and you turn northeast upstream, passing another trail to Taboose Pass in ⅓ mile. Climbing steadily, you cross several unnamed tributaries that can slow you down at the height of the melt, and then ford the infant South Fork (10,840-2.2) near some good campsites. East of the trail, on the Sierra crest, looming Cardinal Mountain (13,397′) is named for red but is in fact half white and half dark, in a strange mixture of metamorphosed Paleozoic rocks. West of this peak you cross grassy flats and hop over numerous branches of the headwaters of South Fork Kings River. Every camper can have his own lake and lakelet in this high basin—though the campsites are austere.

This ascent finally steepens and zigzags up to rockbound Mather Pass (12,100-3.0), named for Stephen Mather, first head of the National Park Service. The view ahead is dominated by the 14,000′ peaks of the Palisades group, knifing sharply into the sky. Your trail now makes a knee-shocking descent to the poor campsites ¼ mile southeast of long, blue upper Palisade Lake. The route then contours above the lakes until it drops to the north shore of the lower lake (10,600-3.5), with its poor-to-fair campsites. Knees rested, you descend again, down the "Golden Staircase," built on the cliffs of the gorge of Palisade Creek. This section was the last part of the Muir trail to be constructed, and it is easy to see why. In ¾ mile from the bottom of the "staircase" you cross multibranched Glacier Creek and immediately arrive at Deer Meadow (8860-3.0), which is more lodgepole forest than meadow, but pleasant enough anyway. Beyond the campsites here, the downhill grade continues, less steeply, across the stream draining Palisade Basin and several smaller streams to reach Middle Fork Kings River (8020-3.7), where a trail takes off downstream for Simpson Meadow. Turning north, you ascend past a series of falls and chutes along the river to Grouse Meadows, a serene expanse of grassland with good campsites in the forest along the east side. Up the canyon from these meadows, you can see repeated evidence of great avalanches that crashed down the immense canyon walls and wiped out stands of trees. The trail climbs gently to turbulent Dusy Branch, crossed on a steel bridge, and immediately encounters the

H6, H7, H8, H9

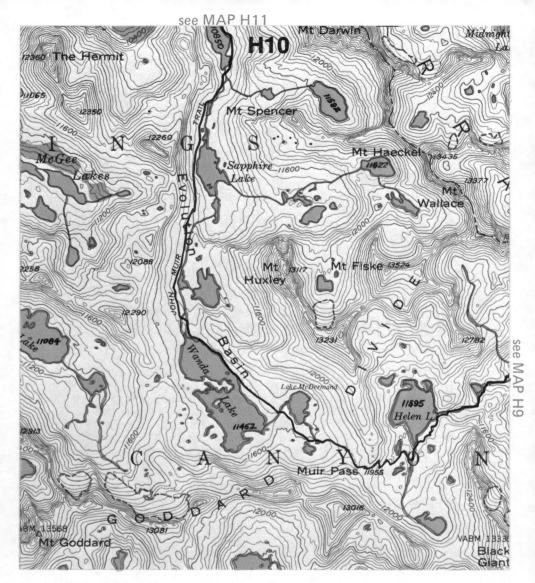

Bishop Pass trail (8710-3.3) to South Lake. Near this junction is a ranger station manned in summer.

Our route up-canyon from this junction ascends between highly polished granite walls past lavish displays of a great variety of wildflowers. The trail passes through sagebrushy Little Pete and Big Pete meadows, and swings west to assault the Goddard Divide and search out its breach, Muir Pass. Up and up the rocky trail winds, passing the last tree long before you reach desolate Helen Lake (11,595-5.7)—named, along with Wanda Lake to the west, for John Muir's daughters. This east side of the

pass is under snow throughout the summer in some years. Finally, after 6 fords of the diminishing stream, you haul up at Muir Pass (11,955-1.3), where a stone hut honoring Muir would shelter you in a storm. The views from here of the solitary peaks and the lonely lake basins are painted in the many hues of the mostly Jurassic-age metamorphic rocks that make up the Goddard Divide.

From the hut your trail descends gently past Lake McDermand and Wanda Lake, the latter having fair campsites near the outlet. (Wood fires are banned from Muir Pass to Evolution Lake.) You then ford Evolution Creek (11,400-

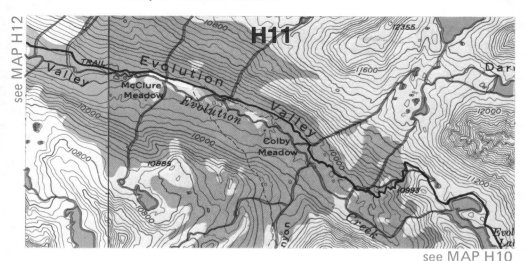

see MAP H12

see MAP H10

2.2) and descend into the Sapphire Lake basin, where there are fair campsites at the north end of Sapphire Lake. The land here is nearly as scoured as when the ice left it about 10,000 years ago, and the aspect all around is one of newborn nakedness. To the east is a series of

Grouse Meadows

tremendous peaks named for Charles Darwin and other major thinkers about evolution, and the next lake and the valley below it also bear the name "Evolution." The trail fords the stream at the inlet of this lake (10,850-2.4), skirts the lake, which has some campsites in clumps of stunted whitebark pines, and then drops sharply into Evolution Valley. The marvelous meadows here are the reason for re-routing the trail through the forest, so the fragile grassland can recover from overtromping by the feet of earlier backpackers and horsepackers. At McClure Meadow (9650-4.9) you will find a summer ranger midway down the meadow on the north side of the trail. After several tributary fords on boulders or logs, you wade Evolution Creek (9240-2.2)—difficult during high water—and soon descend steeply to a bridge across South Fork San Joaquin River (8470-1.3). Past numerous campsites you recross the river on another bridge and roll on down and out of Kings Canyon National Park at the steel-bridge crossing of Piute Creek. Here, where we enter John Muir Wilderness, the Piute Pass trail (8050-3.8) starts north toward North Lake.

The Pacific Crest trail continues down the South Fork canyon, away from the river, to a junction with the Florence Lake trail (7890-1.8). The Florence Lake roadend is 11 miles west down this trail; the Muir Trail Ranch is 1½ miles down it. (The latter is a possible package drop; inquire of the owner by writing Box 176, Lakeshore CA 93634.) Shortly before the ranch, and just west of signs that indicate the John Muir trail is 1½ miles away, both to the

H10, H11, H12, H13

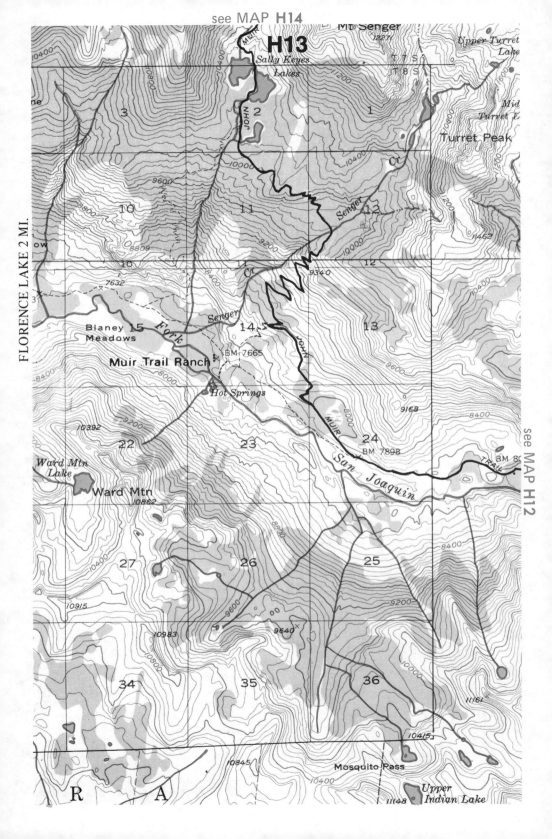

Mt Senger
12271

Upper Turret
Lake

Sally Keyes
Lakes

11200

7 1 S
7 8 S

Mid
Turret L

3

2

1

Turret Peak

JOHN

MUIR

10000

Ct

Senger

12

11462

10

11

9600

9200

10000

9340

8800

8809

8400

10400

Ct

10

11

12

7632

Senger

Fork

Blaney
Meadows

15

14

13

3

JOHN

9600

Muir Trail Ranch

BM 7665

8000

8400

Hot Springs

9163

MUIR

10392

9200

22

23

24
BM 7898

8400

San Joaquin

8000

TRAIL

BM 8

Ward Mtn
Lake

Ward Mtn
10862

27

26

25

10400

10915

9600

9200

10983

9640

8800

10000

8400

34

35

36

11161

10900

10415

R

A

10845

Mosquito Pass

10400

11148

Upper
Indian Lake

east and to the north, an unsigned trail goes south ⅓ mile down to riverside campsites. From the campsites on the south side of the river a faint trail goes 150 yards southwest to a natural hot spring—great for soaking off the grime—and a warmish small lake.

From the Florence Lake trail junction, the PCT-John Muir trail veers right to climb the canyon wall. It rises past a lateral trail down to the Florence Lake trail (8400-1.7), crosses little Senger Creek (9740-2.2), levels off, and below Sally Keyes Lakes meets another trail (10,150-1.6) down to the river valley below. Then your route passes the fair campsites at these lakes, crossing the short stream that joins the two. Leaving the forest below, the trail

H13

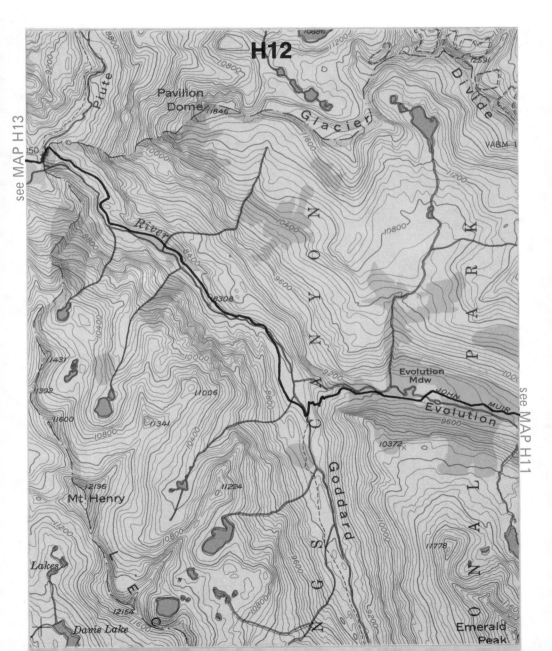

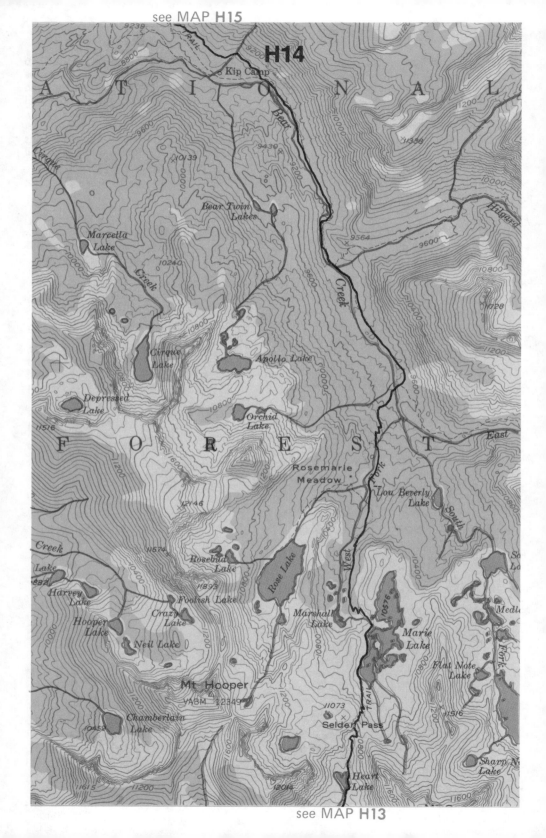

see MAP **H15**

H14

see MAP **H13**

skirts small Heart Lake and reaches barren Selden Pass (10,900-2.1). At this pass, many-islanded Marie Lake is the central feature of the view northward, and soon you boulder-hop its clear outlet (10,570-0.9), then descend moderately to the green expanses of Rosemarie Meadow (10,010-1.6). From this grassland a trail forks left, soon climbing southwest to Rose Lake, and about ¼ mile beyond another trail departs east for Lou Beverly Lake. Both these lakes provide good, secluded camping. About 200 yards past the last junction we bridge West Fork Bear Creek, and then we make a 1-mile descent in lodgepole forest to a boulder ford of Bear Creek (difficult in early season).

On the creek's far bank you meet a trail (9530-1.4) that goes up East Fork Bear Creek, but you turn down-canyon and descend gently to the log ford of refreshing Hilgard Creek. Immediately beyond, the Lake Italy trail (9300-1.2) climbs to the east, and our trail continues down through the mixed forest cover, always staying near rollicking Bear Creek. You pass campsites near the trail, but for more wood and more solitude it is better to find a place to camp across the creek. Below Hilgard Creek, where the old trail veered west, we begin (9040-2.0) a new trail segment that bypasses the former site of Kip Camp. This new segment gradually veers west as it follows the contour line, then turns north at the foot of a tough series of switchbacks. The south-facing hillside here gets plenty of sun, but it is surprisingly wet even in late season, so that you can pleasure your eyes with flowers in bloom and pleasure your throat with cold draughts. Your route then levels off, and at the crest of Bear Ridge passes

a trail (9980-1.6) that descends to Mono Hot Springs.

The north side of Bear Ridge is incised with 53 dusty switchbacks, which begin in a pure lodgepole forest but successively penetrate the realms of mountain hemlock, western white pine, red fir, Jeffrey pine, aspen, white fir and, finally, cottonwoods at Mono Creek (7750-4.6). Campsites lie several hundred yards west down the trail after you cross the bridge over the creek, and Vermilion Valley Resort, 6 miles away, is at the end of this trail. Beyond the bridge, the PCT turns right, soon crosses North Fork Mono Creek, and climbs to a junction with the Mono Pass trail (8270-1.6). Your steep trail levels briefly at lush Pocket Meadow (good campsites), crosses North Fork Mono Creek on rocks (8940-1.4) and then resumes climbing as the route turns up the west canyon wall. The first ford of Silver Pass Creek, on this wall, may be difficult in early season, and it is at the head of a fatally high cascade.

From here to Silver Pass the trail was extensively rerouted and overly constructed in 1980–81. Above a large meadow we reford the creek (9640-1.2) and then rise above treeline. The new trail bypasses Silver Pass Lake and then ascends past the actual pass (low point) to the sign SILVER PASS (10,900-2.8) at a glorious viewpoint. The descent northward passes Chief Lake and then the Goodale Pass trail (10,550-1.2), switchbacks northeast down to ford the small outlet of Squaw Lake, and then makes a long, hemlock-lined descent to beautiful Cascade Valley, where there are good campsites near the junction with the Cascade Valley trail (9130-2.5). Via the PCT, you are now 19.0

H14, H15, H16

Marie Lake, from Selden Pass

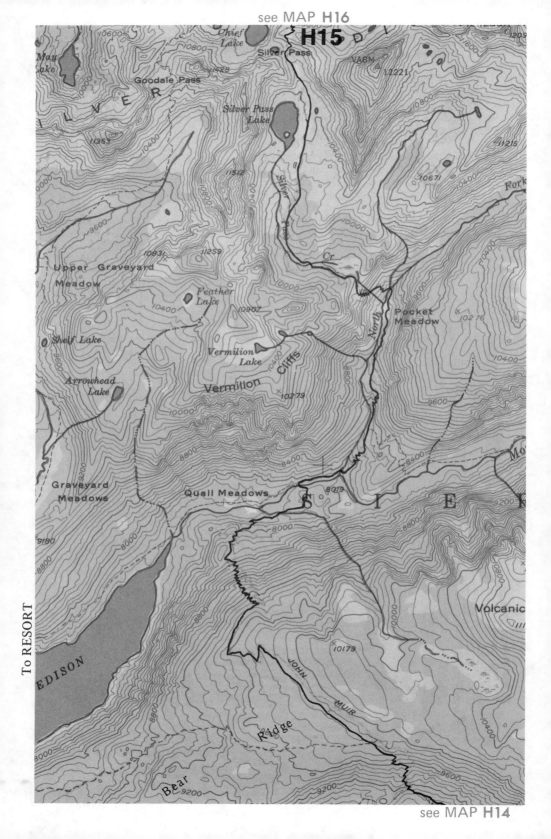

To RESORT

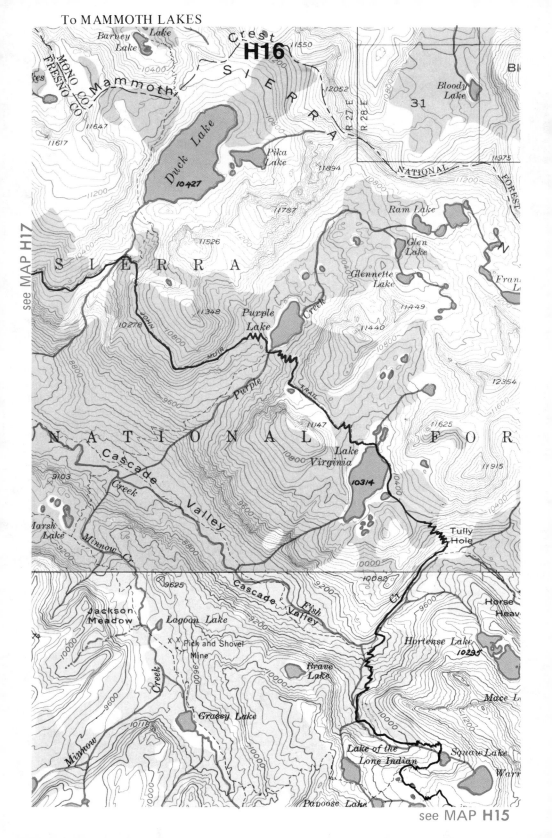

see MAP H17

see MAP H15

Silver Pass Lake

miles from the Rainbow Falls trailhead parking lot near Reds Meadow. Via the Cascade Valley-Fish Creek-Rainbow Falls trail, you are 19.4 miles from it. Some backpackers who aren't committed to following the PCT every step of the way prefer this lower, easier, mostly downhill, less-crowded route. Camping opportunities are greater and, if you're experiencing bad weather, you'll find this lower, well-forested route far more hospitable.

If you stay on PCT, turn right from the Cascade Valley trail junction and ascend northeast, soon crossing Fish Creek on a steel bridge. Staying above this good-sized creek, the route ascends gently to the campsites at Tully Hole (9520-1.1), a well-flowered grassland where the McGee Pass trail departs eastward. Now the PCT climbs steeply north up a band of Mesozoic metavolcanics which sweep east and grade into the Paleozoic metasediments of dominating Red Slate Mountain (13,163'). Beyond the crest of this ascent you reach deep-blue Lake Virginia (10,314-1.9), with several somewhat exposed campsites. In early season you will have to wade across the head of the lake or detour rather far north. From this boggy crossing your trail climbs to a saddle below the vertical northeast face of Peak 11147 and then switchbacks down to heavily used Purple Lake (9900-2.1), at whose outlet a trail begins its descent into deep Cascade Valley. No camping is allowed within 100 yards of the lake's outlet, so if you want to camp in this vicinity, use the sites by the lake's northwest shore. In late summer and in dry years, you may not have any trailside water until Deer Creek, 7.8 miles ahead, so plan accordingly.

From Purple Lake the rocky trail climbs west and then bends north as it levels out high on the wall of glaciated Cascade Valley. Soon you reach a trail (10,150-2.3) to Duck Lake and beyond, which could be used to escape bad weather or to resupply at Mammoth Lakes.

Just beyond the Duck Lake trail, you ford Duck Creek near several undistinguished campsites before traversing first southwest and then northwest. If you sharpen your gaze, you will see both red firs and Jeffrey pines above 10,000' on this north wall of Cascade Valley, well above their normal range. You also have fine views of the Silver Divide in the south as you slant northwest and descend gradually through mixed conifers. From your last set of excellent views, which are along the south slopes of Peak 10519, the trail begins a westward descent, crossing about a mile of lava-flow rubble before turning north for a rambling drop to Deer Creek (9090-5.5). Here you'll find fair, lodgepole-shaded campsites. By the time you reach Deer Creek, you are definitely in Bear Country. Yosemite's black bears have spilled beyond the Park's boundaries, and you can expect to have these nighttime visitors harass your food supply as far north as Kennedy Canyon, north of Yosemite. See the introduction to Section G for hints on bear-bagging your food.

In the next ⅔ mile the trail starts west, climbs briefly over a granitic ridge, and then descends north to a creek crossing in a long, slender meadow. Heading north through it we have views of The Thumb (10,286'), then leave this county-line meadow as we cross a seasonal creeklet. This freshet we parallel for about a mile as we descend a bit to Upper Crater Meadow (8920-2.0). From it, a trail rolls and weaves 3.6 miles over to a trailhead by the northwest shore of very popular Horseshoe Lake. From it, the Lake Mary Road starts a 4.9-mile descent to a junction in with Minaret Summit Road in congested Mammoth Lakes, which is a year-round condo-town similar to

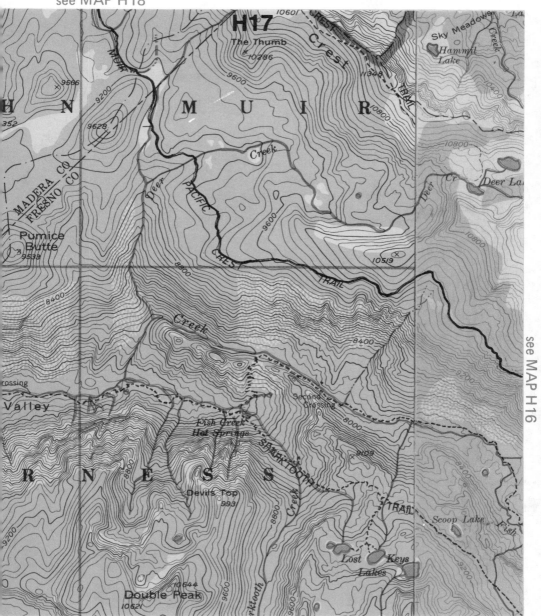

Tom and Jason Winnett at Silver Pass

those around Lake Tahoe, minus the lake and the casinos.

In about 100 yards, by the meadow's north edge, we meet a former section of the John Muir Trail, along which a hiker would have two more opportunities to branch over to the Mammoth Lakes area before the old section

H18

see MAP H19

see MAP H17

Ritter Range, from northern Red Cone

Tully Hole

drops to the Reds Meadow area. With that goal in mind, we take the newer route down along the creek we've been following, cross it in ½ mile, and then descend to a recrossing with a good campsite (8660-0.8), the last one before Reds Meadow. Here we leave John Muir Wilderness for good and enter Ansel Adams Wilderness for a short spell. This creekside campsite lies between the two Red Cones, products of very recent volcanic eruptions. The northern one is easy to climb and offers a fine view of the Ritter Range and Middle Fork San Joaquin River's deep canyon. You'll also see Mammoth Mountain (11,053') in the north-northeast, on whose north slopes as many as 20,000 skiers, most of them from southern California, may be found on a busy day. This mountain is a volcano which began to grow about 400,000 years ago. The area around it, including the upper canyon of Middle Fork San Joaquin River, has been volcanically active for over 3 million years, and the last eruption here occurred less than 1000 years ago. It is the Sierra's "hot spot"—ironically, considering that it is also a mecca for skiers due to its large, late-melting snowpack.

Beyond the creekside campsite between the Red Cones the PCT makes lazy switchbacks down to Boundary Creek (7910-2.3). Roughly midway between it and the next junction, we cross a smaller creek, where we exit from an east lobe of Ansel Adams Wilderness. Through a fir forest our well-graded route descends to an abandoned stagecoach road (7700-0.7), now a broad path, up which you can walk about 300 yards north to Reds Meadow Pack Station. Another 230 yards north along a paved road takes you to Reds Meadow Resort, with a store and cafe, at road's end. The food selection is aimed at campers with ice chests, not at hikers with backpacks. From here and from a number of roadside stops as far north as Agnew Meadows, you can take a shuttle bus to the Mammoth Lakes area (see **Supplies** at the start of this chapter).

Past the abandoned stagecoach road you immediately cross a horse trail that climbs briefly north to the pack station, reaching it at a switchback in the paved road. Just past this horse trail the PCT descends to a crossing of the Rainbow Falls-Fish Valley-Cascade Valley trail (7600-0.2), on which you'd be ascending if you took the alternate route to here mentioned earlier. This popular trail starts from the Rainbow Falls trailhead parking lot about 250 yards north of the PCT. If you've got the time, hike 1.0 mile south on this trail for a view of Rainbow Falls. Afternoon is the best time to see and photograph this waterfall, as well as the columns of Devils Postpile just ahead.

H18

see MAP H20

see MAP H18

Rainbow Falls

Beyond the Rainbow Falls trail, you curve southwest over to a low, nearby crest from which an old trail, essentially abandoned, heads north, and then you meander northwest down to a trail junction (7430-0.5) by the east boundary of Devils Postpile National Monu-

ment. Here we recommend you leave the PCT and head ½ mile north to a junction, crossing a creek from Sotcher Lake just before you reach it. From this junction, at the base of a Devils Postpile lava flow, you can head ¼ mile east to the paved road, mentioned earlier, then hike a few yards north on it to the entrance to Reds Meadow Campground. In it you can get a free, luke-warm shower at the bathhouse by the campground's "hot" spring. From the lava-flow junction the alternate route climbs ¼ mile northwest to a ridge, from which you can take a short trail up to the glacially polished top of the Devils Postpile. The main trail skirts along the base of this columnar lava flow, reaching a junction in about ¼ mile, just beyond a junction with a trail from the top of the lava flow. If you were to continue straight ahead from this second junction, you'd reach the monument's small visitor center and its adjacent campground in about ⅓ mile. Instead, to regain the PCT, you turn left at the second junction, descend to a nearby bridge over the San Joaquin River, and in a minute reach a junction. From here, head 0.4 mile north to the PCT.

Back at the monument's east boundary, PCT purists immediately cross the San Joaquin River on a sturdy bridge, wind westward past two seasonal ponds, then make a struggling climb north through deep pumice to an intersection with the old, trans-Sierra Mammoth

H18

Mt. Ritter, Banner Peak and Shadow Lake, from ridge near the John Muir Trail

Trail (7710-1.0). This relatively unscenic one-mile slog was built to keep PCT equestrians away from the Postpile. Northbound, the old trail descends ¼ mile to meet the alternate route, while the PCT contours along pumice-laden slopes, soon reaching the end of the alternate route (7660-0.6). Here the John Muir and Pacific Crest trails, which have coincided through most of this hiking chapter, diverge for a few miles, becoming one tread again near Thousand Island Lake. On their divergence both quickly re-enter Ansel Adams Wilderness, though the PCT briefly leaves it in the Agnew Meadows area.

*   *   *   *

Briefly, the 12.9-mile JMT segment—the more popular of the two—climbs up to a trail junction near Minaret Creek, quickly crosses the creek (with adjacent campsites) and winds over to another junction by Johnston Meadow (more campsites), 1.4 miles from the PCT junction. The JMT climbs up past knee-deep Trinity Lakes, then later makes a three-stage descent to Shadow Lake, dropping to shallow Gladys and ideal Rosalie lakes along the way

(respectively 6.1 and 6.8 miles from the PCT junction). You can camp at either lake but not at Shadow Lake, except near its southwest shore. However, good-to-excellent, popular campsites abound in the ⅔ mile JMT stretch west of the lake, up along Shadow Creek. No campfires are allowed along this stretch, but stoves are okay. From the creek the JMT climbs 1.9 miles up to a high ridge, then drops ¾ mile to the east end of Garnet Lake, which is off-limits to camping. Ruby Lake, about 1⅓ miles farther, offers one campsite, as does Emerald Lake, just beyond it. Emerald, however, is probably the best lake along this 12.9-mile route for swimming. Finally, no camping is allowed near the east end Thousand Island Lake.

*   *   *   *

Back where the JMT and the PCT split, the pumice-lined PCT winds down to the distributaries of Minaret Creek (7590-0.6), which must be waded except in the late season, just below dramatic Minaret Falls. Still in pumice, the trail bends northeast and almost touches Middle Fork San Joaquin River before climbing north

19

see MAP H21

see MAP H19

10287

10000

10253

10265

9600

Billy Lake

8052

971

Gem

30

RUSH CR TR

Waugh Lake

9424

9424

Rush

Lake

Rush Cr

Rush Creek

Waugh Lake

9600

Rush Cr

8052

PACIFIC

9600

10181

Sullivan
Lake

Island
Pass

Weber
Lake

10508

10495

CREST

10587

10474

No Camping
No Campfires

31

Badger
La

10400

Thousand Island
Lake

TRAIL

RIVER

Emerald
Lake

JOHN

Ruby
Lake

10365

1150

9834

x

akes

Davis

2311

N

S

E

10512

10000

L

MUIR

FOOTPATH

10400

Garnet
Lake

No Ca
No Ca

Lake
Catherine

11158

11200

10324

TRAIL

10

11034

10000

10736

Banner Peak

12945

10704

x

Nydiver
Lakes

10800

9600

Mt Ritter

13157

12000

Shadow

Ediza Lake

No Camping
No Campfires

Cabin

3604

12944

R

Volcanic

Rid

122

10000

No Campfires

FOOTPATH

1150

MUIR

Aceberg
Lake

11711

T

Z

9600

10800

No Campfires
Cecile Lake

H22

away from it over a lava-flow bench that overlooks Pumice Flat. In a shady forest of lodgepole pines and red firs, we make a brief descent to a bridge across the Middle Fork. From the far side of the bridge (7680-1.4), a trail heads just around the corner to the west end of Upper Soda Springs Campground. Beyond the bridge we head upriver, having many opportunities to drop to nearby eating, drinking and chilly-swimming spots along the dashing Middle Fork. After crossing a permanent stream (7810-1.0), our trail bends from north to northwest and crosses a second stream (7910-1.1). Then, just past a small knoll, it reaches a junction (8000-0.2). Here the PCT branches right for a climb to Agnew Meadows. If you were to continue straight ahead, upriver, you'd have many camping opportunities before rejoining the PCT in 5.9 miles, at a point about ⅓ mile west of the Badger Lakes.

Leaving the river route, the PCT first parallels it northwest, then climbs via short switchbacks to a junction with the River trail (8280-0.5). We start east up it and in 80 yards meet a fork. The left (east) fork goes 0.4 mile to Agnew Meadows Campground, from which you can walk 0.4 mile east on a winding dirt road, along which you'll find the PCT's resumption by a trailhead parking area. Taking the right (southeast) fork, we hike through a long, narrow trough before curving northeast around a meadow, almost touching the ranger's trailer (with a parking area) before reaching the Agnew Meadows road (8360-0.9), which has water and an outhouse by a trailhead parking area. The main road to Reds Meadow lies ¼ mile east, and at that junction is the first of 10 stops made by shuttle buses from the Mammoth Mountain Ski Area (see **Supplies** at start of this chapter).

From the Agnew Meadows road the PCT route follows the signed High trail, which switchbacks upward for about 400 vertical feet before climbing northwest. Creeks, creeklets and springs abound along the High trail, for the volcanic-rock formations above us store plenty of water, which they slowly release throughout the summer. Views are relatively few until just before the signed boundary of Minarets Wilderness (9680-2.8), and then the Ritter Range explodes on the scene, with Shadow Lake and the Minarets, both across the canyon, vying for our attention. Views and water abound over the next 2 miles of alternating brushy and timbered slopes, then our traversing route comes to a

junction (9710-2.4) with a trail that climbs easily over Agnew Pass to good camps near the largest of the Clark Lakes, about 1.1 miles distant. Summit Lake, just before the pass, is good for swimming but a bit short on level camping spots. The High trail, our route, now descends, crossing Summit Lake's seasonal outlet creek before climbing briefly to an intersection of a steep Middle Fork-Clark Lakes trail (9500-0.8). Westward, our climb abates and we soon reach a *de facto* trail (9590-0.3), which you'll find just past a lakelet on your left. This trail goes 0.2 mile southeast to good camps beside the largest of the Badger Lakes, which is the only one that is more than waist-deep. It is one of the best lakes in the entire Ansel Adams Wilderness for swimming.

Leaving the Badger Lakes area and last legal campsites this side of Rush Creek, we continue westward, passing a third trail to the Clark Lakes in ¼ mile. Soon we make a brief descent to a junction with the River trail (9560-0.5), then climb moderately northwest before rambling southwest to a reunion with the John Muir trail near the east end of spreading Thousand Island Lake (9840-1.0). Camping is prohibited within ¼ mile of this lake's outlet, but is legal elsewhere. Particularly look along the lake's southeast shore.

The PCT climbs moderately through a thinning forest to two lakelets, reached just before Island Pass (10,200-1.8). The trail then traverses ⅓ mile to a ridge before descending to a sometimes obscure junction (9690-1.0) with a trail climbing 0.8 mile south to the tip of lower Davis Lake. Campsites by it are small and quite exposed, but the beauty of this lake and its surroundings make them a worthy goal. About 250 yards past the Davis Lakes trail junction you reach the first of several Rush Creek forks. Along the ½-mile trail segment that ensues, the early-season hiker may have three wet fords to make. You may therefore want to keep your boots off until the last ford, just before a junction with the Rush Creek trail (9600-0.4). This trail descends 9.5 miles to popular Silver Lake, on well-traveled Mono County road 158 (June Lake Loop road). In the Forks area, small camps abound, virtually all of them illegal since they are within 100 feet of a creek or a trail. A seasonal ranger, sometimes camped 200 yards southeast of the junction, may enforce the rules.

Leaving the Forks, we quickly engage some short, steep switchbacks that we follow north-

H18, H19, H20

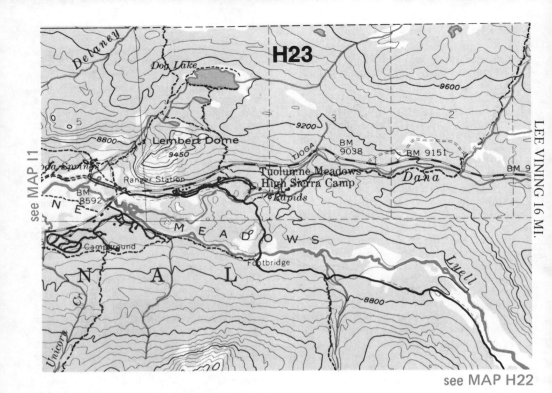

see MAP I1

see MAP H22

west up to a ridge, then cross it and ease up to a junction with the Marie Lakes trail (10,030-0.8). The lakes' outlet creek, just beyond the junction, is best crossed at an obvious jump-across spot slightly downstream. After the ford our trail winds excessively in an oft-futile attempt to avoid the boulders and bogs of the increasingly alpine environment. Whitebark pines diminish in number and stature as you climb toward a conspicuous saddle—easily mistaken in early season for Donohue Pass. After a wet slog across the tundra-and-stone floor of our alpine basin, we veer southwest toward a prominent peak and ascend a some-times obscure trail past blocks and over slabs to the real, signed, tarn-blessed Donohue Pass (11,056-2.6), where we leave Ansel Adams Wilderness.

The Yosemite high country unfolds before us as we descend northwest, partly in a long, straight fracture (southbound hikers take note). We then curve west to a sharp bend southeast, a few yards from which we can get a command-ing panorama of Mt. Lyell, at 13,144′ Yo-semite's highest peak, and deep Lyell Canyon. Leaving the bend, we now descend southwest ½ mile to the north end of a boulder-dotted tarn that occasionally reflects Lyell and its broad glacier—the largest one we'll see in the Sierra. Here a tantalizing trail starts north but this route down large talus blocks should not be attempted with a heavy pack. Rather, contour along the tarn's west shore, then briefly climb southeast to a gap in a low ridge. Next, wind north and soon begin a steep northeast descent that ends at the north end of a small meadow, where you ford the Lyell headwaters (10,220-1.8). Among the whitebark pines in this area you'll find the first adequate campsites since Rush Creek Forks.

Larger campsites appear on a forested bench by another Lyell Fork crossing (9700-0.8), via a bridge. Now we'll stay on the west bank of the river all the way to Tuolumne Meadows. Beyond the bench we make our last major descent—a steep one—down to the Lyell Fork base camp (9000-1.4), at the southern, upper end of Lyell Canyon. This camp, a 3-hour trek from Highway 120, is a popular site with weekend mountaineers. Our hike to the high-way is now an easy, level, usually open stroll along meandering Lyell Fork. A major camp-ing area is found at the junction (8880-2.8) with a trail to Vogelsang High Sierra Camp. Note that some of these campsites have steel cables strung between trees. On these cables

Banner Peak, Mt. Ritter and three unnamed peaks

you can hang a bag of food, counterbalanced at the other end of your short rope by a rock or other weight.

Past the junction, occasional backward glances at receding Potter Point mark our progress north along trout-inhabited Lyell Fork. With the oft-looming threat of afternoon lightning storms, one wishes the trail would have been routed along the forest's edge, rather than through open meadow. Typical of meadowy trails, ours is multitreaded. Numerous treads arise mainly because as the main tread is used, it gets deepened until it penetrates the near-surface water table and becomes soggy. Odds are great that you'll have to leave the tread at least once, thus helping to start a new one.

Shortly after Potter Point finally disappears from view—and beyond half a dozen campsites—we curve northwest, descend between two bedrock outcrops, and then contour west through alternating soggy meadows and lodgepole forests. Both abound in mosquitoes through late July, as does most of the Tuolumne Meadows area. Two-branched Rafferty Creek soon appears, its second branch being a wet ford in early season. Just beyond it we meet the Rafferty Creek trail (8710-4.4), part of the very scenic and very popular High Sierra Loop trail. We continue west and soon meet another junction (8650-0.7), from where a trail goes ¾ mile west to a junction immediately east of the Tuolumne Meadows Campground. From there, the left branch skirts around the camp's south perimeter while the right branch quickly ends at the camp's main road. This road leads ½ mile west to Highway 120, and just southwest on it you'll find services.

Rather than head for the campground, we turn north and soon come to bridges across the Lyell Fork. A photo pause here is well worth it, particularly when clouds are building over Mts. Dana and Gibbs in the northeast. A short, winding climb north followed by an equal descent brings us to the Dana Fork (8690-0.7) of the Tuolumne River, only 130 yards past a junction with an east-climbing trail to the Gaylor Lakes. Immediately beyond the bridge crossing we meet a short spur trail to the Tuolumne Meadows Lodge. Here you'll find both showers and meals, but on busy weekends you must make dinner reservations early in the day.

We parallel the Dana Fork downstream and soon hear the stream as it makes a small drop into a clear pool, almost cut in two by a protruding granite finger. Just beyond the pool we approach the Lodge's road (8650-0.3), where a short path climbs a few yards up to it and takes one to the entrance of a large parking lot for backpackers. Now we parallel the paved road westward, passing the Tuolumne Meadows Ranger Station and quickly reaching a junction. The main road curves north to the sometimes-noisy highway, but we follow the spur road west, to where it curves into a second large parking lot for backpackers. In its east end you'll find a booth from which a summer ranger dispenses wilderness permits. Our road past the lot becomes a closed dirt road and diminishes to a wide trail by the time we arrive at this section's end, Highway 120 (8595-0.8), across from the start of the Soda Springs road. A campground, store and post office lie on Highway 120 just southwest of the Tuolumne River bridge.

H22, H23

Tower Peak (right) and the Sierra crest, from the jeep road above Kennedy Canyon

Section I: Tuolumne Meadows to Sonora Pass

Introduction: Deep, spectacular glaciated canyons, crossed one after another, characterize this short section. The hiker sometimes feels he's doing more vertical climbing than horizontal walking. Unlike the previous John Muir Trail section, which also has pass after mountain pass, this section has passes that are all below timberline, and the canyon bottoms can be quite warm and enjoyable—if proper bear-prevention measures are taken (see below). Nearing the north end of this section, you leave the expansive granitic domain behind and enter Vulcan's realm—thick floods of volcanic flows and sediments that buried most of the northern Sierra Nevada before it rose to its present height.

Declination: 15°E

Mileages:	South to North	Distance between Points	North to South
Highway 120 in Tuolumne Meadows...............	0.0		76.4
		6.0	
Glen Aulin	6.0		70.4
		8.0	
Virginia Canyon trail...........................	14.0		62.4
		3.6	
Miller Lake.....................................	17.6		58.8
		2.2	
Matterhorn Canyon trail.........................	19.8		56.6
		4.5	
Benson Pass....................................	24.3		52.1
		1.9	
Smedberg Lake	26.2		50.2
		4.6	
Benson Lake*...................................	30.8		45.6
		3.1	
Seavey Pass....................................	33.9		42.5
		4.4	
Lower Kerrick Canyon..........................	38.3		38.1
		7.4	
Wilmer Lake	45.7		30.7
		10.5	
Dorothy Lake Pass.............................	56.2		20.2
		5.5	
West Fork West Walker River bridge...............	61.7		14.7
		6.6	
leave jeep road at switchback	68.3		8.1
		8.1	
Highway 108 at Sonora Pass.....................	76.4		0.0

*Although off the official route, Benson Lake is included as part of the PCT since virtually every PCT hiker visits it.

Supplies and Permits: Once you leave Highway 120 at Tuolumne Meadows, you won't encounter an on-route supply point until you reach Little Norway on Highway 50, about 150 miles farther. However, closer, off-route resorts lie on Highways 108, 4 and 88, as mentioned in "Supplies" of the next trail chapter.

Immediate supplies are obtained at the Tuolumne Meadows store, cafe, post office and gas station, which are just west of the Tuolumne Meadows Campground. Don't send any parcels to the post office if you expect to arrive at Tuolumne Meadows before mid-June or after mid-September, for then all these facilities will be closed. Parcels to be picked up then should be mailed to the Lee Vining Post Office. The town is reached by following Highway 120 east 7 miles up to Tioga Pass (9941'), 12 miles down to Highway 395, and then ½ mile north on it into town. Just one long mile before you reach Highway 395, you'll pass the Lee Vining Ranger Station, where you can obtain wilderness permits if you plan to return to the PCT via the Hoover Wilderness.

In Tuolumne Meadows the Visitor Center dispenses only information, not wilderness permits. Leave messages there but get your permits from a booth in the parking lot near the west end of the Tuolumne Meadows Lodge spur road. The Park Service realizes that a lot of Yosemite hikers are weekend visitors, so from late June through the Labor Day weekend they keep the booth open on Friday nights and open it early (sometimes 6 a.m.) on Saturday mornings. Reservations for backcountry trips may be made by mail between February 1 and May 31 by writing to: Backcountry Office, P.O. Box 577, Yosemite National Park, California 95389. The reason you should get a reservation is that only a certain number of hikers are allowed to backpack in from a given trailhead on each day. Weekends, with their flood of visitors, could be a bad time for you to depart from Tuolumne Meadows if you don't have a permit. If you are passing through Yosemite Park rather than starting from Tuolumne Meadows, you should already have your permit. See the section on Wilderness Permits in Chapter 2.

East of the wilderness-permit booth is the Tuolumne Meadows Ranger Station, followed by another parking lot for backpackers. If you are starting south from Tuolumne Meadows, park your car here and, as at any Yosemite location, roll your windows *completely up* unless you want a bear to rip them out. East of this parking lot, at the end of the spur road, is Tuolumne Meadows Lodge and its parking lot, which is for *guests only.* Meals can be obtained here if you make reservations for them at least a few hours, if not a day, in advance. They are, as you might expect, relatively expensive, since the food has to be shipped in from a long distance. Hot showers, supplied with soap and towels, can be had for a small charge.

Wilderness permits are required only for overnight stays in Emigrant Wilderness, which you encounter near the end of this section. However, the PCT barely enters the wilderness, and since there are no campsites along your 2-mile-high, windswept traverse in it, you won't need a permit.

Creek fords: This section contains some difficult creek fords. If you are attempting the entire tri-state route, then you will probably hit this section during its period of maximum runoff. A strong, lightweight rope, 60 feet or longer, is certainly a necessity for early-season hikers and is also recommended for July hikers. However, if you slip while roped up, the rope can hold you under (some people have drowned). Therefore, make sure you can quickly release your rope, if necessary.

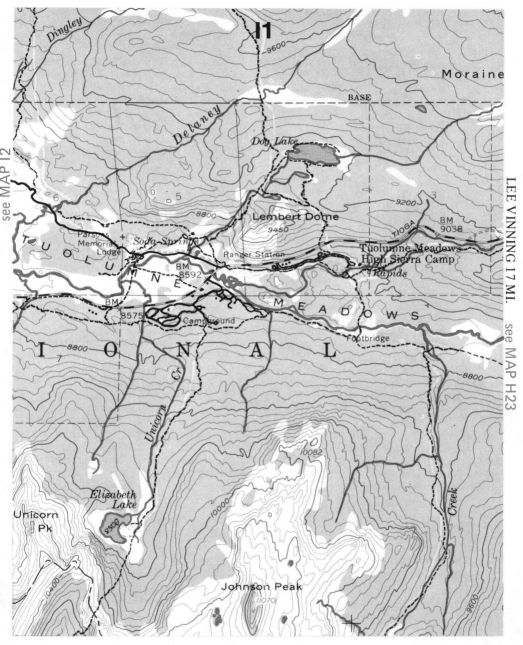

Before leaving the parking lot below imposing Lembert Dome, look at the large feldspar crystals in the rock of the dome's base. This rock, called Cathedral Peak granite (granodiorite), solidified as a single unit several miles below the earth's surface about 80 million years ago. The large, blocky crystals make outcrops of this particular granite—a pluton—very easy to identify.

From Tuolumne Meadows north almost to

I1

the Park border, the Pacific Crest trail coincides with the Tahoe-Yosemite trail. On the Soda Springs road we walk ⅓ mile west and reach a gate where a north fork climbs up to the Tuolumne Meadows Stable. On the closed road we continue west to a fork (8590-0.7) just beyond a minor gap, from where the left branch—the John Muir Trail—traverses southwest to a bridge across the Tuolumne River, bound for Yosemite Valley.

At the fork we keep right, climb a few paces, and take a shortcut trail due west to the road again, intersecting it at the Soda Springs area (8600-0.1). The effervescent, rust-tainted soda springs are obvious, and if you have some powdered soft drink along, you can stir up a soda pop. Nearby Parsons Lodge, once owned by the Sierra Club, is now Park property.

From the springs area our well-signed trail starts a rolling traverse northwest from the road. Heavy use over loose soils has created numerous parallel paths. Just 50 yards before we reach multibranched Delaney Creek (8570-0.8), a trail from the stable comes in on the right. No fishing is allowed here or upstream due to a planted population of endangered Piute cutthroat trout. Not far beyond the creek, near two small granite knolls, the Young Lakes trail (8650-0.4) continues north, straight ahead, but we turn west, then continue northwest. In about a mile our trail approaches the Tuolumne River, and then parallels it, sometimes at a distance, eventually making a short but noticeable climb up granite bedrock. In a gorge below, you may see, on the south side of the river, a dark mass, locally known as Little Devils Postpile—a plug of basalt that was forced up through the adjacent granite 9.4

million years ago. Despite repeated attacks by glaciers, this extrusion still remains.

Now we descend north steeply to a forested flat and traverse southwest to bridge the Tuolumne River (8310-2.7). Here, on the south bank, an abortive spur trail starts southeast, misleading unwary southbound hikers. Continuing northwest, we pass Tuolumne Falls, some minor cascades, and then the high White Cascade, before our rocky trail meets a junction (7920-1.1) with a trail to McGee Lake. Although it is easily reached, the lake is not worth the effort. The PCT bends north—a direction we'll now pursue for miles—and descends to a bridging of the Tuolumne River. During maximum runoff, you may have to wade to reach the bridge! Just beyond it, the PCT meets a trail (7840-0.2) that immediately bridges Conness Creek to arrive at Glen Aulin High Sierra Camp. Just north of it is the heavily used Glen Aulin campground. Only 15 yards beyond the Glen Aulin spur trail is the Tuolumne Canyon trail, and ½ mile down it are less-used campsites. An extremely rewarding side trip during high water is to continue downcanyon past California and LeConte Falls to amazing Waterwheel Falls, 3.4 miles from the PCT.

The PCT climbs north, sometimes alongside Cold Canyon creek, to a forested gap (8800-2.9), then descends ½ mile to the south edge of a large, usually soggy meadow. Midway across it you'll notice a huge boulder, just west. Its overhanging sides have been used as an emergency shelter, but in a lightning storm it is a prime strike target. Beyond it our multitracked route continues north, first for a mile through meadow, then on a gradual ascent through

I1, I2, I3

Tuolumne Meadows panorama, left to right: Unicorn Peak, The Cockscomb, Echo Peaks, Cathedral Peak, Fairview Dome

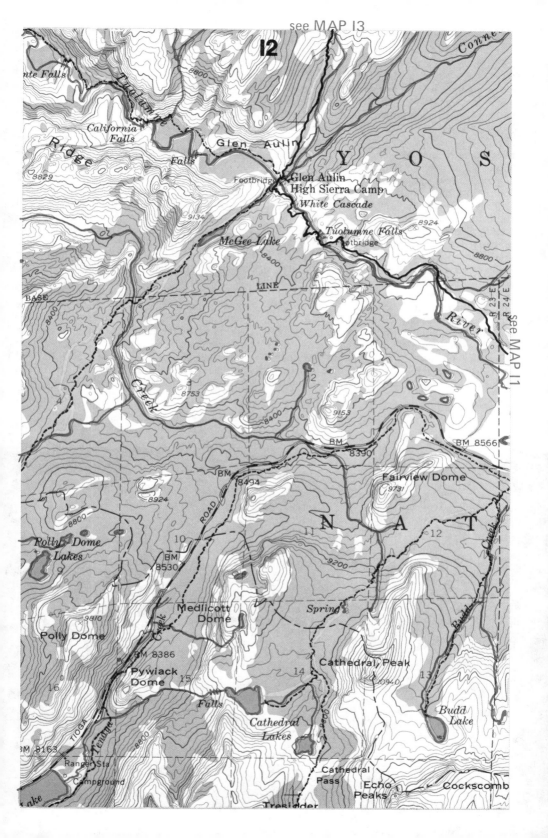

12

Conne

California
Falls

Tuolumne

Glen Aulin

Y O S

Ridge

Falls

8829

Footbridge Glen Aulin
High Sierra Camp

White Cascade

9134

Tuolumne Falls
Footbridge

8924

McGee Lake

8400

8800

LINE

River

BASE

R 23 E

R 24 E

8400

Creek

2

1

3
8753

8400

9153

BM
8390

BM 8566

BM

Fairview Dome

8494

9731

8924

N   A   T

ROAD

11

12

Polly Dome
Lakes

10

9200

9

BM
8530

Spring

Budd

9810

Creek

Medlicott
Dome

Polly Dome

BM 8386

Cathedral Peak

13

Pywiack
Dome

15

14

0940

16

Budd
Lake

Falls

Cathedral
Lakes

TIOGA

Tenaya

8800

BM 8163

Ranger Sta

Campground

Cathedral
Pass

Echo
Peaks

Cockscomb

ake

Tresidder

forest to a crest junction with the McCabe Lakes trail (9080-3.9). A long-½-mile walk northeast up it will get you to a small campsite just above McCabe Creek; an hour's walk up it will get you to larger, better campsites at scenic lower McCabe Lake. The most popular campsites in this vicinity, however, are along Return Creek and lower McCabe Creek, down in Virginia canyon. We switchback down to this canyon's floor, cross McCabe Creek—a wet ford before July—and quickly come to a junction. A spur trail continues up-canyon past campsites, but we turn left to ford powerful Return Creek, which is usually a wet ford and in early season can be a dangerous ford if you're unroped.

On the west bank we walk but a few steps southwest before our trail veers right and meets the Virginia Canyon trail (8540-1.2), which climbs northeast out of Yosemite and into the Hoover Wilderness. On the PCT we start down-canyon, climb west up into Spiller Creek canyon, and then, halfway to a pass, cross the canyon's high-volume creek. Beyond it we soon start up two dozen switchbacks that transport us up to a forested pass (9560-2.2), which

offers fair, reasonably bear-free camps when there is enough snow to provide drinking water. Most hikers, however, continue southwest down to shallow Miller Lake (9490-1.4), with good campsites along its forested west shore. From the lake we parallel a meadow north up to a low gap (9680-0.6), then execute over two dozen often steep switchbacks down to a canyon floor and a junction with the Matterhorn Canyon trail (8510-1.6). On it we descend southwest, reaching this majestic canyon's broad creek in 80 yards. Immediately beyond the often-wet ford lies a large, lodgepole-shaded campsite.

Heading down-canyon for a mile, we pass less obvious, more secluded campsites, then soon leave the glaciated canyon to begin the usual two dozen, short, steep switchbacks—this time west into Wilson Creek canyon, a typical glaciated side canyon that hangs above the main canyon because its smaller glacier couldn't erode the landscape as rapidly as the trunk-canyon glacier did. We twice ford Wilson Creek, then ford it a last time (9500-3.3) and start a switchbacking climb up to windy, gravelly Benson Pass (10,140-1.2).

I3, I4

A rewarding side trip: Lower McCabe Lake

Evening comes to Smedberg Lake

As the passes have become steadily higher, so too have the canyons become deeper, and our multistage descent down to and up from Benson Lake can only be described as incredible. We begin uneventfully with an easy descent to a large meadow, reaching its peaceful creeklet just before a dropoff. Veering away from the creeklet, we soon begin a switchbacking descent that ends at a south-shore peninsula (9250-1.9) on Smedberg Lake. Most of the campsites, however, lie along the lake's west and north shores.

From the lake's south-shore peninsula—below the steep-walled sentinel, Volunteer Peak—we continue west, passing a spur trail to the west-shore campsites before winding southwest up a poorly defined slab-rock trail to a well-defined gap (9340-0.3). From it the trail switchbacks down joint-controlled granite slabs, only to climb south high up to a meadowy junction (9480-0.7) with a trail to Rogers Lake—an easy half-hour walk south that yields a far better camping alternative to crowded Smedberg Lake. Starting southwest up from this junction, we soon cross a low moraine and descend northwest to a junction (9390-0.3) with a trail climbing southwest to a broad saddle that harbors shallow, mosquito-haunted Murdock Lake. Our next step down to Benson Lake is a typical two-dozen-short-switchback descent to a ford (8720-0.8) of Smedberg Lake's outlet creek. The PCT from that lake to here will be virtually impossible to follow in the snowbound early season. Hikers then will want to make a steep cross-country descent west down to this spot on an almost level canyon floor.

Now on the creek's north bank, we pass a small pond before commencing a steady, moderate, creekside descent to a second ford—a slight problem in early season. Back on the south bank, we make a winding, switchbacking descent over metamorphic rock down to our last, sometimes tricky ford of the creek. The next ⅓ mile sees us climbing up to a brushy saddle just east of a conspicuous knoll, then descending into a shady forest of giant firs before crossing wide Piute Creek and reaching the Benson Lake spur trail (7560-2.1). Piute Creek—almost always a wet ford—can usually be crossed via one or more large, fallen logs. No one in mid or late season should make this long descent from Benson Pass without visiting the "Benson Riviera"—the long, sandy beach that forms along the north shore of Benson Lake once the lake's level falls. Our spur trail

I4, I5

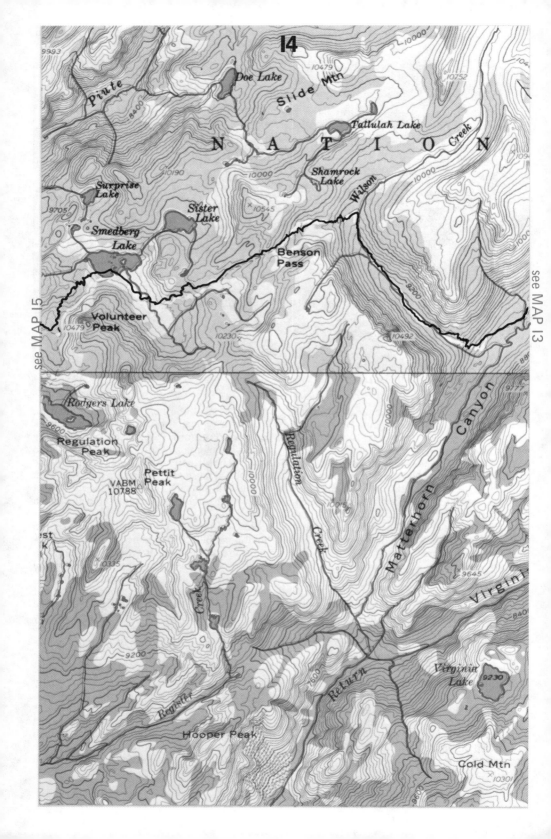

see MAP 15

see MAP 13

Piute

Doe Lake

Slide Mtn

10479

10752

Tallulah Lake

N A T I O N

Creek

10000

Shamrock Lake

10190

10000

Surprise Lake

10545

Sister Lake

Wilson

Benson Pass

Smedberg Lake

9200

Volunteer Peak

10479

10492

10230

Rodgers Lake

9777

Regulation Peak

Regulation

Matterhorn

Canyon

Pettit Peak

VABM 10788

10000

Creek

9645

est

10335

Virginia

Creek

9200

Return

Virginia Lake

9230

Regulation

Hooper Peak

Cold Mtn

10301

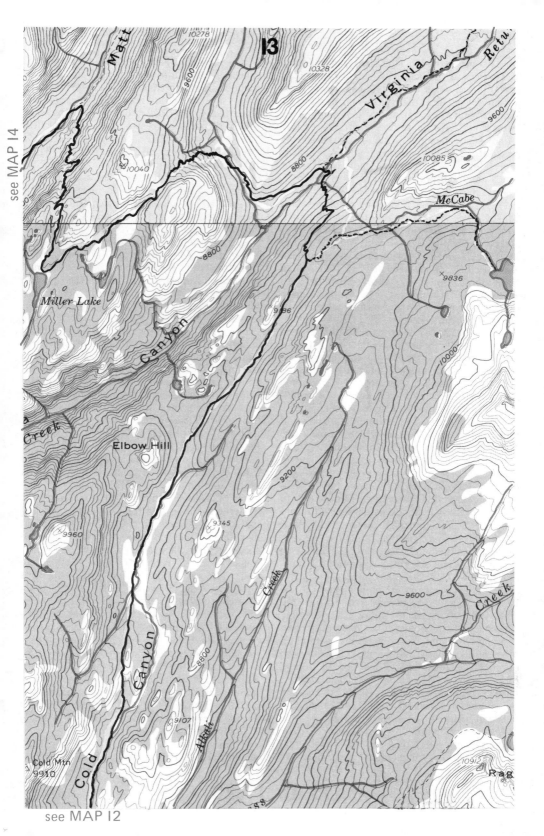

see MAP 14

see MAP 12

13

10278

10328

9600

Matt

Virginia

Retu.

9600

10085

10040

McCabe

8800

9836

8800

Miller Lake

Canyon

9136

10000

Creek

Elbow Hill

9200

9960

9345

9600

Creek

Canyon

8800

Alkali

9107

Cold Mtn
9910

Cold

1091

Rag

winds southwest along the shady, often damp forest floor to a section of beach (7550-0.4) near Piute Creek's inlet. *Remember this spot,* for otherwise this route back can be hard to locate. Numerous campsites just within the forest's edge testify to the popularity of this broad, sandy beach. Swimming in the lake is brisk at best, but sunning on the beach is superb. However, strong, up-canyon afternoon winds can quell both activities.

After your stay, return to the PCT (7560-0.4) and prepare for a grueling climb north to Seavey Pass. At first brushy, the ascent northwest provides views of pointed Volunteer Peak and closer, two-crowned Peak 10060. We cross the creek, continue switchbacking northwest along the base of spectacular Peak 10368, then climb north briefly, only to be confronted with a steep 400' climb east. We are eventually funneled through a narrow, steep-walled, minor gap which rewards our climbing efforts with the sight of a relatively wind-free, sparkling pond (8970-2.1). Just past its outlet you'll find a trailside rock from which you can dive into its reasonably warm waters. The PCT parallels the pond's shore, curves east around a miniscule pond, then climbs northeast through wet meadows before switchbacking up to our second gap. At its north base lies a shallow rockbound pond, immediately beyond which we meet gap #3—signed SEAVEY PASS (9150-0.6). A small meadow separates it from gap #4, beyond which we reach a more noteworthy—the highest—gap (9180-0.2). Now we bend northwest, traverse past the head of a linear lake to gap #6, and switchback quickly down into a southwest-trending trough, spying a shallow pond 200 yards off in that direction. We turn right and immediately top our last gap, from which we descend northeast ¼ mile to a junction (8930-0.5) in Kerrick Canyon.

A cursory glance at the map suggests to the hiker that he now has an easy 3-mile down-canyon walk to the Bear Valley trail junction. Closer scrutiny, however, reveals a longer, winding too-often-ascending route. After 1½ miles of hiking on it, we parallel a moraine, on our right, which dies out in outwash around 8350' elevation. The glacier that left this debris retreated up-canyon about 10,000 years ago. Below the outwash, our trail passes glacier-polished bedrock, left slightly earlier.

A short northward jog of our Kerrick Canyon trail segment ends at the Bear Valley trail junction (7960-3.7). Immediately beyond it, we cross voluminous Kerrick Canyon creek, which can be a rough ford through mid-July. On the north bank a spur trail east leads up to campsites—popular with both backpackers and black bears. The PCT, however, climbs west, affording dramatic cross-canyon views of Bear Valley peak and Piute Mountain. The PCT eventually climbs north to a shallow gap (8720-1.4), and just east of it you'll find a generally bear-free campsite near the west end of a small lakelet. Proceeding north from the gap, we have the usual knee-knocking descent on a multitude of short, steep switchbacks down to the mouth of Thompson Canyon. Here we make a shady, easy descent west to a large camp beside Stubblefield Canyon creek (7740-1.1). The main trail meets the creek just below the camp, and across from it a spur trail up the opposite bank soon meets the main trail. (Most southbound hikers will not see this spur trail; rather, they will continue beyond it in a large creekside camp. From here they can rock hop—in late season only—to the north end of *our* large camp.) Cross where you will, locate the main trail near the opposite bank, and start downcanyon. In ¼ mile we leave the shady floor for slabs and slopes, in an hour arriving at a false pass. A short, steep descent west drops us into a corn-lily meadow, from which we wind ¼ mile northwest up to the true Macomb Ridge pass (8910-2.4).

With the deep canyons at last behind us, the 500' descent northwest into Tilden Canyon seems like child's play. Just beyond the west bank of Tilden Canyon Creek, we meet the Tilden Lake trail and follow it 110 yards up-canyon to a signed junction (8390-1.0). From here the PCT heads west to Wilma Lake and then goes up Jack Main Canyon; a slightly longer alternate route continues north up to huge, linear Tilden Lake—with lots of campsites—then west past domineering Chittenden Peak down to the PCT. Faithful PCT adherents, however, turn left at the junction and wind northwest past several ponds, nestled on a broad gap, before descending west to large, shallow Wilma Lake (7930-1.5). Good campsites are found just beyond it, alongside broad, tantalizing Falls Creek. A few minutes' walk northwest up-canyon takes us to a shallow, broad ford of the creek, then past spacious campsites to a junction (7970-0.3) with the Jack Main Canyon trail.

From our junction, below the site of a 1986 avalanche, the PCT winds northward up-can-

I5, I6, I7, I8

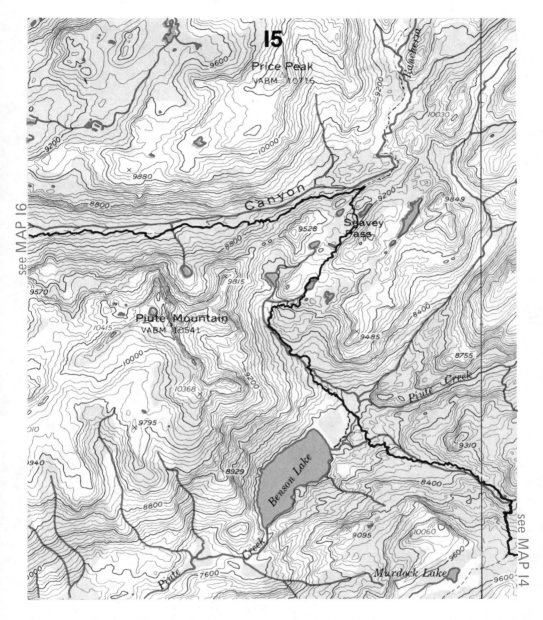

yon, touching the east bank of Falls Creek only several times before reaching a junction (8160-1.9) with a trail east to Tilden Lake. At the creek's bank, 80 yards down this trail, is a good campsite. Chittenden Peak and its north satellite serve as impressive reference points as we gauge our progress northward, passing two substantial meadows before arriving at the south end (8630-3.7) of even larger Grace Meadow. The upper canyon explodes into plain view, with—east to west—Forsyth Peak, Dorothy Lake Pass and Bond Pass being our guiding landmarks. Under lodgepole cover along the meadow's edge you can set up camp. Leaving Grace Meadow, we soon pass through a small meadow before the ever-increasing gradient be-

I8

comes noticeable. People have camped at small sites along this stretch, perhaps hoping to avoid bears, which are usually found lower down, but, alas, no such luck. Our upward climb meets the first (9280-3.1) of two trails that quickly unite to climb to Bond Pass—the route the Tahoe-Yosemite trail now takes. Just beyond these junctions, volcanic sediments and exposures are noticed in ever-increasing num-

bers—a taste of what's to come—before we reach large, exposed Dorothy Lake. Clumps of lodgepoles provide minimal campsite protection from the winds that often rush up-canyon. A short climb above the lake's east end takes us up to Dorothy Lake Pass (9550-1.5), with our last good view of the perennial snowfields that grace the north slopes of Forsyth Peak.

Leaving Yosemite National Park behind, we

I8, I9

see MAP I8

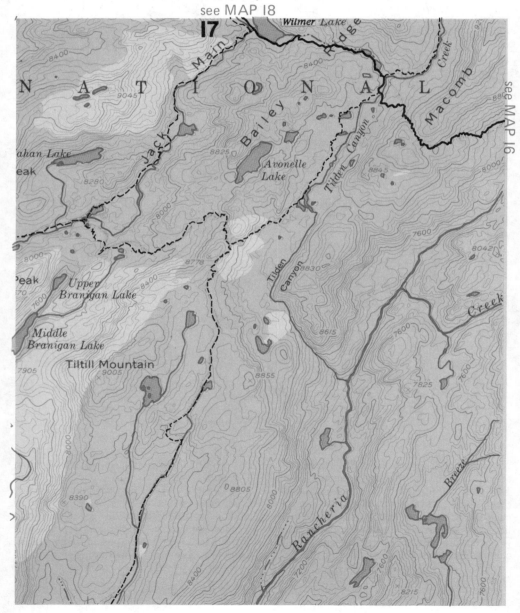

enter Toiyabe National Forest, pass rocky Stella Lake, approach tempting Bonnie Lake, and then switchback east down to campsites along the west shore of Lake Harriet (9210-1.1). Larger, more-isolated camps are on the east shore. The PCT crosses Cascade Creek just below the lake, and then it makes short switchbacks down confining terrain, reaching a large campsite in about ½ mile. Just 50 yards

see MAP 18

beyond it, we cross the creek on a footbridge (9040-0.7). Ahead, the way is still winding, but it's nearly level, and we soon reach—just past a pair of ponds—a junction (9000-0.6) with a trail that descends 1.5 miles to the West Walker River trail. Onward, we start north, then bend west and pass three ponds before winding down to a creek that has a junction (9320-0.9) just past it. West, the original PCT route contorts 1.0 mile over to Cinko Lake, which has adequate campsites. The former PCT route then descends 0.5 mile to the West Fork West Walker River trail and follows the river, making wet fords, 1.5 miles down to a junction with the present route.

On this official, lackluster segment, we first parallel the creek we've just crossed, and soon pass several gray outcrops of marble, which differ significantly in color and texture from the other metamorphic rocks we've been passing. Beyond them we curve left into a small bowl, with lots of snow in early season, then make a short, steep climb through a granitic notch before dropping west to a seasonal creeklet, After winding briefly northwest from it, our trail turns northward, taking almost ½ mile to descend to the West Fork West Walker River trail (8670-2.0). On it we descend to a nearby junction (8610-0.2) by paltry, sedge-choked Lower Long Lake. Here we take a steel bridge across a small gorge that confines the West Fork West Walker River, and we find a large, lodgepole-shaded campsite immediately past it. If you're lucky, you've left Yosemite's bears behind by the time you reach this site, though bearbagging might not be a bad idea here.

Most of your California trek, particularly in the High Sierra, has been across granitic landscapes. That is now about to change, for quickly you'll enter one of many volcanic landscapes, and these will dominate your trek for about the next 500 miles, ending just before Interstate 5 near Castle Crags State Park. First you meander ⅓ mile west to an ephemeral stream bed, then bend north and walk past one of the Walker Meadows to a seasonal creek laden with volcanic sediments. About a half mile past it you approach another creek (8610-1.6) with more staying power, and its two-step waterfall invites you to pause for a break. Below is another Walker Meadow, and you'll find more campsites (and often cows) both north and south of it. The trail briefly reverts to a granitic tread as you enter avalanche-prone Kennedy Canyon, up which you hike west to a

I9, I10

ford of its creek (9060-1.9). This spot is just about your last chance to make a decent camp this side of Sonora Pass. An exposed, alpine traverse lies ahead. Now you face a 1500-foot climb, first curving southwest up to a closed jeep road (9670-1.2), reaching it about 0.2 mile north of the saddle above Kennedy Canyon. Up this road one switchbacks above timberline, leaving virtually all the whitebark pines behind and obtaining fantastic panoramic views just before leaving the road at a switchback (10,580-1.9). Here we're just inside Emigrant Wilderness, whose boundary runs along the crest. We'll weave in and out of the wilderness until we finally leave it where we start a 1200+ foot drop to Sonora Pass.

Before mid-July, short parts of the remaining stretch to Sonora Pass can be potentially dangerous. Hence in the mid-'80s the Forest Service began work on an early-season alternate route. However, due to lack of money and to lack of volunteers, this worthwhile project had to be abandoned. If you've been encountering lots of snow, you might consider the following alternate route.

*   *   *   *

Continue up the road to a gate on a saddle (10,640-0.2), then take the main jeep road down to the outlet creek of Leavitt Lake (9556-1.5). Here you can find campsites among small stands of whitebark pines. You may find more-protected sites along the closed road descend-

ing from the lake to Highway 108 (8440-2.9). Note that here you are 4.0 miles from Leavitt Meadows Lodge, which has a few cabins, a small store and a cafe, but no phone. Just past it lies Leavitt Meadow Campground. The next *near-route* supplies will be in the Carson Pass area, about 62 miles ahead. The alternate route turns left, climbing northwest to a junction with Road 062 (9100-2.4), by which you could camp, and then continue west up to Sonora Pass (9628-1.3). You could also camp near the pass, obtaining water from the headwaters of either Sardine or Deadman creek.

*   *   *   *

Back on trail again, we have a stark, yet stunning, often-windblown traverse along a 2-mile-high volcanic ridge. Heading northwest, we pass several crest saddles before our trail turns north and finally crosses the Sierra crest (10,640-2.3). Should you want to "bag" Leavitt Peak, ¾ mile to the northwest, you can start up the crest or else hike ¼ mile farther along the trail and, in a bowl, start west up a talus slope. About ½ mile beyond the bowl we cross a ridge (10,880-0.7), which is the PCT's highest point since the previous chapter's Donohue Pass area. Latopie Lake lies well below us, and is difficult to reach because of steep slopes. In early season this short stretch of trail across steep slopes is snowbound and dangerous.

I10, I9, I10

Bond Pass, Dorothy Lake Pass (center) and Forsyth Peak above Grace Meadow

see MAP 19

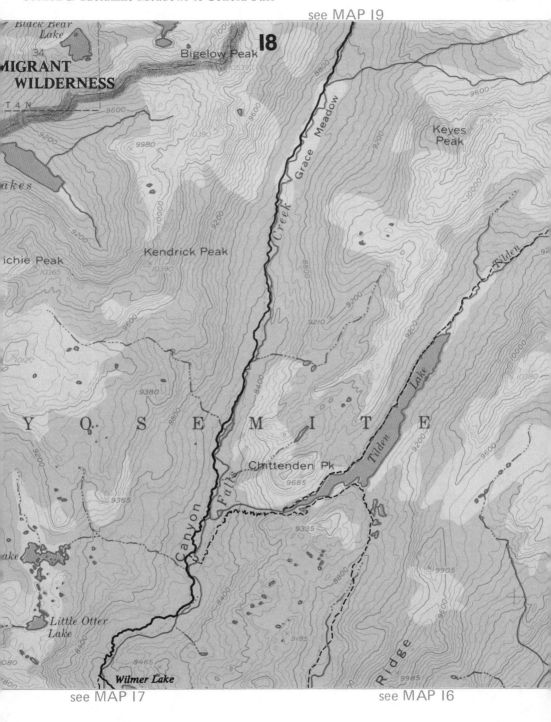

see MAP 17

see MAP 16

see MAP J1

see MAP I9

Ahead, beyond a nearby gully, we traverse along the base of an overly steep wall that is avalanche-prone in early season. We head through a notch in this wall (10,780-0.7) and bid farewell to the last of our excellent views of the Yosemite hinterlands. Our route drops ¼ mile north, then angles northwest, passing two very youthful glacial moraines before climbing to another crest crossing (10,780-0.8). Because volcanic rock is so porous, no lake ponds up behind the moraines. From the crest crossing, our route north hovers around timberline, passing dense, isolated clumps of prostrate whitebark pines before we once again cross the crest (10,870-1.2). We now tackle a 1200+ foot drop to Sonora Pass. In early summer the first ¼ mile of this descent—across steep slopes—is snowbound and potentially lethal if you fall.

Near the end of our descent we cross some closely spaced gullies, with one usually containing water (9820-1.7)—the first creek since Kennedy Canyon. Now in open lodgepole forest we meander slightly up to the Sierra crest, then wind down it to cross Highway 108 (9620-0.7) immediately north of signed Sonora Pass. In the last ½ mile, several trails of use make shortcuts over to the pass, but if you choose the left-hand fork every time you will stay on the PCT. From the pass a jeep road climbs northeast up the crest to a nearby, fairly level area, which serves as an emergency, if windblown, dry campsite, should you not be able to reach an acceptable campsite farther on by dark. Less windy sites lie ¼–½ mile down either side of the pass beside the road.

I10

Northernmost view of Tower Peak (far left) and the Yosemite hinterlands

Section J: Sonora Pass to Echo Lake Resort

Introduction: By the time the hiker has reached Sonora Pass, he'll notice that the Sierra crest has taken on a new character. Virtually all the peaks he'll now see in this section are volcanic in origin—either plugs of pre-glacial volcanoes or remnants of volcanic flows. The erosion of these flows and their associated volcanic sediments has created an impressive, even sometimes surrealistic, landscape, particularly between Ebbetts Pass and the Blue Lakes Road. As in the High Sierra to the south, glaciers flowed down virtually every canyon along this crest route. However, unlike the High Sierra, this landscape is lake-deficient, and the reason for this character lies in its volcanic rocks. The High Sierra is composed mostly of granite rocks, which can be almost 100% resistant to glacier action if they are free of *joints*—a geologist's term for cracks. The joint pattern varies so that in any given area you might see, as you hiked down-canyon, an abundance of joints followed by a paucity of joints. Glaciers cut deep into the abundant-joint sections but then rode over the relatively joint-free sections, which served as effective dams for the basins. In contrast, volcanic flows and sediments lack the joint patterns of granitic rocks, and they are also intrinsically less resistant to glacier attack. In this volcanic landscape, then, a glacier usually advances smoothly down-canyon without carving any basins. The few lakes that do form tend to be small, and most of them are dammed behind moraines, which are deposits left by a glacier. If you were to explore the expansive landscape between Sonora Pass and Echo Summit, you would find that most of its lakes lie in glacier-carved granite basins that are situated below the younger, overlying volcanic ridge-and-crest sediments.

Declination: 15¼°E

Mileages:

	South to North	Distance between Points	North to South
Highway 108 at Sonora Pass......................	0.0		75.2
Wolf Creek Lake saddle...........................	4.1	4.1	71.1
East Carson River trail...........................	9.3	5.2	65.9
Golden Canyon	17.6	8.3	57.6
Asa Lake's outlet creek	24.1	6.5	51.1
Noble Lake......................................	27.0	2.9	48.2
Highway 4 near Ebbetts Pass	30.8	3.8	44.4
Eagle Creek	35.9	5.1	39.3
Raymond Lake trail	40.3	4.4	34.9
Blue Lakes Road.................................	48.5	8.2	26.7

271

Lost Lakes spur road	....	52.7	22.5
		4.2	
rejoin the Tahoe-Yosemite Trail near Frog Lake	......	58.6	16.6
		5.9	
Highway 88 at Carson Pass	....	59.4	15.8
		0.8	
east shore of Showers Lake	....	64.7	10.5
		5.3	
Highway 50 near Little Norway	....	73.7	1.5
		9.0	
Echo Lake Resort	....	75.2	0.0
		1.5	

Supplies: At Sonora Pass you are a long way from any town. From the pass Highway 108 descends 7.8 miles east to Leavitt Meadows Lodge, with meager supplies, then continues 7.5 miles east to a junction with busy Highway 395. This takes you 17 miles south to Bridgeport, which should have any kind of food and equipment that you might need. On the far side of town is the Bridgeport Ranger Station.

After 31 miles of PCT hiking north from Sonora Pass, you'll cross Highway 4 almost at Ebbetts Pass. The closest supplies are at Lake Alpine Lodge, open during the summer, which lies 14 miles southwest down the highway. However, we recommend you go 18 miles northeast down the highway to Markleeville, a peaceful little town with a few eating establishments, a post office and the Forest Service Markleeville Guard Station. If you want to have an enjoyable layover day, hike 4 miles west up Alpine County Road E 1 to Grover Hot Springs State Park, where, for a small charge, you can get a hot bath or a warm swim.

From Ebbetts Pass the PCT continues 28½ miles to Highway 88 at Carson Pass. Like every pass along Section J, this one lacks on-route supplies. Caples Lake Resort, about 4 miles west down the highway, is your closest point for aid and minimal supplies.

It is an easy day hike—14 miles along the PCT—from Highway 88 at Carson Pass to Highway 50 near Little Norway. The Little Norway post office/store/cafe is just 100 yards northwest on Highway 50, and Echo Lake Resort, also with a post office, is only 1.5 miles north of the highway. Because Echo Lake Resort caters to a large backpacker population, it keeps its store well stocked with trail food. However, if you need new boots or other major equipment, follow Highway 50 10 miles northeast from Little Norway down to bustling South Lake Tahoe.

Permits: Unfortunately, to enter Carson-Iceberg Wilderness, just north of Sonora Pass, you'll have to get a permit at the Summit Ranger District office, along Highway 108 at the Pinecrest Lake road junction, which is about 36 miles west of Sonora Pass. Their address is Star Route 1295, Sonora, CA 95370; their phone is (209) 965-3434.

In Mokelumne Wilderness, as in Carson-Iceberg Wilderness, permits aren't required for day hikers. If you start your hike from Highway 4 near the south boundary of Mokelumne Wilderness, you will be in the Carson Ranger District, which has the user-friendly policy of self-service permits at the trailheads—no need to write, phone, or go out of your way. Unfortunately if you are starting a hike south from Highway 88's Carson Pass near the north boundary, you'll be in the Amador Ranger District, whose office is at 26820 Silver Drive in Pioneer, an inconvenient hour's drive southwest from the trailhead (ZIP: 95666; phone: (209) 295-4251). The staff prefers that you pick up your permit in person. Because this office is out of the way for those *not* driving northeast up Highway 88, the Forest Service operates, seven days a week during the summer season, a tiny station at the south end of the Carson Pass parking lot.

From Sonora Pass (9620') the PCT starts north, paralleling westbound Highway 108, and it quickly crosses a trailhead-parking spur road (9610-0.2) at a point about 70 yards from the highway. On a generally northward course, it then winds in and out of more than a dozen gullies before reaching a switchback (10,080-1.7). Ahead, the eastern traverse can be made impassable in early season by steep snow-banks. Also, in some years, the tread virtually disappears in one steep-sloped spot just before a crest saddle. So if you encounter intimidating problems, backtrack and take a cross-country route around them.

To do this, start from the switchback and take the path of least resistance down a bit to where you can contour west to a highly visible old jeep road. Follow it north, the road soon giving way to a trail that you take for a short, steep climb to St. Marys Pass. From it you climb northeast up a ridge to a nearly flat bench just below the west slope of Sonora Peak. You could climb straight up the slope to the summit, and then descend northeast, staying just east of a county-line ridge. This route provides spectacular views, but it requires a lot of effort even with just a day pack. Therefore, head about ½ mile north along the bench to a conspicuous saddle and then head northeast down a cirque to the PCT, about 1200' below. In early season, this 25%-gradient descent can be an enjoyable snow slide.

If the trail is passable, then from the switchback you make an ascending traverse east to a county-line ridge (10,420-0.7), recognized by a group of prominent pinnacles. The sweeping panorama achieved from the nearest summit is well worth the short scramble to it. Dark, volcanic Leavitt Peak dominates the southern skyline, while more-distant, mostly granitic Tower Peak pierces the sky in the south-southeast. Leaving the pinnacles on a gently-climbing trail, we wind in and out of stark gullies, then top the Sierra crest at a saddle (10,500-0.3).

Now we traverse across steep slopes well above the floor of Wolf Creek canyon. Iced-over snow patches can be a real hazard in at least one spot, so be prepared if you're passing through before late July. In about ¼ mile these slopes give way to gentler ones, across which we make a safer, more-relaxing traverse that has whitebark pines reduced to shrub height by winter's freezing winds. As little as 12,000 years ago there would have been no vegetation at all, just a thick river of ice slowly flowing east down Wolf Creek canyon.

Our trail continues to traverse north along the bleak, volcanic lower slopes of Sonora Peak, and below us we soon see Wolf Creek Lake, with the first campsites since Kennedy Canyon, south of Sonora Pass. Well into August this part of the PCT can be obscured by snow, hiding the spot where our trail bends

J1

Wolf Creek Lake and the West Walker River canyon

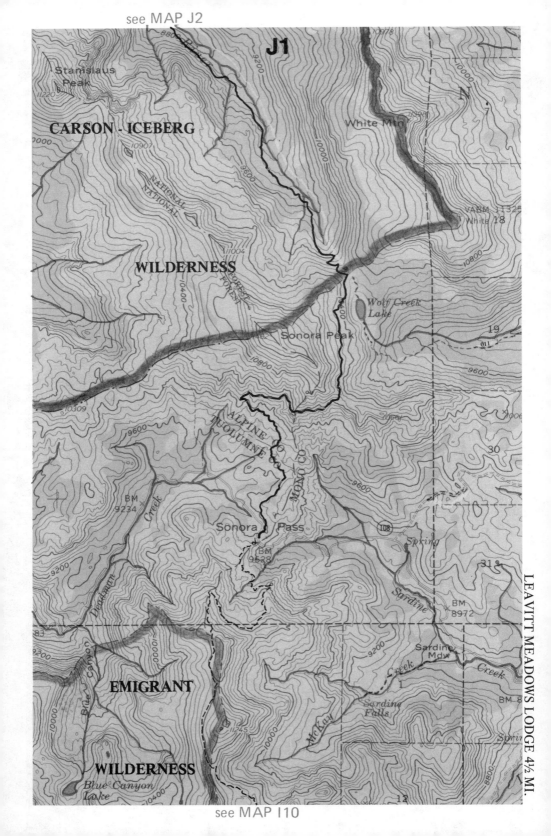

J1

Stanislaus Peak

11220

CARSON - ICEBERG

9000

10907

NATIONAL

NATIONAL

WILDERNESS

11004

FOREST

10400

10309

9600

ALPINE CO
TUOLUMNE CO

BM
9234

Creek

Sonora Pass

BM
9528

9200

Deadman

9200

Blue Canyon

EMIGRANT

10000

WILDERNESS

Blue Canyon
Lake

10400

11245

10000

White Mtn

8598

10000

10000

10000

VABM 11325
White 18

10800

Wolf Creek
Lake

Sonora Peak

10800

10800

10661

MONO CO

9600

9600

108

30

9600

Spring

31

Sardine

BM
8972

Sardine
Mdw

Creek

9200

McKay

Creek

Sardine
Falls

BM 8

Spring

9800

8800

12

right and quickly reaches a granitic ramp. This bend is located near two creeklets found immediately beyond a cluster of wind-cropped willows. Hikers who want to climb easily accessible Sonora Peak can leave the trail here. The rest of us head down the steep, usually snowbound ramp, which is bordered by a granitic cliff on its west side. At its base we exit onto a field of fractured granitic blocks, then snake among them to a junction (10,250-1.2) atop a windblown saddle. From it one or more use paths descend ⅓ mile south to campsites at the west edge of the sedge meadow that contains shallow Wolf Creek Lake.

The PCT enters Carson-Iceberg Wilderness as it leaves the saddle, and then it switchbacks steeply down past sharp, ice-shattered boulders, lingering snow patches and windswept whitebark pines. We quickly drop below the 10,000-foot level, never again to reach it on our trek north to Canada. The trail's gradient then eases considerably before we ford a permanent stream, along which those taking the alternate cross-country route will descend. Continuing down the East Fork Carson River canyon, we pass exposures of glaciated, granitic rock that contain large feldspar crystals, as did the Cathedral Peak granodiorite of Yosemite. Beyond these exposures we cross several avalanche tracks. After a couple hours' descent from the saddle, we reach a small flat, with fair

camping, on which the East Carson trail forks right, and in about 150 yards cross to the east bank of East Fork Carson River.

We veer left, immediately cross two creeks, and then embark on a steep though well-planned tread up the canyon's west wall. Our gradient soon levels, contours to a shallow bowl, and then drops to a larger, forested one. A moderate ascent northeast out of it brings us to the canyon's crest, from which we make a short, increasingly steep descent north to a small flat with an east-end pond. A low knob separates this flat from a prominent crest saddle ¼ mile north of us (8590-3.1). From it a trail descends 1.5 miles through a scenic side canyon to Boulder Lake (a recommended site for a layover day), and then it continues 4.2 miles out to the end of the Clark Fork Road. If you need help, head out to it; you'll certainly encounter people along it, since it parallels Clark Fork Stanislaus River, a fishermen's mecca.

From this saddle we switchback steeply north, soon following an easier gradient west up the crest and then north to a saddle just south of Boulder Peak. A straight, joint-controlled canyon lies below us, which we descend west, and then we curve north around Boulder Peak's lower flank to step-across Boulder Creek (8600-1.6). From it our path climbs northwest briefly, then quickly jogs

J1, J2

Stanislaus Peak, from the East Fork Carson River canyon

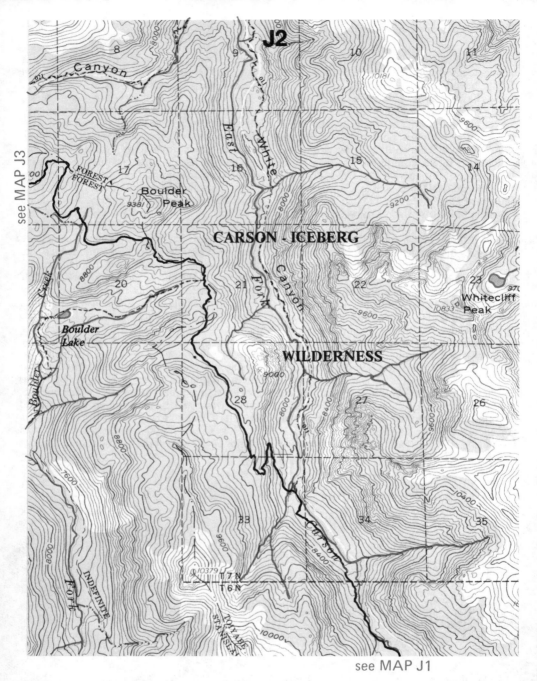

see MAP J3

see MAP J1

southwest—an easily missed switchback for southbound hikers. We soon climb northwest again, quickly spying shady campsites, then continue north back up to the crest. This you promptly leave for a curving traverse around volcanic Peak 9500, staying above the soggy cow meadow at the peak's southwest base. A traverse around the meadow's north end is followed by a climb southwest up to a granite summit, from which we descend an easy ¼ mile to a saddle (9170-2.4). Here an abandoned trail starts southeast, but we make a brief walk

J2, J3

northwest to camps just east of a willow-fringed, seasonal lakelet, Golden Lake. We curve northwest, crossing its outlet creek, which can be buried under early-season snow. Now we contour in and out of gullies to Golden Canyon creek, a large campsite and, shortly beyond it, a trail intersection (9170-1.2). From this spot, the Paradise Valley trail climbs initially, and *invisibly,* northwest to a descending ridge, on which tread appears and climbs steeply southwest up to a well-defined saddle. Also from the spot, the Golden Canyon trail starts a 3.8-mile descent to the East Carson trail.

The PCT climbs northeast across sagebrush slopes and past old paths before topping a saddle (9340-0.6), with a view toward conspicuous Peak 9500 and beyond to dominating Stanislaus Peak. The buff-colored outcrop you see on this saddle is composed of rhyolite, a volcanic rock that is common east of Yosemite but rare here. An ensuing minor descent northwest winds past several campsites near the headwaters of Murray Canyon. It then climbs up to another saddle (9080-1.4) immediately south of a highly fractured, steep-sided volcanic butte. Descending northwest from the saddle, some hikers may momentarily notice a faint trail that starts a traverse north around the butte. The PCT, however, continues northwest, skirts above a large, open bowl, and then curves southwest, ducking into a small but deep side canyon before descending to the slightly cloudy east fork of Wolf Creek (8320-1.5), with a nice camp nearby. A westward traverse takes us past caves and pinnacles in the volcanic sediments above us to the wide, rocky middle fork. Harmless, near-microscopic volcanic particles make this fork quite cloudy. We now climb north past several western forks of Wolf Creek, then switchback west before we cross a poorly defined ridge (8000-1.6). Midway down to Wolf Creek Pass our trail curves north down to a flat saddle, from where the unwary early-season hiker might just continue ahead. The PCT, however, turns abruptly west, descends a small gully and stays close to the crest as it descends northwest past a large lobe of cow-dotted Lower Gardner Meadow. The meadow's creek splashes noisily into a small gorge, and a few moments later we reach an intersection with a trail on Wolf Creek Pass (8410-0.9). A 1.7-mile hike west on it will get you to a trailhead near the Highland Lakes, a popular spot with fishing-oriented car campers.

The PCT parallels this trail north, first staying just west above it, but then climbing northeast to Asa Lake's outlet creek (8520-0.5). Here you can follow the boggy, spring-fed stream up to the nearby 2-acre lake. Like its creek, the lake is spring-fed, and hence too cold for comfortable swimming. However, local beavers don't mind.

From the outlet creek, the PCT arcs west above Asa Lake's spacious north-shore campsites, then soon curves north into a shady bowl, before resuming a steady climb north across sagebrush slopes to a saddle (9330-1.7). Along this ascent you'll have numerous views of the Highland Lakes area, to the southwest. Now the PCT meanders northeast down past whitebark pines to a junction (9110-0.6) with the Noble Canyon trail, which climbs east over a saddle and down into Bull Canyon.

The PCT descends ⅓ mile north to a narrow stringer at the head of large meadow. In early season, when snow may still obscure the route, you're likely to continue ¼ mile north across a bench and arrive at a lakelet with acceptable camping. The PCT, however, crosses the soggy stringer and follows the meadow's edge, first southwest and then north, but soon descends to

Canal flowing into Asa Lake

J3, J4

the lakelet's outlet creek (8900-0.6), which you encounter just above the north end of Noble Lake. Here you'll find marginal campsites crammed between the trail and the lake's outlet.

The trail continues north, then soon switchbacks down juniper-dotted slopes to cross the lake's outlet creek. About ¼ mile beyond it we reach a junction (8360-0.9) with the northern part of the Noble Canyon trail. We then immediately curve west across a ridge and descend to a nearby ford of boulder-choked Noble Creek, which is carving a dramatic landscape out of volcanic sediments. The PCT now climbs northwest, passing five seasonal creeklets before reaching a granitic knob, which it rounds counterclockwise. Then it passes a second knob, just southwest, via a clockwise curve. With a granitic canyon below us and spectacular eroded cliffs above, we follow our cow-trodden path west, shift gears north up to a spur ridge, and then briefly descend west to a junction. From here a spur trail descends ⅓ mile north to a PCT trailhead parking lot, but we wind ⅓ mile, first southwest and then northwest, to Highway 4 (8700-2.9), at a road bend only 200 yards northeast of Ebbetts Pass.

With a surrealistic volcanic landscape awaiting us, we eagerly push northward from Highway 4, crossing an old spur road before climbing quickly northeast to an overlook of the Ebbetts Pass area. With ⅓ mile behind us, we strike northwest to a notch just west of a crest pond, and descend steeply west to a pond and a

lakelet (8760-0.6), the latter, known as Sherrold Lake, providing an adequate campsite. Our often faint tread gradually snakes northwest from the lakelet, ducking in and around obstacles of this granite landscape, then traverses west between a shallow pond and a granite knob just north of it. Following the path of least resistance, we traverse granite benches and then curve northwest to a forested ridge just above and 150 yards south of upper Kinney Lake—an oversized pond in late season when this reservoir is low. Nevertheless, you can camp by it. A westward ¼-mile traverse through a shady forest of lodgepole pines, western white pines and mountain hemlocks brings us to a small broad-crest pond, beyond which our trail curves north, and over the next 1½ miles skirts along the boundary of Mokelumne Wilderness before entering it in the Raymond Meadows area.

The distance from here to the Indian Valley area could be cut by two-thirds if our route were to go northwest to it. Instead, our trail bends northeast up to a broad ridge to begin an incredible route past one of the most bizarre, yet beautiful, landscapes to be seen along the PCT. We descend to a sloping meadow, cross its lower end, and start a sagebrush traverse north past colorful pinnacles and clefts in the flank of Peak 9540. Two more broad spur ridges are crossed before we descend west to the headwaters of Raymond Meadows Creek (8640-3.4), below the rugged, serrated Sierra crest. Since the creek dries up by early August,

J4, J5

View northwest across upper Noble Canyon

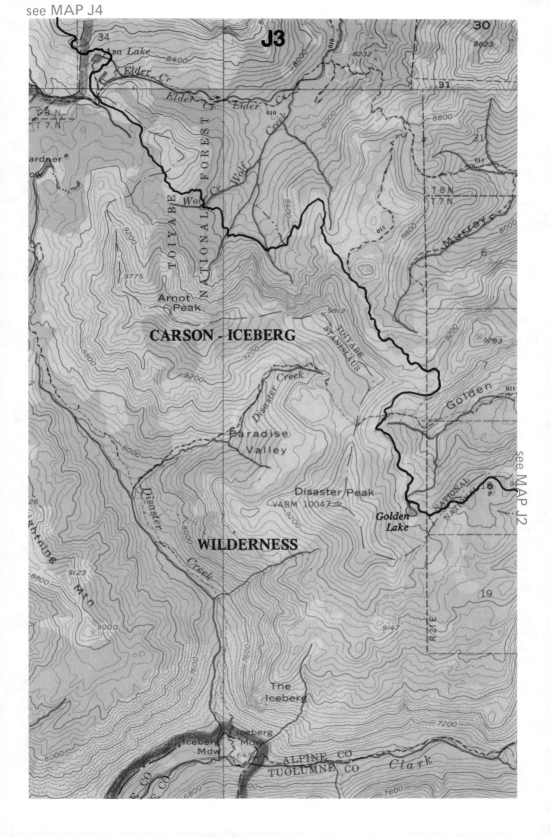

J3

30

34

sa Lake — 8400 —

Elder Cr

Elder Cr

Elder Cr

Creek

8232
×

9823

31

31

015

ardner

ow

T 8 N
T 7 N

9200

TOIYABE

NATIONAL

FOREST

Wolf

Cr

Wolf

8400

8000

8000

8800

010

010

8000

015

8800

8800

Murray

8000

6

T 8 N
T 7 N

9200

9783
⊗

9775

Arnot
Peak

CARSON - ICEBERG

9812

TOIYABE
STANISLAUS

9200

7

8800

Disaster Creek

9200

Golden

021

8000

9200

8000

9200

Paradise
Valley

Disaster

Disaster Peak
VABM 10047

Golden
Lake

8000

NATIONAL

8

95

8000

26

WILDERNESS

9200

Creek

R 21 E

19

8800

9123

Mtn

ahtaline

9000

9147

8000

7600

The
Iceberg

7200

Iceberg
Mdw

Iceberg
Mdw

645

ALPINE CO

TUOLUMNE CO

Clark

CO

CO

6800

8000

7600

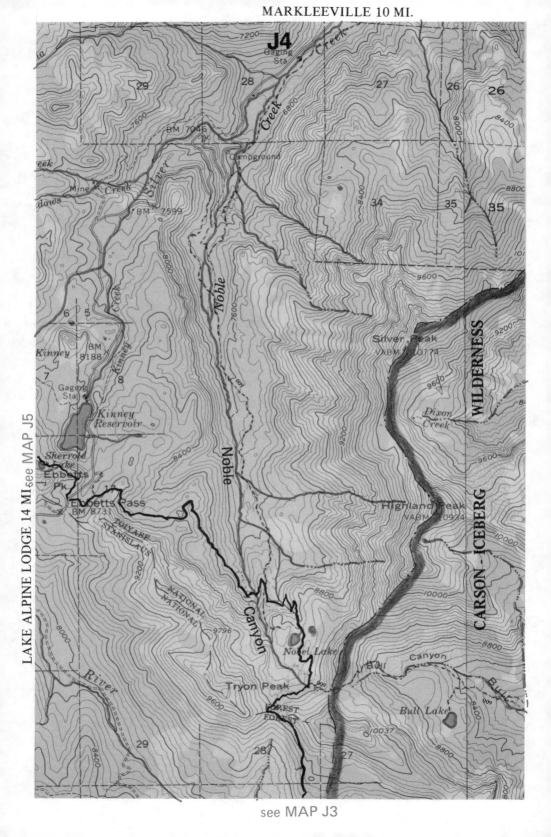

we continue north to another spur ridge, engage a northwest-ascending jeep road at the crest, and parallel the road north to where it begins a steep descent northeast.

Before following our trail west, we're overwhelmed by the symmetry and beauty of a huge dome looming before us. Surpassing any manmade dome in stature, it, together with towering, cathedral-like Peak 9700, on the far skyline, can be a very humbling sight, particularly when they are glowing in the warm rays of early evening. Here, in nature's Holy City, is *the* place for PCT pilgrims to camp, so we hasten west down our trail to barely flowing Eagle Creek (8460-1.1) and a campsite just beyond its step-across ford. Late-season hikers will find water flowing just downstream, where a tributary joins this creek.

We cross this tributary and, engulfed by forest, cross many more as we traverse northeast along the lower slope of the largely unseen dome. This dome sits atop the west end of a ridge, which, eastward, takes on a new appearance. Crowned by high Point 8850, this section of ridge displays an incredible army of sentinels—pinnacles that challenge the rock climber to lay down his pack and try them. The temptation lingers all the way to a deep crest saddle (8510-1.3), from which we switchback through forest down to always flowing Pennsylvania Creek (8140-0.6). Here a small camp could be established just before the jump-across ford. Our odyssey continues with a diagonal climb north to a wind-cropped sagebrush saddle (8660-1.0), followed by an easy descent to seasonally numerous tributaries of

highly gullied Raymond Canyon. Our rollercoaster route winds in and out of these before climbing to a broad east-west crest. Here our faint tread strikes west into a forest that is thriving on the long, north-descending spur from Raymond Peak. We begin to descend northwest across this spur, then meet a trail (8640-1.5) that climbs 0.7 mile south up to tightly confined Raymond Lake. Camping on its shoreline by whitebark pines is fair at best, though the lack of level ground is partly compensated for by the next morning's sunrise, which once again fires up this Vulcan landscape.

From the junction a switchbacking descent, with far-ranging vistas, guides us down to a ford of refreshing Raymond Lake creek (8150-1.0), immediately followed by fords of two smaller creeks. Now we traverse across open, eroded slopes to a saddle, noting along the way the old PCT route below us, Trail 049, which switchbacked 500 feet down before switchbacking up to a junction only 30 yards before we reach the conspicuous saddle (8230-0.8). On west-facing slopes we switchback down to a junction with Pleasant Valley trail 008 (7820-0.6), enter cow country, and climb gradually southwest to a campsite near a tributary (7860-0.4) of Pleasant Valley Creek. On its west bank we start northwest, then angle southwest in and out of gullies up to a crest jeep road, which we follow south 70 yards to a saddle (8200-0.5), where we leave the eastern part of Mokelumne Wilderness. We swing southwest to parallel a road, just above us, cross it in a few minutes, and soon reach a large trailside juniper. The

J5

Sunset in the Eagle Creek area

trail now curves south, levels, and passes the east shore of a pond in the aptly named Wet Meadows area. Early-season hikers, trying to follow a snowbound trail, will be frustrated as their compass rebels to give false readings that are influenced by a close-lying magnetic body. Not until you cross the Blue Lakes Road will your compass *begin* to behave.

From the pond our trail curves west at the north edge of a small meadow, beyond which lies a large lake with fair campsites. Our westward traverse—looking easy on the map—is actually complicated by numerous ups and downs that lie well hidden between the contours. We bend southwest where we cross a narrow road that climbs from a nearby road going to visible Lower Sunset Lake. In a couple of minutes we reach that road (7900-1.6) at a point 200 yards north of a junction with a southeast-climbing road. This road is the same saddle road we briefly paralleled and then crossed before reaching the juniper. It is recommended as an alternate route if you've been having route-finding problems due to lingering snow patches.

Bearing generally west, the PCT crosses the road, avoids the damp soils around Upper Sunset Lake, flirts with an ill-defined Sierra crest, then descends to a spur road, which it follows a few yards west to the road's terminus, a car-camping site (7860-0.6). Immediately beyond it lies a serene lakelet, Lily Pad Lake, whose northeast corner the PCT passes before winding northwest through viewless forest. Midway to the Blue Lakes Road we climb north above the west shore of a shallow lake, with possible camping, then continue northwest, dropping to cross the outlet creek of unseen Tamarack Lake. Soon the forest briefly opens, and almost due north of us stands defiant, steep-sided Jeff Davis Peak—our best beacon to guide us through Blue Lakes country. In the next ½ mile we twice cross the headwaters of Pleasant Valley Creek, the second time immediately before a junction with a short spur trail to an oversized PCT parking lot. An even larger lot, for horsemen, is on the south side of the road. A creeklet, usually lasting through July, bisects the short spur trail, and it provides water of questionable purity to those who might

J5, J6

The Blue Lakes, from slopes west of The Nipple

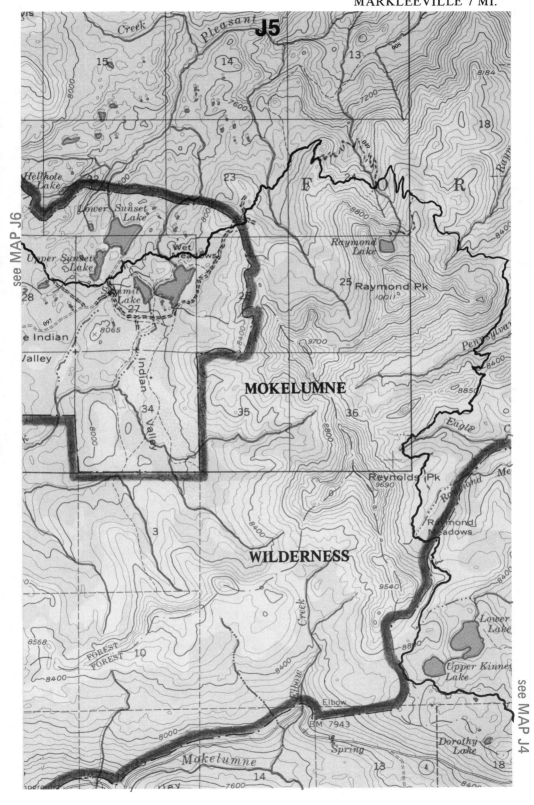

see MAP J6

see MAP J4

Creek

Pleasant

15

14

13

8/84

18

Hellhole
Lake

22

23

F   O   W

R

Lower Sunset
Lake

8800

Raymond
Lake

Upper Sunset
Lake

Wet
Meadows

25   Raymond Pk
1011

28

Summit
Lake

097

26

Pennsylvania

8850

8065

Indian

9700

8400

Eagle

Valley

34

35

36

MOKELUMNE

Reynolds Pk
9690

Raymond Me

3

8400

WILDERNESS

Raymond
Meadows

9540

8568

Lower
Lake

FOREST
FOREST

10

Upper Kinney
Lake

8400

Elbow

Creek

8800

Elbow

BM 7943

Dorothy
Lake

8000

Spring

Mokelumne

4

13

18

14

7600

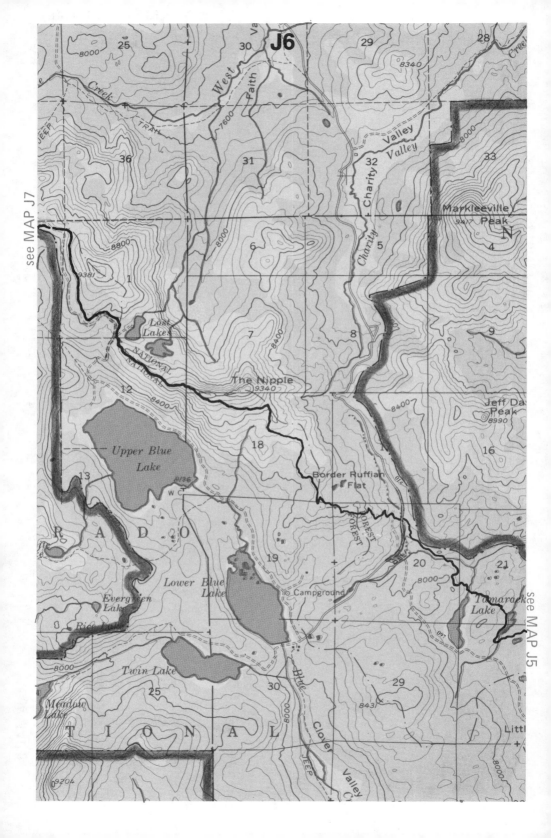

want to camp at the parking lot. The PCT turns north and winds ¼ mile up to the Blue Lakes Road (8900-2.7), crossing it at a bridge over the creeklet. This road gets a lot of use during summer, so if you have to hitch out for help or supplies, here's a good spot to do it.

From the creeklet's west bank we meander 140 yards northwest to the *old* Blue Lakes Road, along which we stroll 60 yards north before leaving it at a bend. You could camp in this vicinity. Back on trail, we make a convoluted climb westward, our trail weaving around a myriad of granitic bedrock outcrops. On this disorienting climb, one can glance east at monolithic Jeff Davis Peak. Listed at 8990 feet on our topo, this volcanic peak is listed at 9065 feet on a newer topo. Either the peak is growing at 4 feet per year or one of the maps is wrong— undoubtedly the latter. The contour lines on any given map are the expression of the cartographer's best effort or guess. Therefore if you try to do precise field work using a topo as a base, you often run into problems. Mapping the PCT in detail is much more difficult than one would guess!

Our trail skirts between two stagnant ponds, then soon heads north up a definable crest, quickly leaving it for a mile-long climb up toward The Nipple. From the saddle at its southeast base (8830-2.4), we see distant Freel Peak in the northeast, this granitic massif standing sentinel above the south shore of

unseen Lake Tahoe. Soon, views of the Ebbetts Pass landscape give way to those of the Blue Lakes, which serve to mark our progress to the Sierra crest west of The Nipple. Along the crest we descend one mile to a closed jeep road, then go 100 yards past it to the Lost Lakes spur road (8660-1.8). Here, by the western lake are your best campsites this side of Carson Pass, though the lake's snags and the presence of car campers do little for wilderness ambience.

Now our famous trail parallels the Blue Lakes Road along the slopes of Peak 9381, which at first are forested, but then open. The open slopes give us views down severely glaciated Summit City Creek canyon and up at hulking Round Top, the highest summit between Ebbetts Pass and Echo Summit. Our trail almost reaches the Sierra crest, but instead veers west, soon crossing Blue Lakes Road and reaching, in about 200 yards, a muddy pond (8830-1.6). You can camp here, though better possibilities lie ahead. Just past the pond we cross a closed jeep road and, momentarily, cross Summit City Canyon trail 18E07 (8880-0.2). Immediately past it we top Forestdale Divide and put the popular Blue Lakes country behind us. We now re-enter Mokelumne Wilderness, and generally will stay within it until just south of Carson Pass. Botanists will appreciate the wonderful wildflower assemblage along the switchbacks down toward several lakelets. Camping is best near the

J6, J7

Round Top, Elephants Back and the Blue Lakes road

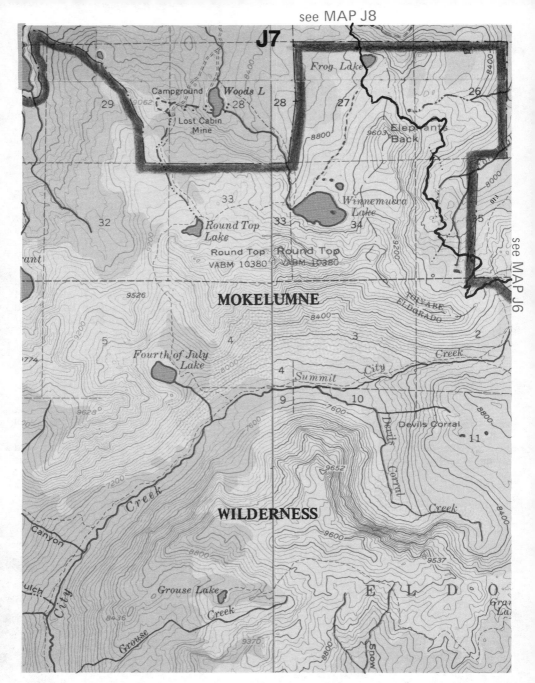

see MAP J6

largest one, which is about 200 yards from the trail. The PCT approaches a second one, only knee-deep, then circles a third (8630-0.8), a tiny pond. Immediately past it we spy a fourth, equally small, then cross a creek coming from the fifth, which is unseen. Our trail crosses two more creeklets before it initiates a winding climb among granitic outcrops. At last we mount a flat, brushy ridge, from whose west end we make a generally moderate climb northwest to the Sierra crest, crossing it just north of dome-shaped Elephants Back. After descend-

Day hikers on the PCT in the Upper Truckee River canyon

ing for a few minutes, we reach a junction (8860-3.1) with a trail that leads south to large, windy Winnemucca Lake and beyond.

Now reunited with the Tahoe-Yosemite trail, which we left below Bond Pass in northern Yosemite National Park, in about 250 yards we reach the corner of shallow Frog Lake, with limited campsites. Beyond this crest lake, we hike ½ mile, making a short, steep, rocky descent north to a parking area, the trailhead for southbound hikers, on *old* Highway 88. This we follow 100 yards up to new Highway 88 and in 120 more yards reach Carson Pass, with two historic markers in a long parking lot (8580-0.8). From the lot's north end we cross the sometimes busy highway and parallel it on an abandoned road to a flat parking area—the trailhead for northbound hikers (8550-0.2).

From the northwest corner of the parking area trekkers first climb southwest and then round a ridge to make an undulating traverse northwest past junipers and occasional aspens to a gullied bowl. After winding in and out of several gullies, we follow short switchbacks north, then traverse west to a junction with a steep trail that descends south to the highway. In 110 yards our north-climbing trail tops a pond-blessed saddle (8800-1.4). In early

season its water is quite fresh, but with time, horses and cattle muddy the situation. Our route follows jeep tracks ⅓ mile north to a junction, where we turn left and descend tracks to a campsite (8460-0.8) by the infant Upper Truckee River. We now make an easy descent northwest, cross the river, and on level terrain pass a trail branching left to two cabins only 200 yards before we meet another one branching right (8380-0.7). Starting as jeep tracks, this trail, the Meiss Meadow trail, traverses 2.3 miles to the northeast corner of Round Lake. You can follow this trail over a low, broad ridge to reach a lodgepole-fringed meadow in 0.5 mile. From it you can then leave the trail and head cross-country 0.6 mile northwest down gentle slopes to the southeast shore of shallow, warm Meiss Lake.

The PCT continues northwest from the Meiss Meadow trail junction, passing another set of northbound tracks in ¼ mile—these to the meadow south of Meiss Lake. Just before we meet a major ford of Upper Truckee River (8310-0.6), we see that lake, and immediately before the ford a faint trail provides the hiker with an easy half-mile meadow traverse to Meiss Lake. The cow-dotted meadow, however, is often damp, if not downright boggy, particularly near the south end of the lake, and until early August this wet environment nurses a multitude of mosquitoes. Before mid-August take the cross-country route to Meiss Lake. From mid-August through mid-September this chest-deep lake is ideal for swimming or just plain relaxing.

After jumping across the Upper Truckee River for the last time, we continue northwest along a meadow's edge and, just before crossing a shallow gap, see a faint trail, on our left, which comes 2.1 miles from Schneider Camp. Just beyond the gap we descend north to a pond and resume our lodgepole-and-meadow traverse. Our jeep tracks soon curve left up an increasingly steep slope on which they narrow to a trail. Nearing a crest, this trail is joined by an abortive set of jeep tracks. We then cross the broad crest and, as we start a descent to nearby Showers Lake, we see a second trail (8650-1.5) from Schneider Camp. Momentarily we reach the east shore of granite-bound Showers Lake (8620-0.1). An old trail may still be seen

traversing northwest across willowy slopes west of the lake, but the time you save by taking this shortcut route will be negated by the mud you'll collect on your boots and socks.

Leaving the lake's campsites, sheltered under western white pines, mountain hemlocks and lodgepole pines, we make a steep descent to the lake's outlet creek, only to make an equally steep ascent up its opposite bank. This, unfortunately, is necessary because a linear wall of granite on the lake's north shore prevents an easier alternative. Behind the linear wall we climb easily west to a junction with the old trail—kept alive by horsemen—then continue onward, passing just beneath an impressive, overhanging volcanic point. Gradually curving northward, we stay just above a granite bench as we cross numerous creeklets. Leaving the bench, we climb steeply north for a moment to a broad, gently sloping area, which we must cross on a mucky traverse northwest through a soggy, deteriorating meadow to a junction (8960-1.9) with Trail 17E16, which

J8, J9

Meiss Lake and volcanic hill

eventually descends to Schneider Camp.

Our forested crest route north now quickly descends to a shallow gap (8890-0.2), from which a faint, discontinuous path strikes east 250 yards down a linear meadow to a camp with a fine view, just beyond the meadow's far end. To the west, a similar tread descends 330 yards to the upper edge of a large meadow, then angles at 330° for 130 yards to a cow camp among a cluster of lodgepoles. Both camps usually have water nearby through July.

From the shallow gap the PCT climbs briefly, and then descends a rocky way to a soggy creek crossing in a small meadow. A short climb from it soon turns into a gradually increasing descent to a saddle junction (8630-1.4) with Sayles Canyon trail 17E14, starting west. Another easy crestline ascent and descent take us to a trail junction in the upper end of Bryan Meadow (8540-0.9). An old trail once cut straight down the meadow, and you can follow it 50 yards west to a small, poor campsite in a cluster of lodgepoles. The new trail starts north before curving west. The PCT climbs 200 yards east to a saddle, crosses it, briefly descends, and then makes a generally viewless climb northeast to the east spur of Peak 8905.

Now begins a fairly continuous descent to Benwood Meadow. First we drop northwest

J9

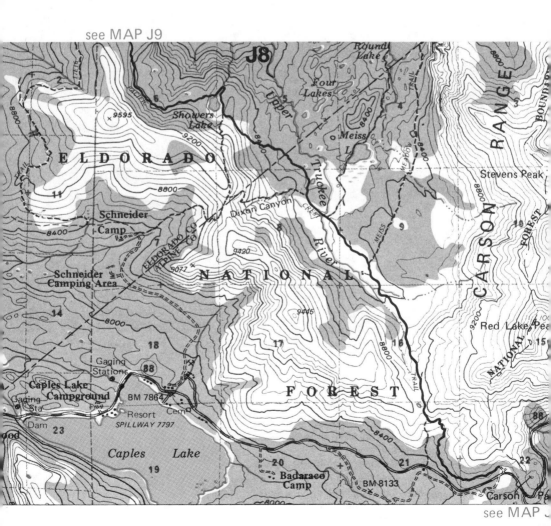

see MAP J9

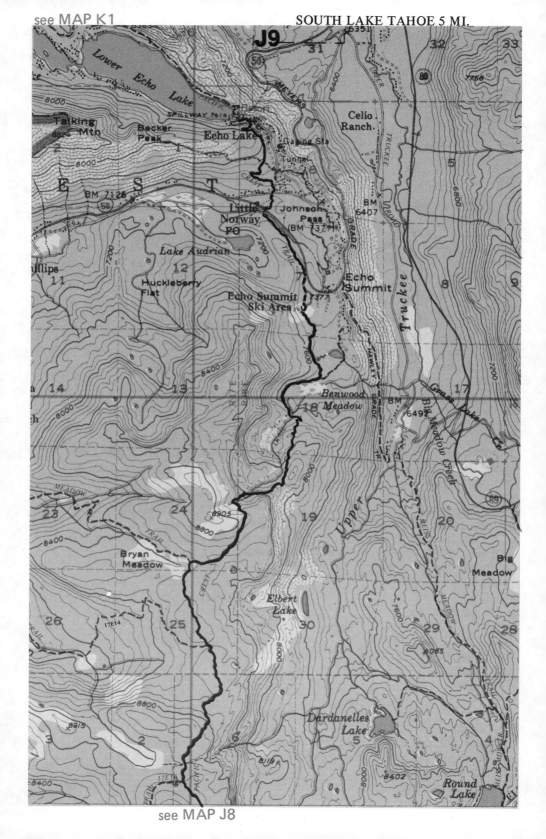

see MAP J8

into a lovely cove, cross its refreshing creek, and then in 0.2 mile recross it (8340-1.1). On a small flat just above the east bank is camping room for six. The trail descends northeast along the base of some intimidating cliffs to reach, in ⅓ mile, a saddle with a view south and east of the Upper Truckee River country. It then descends moderately northward, snaking considerably in its lower part before recrossing the creek. Shortly thereafter, the trail arcs clockwise around Benwood Meadow, staying high enough to avoid the meadow's boggy soil. After the trail traverses along the meadow's north edge, it comes to a junction (7475-1.8).

*   *   *   *

The current, official PCT route goes through the Echo Summit Ski Area, but besides being unattractive, it can be hard to follow. Therefore, some folks still prefer taking a 1.3-mile alternate route. From the junction this initially heads east, then traverses northeast to cross the outlet creek of a lily-pad pond that is dammed behind the crest of the huge west-side lateral moraine of the Upper Truckee River canyon. Onward, the trail winds north up past large boulders to reach a trailhead, ⅔ mile from the junction, on the crest of the moraine. The last 100 yards can be hard to follow, but the crest road and its attendant cottages are obvious. This narrow, paved road goes ⅓ mile north to Highway 50 at Echo Summit, from which one then walks 0.3 mile northwest, passing a highway-maintenance station, before reaching the ski area's entrance.

*   *   *   *

Showers Lake   **J9**

Beyond the Benwood Meadow junction, the newer PCT route meanders north, passing a spring in 0.2 mile, then soon reaching a ski run. This it crosses and then descends about ¼ mile north to the base of another ski run. In past years, the tread has been hard to follow, so to play it safe, you can just descend the first ski run, which narrows to a road, and then take that road down to the ski area's lodge. From its adjacent parking loop, head ¼ mile north along the paved entrance road (Road 1N03) to a resumption of PCT (7390-1.0), this spot being only a few yards before you reach the highway. Note that just 100 yards before this highway, you'll pass a trailhead parking area, with room for about a dozen vehicles.

The PCT winds northwest, staying near the highway and eventually paralleling an alder-lined creek down to a road that bridges it. From the other side of the creek the trail resumes for a few yards up to busy Highway 50 (7220-0.7). Little Norway, with a post office, tiny store, small cafe, rooms, gas and a Greyhound bus stop, is just 100 yards northwest, on the opposite side of an artificial creek from Echo Lakes. The right to water from these lakes is owned by Pacific Gas and Electric Company, which has diverted the outflow westward, away from the Lake Tahoe Basin.

From Highway 50 the PCT crosses the Echo Lakes road in 0.2 mile, the artificial creek in 0.1 mile, and a two-road junction in 0.5 mile, then skirts above Echo Lakes summer homes before making a switchback down to the east end of a backpackers' parking lot above Echo Lake Resort (7525-1.3). Cross Echo Lakes road and follow a tread of sorts down to the resort and its boat dock at Lower Echo Lake (7414-0.2).

In Desolation Wilderness, the PCT skirts Dicks Peak and drops to Middle Velma Lake; view is from the Tahoe-Yosemite Trail

Section K: Echo Lake Resort to Interstate 80

Introduction: Of all the roadless areas in California, compact Desolation Wilderness probably ranks number one in popularity—at least, it has a greater density of hikers per square mile than any other roadless area. The reason for its popularity is simple: it is a beautiful area and it is incredibly easy to reach, lying north of busy Highway 50 and just west above sprawling, urban South Lake Tahoe. It also competes for the number-one spot in density of mountain lakes. From Echo Lake north to Middle Velma Lake you're never more than a few minutes away from a lakeshore or a lake view. The glaciers that scoured out these lake basins, lasting until about 10,000 years ago, also removed the pre-existing soils and loose rocks. Hence in some areas, particularly Desolation Valley, the landscape has a pronounced lack of trees—whence the name *Desolation.* Desolation Valley has been made even more desolate by large Lake Aloha, a Sacramento City reservoir, which floods it. A stand of lodgepoles once greened the south end of this flat-floored valley, but today you'll see only gray snags rising out of the shallow lake, a stark complement to the valley's gray granite walls.

North of Middle Velma Lake, you hike a few miles through viewless forest on a wandering, non-crest trail that certainly deserves replacement by a high-standard crest route. Better tread appears before you leave Desolation Wilderness, and not far north of it you reach Richardson Lake, which offers lakeshore camping and a nice swim. Onward, you enter Granite Chief Wilderness and can make a short diversion to the popular Five Lakes basin or, a few miles farther, make a 20-minute diversion to lightly used Little Needle Lake. Beyond, you climb to a saddle, and if you're not too exhausted, you can take a use trail from here up to nearby Granite Chief for panoramic views of the Tahoe area. After a considerable drop, you climb up to the base of Tinker Knob, which also offers a 360° panorama of the Tahoe area. Good crest views continue as the northbound PCT stays on or close to the volcanic, windswept crest for about 5 miles, then another group of views—of the Donner Pass area—urge the hiker onward for a 2-mile drop to Old Highway 40. You conclude the section with a 2-hour, rambling hike over to bustling Interstate 80, one of the nation's busiest arteries.

293

Declination: 15½°E

Mileages:	South to North	Distance between Points	North to South
Echo Lake Resort.............................	0.0	6.1	63.7
reach Lake Aloha	6.1	7.2	57.6
Dicks Pass........................	13.3	3.8	50.4
jct. above s. shore of Middle Velma Lake............	17.1	9.0	46.6
Richardson Lake's northwest corner	26.1	1.9	37.6
McKinney-Rubicon Springs Road..................	28.0	4.3	35.7
Forest Route 3 near Barker Pass	32.3	2.4	31.4'
North Fork Blackwood Creek campsites	34.7	9.0	29.0
Five Lakes Trail............................	43.7	5.9	20.0
Granite Chief Trail to Squaw Valley................	49.6	3.7	14.1
Tinker Knob saddle...........................	53.3	7.4	10.4
Old Highway 40 near Donner Pass	60.7	3.0	3.0
trailhead-parking lateral near I-80	63.7		0.0

Permits and Supplies: You'll need a wilderness permit to enter Desolation Wilderness but won't need one to enter Granite Chief Wilderness. For the former, write the Forest Service within 90 days of the date you expect to enter the wilderness. Write the Lake Tahoe Basin Management Unit at P.O. Box 731002, South Lake Tahoe, CA 95731-7302, or phone (916) 573-2600. They are located in the *Plaza 89* center at 870 Emerald Bay Road in South Lake Tahoe. (Emerald Bay Road is also Highway 89.) You'll find Plaza 89 on the southwest side of the highway, 0.3 mile northwest of the South Lake Tahoe **Y**, at which Highway 50 branches northeast. If you are driving up Highway 50 from the west, get your permit at Eldorado National Forest Information Center, 3070 Camino Heights Drive, Camino, CA 95709 (phone: (916) 644-6048). Watch for the signed exit a few miles east of Placerville.

This section starts at Echo Lake Resort, which has a store well stocked with trail food and miscellaneous supplies. It also has a post office that is open only a few hours a day. Major supplies are obtained in South Lake Tahoe, 9 miles northeast down Highway 50 from Echo Summit. Ahead, you won't find any on-route supply points in Section K. However, virtually every trail and road east from the PCT will eventually take you, in less than a day's hike, to Highway 89, the Lake Tahoe shoreline, and some nearby highway settlement. Two communities are recommended for emergencies only; under ordinary circumstances they aren't worth the effort. The first is reached by detour after 28 miles. Follow the dusty McKinney-Rubicon Springs Road 8 miles east to Tahoma. The second is Squaw Valley, which can be reached by three routes of nearly equal length, starting from the vicinities of 1) Five Lakes, 2) Emigrant Pass, and 3) Mountain Meadow Lake. Due to esthetics and to private-property constraints, only the last route, Granite Chief Trail 15E23, is recommended.

When you reach Old Highway 40 near Donner Pass, 3 miles before this section's end, you have two choices to resupply. The closest is at Norden House, about 1.5 miles west on the highway. It is a year-round bed and breakfast establishment that also serves lunches and dinners. It has a small but surprisingly well-equipped store. More important, the owner accepts and holds—without charge—United Parcel packages sent by PCT hikers. First contact the owner by writing to P.O. Box 94, Norden, CA 95724, or by phoning him at (916) 426-3326. The second choice is to continue about 1.7 miles west to the Donner Trail Grocery, a relatively complete store that is adjacent to the Soda Springs Post Office.

These are about 0.4 mile west of a junction with Soda Springs Road, at which you'll find a laundromat. There is one more establishment you ought to know about, the Ski Inn. It is located only ¾ mile west of the PCT, just past the Sugar Bowl ski area's entrance, and it has reasonably priced dormitory accommodations (showers included) and relatively inexpensive meals.

Over half the distance to and from the Ralston Peak basin lakes area can be eliminated by taking the Echo Lakes water taxi. Since the Pacific Gas and Electric Company owns the top 12 feet of the lake (because they dammed it that high), they have the right to lower the water by that amount, and by mid-September they usually have done so. Then the lake reverts to its natural, upper-lower pair of lakes, and the taxi service stops.

The Pacific Crest trail coincides with the Tahoe-Yosemite trail (17E01) through most of Desolation Wilderness, the two splitting just north of Middle Velma Lake. We begin this PCT section by crossing Lower Echo Lake's dam. Then we make an initial climb south before heading west on our sparsely treed, rollercoaster trail. The trail traverses below some prominent granodiorite cliffs, and then switchbacks twice and climbs high above lakeshore summer homes. Scattered Jeffrey pines give way to thick groves of lodgepoles as we descend toward the lake's north shore. Then we traverse to a rusty, granitic knoll, round it to forested slopes above Upper Echo Lake, and continue westward. The tree cover is thick enough to blot out any possible view of the public pier at which the water taxis land, and several short trails down to the lake add to the confusion. (The proper one is usually signed.) One can follow any of them down to the shore, then follow a shoreline trail to the obvious pier

K1

Ralston Peak reflected in Ralston Lake; pond lilies invading Cagwin Lake

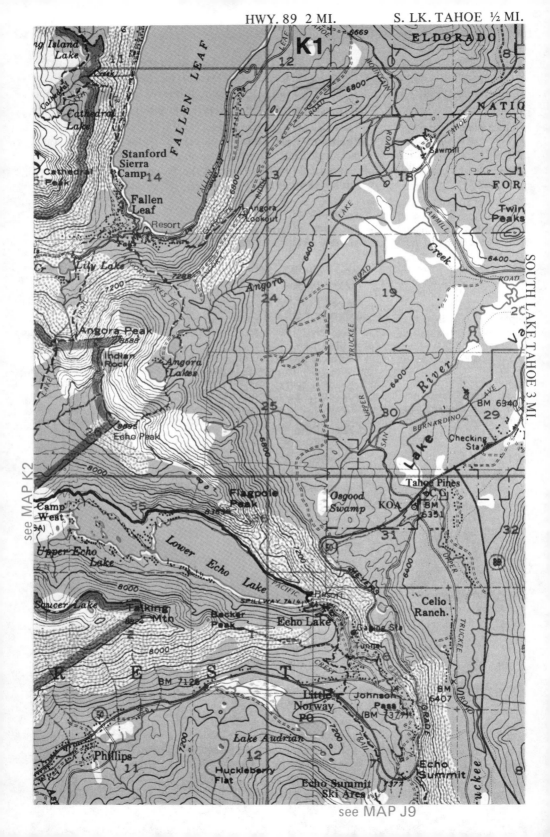

K1

ELDORADO

NATIO

FOR

Twin
Peaks

FALLEN LEAF

Cathedral
Lake

Cathedral
Peak

Stanford
Sierra
Camp 14

Fallen
Leaf
Resort

Angora
Lookout

Sawmill

Creek

6400

Lily Lake

7288

7200

Angora
24

6800

6400

6400

ROAD

19

18

12

13

3

UPPER

SAN

BERNARDINO

River

Lake

BM 6340

29

TAHOE

ROAD

SAWMILL

30

20

Angora Peak
8588

Indian
Rock

Angora
Lakes

8998

Echo Peak

8000

Camp
West
(3A)

Upper Echo
Lake

Saucer Lake

Talking
Mtn

Flagpole
Peak
8218

25

6800

7200

30

Checking
Sta

Tahoe Pines
KOA
CL
BM
6351

Osgood
Swamp

6400

31

32

Celio
Ranch.

Lower Echo Lake

Becker
Peak

Echo Lake

Gaging Sta
Tunnel

PACIFIC

SPILLWAY 7414

Resort

8000

R   E   S   T

BM 7128

Little
Norway
PO

Johnson
Pass
(BM 7377)

BM
6407

Lake Audrian
12

Phillips
11

Huckleberry
Flat

Echo Summit
Ski Area

Echo
Summit
7377

CREST

TRUCKEE

TRUCKEE

UPPER

ROAD

see MAP K2

see MAP J9

View southeast across Lake Aloha

on the lake's north corner. If you've taken the taxi, you'll know which trail to take to get back on the PCT.

Beyond the lake we climb a rocky tread up open slopes and quickly reach a cryptic junction (7700-3.1) with a lateral trail north to a saddle and Triangle Lake. At the Triangle Lake lateral, our trail enters Desolation Wilderness and then it rounds a bend and reaches another trail junction (7865-0.5). From here a ducked trail descends south over barren bedrock to Tamarack Lake, largest of the Ralston Peak basin lakes. Camping is prohibited at all of them. We continue west up the Tahoe-Yosemite

trail to a tiny creek in a gully. Rather than shortcut up the gully, we follow two switchbacks up to a bench, from where we see a lateral trail (8250-0.7) traversing east across a slope to the saddle above Triangle Lake. Just ⅓ mile past this lateral, our trail brings us to the east fringe of Haypress Meadows, rich in wildflowers. Here a trail forks southwest, going ⅔ mile to justifiably popular Lake of the Woods. After an easy stroll northwest, we reach a north-facing-slope junction (8350-0.5) with a second trail to Lake of the Woods.

From this junction we contour only 150 yards before we come to yet another trail, this

K1, K2

Pyramid Peak above Lake of the Woods

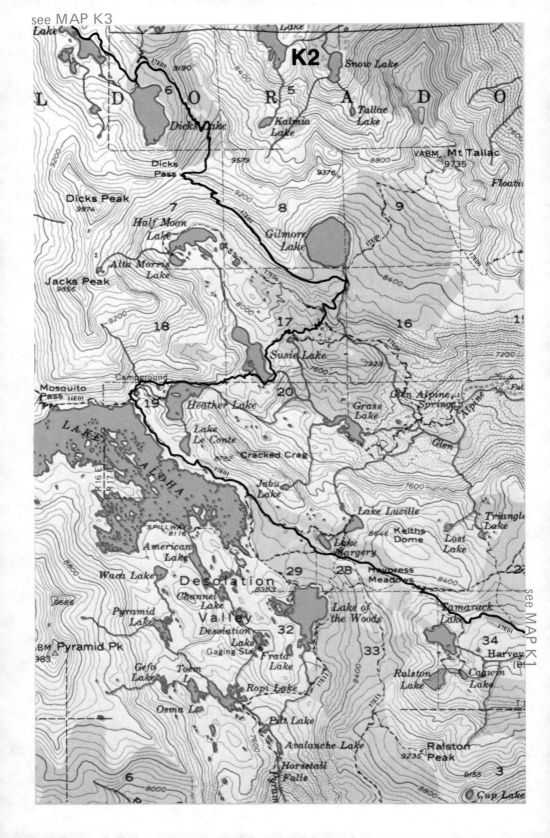

see MAP K3

K2

see MAP K1

one veering right and winding ⅓ mile down to Lake Lucille. After a pleasant traverse above Lake Margery—except for snowbound early-season hikers—we pass a trail (8340-0.5) that leaves our crest and descends to the southeast corner of Lake Aloha, an alternate route with good swimming and several campsites. We descend our amorphous crest northwest to an indistinct saddle, where, by the westernmost of three ankle-deep ponds, we meet a trail (8310-0.2) going first east to Lake Margery then northeast down to Lake Lucille. Both lakes have good camps near them.

Now we enter a thick forest and soon descend on a broad trail down to a junction (8140-0.6) above Lake Aloha. We join the lake's shoreline trail and parallel the lake's unsightly northeast edge, which has hundreds of dead

K2

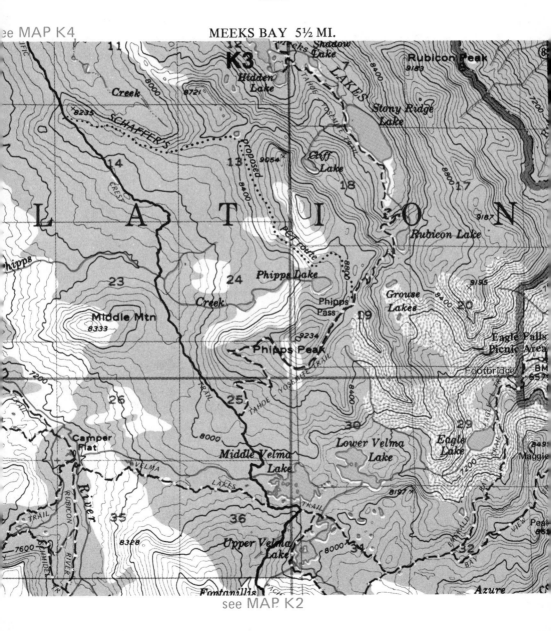

MEEKS BAY 5½ MI.

see MAP K2

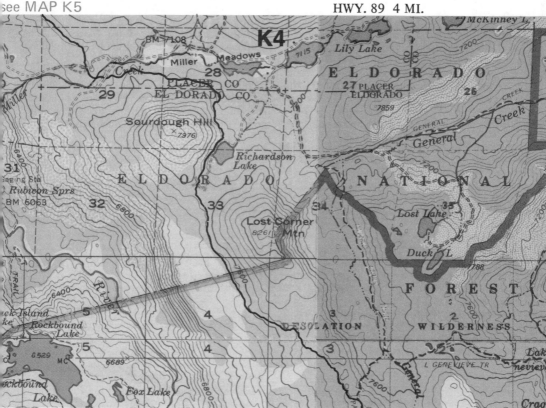

see MAP K3

lodgepole snags that once grew in this basin, Desolation Valley, before the city officials of Sacramento decided it had to be flooded to supply water for their growing population. As we traverse northwest along the lake's shore, we can glance across the lake and see ragged, domineering Pyramid Peak, crowning the south end of the snow-mantled Crystal Range.

Soon our trail takes us alongside a fairly clear, chest-deep, large pond, which like Aloha is good for swimming. Walking 150 yards beyond it, we reach a gully (8190-0.5) up which our trail may seem to head. A snowbank, lasting through July, obscures the correct route, which makes a brief climb southwest before traversing northwest again. Had you gone straight ahead, you would have reached chilly, rockbound Lake LeConte—very scenic, but lacking campsites. Continuing northwest just above Lake Aloha, we now traverse along a nicer, snag-free section, and then reach its

northeast corner, which has a 2'-high retaining wall to prevent the lake from spilling over into Heather Lake, below us to the east. Don't take the abandoned trail at the east end of this wall; rather, climb a few yards west beyond the wall to a junction (8120-0.9) with the Rubicon River trail, which climbs west over Mosquito Pass.

The PCT leaves this junction and descends east, giving us views of the Freel Peak massif to the east. A switchback takes us to a delicate 20'-high waterfall just above deep Heather Lake's northwest shore (7900-0.7). Near a large red fir and the fall's creek is an adequate campsite. Our trail leaves Heather Lake at its low dam, climbs a low, barren ridge, and descends to a cove on the southwest shore of heather-ringed Susie Lake. On a weekend several dozen backpackers may be seen camped at poor, tiny campsites along this easily accessible, dark-shored lake below the towering, rusty, metamorphic shoulder of Jacks

Rusty, metamorphic Jacks Peak looms over Susie Lake

Peak. The best campsites are on a small bench 70 yards down the lake's outlet creek. Perhaps camping wouldn't be so popular around the lake if hikers knew about a 1984 U.S. Geological Survey *Giardia* study. Of 69 High Sierra sources checked for *Giardia,* this lake's outlet creek was the *only one* to have a significantly high level of *Giardia* cysts. We cross the outlet creek (7790-1.1), follow the rocky trail over a low ridge, pass two stagnant ponds, and descend to a flowery, swampy meadow, where the trail forks (7680-0.6). From here a well-used trail to popular Fallen Leaf Resort branches southeast across the meadow. This resort, at the lake's south shore 4½ miles away, has a store and other amenities.

The PCT, now all uphill to Dicks Pass, first switchbacks northeast up to an intersection (7940-0.5) with a second trail southeast down to the Fallen Leaf Lake area. This trail (17E06) also continues northwest to Half Moon and Alta Morris lakes. Beyond this intersection the PCT switchbacks up to a junction (8290-0.6) with Trail 17E09, which leads ¼ mile to good campsites above the south and east shores of orbicular Gilmore Lake. This lateral then continues 1¾ miles up to Mt. Tallac's summit, which gives you perhaps the best view of Lake Tahoe you'll ever see.

As we start west up toward Dicks Pass, we get a peek through the lodgepole forest at Gilmore Lake, and then we ascend steadily northwest, climbing high above the pale brown metavolcanic-rock basin that holds Half Moon and Alta Morris lakes. Lodgepoles, mountain hemlocks and western white pines are soon joined by whitebark pines, the harbinger of timberline, as we approach a saddle east of Dicks Peak. From it, a faint but popular unofficial trail leads up a ridge to the rusty peak's summit.

Rather than descend north from the saddle, our trail climbs ¼ mile east up alongside the ridgecrest in order to bypass the steep slopes and long-lasting snowfields that lie north of the saddle. Our trail reaches Dicks Pass (9380-2.3), an almost level area on the ridge where clusters of dwarfed, wind-trimmed conifers serve as windbreaks or shelters for those who want to camp overnight here to experience the

K2

glorious sunrise falling upon the richly hued metamorphic massif to the west. Lingering snowpatches usually provide campers with a water source. Here, on the highest pass in Desolation Wilderness—and also the highest pass on the PCT north of Sonora Peak's Wolf Creek Lake saddle—we get far-ranging views both north and south.

Ducks guide us across Dicks Pass, the boundary between metamorphic rocks to the south and granitic rocks to the north, and then we descend on hemlock-lined switchbacks, rich in thick gravel from the deeply weathered bedrock. After descending northwest to a rocky saddle, we reach a junction (8500-1.7). Note that one can descend north to another trail junction, traverse northeast over to the Emerald Bay Trail, and take it down to the Eagle Falls Picnic Area, along Highway 89 (right edge of Map K3). From your junction, the route is 4.0 miles long. There are no settlements for miles around, but if you needed help, you could hitchhike along the busy highway either north to several small Lake Tahoe settlements or south to metropolitan South Lake Tahoe.

We descend south from the rocky saddle and quickly reach a spur trail (8450-0.2). This in turn descends 100 yards to a shoreline trail that leads you to campsites along the north shore and east peninsula of Dicks Lake. From the spur-trail junction, we follow the PCT northwest down to a large tarn with a good campsite. Soon we descend a gully to a small cove on Fontanillis Lake's east shore and parallel this shore northwest to the outlet creek. Campsites are fair to poor around this lake but, like most of the Desolation Wilderness lakes, it is stocked with trout.

To leave this rockbound lake, we cross its outlet creek, make a brief climb north to a shady lateral moraine, and then descend part way along its crest before curving left, jumping an intermorainal creek and descending a slightly older lateral moraine to a trail junction (7965-0.9) above the south shore of Middle Velma Lake. From this junction you could also head out to Highway 89, mentioned above, but the first part of that hike—east—is uphill, and the overall route is 4.4 miles long.

From the junction we reach, in only 70 yards, a good view of Middle Velma Lake, and here you'll probably want to descend to campsites by the lake's shore, which are about the best you'll find in Section K. On weekends this lakeshore is crowded, since it is readily acces-

sible from Emerald Bay and it has inviting water that tempts hikers to swim out to and dive from or sunbathe on the lake's rock-slab islands.

Westward, the PCT reaches, only 35 yards beyond a sluggish creek, a trail (7940-0.3) that descends west to Camper Flat. (If you're hiking the PCT in early season, you may find the PCT over Dicks Pass too snowy. Then, you should consider an alternate route to Middle Velma Lake. From the northeast corner of Lake Aloha, head ¾ mile west over to low Mosquito Pass, drop 6½ miles north to Camper Flat, then climb 2¼ miles east to our junction near the southwest arm of Middle Velma Lake.)

The PCT makes a brief descent north to the lake's southwest arm, then it negotiates a muddy traverse across the lake's swampy outlet before it heads north again to an abrupt change in gradient. An old trail used to continue ahead, but now our route first climbs east and then curves northwest to a junction with the old one, from which we climb ⅓ mile north to an important junction (8090-1.1). Here, the Tahoe-Yosemite trail, which has often coincided with the Pacific Crest trail since its start in Tuolumne Meadows, forks northeast and climbs 2.7 miles, via lazy switchbacks, to Phipps Pass before descending 9.1 miles on a lake-blessed route to Lake Tahoe's Meeks Bay.

Leaving the TYT for good, the PCT forks northwest, briefly ascends a shallow gully to an almost imperceptible spur ridge, and then makes a long descent to seasonal Phipps Creek (7620-1.5). On glacier-polished granodiorite slabs just north of the sluggish creek you can find campsites that are relatively mosquito-free. Beyond the creek we climb moderately to better water, which flows down a rock slab into a small pool. We cross its outlet, make a gentle climb to a forested spur-ridge saddle, and descend a shallow gully along the edge of a narrow meadow that runs down it. Our trail passes northeast of a 50-yard-long pond, crosses a boggy meadow beyond it, and then commences a 200-foot climb almost to the top of Peak 8235. From our trail's high point (8120-2.0) one can take a 40-yard spur trail southwest to some rocks from which you see Rubicon, Rockbound and Buck Island reservoirs in the deep canyon to the west.

From this spur-trail junction the PCT descends to a level, northwest-trending ridge, on which we go ½ mile through an open forest to a

K2, K3, K4

junction (7880-0.9). From here the Lake Genevieve Trail forks right and plunges via short switchbacks down to General Creek. We fork left, and in about ½ mile have a good view before we drop into a shallow basin. We then descend a shallow gully, and after the trail levels off, one can leave it at any point for an easy, short descent west to a very open bedrock bench that provides usually dry, relatively mosquito-free camping. Along this level PCT stretch you leave Desolation Wilderness and then, about 0.7 mile later, you reach a snow-depth indicator in a small meadow. From it you climb about 200 yards to a jeep road junction

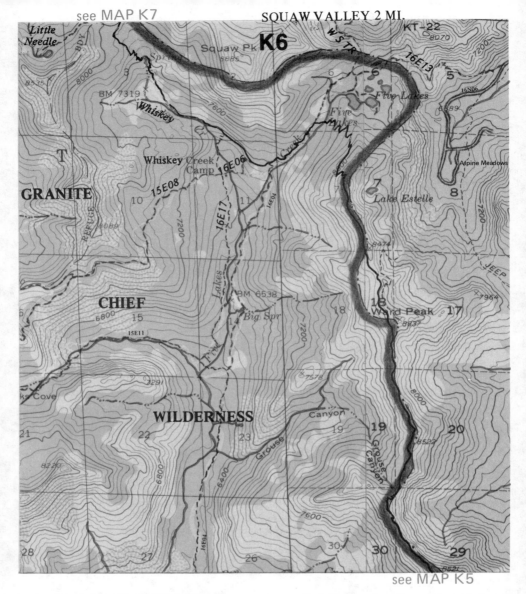

see MAP K5

atop a forested saddle (7570-2.7). The eastbound jeep road drops to shallow Richardson Lake, as does the more-direct, better graded PCT. Along the lake's west shore both nearly touch, and then they diverge at the lake's northwest corner (7400-0.5). Ample space for camping lies along the north shore.

Beyond the lake, the forest is usually so dense that you are unaware you are circling Sourdough Hill. In about ¾ mile, where the trail turns from north to west, you come to within 250 yards of unseen Miller Meadows lake, which is probably for the better, since this oversized lily pond, with questionable water, deserves avoidance. Also, this Miller Meadows area is private land. After ½ mile of westward traverse you approach the western Miller Meadow and then, in another ½ mile, cross a lightly used road (7020-1.7). In 100 yards you re-enter USFS land as you cross Miller Creek, so, if necessary, you can camp nearby or at points north. Past the usually flowing creek, the trail quickly reaches the McKinney-Rubicon Springs Road (7000-0.2), which takes one about 8 miles east to Tahoma, on Lake Tahoe's shore.

K4, K5

PCT parallels this road northwest, keeping within a stone's throw of it. Where the trail curves away from the road, you can drop to it and follow it about 200 yards over to Barker Creek, with abundant camping space frequented by car campers. About ¼ mile past the road the PCT crosses a sloping meadow whose north edge is demarcated by a spring-fed creek. You pass a trickling spring midway to a second sloping meadow, which is about ⅓ mile past the first one. After a couple of minutes' walk beyond that one, you see an old logging road just below the trail, and it parallels your route northeast for about ½ mile. Along this trail stretch at least three springs flow through midsummer, and you could get water at one and then descend to the nearby road and make a *de facto* camp. Past the last spring, which is near a deadend logging spur, the trail climbs ⅓ mile to cross Road 15N03—Forest Route 3 (7650-2.4) near Barker Pass. This well-used road climbs ½ mile south along the crest, then descends 7 miles east to Kaspian Picnic Ground, on the west shore of Tahoe. Tahoe Pines is about ½ mile south on Highway 89; Tahoe City, with major supplies, is about 4½ miles north. Public-transit buses (TART) run along the highway.

Immediately beyond wide Road 15N03, you cross a jeep road, which vaults Barker Pass proper. If you've got enough water, you can make a dry camp at this turf-and-forest pass.

Leaving camp lands behind, we climb west, having views of past and present logging operations in and around the Barker Creek basin, below us. In a short while we top a ridge and view Lake Tahoe to the east and two small volcanic buttes to the north. Our trail switchbacks into a spring-fed gully, then traverses ½ mile over to a saddle (8240-1.6) by the southwestern butte. Here we see, among other sights, conical Barker Peak in the foreground, with Dicks Peak, 14 miles away, on the skyline just above it.

Beyond the buttes the PCT swings past seasonal springs along its drop to a nearly level camping area along the headwaters of North Fork Blackwood Creek (7960-0.8). The possible sites here are the most isolated trailside camps along the PCT in Section K. Onward, you descend north for ½ mile, contour northeast for another ½ mile, then climb switchback legs of differing gradients almost to the Sierra crest, which you reach after rounding minor Peak 8434. Here you enter Granite Chief Wilderness. About 100 yards later, on the north side of a low knoll (8370-2.4), you have excellent views in almost all directions. Of course, those from Twin Peaks, about ½ mile to the northeast, are even better. To reach Twin Peaks, start here, where the PCT traverses north from the crest, and climb northeast up the peaks' south ridge. The gradient increases as you approach the base of a lava knoll, and you

K5

PCT heading southeast toward Twin Peaks

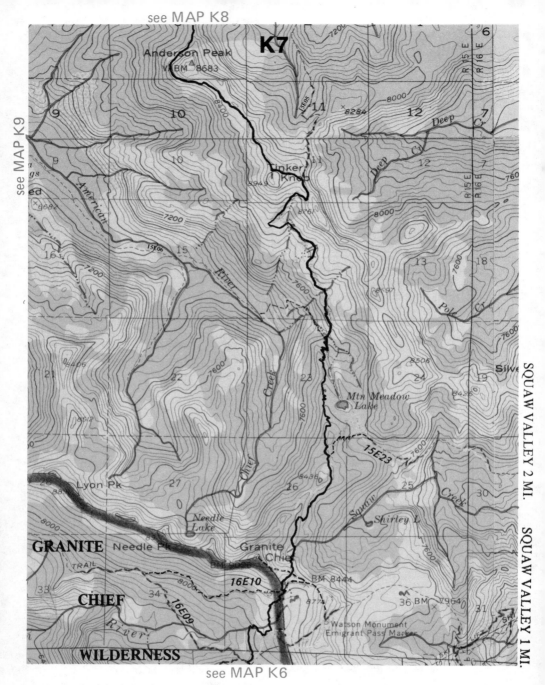

see MAP K9

see MAP K6

leave the ridge, veering left (north) and climbing steeply up behind it. You then see the easy, obvious route up to the west summit of Twin Peaks. The east summit can be tackled by a number of routes, all requiring extensive use of hands. Do note that all routes up to this summit require caution, since all are fairly steep and loose rocks abound.

The PCT contours past Twin Peaks back to the crest, then stays on or very close to it for the next 4 miles. Classic crest-views prevail. Early on this crest traverse you see massive,

K5, K6

columnar lava flows on the flanks of Powder-horn and Little Powderhorn canyons, to the southwest. These flows dwarf the one seen at Devils Postpile, south of Yosemite National Park. Beyond Peak 8522, a remnant of a lava flow perched high above Grouse Canyon, you pass beautiful, trailside hexagonal columns like those at Devils Postpile. As you head north toward Ward Peak, note how the lava flows dip away from deep Ward Creek canyon, to the east. Evidently, there was once a volcano situated there and today all we see are parts of its western flank. The PCT nearly tops Ward Peak, and just northwest of it the trail closely approaches the peak's maintenance road (8470-3.5). On it you can descend to Alpine Meadows Ski Area (which you'll see ⅓ mile farther along the PCT), then head 3½ miles out to Highway 89. Tahoe City is 4 miles south-east up it.

Past our view of Alpine Meadows, our trail, which has been mostly across volcanic rocks since Barker Pass, completes its crest traverse on older rocks, first metamorphic and then granitic. Beyond the last crest knoll the trail switchbacks 16 times as it descends to Five Lakes Creek. If you want to reach the largest and westernmost of the Five Lakes, leave the trail at its ninth switchback, traverse on a slight

descent north for a minute or two, and you should find yourself on a crest about 100 feet above the lake. Continue down the crest to campsites by this warm, shallow lake.

If you stay on the PCT, you'll cross Five Lakes Creek with a bathtub-size pool, about 130 yards before you meet Trail 16E04 (7430-3.1). Here's another opportunity to head over to Lake Tahoe to resupply. First, climb 0.6 mile northeast to a junction with the unmaintained W S (Western States) Trail, and then in a minute or two pass a spur trail south to the nearby Five Lakes. Continue eastward on Five Lakes Trail 16E13 1.9 miles down to Alpine Meadows Road, the trailhead located just opposite the road's junction with the upper end of Deer Park Drive. Take Alpine Meadows Road 2.1 miles down to Highway 89, and follow this busy highway just under 4 miles up along the Truckee River to bustling Tahoe City.

Continuing along the PCT, we parallel Five Lakes Creek down-canyon as we cross generally brushy, flowery slopes. As we're about to curve west through a forest, we come to a junction. Here an old trail starts south, bound for Diamond Crossing. On the PCT we make a forested 250-yard traverse west to a junction with Whiskey Creek Trail 16E06 (7170-1.0). This

K6

Tinker Knob saddle and Peak 8761

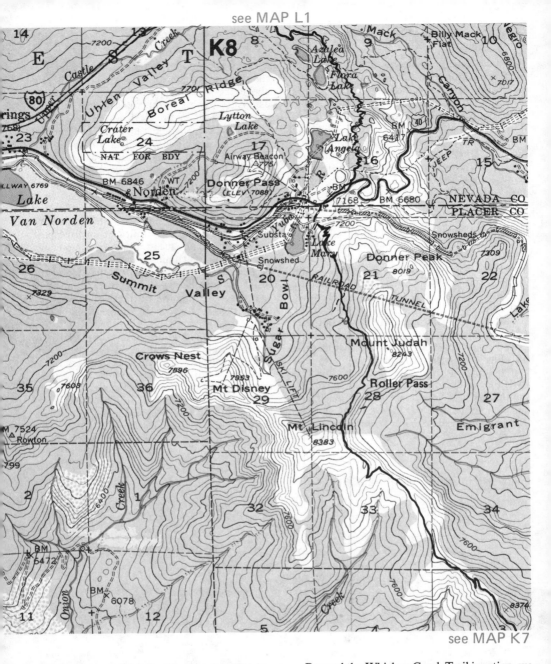

see MAP K7

trail makes a 0.4-mile descent to Whiskey Creek, above whose west bank one finds Whiskey Creek Camp. The spacious camp, with bunkhouse, storage shed and a roofed stove, is popular with equestrians, as attested by abundant horse manure. Hikers can head west or north 100–200 yards and find more-sanitary sites.

Beyond the Whiskey Creek Trail junction, we soon start a ½-mile traverse across steep, brushy slopes, which ends just before our trail reaches the floor of a hanging valley. Here you can walk a few paces over to Whiskey Creek and get its refreshing water before the creek plunges over the valley's brink. Anywhere over the next ⅓ mile you can leave the PCT and

K6

make a camp near this creek. The trail then climbs, moderately to steeply, above a 50-acre field of mule ears to a spring among some alders. Short switchbacks follow, giving way to a meadowy climb that in turn yields to a brief, rocky traverse to a forested saddle. On slopes immediately north below it we meet the Tevis Cup Trail (7915-2.1). For isolated camping, you can head 100 yards northwest down this trail to where, by the edge of a meadow, you find a faint, unmarked trail climbing west-southwest upslope. This ¾-mile long trail becomes more prominent higher up, then dies out past a campsite above the northwest shore of Little Needle Lake.

Northward, the PCT doubles as the route of Tevis Cup Trail 16E09, and we cross and recross the headwaters of Middle Fork American River before the two routes split (8140-0.6). The Tevis Cup Trail climbs rather steeply 0.6 mile east to Emigrant Pass, from which one could descend a road about a mile to the top end of an aerial tramway. Both the road and the tramway descend to Squaw Valley. In summer, the tramway receives quite a bit of use by day hikers bound for the summit of Granite Chief.

Leaving the junction, we cross the miniscule headwaters of Middle Fork American River in 100 yards. Northward, we make a switchbacking climb to an intersection of Western States Trail 16E10, which eastward contours 0.2 mile over to a trail junction on a Sierra-crest saddle before climbing southeast to Emigrant Pass. From that saddle, a trail (used by Squaw Valley tram riders bound for Granite Chief) parallels the crest west-northwest, and we intersect it about two minutes past a spring and only a few heartbeats before the PCT crosses the Sierra crest. This trail climbs steeply 0.4 mile to the summit of Granite Chief—a worthy side trip, for it is the highest point (barely) for miles around.

The PCT crosses the Sierra crest at a minor gap (8550-0.7) immediately beyond this trail, which lies just outside Granite Chief Wilderness. The wilderness setting is disrupted here by the presence of a ski tower just above the trail. We have a hemlock-filtered view of Mt. Rose, which rises above the north shore of Lake Tahoe, but it disappears as we descend short, steep switchbacks—snow-covered in early summer—down to a fragile, subalpine meadow. At its east end we cross the headwaters of Squaw Creek (8270-0.4), and 200 yards northwest of it encounter a small gravel

flat, which makes an adequate campsite. The PCT makes a short traverse north, before crossing beneath granite cliffs and then later descending to an important junction with Granite Chief Trail 15E23 (8170-1.1). This trail winds 3.8 miles down to the north side of a fire station, along Squaw Valley's main road. For supplies, follow the road a short way down-valley to a small shopping center, where you'll also find the Olympic Valley Post Office.

Continuing, the PCT first crosses a minor saddle, then it follows a descending ridge north, offering views south toward Granite Chief, southwest toward Needle and Lyon peaks, northwest down the North Fork American River canyon, and north across the canyon toward our next main goal, Tinker Knob. The views actually improve as we get lower, and then we leave the crest and switchback down to a junction with Painted Rock Trail 15E06 (7550-1.5). Along the last part of this stretch you may see signs of an old trail that once went to Mountain Meadow Lake. This lake lies on private land and is part of an ecological study area that is closed to public entry.

From the junction the PCT descends a few yards to cross the North Fork's headwaters, then it climbs around and over granitic outcrops, reaching a bowl with water and a campsite in ⅔ mile. About ⅓ mile past this bowl, the trail enters a larger one, with more-spacious camping on a waterless flat below the trail. Beyond the bowl you contour past two usually flowing springs and then, in ¼ mile, switchback for a sustained 0.6-mile climb to Tinker Knob saddle (8590-2.2). Sharp-crested Peak 8761, just south of us, divides the impressive panorama we have to the south and east.

For a 360° panorama of the Lake Tahoe Basin/Donner Pass area, head ⅓ mile northwest on the PCT, to where it starts to drop along the Sierra crest. Leave the trail and climb south carefully up to the highly fractured summit of Tinker Knob, reached in 5 to 10 minutes. Inspecting the terrain seen from today's summit, we view a volcanic landscape that has undergone severe erosion, partly due to glaciers, and this erosion has exposed the underlying granitic and metamorphic bedrock. Among the more prominent landmarks is Mt. Rose (10,776'), which stands high above Lake Tahoe's north shore. To the south stands aptly named Granite Chief, devoid of volcanic rock, and in the distant south shines the snowy, granitic Crystal Range, which forms the backbone of Desolation Wilderness.

After you've had your share of views, return to the PCT and head north along the open, windswept crest, with drought-resistant wildflowers. As you drop west around Anderson Peak, note how its massive lava flow dips to the southeast, indicating its source was a volcano standing in the northwest. The PCT momentarily returns to the crest at a saddle just north of Anderson Peak, and here it passes below the Sierra Club's Benson Hut. It then rounds Peak 8374 to a shallower saddle (8170-2.6), from which we have excellent views of the Truckee basin, to the east.

Backward glances toward Anderson Peak mark our progress northward, and after a while we have our first views of Donner Lake, seen as we approach a broad saddle in Section 33. In this section, most of the land west of the crest is private property. We enter USFS land where the PCT leaves the crest for an arc north across steep, gullied slopes of Mt. Lincoln. Past the mountain we enter a sheltering pine-and-fir forest as we descend easily to another broad saddle, Roller Pass (7900-2.8). From here, one can take a recommended USFS cross-country route 0.4 mile northeast up to the summit of Mt. Judah for your last and best view of Donner Lake. This summit also provides the best view of the Donner Pass environs.

On leaving Roller Pass we have our first view northwest down into a popular skiers' playland: Soda Springs, on Old Highway 40, just beyond Lake Van Norden. At first the PCT contours around Mt. Judah, but after ¼ mile it begins to drop, rather moderately, and it crosses a one-lane road (7520-0.8). Soon the forest is replaced by open slopes covered with dense huckleberry-oak scrub. The trail then reaches a rocky bench above a talus slope, From a switchback, the trail makes a short, steep descent west—a stretch that can be snowbound well into July. The descent ends at a road junction (7060-1.0), from where a private road to some Lake Mary homesites branches southwest from an eastbound road. Pace 40 yards northwest on this road to a better road, turn right, and walk north up to nearby Old Highway 40 (7090-0.2). See the last paragraph of this section's "Permits and Supplies" for PCT services available west along this road.

Across the highway, PCT tread resumes by first traversing northeast, part of this short stretch blasted out of bedrock cliffs. It then turns north and soon passes other cliffs popular with rock climbers. Next it winds north through a bowl and then, with a plethora of switchbacks, climbs to a divide that is about ¼ mile due east of Lake Angela's northeast corner. You then descend north to a Section 16 pond, cross under powerlines, and arrive at a Section 9 pond. About 0.2 mile past this pond you cross the brush-lined creek draining Flora Lake. The trail then climbs to the base of some prominent cliffs, heads north past them through a shallow saddle, and then turns west. After about ¼ mile, the trail abruptly turns north and almost tops a higher, shallow saddle. On the other side of the saddle is a shallow basin that holds Azalea and Flora lakes. Be aware that both lakes are on private land and are sources of domestic water supply. The PCT was routed around them so that the water supply wouldn't be contaminated.

From the higher shallow saddle, we begin a ¼-mile descent, which momentarily enters a shady forest. This can have snow through mid-July and hordes of mosquitoes through mid-August. The PCT levels off at the edge of a meadow, where there is a junction (7190-3.0). Here, ¼ mile south of Interstate 80, is where we've chosen to end Section K's PCT, since where the trail crosses *under* the busy highway, there is no legal parking.

To reach I-80's trailhead parking lot, branch 200 yards west along a trail to a junction just above a shallow, murky lakelet. Here you join the 0.6-mile-long Glacier Meadow Loop Trail 15E32, a nature trail with signs. Northwest, it goes 250 yards to eastbound Interstate 80's Donner Summit Safety Roadside Rest Area, which receives heavy use by motorists. Continue west, then southwest on the nature trail. It then turns north, and you immediately reach another junction, ¼ mile from the last. Here you leave the nature trail, which continues 230 yards north to the safety roadside rest area. You take a westward-meandering trail for 300 yards over to the east end of the trailhead parking lot.

To reach this lot by vehicle, take the Interstate 80 exit signed for Castle Peak and Boreal Ridge. This is the first exit west of the interstate's two safety roadside rest areas, and it is the first exit east of the Soda Springs exit. Immediately south of the eastbound lanes' onramp and offramp, you'll reach an obvious road which you follow 0.3 mile east to its end at the trailhead parking lot.

K6, K7

Section L: Interstate 80 to Highway 49

Introduction: Only 38.4 miles long, this section is easily the shortest one in this guide. It is actually short enough for strong day hikers to complete it in one long day. Heavily laden tri-state backpackers can do it in two. The first two-thirds of the distance is mostly on or close to a sinuous crest of volcanic rocks, and you have abundant views of Sierra crest terrain from Tinker Knob northwest to the Sierra Buttes. But then you drop toward Jackson Meadow Reservoir, hiking generally on metamorphic rocks, and views are few. The stretch descending along Milton Creek is about as far from the crest as one can get, but after going miles between reliable water sources, this chorusing creek is music to one's ears as well as relief for one's dry throat.

Declination: 15¾°E

Mileages:

	South to North	Distances between Points	North to South
trailhead parking lateral near I-80	0.0		38.4
		4.2	
Peter Grubb Hut	4.2		34.2
		4.1	
Magonigal Camp jeep road	8.3		30.1
		7.6	
Meadow Lake Road 19N11......................	15.9		22.5
		11.6	
Road 07 near Jackson Meadow Reservoir	27.5		10.9
		6.3	
first (southern) Milton Creek crossing	33.8		4.6
		2.0	
closed road to Wild Plum Campground.............	35.8		2.6
		2.6	
Highway 49 near Sierra City......................	38.4		0.0

Supplies: There are no post offices along the route at which to pick up your parcels. See the last paragraph of the previous section's "Permits and Supplies" for services available along Old Highway 40, about 3 trail miles south of the start of Section L. You can get a few minor items at a gas station's minimart at Boreal Ridge Ski Resort, which lies along the south edge of Interstate 80 about ¾ mile west of where the PCT tunnels under this highway. Near the section's north end you can head over to Highway 49 and follow it down to nearby Sierra City, which has a post office, motels, restaurants and stores.

We begin this section just south of Interstate 80. If you're starting your trek in this vicinity, consult the last paragraph of the previous section for driving directions to the trailhead parking lot. Then follow in reverse the next-to-the-last paragraph for trail directions to the PCT. Basically, you go 300 yards east to a nature trail, ¼ mile up it, then 200 yards east to the PCT (elev. 7190). Here is where Section L's mileage begins.

From the junction the northbound PCT skirts the west edge of a wet, willowy meadow and in ¼ mile reaches Interstate 80. A horse-and-hiker tunnel had been constructed under both the westbound and eastbound lanes—a decided plus for equestrians. However, a stream also goes beneath the lanes, and at times of high runoff, it backs up and overflows through the horse tunnel. Under these circumstances, hikers may opt for a dash across I-80. The PCT then heads 0.2 mile upstream before intersecting Summit Lake Trail 15E09. This descends about 400 yards southwest to the east side of a building at westbound I-80's Donner Summit Safety Roadside Rest Area. The PCT makes a brief climb west, then turns southwest to descend, like the Summit Lake Trail, to the grounds of the rest area. Just northwest of the building, the PCT joins a loop trail that circles a lakelet lying immediately west of the building. Walk about 150 yards along this trail to a junction (7230-0.9), by the lake's west shore, where the loop trail turns south.

Now we leave the confusing array of trails of the I-80 rest areas by starting a climb west-southwest across glaciated granitic slabs, then soon turning northwest and paralleling a major fracture in the bedrock. Beyond it the PCT veers west toward Castle Valley and, staying within tree cover, follows the valley's meadow northwest to a road (7440-1.0). Onward, the early-season hiker is likely to encounter at least a dozen seasonal streams, some of them quite impressive. And before mid-July you just might get wet feet—and find much of the trail under snow. From the last seasonal stream the PCT curves southwest up to a junction with an abandoned jeep road where it crosses Castle Pass (7910-1.4). This road descends 1.9 miles to the on-and offramps of westbound I-80, and in former days it was a temporary part of the PCT route.

From Castle Pass the PCT stays just above the old jeep road for ¼ mile, coincides with it for 100 yards, then stays just below it. Soon both drop into Round Valley, the PCT switchbacking down to Peter Grubb Hut (7820-0.9), which is one of several Sierra Club cabins in the Sierra Nevada. It is open for public use, but please treat it properly. A minute past the hut we jump across Lower Castle Creek, and a minute later we reach westbound Sand Ridge Lake Trail 14E11. Soon we start to climb again, shortly reaching the back side of a glacier-smoothed-and-striated granitic outcrop, from which one has westward views of the Sand Ridge environs. Your climb continues, first up along a persisting creeklet, and then you cross and recross the old jeep road. The PCT then takes an undulating course north, staying below the road but then crossing it (8270-2.2). Apply the repellent, folks, for you're about to enter prime mosquito land.

At first your trail descends alongside the road, but then you switchback down through a forest dominated by mountain hemlocks, which

L1, L2

Glacier-carved Paradise Lake canyon

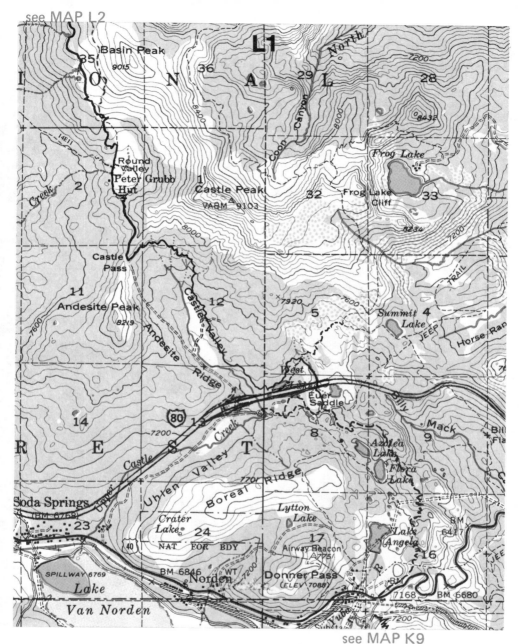

see MAP K9

can be snowbound well into July. Later we leap across North Creek, and quickly pass mosquito ponds for a short traverse to the Magonigal Camp jeep road (7580-1.9). This junction is immediately west of a large, boggy meadow—something to look for if you plan to head east 1.1 miles up to Paradise Lake and then back again. The jeep road to it is open to ORVs, and mosquitoes abound along the west shore. How-

ever, the rocky east shore, reached by a cross-country traverse around the south tip, does merit a layover day. Just before the south tip you'll hit some bedrock cliffs, but these are quite safely negotiated with a bit of prudent route finding.

From the jeep road junction, we first head north past a stagnant pond, then make a climbing effort northwest, emerging from forest

L2

shade to soon reach a knoll (8120-1.1), where a rest is in order. Next we round a nearby ridge and then switchback down steep slopes cloaked with a dense, snow-harboring forest. The gradient abates, and soon we reach White Rock Creek (7630-1.2), which is likely a wet crossing for all but late-season hikers.

Due to the presence of jeep tracks and cow tracks and to a dearth of trees suitable for blazes, the stretch ahead can be hard to follow, particularly for those southbound. In essence you go about 120 yards north-northwest to a meadow, slog through a boggy stretch near its lower end, then soon parallel the northeast edge of a larger meadow, on your left, as you climb northwest. A road climbs north from this meadow, and you almost touch it as your trail

snakes briefly north up to a bend in Road 19N11A (7760-0.7). This bend is 100 yards north of Road 19N11A's junction with the meadow's road.

With the meadowy mess behind us, we climb generally west, ducking in and out of many gullies cleft in steep volcanic slopes. The soil is rich in clay, and when wet the route can be quite slippery—something to watch for over the stretch to Jackson Meadow Reservoir. Without too much effort we cross a saddle (8140-0.8), and have our first of many views to the north. We continue west on slopes below Peak 8450, first past meadows with springs, and then through a forest of mountain hemlocks, which in years of heavy snowfall can retain snow patches into September. The trail then curves

L2, L3

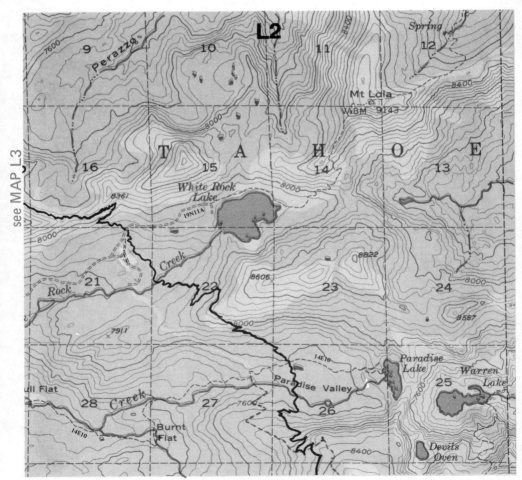

see MAP L3

Meadow Lake Hill separates Fordyce Lake (left) from Meadow Lake (right)

Heading northwest toward Jackson Meadow Reservoir and the Sierra Buttes

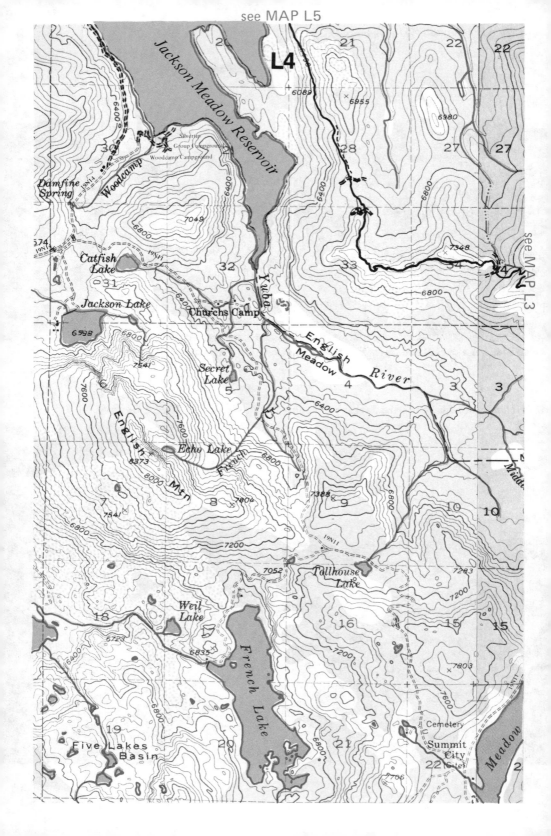

L4

see MAP L3

Jackson Meadow Reservoir

Damfine
Spring

Woodcamp

Silvertip Group Campground
Woodcamp Campground

Catfish
Lake

Jackson Lake

Churchs Camp

Yuba

English Meadow River

Secret
Lake

Echo Lake

English Mtn

French Cr.

Tollhouse
Lake

Weil
Lake

French Lake

Five Lakes
Basin

Cemetery

Summit
City
(site)

Meadow

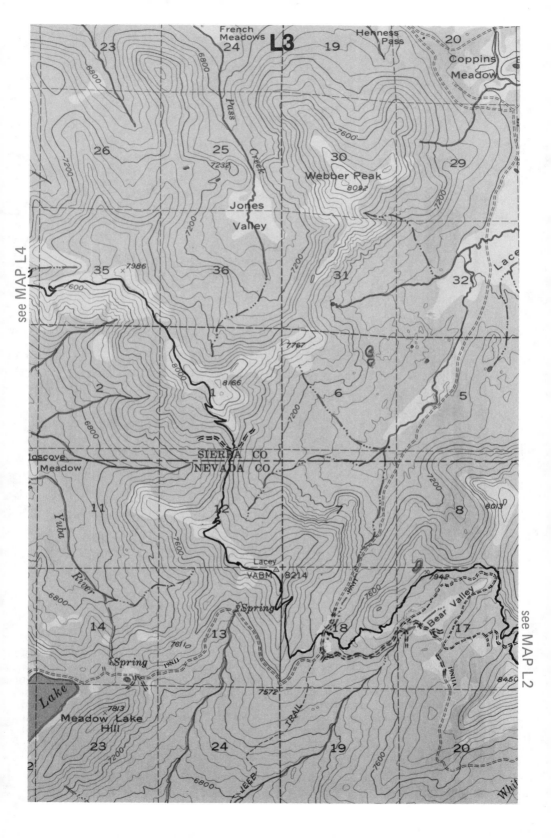

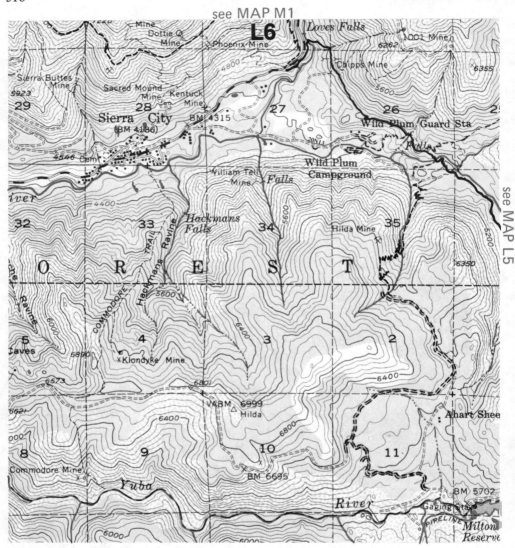

see MAP M1

see MAP L5

to descend a north-trending ridge, and we quickly reach its low point, where we cross a road on a viewless saddle (8060-0.7).

We climb north-northeast for a few minutes to reach an 8086′ knobby, precarious viewpoint, the top of an autobrecciated lava flow. This offers superb views to the north and northeast of the extensively glaciated, volcanic landscape. We descend briefly southwest from the

viewpoint, almost touch the road we just crossed, and then head north to another ridge saddle (7830-1.0), this one at the head of Bear Valley. Now both ridge and trail turn west, and you have some views as you head over toward point 7942 on a volcanic ridge. For views as far northwest as the Sierra Buttes, make a brief climb north to that point. Ahead, the ridge turns southwest, as does the trail, which soon starts a

L3

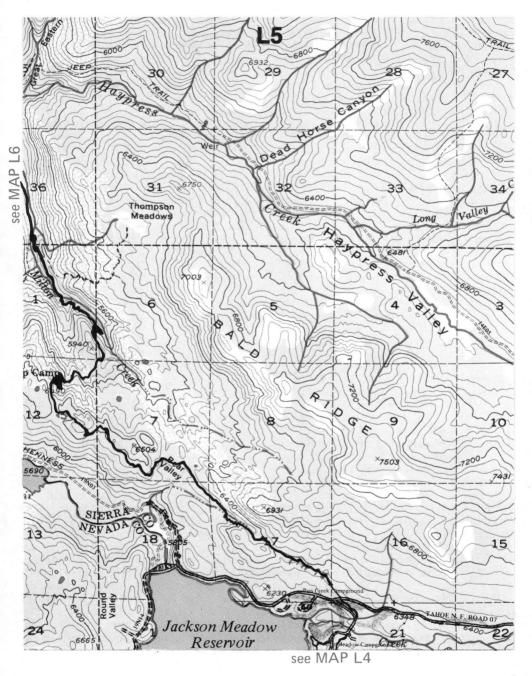

see MAP L6

see MAP L4

1¼-mile descent. We drop into a selectively logged forest of red firs and western white pines, and eventually turn northwest for a short traverse over to Meadow Lake Road 19N11 (7530-2.1). This spot is immediately past a usually flowing creek, which drains a meadow you'll see beginning just south up the road. One could camp hereabouts, though mosquitoes can be fierce through early August.

North, this road goes 6½ miles to Tahoe N.F. Road 07, the same road that skirts the north shore of Jackson Meadow Reservoir. We, however, go a few yards south to find the PCT beginning southwest from the road. Past a small meadow the trail soon turns north and climbs to a ridge (8000-1.1). This it ascends, giving us views of Fordyce and Meadow lakes plus views of the peaks along the PCT north and south of Donner Pass. The trail then curves west, reaching its zenith just beneath Peak 8214, from whose summit you get an unrestricted 360° panorama of the Section L area. Just west of the summit, those keeping to the trail have their first view of Webber Lake. About ¾ mile past Section L's high point, the trail starts a descent along a lower, north-trending ridge, leaving views behind as it heads over to a logging road (7640-2.1).

A switchbacking climb ensues, with views improving once again as we strive for, but do not attain, the summit of Peak 8166. Now the route is essentially downhill all the way to Jackson Meadow Reservoir. Views along our descending, volcanic crest are plentiful and interesting, though not on a par with those near Peak 8214. After a descent west past knobs of autobrecciated lava, the PCT heads north, descending 0.2 mile almost to a creek (7330-3.6) that flows through most of the summer. We switchback almost to it a second time, then descend to a major road that crosses a minor saddle (7135-0.4). You could camp in this vicinity and get water from the seasonal creek, reached by walking about 0.2 mile north down the road.

Westward, we climb just a bit before skirting past autobrecciated lava buttes on Peak 7348. As our descending route curves north down a ridge, we enter an area of selective logging, cross a good road, and in ⅓ mile cross another good road (6740-2.3). Now hiking on slopes of metamorphic rocks, we leave the ridge, parallel the west edge of an old road for 0.4 mile, then drop ever closer to the northeast shore of spreading Jackson Meadow Reservoir. Nearing

the reservoir, the PCT almost touches a south-climbing road, and if you plan to visit East Meadow Campground, head 0.1 mile down this road to the paved campground road. The PCT curves northeast away from the campground, then quickly reaches its paved road (6170-1.7) only a few yards west of a junction with southeast-climbing Pass Creek Loop Road. East Meadow Campground lies ⅓ mile west along the paved road, and it is perched just above the welcome, fairly warm waters of Jackson Meadow Reservoir, a boaters' mecca.

On the paved road walk north across nearby Pass Creek to the north bank of its tributary, from which the trail resumes, curving northwest ¼ mile over to paved Tahoe N.F. Road 07 (6200-0.4). If you head ¼ mile west along it, you'll reach the entrance to Pass Creek Campground, which is also used by PCT trekkers.

From Road 07 the trail continues northwest, passing by springs emerging from volcanic soils as it climbs through an old logging area to a minor saddle (6450-0.8). The Sierra Buttes loom dead ahead as we descend through a linear minicanyon. A series of short, descending switchbacks take us out of the minicanyon, and then we cross its usually dry creek. Water here may flow underground, for rocks on the southwest wall appear to be marble (the stuff caves are formed from).

Next we contour across slopes above miniature Bear Valley. Today, "Cow Valley" would be a more accurate name, and besides, we already passed another Bear Valley about a day's hike ago and don't need the confusing name duplication. Beyond a ridge west of and above Bear Valley we traverse northwest, reaching in ½ mile a view of the canyon we'll soon drop into. After another ½ mile we circle a knee-deep lily-pad pond. Then in ¼ mile we breach the canyon's rim and start down an intricate route with over two dozen switchbacks in it. If you're heavily laden and heading south up the PCT, you'll appreciate the trail's easy gradient; northbound hikers are typically unappreciative. At last we cross Milton Creek (5240-5.5), and just past it spy a small campsite.

We're now entering a lower forest, one dominated, to be sure, by white firs, which we've often seen before. However, now some of its low-elevation associates appear, notably incense-cedar, sugar pine, ponderosa pine, Douglas-fir and black oak, all of which have been infrequent along the PCT. After a descent

L3, L4, L5

north, we make a short jog southwest to bridge Milton Creek (4990-0.8). Now on the creek's west bank, we pass several spots with creekside camping as we leisurely stroll northward down to a closed road (4810-1.2), today just a broad trail. Eastward, the road ends at Milton Creek in a few paces. A fallen log or two provides access to the east bank. Here, on a large, flat stream terrace near the confluence of Milton and Haypress creeks, there's room for dozens of campers. Stay here rather than down at Wild Plum Campground, which can have some rather noisy car campers.

Since 1980 the permanent PCT has existed over to Highway 49. Nevertheless, many PCT hikers still take the "supply" route to Sierra City, descending 0.9 mile along the closed road to the east end of Wild Plum Campground, hiking 0.3 mile through it to Milton Creek, and traversing 1.4 miles west to Highway 49. "Downtown" Sierra City is 0.5 mile southwest down the highway; the PCT is 1.0 mile northeast up it.

Those hikers adhering strictly to the PCT follow the closed road only 40 yards west, branching northwest from it down a sometimes indistinct tread. Heading toward the Sierra Buttes, you quickly reach a bridge (4720-0.3), which spans Haypress Creek about ¼ mile above its low but roaring falls. A westbound trail at the bridge's south end gives hikers a second chance to head out to Wild Plum Campground.

Nearing the end of this section's short hike, we traverse across dry slopes that are often hot and fly-ridden in summer. The PCT runs along or close to an old trail that still climbs from Wild Plum Guard Station east up Haypress Creek canyon. After leaving this trail just beyond a gully with a seasonal creeklet, we contour over to a bedrock ridge, cross over it, and traverse past live oaks and their seemingly omnipresent flies to an old jeep road. From it the PCT descends to a seasonal creek, then drops, with the aid of short switchbacks, to a prominent bridge (4600-1.9) that vaults the North Yuba River. Here the river has cut a minigorge through the resistant Mesozoic-age metavolcanic rocks. By late summer the river's volume diminishes sufficiently to allow safe swimming in its inviting, though nippy, pools. The trick is descending safely to them. If you are low on water, get some from the spring you pass between the bridge and Highway 49 (4570-0.4). Your route ahead is usually dry in summer until you reach some springs about 7½ miles ahead, just past the PCT's crossing of the Sierra Buttes jeep trail.

L5, L6

View south toward Jackson Meadow Reservoir and English Mountain

Sierra Buttes Fire Lookout

Section M: Highway 49 to Highway 70

Introduction: Great diversity characterizes this rather long section. Glaciated lake-basin environments contrast strongly with those of Feather River's deep Middle and North fork canyons. Red firs, mountain hemlocks and western white pines give way at lower elevations to other trees, which in turn give way to others until finally, along the forks of the Feather River, Douglas-firs, California nutmegs and ponderosa pines—among others—are seen. Cool snow patches yield to hot canyon bottoms, and mosquitoes are replaced by flies. Many types of rocks abound, ranging in age from late Paleozoic ocean sediments to volcanic flows that are only a few million years old. These flows generally make up most of the crests and ridges along the PCT, but they have been largely eroded away in the highly glaciated Sierra Buttes/Lakes Basin area, where underlying metavolcanic rocks have been exposed. These metavolcanics in turn give way northward to granitic rocks of the Bucks Lake-Three Lakes area. Between these two areas the PCT route is mostly along relatively youthful volcanic sediments when it is near the crest along ancient, usually metamorphosed marine sediments when it traverses the Middle Fork Feather River canyon.

Most of Section M's lakes are passed along the first quarter of the trail. The trail, however, stays high on the crest, avoiding all but Summit Lake, which is more of a pond than a lake. Lakes Basin—a miniature Desolation Wilderness—is barely seen, and when it is, you see it from along a portion of crest with such steep slopes that descent into the basin is dangerous and impractical. The basin is day-use only, so the Forest Service routed the PCT well away from it, to prevent PCT hikers from camping in it. This may be unfortunate for you, but it is fortunate for the basin, which now receives much less human impact than it would if camping were allowed, as it was in the past.

Declination: 16°E

Mileages:	South to North	Distance between Points	North to South
Highway 49 near Sierra City......................	0.0		96.2
		7.2	
Sierra Buttes jeep trail	7.2		89.0
		2.6	
Packer Lake Saddle	9.8		86.4
		4.4	
Summit Lake road...............................	14.2		82.0
		9.0	
saddle with a diminutive pond....................	23.2		73.0
		3.6	
A Tree saddle...................................	26.8		69.4
		7.6	
Johnsville-Gibsonville Road......................	34.4		61.8
		4.5	
unnamed lake below Bunker Hill Ridge..............	38.9		57.3
		3.6	

Quincy-LaPorte Road.	42.5	7.3	53.7
Black Rock Creek Road 22N56	49.8	1.2	46.4
leave PCT for Fowler Lake	51.0	7.4	45.2
Middle Fork Feather River	58.4	3.5	37.8
Bear Creek	61.9	6.8	34.3
Lookout Rock	68.7	3.6	27.5
Big Creek Road 33N56	72.3	4.8	23.9
Bucks Summit	77.1	5.6	19.1
Silver Lake trail	82.7	4.4	13.5
Clear Creek	87.1	9.1	9.1
Highway 70 at Belden Town bridge	96.2		0.0

Supplies: Sierra City, 1½ miles southwest along Hiway 49 from the start of this section, is a small town with post office, motels, restaurants and adequate, though not trail-oriented, supplies. At the opposite end of this section is Belden, which is little more than a pleasant resort. However, it does have, besides scant supplies, a post office. Between these two settlements you'll find no on-route supply points. However, a supply route many hikers take is our alternate route along the shore of sizable Bucks Lake. Along this route you can get lodging, meals or foodstuffs at Bucks Lake Lodge and at Lakeshore Resort. At the start of this alternate route you could also take Big Creek Road 6.9 miles down to Bucks Lake Road, then follow that road 2.2 miles down to the Meadow Valley Post Office. (If you need major supplies or boot repairs, continue east on this busy road 7.2 miles to Quincy, your last sizable near-route town until Chester, in Section N). From Meadow Valley, return to the Big Creek Road junction and continue 3.4 miles past it up Bucks Lake Road to the PCT at Bucks Summit.

Rattlesnakes: These are common at lower elevations, generally below 5000′, so watch where you step when you descend and ascend the Middle Fork canyon, and when you descend the North Fork canyon to Belden. At these lower elevations, however, you are more likely to pick up ticks or get poison-oak rashes than meet rattlesnakes.

This section begins on Highway 49, about 1½ miles northeast of Sierra City and 1.0 mile northeast of a road branching east to Wild Plum Campground. During the summer, your first reliable water is 7½ miles away, at a spring about ¼ mile beyond the Sierra Buttes jeep trail. The climb around Sierra Buttes is mostly sunny, so try to get an early start so that you won't be guzzling water. If you need some immediately, cross Highway 49 and follow the southbound trail about two minutes to a creek-let that originates at a spring just below the highway. If by chance that is dry, then continue ¼ mile farther to the North Yuba River.

The first part of this trail section is on a narrow, abandoned road through a forest of black oak, ponderosa pine and incense-cedar. Mountain misery, a low, sticky shrub, per-meates the air with a subtle fragrance as the day's temperature rises. After the PCT bends north onto cooler east-facing slopes, we meet Douglas-firs and their associated vegetation. About a mile from the start, our sporadically switchbacking trail leaves noisy Highway 49 and switchbacks relentlessly upward to a flume (5720-2.7) that today is bone-dry. About ¼–½ mile north lie smooth, bushy ridges, a smaller set within a larger one. These are lateral moraines left by glaciers that descended east from the Sierra Buttes. The earlier glacier left the outer ridges; the later, smaller glacier left the inner ones.

Our well-graded ascent has mostly been a forested one, but we leave all the trees behind just before the switchbacking ascent tops off on a ridge (6070-0.7). From it we have views both

M1

up and down the North Yuba River canyon and views up at the east buttress of the Sierra Buttes. Now shrubs line the trail, mainly huckleberry oak, greenleaf manzanita, tobacco brush and bitter cherry, but also a dab here and there of snow bush and squaw carpet. The shadeless route west is an easy one, which is fortunate, for if the climb were steep, it would be miserable on a hot summer day. After weaving around several ridges and gullies and getting saturated with views, we finally arrive at a saddle and the Sierra Buttes jeep trail (7150-3.8).

The Sierra Buttes Fire Lookout stands over 1400' above this junction, and normally we wouldn't recommend such a strenuous side trip. However, the Sierra Buttes rise so far above other local summits that one has non-pareil views which extend, on clear days, from the Tahoe area north to Lassen Peak. And nowhere along the tri-state PCT route will you find such a narrowly perched (though safe) lookout. We recommend you leave your heavy pack behind at the junction and travel as lightly as possible to the lookout.

Start up the steep jeep trail, partly shaded by red firs and western white pines, then after ¾ mile reach a junction at 7910' elevation. From here you could follow a winding trail north-west down a ridge to the PCT, but only if you've carried your backpack up to this spot. If you're traveling lightly, continue ¾ mile up the switchbacking jeep trail to the base of the lookout, and after soaking up the views, return the way you came.

By the time you reach the base, you'll have left trees behind and will have some alpine wildflowers for companions. The lookout sits atop a Sierra Buttes crest pinnacle, and you'll have to climb about 176 steps to reach it, most of the steps on steep, airy ladders—no place for the faint-hearted. The pinnacle's summit is so small that the lookout actually projects out into space, and through the iron-grating view deck you stand on, you can look straight down the 600' nearly vertical northeast escarpment. The deeply glaciated Sardine Lakes canyon to the northeast contrasts strongly with the barely eroded slopes up which your jeep trail climbed. To the south lie slopes of intermediate erosion, cut by tributaries of the North Yuba River. The views are far-ranging. On the distant north-west horizon stands snowy Lassen Peak, about a two-week backpack trip away. Numerous high peaks dot the Lake Tahoe environs to the

Stairway up to the Sierra Buttes fire lookout

southeast. With compass in hand you can identify Mt. Rose (10,776'), 114°; Mt. Lola (9143'), 126°; and the light-gray Crystal Range of Desolation Wilderness (9983' maximum), about 155°. Many lower summits and ridges, both near and far, are seen in every direction.

*   *   *   *

Back at the Sierra Buttes jeep trail junction, the PCT traverses ¼ mile over to a spring, then in about two minutes we pass another one, both lying just below the trail. About ½ mile farther we start a traverse northeast across a bowl that can be snowbound into early summer, and then we quickly arrive at a ridgecrest trail junction (7350-1.1). South, a trail soon curves southeast as it climbs almost one mile up to the 7910' junction mentioned in the side trip to Sierra Buttes Fire Lookout. North, the PCT traverses along the ridgecrest. Before describing it, we'll first mention a lake-blessed alternate route.

*   *   *   *

M1

see MAP L6

The PCT, unfortunately, too often has a "look but don't touch" character to it: you'll see a number of lakes, but they'll be too far away for easy access. This is unfortunate, in terms of both esthetics and campsites. There-fore you might consider this well-watered alternate route.

It begins as a steep trail that makes an initial jog southeast from the crest. Then it switch-backs and continues steeply ¼ mile north down

M1

to a logging road that climbs northwest back to the PCT. Straight ahead, you now descend moderately on a closed jeep road, passing just west of and above upper Tamarack Lake. You'll spy a jeep road that leads over to it. Just past this spur, you come alongside lower Tamarack Lake, which has a very shallow west half, but a swimmable, fishable east half. Camping is discouraged due to the area's heavy use.

Just past the lower lake you reach a junction (6700-1.0), from which a closed jeep road heads over to the Sardine Lakes. Keep descending north on your closed jeep road, whose tread splits and then rejoins before passing an eastward, gated road only ¼ mile before you reach paved Forest Route 93. From here you could head 1½ miles up the road to Packer Lake Saddle and the PCT. Rather, follow it about 250 yards north down to the Packer Lake Picnic Area (6230-1.0). Here you'll find the entrance road to Packer Lake Lodge. The lodge serves good meals and PCT trekkers are welcome. After a refreshing swim in warm, fairly shallow Packer Lake, continue down Road 93 to Packsaddle Camping Area, on your right. Just 70 yards beyond it, you leave the road at the start of Deer Lake Trail 12E02 (6130-0.3).

The trail traverses northwest past four unequal-sized creeks that drain Packer Lake and the slopes north of it. Departing from the lush, streamside vegetation, we begin to climb up-

ward, mount two well-graded switchbacks, and swing past a two-stage lateral moraine—an indication of two separate glacier advances. Our comfortable trail underfooting becomes rocky as we curve over to the first Grass Lake's outlet creek, and it remains so almost to the lateral to the second Grass Lake. The first Grass Lake turnoff is about ¼ mile up the trail from the outlet creek. Where you encounter a ridge jutting 10–15' above the trail's west side, you can climb up it, and from it an easy, 100-yard, cross-country descent to the east shore will become immediately apparent. There are four Grass Lakes in this part of the Sierra, and this one is the smallest, diminished by invading grass. Two small flats provide adequate campsites. One is above the lake's east side, the other just southwest of its outlet creek.

From the trailside ridge, we confront a steady, bush-lined ascent. Eventually our trail levels off at an open-forested flat (6830-1.5), on which you may see a sign to the second Grass Lake. If you wish to hike ¼ mile to it, start northeast, cross a seasonal creek in 30 yards, then follow a faint, ducked trail that crosses a gentle ridge and gradually descends its north slope to the willow-lined lake, which provides warm midsummer swimming. Larger and deeper than the first Grass Lake, this chest-deep, grass-bottomed lake also differs in that its water is not crystal clear. Should you decide to camp near this somewhat-hard-to-find lake, obtain fresh water from audible

M1

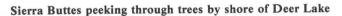

Sierra Buttes peeking through trees by shore of Deer Lake

Sawmill Creek, which is 300 yards from the lake's north shore.

Only 60 yards north of the Grass Lake route junction you can bear west-northwest across a small flat toward a conspicuous gully. From its bottom a rocky path, ducked and blazed, goes ½ mile northwest to Deer Lake. Small campsites can be found along the west, south and east shores, and diving and swimming are best on the east.

Past the lateral we climb northeast briefly up to a low ridge, then veer northwest over a ford of Sawmill Creek just below its small pond. Continuing northwest, we quickly reach a saddle (7100-0.6) and a trail to Salmon Lake. A second trail to Deer Lake starts just before this junction. It is essentially a use trail that bears west-southwest, ending near the lake's northeast shore.

Leaving the Salmon Lake Trail only 15 yards north of the saddle, our trail continues by first starting west up a shallow gully. The trail then climbs and descends a slab into a larger gully, follows it to its head, and bends southwest across a slope to a jeep road. Downslope, you can take it ¼ mile to the lake, but we take it ¼ mile up to the PCT (7440-0.7-5.1).

*   *   *   *

From the 7350′ trail junction high above the Tamarack Lakes, the PCT traverses ⅓ mile along a ridgecrest, then trail tread ends at a rough road where it cuts southeast through the ridgecrest. This is the logging road mentioned early in the above alternate route. The road is now part of the permanent PCT route, and on it we wind northward down to a gap (7010-0.9), where we meet a good road, which curves west. We take it 0.2 mile north along the ridge up to paved Forest Service Road 93—also part of the permanent PCT—and we follow it down to a second ridge gap, Packer Lake Saddle (7020-0.6). Here you have a second chance to drop to Packer Lake.

Now back on PCT trail tread, we climb north along the ridge, staying just east of a crest road. Past a jeep road to the Wallis Mine, the trail curves northeast, switchbacks twice, and then climbs northwest to the edge of a clearcut. A two-minute walk north through it to a hemlock-adorned crest saddle saves you ¼ mile of walking. PCT purists head east to a point, are rewarded with excellent views, then head west to the crest saddle. The PCT stays imme-

diately west of the crest for ¾ mile, then runs more or less along it, giving you views of alluring Deer Lake. After ⅓ mile we reach a jeep road (7430-2.6) that drops ⅓ mile and 300 feet to west-shore campsites. After the snow melts away in early or mid-July, you can expect to see 4WDs driving down to these sites.

Over the next ¼ mile the PCT crosses and recrosses an abandoned jeep road, then crosses a west-climbing jeep road, the one you'd be ascending if you had taken the alternate route past Packer, Grass and Deer lakes. Red firs at first obscure our views, but they soon reappear and are particularly good near Peak 7503, where we can see the Sierra Buttes, the Salmon Lakes and giant Gold Lake. Forest cover returns north of the peak, though we end our descent in a clearcut that extends down to Summit Lake road (7050-1.8). This road tops out at a jeep-road junction about 150 yards to the southeast. Small, shallow Summit Lake is immediately south of that junction, and if you drink the lake's water, you might treat it before doing so. Camping space is plentiful in this vicinity.

North of the Summit Lake road the PCT parallels the jeep road, at first at a distance, then alongside it. Near the north end of a fairly level ridge, a jeep road cuts northeast across the crest (7290-1.3), and we have three route choices. First, we can head a few paces west to the jeep road we've been paralleling and take it 0.3 mile northwest down to Oakland Pond, which is like Summit Lake in water purity and camping potential. About 200 yards past the pond, where the road turns west, a trail climbs moderately north 0.3 mile back to the PCT. Second, one can follow the northeast-heading jeep road. The PCT route does this for a few yards before leaving it, but you can continue onward and drop to Round Lake. The road soon narrows to a trail and the route down to the lake isn't very obvious. Make sure you pass a nearby pond on its west side. Furthermore, 300 yards below the pond, be sure you curve northwest to a 5′ deep gap rather than descend a gully northeast toward the broad saddle above Gold Lake. Camping is *not* allowed in Lakes Basin, but you might take a layover day, staying at Lakes Basin Campground, then later rejoining the PCT at a saddle in Section 11 (in the west part of Map M2). Third, we could follow the lakeless PCT.

This route leaves the northeast-bound jeep road in a few paces, then climbs almost to Peak

M1, M2

7550, switchbacking needlessly several times just south of it. From the switchbacks you get excellent views of the western Sierra, particularly of the closer terrain that includes Snake Lake, Little Deer Lake and PCT campers at Oakland Pond. North of Peak 7550 we have views down into well-named Lakes Basin, which has been severely glaciated. Glaciation in the entire Sierra Buttes-Lakes Basin area was quite extensive. From the Sierra Buttes, glaciers descended first northeast to the North Yuba River canyon, and then down it to the 4300' level, just east of Sierra City. From the Lakes Basin and the canyons both east and west of it, glaciers extended north down to Mohawk Valley (4400') and dammed the upstream part of the Middle Fork Feather River, which led to the creation of a 200-square-mile lake.

Steep slopes of granitelike rock prevent us from dropping into the sparkling Lakes Basin. The bedrock here, as along most of our chapter's hike so far, is metamorphosed volcanic rocks that were erupted perhaps 300–400 million years ago, roughly 100 times earlier than the eruptions of the volcanic rocks we traversed in the previous chapter's hike. At a nearby saddle, our views of the Lakes Basin disappear, and we drop back into forest cover and reach a junction (7355-1.0). Had you taken the Oakland Pond route, you'd be climbing northwest to meet the PCT here.

The PCT heads briefly west to a ridge that provides views to the south and west, then enters viewless forest for a traverse almost a mile long. Next, it curves southwest through a shady forest growing on a flat, ill-defined crest that can harbor snow patches into July. Momentarily we cross a jeep road that heads north to a ridge above the west edge of Lakes Basin. The PCT curves south to a ridge, then curves west to an excellent viewpoint above Hawley Lake. We re-enter forest again and descend ⅔ mile to a jeep-road crossing at a county-line crest saddle (7050-2.3). Those who made excursions through Lakes Basin rejoin us here. Immediately west of the saddle is a diminutive pond that nevertheless has enough staying power to hold water through most, if not all, of the summer. You could camp here, but get water at a spring-fed creek, reached by following the jeep road about 200 yards east.

Our trail briefly parallels the road west, then swings north, taking a tortuous course that has to be hiked to be believed. (More such diversions lie ahead between here and the Middle Fork Feather River.) Twice we almost touch the jeep road, only to veer away, but we finally cross it (7330-1.3) near a high point on the Sierra crest. A moderate descent, just over ⅓ mile, brings us back to the road, and then we leave it for an increasingly easy descent across open slopes that provide views of Spencer Lakes, too far below the trail to be of any use to us. After heading west for a spell, our trail hits an old jeep road that descends to the lakes. We, however, contour northwest ¼ mile along it,

M2, M3

Mt. Elwell, Long Lake and Silver Lake

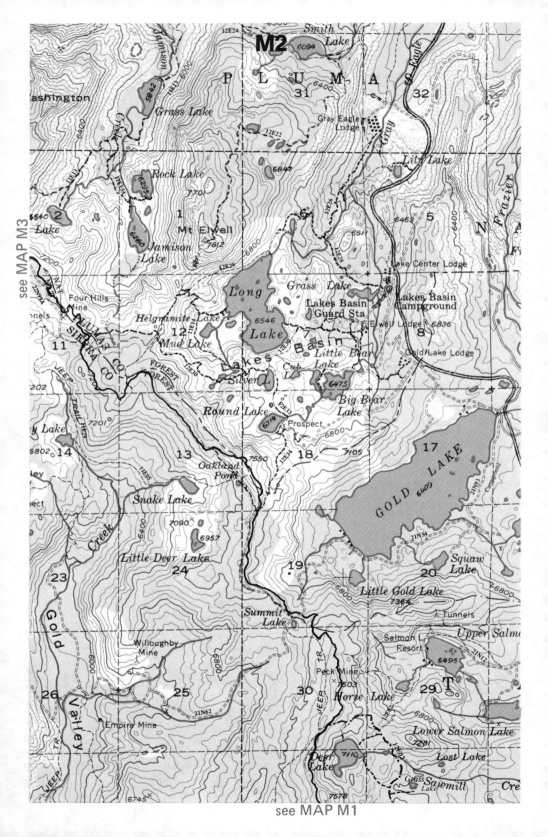

see MAP M3

leave it, and then parallel it through forest down to a saddle (6630-1.8), where you almost touch the jeep road. We then curve around the south and west slopes of Peak 6822 down to a second saddle, the A Tree (6550-0.5), a focal point for five roads. By starting southwest down a jeep road, you should quickly find a spring, the first *fresh* trailside water since the two springs on the west flank of the Sierra Buttes, about 19¼ miles back. Here is your last chance for a while for a rather short exit to "civilization." You can take the main road, 22N99, first north and then northwest 2.3 miles out to a junction with the Johnsville-Gibsonville Road. Just before this junction is a popular car-camping area centered on Jamison Creek. Emergency aid can be obtained at bustling Plumas Eureka State Park, about 5 miles east down the road.

The stretch of PCT northward to the Johnsville-Gibsonville Road was the last part of California PCT north of southern California to be completed—in September 1985. From the A Tree saddle the PCT at first parallels the Cowell Mine road west, but soon diverges from it to rise to a saddle (6920-1.1). Just beyond it we have some brushy terrain, which gives us open views southeast to the Sierra Buttes, to the right of the much closer Spencer Lakes. To the south lies Lavezzola Creek canyon, largely ravaged of its forest cloak. Ahead, the trail should have contoured across Gibralter's relatively gentle south-facing slopes. Indeed, most of the stretch from the Johnsville-Gibsonville Road southeast to the A Tree had been built, only to be aborted by the refusal of right-of-way by the Cowell Mine's owner. A less practical new route had to be built, and you could find it quite snowbound before early July.

This route starts out uneventfully enough by climbing moderately to the county-line crest, proceeding west up it to a jeep road, and then paralleling it 280 yards northwest over to a saddle (7380-0.8) at the south end of McRae Ridge. Now the "fun" begins. Leaving the road, we descend southwest across steep slopes to a switchback, from where we have a superb view of Gibralter's foreboding, pock-marked face. Several more switchbacks lead us down to the base of a towering trailside pinnacle, from which we make a gentle descent south toward Gibralter's massive face—a cliff composed of layer upon layer of volcanic mudflows. We turn west and skirt just below this cliff, crossing

several gullies, none of them with a reliable creek. From a switchback you may note where the aborted PCT segment once began a climb south-southeast to a county-line saddle.

Our route next descends to gentler slopes, and we cross one usually flowing creeklet just a few minutes before reaching a gully in which our route turns northward. Soon we make a short switchback and almost touch the headwaters of West Branch Nelson Creek. We then turn northward and descend 300 yards to a spot (6150-3.2) from which you can meander a few yards northeast to the first possible campsite in some time. From this spot, about 100 yards north of Section 31's south edge, we follow the creek down-canyon, always keeping well above it, due to the rather steep-sided gorge the creek has cut. From about the middle of Section 31 onward for ⅓ mile, you'll be able to reach any of about a half-dozen campsites by scrambling down to the creekside. You'll see a road paralleling the creek's far side, and at the road's upper end (near the east edge of Map M4) there is a fine campsite with lots of level spots. In the past, it has been complete with table and shelves.

We barely enter Section 30, and where we leave it (5790-1.3), we also leave West Branch Nelson Creek. Be sure you have plenty of water, for after midsummer the route ahead will usually be waterless for 24 miles, until just before Middle Fork Feather River. However, there are places along the way where you can find water by detouring ½ mile or less. Beyond Section 30 our descent ends, and soon we traverse west in and out of gullies, then make a moderate climb from the last one up to a crossing of the Johnsville-Gibsonville Road (6065-1.2) at a minor county-line saddle.

Mt. Etna is about 1¼ miles away, but we'll take twice that distance to reach it, for we're faced with another intricate trail route. Weaving in and out of gullies and microgullies, the trail takes almost a mile to reach a saddle that is barely ½ mile away from the previous one. Skirting the back side of Stafford Mountain, we have pleasant views even though part of the area has been logged. After nearly one more mile we crest another saddle, which is just over ½ air mile from the previous one. We pass gully after gully as we traverse west beneath the crest, and some of them provide snowmelt water through early July. On our traverse we skirt below volcanic pinnacles and then, below Mt. Etna proper, beneath volcanic cliffs. Mt.

M3, M4

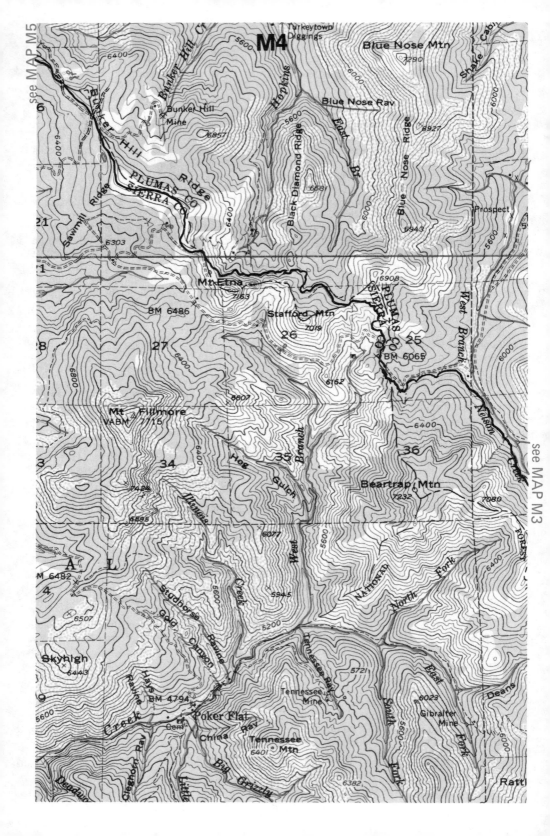

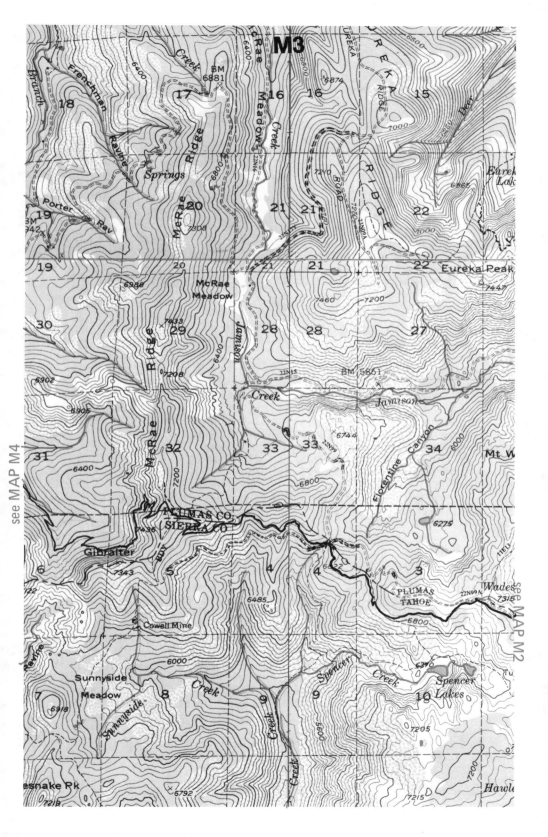

Etna and Stafford Mountain appear to be two resistant plugs that were once part of a large volcano. Much of the layers of volcanic rocks we see in this vicinity probably came from this source.

The route ahead is now direct, and once atop Bunker Hill Ridge proper we can enjoy leisurely walking and panoramic views (see title-page spread). Pilot Peak, Blue Nose Mountain, Stafford Mountain and Mts. Etna and Fillmore are readily identified. As our crest route descends into a red-fir forest, we view a small, unnamed lake on a bench just below and west of the trail. You can camp at it, but as ususal, consider treating the water. On a saddle just over ⅓ mile north of the lake we cross two intersecting roads, then we contour an equal distance to a second saddle (6700-2.2). If you start north on a road crossing this saddle, you should locate, in a minute or two, seasonal springs just below you.

Rather than head directly over to Pilot Peak, the trail soon veers left off the crest, traverses needlessly west to the north end of Gibsonville Ridge, and then heads back to the crest proper. The Pilot Peak Fire Lookout provides far-ranging views, but since the jeep road to its summit is on the other side of the mountain, we just angle northwest and descend its lower, forested slopes to a road (6680-1.9), which we come to immediately before a crest saddle. If you are low on water, then you should take a 1¼-mile alternate route. Head southwest down the road to the Quincy-LaPorte Road, follow it 100 yards east to the headwaters of the South Fork Feather River, backtrack to the junction, and continue ¼ mile past it to a PCT saddle. Those with an adequate supply of water stay on the PCT, descending it to a trailhead, then heading 0.1 mile west on a level spur road out to the aforementioned saddle (6474-1.0). The Quincy-LaPorte Road, crossing the saddle, heads north to Quincy, a long day's walk away, should you have to get out. However, you could probably hitchhike out. To the south, the road goes 11½ miles to LaPorte, a hamlet with minimal supplies and a post office. It is too far away to be a practical resupply point.

Leaving the saddle, we head southwest 0.1 mile on paved Kenzie Ravine Road 22N60, then branch right, back onto trail again. In a minute we hit the Fowler Peak trail, a closed, crest-running jeep road that we'll follow most of the way to Fowler Peak. On this jeep road we cross Road 22N60 at a saddle (6510-0.9),

Chimney Rock

then ½ mile past it, we drop northwest off the crest on a mile of trail tread. In a logged-over area near the bottom of our descent, we regain the jeep road and follow it almost ½ mile west down to a recrossing of Road 22N60 at another saddle (5900-1.9).

Our Fowler Peak trail climbs ⅓ mile almost to a volcanic crest summit (6045'), traverses over to a second one (5948'), then drops to a saddle crossed by Bear Wallow trail, a jeep road (5755-1.4). You should be able to find water by dropping about ½ mile south along it. The Fowler Peak trail continues southwest along the crest, and a fragment of PCT tread parallels this jeep road's north side, crossing the road just as it starts a short, steep climb. Our path takes an easier, albeit longer, route, looping around summit 6031 before rejoining the jeep road immediately west of the summit. Eastbound hikers may miss this brushy junction and continue along the jeep road, which is fine. Views of distant Lassen Peak and of massive, not so distant clearcuts reappear, as they have in many places along our westward traverse. After about a ¼-mile descent, we reach Chimney Rock (6000-1.0), at a bend in the road. PCT tread branches left a few paces before this bend, only to end at the road where its gradient slackens. Steep-sided, blocky, easily climbed Chimney Rock is a remnant of a lava flow that once rumbled down a valley floor. Today it sits atop a ridge, an example of reversed topography. Ancient streams cut along the sides of the resistant flow, and in several

M4, M5, M6

million years cut Onion Valley canyon to the north and South Fork canyon to the south.

From where the PCT rejoins the Fowler Peak trail below Chimney Rock, we have an easing ⅓-mile descent to a saddle. From it you can head ¼ mile south, down to the headwaters of Black Rock Creek, for water. On the jeep road we climb for a minute or two to a crest high point, then have a pleasant, occasionally shaded one-mile descent to the base of a minor ridge point. The road angles northwest over the point while the PCT tread branches south and goes ⅓ mile, mostly through forest, down to a recrossing of the jeep road immediately east of an important saddle (5460-2.1). From here Black Rock Creek Road 22N56 descends south, and about ¼ mile down it you should be able to find water. A major logging road contours west, giving rise to a newer Black Rock Creek Road in about a mile. Both of these descending roads take you close to a north arm of Little Grass Valley Reservoir. Head along its west shore if you have to go out for aid.

The PCT heads northwest across the saddle and briefly goes along the Butte Bar trail, an old jeep road now closed to motor vehicles. This it leaves at the northeast base of Fowler Peak, and we have a relaxing, increasingly shaded descent west. Where the trail bends northwest in dense forest to descend along the east side of a minor ridge, you can leave the trail (5500-1.2) and head ¼ mile down to Fowler Lake,

crossing a second ridge halfway to it. Shallow and adorned with water lilies, it nevertheless offers the best campsites between the earlier nameless lake and the Middle Fork Feather River, 7½ miles ahead. To rejoin the PCT, follow the lake's outlet creek down to a road and hike north briefly down it to a ridge junction with another road, the PCT route.

If you don't visit Fowler Lake, you descend northwest along the minor ridge, which happens to be a glacial moraine. Within the last 100,000 years, perhaps three glaciers developed in the cirque containing the lake. The youngest barely flowed past the lake, an older one advanced ¼ mile beyond it, and yet another one (or perhaps an earlier stage of the older one) advanced almost a mile past the lake. What is remarkable about these glaciers is that they originated in a cirque whose headwall was below 6000' elevation. To Schaffer's knowledge, no other cirque in the mountains of California has a headwall below 6000'—though a few have floors below it.

The trail's tread ends about ¼ mile down the glacial moraine, and then we make a fairly steep descent about 150 yards northwest along a narrow, abandoned road to a crest junction with a second road (5280-0.3). Slate Creek usually flows through most of July, and you can reach this lake-fed creek by heading a bit south up the road to it.

From the junction we continue on a lesser

M6

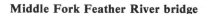

Middle Fork Feather River bridge

see MAP M7

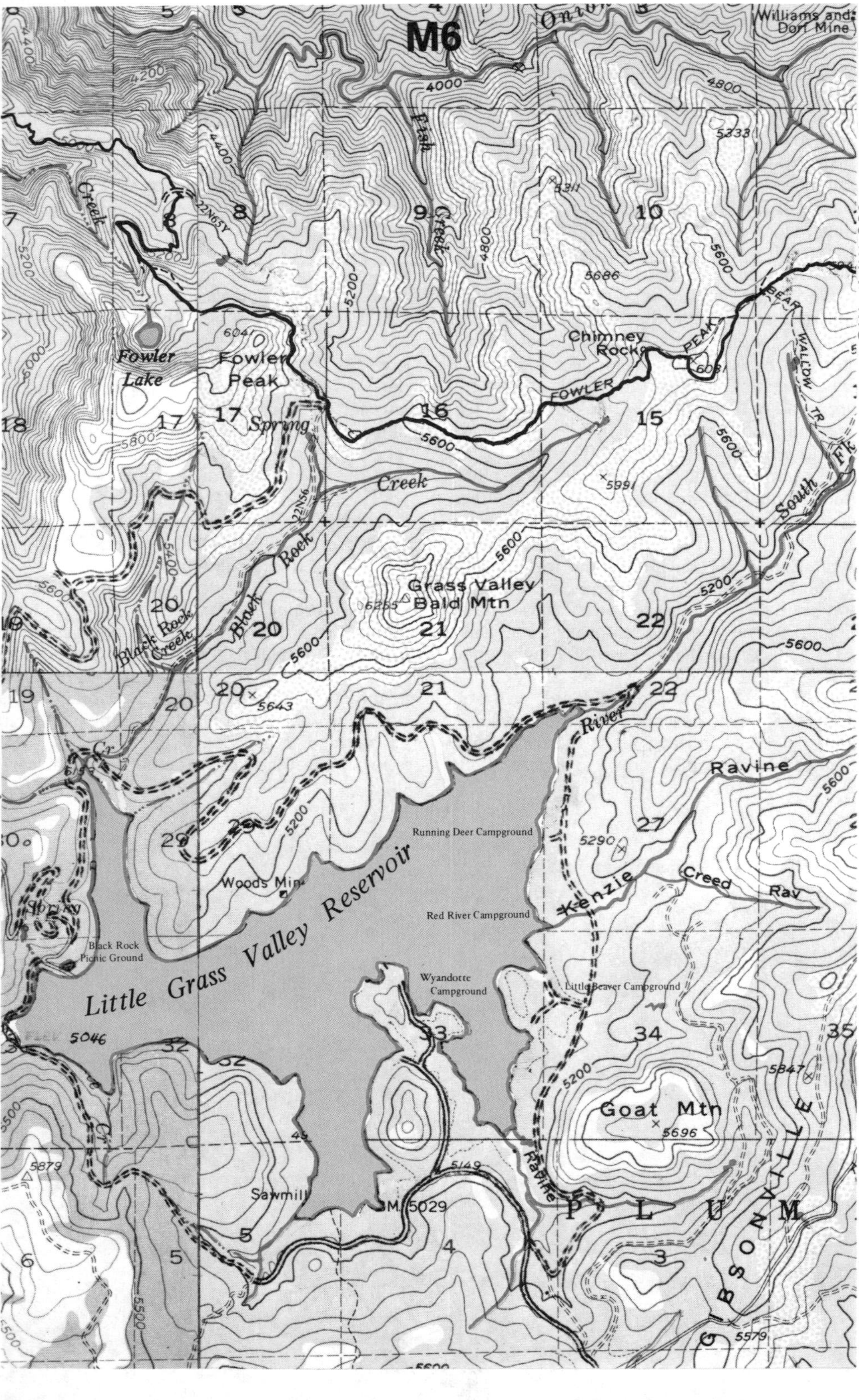

see MAP M5

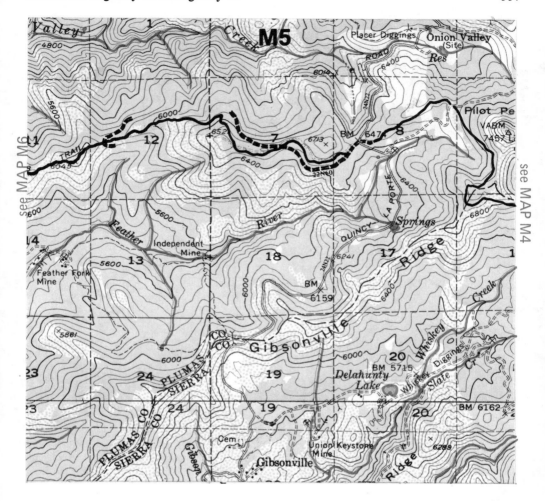

gradient down the closed road, leaving it in 0.2 mile for an unnecessarily long traverse east. On a major crest, which we'll be descending to the Feather River, we cross broad Sawmill Tom Creek Road 23N65Y (5060-1.0), then make an uneventful 0.4-mile traverse along the northwest side of the crest. The crest bends west and, being logged, is not a beautiful sight. Therefore the trail runs immediately below and south of the crest, crossing an incredible array of gullies that drive PCT *mappers* crazy. You only have to *hike* along this convoluted route, though you could take the road you see below you. We almost touch the road at a saddle (4910-1.8), then almost touch it again ¼ mile later. After switchbacking down the ridge, we finally cross this road, known as Dogwood

Creek Road, Butte Road and Road 23N29X (4240-1.6). Here the road crosses to the northeast side of the ridge while the PCT crosses to its southwest side, thereby avoiding—temporarily—an unsightly logged-over area.

After a mile of easy descent northwest, our trail abruptly bends east and we can gaze down at the churning Middle Fork Feather River, about 850′ below us. Only ½ mile to the northwest lies Deadman Spring saddle; our trail will take 3.0 miles to reach it. Shortly, our trail bends again and we descend southeast along the lower part of a ravaged, clearcut area. We then switchback three times under forest cover, the last time at a delicious spring (3180-2.3). Southbound hikers should tank up here, for their climb out of the canyon is waterless and

M6, M7

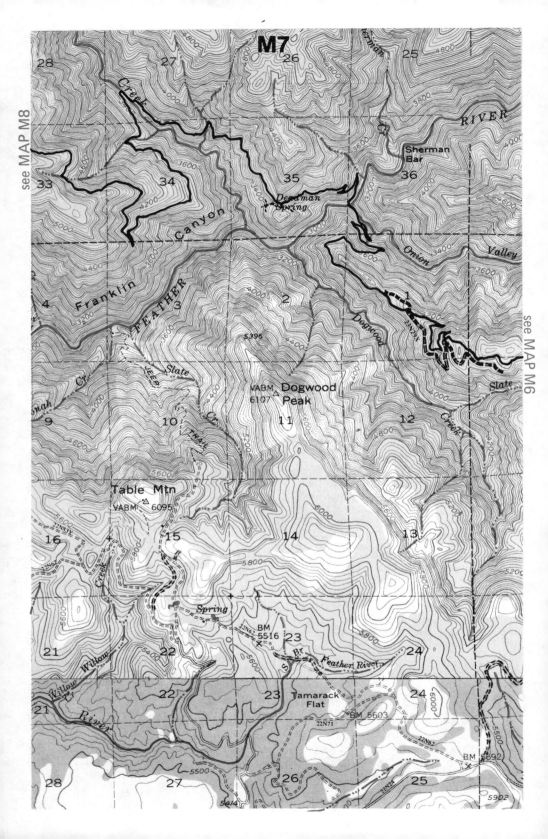

summer afternoon temperatures can soar into the 90s. Northbound hikers draw even closer to the pure waters of Onion Valley Creek. Among Douglas-firs, maples and dogwoods that line it, you'll find a lovely campsite.

Our long descent ends near Middle Fork Feather River (2900-0.4), which you cross via a massive arch bridge, the largest equestrian bridge on the entire PCT. Immediately beyond the bridge is one of the river's many fantastic pools, and a small outcrop of water-polished granite provides smooth, warm slabs for sunbathing. Metamorphosed, Paleozoic-age marine sediments prevail elsewhere throughout this part of the river gorge. From late July through mid-August, when summer temperatures are at their maximum, the pool warms to 70°F or more by midafternoon. In early or late summer or early in the morning, the temperature can be 60°F or less. To reach this pool, leave the PCT just before it climbs up to the bridge.

Campsites abound along the river's north bank, but the river's slightly cloudy water makes these sites less attractive than the one on Onion Valley Creek. Our well-graded trail climbs up-canyon past the sites, then switchbacks for a climb west to Deadman Spring saddle (3590-1.4). In early summer, you're likely to find it, but it seems to dry up later on, so don't count on it. Hikers descending a jeep road southwest to the river have been run off

private land by the armed owner, so don't stray too far looking for the spring. Onward, we contour along the forested east wall of Bear Creek canyon, swatting flies that are so prevalent below 4000' elevation. We cross a refreshing tributary in a deep gully, then continue over to Bear Creek (3240-2.1), which we cross via a large steel bridge. Look for a camp about ⅛ mile northwest of this bridge.

We now confront a 2700-foot, 7-mile climb to Lookout Rock. Fortunately, the trail is well-graded and generally well-shaded, and there's water along the route. Our trail heads briefly up-canyon, then climbs about ½ mile south to a permanent creek before heading southeast to a prominent east ridge. From it we climb southwest to a switchback on another ridge (4250-2.5), and leave behind most of the river views, poison oak and fly-harboring live oaks. Conifers prevail by the time we recross the east ridge, and we're shaded by Douglas-firs, ponderosa pines and sugar pines. We climb west, cross a large, often-dry gully, round a smaller ridge, and in ½ mile arrive at a seasonal spring (5350-2.3), flowing among dogwoods, alders and moss. In normal-rainfall years, you can count on it through early or mid-August. If you don't mind dry camping, you can fill up here and then, about 0.9 mile later, set up camp on a broad, white-fir forested ridgecrest that the trail almost tops.

An outcrop of granitic rock now lies just

M7, M8

Spanish Peak, from Lookout Rock

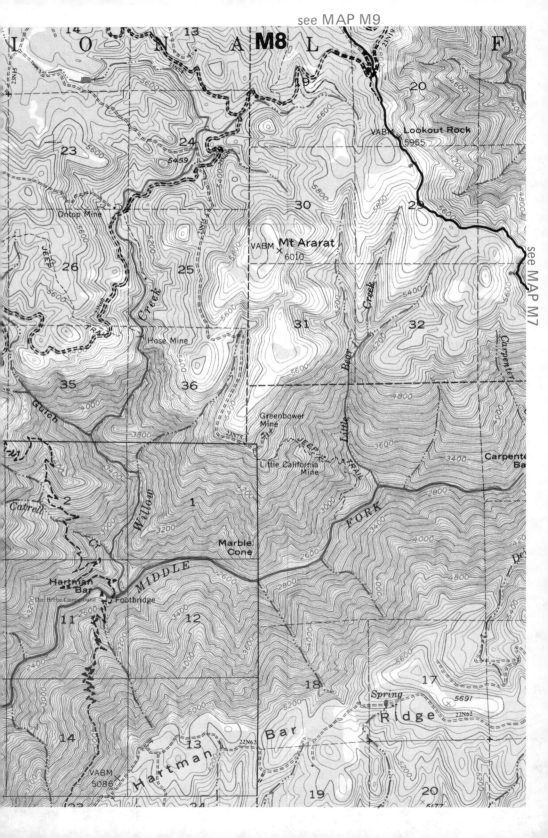

see MAP M7

Aspens along east shore of Bucks Lake

below us as we climb northwest across dusty volcanic rock to a sunny crest saddle (5750-1.4). Bending north, we continue upward and in ⅓ mile meet a willow-lined spring with staying power through midsummer. Southbound hikers can get water here and dry-camp on the sunny saddle. Treading the contact between volcanic rocks above and granitic ones below, the trail climbs ⅓ mile to Lookout Rock (5955-0.6), a resistant outcrop of tonalite. For southbound hikers, it provides the first good views of your descent ahead. For northbound hikers, it shows you Spanish Peak, the eastern point of a flat-topped highland rising northeast above unseen Bucks Lake.

Leaving Lookout Rock, our route descends to a nearby crest gap, goes about ¼ mile north on the Lookout Rock jeep road, and then parallels its east side down to a saddle crossed by Road 23N19 (5870-0.7). Northbound, this road drops 1¾ miles to Road 33N56. Keeping just northeast of the crest, we parallel old, crest-hugging Road 23N74Y northwest, and after we descend to a saddle, we quickly arrive at a road branching north (5880-1.3). This shortcut road switchbacks 0.7 mile down to the PCT and paved Road 33N56, but our tread takes a much longer route, heading northwest for tempting views of Bucks Lake before circling east for a forested descent to Road 33N56 (5505-1.6). You should get water at either of two near-road, spring-fed creeklets,

the eastern one located where the trail crosses the road. By the road's north shoulder you'll find a 40′ wide pond, fed by the creeklet. You can camp nearby.

*   *   *   *

Many hikers prefer to head west down to Bucks Lake either for supplies or for a lazy day at the lake. Should you wish to take this 6.8-mile alternate route, first walk west along paved Big Creek Road. After 2.5 miles you meet the Bucks Lake Road, also paved, and head 0.2 mile north to Haskins Valley Campground, operated by Pacific Gas and Electric. The utility company uses Bucks Lake water to power one of their generating plants on North Fork Feather River, about 2000′ below us. By late summer they've released quite a bit of water from Bucks Lake, and then it loses its attractiveness.

Just 0.3 mile up the road past the campground you reach Bucks Lake Lodge, which has a market, restaurant, RV campground, cabins and marina. Bend northeast along the lake 0.7 mile to Lakeshore Resort, which has the same facilities. Continue east past private summer cabins, and perhaps drop to the lake's east tip for a swim. In 1.0 mile from the resort you bridge Bucks Creek, then amble 0.5 mile over to Whitehorse Campground's entrance. Since this USFS Campground is your last

Lassen Peak, from Spanish Peak environs

source of reliable water until Clear Creek, 11.6 miles away, you ought to spend the night here or at least tank up. To regain the PCT, hike 1.6 miles up Bucks Lake Road to Bucks Summit.

*   *   *   *

If you're in a hurry, be aware that the PCT route from Big Creek Road north to Bucks Summit is 2.0 miles shorter than the supply route. A few paces east of the 40′ pond, you'll hit the bottom end of the shortcut road, mentioned earlier. From this junction, you descend 200 yards northeast on a closed road toward a meadow, then fork right on trail tread. This path skirts around the meadow's east end, staying just within the forest. In ¼ mile it slants across Road 24N29Y, the old temporary PCT route before this section of trail was completed. The road ends at Bucks Lake Road only 0.2 mile southwest of Bucks Summit, and the temporary route may be a better route than the trail when there's lots of snow.

Just beyond the road our path curves east to a creeklet, crosses it, then climbs about ½ mile north to several seasonal springs. About ⅓ mile farther, in a gully past a definable ridge, we have two more springs, then ¾ mile farther, after we jog west down into a deep gully, we reach our final water supply, a creeklet (5520-2.4). Midway between Haskins Valley and Bucks Lake roads, we now face 12.4 miles to Clear Creek, our next reliable source. Our mile-high trail contours northward in and out of gullies, eventually merges with an old logging

road, and follows it 200 yards north down a ridge before turning sharply west. We stay on this old road as it traverses a rejuvenating logged-out flat, then fork right for a 150-yard climb northwest to Bucks Summit (5531-2.4), which presents us with a good view to the east.

Across Bucks Lake Road we start up the closed Spanish Peak road and enter Bucks Lake Wilderness. This narrow, rutted road switchbacks up slopes covered with shallow, granitic soils. Once forested, these slopes were logged over before 1950, and for three decades they supported a thick, mature mantle of chaparral. Jeffrey pines are finally establishing themselves, and perhaps by the turn of the century there will be sufficient shade along this once shadeless route. It's still a good idea to ascend this moderately graded climb quite early in the morning. Switchbacking upward, we twice cross the often-flowing headwaters of Bucks Creek, then climb to another switchback, from where we get a view northeast down into Meadow Valley, a once rural setting that is increasingly becoming a retirement community—sort of a western extension of Quincy. From it our western route jogs north after ½ mile, enters the forest's fringe, keeps right at a fork, and soon arrives at a path (6550-0.6) on a shady flat where the road turns sharply counterclockwise from northwest to south, and we take the path.

The path begins by skirting along the base of the north-trending volcanic ridge, staying just high enough above meadows to keep one's feet dry. Snow doesn't finally melt in this vicinity until mid-July, and until at least then you'll encounter two large, shallow ponds that give rise to thousands of croaking tree frogs. Even before snow melts from the ponds' edges, corn lilies sprout and begin to grow skyward through the freezing water.

Our gradual climb north soon leaves the meadows behind, passes through a dense forest, and emerges high on fairly open slopes garnished with clusters of magnificent red firs. Our route traverses above a conspicuous granitic bench, whose low, brushy cover permits us to look east 3000′ down on serene Meadow Valley.

Beyond the bench, our trail gradually becomes a faint, old road, which passes a cluster of water-loving shrubs and trees that tap a near-surface water table. Our road comes to an open gully, and beside it we see a deteriorating log

shelter, which, during a rainstorm, would provide only minimal protection. Above it, we enter a pure stand of mature red firs, whose tall, straight trunks are embellished with a chartreuse cloak of staghorn lichen. Note that the lower 10–15′ of each tree is devoid of lichens, for this part of the trunk is annually buried by snow.

A brief stroll up our road along the shady, forested, gentle slope brings us to a shallow saddle (6920-1.6), on which we again meet the Spanish Peak road. The ⅓-mile hike east to its end provides rewarding views. The shallow saddle approximately marks the boundary between ridgecrest volcanic mudflows and much older granitic rocks on which the flows were deposited. From the saddle we take a path initially north, then make a relaxing traverse along the crest above usually unseen Gold Lake. As we curve northwest along the rim of a

M10

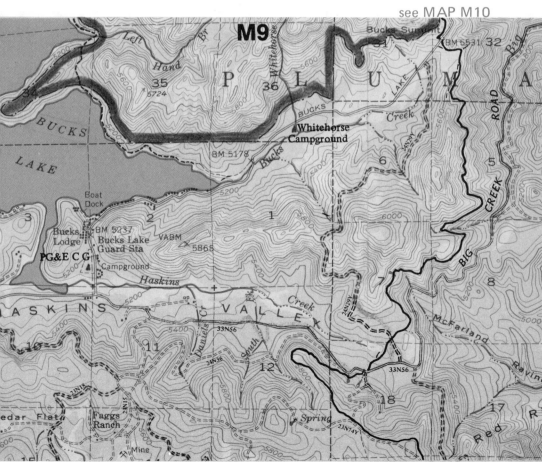

see MAP M10

see MAP M8

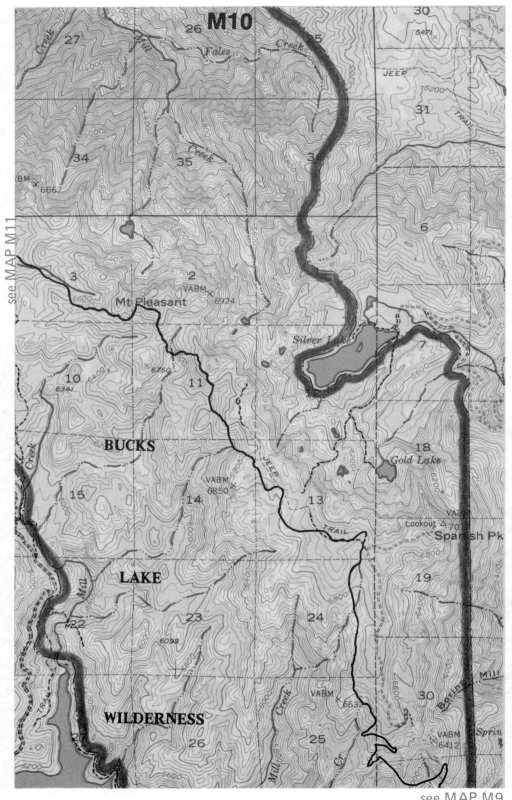

see MAP M11

see MAP M9

cirque wall, we can see large, shallow Silver Lake in the distance below. Partly obscuring it is a smooth, rounded, brushy moraine that the conspicuous Gold Lake trail traverses. This lateral moraine buries a bedrock ridge that separated the Silver Lake glacier from the Gold Lake glacier. Abundant red firs, together with some western white pines and a few Jeffrey pines, filter this view.

Our rim trail gradually curves north, then turns to descend west to a trail junction (6870-1.4) on the west side of the head of a steep gully. The faint, steep trail descends to the popular, highly visible Gold Lake trail, starting from the north end of Silver Lake. Our scenic rim route continues northwest through open forest, ascending and descending increasingly larger ridge knolls. The first is barely noticeable; the second we breath a little heavily to top; on the third we begin to wonder why our trail doesn't contour around them. On the third we cross a jeep road (6880-1.2), which climbs up to its bouldery summit. This road has more-or-less paralleled our path ever since we began it. This area's snow pack lasts well into July, and before then you may want to follow the road, although much of it too is then snow covered. We climb the fourth and last knoll almost to its very top, only to start on a 250' descent to a forested saddle (6710-1.0). Now below the east end of Mt. Pleasant—the high point of our ridge—we traverse west across its slopes, cross its low west spur ridge, and descend northwest to cross the headwaters of Clear Creek.

Our route west—faint at times—descends to within sight or hearing of this refreshing creek, almost levels off, and crosses an unsigned north-south trail. Not far beyond this intersec-

tion, our trail crosses Clear Creek (6190-2.2) where it turns north to flow down through a deep gap. Before leaving this creek you might consider establishing camp on the nearly level ground east of it. Campsites in this area are about as isolated as one can expect to find in California.

We head west across Clear Creek, then follow the Pacific Crest Trail northwest up to its junction with the old California Riding and Hiking trail (6240-0.5). Just west of this junction we pass a shallow pond choked with grasses and pond lilies. Our gently undulating trail then skirts the base of a granitic ridge and along our traverse we pass a second, larger but shallow pond. Late-summer hikers will see only a wet meadow. Beyond it our fir-lined trail passes a more distant pond, but white and red firs hamper our efforts to see it. Then we come to a trail junction (6270-1.0), from which a newer segment of the PCT climbs right but the older CRHT descends left.

If you want to descend to Three Lakes, head down the CRHT. This recommended side trip starts a southwest descent, quickly encounters a short lateral trail that climbs northwest back up to the PCT, then makes a fairly steep, fern-lined descent past large boulders before dead-ending at a curve in a road. To get to nearby Three Lakes from the end of the CRHT segment, turn left and follow the road southeast to the north arm of the lower lake. This lower lake, when full, extends all the way up to the middle lake, but in late season its level falls at least 15 feet, turning it into an unattractive mudhole. From the north arm a muddy, rutted road curves east over to the northwest shore of the more scenic middle lake, which has trout—ranging up to at least 16 inches—jumping from

M10, M11

Three Lakes' rocky, brushy middle lake

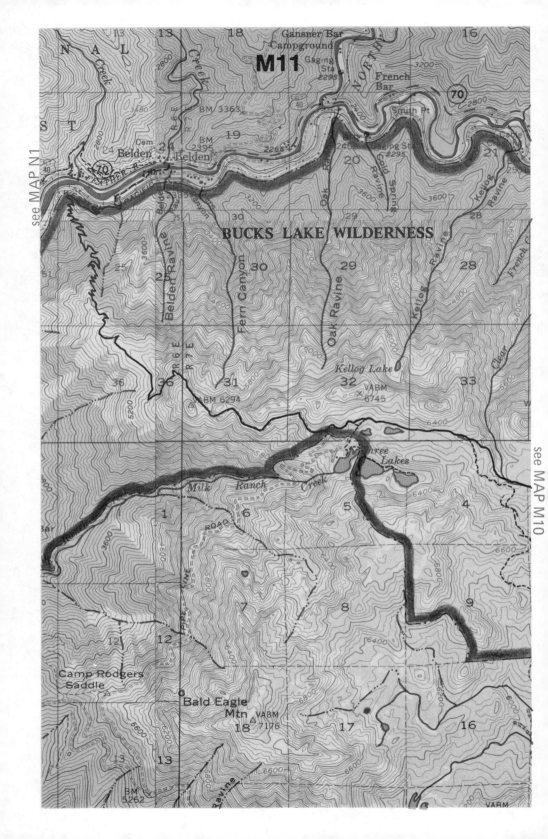

see MAP N1

see MAP M10

BUCKS LAKE WILDERNESS

its warm waters. Like the lower lake, this one drops considerably, but not drastically, in late season. Unlike the lower lake, this one is not dammed, and the Bucks Lake Wilderness boundary runs between the two. Our road traverses to the lake's east end, from where a trail starts up the north side of the refreshing outlet creek from the upper lake.

Starting on a terrace at a point about 12 yards north of this creek, this trail climbs up a brushy slope of huckleberry oak, tobacco brush, manzanita and chinquapin. Nearing the upper lake, we pass scattered specimens of sugar pine and white fir, then encounter more luxuriant growth in the form of mountain ash, dogwood and bracken fern. The upper lake is a pleasant surprise in that it is natural and its level stays high. In late summer, however, its fairly warm water becomes slightly cloudy, and purification may be advisable. Rock climbers will find prominent crack climbs on a band of diorite cliffs above the lake's south shore. Finding a good campsite is another matter. Because this lake is so hemmed in, there is very little level ground. Nevertheless, small sites can be found just above the lake's north, east and southwest shores.

Back where the PCT and CRHT fork, we follow the PCT right and make a brief climb, then come to another junction, from which a lateral trail descends back to the CRHT. This spur is for the convenience of southbound PCT trekkers who want to camp in the Three Lakes area. From the junction we have an easy ⅓-mile traverse to a shady bend on an old fire road (6260-0.4). If you descended to Three Lakes, you can rejoin our route at this bend by following Three Lakes Road ("Pipe Line Road" on Map M11) ¼ mile down-canyon from the lowest lake, then veering west up a closed, brush-lined jeep road, which quickly switchbacks northeast up to the bend. (If you encounter a fair number of people at Three Lakes, it's likely because the people have driven to them via the Three Lakes Road, which became a popular RV route in the '80s.) From the shady bend we climb west out onto sunny slopes which are clothed with manzanita and chinquapin, and lesser amounts of wild cherry and aromatic tobacco brush.

Our sunny, curving road descends northwest toward a crest saddle and, approaching it, we see snowy Lassen Peak (10,457') on the horizon ahead of us. Leaving the saddle, we pass some low, granitic blocks and pinnacles that cover the broad crest and tempt rock climbers to boulder a while. A second northwest descent takes us to another saddle and another view of Lassen. Seen in the north-northeast is a fire lookout atop well-named Red Hill (6330'), whose rusty color is derived from an iron-rich belt of ultramafic rocks—the same fault-bounded belt that underlies Meadow Valley. Our road continues beyond the saddle, descends the north slopes of Peak 6294, then crosses its west ridge just before a secondary summit and dead-ends in 200 yards (5900-1.8). From the road's left side, the Belden trail segment of the PCT begins.

A long switchback leg starts south on a moderate-to-steep descent, then quickly bends southwest and maintains its gradient across brushy slopes. We pass a trickling spring before reaching a ridge and switchbacking north past a few scattered pines. The descent ahead of us is perfectly clear, and we soon pass a second trickling spring before our trail curves northwest and descends toward Chips Creek canyon, which is a prominent cleft in the opposite wall of the Feather River canyon.

Our rapidly descending section of the PCT reaches a prominent ridgetop, briefly curves northeast across it, and then quickly rejoins it. The ridgetop descent is only momentary, for we soon leave brush behind and switchback under verdant forest cover north down toward the Feather River.

As our trail approaches the river, bay trees and live oaks appear. Nearing the end of our route, we traverse eastward and cross an ephemeral creeklet. Not far beyond, we leave Bucks Lake Wilderness and our trail reaches a trailhead beside Western Pacific's two railroad tracks (2310-4.7). Sometimes a freight train stops for about ½ hour on one track to let another train pass. If so, cross with caution or wait for the parked train to move. About 0.1 mile down a paved road from the tracks you'll pass a trailhead parking area on your left, then 0.2 mile farther you'll pass the entrance road to former Belden Campground, which was eradicated by a 1986 flood. Still, PCT hikers and equestrians camp there beside the Feather River. Not much farther on you reach Belden Town (2310-0.6), which has a small store, a saloon, a motel, RV sites, a laundry, a PCT register, and most important, a post office (ZIP 95915). This section of PCT ends as you follow the road across North Fork Feather River to adjacent Highway 70 (2330-0.1)

M11

June wildflowers on Hat Creek Rim

Section N: Highway 70 to Burney Falls

Introduction: After only a few hours' walk on this section, you leave a few scattered outcrops of granitic rocks behind and then belatedly say goodby to the 400-mile-long Sierra Nevada. Challenging you ahead are the snowbound slopes of the Cascade Range and the dry slopes and escarpments of the Modoc Plateau. The overall geologic character is unquestionably volcanic, but the plant life is quite diverse. Not only do you see differences due to elevation change, as you did in the previous section, you also see longitudinal changes: the landscape is progressively drier to the east. The best example of this is Hat Creek Valley. Its west rim is cool, lake-bound and forested—the ideal terrain for the Pacific Crest Trail. The *trail,* however, has been built on the east rim, a faulted escarpment, which is hot, virtually waterless, and offers only token shade under its open, woodland cover. Lassen Peak, the southernmost volcano of the Cascade Range, is the highlight of this section, and you may want to spend some extra time exploring the thermal wonders of Lassen Volcanic National Park.

Declination: 16½°E

Mileages:	South to North	Distance between Points	North to South
Highway 70 at Belden Town bridge	0.0		136.0
		6.2	
Williams Cabin flat.............................	6.2		129.8
		6.8	
Poison Spring..................................	13.0		123.0
		6.3	
Humbug Road at Cold Springs	19.3		116.7
		6.8	
Humboldt Road at Humboldt Summit	26.1		109.9
		6.2	
saddle south of Carter Meadow	32.3		103.7
		10.5	
Soldier Creek springs	42.8		93.2
		3.7	
Highway 36	46.5		89.5
		3.2	
Stover Camp...................................	49.7		86.3
		6.7	
Chester-Childs Meadows road....................	56.4		79.6
		8.5	
Warner Valley Campground......................	64.9		71.1
		7.6	
Lower Twin Lake, north end.....................	72.5		63.5
		5.6	
Badger Flat, east end	78.1		57.9
		5.4	
Road 32N12....................................	83.5		52.5
		9.0	
spur trail to Baker Spring campsite................	92.5		43.5
		4.5	
Highway 44's trailhead parking area	97.0		39.0
		4.3	
route northwest to Grassy Lake	101.3		34.7
		6.8	
Hat Creek Rim Fire Lookout.....................	108.1		27.9
		2.8	
Road 22	110.9		25.1
		8.8	
Cassel-Fall River Mills Road	119.7		16.3
		4.3	
PG&E road south to Cassel	124.0		12.0
		4.2	
Highway 299	128.2		7.8
		7.8	
Burney Falls...................................	136.0		0.0

Supplies and Permits: Although this section is the second longest one presented in this two-volume guidebook, its topography is gentle, and therefore most backpackers can do it in 8 days or less. This is fortunate, since there are no supply points along the route. Where you cross Highway 36, about 46½ miles along your way, you can head 8 miles northeast into Chester, where you can get virtually any trail item you might need. North of Lassen Volcanic National Park, many hikers leave the PCT at Road 32N12 and head over to the Old Station Post Office, Hat Creek Resort and other attractions, which are mentioned in our alternate-route description. The resort's store is camper- and fisherman-oriented, so don't expect much in the way of supplies. If you're heading past Burney Falls, your last near-route post office before Interstate 5 will be in Cassel, about one mile south of Baum Lake. From it you can leave the PCT and head south up a road, passing a good campground only minutes before reaching the Cassel Post Office and a small store. Later, when you reach Highway 299, you can take it 2½ miles southwest to its Highway 89 intersection, 2 miles farther to Johnson Park, with a store and a couple of cafes, and then 3 miles more to Burney, which has virtually all the supplies you'll likely need.

You'll need a wilderness permit to camp overnight in the backcountry of Lassen Volcanic National Park. Write for one several weeks in advance. However, note that if you camp overnight *only* at the park's Warner Valley Campground and not in its back-country, you won't need a permit. Equestrians are *not* allowed overnight in the back-country, so if you plan to have horses overnight, you'll have to make advance reservations with the park service. You have only three choices, and the Juniper Lake corral is too far off the PCT to consider. The other two corrals are at Summit Lake, about 4½ miles west of the PCT from Lower Twin Lake, and Butte Lake, about 4½ miles east of the PCT along the Nobles Trail.

Rattlesnakes: These may be encountered at a number of stretches along this route, particularly in lower Chips Creek canyon and on the Hat Creek Rim escarpment. However, they'll stay out of your way if you'll stay out of theirs. Ticks are likely in the same areas.

Water: Although this section is in northern California, it can be quite dry by midsummer and pose drought problems similar to those of southern California sections. North of Cold Springs you have to walk 23½ miles before you reach Soldier Creek springs. Between the two, your route is dry once the snowmelt creeks and seeps disappear, usually by late July. However, about halfway along this dry stretch you can head north on the Carter Meadow Trail and find water (and campsites) in ½ mile or so.

A more serious problem is lack of water along the Hat Creek Rim escarpment. The Forest Service spent thousands of dollars trying to provide fresh water to this often hot, usually shadeless stretch. At Baker Lake and Porcupine Reservoir they drilled exploratory wells hundreds of feet deep—to no avail. A few years later, they developed a campsite near Baker Spring, but the spring proved to be unreliable. Then in 1987 a major fire torched much of the rim, which exacerbated the water-shortage problems and also obliterated miles of PCT. The trail is supposed to reopen in 1990, and water is supposed to be stored at a tank by the Hat Creek Rim Fire Lookout, which was also torched. Before you do the Hat Creek Rim between Highway 44 and Road 22, first check with Lassen National Forest's Hat Creek District office about the trail's condition and water availability. Write to the office at P.O. Box 220, Fall River Mills, CA 96028, or phone them at (916) 336-5521.

This section starts on Highway 70 at the Belden Town bridge, by the PG&E Belden Power House, which empties into Yellow Creek. Immediately west of the creek we come to the Belden Rest Area, and from its west end, by the Ely Stamp Mill, we start west on PCT tread. The trail parallels the highway and some powerlines for about ½ mile, then swings northwest for a traverse to a bridge over Indian Creek (2370-1.1). Shaded by Douglas-fir, big-leaf maple, black oak, live oak and bay tree, we traverse out of the creek's canyon, meeting a trail (2400-0.3) immediately after turning west to parallel the busy highway. Should you want to take a last swim in the Feather River—here an inviting reservoir—take this trail ¼ mile down to the highway. We now face a shade-less, rocky traverse above Highway 70 as we cross nearly vertical beds of the Calaveras formation.

Beneath the buzzing of giant powerlines, we cross a low ridgecrest, quickly spot Chips Creek below us, and once again enter shady forest. After a pleasant traverse through the forest, we reach a junction (2470-0.6) from which a trail descends briefly northwest to a short, nearly level segment of an old road. This road is wide enough to pitch a tent on, and trekkers have certainly camped here in the past. Get water—and perhaps a brisk, refreshing bath—from Chips Creek, not too far below the road. If you were to wade or boulder-hop a few minutes downstream, you'd see the site where the road once bridged the creek. Today only a fine swimming hole—a worthy goal—remains.

From the trail down to the old road, our Chips Creek trail continues its shady traverse, begins to climb, and then executes four switchbacks to get us high above the creek. Beyond the last switchback, our ascent northwest is a moderate one, across metamorphic rocks that were metamorphosed in part when a granitic pluton—partly seen across the canyon—intruded them. In several places along our trail, we cross small bedrock exposures of this granitic pluton, and these mark the northern boundary of the granitic Sierra Nevada. From the headwaters of Chips Creek, volcanic rocks extend northward in a continuous mantle to central Washington, where granitic rocks once again appear.

After a protracted, moderate ascent, our trail levels off, then even descends, crossing several welcome seasonal creeks. Beyond them several more creeklets of varing size and duration are crossed on a traverse west, and then we arrive at a small cabin on a white-fir-shaded flat (3700-4.2). This level area, only 100 yards north of bounding, noisy Chips Creek, makes a lovely campsite, and Rex and Conrad Williams extend an invitation to PCT hikers to use their cabin. They only ask you to observe a few rules: Build fires only in the stove or in the fire pits. Make sure all fires are completely out before leaving. Make sure the cabin door is closed and latched. You can use anything in the camp, but please replace any wood you use, and if you use their pots, pans and dishes, please wash them. Unfortunately, their open hospitality has been countered at times with vandalism.

Our west-climbing trail crosses a creek—sometimes a touchy ford via slippery boulders—then soon climbs to Myrtle Flat Camp (4180-0.9), with a roofless cabin. A steep, narrow trail behind it descends west to a small, cold, invigorating pool on Chips Creek. As we make a protracted climb west, passing ephemeral creeklets on the way, we note that ponderosa pines give way to sugar pines and white firs. You may find one or two flat spots to camp at before reaching the canyon's headwall, where we switchback up, crossing and recrossing an old jeep road, to a ford of a creek from Poison Spring (5650-3.8) just above a series of small waterfalls. Hikers have camped on the old road just beyond the crossing. We start up it, then follow a switchbacking trail up to the lip of a glaciated bowl, in which our trail ends at a junction with the old road (5920-0.4). On this gently climbing road we hike west, passing an aspen-bordered campsite where a seasonal creek curves north toward Poison Spring. As we approach the headwall of Chips Creek canyon, we leave the old road, forking right on trail tread (6100-0.5) and then climbing up to the vicinity of Poison Spring (6680-1.2). The spring flows into a nearby pond, which lies about 60 yards below the trail. If you descend to this pond and its adjacent road and campsite, you'll become acquainted with stick-seeds, at least from midsummer onward. These plants produce barbed seeds that tenaciously cling to your socks. The few plants here are nothing compared to the numbers you'll meet on the Hat Creek Rim.

Beyond the spring we climb north to a wide lumber road (6900-0.4), from which our trail continues northeast. Now we climb ¼ mile up to a crest, follow it east ½ mile, and then

N1, N2, N3

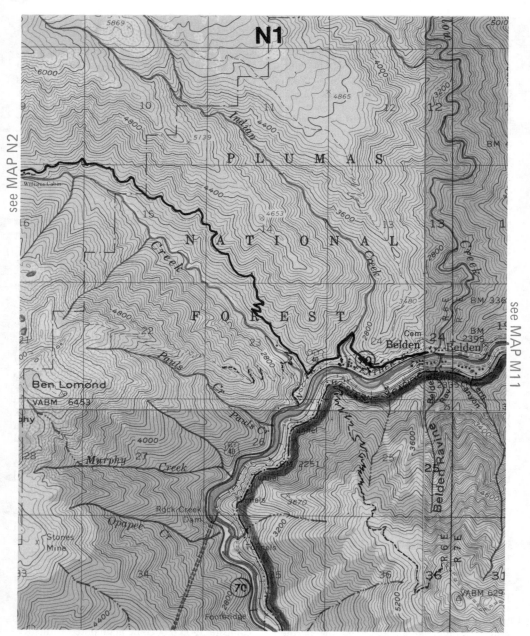

switchback down its north-facing slopes, passing a spring before curving north across a lower spur ridge to a roadend (6620-2.5). On this closed road we amble north for about 10 minutes to another PCT trail segment (6610-0.7), on our left, beginning just after our road curves right and starts a noticeable descent. From this junction the PCT makes a somewhat confusing descent north gently down through a

partly logged-over area, then around a forested slope to two crossings of an old jeep road. Only 150 yards north of the second crossing, the trail segment ends on the road's east side, and you walk 50 yards north-northeast on it to a junction where the east-west trending Road 26N02 (6380-1.0) intersects the north-south trending Humbug Ridge Road.

From the northwest corner of the intersec-

N3, N4

tion we follow a signed trail segment 0.3 mile northwest to an old road and walk northwest on it less than 100 yards, to where it starts to curve northeast. Here a short trail segment bears northwest to the south end of a long, mule-eared meadow. Rather than taking an obvious, but erroneous, short trail north, we follow PCT diamonds west across the south edge of the meadow, and, 30 yards into a lodgepole forest on an old westward logging road, we reach yet another trail segment. Following it north, we parallel at a distance the long meadow's west edge. Our trail ends at another old logging road, and on this we hike north, still parallelling the meadow, then leave it on another trail segment that climbs above the meadow's northwest corner, switchbacks west and reaches, on a low ridge, yet another old logging road. This we follow ¼ mile northwest to an intersection of Humbug Road 27N01 (6450-1.7). We walk a few paces west and find Cold Springs, from which the trail angles right. Among conifers just below the springs you'll find a car-camping area. You are 23½ miles from your next reliable trailside water, Soldier Creek springs, and about 30½ miles from your first decent campsite with water, Stover Camp. The latter destination is quite a far day's hike away. Fortunately, you can get water and make camp in the Carter Meadow area, about ½ mile from the PCT after you hike 13 more miles.

From Cold Springs the PCT climbs past two roads, the second one (6710-0.7) heading southeast across a clearcut to nearby Humbug Summit. Continuing north, we attain a minor ridge that is a drainage divide between east- and west-flowing creeks. Up it we wind northwest, largely under the shade of mature red firs, then traverse north across an open flat. A pond lies just west of the trail (7100-1.6) but it usually evaporates by mid or late July. From the flat's north end we traverse northwest on an old jeep road and have our first views of the Lake Almanor area and the Lassen Peak environs. The closed road then switchbacks down to a narrow ridge and our views disappear. Near the north end (7000-0.9), a blocked-off jeep road forks right and drops about 500′ as it descends to the Lost Lake environs. Our jeep road ends in 0.1 mile and we fork left down a bush-lined trail. We quickly re-enter forest and stay within it until just before our crest route starts to curve west. We now have views, with the dark, prominent Eagle Rocks (7063′) looming ½ mile to the northeast. We can scan the Cascade crest that rims the upper Butt Creek basin. A prominent gap on the north rim is the saddle south of unseen Carter Meadow. The gap is 2¾ air miles away, but the PCT will take 7½ miles to get to it. As we progress west, we pass two volcanic pinnacles, just to the north, then pass smaller trailside pinnacles and blocks. We leave the crest and our panoramic views disappear as we enter a forest on the northwest steep slope of Humboldt Peak (7087′). Snowbound at least

N4, N5

Butt Mountain and distant Lassen Peak

until early July, this stretch first drops, then climbs to the Humboldt Road at Humboldt Summit (6610-3.6).

Under a cover of stately red firs are several short roads that more less delimit a *de facto* car-camping area. Here, lingering snow patches may provide you with water through mid-July. Following the westbound road for 80 yards, we spy a trail—the PCT—on which we now parallel the road a few yards, and then we veer right and descend an arcing path to a spur ridge before switchbacking down to a saddle on the county-line crest. Leaving the old logging scar of this area, our well-graded trail stays close to the crest without any unnecessary climbing or descending. Shady forest cover alternates with shrubby slopes that provide views of Lassen Peak and, on clear days, Sacramento Valley. One-half mile beyond a crossing of a set of old jeep tracks, we descend to the lowest of several saddles (6155-3.9). Our climbing trail now turns gradually eastward, passes an interesting outcrop of volcanic rocks, and veers north to cross a long spur ridge before descending southeast to the Carter Meadow trail junction, on a saddle (6600-2.3). The trail goes only about a mile north to a logging road. Along it, you should only have to go about ½ mile to find water and campsites. If you need to get out of the mountains, follow the road 7½ miles down

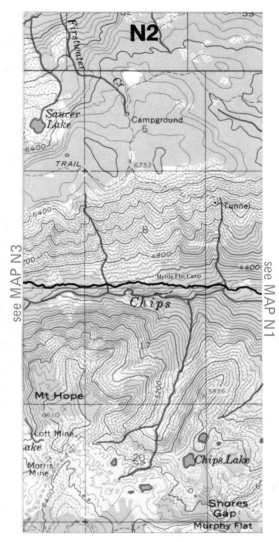

see MAP N3

see MAP N1

we make a moderate climb of ½ mile, skirt the south end of Butt Mountain, and reach the west end (7580-3.9) of another long, nearly level crest. Along it we see not only Lassen Peak, but also Brokeoff Mountain, west of it. Brokeoff Mountain (9235′), second only to Lassen in height, is the southwest remnant of a now-eroded stratovolcano that may have stood 11,000 feet high about 300,000 years ago. Lassen Peak, at 10,457 feet, is considerably smaller than the older, spreading stratovolcano. Lassen, a huge dome of pasty lava, is also considerably younger, having been squeezed onto the surface roughly 11,000 years ago.

Leaving the east end of our crest, we descend almost a mile east across brushy slopes that give us ample opportunities to survey the south end of Lake Almanor to the east, and past and present logging operations to the south. Our route enters a red-fir forest as it begins to curve north, and then it descends ½ mile to a secondary ridge, which it rounds before descending ½ mile northwest to a shallow gully (6920-2.4). Before mid-July you may find water in this gully, but it quickly disappears after the snow melts. We start east down the gully, but soon veer away and, on a southeast-facing slope, see our first sugar pine on this descent. White firs clothe the slopes as we continue our descent, though ¼ mile before our second major gully we have an opening with our first good view of giant Lake Almanor. Beyond the second gully we descend ¾ mile northeast to a ridge, then more than a mile west to the seasonal headwaters of Soldier Creek. We cross its gully and then descend, in just under a mile, to its recrossing (5480-4.2). The creek is flowing here, for our ford lies just below permanent Soldier Creek springs. Unfortunately, topography limits camping space to just one tent site. Don't expect any decent camping until Stover Camp, still 6.9 miles away.

Ponderosa pines and incense-cedars are now commonplace among the white firs as we traverse east and drop into private property just before crossing an old road (5150-1.5). We continue ¼ mile east to a newer road, then switchback and parallel it ¼ mile northwest before crossing it. On nearly flat ground we head north to a grassy trough (4870-0.7), which becomes Soldier Creek only during flooding. The grass grows on porous, scoriaceous basalt, so the creek along this stretch is

to Highway 32. Lots of logging roads complicate this exit, but generally head north down to Deer Creek Meadows, then 2 miles west out to the busy highway.

The PCT climbs east up the divide to some interesting rim volcanics, then switchbacks across forested slopes to climb above rugged cliffs. About 1½ miles from the saddle our route starts climbing northeast on a moderate grade, and then it descends a bit through brush to a long, nearly level crest. Along it we have views south of logged-over Ruffa Ridge and views north of Lassen Peak, which stands in the distance above the glaciated canyon lying below us. From the northeast end of the crest

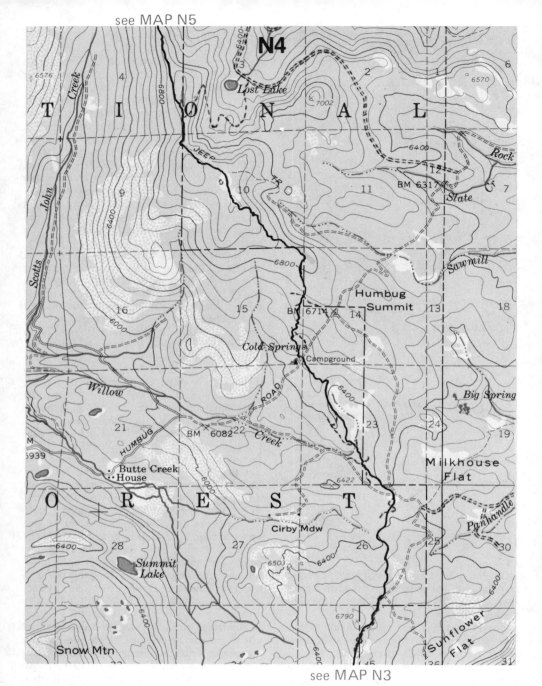

see MAP N3

largely subterranean. Lodgepole pines, taking advantage of this underground source, line the trough. This stand of water-loving conifers is near its lower-elevation limit; you see few lodgepoles below 5000 feet. Along the northeast side of the grassy trough runs a dirt-bike path, which is a remnant of the Lassen Trail. Danish immigrant Peter Lassen pioneered it back in 1847, providing settlers with the first route into northern California. The route, however, was not efficient, and it fell into disuse after William H. Nobles pioneered a shorter,

N7

better route in 1851. We'll hike several miles of his route in the northern part of Lassen Volcanic National Park.

Leaving the grassy trough and the lodgepole pines which tap the near-surface water, we climb just a bit into a dry, open forest of Jeffrey pines. The soil derived from the geologically young basalt is extremely dusty, and your boots and socks get covered with it by the time you reach a minor road. Immediately past it you cross a heavily used logging road, then climb ½ mile across less dusty terrain to Highway 36 (4990-1.5). The highway lacks parking, which is unfortunate for those wanting to do just the enjoyable Highway 36-Highway 44 stretch. The St. Bernard Lodge lies 1.5 miles west along Highway 36 and the Black Forest Lodge, with the menu preferred by Schaffer and Schifrin, lies 0.2 mile past it. Chester, a "full-service" community, lies 8 miles to the northeast.

North from Highway 36 you cross three roads in one mile, the third one a major road. Just 130 yards past it you cross a fourth, then weave ½ mile over to Marian Creek (5060-1.6), which is usually dry during most of the summer. We then climb 0.4 mile to another major road, cross it, circle counterclockwise ½ mile to a similar road, cross it and in 110 yards cross yet another one. Quickly we start a climb up the west side of a gully, cross it midway up, then continue our climb to Stover Camp (5660-1.6). With gushing, spring water, this undeveloped Forest Service campground, halfway between Highway 36 and North Stover Mountain, can be one of the section's nicer camps—if it hasn't been recently trashed when you pass through.

We leave the camp by a short climb east, then resume our northward ascent, crossing an abandoned road in ½ mile. An old clearcut lies between it and a low divide, a county boundary. After ⅓ mile of traverse, we cross a major road (5810-1.1) just west of the county-line crest. We parallel it briefly west, then traverse across logged lands to an abandoned road, which we cross ½ mile past the major road. This we parallel almost a mile northwest back up to the county-line crest (5920-1.4), the last 125 yards being on private logging land in the southwest corner of Section 31. A gentle climb ensues, taking us north-northwest through a logged area to flat, viewless North Stover Mountain (6050-0.7), clothed in firs and sugar pines. A well graded, shady descent follows, and it provides us with several views of Lassen

Peak before we cross a major logging road (5400-1.6) on a ridge.

From the ridge our trail first descends to a large bridge over North Fork Feather River (5020-1.0), making an unnecessary climb along the way. From the bridge's north end the trail jogs a few paces west before climbing east out of the small gorge. You'll find good campsites just upstream from the jog in the trail. Out of the gorge, we have a level route north and cross a long, narrow clearcut a minute before crossing a major logging road. About two minutes past it we meet a minor road, and if you want to visit Domingo Spring Campground, follow this road northeast to a quick junction with a major road going 0.3 mile east to the campground. After another two-minute walk on the PCT, we cross this major road, the Chester-Childs Meadows road (5110-0.9). This road goes 8.0 miles west, ending at Highway 36 as Wilson Lake Road. It also goes 8.8 miles east to Chester, ending at Highway 36 as Feather River Drive. If you went to Chester for supplies, you could return to the PCT along this road, bypassing one of the less attractive sections of the PCT.

The PCT north of this road begins along a short, abandoned road spur, which makes a convenient trailhead parking area. Staying quite level, the trail traverses along the base of a volcanic-rubble slope, then climbs briefly onto a closed road. Up it you count off 110 yards before the trail resumes. It switchbacks once across this steeply ascending road, then joins it where the road's gradient reduces to moderate. We now follow the road for 0.4 mile to where it ends at a 1986 clearcut, which was to be planted in 1989. Judge for yourself how fast the forest is regenerating. At least you do get a view of Stump Ranch meadow and, in the distance beyond it, Butt Mountain. Just after you pass it, you cross a second, smaller clearcut of similar vintage, this one extending downslope from a shallow saddle. Just above it the PCT crosses and immediately recrosses the crest, then crosses it about ½ mile later. It soon arrives at the brink of an east-west trending secondary ridge, from which we can see Willow Lake northeast below us and Lassen Peak northwest above us. From this viewpoint you can't see the conspicuous lakelet about ¼ mile to the east. Neither it nor the pond west of it is worth a visit.

Beyond the viewpoint the trail contours west, descends to a saddle on the main ridge, crosses

see MAP N6

see MAP N4

Carter
Meadow

Butt Mtn
VABM△7866

Carter TRAIL

Elam Creek

Creek

Creek

MEADOW

CARTER

L A S S E N

Ruffa Ranch

HUMBOLDT

Butt

Eagle Rocks
VABM△7063

Robbers Roost

Humboldt Summit
VABM△7087
Humboldt Pk

PLUMAS CO

Yelle

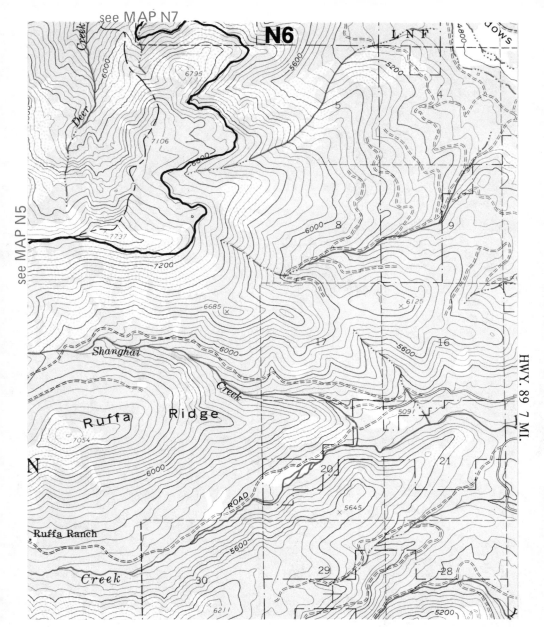

it, and traverses northwest across the west slope. Up the canyon to the west, a private road climbs to a broad saddle, where your now-descending trail almost touches it, then finally diagonals across it after a 0.1-mile paralleling descent northwest (5960-4.1). Here you'll see an abandoned road branching left, and you walk along it but 45 yards to where trail tread resumes, along the road's left (south) side. The trail quickly curves north, soon reaches Little

Willow Lake's outlet creek, and then climbs steeply up this seasonal creek to a junction along the east fringe of swampy Little Willow Lake (6100-0.7). Since its basin is your first potential camping area in Lassen Park, you should remember that in the park no camping is allowed in meadows or within 100′ of a lake or creek. You'll also need a wilderness permit to camp outside the park's campgrounds. Since the Little Willow Lake marsh is prime mos-

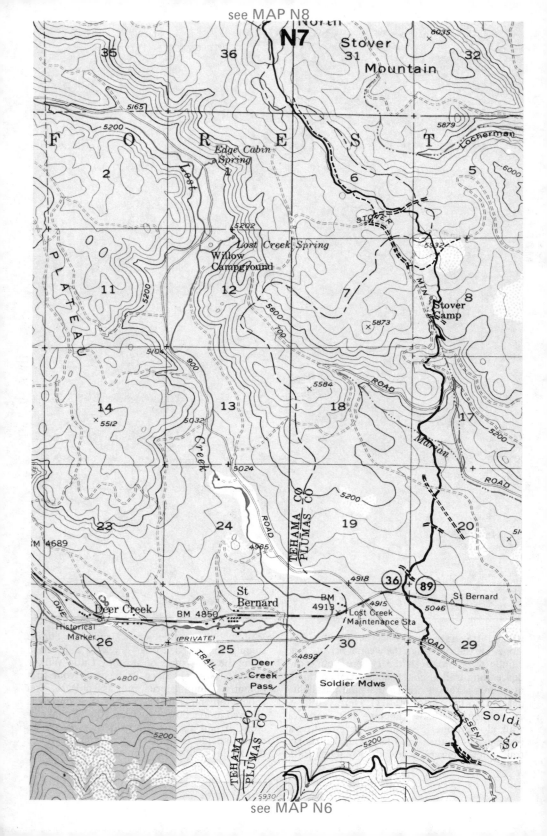

quito land, at least before August, you'll probably want to push on to Warner Valley Campground, our first real camping opportunity.

Like trails of old, our next stretch of northbound PCT climbs over a ridge and drops to a junction rather than contour over to it (6030-1.0). Here you can make a short side trip, descending ¼ mile to a road going briefly north to Terminal Geyser. Midway along this descent you'll meet a spur trail that goes east to a nearby overlook of the Terminal Geyser bowl, but the geyser is better viewed from below. Therefore, follow the road north 180 yards to the roaring geyser, at road's end. Continually churning out steam, it is technically a fumarole, not a geyser. Observe it with caution. On the broad area at road's end you'll see a capped well, drilled in 1978 by Phillips Petroleum Company, which was doing geothermal exploration.

Back at the PCT junction, your trail splits in just 25 yards. If you are on horseback, you have to take the right trail, which goes 1.6 miles to a junction just north of Boiling Springs Lake. If you are on foot, take the more scenic left trail which in 1⅓ miles climbs over a divide and drops to a junction by a ravine just above Boiling Springs Lake. Again here, you can go either right or left, though the official, more scenic PCT route goes left. On the park's Boiling Springs Lake Nature trail, we head northwest past the scalding hot lake's fumaroles, mudpots and rotten fumes. Just beyond the lake we cross its short-season outlet creek and by its east bank meet the end of the counterclockwise nature trail around the lake. Then, in about 0.2 mile, we meet the horse trail

Terminal Geyser

(5800-1.8). Our well-traveled route descends ¼ mile to a trail climbing west to Drake Lake, then a few muddy paces later passes a trail northwest over to nearby Drakesbad Guest Ranch. We start east and immediately see this resort's tempting pool, heated by hot springs. The pool, unfortunately, is for guests only, and the resort is usually booked several *years* in advance. However, you can get a meal at the lodge if you give them sufficient warning; their supplies are limited.

Beyond a couple of hot springs our trail descends to a bridge across Hot Springs Creek. Despite its name, the creek is very, very cold. Between creek and meadow, we walk a few minutes east to a picnic area, head over to the

N8, N9

Marshy Little Willow Lake

CREST TRAIL

Terminal
Geyser

Sifford
Mountain

6800

6726

35

36

31

6400

Kelly
M
8919

Little Willow
Lake

5837

Willow Lake

3

2

6201

6350

6000

6400

PACIFIC

5600

6

6157

5988

STUMP

6000

10

11

12

7

6136

6000

3786

5633

5866

I
5681
5711

O

5589

N
Cinder
Pit

A

L

18

CREST

ROAD

CREEK

5600

Cinder
Pit

15

Buzzard
Springs

14

RANCH

13

ROAD

5200

5355

ROAD

5240

5150

TRAIL

Sawmil

5410

5272

5200

Domingo
Spring

22

23

Stump
Ranch

24

19

Domi
Spr C

North

Fork

Feather River
Rod & Gun Club

5263

Feather
TRAIL

Fe

5444

PLUMAS CO
TEHAMA CO

27

5853

26

Ice   Cave

25

5702

CREST

30

ilson
Lake

Ice
Cave

Mountain

34

35

36

PACIFIC

31

5800

nearby Drakesbad road, then make a short walk east on it to a fork. We branch left, climbing past a few campsites to the east end of Warner Valley Campground (5670-0.9), where PCT tread resumes near a spring-fed creeklet. If you camp here and not in the park's back-country, you won't need a wilderness permit.

From the campground, the trail crosses the creeklet in less than 40 yards, then soon switchbacks twice. It makes a very well-graded ascent northwest on glaciated lava flows, one thick flow forming a prominent band of nearly vertical cliffs. We started in a forest of white firs, Jeffrey pines, incense-cedars and sugar

N9

see MAP N10

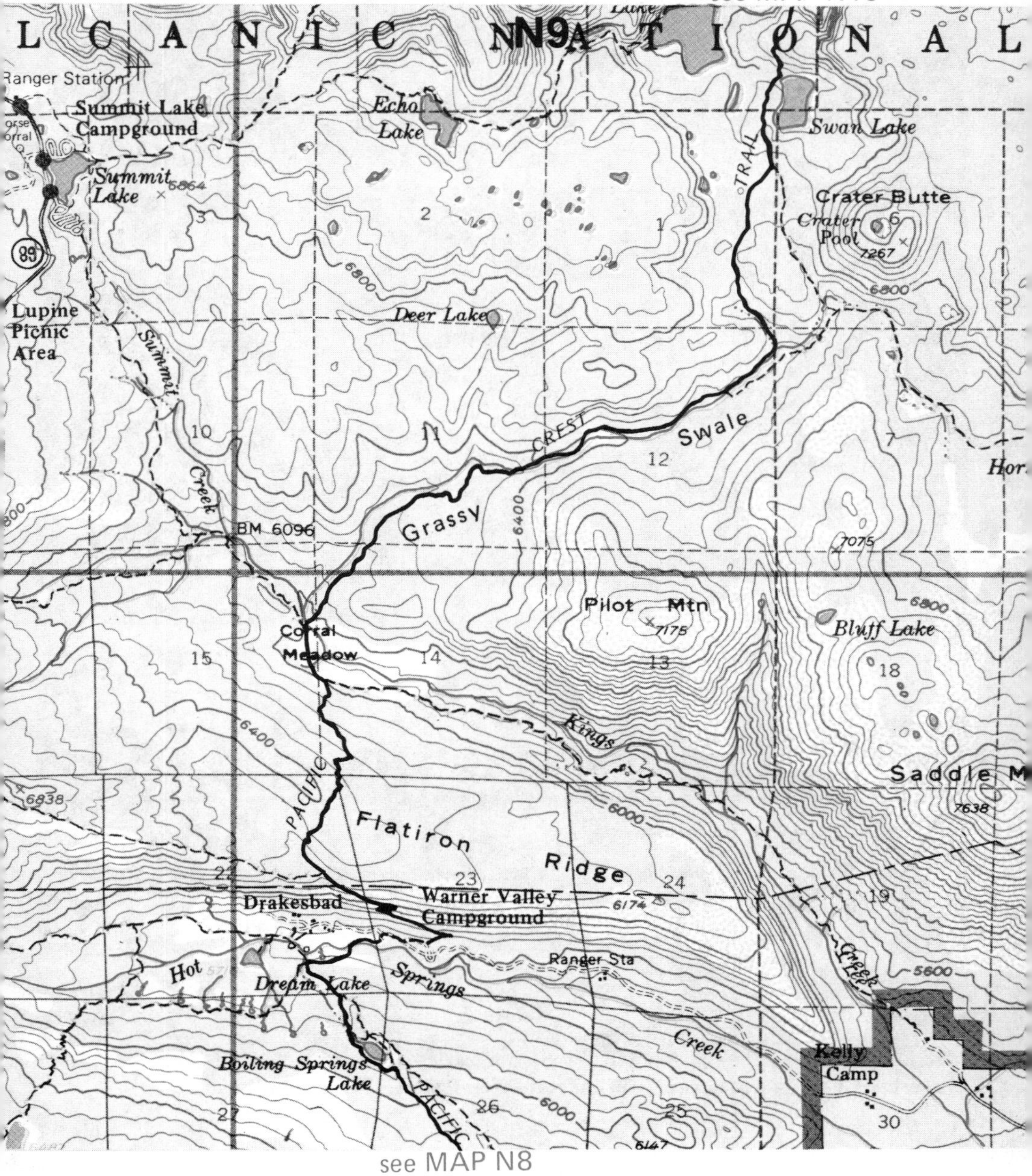

see MAP N8

Drakesbad Guest Ranch, Lower Twin Lake and West Prospect Peak, Silver Lake

pines, and when we re-enter forest higher up, the last two species are no longer with us. Until that re-entry, we have some fair views of the Drakesbad area, and we pass some drought-resistant wildflowers and ferns. We gradually leave the cliff escarpment and ease into a fir forest, shortly arriving at a junction (6180-1.0). The trail branching left leads to others climbing to Bench Lake, Sifford Lake, Kings Creek Falls and the Lassen Park Road.

As we continue upward, white firs disappear, red firs become dominant, and western white pines join them. Our trail crosses the western part of Flatiron Ridge, which is composed of relatively flat layers of lava flows topped with glacial sediments. The flows are among the park's older volcanic rocks, probably being on the order of ½–1 million years old. From the crest of a glacial moraine we wander down the gullied north slopes of Flatiron Ridge and arrive at a trail junction at the outskirts of Corral Meadow. Here, a trail takes off down Kings Creek. This infrequently used trail offers hikers some pretty impressive views of the Kings Creek gorge. The PCT quickly crosses two seasonal creeks, the second one the more persistent of the two, and ¼ mile past the previous junction reaches another junction in the midst of a plethora of campsites (5990-1.4). Perhaps no other area in the Lassen Park backcountry receives such heavy use. Summit Lake and the Lassen Park Road are about 2½ miles away along the trail climbing left from the junction.

From the spacious west-bank campsites our trail crosses to the east bank of Kings Creek—definitely a wet ford. However, you might find a log bridge just upstream, providing a dry crossing. From the log you then head back down to the trail's resumption, although a misleading *de facto* trail continues upstream, leading hikers astray. The trail goes a bit over 100 yards to the confluence where Grassy Swale and Summit creeks become Kings Creek. You can find an additional campsite in this vicinity. Immediately above the confluence, Grassy Swale creek noisily cascades 30′ down into a small, shallow pool, which in turn spills into a deeper one—this one a cozy, if chilly, swimming hole.

In July the stretch of trail from Corral Meadow northeast through Grassy Swale abounds with mosquitoes, and you'll probably want to wear long pants and a long-sleeved shirt here. Our trail makes an initial climb, then wanders through a variable red-fir forest, arriving after one mile at a small, wet meadow, which is an excellent place to look for diminutive wildflowers, including the rather uncommon round-leaved sundew. We loop around the meadow's south border and then, about ⅓ mile beyond it, we log-cross or boulder-hop Grassy Swale creek. For the next ⅓ mile, we stay close to the creek, yet just far enough above its bank to be on dry, gravelly soil. We then return to mosquitoland, a marshy meadow lined with western blueberries, which extends for several hundred yards. Almost ½ mile past the marshy Grassy Swale creek meadow, we come to a junction (6470-2.5). Here a trail follows boggy tread across the swale before continuing 0.6 mile up the swale to another junction. From the junction one trail climbs 0.8 mile north up to the PCT while another, eastbound, takes you 1.4 nearly effortless miles over to the northwest arm of Horseshoe Lake.

Our trail continues ⅓ mile up the northwest bank of Grassy Swale creek before leaving it for a moderate, one-mile climb to meet the previously mentioned trail (6710-1.3). Should you want to climb a small volcano with a lake in its crater, then climb nearby Crater Butte, rising 500′ above you to the southeast. This "cinder cone" is—like its northern neighbor, Fairfield Peak—more lava flow than cinders, and both probably originated during the last episode of glaciation.

About 250 yards past the junction we crest a low divide and leave behind the headwaters of the North Fork Feather River. Entering the headwaters of the Pit River, you'll quickly note Swan Lake, a short distance below you. If you plan to camp at this typical backcountry lake, leave the trail here and look for a site above its south shore or ones on its east-shore bench. Our trail almost touches the lake at its northwest corner, then immediately crosses its barely discernible outlet creek (6620-0.5) before dropping ½ mile to a junction on the southeast shore of lodgepole-fringed Lower Twin Lake. Westward, a 4¼-mile route skirts along the lake's south shore, then climbs past Upper Twin and Echo lakes to Summit Lake's north-shore campground. On a ¼ mile stretch, we start east, immediately passing a campsite before curving north to an east-shore junction with a trail that climbs ⅔ mile to Rainbow Lake. After several more minutes of east-shore walking, we reach Lower Twin Lake's north shore and a trail (6545-0.9) that skirts along it.

N9, N10

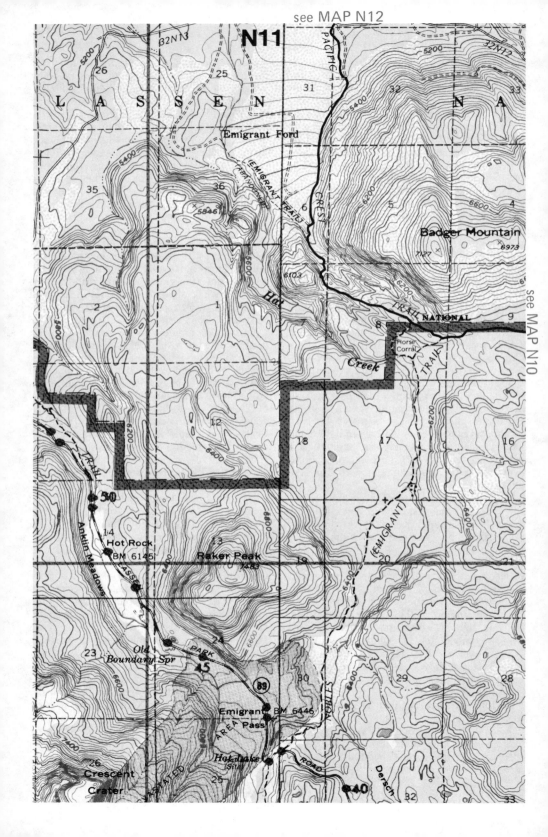

see MAP N10

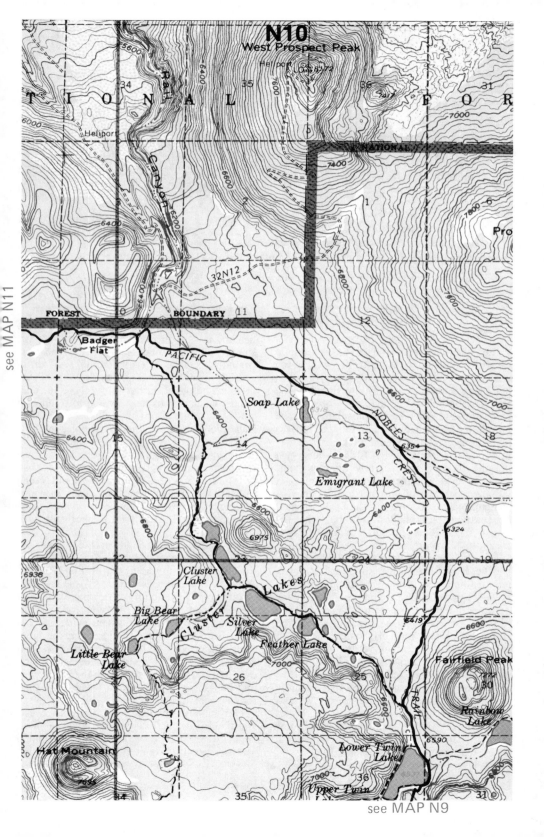

see MAP N11

Cinder Cone, lying 3½ miles northeast of Lower Twin Lake, is a very rewarding trip

Just a short hike past this junction, our route, now a closed road, gives rise to a trail descending left (6520-0.4).

*   *   *   *

The Pacific Crest Trail takes a 5¼-mile waterless route along old, gravelly roads to the east end of Badger Flat. If you'd rather take a lake-blessed route, then follow the 4⅔-mile trail that branches left here. Be forewarned, however, that before August mosquitoes can be quite fierce along it. In ¼ mile the trail crosses Twin Lakes creek and then it traverses nearly ½ mile over to a pond, which is chest-deep, just like the one we meet a few minutes later. Feather Lake lies immediately beyond it, and is perhaps the nicest of all the Cluster Lakes. A triangular lake 200 yards north of it is pleasant too, for though it is shallow, it probably has the fewest mosquitoes of any of the Cluster Lakes—an important consideration before August. By early August all the Cluster Lakes, like the Twin Lakes, drop about a foot or so, and then a narrow yellow ring of tiny primrose monkey flowers circles each lake. A low divide separates Feather Lake from Silver Lake, and ¼ mile past that lake we come to a junction with a trail that climbs 4¼ miles to Summit Lake's north-shore campground. Continuing northwest, we skirt past Cluster Lake, with a couple of campsites near its north end, then circle around an unnamed lake that severely shrinks in volume by late summer. We next descend along the seasonal Cluster Lakes creek, cross it where it bends east, vault a low divide, and descend 1⅓ miles to a reunion with the PCT at the east end of Badger Flat

*   *   *   *

If you're adhering to the official PCT, then descend along the lodgepole-pine-lined road, heading toward Prospect Peak, a late-Ice Age shield volcano. About 1¾ miles beyond the beginning of the alternate route, you cross gravelly Twin Lakes outlet creek, which often dries up before the Fourth of July. The road, almost level, climbs near its end to a junction with the Nobles trail (6354-2.6). Now on the route pioneered by William H. Nobles in 1851, we climb briefly northwest to a minor divide, then traverse through viewless terrain until we reach an opening (6320-1.0), from which we see shallow Soap Lake just to the south. Being rather low in elevation, this lake provides acceptably warm swimming even in early July, when most of Lassen Park's lakes still have snow nearby.

A forested, viewless traverse continues all the way to the east end of Badger Flat, where the alternate route rejoins the PCT (6270-1.6). A creek draining this meadow usually flows through mid-July, and if it's flowing, you might want to camp nearby. As you follow your climbing road west, you'll note evidence of a 1984 fire. After about ½ mile from the junction, you cross a low ridge and then descend briefly to a shallow pond, on the right. If it's dry, so too will be the springs in the upper west end of Badger Flat, so don't waste your time looking for them.

Our mainly viewless route traverses westward until just before the old emigrant road begins a moderate drop. On a flat, we branch northwest on trail tread, then in ¼ mile reach a trail junction by the park's north boundary (6200-2.1). From here a trail winds 0.4 mile southwest across glacial moraines to a former horse camp. Located beside Hat Creek, it is still a fine site for backpackers, certainly one of the best in water-and-camp-deficient Section N. Consider: from the park boundary, if you adhere to the official PCT you are about 44 miles from your next source of reliable water, Rock Spring Creek, near Baum Lake. This is too far to hike in one day. So if you plan to take the PCT route along Hat Creek Rim, don't camp here, but rather do so at Twin Bridges Dispersed Recreation Area, about 1½ miles out of your way—see the following alternate route. Then, laden down with perhaps two gallons of water, backtrack to the PCT and continue onward.

From the park boundary, the PCT descends the crest of a glacial moraine. After about ½ mile of crest descent, with views south of Lassen Peak above a dry gorge below, the manzanita-and-tobacco-brush-bordered PCT descends ¼ mile through a gully, then continues a similar distance on an easier gradient to a section of the Plantation Loop Road (5560-1.5). We start east and follow this still-driven-on RV road—this is the PCT? The road momentarily turns north, and is shaded somewhat by a rejuvenating plantation of Jeffrey pines. The pines are also making a comeback on adjacent Badger Mountain, which like lands to the west was ravaged decades ago by a large fire. Eventually the road angles north-northwest in a moderate descent to a junction (5120-1.3) at the edge of a shady forest. We start west on an old lateral road, but in 30 yards turn right

and follow a trail north which stays within the forest's fringe. Soon our trail intersects Road 32N12 (5010-0.5) at its bend, which is just 40 yards west of the north end of the Plantation Loop Road.

*   *   *   *

From Road 30N12 you can take any of several alternate routes, all easier and better watered than the PCT. However, we hope some adventurous souls will take the PCT, if only to prevent the trail from becoming overgrown with wildflowers, grasses and shrubs. In late spring, parts of the trail are ablaze with colorful wildflowers, though by early summer most of them are going to seed. Annuals are particularly plentiful along Hat Creek Rim's lower elevations north of Road 22, and many produce seeds that either cling to your socks or penetrate through them. In one meadow, Schaffer got hundreds of them on his socks in a matter of minutes. Wear long pants to protect your socks, or if the rim route is just too hot for that, wear a pair of gaiters, which are normally used to keep snow off your legs—they work quite well against seeds. The foregoing certainly doesn't make the PCT sound appealing, and it doesn't help to add that the prime weedy stretches, through which the trail is sometimes hidden, are also prime rattlesnake territory, due to lots of seed-gathering mice. It's quite unnerving to blindly push through a field of annuals and be buzzed by a rattlesnake. However, if you started your hike in southern California, you may have grown accustomed to this sort of thing.

N11, N12

see MAP N13

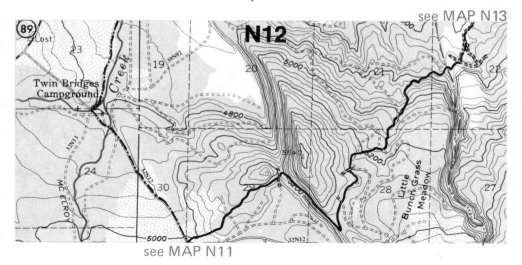

see MAP N11

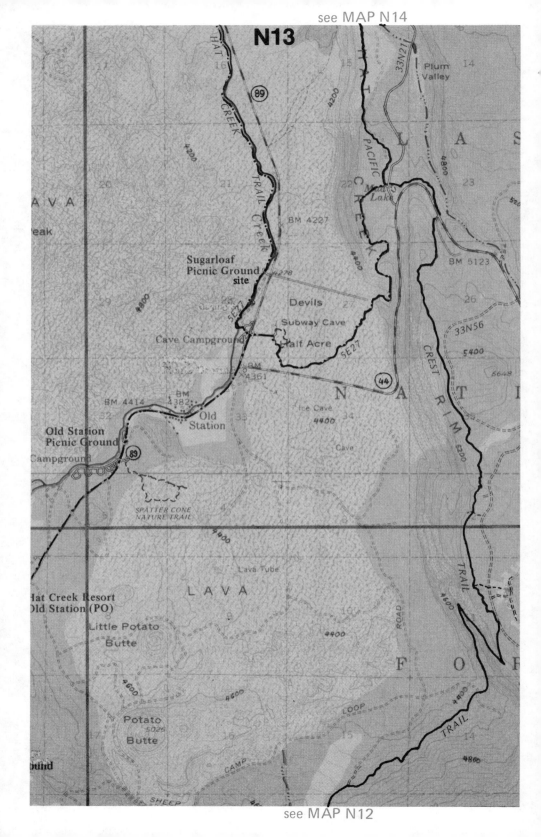

N13

Those who haven't should take an alternate route. Hike northwest on Road 32N12 to Road 32N13 (4830-1.5), just beyond the Lost Creek bridge, the second of the two Twin Bridges. Go north on Road 32N13, which first parallels Lost Creek to its quick union with Hat Creek,

then parallels that creek through the Twin Bridges Dispersed Recreation Area (read "undeveloped campground"). Your road reaches Big Pine Campground (4650-1.3), which is the only Forest Service campground near Hat Creek that is not packed with fishermen during the summer. Your road then bends west and heads ½ mile to a junction with Highway 89, which you follow northeast to a turnoff by unbelievably large Big Spring (4600-1.4). By itself it approximately doubles the volume of Hat Creek. Descending northeast along Highway 89, we soon cross Hat Creek and in 50 yards arrive at Hat Creek Resort, with cabins, a small store and cafe, and the Old Station Post Office (4560-0.7). Continuing northeast, we pass Hat Creek Campground (4460-1.5), from whose east-side trailer sewage dump a nature trail climbs up to some nearby spatter cones. These gave rise to the extensive lava flows that flooded Hat Creek Valley less than 2000 years ago. Old Station Picnic Ground lies immediately past the campground, and then we curve east to Old Station (4380-0.9), its high point being Uncle Runts restaurant. Leaving this small settlement, we curve northeast again to a junction with Highway 44 (4360-0.6), 7.9 miles from the start of the alternate route. You could hike up it back to the PCT atop Hat Creek Rim, but that would be unimaginative. Rather, we propose five choices. All go north

N12, N13

A Hat Creek cascade (above) and Subway Cave (below).

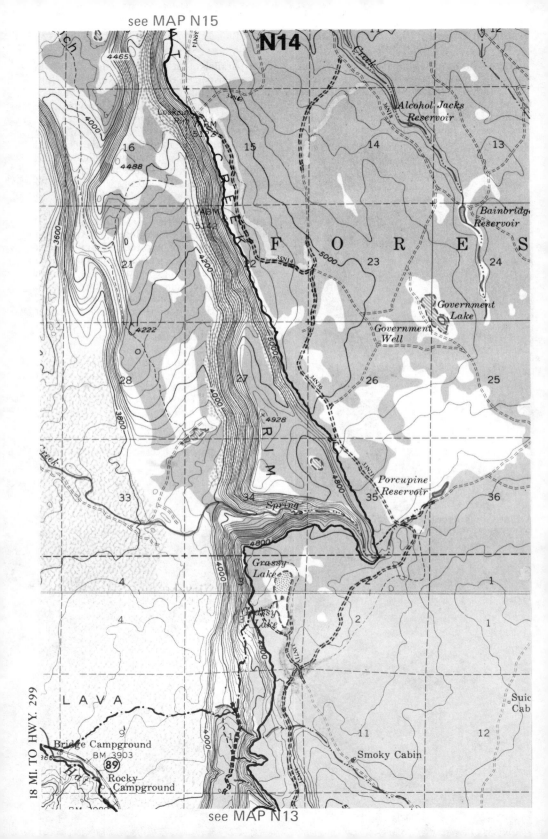

N14

3N14

Alcohol Jacks
Reservoir

Bainbridge
Reservoir

16

4465

Lookout
RM
5128

15

14

13

21

VABM
5142

22

3N14

23

5000

24

4488

4200

Government
Lake

Government
Well

28

4222

27

4000

26

25

5000

4928

R
I
M

4800

3N1

Porcupine
Reservoir

33

34

Spring

35

36

4800

4000

Grassy
Lake

4

3

2

1

4800

4000

4

3
Lake

2

1

3N14

L A V A

3N14

9

11

Suic
Cab

12

Bridge Campground
BM 3903

89

4000

Smoky Cabin

Rocky
Campground

F   O   R   E   S

C
R
E
E
K

18 MI. TO HWY. 299

on Highway 89 to a paved intersection (4345-0.3); then the first route goes east to Subway Cave and the other four go west into Cave Campground.

On the first route, head east to the Subway Cave parking area (4350-0.2), where you'll find a water faucet. Visit Subway Cave if you have the time, then tank up for the long, dry rim route ahead. Where the cave's entrance road bends north at the start of the parking area, you'll see a trail heading southeast. Take it about 0.1 mile to another trail and follow that one 0.2 mile south to an old road that is blocked off at its west end. On this closed road you arc 1.1 miles counterclockwise northeast to the blocked-off east end of a linear road, old Highway 44. Turn right and follow it 0.7 mile up to where the road is again blocked off. Here you start up a trail that meanders 0.9 mile north to the PCT's Highway 44 trailhead parking area (4870-3.0-11.4).

The second route heads across Cave Campground to the Hat Creek trail, which starts from the west end of a bridge over the creek. Always near the creek's west bank, you descend 0.6 mile to the site of former Sugarloaf Picnic Ground, which is still popular with fishermen. A sturdy bridge would take one across the creek to nearby Highway 89. Keeping to the trail, you go 2.7 miles to a bridge over to Rocky Campground, and then 0.5 mile to the east end of Bridge Campground, which you walk through to Highway 89 (3860-4.0-12.2). Start

east, crossing Hat Creek in 0.1 mile and tanking up on water if you didn't do so at the campground. In another 0.1 mile you branch left on Road 5E03. Be forewarned that the lands east of Highway 89 were severely burned in 1987, and that much of the route is essentially cross-country. Don't attempt to hike it until you've verified the following route's condition with the Forest Service (see this section's "Water"). Road 5E03 narrows to become Trail 5E27, which you take east to the base of the Hat Creek Rim escarpment (3960-1.5). Climb ¼ mile via short, steep switchbacks to a fork, branch left, away from Trail 5E27, and traverse 0.1 mile over to a nearby road in a trough. From it your trail climbs moderately to steeply north up to the rim and the PCT, meeting it at a point (4820-1.3-15.0) from which a spur trail once went to Grassy Lake.

Your third route is a much more desirable route, even if it is along a busy highway, for it has water, shade and supplies. It leaves the second route at mile 12.2, the entrance to Bridge Campground. Hike northwest down Highway 89, passing Honn Campground (3410-5.0), then the Hat Creek Work Center, which you pass just 0.2 mile south of the start of a loop road, with a gas station and restaurant (3440-2.0-19.2).

From here there is a fourth route: you can return to the PCT by going 1.4 miles along this road to Road 22, then taking that road 6.0 miles east up to the PCT along the Hat Creek

N13, N14

Burney Mountain, from PCT just north of small reservoir

Rim (4660-7.4-26.6) This may be your best choice, since you get to sample about 6 miles of the Hat Creek Rim that were untouched by the 1987 fire, and you don't have to worry about water—if you carry about a gallon with you. Along this stretch, your pack will probably be low on food, so the added bulk and weight of the water won't be such a burden. Plan to spend the night at Honn Campground, hike all the way to the Baum Lake area the next day, and then leave the PCT for a short jaunt to the PG&E campground. This stretch amounts to about 23½ miles, which is on the long side for one day, but then you'll have only one major climb along it—up to the rim—which isn't much of a climb compared to the daily climbing you've done in the High Sierra.

If you keep to the third route, you continue north on Highway 89, passing the north end of the loop road in 1.7 miles and reaching the Hat Creek Post Office and a general store (3300-1.8) just past it. By the edge of a lava flow your highway crosses Hat Creek (3260-1.5), and then recrosses it (3210-1.7) before coming to a junction with Cassel Road (3203-0.8-25.0).

Here you have a possible fifth route, which is not recommended unless you need to go to the town of Burney for major supplies. If so, continue 4.8 miles northwest on Highway 89 to Highway 299 and take it about 5 miles southwest into town, then backtrack to 89. Ahead on 89, you'll go 5.3 miles to a cryptic crossing of the highway by the PCT. If you miss the trail, you'll reach the entrance road to Burney Falls State Park in ½ mile.

To conclude the third choice, you leave Highway 89 and follow Cassel Road north, crossing Rising River (3198-1.9) before reaching Cassel-Fall River Mills Road in Cassel (3199-1.3). Head west through this tiny settlement, which has a small general store, to Cassel Post Office (3195-0.2). This is immediately west of a PG&E road starting north. Take this road, and in 0.1 mile reach the south end of PG&E's Cassel Campground. The campground lies on both sides of the road and stretches north for about 0.2 mile. Beyond the campground you soon start a ½-mile drop to the PCT (2990-1.0-29.4).

*   *   *   *

Meanwhile, back on the Pacific Crest Trail at Road 32N12, south of Old Station, you should stick to the dry, often shadeless PCT if you are a purist or a desert rat. There will be some rewarding views to justify your trials. The trail's grade is sympathetic to your struggle: it is mostly level in either direction. From Road 32N12, head east-northeast through a selectively logged forest, crossing several old roads before finally reaching a more used one (5160-1.1) just below a saddle southwest of point 5640. Up this road we walk but 40 yards, almost to atop the saddle, where we locate our trail once again as it starts a very long, gentle switchback leg southeast. Along this leg the avid photographer will stop many times to capture the beauty of Lassen's north face exquisitely framed by trailside ponderosa, Jeffrey and sugar pines, plus white firs and incense cedars. Don't use up all your film here, for there are more views to come.

Eventually we reach a low point (5290-0.8) atop this up-faulted escarpment of Pliocene andesite lavas. Now numerous roads in various states of disuse are crossed. From the escarpment we start a traverse north to a low ridge (5360-0.5), then make a winding descent to a usually dry creek. Beyond it we walk northeast through chaparral—mostly chest-high manzanita—for about 200 yards to a major east-west heavily used logging road (4690-1.9). Our trail ends here and we follow a hot, dusty road north. In about 250 yards a similar road, emerging northwest from the forest, joins ours. We continue our sunny, gentle descent north, begin a curve northeast, enter the forest's fringe and soon make contact with the PCT again (4520-0.6).

Now our route is a long, winding traverse past some steeply descending logging spur roads. Along this traverse the observant hiker will notice a subtle change in forest vegetation: the typical forest understory shrubs are now largely displaced by bitterbrush, a woody shrub indicative of drier soils. Another addition to the forest's ledger is the Douglas-fir, which has crept up from the Hat Creek valley floor. Just after we cross the last logging road (4440-1.6), which descends only moderately, we commence a series of long, easy-graded switchbacks that take us almost effortlessly up the faulted Hat Creek Rim escarpment. Once again we see to the south Lassen Peak and its subordinate associate Chaos Crags. Below us to our west lie the basaltic Potato Buttes and related, sparsely vegetated lava flows that may be only several thousand years old. The third switchback leg takes us north up to Hat Creek

N18, N12, N13

Rim, and we quickly reach a gate across a well-maintained logging road (5260-2.0). We head north 20 yards along the road, then start on PCT tread, which branches northwest. The PCT parallels the road a brief distance before meandering over to the escarpment and soon reaching a junction (5260-0.5) with a spur trail. This goes 160 yards east to a crossing of the logging road, then 190 yards farther to the Baker Spring campsite, which is fenced in to keep the cattle out. Should the spigot be dry when you visit it, you can always check its source, Baker Spring, a seep about 125 yards to the east, at the far side of the cow-pasture

meadow. Be forewarned that the spring is *seasonal*. However, if you're hiking before summer or are carrying lots of water, the campsite is worth a night's stay.

Beyond the spur-trail junction the PCT continues along the escarpment for over 3 miles before turning east and then descending north through a logged area to a spur road along Highway 44 (5000-3.8). Along the escarpment you'll see the familiar Jeffrey, ponderosa and sugar pines, but will also notice the appearance of drought-tolerant species: juniper, mountain mahogany, bitterbrush, rabbitbrush and sagebrush. Also for the first time, you'll see

N13

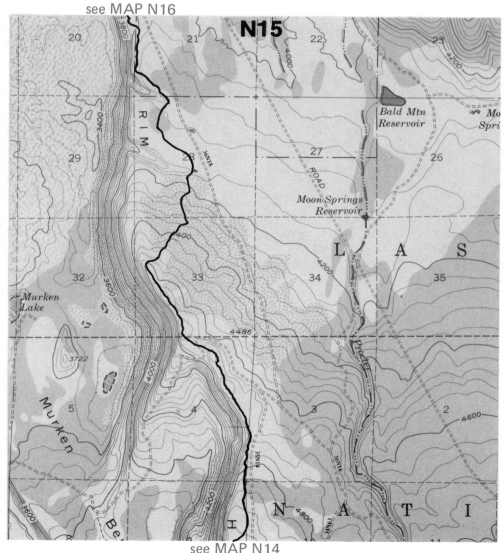

Burnt Hat Creek Rim fire lookout (Lassen Peak at right)

Mt. Shasta as well as Lassen Peak. This rim traverse between these two imposing volcanic monarchs offers a taste of the Cascade scenery you'll see farther north, where you're often between two dominating volcanoes, such as between Mts. Jefferson and Hood in Oregon or Mts. Adams and Rainier in Washington.

We cross Highway 44 at the spur road and then parallel the highway west, skirting the north edge of summer-dry Mud Lake immediately before crossing Road 33N21 (4870-0.7). Immediately after the PCT crosses this road it reaches a spur trail that goes 70 yards south to Highway 44's trailhead parking area. If you took the first alternate route, you'd end up here, at the west side of the parking area's turnaround loop. A short spur road west to this parking area begins about 300 yards north along Road 33N21 from Highway 44. If you're driving to it, don't take the spur road west that begins about 200 yards north from the highway.

In 1987, fire blackened most of Hat Creek Valley lying east of Highway 89 and between Highway 44 and Road 22. Likewise, Hat Creek Rim and lands east of it were also burned, a stretch extending from about 1¼ miles north of the trailhead parking lot to about ½ mile north of the Hat Creek Rim Fire Lookout (which was also consumed in the blaze). Much of the PCT's tread was eradicated by bulldozers fighting the fire, and with debris strewn about, the route became a nightmare to follow. However, it is being rebuilt, and it should be opened once again in 1990 or '91. Before you plan to hike it, check its status by contacting the USFS Hat Creek District—see "Water" in this section's introduction.

Since this stretch of PCT is likely to be rebuilt on an essentially identical route, we'll describe the route as it existed before the fire. From the spur trail south to the trailhead parking area, the PCT starts north and reaches Hat Creek Rim after ½ mile. We follow it almost ¾ mile before reaching the southern edge of the 1987 burn. In addition to being dry, the rim lands were only sparsely forested, and hence there was little shade. Since the burn, shade is essentially nonexistent, so you'll find no protection from the piercing sun of summer afternoons.

In ¼ mile we veer east into a sizable gully and soon cross its usually dry creek (4640-1.8). You can make an easy, 0.3-mile cross-country walk up it to Road 33N21, where you'll find Plum Valley's reservoir. This *almost always* has water in it, and at times it is even stocked with bass. If it has dried up, then you can expect every other source of water along or near the rim to have done likewise. Cattle grazing the rim lands drink from this reservoir and others, and appear to survive. You, however, may get sick. *To minimize your risk, first strain the water with a water-filtration system (see "Water" in Chapter 1), and then boil it for several minutes. Boiling but not filtering the water is risky!*

Northward, the PCT climbs a few yards up from the creek, then descends northwest to the rim, only to veer immediately east into another dry-creek gully. Near the head of the gully, a side trail (4600-0.9) begins a plunge west 0.3 mile to a dirt road, on which you could walk 115 yards north to the trail's resumption. You could then drop 0.3 mile north to a trail junction, where you'd reach the second alternate route to the Hat Creek Rim PCT. A westward

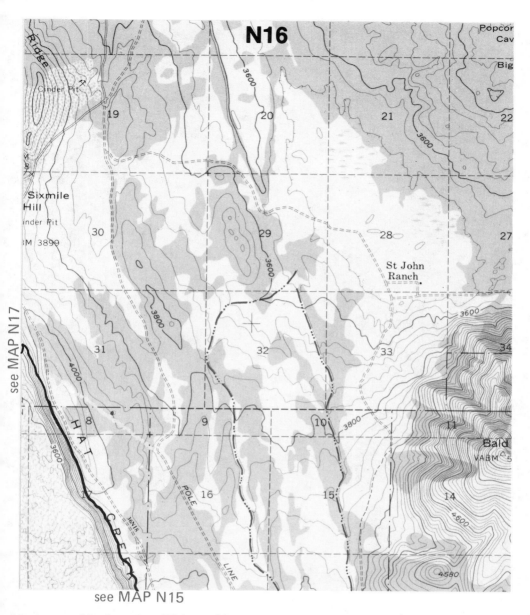

see MAP N17

see MAP N15

descent would take you to Highway 89 near Bridge Campground.

The PCT briefly returns to the rim again, leaves it, and climbs to a higher rim which, like the first, is the result of uplift along a north-south-trending fault. A ½-mile winding traverse on the rim ensues, soon bringing us to a shallow depression (4820-1.6). If you took the second alternate route, you'd end it here. A faint trail (essentially cross-country) strikes northeast ¼ mile to usually dry Grassy Lake, and in its

center is a muddy water hole, though it too can dry up. Filter and boil the water.

The PCT goes to the rim again and winds along it to the brink of Lost Creek canyon, and you may hear a spring-fed creek flowing down its lower section. Rather than descend to it, however, our trail stays high and follows this canyon's rim 1½ miles east to a usually dry crossing of the upper canyon, now just a gully (4810-2.1). In 1982 the Forest Service was going to build a spur trail west down to the

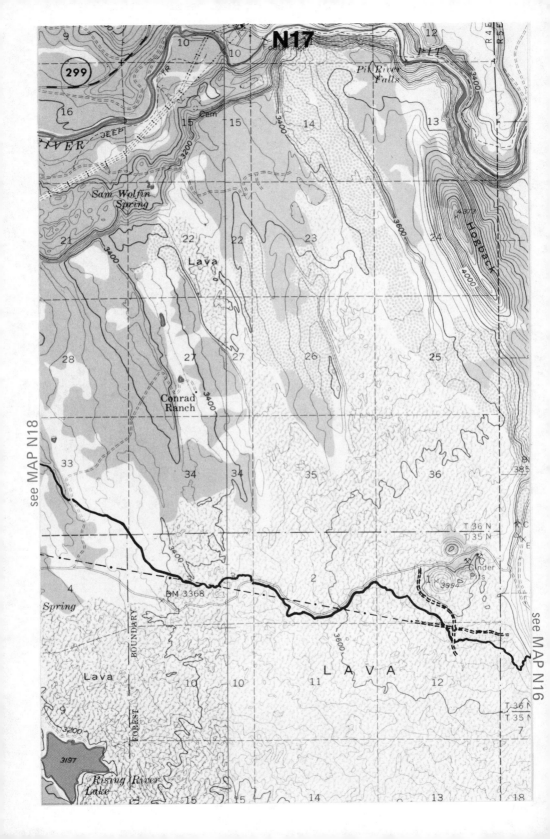

see MAP N18

see MAP N16

spring, but lack of funds stopped the project. All too often those of us working in the mountains heard similar fates of other very worthwhile projects. Lost Creek spring would have been the only freshwater source for the entire stretch between Lassen Park and the Baum Lake area! So instead, you can go ⅓ mile crosscountry up the gully to Road 33N21, walk about 0.1 mile southeast up it to a minor road, and take that ⅓ mile northeast to Porcupine Reservoir. In early summer it's a grassy swamp; later, a dry, grassy meadow.

Northwest, the PCT quickly climbs onto another fault-formed rim, almost touching Road 33N21 where the trail crosses a spur road that heads west down to Little Lake—almost always dry. With one more mile behind us, we continue our dry-rim traverse, fervently believing that distant Mt. Shasta *is* getting noticeably closer while Lassen Peak *is* fading away. After several more miles of winding to and from rim views, we eventually spy and reach the tall metal tower of Hat Creek Rim Fire Lookout (5122-4.7). The wooden lookout cabin atop the tower burned in the 1987 fire, and it is supposed to be replaced, but may not be, due to lack of funds. The Forest Service plans to reopen the PCT here in 1990 or '91, and it plans to place a water tank here for PCT users. If it does, then this *could* be the rim's only reliable source of water. We say *could* because Schaffer saw a water tank along Road 22 that was peppered with rifle holes. How do you prevent a similar attack at this water hole?

Northward, our sometimes weedy tread provides us with an almost continual line of views, for it never veers far from the rim. Every escarpment you see around you is due to faulting, which in this area goes hand in hand

with volcanism. Cinder Butte, a sparsely vegetated conical hill to the northwest is, like Sugarloaf Peak to the south, a young volcano. We leave the scorched lands of the 1987 fire in about ½ mile, and about there the trail begins a serious, lengthy descent before making a shorter traverse to an intersection of Road 22 (4660-2.8) about 100 yards west of a low pass. Here, those taking the fourth alternate route join us.

Ahead, the PCT climbs northwest to a knoll on the rim that evidently has been used as a takeoff spot for hang gliders. And why not, for here the escarpment rises a full 1100' above Murken Bench. This is the highest unbroken escarpment along the entire rim, an inducement to glider pilots. From the knoll the trail makes a drop of its own, nearly 600' down to a small reservoir (4140-1.9), which is just 200 yards west of Hat Creek Rim Road 36N18. Despite the questionable nature of the reservoir's water, it is probably no worse than any other rim reservoir you've visited. You should probably plan to camp here, since you are within a day's hike of Burney Falls State Park, which is about 23 easy miles away. Spring-fed water is only 10.7 miles away. Enjoy a swim, then tank up on water—after you filter, boil and treat it.

Ahead, the trail wanders for almost 1.2 miles before breaking through to the rim at a spectacular viewpoint. The wildflower gardens along the way to it can be fantastic in May, but by late June the flowers turn just plain sticky. After a lengthy rim traverse you come to a closed gate (4030-3.1), which is just 80 yards below Road 36N18. The trail now leaves the rim and descends to an abandoned jeep road, which you briefly follow before switchbacking

N14, N15, N16, N17

Bald Mountain and a small reservoir near Road 36N18

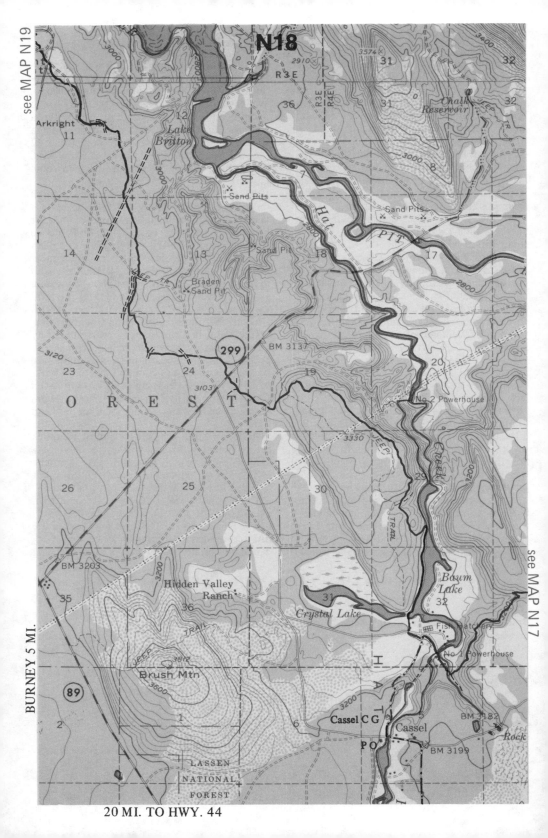

see MAP N17

BURNEY 5 MI.

20 MI. TO HWY. 44

31

3574

2910

R 3 E

32

Chalk Reservoir

31

32

36

R 3 E

R 4 E

3000

8

Arkright

11

12

Lake Britton

7

3000

Sand Pits

Sand Pits

3000

Hat

14

13

Sand Pit

18

PIT

17

2800

Braden Sand Pit

299

BM 3137

19

20

3120

23

24

No 2 Powerhouse

3103

O   R   E   S   T

3330

26

25

30

Creek

29

JEEP

TRAIL

3200

BM 3203

35

36

Hidden Valley Ranch

31

Crystal Lake

32

Baum Lake

TRAIL

89

JEEP

3812

Brush Mtn

3600

1

6

H

Fish Hatchery

No 1 Powerhouse

3200

2

Cassel C G

Cassel

PO

BM 3182

Rock

BM 3199

LASSEN

NATIONAL

FOREST

just beyond a powerline. On a south tack you descend to quickly recross the powerline, then after 40 yards you switchback northwest. The route quickly turns southwest for a 250-yard winding descent across youthful lava to semi-level ground, then arcs northwest to an intersection of a north-climbing road. If you were to hike north on this road, you'd reach an old powerline road in 200 yards. The PCT reaches this road in 250 yards, 1.0 mile from the switchback 40 yards beyond the powerline. You parallel the powerline about 20 yards west, then angle northwest on a faint road that soon narrows to a trail. After 0.8 mile you almost reach Cassel-Fall River Mills Road, then parallel it 1.4 miles westward before crossing it (3480-3.8). If you've mailed yourself supplies to the Cassel Post Office, you could reach it directly by hiking 3.3 miles west down this paved road. However, we recommend a longer, less direct route to it.

Like others, you take the PCT, starting north from Cassel-Fall River Mills Road. The trail quickly veers west and meanders across a youthful lava flow with caves before crossing and recrossing the same powerline you met south of the road. About 0.6 mile past the recrossing you exit from Section 3. If you must camp before Highway 299, do so before you leave this section, the last of Lassen National

Forest land. Private lands now lie ahead and camping is prohibited. Our trail heads northwest through a dry, open woodland of juniper, Digger pine, mountain mahogany and oak, and we have views of Mt. Shasta until we enter a ponderosa-pine forest where we cross Conrad Ranch road (3270-2.1).

Under welcome shade, we climb ⅓ mile northwest to a low gap, drop ¼ mile west to a gully, then wind southwest to a road (3025-1.7) that is just above Rock Spring creek. This is the first *fresh, trailside* water we've had since Lassen Park's Lower Twin Lake, 51 miles back. Undoubtedly, you've made side trips or taken alternate routes to obtain water along the way. Descend the road, which crosses the creek in 100 yards. Your route crosses the creek about 10 yards sooner, though you'll want to walk a few paces upstream and cross it where you can keep your boots dry. The trail then leads northwest, passing between a horse corral on the east and a residence on the west. Immediately beyond them you walk along the east side of a PG&E powerhouse, then cross the adjacent bridge which spans Rising River/Hat Creek. Next you parallel the main road briefly northwest, staying just above it and having oak-filtered views across it toward Crystal Lake State Fish Hatchery (visitors welcome). The trail momentarily curves southwest and you

N17, N18

Baum Lake

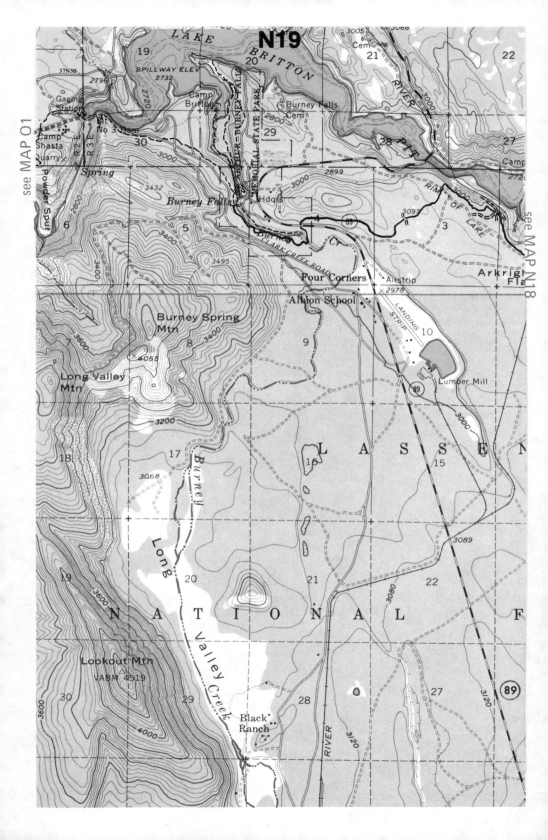

reach a PG&E road (2990-0.5) only a stone's throw from where it reaches the paved Crystal Lake State Fish Hatchery road. We highly recommend that you head south up this road, climbing moderately for ½ mile, and then soon reaching PG&E's Cassel Campground, located on both sides of the road. You might stay there for the night after first walking a couple of minutes farther to the road's south end, at the Cassel-Fall River Mills Road. By this junction, 1.0 mile from the PCT, you'll find the Cassel Post Office and a small general store.

Backtrack along the PG&E road to the PCT and follow it briefly northwest to a crossing of the Crystal Lake State Fish Hatchery road (3000-0.1). Now the PCT skirts along the west side of a long fishery tank, then reaches, just beyond it, a short trail east over to a picnic area. No camping is allowed here along the shore of Baum Lake, at Crystal Lake, or essentially anywhere between here and Highway 299. Crystal Lake drops a few feet down to Baum Lake and we bridge this spillway, then walk 0.9 mile along the west shore of Baum Lake, leaving most of the fishermen behind. Our trail then switchbacks southwest over to a small gully, ascends it, rounds a ridge, and then, in a second gully, crosses a jeep road (3150-1.5). We now stay close to the east rim of a lava plateau and have several oak-and-pine-framed views east toward the Pit River. Midway along our northwest traverse we diagonal under some major powerlines, then at the north end of the plateau make a short descent to another jeep road (3240-1.8). You may note that the plateau's west edge is quite linear, for it has been uplifted along a north-northwest-trending fault. We quickly cross this fault where our trail angles northwest, then in a minute cross a good road. The trail continues along a northwest course, partly following bits of abandoned jeep tracks. Other tracks may lead you astray, so watch for trail markers along this short stretch out to Highway 299 (3110-0.8). The town of Burney lies about 7 miles southwest.

From the highway our trail starts north through Shasta-Trinity National Forest land and quickly turns west to avoid private land. We cross two roads and then, at a third, 0.8 mile past the highway, resume a northward course. We loop around the head of a trough and then parallel a road, just above us, 0.4 mile to a crossing of a road that has been upgraded from "jeep trail" status. With occasional views

back toward Burney Mountain and ahead toward Mt. Shasta, we stroll ¾ mile along fairly level, oak-dominated terrain and slant across a major, straight road (3070-2.3). We cross four more roads in the next mile, then descend for a few minutes to a road crossing that is at the south edge of Arkright Flat (2995-1.3). Since the route ahead is largely across private land, dry camp, if you must, before you reach Arkright Flat. The flat is a fault-formed basin and the cliff on its east side is a fault scarp.

On private land, our trail heads along the west side of the flat, crosses some railroad tracks, then crosses a nearby road (3005-0.4). Paralleling this road, we quickly cross a minor road striking east, and from it we have a walk northwest along the rim of the Pit River canyon. Douglas-firs, climbing up the canyon's cooler slopes, offer us shade along with Oregon oaks, ponderosa pines and occasional incense-cedars. In 0.4 mile we cross two roads where they join a third, then continue along the rim about 0.6 mile farther before turning south and crossing nearby Rim of Lake Road (3010-1.2). The PCT then winds southwest across rolling, logged terrain before turning west and heading over to Highway 89 (2995-1.5), which we cross by the east side of a closed road. Actually, the trail dies out 40 yards before the highway, to hide it from motorcyclists who might take it east onto private land. If you happen to be southbound toward Lassen Park, then from the highway head due north, and you'll quickly find the trail. In the other direction, the trail is very obvious. You are now inside McArthur-Burney Falls Memorial State Park, and you can shortcut by heading nearly ½ mile west along the highway over to the park's entrance road. You'll find a store just past its entrance station and a sprawling campground just beyond that.

You can conclude Section N in either of two other ways. Both cross Highway 89 and follow the PCT 220 yards to a trail junction above Burney Creek. One way leaves the PCT here, taking a trail downstream. This trail starts northwest along usually dry Burney Creek, but in 90 yards, the first springs appear, and in another 90 yards, where the trail and the creek bend west, additional springs have given rise to a sizable creek. Continuing ⅔ mile west along the trail, you'll see Burney Creek metamorphose from a creek to a raging torrent. The trail ends by the east side of a 40-yard-long bridge that is just upstream from Burney Falls. To

N18, N19

view the falls, head right 35 yards up to a parking area, then take a broad, 160-yard-long trail along the west side of the parking lot's road almost to the park's entrance station. Continue 50 yards farther, paralleling the park's main road, to where you'll meet a crosswalk. From it a path goes over to the park's nearby store, which caters mainly to the car campers in the campground just north of the store. You go another 27 yards alongside the main road to the start of a paved trail, on your left. Just 10 yards down it, you'll reach the park's best view of thundering Burney Falls.

The other—and official—way keeps to the PCT, going 35 yards to a sturdy bridge that spans Burney Creek. Although the creek is dry when most hikers cross it, it can be a raging torrent in heavy rains. The trail briefly climbs to flat land above the creek's south bank and then heads about 300 yards to one of the largest backpackers' camps you're ever likely to see (2970-0.4). It is also used by sometimes-large groups of equestrians or bicyclists. Onward, the PCT winds first west, then northwest, usually staying within sound of Burney Creek, but not within sight of it. You then intersect a broad path (2950-0.6) west, which takes you in a minute to a small parking area on paved Clark Creek Road. East, it goes almost 60 yards to Burney Falls Nature Trail, a 1.0-mile loop trail. To reach the entrance station, store and falls' viewpoint mentioned in the previous paragraph, turn right and head just 27 yards over to the also-mentioned, obvious, 40-yard-long bridge.

Arkright Flat

Section O: Burney Falls to Castle Crags

Introduction: Those who hiked through the San Bernardino Mountains of southern California (Section C) may be reminded of that mountain scenery while hiking through Section O. Glaciation was minimal in each, so natural lakes are a rarity. In Section O, glaciation was restricted to the north slopes of Mushroom Rock and of Grizzly Peak. Man-made lakes occur in both sections, although Section O's are milky blue-green in color. During the summer, water—or lack thereof—can be a problem in both sections, even though Section O receives twice the precipitation. This extra precipitation has created denser forests and consequently this low mountain country is prime logging country. Therefore, you may not escape the sounds of civilization, for most of the route lies within earshot of motor vehicles.

Section O makes a long arc, from north to west, connecting the scenic but hot and dry Hat Creek-Burney Falls area with the equally scenic, often hot Castle Crags area. As the route arcs westward, it leaves behind the younger volcanic rocks of the Modoc Plateau and gradually crosses older and older rock units until you are walking across rocks that are as old as 400 million years. No other trail section along the entire PCT displays such a succession of rock strata. Along this arc the Shasta red fir replaces the common red fir we saw throughout the Sierra Nevada, and we'll see this new fir time and again all the way into southern Oregon.

Declination: 16¾°E

Mileages:

	South to North	Distance between Points	North to South
Burney Falls...................................	0.0		82.4
Rock Creek....................................	5.4	5.4	77.0
Peavine Creek	14.1	8.7	68.3
road junction at south base of Red Mountain.........	16.9	2.8	65.5
saddle west of Harlow Flat Road..................	21.5	4.6	60.9
road southeast down to pond.....................	26.1	4.6	56.3
springs at Moosehead Creek's headwaters...........	29.4	3.3	53.0
Tate Creek road................................	34.2	4.8	48.2
Alder Creek Trail...............................	36.8	2.6	45.6
Grizzly Peak Road before Pigeon Hill..............	38.9	2.1	43.5
Grizzly Peak Lookout road	42.1	3.2	40.3
Deer Creek....................................	44.2	2.1	38.2
McCloud-Big Bend Road	52.2	8.0	30.2
Ah-Di-Na Campground road......................	54.9	2.7	27.5
Squaw Valley Creek	66.0	11.1	16.4
Girard Ridge Road	71.7	5.7	10.7
Fall Creek.....................................	76.6	4.9	5.8
Interstate 5 near Castle Crags State Park	82.4	5.8	0.0

Supplies: No on-route supplies exist along this section. If you are hiking north, use the Cassel Post Office, mentioned in the previous section. If you are hiking south, use the Castella Post Office, mentioned in the next section. Ammirati's Market is next to the Castella Post Office, and its fairly large inventory caters to both Castle Crags State Park visitors and local residents.

Rattlesnakes: These can be found in all but the highest elevations in this section, but you probably won't see any. Ticks can be a problem at the lower elevations, though flies will probably pester you more than anything else.

Trail Condition: Section O's PCT steadily degenerated in the 1980s to the point that some of it was little better than cross-country hiking. You can expect one or more ongoing logging operations to confuse you, though the main problem is that brush reclaims sections of the trail. Forest Service maintenance has been virtually zero, and Section O's area is so sparsely populated that there aren't enough volunteers to do the job. Many of the residents work for lumber companies and couldn't care less about the trail. Furthermore, who can blame them for wanting to get *out* of the mountains when the weekends come. We hope the Forest Service once again gets funds to maintain the trail, but until it does, anticipate some really nasty stretches.

Roughly 130′ high, Burney Falls is no match in height for Yosemite Valley's towering waterfalls. But in volume, Burney Falls exceeds most of them, and it rivals Vernal and Nevada falls, both along the Merced River just above the valley. That river's discharge averages, for the year, about 225 million gallons a day, whereas Burney Falls averages about 200 million. However, the Merced River, being largely fed by snowmelt streams, is very seasonal, with high discharge from mid-April to mid-August. For the remaining eight months of the year, Burney Falls ranks as California's most voluminous waterfall, producing enough water to cover one square mile of land one foot deep in water *every day*. Because Burney Falls is fed by a huge, underground reservoir, its volume and its temperature (about 42°F) are very constant from day to day.

If you've just finished hiking Section N, you'll know where to find the Pacific Crest trail. If you're just starting your hike north in Section O, then head over to the McArthur-Burney Falls Memorial State Park's entrance station. The main road goes past a nearby store to a large parking lot and the start of the Burney Falls Nature trail. You branch left at the entrance station and go down to a small parking area just west of the station. The nature trail ends here, and on it you immediately cross a bridge. Before you can say "McArthur-Burney Falls Memorial State Park," you reach a junc-

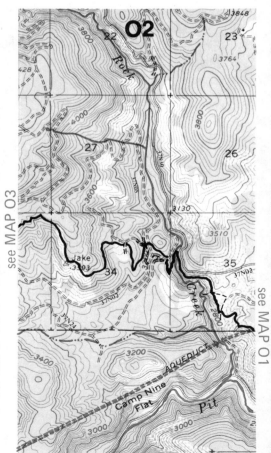

see MAP 03

see MAP 01

O1

tion and climb a few yards west over to an intersection with the broad Pacific Crest trail. A westbound trail from here goes 140 yards over to a small parking area on Clark Creek Road. If you're driving northwest along this road, look for this parking area 1.8 miles after you leave Highway 89.

Because the Pacific Crest Trail is for equestrians as well as for hikers, it was built away from Burney Creek and Burney Falls. Hence, you only hear these features, not see them. Our hike begins by paralleling Clark Creek Road, which it crosses in almost a mile and then continues above the road, finally switchbacking down to it at the east end of Lake Britton's dam. Walk across the dam and find the trail's resumption in about 35 yards (2760-1.9). Before starting up the trail, you might take a swim in Lake Britton.

The PCT climbs 210 yards northwest up to a junction of two roads, then climbs west, paralleling one of them ¼ mile up to another road. Here the trail turns southwest for a while before crossing two more roads just as it starts to climb. We climb into a shady gully, then up to a ridge, from which we have views down into

600′ deep Pit River canyon, with its inviting river. Along the lower parts of Section O's route, such as on this stretch, midafternoon summer temperatures are typically in the 90s. Ponderosa pines are the primary shade trees, although on wetter, cooler slopes you'll find Douglas-firs predominating. Incense-cedars and Oregon white oaks do better on the drier slopes, but we'll leave these behind not long after crossing Rock Creek.

With that destination in mind, we follow the PCT as it winds northwest, descending into Rock Creek canyon to a small bench above an inner gorge. Here we cross an abandoned, south-heading road. Then, 0.2 mile later and a bit higher, we meet a jeep road (2930-2.9), which drops 200 precipitous yards to Rock Creek. You'll find more camping space down there than on creekside gravel where the PCT bridges Rock Creek (2980-0.6). This latter site is more esthetic, however, for it is perched just above two-tiered Rock Creek falls. A somewhat chilly swimming hole lies at the base, and it can be reached by descending *loose, steep* slopes on the west side of the creek. Be extremely careful if you make this descent.

O1, O2

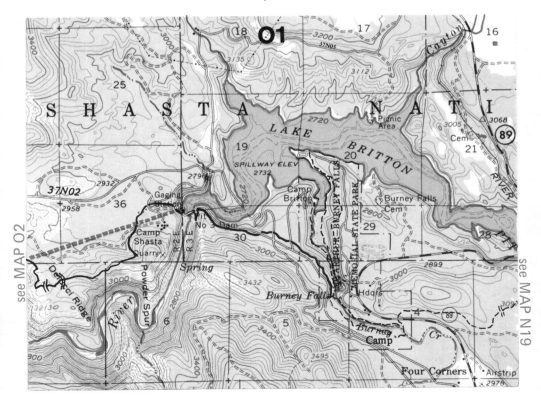

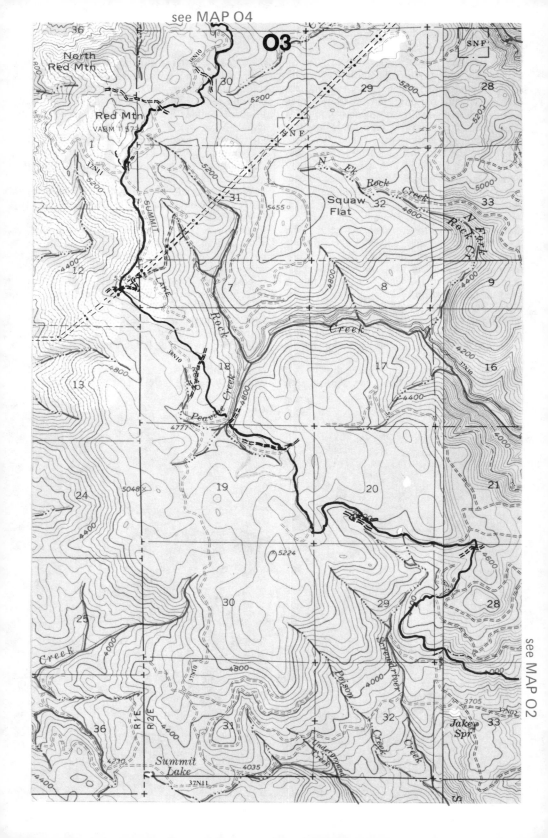

O3

North
Red Mth

Red Mth
VABM 571

SNF

N Fk

Rock

Creek

Squaw
Flat

N Fork
Rock Cr

SUMMIT LAKE

Rock

Creek

Creek

38N10

Peavin

4777

Pea

Road

5048 X

5224

5203

5455

36
30
29
28
31
32
33
12
7
8
9
18
17
16
13
24
19
20
21
25
30
29
28
36
31
32
33

Jakey
Spr

3705
37N02

Summit
Lake

4035

37N11

37N11

37N10

38N10

37N10

38N10

R1E
R2E

Creek

Stringtown

Poison

Creek

Underground
Creek

Creek

4800
4400
4400
4400
4400
4400
4400
4400
4400
4400
4400
4200
4200
4600
4600
4800
4800
4800
4800
4800
4800
4800
5000
5000
5200
5200
5200
5200
5200
5200
800

From the bridge the PCT switchbacks out of the canyon and up to paved Road 37N02 (3100-0.4). On it you can head ⅓ mile up-canyon to Rock Creek Campground, a primitive car-camping area. During most of the summer you won't find a potential campsite with adequate water until you reach the Peavine Creek area, 8.3 miles past Road 37N02.

Beyond this paved road the PCT climbs 0.2 mile northwest to a graded road and a saddle, from which it starts southwest. After 150 yards it hits an abandoned road on which you walk 35 yards south to the trail's resumption. The trail continues southwest to a minor ridge, then climbs up it, first ¼ mile north, then ¼ mile west. Then, starting south, we face a long ascent across slopes up to Peavine Creek. The first part of our ascent is dry and rather open, so we have views of lofty Burney Mountain, standing in the south-southeast, 16 miles away. By the time we cross the 4000′ contour, ponderosa pine, Douglas-fir and incense-cedar have largely replaced oaks. Soon we enter a small bowl and cross its abandoned, southwest-descending road. We climb into a second bowl, then curve clockwise up shady slopes to a west ridge, almost topping it as we cross a road (4480-4.3). Our trail now climbs northeast, crossing a good road in 0.7 mile and then, a bit past it, turning west and traversing over to the southeast edge of an old clearcut (4660-1.4). Here, early-season hikers will find seeping water of questionable quality, the first water since Rock Creek, 6.1 miles back.

In ⅓ mile we cross a major logging road, then traverse over to a gully and climb south to a closed jeep road. This route north is being narrowed to a trail by encroaching shrubs. Tobacco brush and snow bush have replaced deer brush, which is another Ceanothus you've seen, and perhaps smelled, lower down. All three are very aromatic when in bloom. Green-leaf manzanita and chinquapin are also present, and they will be common trailside companions in many places as we make a 1½-day fir-forest crest loop around a large basin.

Our abandoned road crosses another abandoned road, then in 100 yards crosses an active road and parallels it down to a road junction located immediately before Peavine Creek (4760-2.6). You can camp by this creek, pause to refresh yourself in its small pond, or head north over to an adjacent road and follow it 120 yards west to better campsites along Peavine

Rock Creek falls

Creek. Cows roam the area in summer, so you may want to treat the water. Your next trailside water won't be until springs at Moosehead Creek's headwaters, 15⅓ miles ahead. Closer sources, however, lie just off the route. In late summer, Peavine Creek may dry up, but you can always head north on the road down Peavine Creek, tank up at Rock Creek, and take the Rock Creek road north up to the PCT near Red Mountain.

Over the next 22.7 miles we cross, recross and often parallel Summit Lake Road 38N10. If you are hiking in June or in October, you may have some snow problems and therefore may want to take the road instead of the PCT. From the road junction immediately north of Peavine Creek, the PCT winds northwest through a forest of white firs and sugar pines, crossing one road and then Road 38N10 before breaking out to views near a set of giant, crackling powerlines (5200-1.6). Bald Mountain, a Miocene-age volcano standing just above us 3 miles to the northwest, serves as a reference point to mark our progress as we traverse north. Grizzly Peak, which we'll reach in a day or two, stands above and right of Bald Mountain.

O2, O3

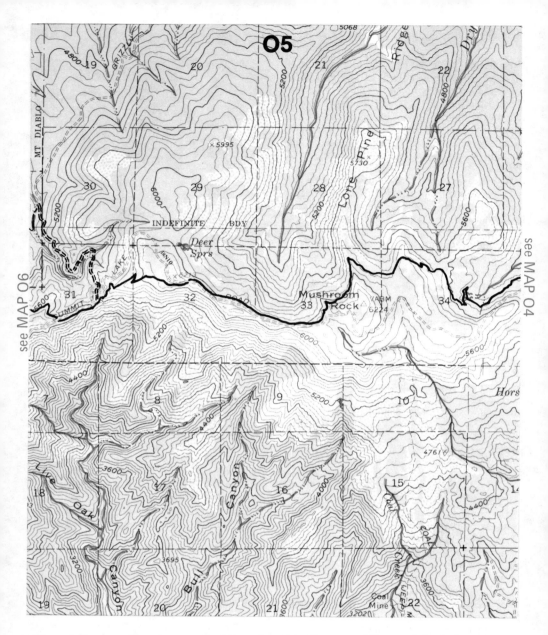

Beyond the powerlines traverse a while and then duck into forest cover for a short spell just before turning northeast and reaching a road junction at the south base of Red Mountain (5380-1.2). If you want to get a 360° panorama of Section O's terrain, follow an old jeep road ½ mile north up to the mountain's summit. From it you can see part of Lake Britton, about 10 miles to the southeast, Grizzly Peak, about 10 miles to the west-northwest, and of course

Mt. Shasta and Burney Mountain, volcanoes which we've seen many times before. You scan about 200 million years of geology. The volcanoes are certainly less than one million years old, and the flat lands around Lake Britton may be that young or slightly older. The volcanic rocks get older toward your viewpoint, perhaps 5–10 million years on lower, eastern slopes and 10–20 million years along your north-trending rim. About 2 miles to the north

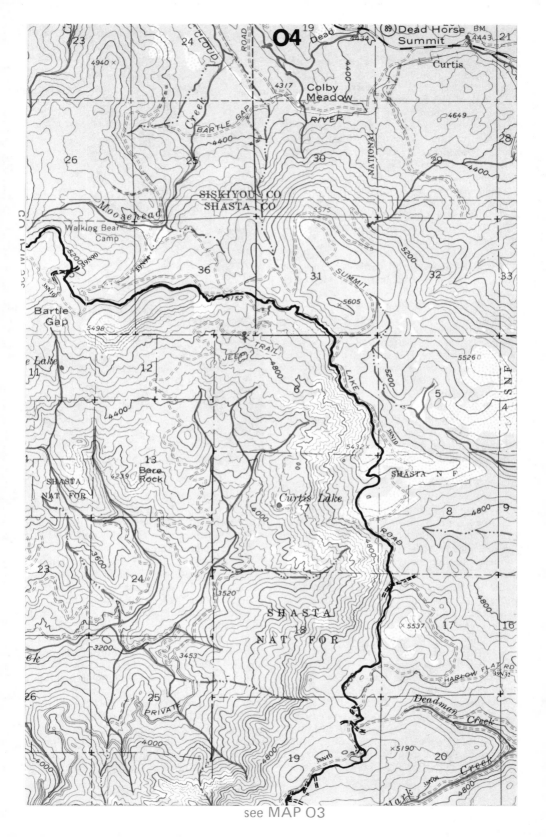

see MAP O3

and northwest lies Kosk Creek, and the rocks extending north from it almost up to Bartle Gap and Mushroom Rock are continental sediments about 40–50 million years old. The rocks of the western half of the basin are much older, deposited on an ocean floor roughly 200–225 million years ago. West beyond Grizzly Peak the rocks get increasingly older. To get back to the PCT, either retrace your steps or continue north ⅓ mile down to a saddle and then east on a logging road to Road 38N10. Walk several yards south on it and then go 80 yards southeast on another road to the PCT.

From the south base of Red Mountain, the PCT heads north-northeast, traversing in and out of gullies before it drops to cross Road 38N10 (5410-0.8). In 60 yards we cross the southeast-dropping road just mentioned, and then we traverse a small, seasonal bog, round a low ridge, and finally drop to another spur road (5290-0.7). We wind for one mile down to a third and in 340 yards arrive at a fourth. Up it we pace 20 yards to the trail's resumption then more or less parallel Road 38N10 over a broad ridge and down to a crossing of two roads by their junction (5060-2.1). The first road quickly ends, but the older one, a few yards north of the first, heads east down to Deadman Creek. In early summer, you can usually find water by hiking ½ mile or less down the road. In late summer, you may have to hike a mile or more. From these roads our trail climbs up to a crossing of Road 38N10 (5140-0.2). If you have to exit to civilization, go one mile along this road, first north up to a saddle, then east down to a fork. Branch right and take Harlow Flat Road 8 miles down to Highway 89 and hitch a ride south to Burney or north to McCloud or Mt. Shasta city.

Our crest trail loops around a broad, fir-forested ridge and in ¾ mile almost reaches a saddle and Road 38N10. Our shady route then climbs north but soon starts descending to a major logging road (5150-1.4), which we cross at the north base of Peak 5537. By heading down it and other roads, you can reach Highway 89 in about 6 miles, should the need arise. Over the next ⅔ mile, Road 38N10 is our constant rim companion; then it veers east to tackle slopes while the PCT winds northward. After a brushy ascent, we cross Peak 5432 in a shady gap just east of the summit and descend about 150 yards to a spot (5390-1.8) from where you can walk a few paces west to gain a panoramic view of coarse volcanic sediments that are deeply gullied and sparsely vegetated.

Road 38N10 forces PCT onto narrow rim

Road 38N10 encroaches upon us again, almost forcing the trail off the sometimes narrow rim. In just over one mile, the first half of it very scenic, the PCT splits northwest and the road splits northeast. In less than ¼ mile from this fork our route crosses an outcrop of unstable volcanic rock, which tends to slide occasionally, wiping out the tread. This is no major problem for hikers but it can be one for equestrians. In ¼ mile we round a small alcove and in another ¼ mile round a second. This one has a seasonal spring about 50 yards below the trail. In one more ¼ mile we cross a descending road (5110-2.2), which you can take ½ mile southeast to a small roadside pond, a suitable campsite.

Our trail, now westbound, presents us with a last view south down into the spreading basin before touching Road 38N10 just after it crosses over to the north-facing slopes of the basin's rim. Across these slopes we make a gentle descent through a cool fir forest back to

O3, O4

Road 38N10 (5070-1.6), crossing it just below Bartle Gap. Here, another camping opportunity presents itself, for if you descend 270 yards north along the road, you'll reach a spring-fed creeklet that usually lasts through July. Northward, the creeklet is longer lasting, and the road goes about 5 miles out to Highway 89.

The PCT climbs to the creeklet's usually dry headwaters gully, crosses it, and then crosses nearby Road 39N90 (5190-0.4). Now we traverse north to a ridge, bend southwest, and climb back into National Forest land. Since the powerlines, we've been hiking mostly on private land. After climbing gently about ½ mile southwest, you'll come to within 200 yards of Moosehead Creek, which is visible just below you. You might plan to camp here, since the next spacious campsite with water is at Ash Camp, on the McCloud River, a lengthy (though easy in this direction) 23½ miles away. Several other off-route camping possibilities exist between these two camps.

The trail continues about ¼ mile up our mildly glaciated canyon, then arcs northwest over to some nearby springs at Moosehead Creek's headwaters (5440-1.3). For late summer hikers, these springs will be your last source of permanent water until you cross Deer Creek, 14.8 miles ahead. Many hikers will find snowpatches burying sections of trail along north-facing slopes, especially if they hike the trail before mid-July.

The PCT switchbacks above the springs, climbs ½ mile northwest to a crest, and then continues ½ mile west up to a higher one. Views up at Mt. Shasta and down into Dry Creek canyon briefly appear, then disappear as we arc through a shady forest. They reappear when we reach a sharp ridge, from which we climb south up into the glaciated, forested bowl just below Mushroom Rock. You can take a viewful breather at a rocky point (6080-2.3), rising ominously above the trail, or at a second one, about a minute's walk past the first. Beyond it, the trail rejoins Road 38N10 and stays just beneath it as both head west.

Our trail crosses Road 38N10 at this section's high point (6120-1.4), which is immediately east of Peak 6213. From our bush-lined trail we have ample views to the south, down Live Oak Canyon, as we descend west to a reunion with Road 38N10 at a road junction (5580-1.1). By descending ½ mile from here on

O4, O5, O6

A late-summer storm visits the Kosk Creek basin

a north-trending road, you'll reach possible campsites at the headwaters of Tate Creek, which flows well into summer.

Westward, the PCT stays along the south side of Road 38N10 for ⅓ mile, crosses it, takes a convoluted course across gullied north-facing slopes, and then twice approaches that road before recrossing it again (5610-1.5). Our rim trail parallels the road—largely hidden by dense brush—for almost ½ mile, then descends southwest another ½ mile, leveling off at the Alder Creek trail (5440-1.1), which climbs south over the nearby rim and descends to lower Alder Creek and the Kosk Creek road. Northward, this "trail" (definitely a road) goes ⅓ mile over to an intersection with Road 38N10. You could camp here, as others have done, and get water from a nearby, seasonal pond, though you'll find better water if you continue 0.2 mile north on the road to the head-waters of Star City Creek. This creek typically dries up in August or early September, even in the Stouts Meadow area.

Our rim route west stays within white-fir cover for ½ mile, then crosses a burned-over stand of knobcone pines, the first you'll see on the Pacific Crest trail. Between here and the dry slopes above Cook and Green Pass, near the Oregon border, you'll see this tree only a few times. Here, the pines are growing near their upper elevation limit. They survive well in

frequently burned areas because fires cause their cones to open, and their seeds do well in freshly burned soil. We see more stands of knobcone pines as we traverse across brushy slopes to a saddle and a crossing of Grizzly Peak Road (5540-2.1). Before August, you can usually find water by descending ½ mile or so down this road. Staying just above the road, the PCT follows it west over to a saddle, then recrosses it (5420-0.6).

*   *   *   *

If you've got your heart set on climbing Grizzly Peak, which you've seen since the east rim of the basin, then start south along the road. It climbs 1.9 miles to the west ridge just below the peak, and then you take a spur road 0.2 mile up to the fire lookout atop the peak. After taking in a sweeping view of the scenery—most of Section O—go back to the west-ridge junction, continue briefly west, and then descend southeast to a south-ridge junction with the PCT.

*   *   *   *

If you don't take the 2.9-mile alternate route, then you face a PCT route almost as long with almost as much climbing, *sans* views. Logically, the trail should have climbed to Grizzly Peak

The PCT route southwest toward Grizzly Peak

or started a descent to Deer Creek. Instead, it contours for about 1.2 miles, and then you round a ridge and face the steep, barren slopes of Grizzly Peak. Confronted with these, the builders dropped the trail almost to their base, then made it climb for more than ½ mile to a saddle on the peak's southeast ridge. From it the trail should have contoured over to another saddle, ¼ mile to the west, then descended to Deer Creek. Instead, it climbs ½ mile northwest to a road on the south ridge of Grizzly Peak (5640-2.6).

Reunited with the alternate route, we now face a 10-mile descent, which—fortunately—is very well graded, making the climb in the opposite direction relatively easy, if lengthy, task. Our trail starts west, crosses the usually dry headwaters of Deer Creek, switchbacks to recross them, then descends southward through a shady forest of white firs and Douglas-firs. After weaving in and out of several dry gullies, the trail switchbacks north and quickly brings us to delightful Deer Creek (4700-2.1). Southbound hikers, be aware that this is your last reliable water along the trail until you reach the springs at Moosehead Creek's headwaters, 14.8 trail miles to the east.

Since camping space is nil, we push on, at first following the creek, though at a distance, downstream, then veering into a side canyon with a refreshing creek (4360-1.4). Umbrella plants, which you'll recognize by their large leaves, line this creek's banks and those of others we'll see on our westward trek through Section O. Again, camp space is nonexistent, so we trek onward, in and out of gullies, and watch Deer Creek drop farther and farther below us. At last we cross a ridge and descend gently north for more than a mile to broad Butcherknife Creek (3300-3.2), also without sites. Now we have the pleasure of weaving in and out of gullies (some with seasonal water) as we parallel the creek and watch it gradually drop away from us. After 1.6 miles we cross a narrow ridge, descend into a nearby gully, and then circle over to usually dry Doodlebug Gulch (3000-2.1). Now on lower, south-facing slopes, we're pestered by flies as we traverse to a second ridge and make a gullied descent northwest past marble outcrops to Centipede Creek. This we cross at the McCloud-Big Bend Road (2404-1.3). If you have to get out to civilization, hitchhike north out to McCloud, about 14½ miles away. You can camp along the road, but it's better to continue west on the PCT and descend to nearby Ash Camp (2390-0.2) along the McCloud River. This small camp is not as pleasant as Ah-Di-Na Campground, ahead, but neither is it ⅔ mile out of the way.

Leaving the campground, you follow the trail 0.1 mile up the McCloud River, then span it on a 50-yard-long bridge. Rather than parallel the river, the trail climbs ¼ mile south to a minor gap, then contours west for 1¼ miles, staying disappointingly high above the McCloud River and its alluring pools. However, there is method to the trail planners' madness: they have purposely kept the trail high to discourage you from reaching the river since it periodically floods when the gates on the McCloud Reservoir dam are opened. Finally your hot route starts to descend, then turns north onto an abandoned road, on which you could camp. You head briefly up Fitzhugh Gulch and come to its creek (2320-2.1), which usually flows through early August. This will be your last trailside water until Trough Creek, 3.0 air miles away. You, however, will walk 8.3 miles to reach it. Most of the rocks we've seen over the last few miles are, like those ahead, volcanic rocks that erupted on the earth's surface about 200–250 million years ago and then were subsequently metamorphosed. However, beyond Bald Mountain Road, to which we're now going to climb, these metavolcanics give way to metasediments, rocks that were originally deposited on a shallow ocean floor. These rocks are older, roughly 300–350 million years old. By the time we approach the Sacramento River, the rocks will be twice as old as those we've just traversed.

From the creek in Fitzhugh Gulch we follow a short trail segment over to a dry gulch and climb up to nearby Road 38N53 (2400-0.4). This descends 0.6 mile to the entrance to pleasing Ah-Di-Na Campground, which is located on the site of an old resort. Here is a good place for a layover day, particularly if you're an angler. Fishing is also supposed to be good at Squaw Valley Creek, our next major goal. Halfway down Road 38N53 you'll find a flowing creek, though the creek is usually dry where the PCT crosses it, about 400' higher.

Just ½ mile past Road 38N53 the PCT crosses this creek, and then it makes a steady, gentle ascent into ravines and out to ridges, presenting us views through live oaks, incense-cedars and Douglas-firs. Flies can be terrible along this stretch, swarming to such an extent that you're likely to inhale a few. They particu-

O6, O7, O8

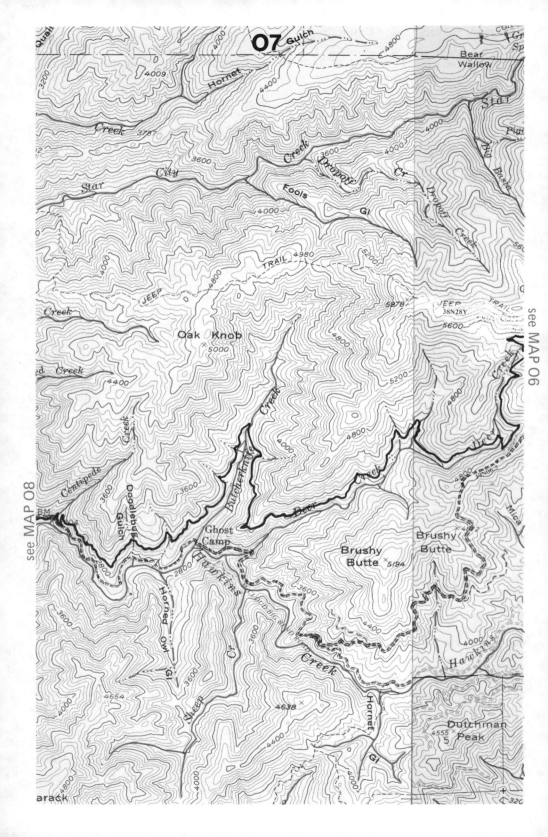

see MAP 06

see MAP 08

Gulch

Bear
Wallow

Star

Pig

Hornet

Creek 3787

Star City

3600

Creek

Dropoff

Cr

Fools

Gl

Creek

Dropoff Creek

4000

TRAIL 4980

5200

JEEP 4800

5878

JEEP
38N28Y

TRAIL

5600

Oak Knob
× 5000

Creek

4800

5200

Creek

4400

4800

Creek

Brushy
Butte

Butcherknife Creek

Deer

Creek

Brushy
Butte

Mica

Centipede Creek

Doodlebug Gulch

3600

Ghost
× Camp

Hawkins

Brushy
Butte × 5194

BM

Hornet Ow Gl

Creek

3600

Creek

Hawkins

4654

× 4638

Sheep Cr

Hornet
Gl

Dutchman
Peak
4555 ×
5

arack

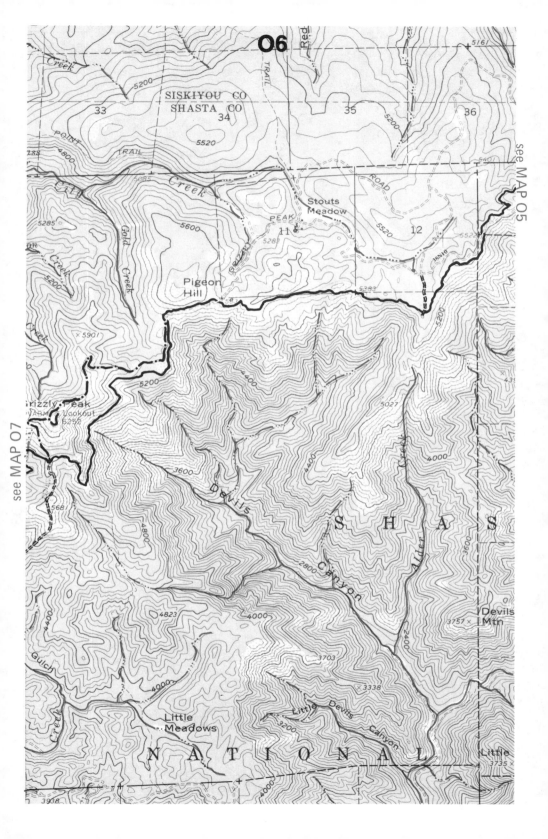

see MAP O5

see MAP O7

SISKIYOU CO
SHASTA CO

33

34

35

36

Red

TRAIL

POINT

TRAIL

City

Creek

Gold Creek

Creek

Creek

5285

5200

5901

Grizzly Peak
VABM
Lookout
6252

5681

Stouts
Meadow

PEAK

Pigeon
Hill

11

12

5200

5027

5200

S   H   A   S

Devils

Canyon

Alder

4000

3600

3600

3757

Devils
Mtn

Gulch

Creek

Creek

4823

4000

3703

3338

Little
Meadows

Little Devils

Canyon

Little

N   A   T   I   O   N   A   L

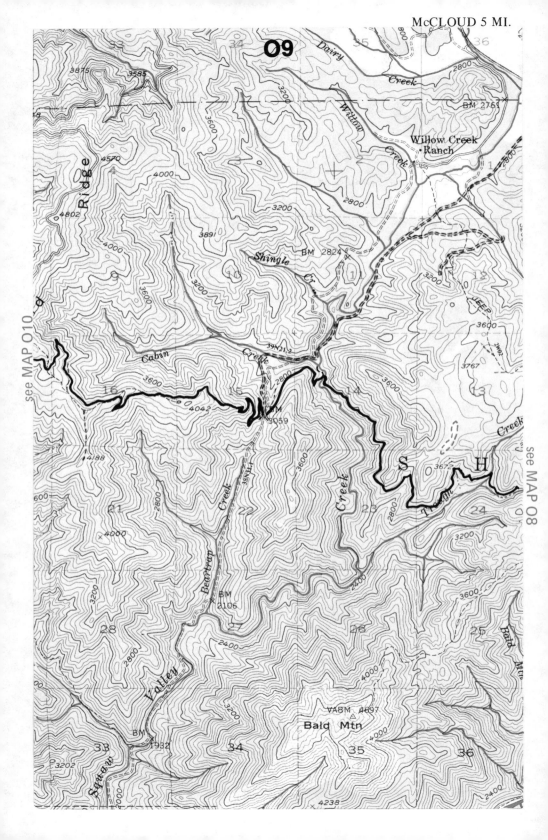

O9

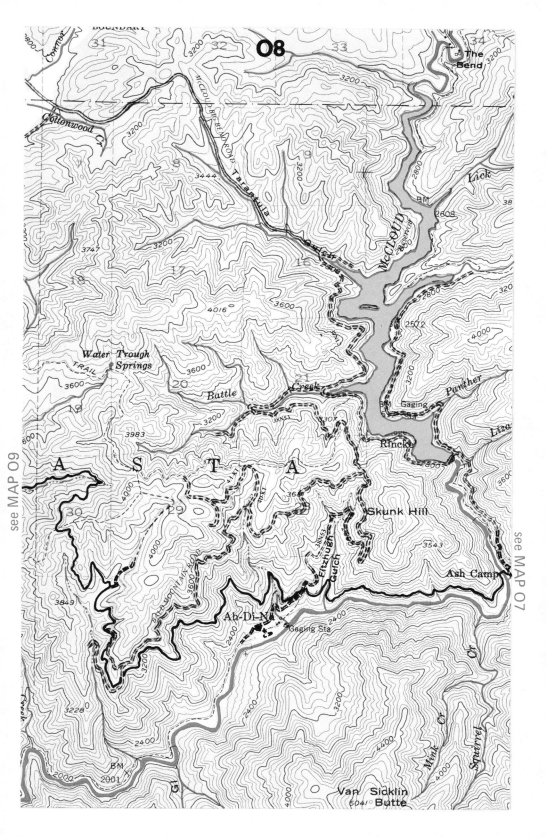

see MAP O9

see MAP O7

BOUNDARY

Connor

The Bend

Cottonwood Cr.

McCLOUD-BIG BEND ROAD

Tarantula

Lick

BM 2608

McCLOUD

RESERVOIR

2572

Water Trough Springs

TRAIL

Battle Creek

Panther

BM Gaging

Rincke

Liza

S   H   A   S   T   A

Skunk Hill

Ash Camp

Fitzhugh Gulch

Ah-Di-Na

Gaging Sta

FLAT MOUNTAIN ROAD

Mink Cr.

Squirrel

BM 2001

Van Sicklin Butte

Bridge over Squaw Valley Creek

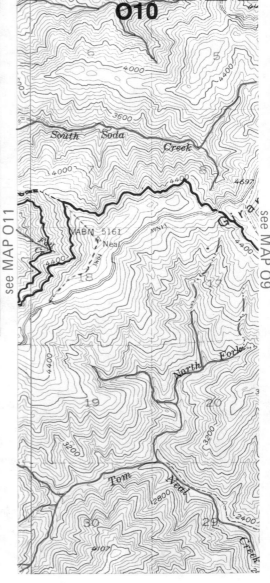

larly love you if you're sweaty, so try and hike this stretch in the morning. You'll have lots more fly problems in the remainder of Section O, particularly when you are hiking across dry, oak-covered terrain. Finally, we cross Bald Mountain Road (3380-3.1), parallel it southwest for a bit, and then turn north and gently climb to another road (3520-0.8)), which we meet at a road bend on a ridge (southbound hikers take note). Ahead, the road is closed to motor vehicles, and we take it around the bend, into two gullies, around another bend, and then into two more gullies. This stretch of road is being overgrown by deer brush, and in early summer these wild lilacs bloom and permeate the air with their sweet fragrance.

The road dies out among brush and we follow a trail segment that first climbs northwest up a dry gully, then south around a ridge. The route then climbs ¾ mile north, veering in and out of minor gullies before topping out on a ridge saddle (3880-1.9). In another ¾ mile we descend to the head of a beautiful, linear canyon. About the only time you'll see water flowing down it, however, is during a heavy rainstorm, for the canyon is lined in marble and the drainage is subterranean. After a mile of hiking through this cool, verdant canyon, we swing over to nearby Trough Creek (3030-2.1), whose water provides a welcome sight.

Beyond it, our shady route contours 0.4 mile west over to a seasonal creek fed by an equally seasonal lake, and then it contours ⅔ mile over

O8, O9

View northeast across the Squaw Valley Creek drainage

to a ridge. Douglas-firs and ponderosa pines begin to thin out by the time we contour over to another ridge, ½ mile away. Then black oaks, live oaks and flies take over as we descend to Squaw Valley Creek (2580-3.2). By late afternoon the creek warms sufficiently to provide an enjoyable swim in the alluring pool by the route's arch bridge. In this minigorge, a west-bank trail runs upstream to nearby Cabin Creek. You'll find several campsites along this trail, and you should plan to camp at one of them, since in the remaining 16.4 miles of Section O there are no more campsites with water. Until you reach the Sacramento River, near this section's end, your only other reliable water source will be spring-fed Fall Creek, 10.6 miles away.

Like the McCloud River, Squaw Valley Creek was flowing even before these mountains started to rise millions of years ago. Hence it cuts across the mountain range and its headwaters originate on the southeast slopes of Mt. Shasta. Before that volcano developed and blocked south-flowing streams, Squaw Valley Creek might have drained a larger area, which would explain how it could have cut such a deep canyon.

We climb out of the canyon, ending our ascent on an abandoned road that climbs southwest to a deep saddle (3059-0.9). From here roads head in all directions, but the one we want starts from the base of a large cut on the west side of the saddle. We head 190 yards north-northwest on an abandoned road, then

spot the PCT and start south on a switchbacking ascent, which takes us to the top of a west-climbing ridge. We follow it momentarily, and then head over to Douglas-fir-shaded north slopes that provide us with occasional views of Mt. Shasta. After about 2 miles, the trail regains the ridge, follows it briefly west, and then switchbacks up south slopes to recross the ridge higher up. Again we traverse shady north slopes, barely climbing to a descending, abandoned road, but then climbing with effort back to a last crossing of the ridge. We conclude our climb by traversing ¾ mile northwest gently up to a saddle crossing of Girard Ridge Road (4600-4.8).

Mt. Shasta now reveals itself for full inspection, a magnificent sight when it is snowy white in early summer or early fall. West of it stands conical Black Butte, a smaller, younger volcano that lies midway between the towns of Weed and Mt. Shasta. Like Section N's Lassen Peak, Black Butte is a plug dome, and it erupted over perhaps a year or two roughly 9500 years ago. Shasta, on the other hand, is a stratovolcano, and it has been building up over tens of thousands of years. Just in the last 2000 years, it has erupted six times.

The PCT contours across brushy, logged-over slopes to a ridge, from which we get our first view of Castle Crags. These are the first granitic rocks we've seen since climbing up Chips Creek canyon back at the start of Section N. We'll see lots of them in Section P. The granodiorite rock comprising Castle Crags

O9, O10

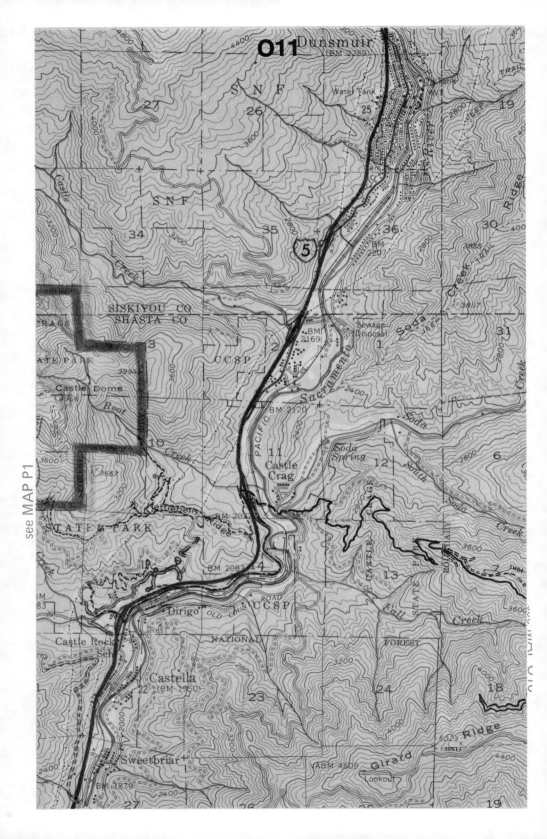

O11

see MAP P1

solidified in the earth's crust roughly 140 million years ago, then tens of millions of years elapsed before the overlying rock was eroded away. In contrast, most of the rocks along the first part of our descent from Girard Ridge originated as sediments laid down on an ocean floor roughly 300–400 million years ago.

Views continue as we contour west to a northwest-descending ridge (4640-1.8). The original, temporary PCT route once plunged across private property down this ridge, allowing hikers to reach the Sacramento River in about an hour. Southbound hikers, however, faced quite a struggle up this steep, sometimes hot ridge. The permanent PCT is too gentle and far too long, but this is partly due to the necessity of routing it around private logging lands. From the northwest-dropping ridge we make a largely open, barely perceptible descent past marble outcrops to a switchback on a prominent ridge (4330-1.8). We then contour ½ mile east before dropping into a gulch containing Fall Creek (4050-1.3). Level ground, unfortunately, is absent, and no camping is allowed on the private land and the state park land ahead.

From the creek, the trail actually climbs a bit, and then descends ever so gently, passing through a logged area before reaching the northwest-descending ridge where a road crosses it (3770-1.5). Here we enter Castle Crags State Park and make a protracted, switchbacking descent in and out of dry, fly-infested gullies. Vegetation ranges from shady Douglas-fir on north slopes to live oak on southwest slopes. As we approach the Sacra-mento River, whose flowing water sounds are drowned out by trucks on nearby Interstate 5, we descend north to a closed road. This we descend ⅓ mile southwest to a ridge, and then descend a trail 140 yards down the ridge to Old County Road (2200-3.7). If you're taking the supply route to Castella, you can either head south on it or head northwest down it to nearby Soda Creek Road (2150-0.1). On this road we stroll a few minutes over to the wide Sacra-mento River, then to Southern Pacific's rail-road tracks. A 4-mile walk north up them would take you to central Dunsmuir, which has just about everything, including boot repair. Just past the tracks we curve over to Frontage Road (2125-0.4), then cross under adjacent Interstate 5, where Section O ends at a locked gate, the eastern boundary of the west half of Castle Crags State Park (2130-0.1).

*   *   *   *

To visit Castella, head south on Frontage Road. In 2.0 miles you'll reach Sam's Market, which is at a junction with a road crossing the Sacramento River. If you decided to take Old County Road south past the park's picnic area, you'll be crossing the Sacramento on this road. If Sam's Market is inadequate, continue 0.2 mile to Road 38N18. This immediately heads under Interstate 5, and on its west side you'll see the Castella Post Office and fairly large Ammirati's Market. Another 0.2 mile farther, you'll come to the entrance to Castle Crags State Park. The next chapter describes the route back to the PCT.

O10, O11

Mt. Shasta and Black Butte, from Girard Ridge

The Statue, upper left, stands above hidden Statue Lake

Section P: Castle Crags to Etna Summit

Introduction: Like the Sierra Nevada, this area we are about to hike has been heavily glaciated. Therefore, lakes abound, although the trail skirts only three: the two Deadfall Lakes and Paynes Lake. Nevertheless, about three dozen lakes lie within a half-hour's walk (or less) from the PCT. The reason the PCT doesn't visit more lakes is that most lie in deep basins that don't become snow-free until mid-July or later. The PCT, routed along many south- and west-facing slopes, becomes mostly snow-free by late June.

Like the area's lakes, its rocks may remind you of the Sierra Nevada. Like that range, much of Section P—an eastern part of the Klamath Mountains—is granitic. Still, about half of the miles we walk will be across ultramafic terrain and a few will be across mafic terrain. Ultramafic and mafic rocks, like granitic rocks, are intrusive rocks, all solidifying within the earth's crust. Granites are light gray, mafics are intermediate, and ultramafics are dark gray—when fresh. This last type, rich in iron and manganese, weathers to a rusty color, as you'll see just north of Toad Lake. This color makes them easy to identify, and you'll see them time and again on your way to Oregon.

As in the previous section, Shasta red firs dominate at the higher elevations, and if you're going to have any early-season snow problems, they will be in these forests and in stands of mountain hemlocks. Loggers are harvesting these firs as well as white firs and Douglas-firs lower down. Though you'll see some clearcuts that are real eyesores, the trail generally avoids such areas and the feeling of wilderness often prevails. Still, loggers and logging roads abound, which are convenient if you have to exit down to civilization.

Declination: 17°E

Mileages:

	South to North	Distance between Points	North to South
Interstate 5 near Castle Crags State Park	0.0		99.8
		6.6	
Sulphur Creek	6.6		93.2
		3.4	
Section 31 tributary of North Fk. Castle Creek	10.0		89.8
		5.7	
crest saddle 5983	15.7		84.1
		6.7	
Trinity Divide.	22.4		77.4
		2.3	
Road 40N30.	24.7		75.1
		5.6	

Porcupine Lake trail	30.3	5.4	69.5
upper Deadfall Lake	35.7	3.3	64.1
Parks Creek Road 42N17	39.0	8.4	60.8
Bull Lake saddle	47.4	7.9	52.4
Masterson Meadow saddle	55.3	4.4	44.5
Highway 3 at Scott Mountain Summit	59.7	8.1	40.1
E. Boulder Lake/Marshy Lakes saddle	67.8	6.0	32.0
Trail 8W07 near Section Line Lake	73.8	5.8	26.0
Forest Highway 93 at Carter Meadows Summit	79.6	6.2	20.2
s.e. rim of South Russian Creek canyon	85.8	4.8	14.0
slopes below Statue Lake	90.6	3.3	9.2
Paynes Lake	93.9	4.2	5.9
Upper Ruffey Lake saddle	98.1	1.7	1.7
Somes Bar-Etna Road at Etna Summit	99.8		0.0

Supplies: Dunsmuir lies a few miles north of this section's starting point. It should have just about any kind of food and equipment you might need. Food and minor supplies can be bought at Ammirati's Market, which lies just east of the main entrance to Castle Crags State Park. The Castella Post Office is next to the store, and you should mail your parcels to it. Plan to make your "CARE" package last all the way to Seiad Valley, at the end of Section Q, for there are no nearby towns, post offices or resorts anywhere in between. Unless you're a strong backpacker, count on 10+ days to do both sections.

If you have to go out for supplies, you can leave the PCT at Scott Mountain Summit. Follow Highway 3 8½ miles to Callahan, with post office, store and ranger station, then climb southwest 12 miles back to the PCT at Carter Meadows Summit. Unfortunately, the 20 miles of PCT you would thus bypass are among the section's best. Later, at Etna Summit, where Section P ends and Section Q begins, you can descend northeast 10½ miles to Etna. Sawyers Bar, 15 miles west from the summit, is too distant to consider.

Permits: There are three wildernesses in Section P: Castle Crags, Trinity Alps and Russian. You'll need a wilderness permit only for Trinity Alps Wilderness. In Section Q, you'll need a wilderness permit for Marble Mountain Wilderness. You hike through Trinity Alps Wilderness in Section P's stretch between Highway 3 and Forest Highway 93, and through Marble Mountain Wilderness in most of Section Q. If you're driving through this general area, pick up a permit for both areas at the Callahan Ranger Station in Callahan or at the Scott River Ranger Station in Fort Jones. As usual, it's best to write in advance. See Chapter 1 for addresses.

Water shortage: After mid-August in normal years and before that in drier years, water may be absent in this section's first 22 miles. If you are hiking this stretch in late summer or early fall, be sure you carry enough water to last until Upper Seven Lake.

Hazards: Particularly watch for rattlesnakes along the first 11 miles. They are usually less common westward, higher up, though they have been relatively common from Cooper Meadow south to Scott Mountain. Ticks and poison oak may be a problem below 4000', but flies will pester you the most. Up by the crest, mosquitoes can be locally abundant before late July.

Castle Crags

Long-distance hikers will start this section at the main entrance to Castle Crags State Park, which is 0.2 mile west of the Castella Post Office. From the entrance station just inside the park, fork left. The pavement quickly ends, and you ascend this road about ½ mile, first northwest and then northeast, up to a tight bend in the road. Here there's a junction with the Milt Kenny Trail, which rambles 1.0 mile eastward in and out of shady gullies to site 25 of the state park's campground. Beyond the trail junction, the rather steep road passes a road branching right in just 40 yards, and then it climbs about ¾ mile to a turnaround loop atop a minor ridge. From here you climb 200 yards up Bobs Hat Trail to the PCT.

* * * *

Section P arbitrarily begins at the west side of an Interstate 5 onramp-offramp, the next one north of the Castle Crags State Park onramp-offramp. Here, by a locked gate, we enter the park and immediately turn left (south) on an old road. North, it goes 80 yards to

refreshing Root Creek. We follow this narrowing road, hiking under the pleasant shade of Douglas-firs, ponderosa pines, incense-cedars, black oaks and big-leaf maples. Although sheltered from the sun, our low-elevation route can get up into the 90s on hot summer afternoons. Characteristic of this environment is a profusion of poison oak, which in Section P grows up to about 3500' elevation.

Our route, after briefly following a one-cable line, leaves it to quickly jog west up to another road (2400-0.3). A section of this road, blocked off at both ends, is now part of the PCT. We follow its amazingly level course west, passing a set of powerlines and ducking in and out of gullies. We then veer north for ¼ mile, crossing under a larger set of powerlines, then briefly switchback up, almost touching a spring-fed creeklet before we climb ¼ mile south to the Root Creek trail (2590-1.5). On it, you can hike ¼ mile to a spring. The trail ends at Root Creek, about 0.4 mile farther.

The Pacific Crest trail was built around the southwest base of Castle Crags, not up over the crest of the crags. In a way, this is unfortunate,

P1

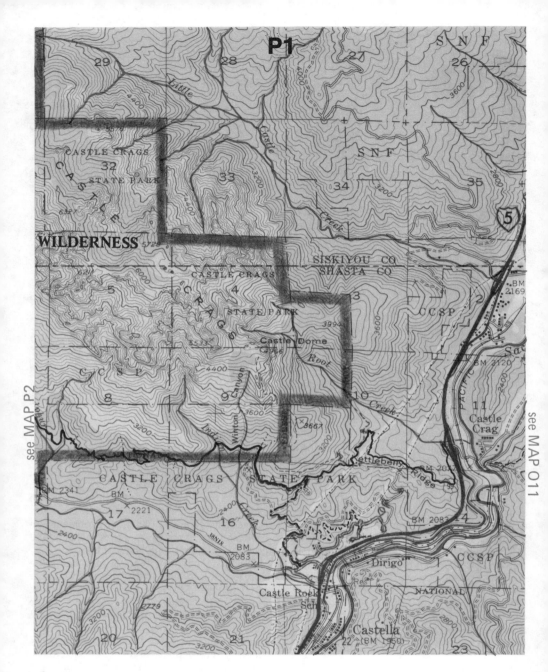

since the crest, studded with pinnacles, blocks and domes, is a far more exciting route. But the park people rightly felt that a trail blasted along the crags' crest would ruin its wilderness character. However, experienced mountaineers can traverse the Castle Crags high country. In 1972, Schaffer and another mountaineer, Bob Ng, made such a traverse, starting up Root Creek and ending on the saddle in the northwest quarter of Section 30. Traveling very light, we didn't have to use ropes. Don't attempt such a route with a heavy, awkward pack. One can avoid the initial cross-country climb up Root Creek by starting cross country from Castle Dome, at the end of the Crags trail. Again: for experienced mountaineers only; others can expect real trouble.

For a short distance south the PCT coincides with the Root Creek trail as it immediately crosses a gully and, midway south to a next one, leaves that trail (2590-0.1). In Castle Crags State Park, camping is allowed *only* in its campground. You can reach it by following the Root Creek trail 0.4 mile east down to a roadend parking lot. From it you can descend to the spacious campground, which is one of the best-designed ones you'll ever find. Unfortunately, Interstate 5 was built right next to it, so the nights are noisy. Campsite 25 is specifically set aside for PCT backpackers, but not for equestrians—they should contact the park in advance to make arrangements. From campsite 25, the Milt Kenny Trail, mentioned in the first paragraph of this section's route description, rambles 1.0 mile westward to a road. Take this road up to regain the PCT. If you need supplies, then from the state park's campground, continue down the paved road to the park's entrance station and just beyond it to paved Whalen Road 38N18, this junction being 1.7 miles from the previously mentioned roadend parking lot. A post office and store are 0.2 mile east.

Beyond the Root Creek trail the PCT goes up to a powerline saddle (2650-0.1), on which it crosses the Crags trail. Eastward, this quickly reaches the Root Creek trail; westward, it climbs to Castle Dome, mentioned above. Leaving Kettlebelly Ridge, we traverse west across gullies to meet the Bobs Hat trail (2820-0.5), where the alternate supply route, mentioned in the first paragraph, ends at the PCT. In about 27 yards the Bobs Hat trail branches right and climbs steeply up to the Crags trail.

The PCT now swings clockwise over to two adjacent creeklets, entering Castle Crags Wilderness. Just 0.2 mile past them we bridge Winton Canyon creek (2875-1.0) and then in ¼ mile cross Indian Creek. Over the next hour we cross two spur ridges, leaving Castle Crags State Park ¼ mile beyond the first one. Before the second one, we cross many gullies and have lots of views up at the Crags, and then the trail drops to the shady east fork of Sulphur Creek. Next it loops around another spur ridge and climbs northwest to Sulphur Creek (2750-3.1). Like all the creeks mentioned so far, this one is usually reliable through early- or mid-August.

California pitcher plants

Knobcone pines briefly join ponderosa pines, Douglas-firs, incense-cedars and manzanitas as we climb southwest up to a spur ridge. Just 120 yards after we round it, we meet the Dog trail (3040-0.6), which descends ½ mile to North Fork Castle Creek and Whalen Road 38N18. Since the road and creek are on Forest Service land, you could camp by them—the first real camping opportunity since the park's campground. The Dog trail is for the dogs—literally. Dogs aren't allowed in the park, so northbound hikers with dogs have to hike west up Whalen Road to the creek and then rejoin the PCT via the Dog trail. Southbound PCT hikers with dogs must exit on the Dog trail. Now if you have a cat. . . .

The PCT climbs north from the Dog trail junction, then contours in and out of about a dozen gullies, some with early-season freshets, before switchbacking briefly down to two converging branches of a North Fork tributary (3110-1.8). During most of the summer, these are either seeping or dry. We then switchback up one of the branches, twice crossing it before winding around a ridge and descending to a refreshing tributary of North Fork Castle Creek (3370-1.0). After mid-July, this could be the last near trail water you'll access to until

P1, P2

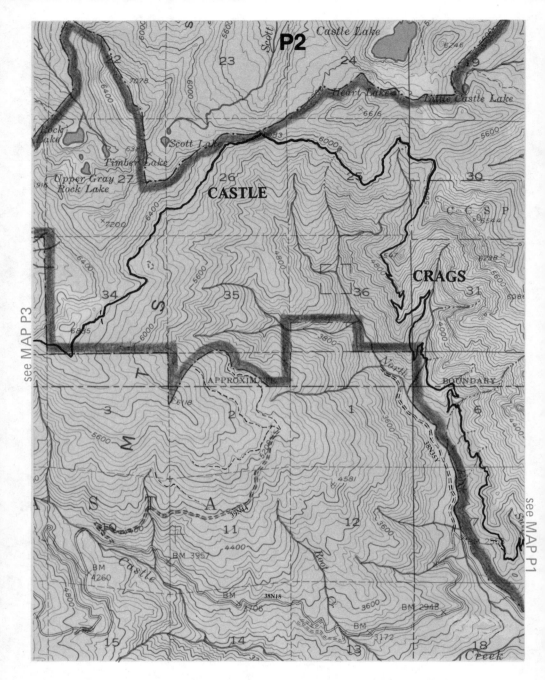

you leave the trail for either the Seven Lakes, about 12 miles ahead, or for Upper Gumboot Lake, about 14½ miles ahead.

The real climbing now begins—about 2500′ of it—up to a crest saddle. In one mile we climb about 500 feet, first away from the creek, then almost back to it. We then climb southwest to a south-dropping ridge, finally leaving the live oaks and their hordes of flies behind us. Ponderosa pines, sugar pines and Douglas-firs offer some shade as we switchback up the ridge, but the vegetation is predominantly

Mumbo Lakes in Mumbo Basin

brush, especially huckleberry oak. The brush, however, lets us have many views, and these improve as we climb. To the east rise massive granodiorite faces, most of them with the same orientation, for this pluton is being slowly eroded along major fracture planes. To the west lie denuded slopes, the first of many logging scars we'll see in Section P.

After crossing the ridge several times, we climb about ½ mile north to a west-dropping ridge, from which we see miles of PCT tread heading westward and see a cascading creek, to the north, that drops well below us. After ⅓ mile of moderate ascent we reach a flat-topped bedrock outcrop, from which the inaccessible cascades are even more tempting. A final ⅔ mile haul, mostly through a fir forest, brings us to a forested saddle (5620-3.6) just beyond the northernmost boundary of Castle Crags State Park. Trees prevent a view of Mt. Shasta, to the northeast, but they don't restrict views to the west. If you've brought along enough water or are willing to descend west to get some, you can camp here. Before August you can also obtain water about 10 minutes up the trail at the headwaters of the cascading creek (5750-0.4). Most of the creek's springs, unfortunately, lie below the trail in extremely dense brush.

Beyond the brush-covered springs and the audible, cascading creek, we contour around a ridge and reach a seasonal, densely vegetated creeklet (5840-1.0). Among other plants you'll see is the California pitcher plant, a cobra-shaped plant that derives part of its nourishment from insects. Flies and other insects, tempted by the alluring odor, venture down its hollow, tubular stem, only to find that downward-pointing hairs prevent their retreat. Other organisms, including bacteria and small invertebrates, digest the hapless insects and the plant absorbs the juices. This bog plant welcomes us to the Klamath Mountains, the only area where it is likely to be seen, though it is occasionally found in a few places outside these mountains. The Klamath Mountains are a collection of smaller mountain ranges that include, among others, the Trinity Alps and the Scott, Salmon, Marble and Siskiyou mountains. This mountain province differs from all other North American ranges in that it has an abundance of ultramafic rocks. In Section P, half of the PCT's length is across such rocks. Ultramafic rocks are related to granitic rocks in that both are igneous in origin and intrusive in nature. That is, both began as molten material within the earth's crust or mantle and solidified there, rather than on the surface. Ultramafic rocks, unlike their granitic relatives, are rich in iron and manganese, and hence heavy. The commonest ultramafic rock in the Klamath Mountains is peridotite, which geologists believe is the kind of rock that makes up the lower part of giant oceanic plates. If so, what we see, up here in the Klamath Mountains, are remnants of rock that once lay beneath an ocean floor. Oceanic plates, colliding with plates carrying continents, buckled and injected huge slabs of their ultramafic rocks into the continental masses. During this process of intense, low-temperature, high-pressure deformation, most of these rocks were altered, with the addition of water, to serpentinite. These rocks weather to

serpentine soils which, when boggy, prove to be very popular grounds for pitcher plants.

On such rocks and soils we contour west over to a saddle (5983-0.7), shaded by white firs, red firs and mountain hemlock. Through the trees we have our first view of Mt. Shasta, which we last saw on Section O's descent west from Girard Ridge. The peak will now appear quite regularly time and time again all the way into southern Oregon. By descending northwest cross country across north-facing slopes, you can reach Scott Camp Creek in less than 10 minutes. The nearly level terrain by it provides sites for small camps.

Beyond the saddle our trail traverses 1¾ miles southwest, providing us with ever-changing perspectives of Castle Crags. Some of the best views are from a scrubby ridge (6320-2.0), which we reach just after circling a basin with a usually dry lakelet. Just beyond the ridge we enter forest cover and climb gently southwest to an intersection of the Soapstone trail (6500-0.5), which descends south to a maze of logging roads that lead down to Whalen Road. Our southwest climbing ends atop Peak 6835's south ridge (6670-0.5), on which we briefly enter and then leave Section 3. Like so many privately owned sections we see along the PCT, this one belongs to the Southern Pacific Company, California's largest private-land owner. With close to 4000 square miles in its domain, this company manages an area about the size of Los Angeles County, about twice the size of the San Francisco Bay Area. Starting northwest, we leave Section 34 in a few minutes, and doing so, leave Castle Crags Wilderness.

Westward to Trinity Divide and beyond, we will now walk across a glaciated terrain of mafic intrusive rocks. These are intermediate between the light-gray granitic rocks of Castle Crags and the dark-gray ultramafic rocks we've just traversed. The latter, due to their high iron and manganese content, weather to a rusty color, which is very conspicuous where the vegetation is thin. Mafic rocks, like granites, intruded older, continental rocks. Ultramafic rocks, in contrast, first formed beneath the ocean floor and only later intruded continental rocks; they are usually older than the rocks they've intruded.

Our westward path skirts across several crest saddles, giving us views to the north down into the glaciated South Fork Sacramento River canyon and beyond it to Mt. Shasta. Most of our traverse is brushy, so we have almost con-

P2, P3

Mt. Shasta peeks over ridge above Toad Lake

tinual views to the south, where the appropriately named Grey Rocks at first hold our attention. This mass of ancient metamorphosed volcanic rock yields to steep-sided Boulder Peak and Echo Lake. After more than 3 miles of westward traverse, our trail bends southwest and Upper Seven Lake, 550′ below, gets your attention, particularly if your route so far has been dry. However, huckleberry oak, cream bush, greenleaf manzanita, chinquapin and tobacco brush grow in such a dense stand that access to the lake is nearly impossible. To reach Upper or Lower Seven Lake, continue a bit farther to a major crest cleft, Trinity Divide (6780-3.7). From this saddle descend cross-country to an obvious jeep road that heads down to the lakes and a selection of campsites. Also leaving this saddle is Trail 6W12, in poor condition, which goes to jeep roads leading down to Lake Helen.

At Trinity Divide we exchange Sacramento River drainage for Trinity River drainage. It's interesting to note that water draining down the two sides of the divide will enter the Pacific Ocean at two points that are 280 miles apart. On a curving traverse from north to northwest, we have ample opportunities to survey a part of the Trinity River basin, one so large that most hikers will take three or four days to circle its headwaters. The shallow Mumbo Lakes, in a glacial cirque below us, serve as reference points to mark our progress. As we continue to descend northwest, our trail vacillates along the crest, providing us with views down into both the Trinity and Sacramento river drainages. Just ¼ mile beyond a notable crest saddle above Upper Gumboot Lake, we come to a

second one, which is breached by Road 40N30 (6460-2.3). To reach the lake, about 250′ below the saddle, head cross country straight down to it. Gumboot Lake, about ⅓ mile below it, has a primitive USFS campground. The campground's road descends ⅔ mile to Road 40N30, which in turn descends about 11 miles along South Fork Sacramento River to Lake Siskiyou, then continues about 4 miles beyond it up to Mt. Shasta city.

From the Road 40N30 saddle, the PCT switchbacks up to a higher one crossed by Road 40N45 (6550-0.8). Our next stretch of PCT starts out as an old jeep road, and we have views west down upon shallow Picayune Lake and its swampy satellite. After ¾ mile, our road narrows to a trail as it contours the forested slopes west of Bear Ridge. It then dallies along the crest for ½ mile before contouring across cow-infested slopes to a major saddle (6770-2.1), crossed by the Little Picayune Trail. About 0.4 mile north of it, as we traverse the slopes west of White Ridge, we meet three springs, one of them with considerable staying power. Twenty-eight miles into Section P, this is your *first* really reliable *trailside* water.

In about 300 yards we cross the crest at a minor saddle, then pass above a small meadow after a few minutes, and in ⅓ mile come to a small spring, immediately below the trail. Typical of such seeps in ultramafic terrain, this spring has its colony of pitcher plants. Our traverse through a shady red-fir/western-white-pine forest continues, and after ⅔ mile we pass another spring, this one seasonal. From it our trail traverses ⅓ mile east-northeast to an east-dropping ridge (7130-2.2), which gives us an

P3, P4, P5

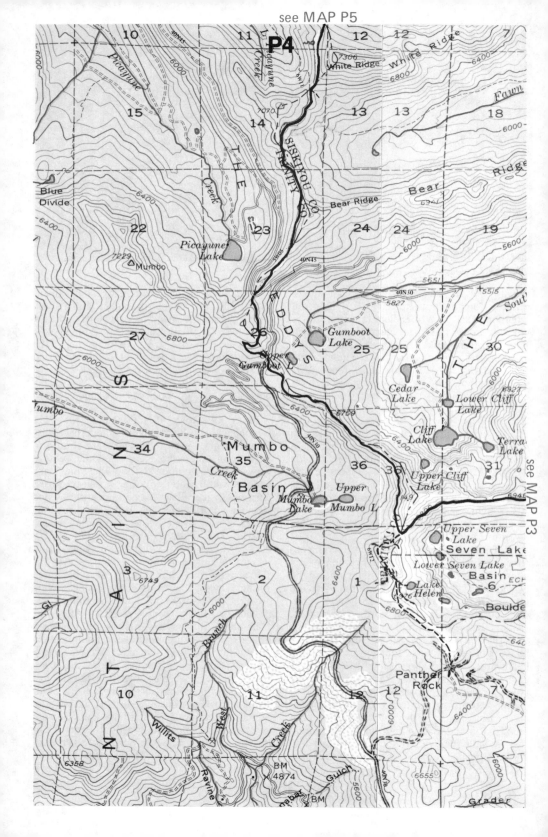

see MAP P3

Upper Deadfall Lake

excellent view of Lake Siskiyou, Mt. Shasta city, and its namesake, Mt. Shasta. Now on mafic igneous rocks such as diorite or gabbro, we contour along a blasted tread, first across a brushy rock field, then through a bouldery forest before arriving at a spur trail junction (7220-0.5). Up it, you have scarcely a five-minute walk to beautiful Porcupine Lake, which is one of Section P's most desirable gems. However, the west-shore area, with level ground, can handle only a few backpacking parties. From the moraine that dams the lake, you see Castle Crags and Lassen Peak—a rare view indeed.

Beyond the Porcupine Lake spur trail, the PCT climbs briefly to a crest (7300-0.3), from where a steep trail descends 350' over a half-mile stretch to the west shore of Toad Lake. Lying at the bottom of an 800' deep cirque, this glacial lake can be fed by melting snow till mid-July or later. Nevertheless, swimming can be quite agreeable in the lake's shallow east waters. Tables dot the lakeshore, for a campground once ringed the lake. Today the jeep road to it is closed, and not too many campers or fishermen walk the steep half-mile route up to it. If you plan to spend a layover day at a lake, consider doing it at Toad Lake.

From the crest above Toad Lake, the PCT traverses clockwise around the basin, intersecting Trail 6W06 (7420-0.9) on the basin's north slopes. Gently climbing, our trail leaves red firs for western white pines, then those for open, view-packed slopes as we climb to a minor gap on the east ridge (7620-0.9). Standing here on Section P's highest point, we can compare the rusty ultramafic rock of Mt. Eddy, 2 miles to the north, with the drab-colored mafic rocks of the ridge just south of us. Light-gray granitic rocks show up on White Ridge, about 3 miles to

the southeast, and on Castle Crags, beyond the ridge.

The geology lesson over, we cross the gap and traverse west for a climatology lesson. Here you'll note samples of whitebark pine and then mountain hemlock. The former we haven't seen since the Dicks Pass vicinity in Lake Tahoe's Desolation Wilderness. Its characteristic habit is one at high elevation where winter winds are extreme. The hemlock, on the other hand, requires some protection from the wind and typically grows where snow accumulation is deep and long-lasting. We can deduce, therefore, that this area is a very inhospitable place to spend a winter.

Our trail circles a small bowl that once spawned glaciers, then descends ⅔ mile north, usually on a gentle gradient, to a trail intersection on a windy saddle (7440-1.2). To avoid inclement weather, you can make a moderate one-mile descent northwest on this trail to a trail junction, then head 0.1 mile north to a roadend. This road descends almost one mile to Road 40N45, which we crossed earlier. On it you go 1¼ miles north to Deadfall Creek, which has many campsites on both sides of the creek just upstream from the road's bridge across it. In 260 yards you'll reach a junction with Road 42N17, which takes you 2 miles up to a saddle and the PCT.

The PCT leaves the saddle separating Bear Creek from North Fork Sacramento River and contours northwest through an essentially viewless fir forest to a crest. Watch for a notable change from ultramafic rocks to granitic ones along this traverse. We then traverse ½ mile southeast across steep, blocky slopes, passing above disappointing lower Deadfall Lake before coming to an 80-yard spur trail (7250-2.1) that goes over to shallow, enjoyable upper Deadfall Lake. Several campsites exist along the northwest shore's granitic rocks; more-secluded ones lie among the shadier southeast shore's ultramafic rocks. Upper Deadfall Lake is Section P's only trailside lake that merits an overnight stay.

Our trail heads north above the east shore of lower Deadfall Lake, which by late summer can lose most of its volume. Just past this view we cross the Deadfall Lakes trail (7230-0.3), which ascends southeast from the switchback on Road 42N17. Our well-graded trail then immediately crosses infant Deadfall Creek and starts an almost imperceptible descent north past springs, views and wildflowers. At a gully

P5

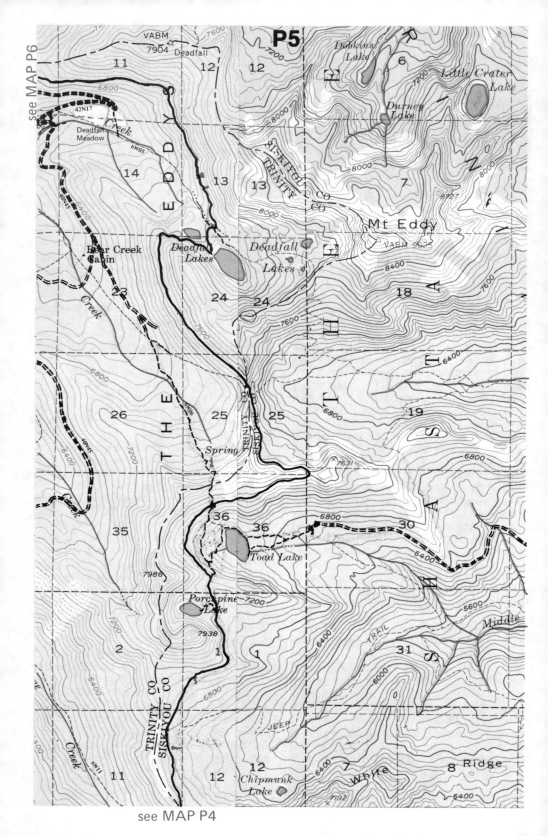

see MAP P6

see MAP P4

Bull Lake, Mt. Eddy and distant Mt. Shasta

with a permanent spring (7080-1.4), granitic rocks yield to ultramafic ones and the trail bends west. Mid-summer hikers may not find water until Chilcoot Creek, about 8 miles away. Late-summer hikers will have to travel even farther, going out of their way to drop to Bull Lake, about 1¾ miles beyond Chilcoot Creek.

The PCT continues its almost imperceptible descent, gradually losing red firs and white firs while gaining manzanitas and Jeffrey pines. Finally the trail curves north and, hemmed in by a jeep road on the right and Parks Creek Road 42N17 on the left, it reaches a shallow crest saddle (6830-1.6). The Parks Creek Road descends 14 miles northeast to Interstate 5, reaching it about 3 miles west of Weed. South this road switchbacks down to the Trinity River and follows it all the way to Highway 3. You won't find emergency help in that direction, except perhaps down at the *de facto* campground.

Ahead, the PCT starts along the east side of a jeep road, quickly crosses it, and then contours 0.4 mile out to a ridge that is ¾ mile due east of Cement Bluff. Your circular route will take 4.2 miles to reach a shallow saddle just west of that bluff. The trail stays almost level, circling around a logged forest in the basin below us. Halfway around the basin, just past a snowmelt creeklet, the trail becomes vague and you head 130 yards at 150°, passing through a small meadow before crossing an old trail by the meadow's edge (6770-3.0). Southbound,

the PCT crosses two more ephemeral creeklets, beyond which it crosses two dry gullies. It turns east in the second one and more or less contours over toward Bluff Lake, situated on Southern Pacific land. The lake has inviting campsites, which are sometimes used by car campers. If you plan to visit the lake, leave the trail before it climbs above steep, loose bouldery slopes. Above these, the trail tops out on an adjacent ridge (6650-1.6). The ridge, like Cement Bluff immediately east, is part of an old, eroded glacial moraine. This moraine is indeed cemented, for calcium, weathered from ultramafic rocks above the moraine, has combined with carbonate to form calcite, a strong cementing agent. Large boulders clinging to the overhanging north wall of Cement Bluff attest to the binding power of calcite.

Our route gently climbs just over ½ mile to usually dry Salt Lick Creek, then finishes its ascent, ⅓ mile later, on another glacial moraine. Now, in almost a mile, the trail gently descends to Chilcoot Creek (6650-1.7) and in 80 yards reaches a spring-fed creeklet. The creek typically dries up by late July, the creeklet by early September.

Past the creeklet, we contour just over ⅓ mile to another glacial moraine that is composed of large, cemented boulders just like those at Cement Bluff. In colder times, glaciers developed in all the canyons we've traversed, including Bull Creek canyon, just to the south. They all flowed down their canyons and con-

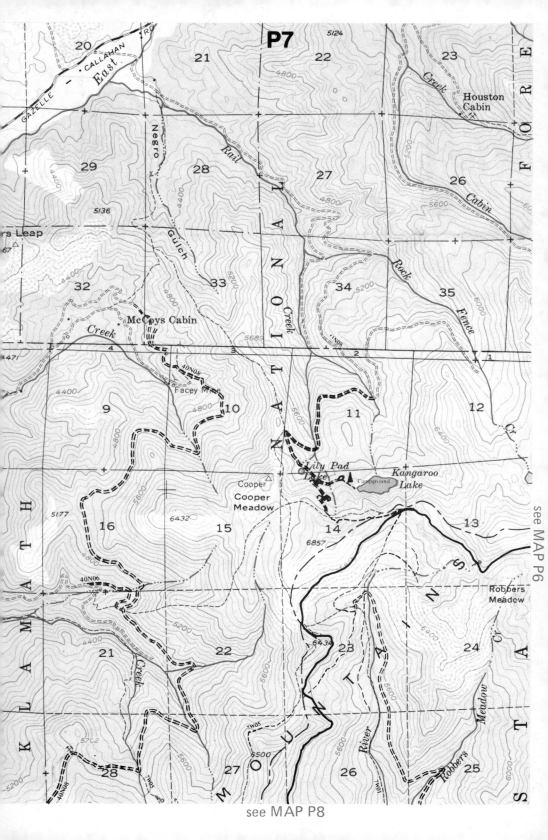

see MAP P6

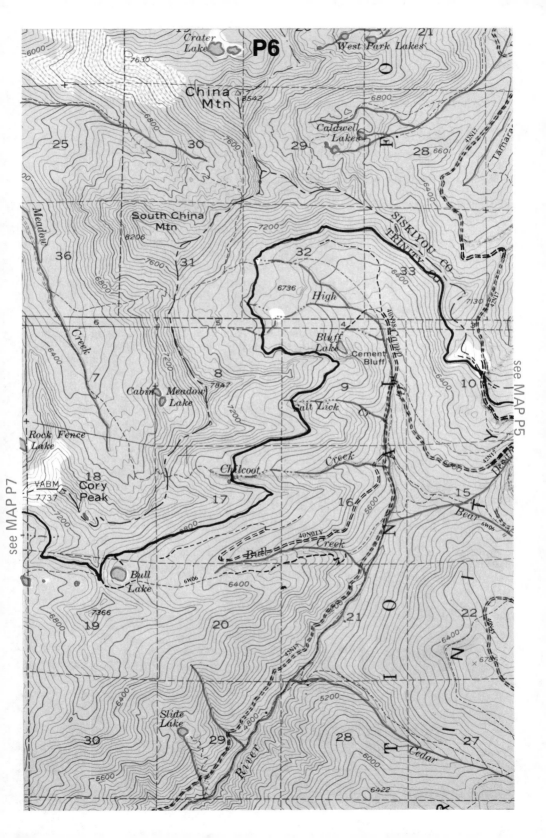

P6

verged to form an ice pack in the upper Trinity River basin. However, unlike Sierran glaciers, they didn't flow very far down-canyon, for they were too low in elevation to produce enough ice to do so. Beyond Bull Creek canyon we'll see dozens of canyons that held short, thick glaciers during the last major glacial advance.

From the bouldery moraine's crest the PCT climbs gently southwest up the north slopes of Bull Creek canyon. If you plan to camp at Bull Lake, which is one of the most accessible along our route, then leave the trail as soon as you see the lake. By the time you climb moderately to a poor, ¼-mile spur trail down to it, you've climbed too high. About ¼ mile past this trail and 10 yards below a crest saddle, you meet the old Sisson-Callahan trail. Eastward, this trail descends to Bull Lake in about ¼ mile. From the saddle (7100-2.1) the old trail descends past three shallow lakelets before turning north and dying out in Robbers Meadow, which is good for camping. This old trail, like so many others in the Klamath Mountains, was meant for stock animals. It goes past lakes and meadows, unlike the modern, freeway-like PCT. Equestrians will find the lack of pasturage very annoying.

Leaving a postcard view of Mt. Shasta over Bull Lake, we start a contour northwest, then gently descend west, staying well above the three lakelets. The middle one, larger in historic times, is now no more than a pond. We round a ridge, enter a glacial bowl and soon cross its seasonal creek. Beyond it, the trail circles the bowl, eventually dropping to a saddle (6770-1.6) on a secondary crest.

We contour from it and meet a seasonal spring in about two minutes. From it, as well as northwest of it on the trail, we have a view of miles of PCT as it threads along the upper west slopes of logged-over Little Trinity River can-

yon—Section P's most unsightly stretch. The tall, granitic mountain rising above the canyon is Craggy Peak, 8098' high and 9¾ miles away. The tiny settlement of Callahan lies at its north base, 5000' below the summit.

Our trail, contouring at first, changes to a gentle descent, then later, as we enter a logged-over area, shifts into a moderate descent as if to speed us through it. The descent momentarily ends on a broad saddle, where we meet two trail junctions (6480-0.9). Here, at Section P's mid-way point, we first meet Little Trinity River trail 7W01, which drops to relatively close logging roads. The second, in 20 yards, is the Sisson trail, which first climbs west and then descends to a road that leads down to Kangaroo Lake Road 41N08. Unseen Kangaroo Lake is scarcely ¼ mile north of our junction. Play it safe and use the trail and road down to the lake's campground, if you go there.

A long, gentle descent, hot on most summer afternoons, takes us southwest across brushy slopes of granitic Peak 6857 to the next saddle (6160-1.3). In ¼ mile we pass the faint Cooper Meadow trail 7W05, which climbs up Peak 6434, then descends into logging debris. We're treated to more views of grand-scale logging as we round the peak, passing outcrops of peridotite and serpentinite before descending to an abandoned logging road on another saddle (6030-0.9). Past it we contour ⅓ mile southeast to a ridge, from which we can look up-canyon and see 2 miles of constant-angle PCT tread. Here we encounter a few Douglas-firs and incense-cedars, which are near their upper-elevation limit. We now contour through an open forest, largely of white firs and western white pines, and through it view logging roads and logging scars. Just after crossing a conspicuous, rusty-boulder field, we meet two

P6, P7

The PCT traverses Peak 6857 while Craggy Peak, at left, rises above unseen Callahan

The sawtooth range above Tangle Blue Creek

springs (6080-1.3), the second one lying among azaleas, ferns and pitcher plants. This one usually lasts through mid-August, several weeks longer than its companion. The PCT quickly rounds a blocky ridge, then contours through a forest punctuated by two boulder fields of ultramafic rocks. Just past the second one, which provides a view of Lost Lake 0.4 mile below us, we cross a secondary ridge (6100-1.1). Now we contour northwest through a shady fir forest to lasting springs at the upper edge of a meadow (6110-0.7). Here, the Masterson Meadow trail begins a descent south along our meadow and the Cooper Meadow trail begins a climb northwest toward Peak 6434.

Immediately past the spring-fed meadow, we enter private land and cross a wide, densely forested saddle. You could camp on it. From its west end (6130-0.2), the Grouse Creek trail descends one mile northwest to Road 40N08, a major logging road that winds southwest to our next major destination, Scott Mountain Summit. The PCT angles southwest and climbs ¼ mile up to a shallow gap in the crest. From it you could go cross country, contouring ⅓ mile west to shallow Grouse Creek Lake. For camping, it certainly beats slimy bottomed, knee-deep Masterson Meadow Lake, ahead. Starting through a willow grove, we traverse southwest across partly logged slopes, entering a swale in about ⅔ mile. Just below us, in a

small meadow, is a spring, and this is a visual clue for those who want to visit Masterson Meadow Lake, which lies 100 yards south, over a low moraine. In a logging mess the trail crosses the lake's seasonal creek (6180-1.1). The lake is a 100-yard walk away, up boulders and logging debris. Fortunately, the lake's shore and the slopes above it are unscathed.

We now make a momentary climb to a minor ridge, then start a contour across Scott Mountain's southeast slopes. Trees give way to brush, and we see Mt. Shasta towering above rusty Mt. Eddy. To the south-southwest we see a sawtooth ridge, in Trinity Alps Wilderness, standing high above unseen Tangle Blue Creek. The PCT contours through an open forest to a rocky knoll on a ridge (6170-1.3), then starts a well-graded descent northwest. About ½ mile past the end of an old logging road, the trail switchbacks (5790-1.3), and then it descends 0.4 mile at a moderate grade to a narrow old road. On it we go 50 yards, then branch right, and in 75 more yards recross it. Immediately west, this road ends at newer, wider Road 40N08, which climbs northeast to Big Carmen Lake, Grouse Creek and beyond.

On an abandoned road we parallel Road 40N08 south for 250 yards, then west for 75 yards. With Scott Mountain Summit in sight, we walk 90 yards west on Road 40N08 to Highway 3 (5401-0.6). Just south of the summit you'll meet the entrance to Scott Moun-

P8

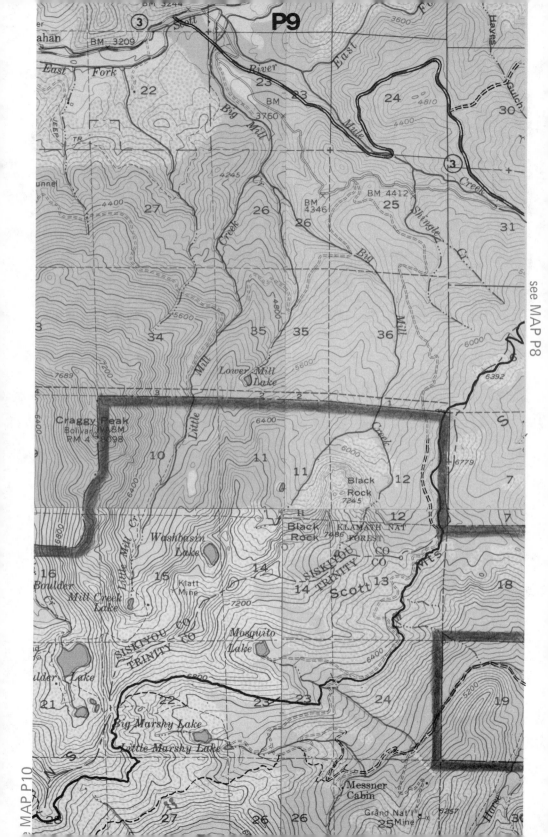

see MAP P8

e MAP P10

Big Carmen Lake

Grouse Creek Lake

Little Carmen Lake

SISKIYOU

TRINITY

CO

6610

3

BM 5192

32

33

34

35

Hayden Cabin

Scott Mtn
6829

Masterson Meadow Lake

Masterson Meadow

Lost Lake

Campground

BM 5401

Scott Mtn Summit

5

4

3

Masterson

Meadow

2

Creek

Scott

Cr

BM 5031

Dan Rice Cr

BM 4515

6227

Miller

Gulch

Mtn

Creek

4400

Miller

8

9

10

11

5873

5200

8

9

BM 4102

Scott

10

11

17

16

Mtn

Cr

15

14

Creek

BM 3296

Tangle

20

21

22

Trumble Ranch
BM 3193

23

3

RIVER

5600

5771

Sunflower Flat
BM 3095

29

28

27

26

Bear

BM 3016

TRINITY ALPS WILDERNESS

Groves

The northbound hiker's first good view of the Trinity Alps

tain Campground, a good if sometimes noisy place to spend the night. Sometimes the camp's water system works; at other times you have to head ¼ mile south to the cow-pied headwaters of Scott Mountain Creek. For better quality water, head ½–1 mile south on Highway 3 before dipping into the creek.

From Highway 3 at Scott Mountain Summit, eastbound hikers face a 700′ climb. Westbound, we face a 1200′ climb, but at least it is on shadier slopes. We walk 50 yards west on a wide road, which forks, with Road 40N63 starting north. We continue west on PCT tread, cross a good road in 300 yards, and shift to a moderate upward grade. Now the PCT switchbacks one mile up brushy slopes to a crest saddle, shaded by red firs, then switchbacks another mile, past firs and brush, to a second shady saddle. We stay on the crest barely ¼ mile before climbing west across a small, logged slope, then turning south to immediately enter the Trinity Alps Wilderness (6370-2.8). Wilderness permits are required. With the bulk of our ascent behind us, we now have an easy stroll south through a shady fir forest. Road 40N63, which we left by Scott Mountain Summit, gradually climbs to meet us, and we touch it on a shallow crest gap (6630-1.1). Mountain scenery opens up here, but after we walk a minute much more scenery explodes into view as we turn a minor ridge. A sawtooth range rises 3–4 miles to the south, and from each of the range's deep cirques a pair of fresh-looking glacial moraines stream either north down to Tangle Blue Creek, 2000′ below us, or

east down toward the Trinity River. Looking east-southeast, we see several waves of increasingly higher ridges, the highest one capped by the unmistakable Grey Rocks (7241′ and 7133′).

We now parallel Road 40N63, keeping below it to minimize its presence. In a few minutes Mt. Shasta comes into view as we continue across bushy slopes on a descending route. About ¾ mile past our crest crossing, we meet a seasonal spring, then about ¼ mile later cross a small meadow with two springs, a creeklet and cows. From it we angle south, crossing a final spring in about 100 yards. You can usually expect all these springs to dry up between late-July and mid-August.

With the road only a stone's throw above us, we parallel it southwest, mostly through dense brush. You'll see a recent landslide on the opposite side of the canyon before your trail curves west and crosses Road 40N63 (6210-2.0). If you have an emergency, you could follow Road 40N63 east to a nearby road junction and then take the westbound road ¾ mile up to Mosquito Lake. There lies a summer camp with leaders who take youths on rigorous backpack trips in this eastern part of the wilderness. From the lake, a use trail climbs southeast over a ridge and then descends southwest to the PCT.

From the road crossing we start toward that trail junction and in 90 yards cross a cow-frequented creeklet. Two minutes later we cross Mosquito Lake creek (6240-0.2), which bears the dubious distinction of being the first truly permanent stream the PCT has crossed since the Sacramento River, about 66 trail miles to the east. Our trail climbs ¼ mile south to a ridge, then turns west and climbs moderately up drier slopes of Jeffrey pine, incense-cedar and brush. Soon we meet the summer camp's primitive trail (6460-0.5), which crosses the PCT and continues southwest toward inviting Big Marshy Lake.

The PCT continues its moderate climb west through an open forest, which becomes dominated by western white pines before the trail starts to curve southwest up to a junction (7020-1.5). Here, a trail climbing from the Marshy Lakes basin crosses our route and pops over a crest saddle, about 70' above us. If you don't mind a half-mile-long, 400' drop, then take this trail down to East Boulder Lake, the largest lake close to Section P's PCT. Hikers with less energy can take this scenic drop halfway and choose a camp near one of three smaller lakes.

From the junction we embark south on an exceedingly curvy, exceptionally scenic stretch of PCT. At 7100' here, we're not at Section P's actual highest point, but we're at the place of highest elevation plants. Here you'll see rock-fringe and other species that grow around 10,000–11,000' in the High Sierra. Before mid-July, snow often buries part of this route. After ¾ mile of winding, we crest an east-trending ridge. A rocky ridge knoll, just east of the trail, provides a very impressive panorama of the Tangle Blue Creek and Eagle Creek canyons. From this ridge we climb ¼ mile southwest across warmer slopes to a notch in a ridge, then climb west a few minutes to the edge of a talus slope (7240-1.3). From here, in a small trough, you could head south cross country down to a knee-deep pond, 130' below the PCT, and camp near it.

Now the PCT climbs southwest, first across a talus slope of large, black boulders which, being ultramafic, will weather to a rust color. However, before that happens, more boulders are likely to break loose from the unstable bedrock above the trail. Our trail continues to climb, heading through a forest of red fir, western white pine and mountain hemlock as it tops out at 7400' elevation. You then descend a bit to a nearby ridge, on which you'll see weeping spruce. This subalpine tree, never common, is found only in the Klamath Mountains, and you can easily recognize it by its long, hanging branches that have hanging cones

up to 6 inches long—considerably longer than those of mountain hemlocks.

Westward, the PCT contours ¼ mile over to the east end of a windswept crest (7400-0.9), at which we enter an extensive granitic realm. From this east end a trail drops north into a glacial bowl that contains two shallow tarns, both quite exposed, though adequate for nearby camping when good weather prevails. With an average grade of 20%, the steep trail continues ½ mile farther down to sheltered campsites at Middle Boulder Lake, which is not worth the effort unless bad weather forces you off the crest.

Protected by wind-sheltering trees, our high route stays just below the crest then soon angles southwest and passes above a small meadow. Beyond it we see the sawtooth range above Tangle Blue Creek and the distant Grey Rocks. In ¼ mile we arrive at another meadow (7260-0.4), this one with a spring-fed creeklet that usually persists through early August. A ⅔-mile-long trail to Telephone Lake once headed west over the nearby crest saddle, but now the route is partly cross country.

The PCT next circles Eagle Peak, passing four springs that usually last through midsummer before reaching a junction above the north end of a crest saddle (7160-0.9). Bloody Run trail 8W04 starts south down the crest, intersecting Eagle Creek trail 7W05 in 130 yards. From this crest our trail climbs gently northwest, and midway along this ascent, the forest opens to give us our first good view of the Trinity Alps. The tallest peak, 19 miles to the southwest, is 9002' Thompson Peak, the Klamath Mountains' ermine-robed monarch. It is the only peak in the entire mountain system to support glaciers—two incipient ones exist.

On a crest at the end of our gentle climb (7300-0.6) we have a view north down West Boulder Creek canyon. The view is quite revealing, for you see all the way down to irrigated fields in the Scott River Valley, over 4000' below. Dry, brown hills line the valley and, closer by, Craggy Peak dominates our canyon's east flank. However, you can't help but notice the barren Cement Bluffs below the peak, whose origin is similar to the Cement Bluff we crossed more than 28 miles ago.

Our trail next descends to a windswept, sagebrush-covered crest saddle (7190-0.4), from which you could traverse cross country about 0.4 mile to unseen West Boulder Lake. The PCT contours west, first passing above a

P9, P10

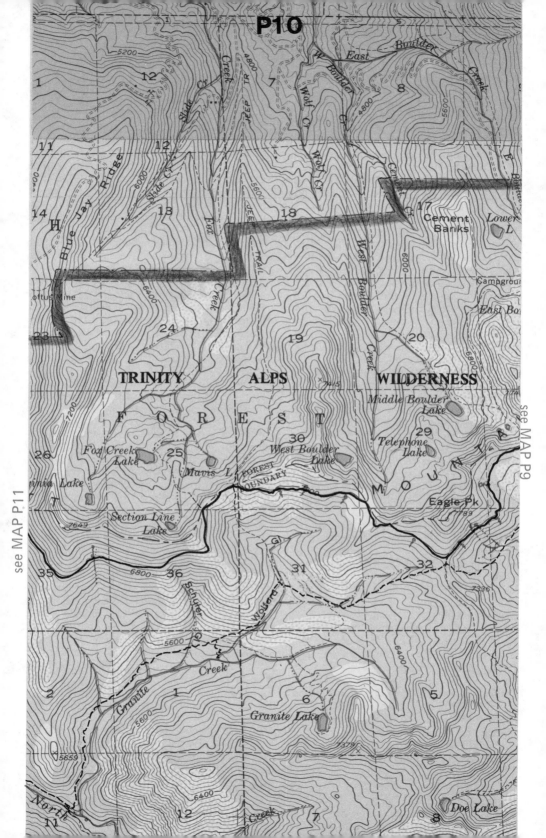

TRINITY   ALPS   WILDERNESS

F   O   R   E   S   T

see MAP P.11

see MAP P.9

View north down West Boulder Creek canyon:
Craggy Peak, Cement Bluffs below it and distant Scott River Valley

spring-fed alder thicket, then just below two others. At the east end of a long crest saddle, we come to a trail junction (7170-1.2). Trail 8W05 descends one mile south to a trail junction by Wolford Cabin Snow Survey Shelter while Trail 8W10 descends 3 miles north to Road 40N17.

We traverse the saddle, then climb southwest to a higher point on the crest (7230-0.3), and here Trail 8W07 starts a ⅔ mile descent to Fox Creek Lake. If you don't mind cross-country travel, aim for Section Line Lake, ¼ mile to the southwest and only 130′ below the trail junction.

Now we begin a long, erratic descent to Carter Meadows Summit. First we descend south to a dry ridge sporting greenleaf manzanitas and huckleberry oaks, then descend west through a forest of red and white firs. A swath of alders (6850-1.4) breaks the forest cover and in it we cross several freshets that provide water through most of the summer. Back in forest cover, we descend past an outcrop of car-size granitic boulders, then round a ridge that supports aromatic tobacco brush. Now we contour northwest past firs and brush, meeting a seasonal spring in an alder patch ¼ mile before we reach a crest saddle (6780-1.2), which generates Trail 9W01, dropping steeply south to Saloon Creek. From the saddle's west end (6780-0.1), another branch of Trail 9W01

drops south, an abandoned trail starts south, and a misleading, tempting trail contours southwest.

Leaving Shasta-Trinity National Forest and entering Klamath National Forest, we head ¼ mile northwest down an old jeep road, leave it in a shallow gully, and follow a poor, winding tread up to a gap in a narrow crest (6660-0.5). From it our poor segment descends too steeply to a switchback, then heads south at a moderate gradient down into a glaciated bowl. You can camp near its alder-lined creeklet. The last glacier to occupy this bowl left conspicuous morainal ridges on both sides of the bowl, and we can estimate by their lengths that the glacier was roughly ½ mile long. Earlier glaciers were longer and joined with others from adjacent canyons to flow north down the upper part of South Fork Scott River canyon.

On poor tread—one of the worst sections of "new standard" PCT—we descend north along the canyon's west slopes, then head west to a rocky point before descending southwest to a junction with South Fork Lakes trail 9W13 (5810-1.5). This trail climbs to South Fork Lakes through a giant, hanging jungle of alders. The exhausting push up through them certainly negates any advantages found at the lakes. These lakes lie in a deep, narrow cirque that shelters long-lasting snow patches which make the alder jungle possible. From the junc-

P10, P11

see MAP P13

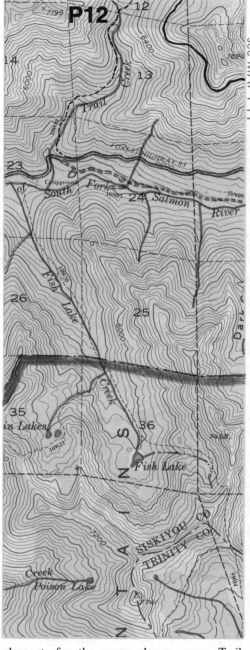

see MAP P11

tion the PCT descends to cross 10' wide South Fork Scott River (5780-0.2), crossing it near the base of the jungle. Early-season hikers can expect a wet ford.

Now our poor tread climbs gently northwest to a shallow gully with an alder-lined creeklet (5880-0.5), this one lasting through most of the summer. From the gully we make an annoyingly steep climb north to a ridge, where we take leave of Trinity Alps Wilderness. Just ahead lies Forest Road 93, which was blasted through Carter Meadows Summit (6160-0.4). From this paved road, a spur road—the old highway—climbs 100 yards southeast to a small flat with room enough for four cars or several hiking parties. If you dry-camp here, get water by descending ½ mile west on the highway to a road that branches southwest over to the adjacent headwaters of East Fork of South Fork Salmon River. Don't take the trail starting southwest from the summit, for it goes up to Hidden Lake, not down to the river. During mid and late summer, your route ahead can be waterless all the way to Bingham Lake's outlet creek, 7.1 miles ahead.

The first few miles of ascent westward are mostly across metamorphosed volcanic rocks that originally formed about 450–500 million years ago. They may have been part of an island chain, like Japan today, which later was crunched against sediments as a major oceanic plate slid beneath a continental one. Our last trail stretch north from South Fork Scott River climbed up a wedge of such sediments.

Climbing northwest, the PCT quickly crosses a road, which it later meets as another road branches southwest from it on a crest saddle (6660-1.1). The views back into deep South Fork Lakes canyon now lie behind us, and as we progress northwest, we can peer first into Long Gulch, then into Trail Gulch and Dark Gulch—all deeply cut by glaciers. In several places our trail almost tops the crest, and short walks to it presents the inquisitive hiker with views northeast across a variegated landscape. As our trail curves west under a crest saddle (6910-1.7), it starts a traverse past a row of ragged outcrops of ancient, metasedimentary rock known as phyllite. The metavolcanic rocks we've just seen are blocky and rather drab whereas the sparkling phyllite is composed of thin, beautiful bands of light and dark crystals. After ¾ mile of traverse below the phyllite outcrops, our trail peaks out at 7150' and starts a descent northwest. Our new views are not too

pleasant, for the upper slopes across Trail Creek canyon were ravaged by a fire. The slopes were then cleared and later terraced to reduce erosion and promote new plant growth.

Beyond more phyllite outcrops our trail levels off and contours northeast. In an old, selectively logged forest, the trail starts a short

CALLAHAN 7 MI.

see MAP P12

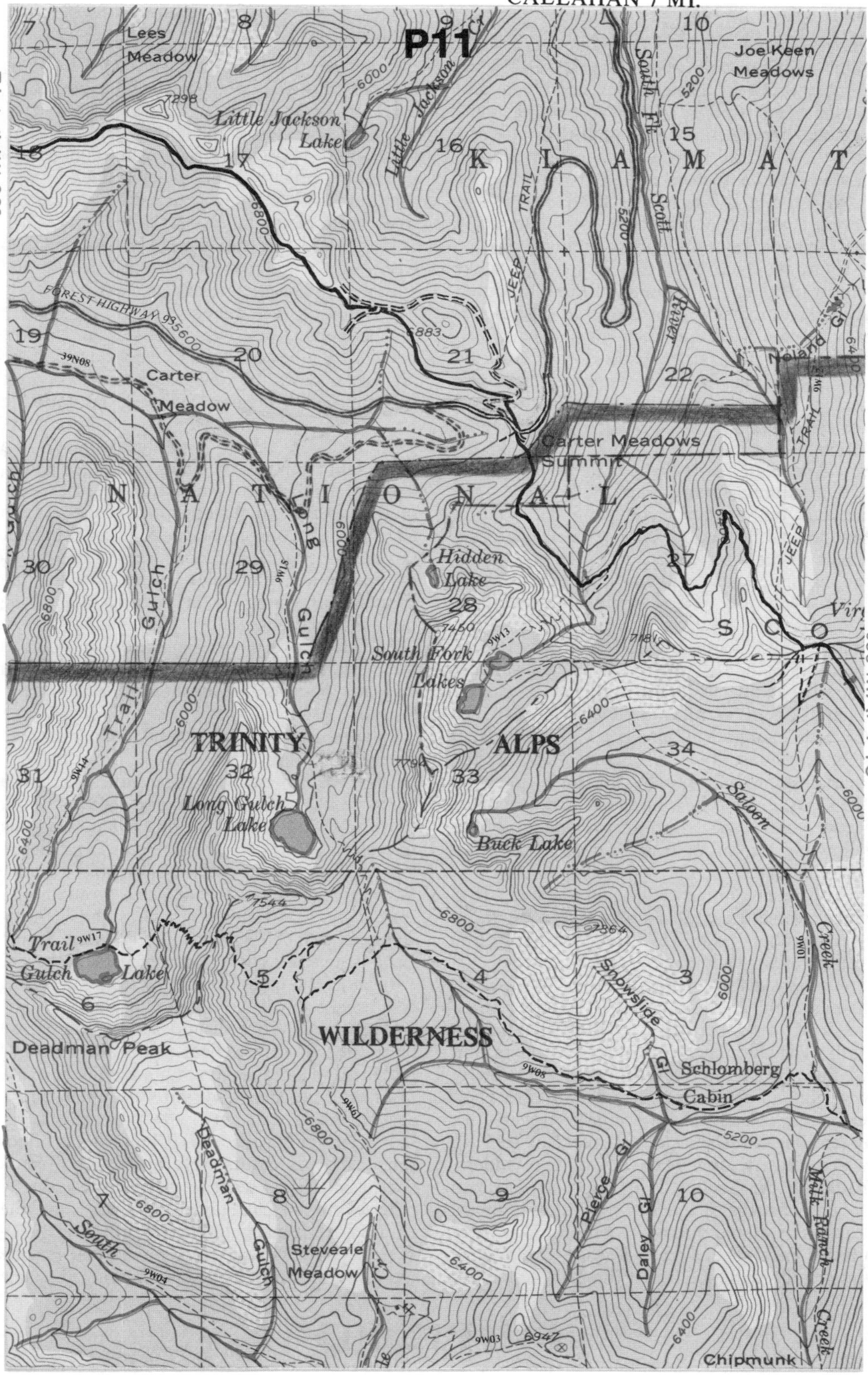

see MAP P10

climb to a jeep trail (6940-2.3). The PCT then climbs northwest through open grazing land to another jeep trail (7030-0.2), passing some seasonal springs along its way. If these are dry, take the jeep trail ¼ mile southeast down to an obvious saddle, then take one of two trails eastward ¼ mile down to the head of Jackson Creek. West, the jeep trail climbs ¾ mile gently up to camping possibilities at Siphon Lake.

From the jeep trail the PCT switchbacks almost to the granitic summit of Peak 7383, but at the last moment chooses to skirt past mountain hemlocks on its steep east slope. Definitely climb 150 bushy, bouldery yards to the peak's summit, for three major streams are born on the peak's three slopes. To the north lies the deep canyon of South Russian Creek, which drains into North Fork Salmon River. You'll soon start a 4⅓-mile traverse high along this granitic canyon's east wall. Above the canyon, the southeast limb of the Salmon Mountains, in Marble Mountain Wilderness, stands in the hazy distance. To the east you'll see large, deep Jackson Lake, on private land, 1200' below you. Fed by our peak's snowfields, the lake spills down to Jackson Creek, which empties into South Fork Scott River. Bits of Highway 3 and the Scott River lie below, about 10 miles away, and to the northeast your view extends about 50 miles to the high peaks of the Cascade Range. You also see Craggy Peak, 9 miles due east, but far-ranging views to the southeast are blocked by the high ridge the PCT has been following. However, we have views south and southwest down into the sprawling canyon of East Fork of South Fork Salmon River.

After taking in the views, go back to the trail and traverse the peak's steep east slope and a north-trending ridge. This stretch may be snowbound in early summer.

At a saddle we enter Russian Wilderness, then switchback southwest, and then resume our northward course, a trail blasted across cliffs. The cliffs give way to large boulders, and we hike through a fir forest interspersed chiefly with chinquapin, huckleberry oak and greenleaf manzanita. After almost a mile of traverse we reach Bingham Lake's outlet creek (6940-1.8), which mostly flows beneath large boulders. Although the Section P PCT passes close to dozens of lakes, it touches only three: Paynes Lake, ahead, and the two Deadfall Lakes, way to the east. The Forest Service could have easily routed the PCT past Bingham Lake, but

instead they chose to drop it 120' below the bouldery moraine damming the lake. Normally, a 120' climb would be an easy side trip but, as you'll find out, this climb is very bouldery, very steep, and very overgrown with almost impenetrable brush. If you're determined to visit this hidden lake, start your climb among the trees south of the lake's creek.

Northward, our trail is more brush-lined than tree-shaded, and we pass several creeks and springs of variable persistence. After nearly two miles of very gentle descent, we cross a distinctive bedrock water chute that is often dry. Just ¼ mile past it we round a ridge and are hit with a powerful view of a massive wall of granitic rock. The hiker can't help but feel that he is again back in the High Sierra. This South Russian Creek canyon certainly appears to be a transplant from that mountain range. In a way, it is a transplant. An extensive belt of granitic plutons was intruded along much of the western edge of Mesozoic-age North America, but later this belt was broken up. One section was transplanted hundreds of miles northwest to the San Francisco Bay area via lateral movement along the San Andreas Fault. The South Russian Creek pluton was transplanted tens of miles to the west. Originally it formed over by the Cascade Range, just north and east of Mt. Shasta.

In another ¼ mile we meet a boulder-strewn, alder-choked creek that usually flows through most of the summer, and then our trail begins a very gentle ascent, reaching Blakes Fork (6700-2.8) in ½ mile. Like an earlier creek, this one slides down a bedrock chute, and hence runs dry well before the alder-choked creek. We are now below the massive, granodiorite wall. Near its northwest crest stands a conspicuous pinnacle, The Statue. Unseen Statue Lake is just 100 yards north and 200' below it. After a gentle climb for about 15 minutes, our trail breaks through a notch in a granitic ridge. Instantly our views disappear, and the dense huckleberry-oak/greenleaf-manzanita brush is replaced by a red-fir/mountain-hemlock forest. Over the next, shady, viewless 1¾ miles, early-season hikers can anticipate snow problems. Our trail gently descends ⅓ mile to a minor ridge, then contours several hundred yards southeast. If you want to visit Statue Lake, ¼ mile away and 250' above the trail, leave the PCT where it starts to curve northeast (6930-1.1). If you pass a seasonal spring, you've gone too far. Despite its tiny size, Statue Lake once

P11, P12, P13

see MAP P14

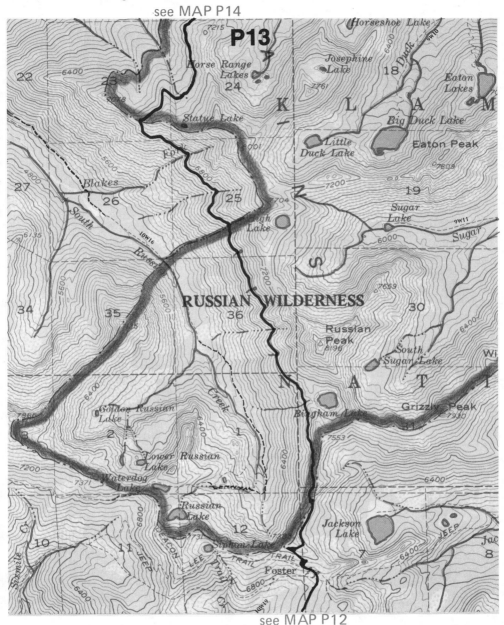

see MAP P12

had great fishing. However, now that the PCT has been built close to it, the lake is likely to be overfished.

Beyond a seasonal trailside spring we traverse a viewless mile to a saddle breached by Trail 9W09 (6710-1.1). West, this goes ½ mile to Road 40N54, which then descends about 9 miles to the Somes Bar-Etna Road, meeting it just east of the entrance to Idlewild Campground. The town of Sawyers Bar lies 5½ miles west down that road. East, Trail 9W09 goes about a mile to roads leading down to a section of Highway 3 between Callahan and Etna.

From the saddle we have a glimpse of Mt.

P13, P14

P14

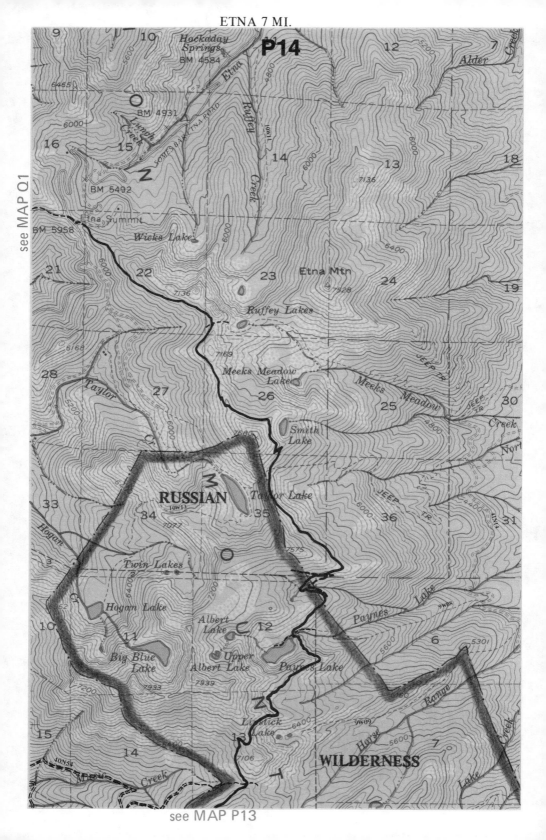

see MAP Q1

see MAP P13

Shasta, and then we have a few views west as we climb about ½ mile to a crest. We then traverse the headwall of a cirque, passing bedrock and tobacco brush, then descend northeast, staying high above Lipstick Lake and its eastern twin. Neither is worth visiting. With Paynes Lake next on our agenda, we turn a ridge, dip across a lakeless, glaciated bowl, then continue northeast down toward another ridge. Nearing it, we have a "top of the world" feeling, for we have excellent views east down into agricultural Scott River Valley. Low, dry mountains rise to its east, and far beyond them rises our old acquaintance, snowy Mt. Shasta. More such views will appear—and improve—until we leave the Smith Lake environs.

We duck around the upcoming ridge and in ⅓ mile reach Paynes Lake Creek, with a descending, north-bank trail (6460-2.2). Paynes Lake is just a few heartbeats up the trail. Hemmed in by steep slopes, the lake is fairly scenic, but it is also deficient in campsites. You might set up camp on the lake's moraine, just south of the trail junction. Better camping lies ahead, so follow the PCT ½ mile northeast to a ridge, from which it parallels an old logging road, immediately below, west to the headwaters in a glacial bowl (6620-0.7). You could establish camp either on the old road or near the trail just before it crosses a permanent creek. Past that one you go 70 yards north to a seasonal one, then make a short, moderate climb to an abandoned logging road that steeply descends to the one we've just paralleled. The road continues to climb, as does our trail, out to a ridge. Here, if you look south, you'll see pairs of glacial moraines descending east from Paynes Lake canyon and the canyons south of it. The glaciers that left these lateral moraines averaged about 2–3 miles long and they descended to about the 4000' level. Though short, they were quite massive, becoming up to 400–500' thick.

We now head northwest across selectively logged slopes, ending our traverse at a trail junction (6970-1.5) by a notch in a knife-edge ridge. The trail crossing the notch makes a steep 550' descent to large Taylor Lake. You might brave this knee-knocking descent, for the lake has ample flat ground at its north and south ends. Over the last 2 miles, the PCT has flirted with the Russian Wilderness boundary,

but now the trail leaves the Wilderness for good as it climbs just over ¼ mile—rising above a tree farm—to a switchback near the crest of a descending ridge. If you want to visit Smith Lake, seen from the nearby crest, leave the trail here and descend the brushy, bouldery ridge.

In ⅓ mile the PCT climbs to a spectacular viewpoint above the lake, and one can see that its steep, bouldery shoreline makes camping likely only at the forested notch above its northeast shore. Our views east to Mt. Shasta and northeast to southern Oregon's Siskiyou Mountains end as our trail turns west to contour through a mountain-hemlock forest. Westward views appear as we cross a granitic crest, and among sagebrush and mountain mahogany we descend ⅓ mile to a level stretch of crest. We then round the west ridge of a crest summit before descending to a jeep-road junction (6910-2.0) immediately beyond a logged area. East, this road immediately tops a saddle, then descends ¼ mile to the small, cow-habited basin of Upper Ruffey Lake. Although the glacier that scoured this lake basin flowed mostly north, today the lake drains east below the south slopes of Etna Mountain. Standing at the brink of the lake's north shore, you'll also note that the former cirque glacier spilled north into another cirque (Lower Ruffey Lake), which in turn spilled north into a third cirque—an interesting arrangement. Given that the next decent camping area with water is in the Shelly Meadows area, 12½ miles away, you should seriously consider camping at Upper Ruffey Lake.

Leaving the nearby saddle and its jeep road, the PCT also leaves the granitic landscape as it descends northwest moderately down toward Etna Summit. The first half is through a shady forest growing in soil derived from mafic intrusive rocks. The second half is through an open forest growing in soil derived from metavolcanic rocks, which we'll tread most of the way to Shelly Meadows. At the southeast edge of Etna Summit, we cross the summit's older road. Immediately beyond it we cross a trailside parking area that can hold a dozen cars, then take a brief trail segment over to the wide, gravel Somes Bar-Etna Road, which we cross at the northwest edge of Etna Summit (5960-1.7).

P14

Summit Lake and a landslide on Peak 7401

Section Q: Etna Summit to Seiad Valley

Introduction: Although this stretch is one of the shortest sections in this California PCT guide, its features are still quite diverse. Little more than half the length of the previous section, it nevertheless has more rock units, each with its own characteristic hue and texture. And with more rock units comes greater diversity of wildflowers and other vegetation. Over the first two thirds of the route, the trail stays high, generally traversing from the head of one glaciated canyon to the head of another. Midway through your journey you pass the crown jewels of the Marble Mountain Wilderness: Black Mountain, Kings Castle and, of course, Marble Mountain itself. With about a half-hour's walk you can make a side trip up to the top of Marble Mountain and survey much of northwestern California. The last third of the route is mostly a long descent through a deep canyon that nurtures a virgin Douglas-fir forest. The walk through it is a refreshing change from your typical crest hiking, which all too often can be deficient in water. If you're hiking this section only, you'll want to end (or start) at Grider Creek Campground rather than at Seiad Valley, for the 6½ miles at the north end are along roads. Then your route is a comfortable 50-mile backpack hike.

Declination: 17¼°E

Mileages:	South to North	Distance between Points	North to South
Somes Bar-Etna Road at Etna Summit	0.0		56.1
		11.2	
Shelly Fork trail/Shelly Meadows trail	11.2		44.9
		4.8	
Kidder Lake trail	16.0		40.1
		4.6	
Red Rock Valley trail/west Cold Spring trail	20.6		35.5
		3.3	
Marble Valley G. S./Canyon Creek trail	23.9		32.2
		5.3	
Paradise Lake	29.2		26.9
		1.6	
Bear Lake-Turk Lake trails	30.8		25.3
		4.0	
Buckhorn Spring	34.8		21.3
		7.8	
Grider Creek trail at Road 46N72	42.6		13.5
		7.0	
Grider Creek trail at Grider Creek Campground	49.6		6.5
		6.5	
Highway 96 at Seiad Valley.	56.1		0.0

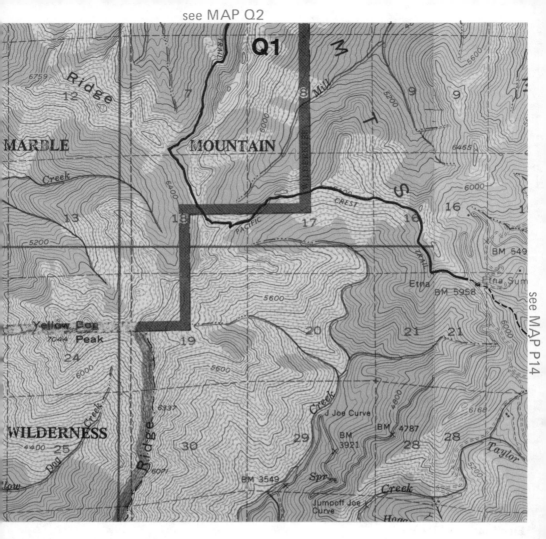

see MAP P14

Supplies and Permits: See "Supplies and Permits" in Section P.

Potential Problems: Until mid-July, snow may obscure parts of the route, as in the Sierra Nevada. Also, because the Marble Mountain Wilderness has become increasingly popular—particularly since the publication of David Green's excellent guidebook to the area—it may develop a bear problem similar to the one in Yosemite National Park (see Section I: "Bears"). As of yet they aren't a major nuisance, but generally don't leave your pack unattended.

From the northwest edge of Etna Summit, the PCT leaves the Somes Bar-Etna Road and makes a usually gentle climb, first west, then north to a crest saddle. After climbing briefly, the trail bends westward down to a longer saddle, from which it contours across a brushy, south-facing slope. South, you'll see snowy Thompson Peak, which at 9002' is the paramount peak in the Klamath Mountains and the only one to sport glaciers—two miniscule ones. We rejoin the crest and in 200 yards enter Marble Mountain Wilderness (wilderness permits required). Staying close to the crest, we have views north down into deeply glaciated

Mill Creek canyon and views south into less glaciated North Russian Creek canyon. Our trail exits from but soon re-enters the wilderness, doing so as it heads northwest toward a saddle. We cross the crest and for just over ½ mile we have views down into Big Creek canyon before we hit our sixth saddle, a notch at the south end of Razor Ridge (6690-3.7).

Here, at the head of Pointers Gulch, we start a forested descent northeast, quickly passing a seasonal seep that drips from a massive, mossy outcrop above the trail. Later, after we traverse open, rocky slopes, we cross an ephemeral creeklet, bend east into a bouldery gulch and cross a more persistent creeklet (6450-1.0). North, our route usually descends almost imperceptibly, rounding two bowls before veering west out to a ridge and north past it to another creek (6170-2.0), the best one so far. Beyond the next ridge, we contour more-open slopes, passing a seasonal creek, then in ⅓ mile rejoining the crest at the head of Babs Fork Kidder Creek (6290-0.9). The trail skims a long crest saddle, which divides metavolcanic rocks to the southeast from metasedimentary ones to the northwest, then climbs gently west and then gently north, coming close to the sum-

mit of Peak 6667 before plunging to the saddle just north of it (6430-1.4). From here you can drop east into the head of a deep canyon and reach Cub Bear Spring, one of several in the canyon that give birth to Glendenning Fork Kidder Creek.

On the PCT we climb ⅓ mile north, almost to the top of another crest saddle, this one dividing metasedimentary rocks to the southeast from younger granitic rocks to the northwest. Starting a descent west, we come upon a short trail that drops to nearby Shotgun Spring, in a meadow below the trail. Continuing on a usually gentle grade, we soon turn northwest and descend brushy slopes that permit us to survey half a dozen major gulches that feed into the canyon of Right Hand Fork of North Fork Salmon River. Crossing a lateral moraine left by a former glacier, we momentarily come to Shelly Lake's outlet creek (6150-1.7), your first usually reliable trailside creek. You could camp nearby or, better yet, just ahead, near the Wilson Cabin ruins, which are immediately past the north tip of southern Shelly Meadow. In a fir-and-hemlock forest, we quickly reach a junction (6220-0.3), from where a lateral trail descends ⅓ mile northwest, meeting the Shelly

Q1, Q2

Deep Cliff Lake and shallow Campbell Lake

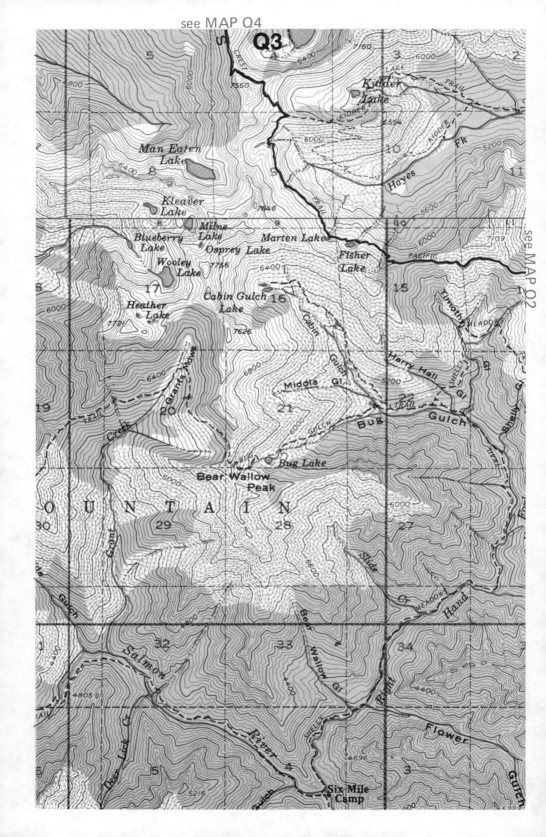

Q3

see MAP Q2

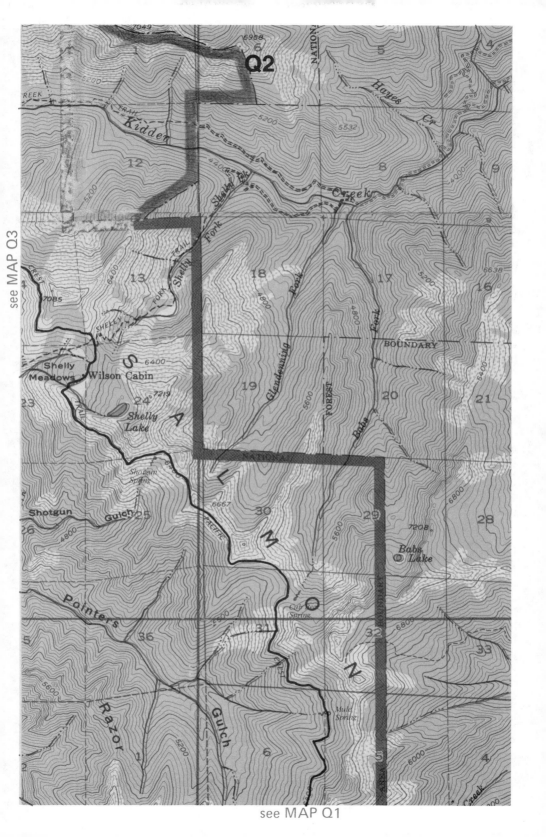

see MAP Q3

see MAP Q1

Light Marble Mountain and dark Black Mountain

Fork trail in northern Shelly Meadow. You can find more water and a possible campsite in this vicinity. Curving north, we make a brief struggle up the PCT to a crest junction with the Shelly Fork trail (6340-0.2), which descends steeply northeast. All the trails you meet in the wilderness that descend east or northeast go to roads that take you ultimately down to paved Scott River Road, on which you can hitch a ride east to the small but growing town of Fort Jones.

In a minute's time we meet the Shelly Meadows trail, which descends 7½ miles to Six Mile Camp, then 6¼ miles south to a wilderness trailhead at Mule Bridge. If you were to head 2¼ miles south from it on Road 41N37, you'd reach Idlewild Campground by the Somes Bar-Etna Road. This highly scenic route was once part of the PCT, and it is preferred by those who get tired of continual crest hiking.

Immediately beyond the Shelly Meadows trail our PCT route turns west to start a contour around Peak 7085 to a saddle, then west below Peak 7109 to another saddle (6410-2.2), this one at the head of Timothy Gulch. After a short descent you switchback down to a permanent creeklet (6190-0.3), with campsites, then continue on to more sites by Fisher Lake (6220-0.4). Climbing up open, metavolcanic bedrock, we soon reach smaller Marten Lake (6360-0.3), with no real campsites, though it provides a swim, as Fisher Lake does, after the snow melts in mid-July. Taking advantage of various bedrock ledges, our trail undulates northwest, passing a pond on a bench just before it makes a ⅓-mile-long climb to a ridge junction with the Kidder Lake trail (6640-1.6). Kidder Lake lies just over one mile down this trail and the trailhead is 3½ miles farther.

You now face Section Q's steepest climb, which switchbacks up to a crest above Cliff Lake. Take lots of rests on this ascent and enjoy the profusion of midsummer wildflowers and the views east down 2000′ deep Kidder Creek canyon. Gem-shaped Cliff Lake, seen from the crest, is 175′ deep—the deepest lake in this wilderness. In the past, glaciers as thick as 800′ developed in this cirque and flowed 6 miles down Shackleford Creek canyon.

Until late summer the hiker faces a traverse west across a snowfield (which is an impassable barrier for stock). Once beyond it we see Campbell Lake, resting below Cliff Lake, and then we traverse past mountain hemlocks up to a shallow gap in a serrated crest (7230-0.9). Leaving Section Q's high point here, we make an initial descent southwest, then turn north and descend to a saddle. Leaving that, we soon lose our spectacular lake views and make a traverse to another crest saddle, this one cloaked with Shasta red fir, mountain hemlock and western white pine. Advancing toward the next saddle, we climb northwest, cross an open field of ankle-high eriogonum, wind through a near-crest forest, and momentarily descend to the first of two scenic switchbacks. Don't get too close to the precipitous edge, for the landslide debris you see scattered around Summit Lake, way below you, came from the area you're standing on. A large landslide scar on the canyon's opposite wall gives further testimony to the instability of this glaciated canyon's overly steep walls.

We now switchback steeply down the crest to its saddle (6590-1.8), from where the Shackleford Creek trail descends 0.4 mile to a bowl 300 yards below Jewel Lake, then switchbacks ½ mile down to Summit Lake. From the junction we engage a northwest traverse through a thinning forest that gradually is replaced with abundant brush and a smattering of Jeffrey pines. The forest cover returns again as we regain the crest and get our first views of the Marble Mountain area, dominated by Black Mountain, named for its dark gray-brown cap of metamorphosed sediments. Closer to us are the burnt-red slopes above Red Rock Valley. These rocks are ultramafic intrusives, and if you were to break open a fresh sample, you would see that it is blackish-green, for it is partly composed of the green mineral olivine. This mineral and its associates, being rich in iron, weather to produce the rust-colored landscape.

A two-minute walk down the crest brings us to an important trail junction (6310-1.6). From this level spot a steep trail winds about 100 yards north, dying out on a ridge just a few feet away from the Red Rock Valley trail, which is a good route out to civilization. To the south, another trail weaves ¼ mile moderately down to a trail junction just above Cold Spring bench. With at least three springs and ample camping space, the bench is a welcome goal for weary PCT trekkers. On the shady crest the PCT continues a traverse to a second set of trails (6370-0.3). The Red Rock Valley trail drops ¼ mile east to the ridge that the north-winding trail died out on, then continues ¼ mile north down this glacial moraine before curving northwest and giving rise to a spur over to a vegetated lakelet. Camping here is definitely inferior to camping by Cold Spring. Southbound trekkers reach the spring by leaving our crest junction and descending 0.3 mile to the previously mentioned junction just above the Cold Spring bench.

Our crest route now climbs a bit west to the east end of the Shadow Lake trail (6480-0.3). This trail, sometimes hard to follow, goes ½ mile northwest over to the lake, which is perched on the brink of a cliff above Sky High Lakes. You'd be hard pressed to find a more dramatic campsite. Westbound, the PCT traverses the southeast slope of Peak 6817, then on its southwest slope encounters a short, sometimes hidden trail traversing over to nearby Soft Water Spring. The PCT passes just a few yards above this seeping spring (6580-0.6), and where it does, the west end of the Shadow Lake trail takes off over the adjacent crest, then drops ¼ mile northeast to that lake.

A deep marble fissure

We now make an easy ¼ mile descent to a crest saddle above the Sky High Lakes, then stick close to the crest as we contour northwest to the first of two Sky High Valley trail junctions (6400-0.9). The first path climbs 60 yards to the crest, where it joins the second, which originates from our trail in 120 yards. Past it we follow the crest down to a saddle with a trail intersection (6232-0.5). From here a wide trail to Big Elk Lake descends west, the Marble Rim trail—a footpath—continues ahead along the crest, and the PCT drops north into deep Little Marble Valley. For perhaps the best view in all of Marble Mountain Wilderness, hike ⅔ mile northwest on the Marble Rim trail, then climb cross country up to the nearby summit of 6880' high Marble Mountain. From it, most of the wilderness spreads below you. You can distinguish the different kinds of rocks: medium-gray marble, light gray granodiorite, brownish metavolcanics and rusty ultramafics. Red Mountain, the hugh ultramafic mass to the east, is capped by 8299' Boulder Peak, which is the highest mountain in the wilderness and one of the highest in the Klamath Mountains.

Back on the PCT, you drop into Little Marble Valley, and in about ⅓ mile your trail levels just before it starts a northeast descent. From that level area an old tread—essentially cross-country—descends 0.2 mile east to a spring. You may wonder why this canyon and other ones nearby don't have glacial lakes, for they were glaciated at least as much as the Sky High, Summit and Cliff lakes canyons. The

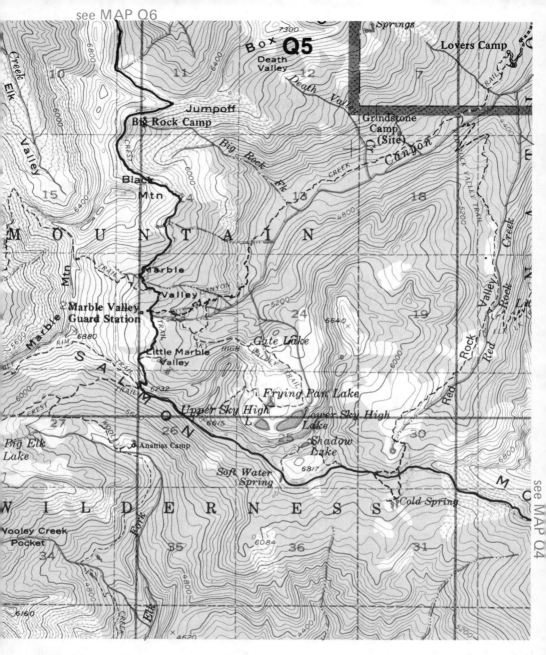

answer lies in the rock—marble—which dominates our area. About ¼ mile before our trail reaches the Marble Valley Guard Station, we encounter an excellent outcrop of these rocks and can see why they can't hold lakes: water percolates right through them. Just east of the trail you can find a number of fissures and caves. This marble is just a 600′ thick stratum

out of a total of more than 10,000′ of sediments deposited on the North American continental shelf during the Triassic period. Most of these sediments were volcanic in origin, for back then the continent's edge was a scene of intense volcanic activity. During a fairly long period of volcanic quiescence, coral reefs gradually built up a thick layer of limestone, which

Q5

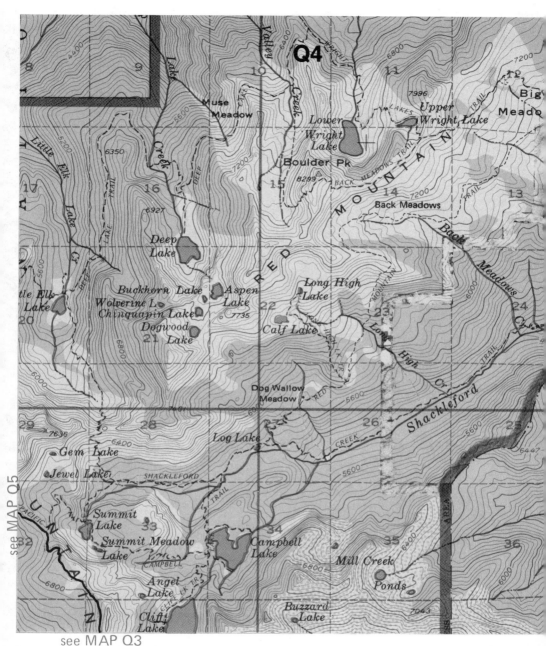

see MAP Q5

see MAP Q3

later was metamorphosed, along with the other Triassic sediments, and it became transformed into marble.

Beyond the marble outcrop we make a brief, steep descent to a creeklet, then climb 90 yards to the Marble Valley Guard Station, which is immediately west of a junction with the Canyon Creek trail (5700–1.0). A two-hour walk northeast down it takes you to the wilderness' principal trailhead parking lot—the starting point for many weekend hikers. You might plan to camp in Marble Valley, for the next site, Big Rock Camp, has limited space. From the junction we make a short climb north-northeast to a low ridge, then angle west-northwest up it for 200 yards to a junction with the Marble Gap

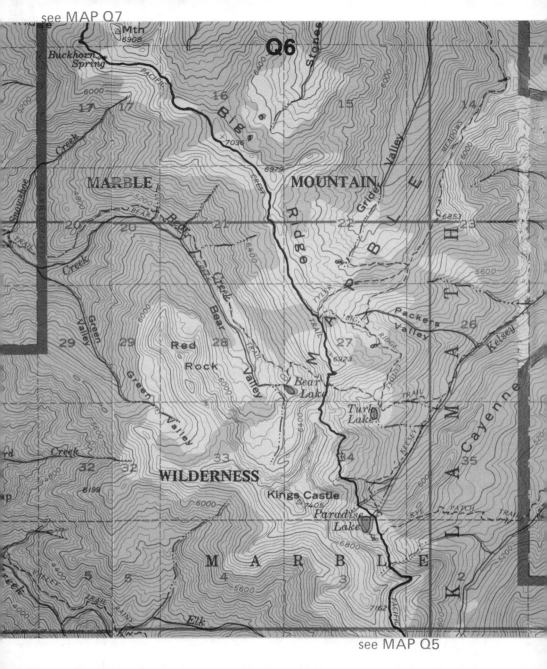

see MAP Q5

trail (5840-0.3), forking left. We fork right, cross the infant Canyon Creek in a couple of minutes, and then wind steeply north before starting a traverse around Black Mountain—the wilderness' most eye-catching peak. Hikers sometimes mistake it for Marble Mountain, which is hardly more than a high crest that one can pass without even recognizing. The PCT climbs northeast through a dense forest to Black Mountain's southeast ridge, traverses the mountain's glaciated east bowl, and then executes short switchbacks northwest up to some prominent trailside caves in a thick bank of marble. On the opposite canyon wall, to the

Q5

northeast, you'll see a continuation of this thick, gray band. Its thickness indicates the maximum depth to which any of our caves descend.

About 200 yards past these caves we pass under a vertical wall of loose, unstable marble, beneath which unsuspecting hikers have camped. Our route soon leaves its cover of hemlock, pine and fir to traverse northwest across a large, glaciated bowl. When the trail bends north, it enters forest cover again, then emerges in a smaller bowl. In it you'll recognize Big Rock, on your left, which has broken off from upper slopes. Immediately beyond it a poor 100-yard-long trail (6640-2.2) descends down-canyon to Big Rock Camp, which can be packed with up to eight persons. Our trail next bends eastward, passing a second poor lateral down to the camp before reaching the Jumpoff (6650-0.4), a low point on a narrow crest. Looking north from it we can see the twin summits of ultramafic Red Butte, which stands just northeast of Kangaroo Mountain and considerably west of Condrey Mountain, the highest peak on the horizon. In about four days you'll pass through this part of the Siskiyou Mountains and enter Oregon.

Starting northwest, we begin a long traverse above the headwaters of South Fork Kelsey Creek, cross a northeast ridge of Peak 7162, then make a minor descent ½ mile to a notch (6190-2.2) in the southwest end of Cayenne Ridge. From the notch a faint tread—the Rye Patch trail—starts northeast along the ridge before making a 1¾ mile drop to Road 44N44. The PCT leaves the notch and descends moderately northwest to the outlet of popular Paradise Lake (6130-0.2). Just beyond the ford is a good-sized campsite by the lake's edge. Others can be found by taking the lake's loop trail to the opposite shore. All these camps are illegal since they are within 200' of the lakeshore. You're not supposed to camp in meadows either, and since the lake is surrounded by meadows, you're stuck. However, you should be able to find a site among red firs about 0.1 mile east of the lakes's outlet. This murky lake will be your last reliable water source until sometimes-polluted Buckhorn Spring 5.6 easy miles farther. Kings Castle, the first major landmark southbound PCT trekkers see in the Marble Mountain Wilderness, is the small marble block atop the high crest above the lake.

Leaving the lake, our trail contours, then makes an increasingly steep ascent to a ridge, from which it traverses northwest under the nearly vertical north end of the Kings Castle

Q5, Q6

Paradise Lake and Kings Castle

see MAP Q6

ridge. In ½ mile we descend the main crest north to a saddle junction (6580-1.6). From it, two ducked trails descend steeply, one ⅔ mile east to very shallow Turk Lake, the other ⅔ mile west to slightly deeper Bear Lake. The latter is more inviting, and the drop to it is "only" 600'; the drop to Turk Lake is 750'.

We switchback north up the rocky crest, which is sparsely covered with Jeffrey pines. Growing on soil derived from ultramafic rock, these trees seem to do better on such soil than do the wilderness' other conifers. Upon approaching Peak 6923 we get an excellent view back at Kings Castle, then onward we keep

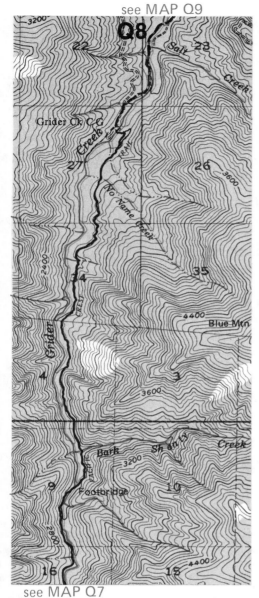

Faint, distant Mt. Shasta above Big Ridge

447

close to the crest and soon reach an open saddle with more views (6800-0.7). Here the Big Ridge Cutoff trail drops east into Packers Valley, seen below, while the Tyler Meadows trail starts a contour northeast to the wilderness boundary and the start of Road 45N77. Continuing along Big Ridge, we contour north, occasionally touching the actual crest and then finally descending its north end to a saddle below Buckhorn Mountain. Here we leave the last of the prominent outcrops of marble and traverse west across the mountain's open, south slope, cross its southwest ridge and immediately encounter Buckhorn Spring (6570-3.3).

Our trail route, largely open for the last few miles, will now be mostly forested all the way to the Klamath River. Leaving the spring, we quickly enter a cover of hemlock and pine and soon descend to a small flat with a tiny pond (6300-0.3). Shasta red firs begin to give way to white firs and incense-cedars as we descend north and pass two springs that run well into August. After a ⅓-mile traverse from the second, our trail comes to a junction with the Huckleberry Mountain trail (6020-1.0), which winds 2½ miles down to a road that goes to Cold Spring and Road 46N77. That road traverses many miles north on Grider Ridge before meeting Road 46N66, which descends east to Grider Creek Campground and Seiad Valley.

After a two-minute walk northeast to a crest saddle, we start a 4400', 13¼-mile drop to that campground. Among red firs, our well-graded trail starts a shady descent southeast, leaving the north boundary of Marble Mountain Wilderness as it turns east. We quickly reach a descending ridge and encounter white fir, Douglas-fir and even sugar pine. At a logged-over area midway along the first leg of our

Q6, Q7

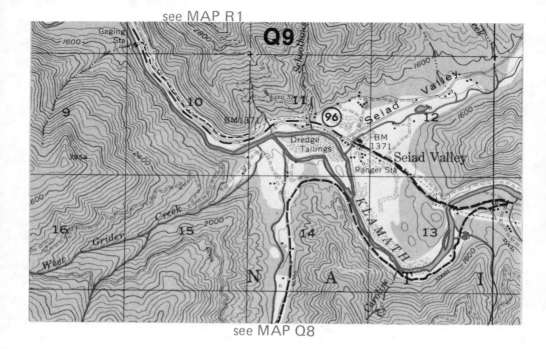

see MAP Q8

descent, we can look north down our **V** canyon and above it see the distant twin peaks, Kangaroo Mountain and Red Butte. In about two days we'll reach the crest of the Siskiyou Mountains in the notch between these two peaks. Cook and Green Pass is the deep gash to the east of Red Butte.

The first leg of our descent ends where we cross a good road (5300-1.5). From it we start north along the ridge on an abandoned road and follow it as it quickly switchbacks southwest into brush fields along a creek. We re-enter forest and parallel another good road, which curves around our descending ridge, and then our trail crosses the road (4800-1.0). We arc

north, passing lots of trailside thimbleberries, which are indicative of our lower elevation, then soon descend southeast on a brush-lined, abandoned road (4820-1.0). In ¼ mile we turn north and descend through an old logging-scar to our last logging-road crossing (4370-0.9). Our trail starts north but quickly curves south, winding ⅓ mile in and out of gullies down to a switchback. Now we have a shady descent north in a virgin forest of Douglas-fir. You may hear Cliff Valley creek, a couple of hundred feet below you, but the slopes are too steep and vegetated to warrant a descent to it. After ¾ mile, we bend southwest into the gully of an early-summer creeklet and then, a few minutes

Q7

Kangaroo Mountain and Red Peak: twin peaks above Grider Creek Canyon

later near a second creeklet, we see our first madrones, with their rusty, slick bark. In ½ mile our trail bends west and momentarily crosses refreshing Cold Spring creek, then in 150 yards ends at the south tip of Road 46N72 (3200-2.0). Along this road you'll find the only spacious campsites that exist in this northern stretch of Section Q.

After 150 yards of northward walking, we leave the road and parallel musical Cliff Valley creek down to Grider Creek, which we cross via footbridge (2870-0.8) immediately beyond the two creeks' confluence. A horse path first crosses Cliff Valley creek, then Grider Creek, then heads northwest to the footbridge. Now above the east bank, our trail starts north down Grider Creek canyon and passes the first of many marble outcrops in ¼ mile. The trail stays fairly close to Grider Creek, but the canyon's slopes are so steep and the vegetation so thick that access to it is usually difficult. After a pleasant walk, we recross the creek on a second footbridge (2640-1.3). We now make a momentary climb, then traverse above a short stretch of marble-walled Grider Creek, which playfully cascades from pool to pool. Just ¼ mile past the bridge, we enter a small hollow in which a creek flows underground through an alluvial fan to nearby Grider Creek. Through the trees you'll see Rancheria Creek also joining our energetic stream.

In another ¼ mile we spy our first trailside poison oak, which is another indicator of our lower elevation. Douglas-firs still predominate, though we pass through a grove of madrones just before we cross our third footbridge (2330-1.7). Next we have a long, eastbank walk, and we weave in and out of gullies—most of them minor—before the trail switchbacks. If you're on horseback, continue momentarily ahead down to the creek, which you cross, and then head briefly up an old road to where PCT trail tread ends. If you're on foot, angle left and follow the PCT over to a nearby bridge that spans Grider Creek (1690-4.1). Then in 40 yards you reach trail's end at the old road. Here, in Grider Creek Campground, we face an all-road route to Seiad Valley. For years the Forest Service tried to piece together a trail route to Highway 96, but private lands and the prohibitive cost of a massive horse-bridge across the Klamath River ultimately scuttled the project. Hence, you can consider the following route as *permanent* Pacific Crest Trail.

Grider Creek

We walk past the small campground, which has most of its sites to the left and upstream of us. To the right are facilities for equestrians. By the campground's entrance you may see, on your left, the start of the old Grider Creek Trail, which parallels the PCT upstream. We then take the campground's entrance road, 46N24X, north to Road 46N66 (1680-0.3), turn right, and take this well-used logging road downstream to our last bridge across Grider Creek (1520-0.8). We continue downstream, then curve east around a nose to a junction with a spur road (1400-1.5) on our left. After a few minutes' walk east we approach the Klamath River and see why a bridge across it would be expensive. We parallel the river, first southeast and then northeast, to Road 46N46, which parallels Walker Creek. Only 35 yards north on this road we meet Highway 96 (1435-2.4). On this we hike west, cross the Klamath River (1430-0.5) and continue to a store and post office in the sleepy settlement of Seiad Valley (1371-1.0). The store, like some other points along or near the PCT, has a Pacific Crest Trail register for trekkers to sign.

Q7, Q8, Q9

Weeping spruces along PCT north toward Red Butte

Section R: Seiad Valley to Interstate 5 in Oregon

Introduction: In this section the hiker makes a long traverse east to get over to the Cascade Range. The long traverse west from Burney Falls to Marble Mountain was quite necessary, though inconveniently long, since a route going north from Burney falls past Mt. Shasta would be a dry, hot one indeed. Before the Pacific Crest Trail route became final, this sun-drenched corridor was the one most hikers followed to the Oregon Skyline Trail—Oregon's section of the Pacific Crest Trail. Section R's route stays remarkably high for most of its length, dropping significantly only at each end. Although high, it has been only mildly glaciated, and because glaciers haven't scoured away the soil, thick forests abound. These, unfortunately, are rampant with logging roads. From Reeves Ranch eastward you are always paralleling one road or another, so you certainly lose the wilderness feeling this high-crest hike is supposed to offer. Views, however, are pleasing enough, and surprisingly few logging operations are seen from the trail. Before early July these roads are an advantage, for significant stretches of trail are still snowbound. The roads, being more open, are quite easy to follow, though they still have enough snow patches on them to stop motor vehicles. As you progress east on trail or road, you walk across increasingly younger rocks, first late-Paleozoic/early-Mesozoic metamorphic rocks, then mid-Mesozoic granite rocks of the Mt. Ashland area and finally mid-to-late Cenozoic volcanic rocks of the Interstate 5 area.

Declination: 17¼°E

Mileages:

	South to North	Distance between Points	North to South
Highway 96 at Seiad Valley............................	0.0		64.5
Lower Devils Peak saddle	6.5	6.5	58.0
Cook and Green Pass	15.1	8.6	49.4
Lowdens Cabin site................................	20.4	5.3	44.1
Alex Hole Camp entrance	27.9	7.5	36.6
Mud Springs spur road	30.2	2.3	34.3
Bearground Spring................................	32.6	2.4	31.9
Wards Fork Gap	33.9	1.3	30.6
California-Oregon border	36.7	2.8	27.8
Sheep Camp Spring................................	41.1	4.4	23.4
Wrangle Gap	43.4	2.3	21.1
Long John Saddle	48.8	5.4	15.7
Grouse Gap	53.8	5.0	10.7
Road 2080	57.6	3.8	6.9
Interstate 5 near Mt. Ashland Road 20	64.5	6.9	0.0

Supplies: No supplies are available once you leave Seiad Valley. Along this crest route virtually all roads south will get you down to Highway 96, which has a smattering of hamlets, and virtually all roads north will ultimately channel you down to the Ashland-Medford area. However, we don't think you should descend either direction since you would then be way off route. Even in an emergency situation, you're likely to get help from people driving along the near-crest roads long before you could reach any settlement. If you're continuing through Oregon, you'll want to end Section R in Ashland, and routes to it are described in this trail chapter. You won't find any more sizable towns within an easy day's walk of the PCT—other than Sisters—until you reach the Oregon-Washington border area, more than 400 miles beyond this section's end. If you think you'll need a new pack, a camera or a pair of boots, certainly stop in Ashland.

We begin this section at the Seiad Store and post office (1371′ elevation, located 46 miles west of Interstate 5 via Highway 96). Walking west along the highway, we immediately cross Seiad Valley Road, which heads northeast up to Horse Tail Falls and beyond to Cook and Green Pass. Not much farther on we reach School House Gulch (1380-0.5), from where the old PCT route once started. Following the road as it curves west, we quickly reach a newer trailhead for Lower Devils Peak Lookout Trail 12W04 (1380-0.3). Since it is an exhausting 4400′ ascent to potential campsites by the Kangaroo Mountain meadows, one is prudent to start this strenuous trek in the cool shade of the morning.

Under a cover of madrone, Douglas-fir, incense-cedar and Oregon oak, our trail curves west and climbs moderately to reach a junc-tion (1600-0.2) with a trail that parallels Highway 96 west for 1.4 miles before ending close to a stream-gaging cable that spans the mighty Klamath River. The PCT was supposed to cross there, rather than on the Highway 96 bridge east of Seiad Valley, before this plan was abandoned.

From the junction with the Highway 96 trail, where we cross under some minor powerlines, our trail heads north into a shaded gully with its poison oak, and we soon reach a junction with the original Devils Peak Lookout trail, now abandoned. About ¼ mile beyond this junction we reach Fern Spring (1900-0.7), a small seep trickling from a pipe into a concrete cistern. You may find a trail register here.

Our well-engineered trail switchbacks up shady, though fly-infested, south-facing slopes, then follows a ridge system northeast up

R1

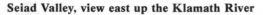

Seiad Valley, view east up the Klamath River

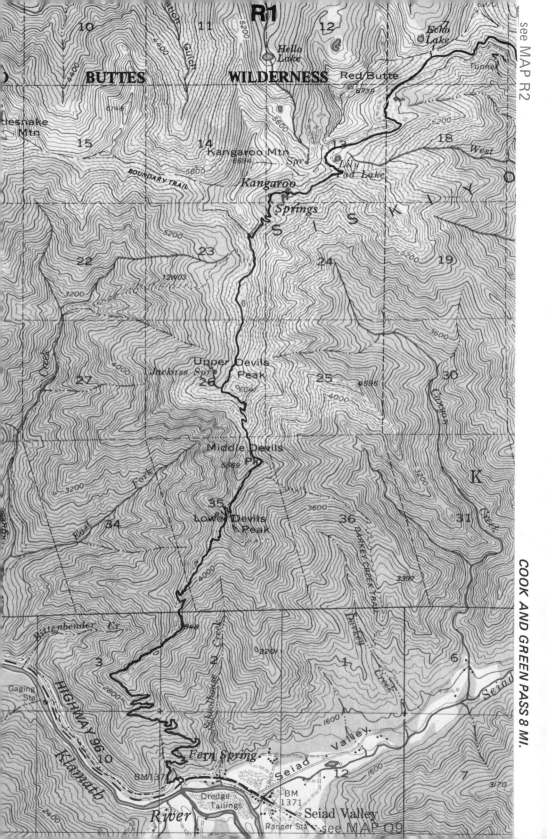

R1

COOK AND GREEN PASS 8 MI.

To APPLEGATE LAKE and MEDFORD

see MAP R1

see MAP R3

HIGHWAY 96 4½ MI.

toward Lower Devils Peak. Along this stretch you'll see some trees scorched in a widespread fire started by lightning in the summer of 1987. The damage here is minor compared to that north of Lower Devils Peak. Where the ridge fuses with the peak's flank, we climb up some short switchbacks, then traverse north across west-facing slopes to a junction. From here a 40-yard-long trail goes over to Lookout Spring. This trickling spring is *usually* reliable, though one has to marvel how any water flows at all, since the spring is so close to the Devils Peaks

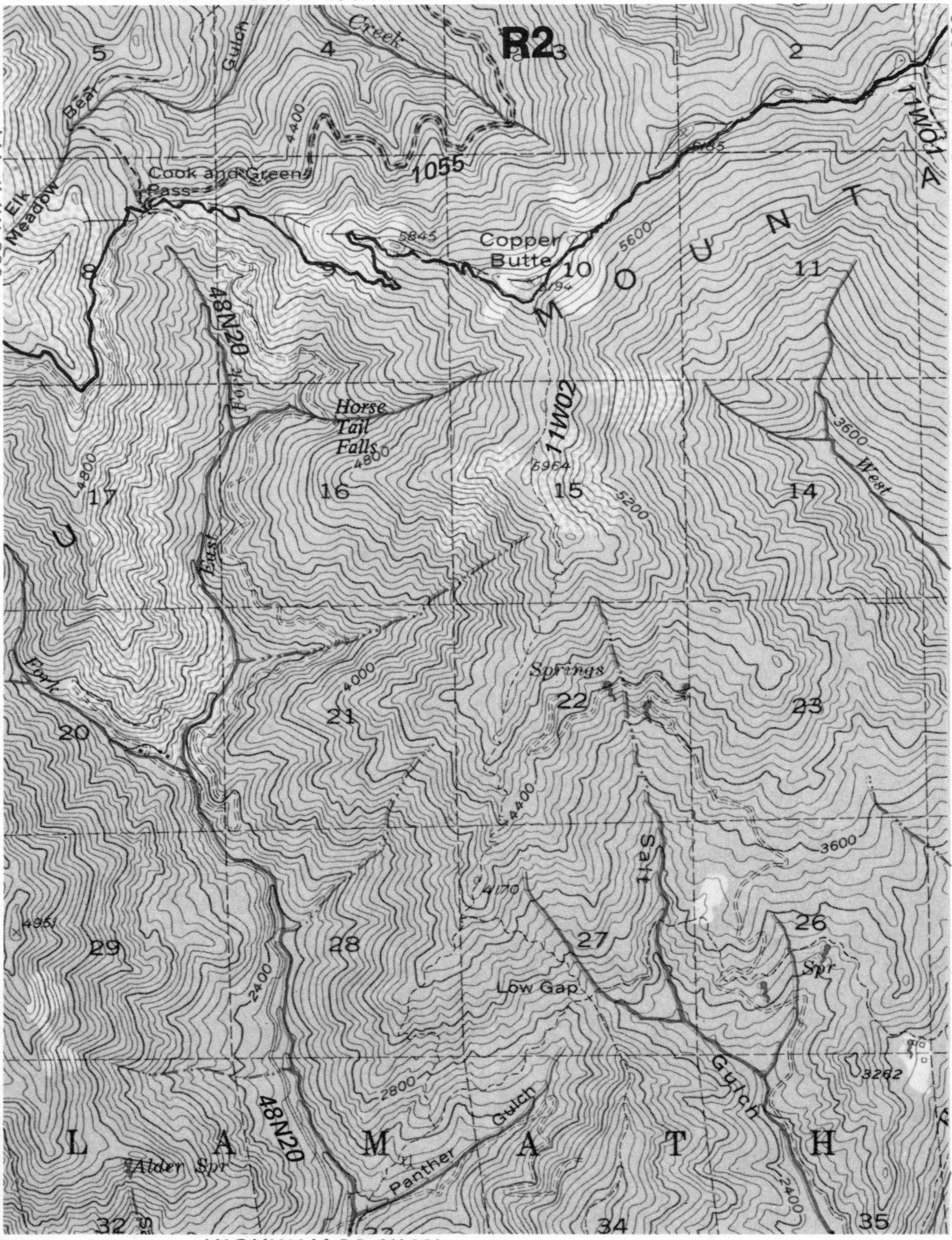

R1

Upper Devils Peak (left) and Kangaroo Mountain, from Middle Devils Peak

crest. From the junction we climb about 300 yards in a final push up to Lower Devils Peak saddle (5020-4.8), on the Devils Peaks crest. From the saddle you can follow a faint, rocky trail ¼ mile over to the remains of Lower Devils Peak Lookout, which was dismantled in 1976. The views you obtain from it are fine, but the many views ahead equal those from the lookout site. The lower room of the lookout still remains, albeit roofless, and it does offer a flat, fairly wind-free campsite.

From the crest saddle we start across the first of several major burns we'll traverse before Lily Pad Lake. Note the charred remains of knobcone pines here. These pines need a major fire, whose heat opens their cones, to release the seeds. These short-lived pines die in the process, but new pines soon sprout. Without periodic fires, the population would die out. On the east ridge of Middle Devils Peak we meet the Darkey Creek Trail (5170-0.6), starting down the burned-over ridge. As we traverse the northeast-facing slopes of Middle Devils Peak, we pass the first of several small groves of weeping spruce, spared from the conflagration. Note the trees' drooping "Douglas-fir" branches, their oversize "hemlock" cones and their scaly "lodgepole" bark.

North of the peak we reach a saddle, and from here, as well as from short switchbacks above it, we can pause for views of snow-capped Mt. Shasta (14,162') to the east and the Marble Mountain Wilderness to the south. Beyond the switchbacks we reach Upper Devils Peak's western arm (5820-1.0), from where a spur trail once descended 330 steep yards past western white pines to a seeping spring amid a cluster of alders. The pines and the trail are

R1

Lily Pad Lake

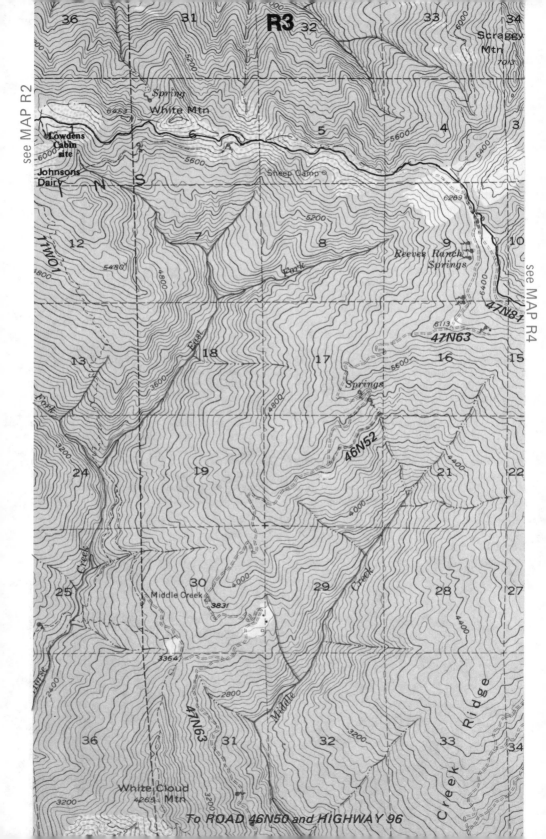

see MAP R2

see MAP R4

36   31   32   33   34
                                    Scraggy
                                    Mtn

Spring
White Mtn   5
Lowdens
Cabin
site   4   3
Johnsons
Dairy   N S   Sheep Camp

12   7   8   9   10
                                Reeves Ranch
                                    Springs
                                            47N81

                                    47N63
13   18   17   Springs   16   15

                        46N52

24   19   21   22

25   30   29   Creek   28   27
    Middle Creek

36   47N63   31   32   33   34

    White Cloud
    Mtn

To ROAD 46N50 and HIGHWAY 96

largely gone, but if you bear about 330° downslope, you should have very little trouble finding the spring.

Our trail now makes a traverse north, and along it we pass the charred remains of a forest before we pass a small grove of weeping spruce. Just past it we descend briefly to a saddle, which has a junction with faint Portuguese Creek Trail 12W03 (5760-1.2). If you need water, you can drop west about 300 vertical feet along it to the seasonal headwaters of Portuguese Creek and then follow the creek down another 300-600' to find flowing water. The PCT next climbs north up to a quickly reached junction with Boundary Trail 12W47 (5940-0.3). Before the creation of Red Buttes Wilderness in 1984, this was known as the Rattlesnake Mountain Trail. As you can see on this section's first map, the trail stays quite close to the south boundary of Red Buttes Wilderness. You'll likely have noted by now a high, often snowy peak along the western skyline, 7309' Preston Peak.

Now we head 100 yards southeast to a minor saddle on nearby Devils Peaks crest, which also happens to be the south ridge of rusty Kangaroo Mountain. The mountain's glaciated, broad-floored basin greets us as we start a short, switchbacking descent, and along it you may see two tiny ponds, each having a nearby campsite. Heading north from the switchbacks, we discover a creek that disappears into a sinkhole dissolved from a layer of light-gray marble that contrasts strongly with the orange, ancient, ultramafic intrusives of this area. These rocks are likely the northern extension of the rock types one sees along the PCT in the Marble Mountain Wilderness, on the distant southern skyline.

Likely because of the often damp nature of the basin's floor, the basin was largely spared from the 1987 fire. The basin's western lands are drier, and if you need to camp, look for a site there. Heading east, we reach a spring (5760-0.8) in spongy ground. From this spring—the easternmost of the Kangaroo Springs—the trail soon reaches a southeast slope. This the trail traverses, and soon you reach Kangaroo Mountain's east ridge (5900-0.5) and leave burned, *trailside* vegetation behind, although you'll see burned slopes on lands south of you all the way to Cook and Green Pass.

From the east ridge we can gaze down at Lily Pad Lake, with its small, poor, adjacent camp-sites and its multitude of frogs. Our trail stays high above this lake and arcs northwest over to a narrow ridge, which is a small part of the Red Buttes Wilderness boundary. Along this ridge you may find a trail register, and just past it is a junction with a spur trail (5900-0.2). This goes 115 yards north along the boundary ridge to a jeep road, on which you could pitch a tent. Westward, within the wilderness, the jeep road is closed, but eastward it is still open and is definitely used. The PCT will parallel it at a distance down to Cook and Green Pass.

With that goal in mind, we go but 200 yards northeast on the PCT before intersecting an old trail that starts from the jeep road just above us and drops to Lily Pad Lake. Now we descend gently east to a ridge that provides views down into the lake's glaciated canyon. From the ridge we circle a shallower, mildly glaciated canyon and cross the jeep road (5710-1.0) which has been staying just above us. The trail has kept below the road to avoid the Chrome King Mine, which lies just southwest of the road crossing. Next we traverse through a stand of timber, then climb past more brush to a junction on a crest saddle (5900-0.5). From it Horse Camp Trail 958 descends northeast toward nearby Echo Lake, whose environs provide camping superior to that at Lily Pad Lake.

Leaving the saddle and the last outcrop of marble we'll encounter on our northbound trek, we make a long, mostly brushy descent, first east and then north, down to Cook and Green Pass (4770-2.5). There is room for at least several hiking parties on the forested, nearly flat crest immediately west of the road that crosses the pass. Get water by going along a trail that leads northwest from the pass. You'll reach a spring in 150 yards; if it's dry, continue another 225 yards to a creeklet. Here, along the crest border between Klamath National Forest to the south and Rogue River National Forest to the north, a major USFS road crosses the pass and then descends about 10½ miles to the start of this section's route, Seiad Store. The PCT route is about 4½ miles longer. North-bound from Cook and Green Pass, the USFS road snakes its way about 10 miles down to Hutton Campground, which is situated about a mile from a large reservoir, Applegate Lake.

From this pass we follow an obvious trail east up the ridge toward Copper Butte. On it we pass scattered knobcone pines in a vegetative cover that includes manzanita, western ser-viceberry, tobacco brush and Sadler's oak. Like

R1, R2

Deer on crest near Mud Springs

tombstones, slabs of greenish-gray, foliated mica schist stand erect along the trail and, in the proper light, reflect the sun's rays as glacially polished rocks do. Our trail makes a long switchback up to the crest, passing a clearcut in the process. There are other clear-cuts to the south, on slopes east of Seiad Creek, and this patchwork landscape of forest and clearing contrasts with the burned slopes, which are mostly west of the creek. We must remember that this section is logging country, and one may run into ongoing logging operations along the route east.

Once back on the crest, the PCT enters a stand of white fir, red fir, mountain hemlock, Douglas-fir, ponderosa pine and knobcone pine—a combination we'd never see in the Sierra Nevada, where these trees are altitudinally zoned to a much greater extent. On the north slopes just below the crest, you'll also find weeping spruce. Rather than struggle to the top of Copper Butte, as early PCT hikers did on the old trail, we make a slight ascent to its south ridge, on which we meet Trail 11W02 (6080-2.8), which descends south to Low Gap, Salt Gulch and Seiad Valley. Our course now becomes a northeast one and we keep close to the crest, crossing several forested crest saddles before arriving at an open one (6040-2.2), from which Horse Creek Trail 11W01 begins a brushy descent south to Middle Creek Road 46N50. This road descends southeast to the hamlet of Horse Creek on Highway 96. We continue northeast to another saddle (6040-0.3), where you'll find a spur trail, hopefully marked, which heads 130 yards southeast to a small spring with an equally small campsite at the Lowdens Cabin site. It is better to camp at

the saddle, where there is more room. Leaving it, we start a contour east and from brushy slopes can identify the spring area, across the meadow south of us, by noting a large log near the forest's edge.

Our brushy contour becomes a forested one of Douglas-fir, Jeffrey pine and incense-cedar,

R2, R3

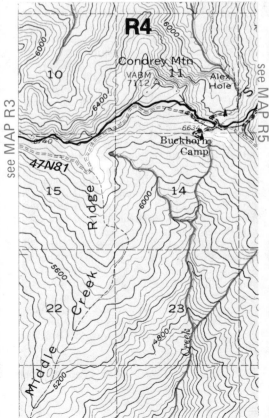

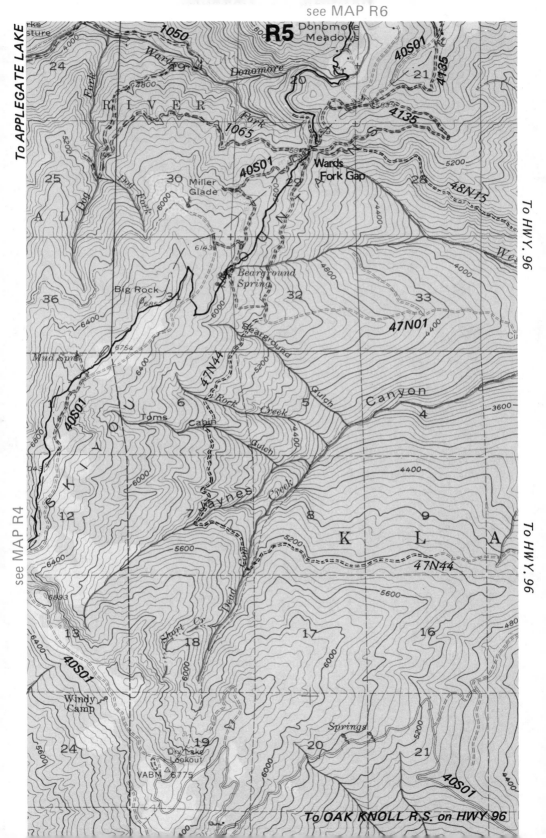

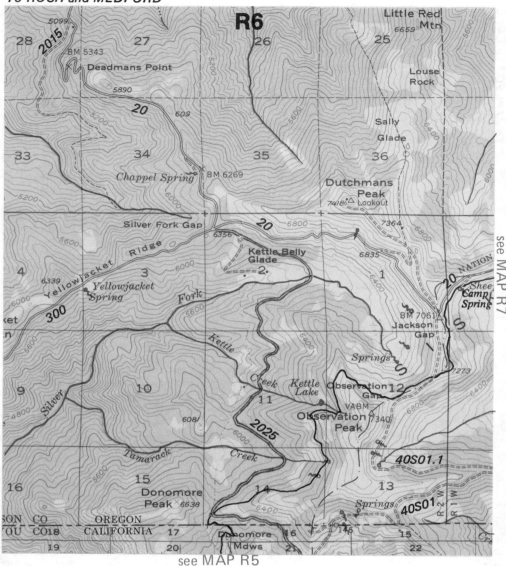

see MAP R6

see MAP R7

see MAP R5

and before we reach a deep crest saddle, we pass just above Beardog Spring. Along the south slope of White Mountain we cross somewhat open slopes again, reach its spur ridge, and then arc east across the upper limits of a meadowy hollow. At its east end is a junction (5950-2.0) with the old PCT, which will lead you to a seep near the hollow's west edge. Late-season hikers will have to descend the hollow a short distance to get their water. Just beyond this junction we reach another saddle and from it we climb east up to a higher crest. We stay close to it on a path that glitters with mica

flakes before we eventually curve southeast and descend an open slope. On it we cross, then parallel, a crest road that takes us across a long saddle, passing a *de facto* car-camping area below us, then almost touching the hairpin turn of Road 47N81 (6310-2.4). You can take the lower road branch south ½ mile to Reeves Ranch Springs, located below the road.

The Pacific Crest Trail parallels the east side of the road's upper branch, climbing first south, then east, and eventually traversing the south slopes of Condrey Mountain before descending ¾ mile to a saddle (6630-3.1). On it, a spur

R3, R4

Misty sunrise near Observation Gap

road leaves Road 47N81 to descend west-southwest 0.3 mile to Buckhorn Camp, a poor campsite beside a trickling spring a few yards farther east. Another spur road leaves the saddle, this one descending north ¼ mile to delightful Alex Hole Camp, located near a willow-lined spring. Here, where your far-reaching view north is framed by cliffs of mica schist, your only neighbors may be deer, chipmunks and mountain bluebirds.

Back on the PCT, we start to parallel ascending Road 47N81, then veer north away from it to climb the main Siskiyou crest. We almost top Peak 7043 before descending into a mountain-hemlock forest. Long-lasting snow patches can make the next mile to the Mud Springs spur road difficult to follow, but if so you can take the crest road, just east of us, to the same destination. Just yards away from Road 40S01, the PCT crosses the Mud Springs spur road (6730-2.3), and you can continue northwest 0.2 mile down this road to its end, where there are several very refreshing clear-water springs—a good camping spot.

Past the spur road we have a wonderful, open, near-crest traverse that passes a prominent rock midway in our approach to less imposing, misnamed Big Rock. We descend

R4, R5

View northeast from Jackson Gap

northeast across its open, gravelly east slope of glistening mica, briefly enter a patch of firs, leave it, and head south back into forest as we descend to a crossing of Road 40S01 (6250-1.6). Our trail now enters an old logging area as it first continues southward, then turns northeast and descends to cross a road (5930-0.8), which lies immediately north of Bearground Spring. As you'll see, this is an area of several springs. In this vicinity, which in former days was heavily used by car campers, you should be able to find a decent campsite.

From the Bearground Spring road you start among shady Shasta red firs and make a steady descent northeast, crossing an abandoned logging road midway to a saddle. Nearing this saddle, you cross narrow Road 40S01 at its hairpin turn, immediately recross the road, and in a couple of minutes reach a 6-way road junction on the saddle, Wards Fork Gap (5317-1.3). Southbound Road 47N01 traverses over to Road 47N44, and from that junction both descend to Beaver Creek. Along the creek, Road 48N01 descends to Highway 96, reaching it just 0.7 mile northeast of Klamath River, a small community with store and post office. Road 48N151, descending east from the saddle, also will get you to Beaver Creek. Road 1065 traverses west from the saddle, but later drops to Road 1050, which makes a long, leisurely descent west to Hutton Campground and the nearby Applegate Lake area.

Between north-climbing Road 48N16 and east-climbing 40S01, the PCT starts to climb northeast from Wards Fork Gap. This short stretch is usually overgrown and hard to follow. If you can't, then from the saddle head north briefly up Road 48N16 to a bend, from which a logging spur continues north. You'll see the PCT just above it, paralleling it first north, then west. Walk south up Road 48N16 midway to its second bend, and you should be able to find the northbound PCT without much trouble.

On it we make a short climb north before embarking on a long traverse that circles clockwise around a knoll to Donomore Creek. This you parallel east to within 100 yards of the Donomore Meadows road, then bridge the creek (5600-1.5) and wind northward up an amorphous ridge that may be crisscrossed with misleading cow paths. In ½ mile we cross this road at a point about 80 yards east of a cabin, then parallel a jeep road, immediately below us, which follows the meadow's edge north. At the meadow's upper end, our trail curves east

To TALENT and MEDFORD

R7

above it, then switchbacks west for a short, partly steep ascent northwest into Oregon, and soon veers north up to a logging-road saddle (6210-1.4).

Here we cross wide Road 2025, then climb east up a clearcut crest, and leave it to make a long, curving traverse northward to the west ridge (6750-1.6) of twin-topped Observation

R5, R6

Sheep Camp Spring area

Peak. Kettle Lake, below us, immediately comes into view as we start an uphill traverse east; if you want to camp at it, then descend directly to it. We climb east to Kettle Creek, then climb north from it high above Kettle Lake before rounding the large northwest ridge of Observation Peak. A southeast traverse through stands of mountain hemlocks—snowbound until mid-July—gets us to Observation Gap (7030-1.2), a shallow saddle just west of and above 40S01.1. From the gap we go ½ mile on our crest trail, cross Road 40S01.1, traverse around the east slopes of Peak 7273, and then parallel the crest north to Jackson Gap (7040-1.2). Before reaching this gap you'll certainly notice landscape terracing in the Jackson Gap area, done to prevent erosion on the burned-over slopes. Crossing this gap just a few feet above us is broad Road 20, which we'll parallel all the way to the end of Section R. Before mid-July, snow drifts will probably force you to take this road rather than the PCT.

Leaving the cover of hemlocks and firs, we arc clockwise across the upper slopes of a huge open bowl, soon reaching a spur road (6920-0.3) to Sheep Camp Spring, located 10 yards south on it. Camp space is very limited, and since it lacks tree cover, you would probably greet next morning's sunrise from a very wet sleeping bag. Departing east from the spur road, we gradually descend, with unobstructed views, to a spur ridge, then arc northeast to Wrangle Gap (6496-2.3), reaching it ¼ mile

after we cross to the north side of Road 20. From here a spur road descends steeply west to Wrangle Campground—the answer to an exhausted hiker's prayer. This little-used recreation site, nestled among Shasta red firs, has a large stone shelter complete with fireplace, two stoves and tables. In the '70s it also had tap water, and old-time hikers lament its loss. Unless the USFS decides to reinstate piped-in water, you'll have to get some from a nearby spring or lower down, from Wrangle Creek.

From Wrangle Gap the PCT route could have gone east, but instead it makes a long climb north to the end of Red Mountain ridge and starts to wind southeast up it. The route does have the advantage of giving you sweeping panoramas of southern Oregon and its pointed landmark, Mt. McLoughlin—an Ice Age volcano. After crossing the ridge we contour south and then east, leaving Red Mountain's slopes for a winding, moderate descent to the west end of open Siskiyou Gap (5890-3.8), where we cross Road 20. The northeast quarter of Section 34 lies in private land, and for many years the owner resisted attempts at building a direct trail, paralleling Road 20, over to nearby Long John Saddle. Finally in desperation, the USFS built a trail twice as long to that goal. It first parallels Road 20 briefly over to its junction with Road 40S12, then parallels that road briefly over to a crossing (5800-0.3). Then it makes a long swing around a hill, offering us some Mt. Shasta views in partial compensa-

R6, R7, R8

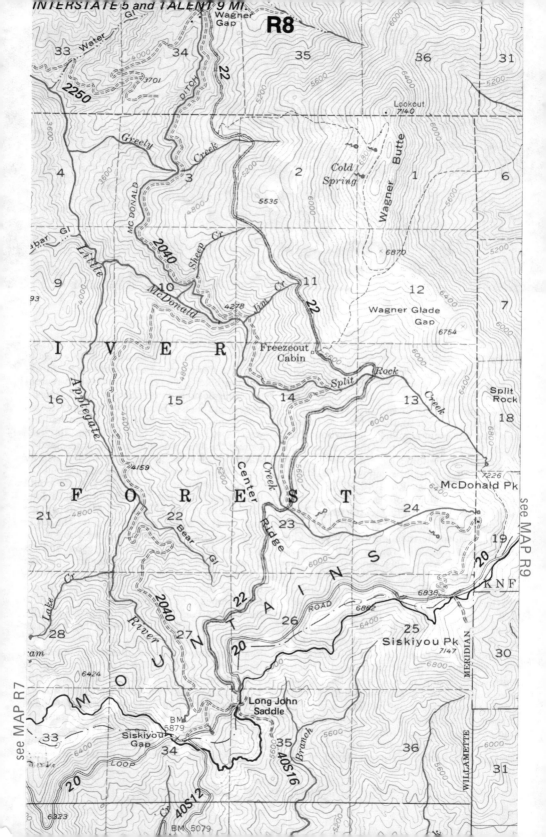

Mt. Shasta, from Mt. Ashland Campground

tion for our added hiking effort before finally reaching a 5-way road junction (5880-1.3) on forested Long John Saddle.

Road 20 traverses north across the level saddle and a minor logging road descends northeast back the way we came. Between the two the Pacific Crest Trail starts to parallel Road 20 north, then climbs northeast through an old logging area. After a mile of progress, we come to a spur ridge and exchange this scarred landscape for a shady forest climb north. From a gully our gradient eases to give us a pleasant stroll northeast to an open crest saddle (6710-2.1). On it, our tread almost disappears as it parallels Road 20 for a few yards, then it becomes prominent again and climbs a short ½ mile up to a saddle just north of Siskiyou Peak. From this saddle you'll see chunky Pilot Peak on the eastern skyline—a guiding beacon for early pioneers and for us. If you're continuing through Oregon, you should pass by it in a few days.

Our road now winds ⅓ mile northeast toward a saddle on the main crest, crossing a spur road (6900-0.8) that is just 25 yards below its departure from crest-hugging Road 20. The saddle is signed as the Meridian Overlook, since it is a viewpoint close to the Willamette Meridian.

We parallel Road 20 northeast, sometimes below it and sometimes above it, to another saddle (7030-1.1) which is south of the main crest. Here the road bends north to descend,

but we first go south briefly before switch-backing to descend northeast to reach Road 40S30 (6630-1.0) at its junction with Road 20 on expansive Grouse Gap. This road takes you 0.2 mile south to a fork, from where you branch left on Road 40S30A for a minute's walk to Grouse Gap Shelter, built in the mid-70s. The shelter provides protection from the elements and it offers dramatic sunrise views of Mt. Shasta. You can usually get water from the creeklet just northeast of and below the shelter, however, late-season trekkers will likely have to backtrack on 40S30A to 40S30, and then take that road ⅓ mile southwest down to an obvious gully with a spring-fed creeklet.

From Grouse Gap the PCT parallels Road 20 and passes several seeping springs before it gradually drops away from it down to a crossing of Road 40S15 (6480-1.9), which climbs ½ mile northeast up to this crest road. From their junction, Road 20 contours ½ mile northeast to the Mt. Ashland Ski Area, and eastward, the road is paved. An alternative to camping at Grouse Gap Shelter is to camp at Mt. Ashland Campground, which straddles both sides of Road 20. To reach it, leave the PCT and follow Road 40S15 about 250 yards up to its bend left, from where you'll see an abandoned logging road that climbs directly upslope to the campground. The piped water isn't always flowing, and when it's not, get water in a little gully just above the camp-ground's upper (north) sites. From Road 40S15

R8, R9

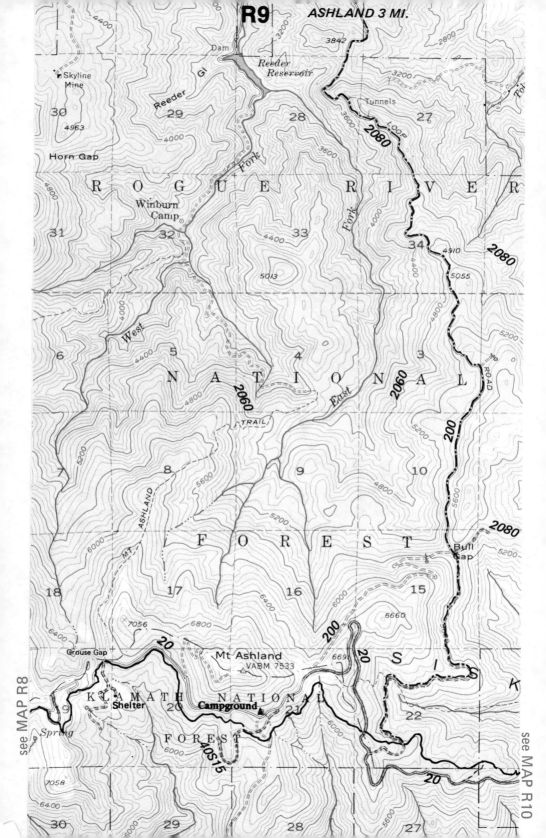

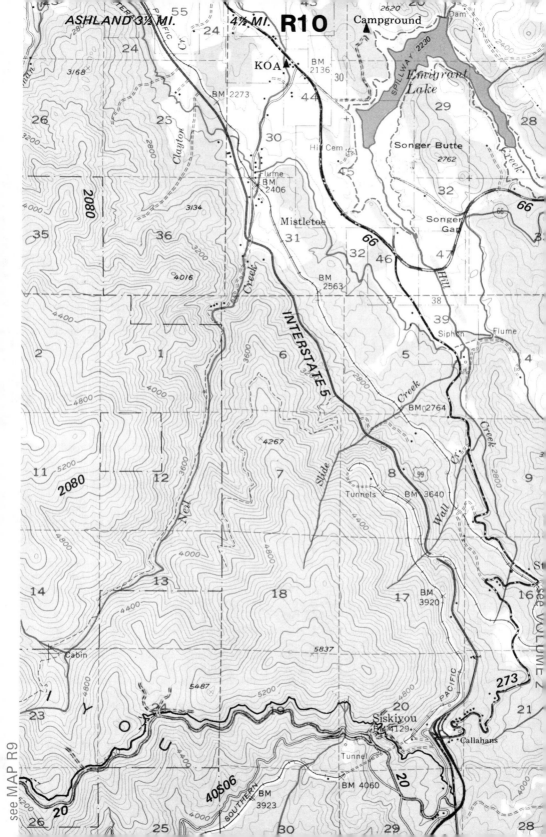

the PCT contours southeast to the bend and then traverses northeast to an open bowl below the ski area. From this it traverses southeast to a saddle, where we cross Road 20 (6160-1.5). Continuing southeast down-ridge, we follow the PCT down to Road 2080 (6060-0.4).

*   *   *   *

From our ridge you can take a supply route by following Road 2080 north down to Bull Gap (5500-2.8), where you meet Road 200, which climbs southwest up to the Mt. Ashland Ski Area. Continuing north, take Road 200, which in 3 miles rejoins Road 2080, all the way down to Glenview Drive (2200-8.5) in Ashland. Descend this road north, then descend Fork Street. You quickly reach Pioneer Street and follow it two blocks to C Street. The Ashland Post Office is one block southeast on it, at the corner of First and C streets (1920-1.1). To get back to the PCT, head southwest one block to East Main and walk southeast. It quickly becomes two-way Siskiyou Boulevard (1950-0.3), and you continue southeast on it to Highway 66 (Ashland Street) (2010-1.1). Take this east past the Ashland Shopping Center to Washington Street, which has the Ashland Ranger Station at its end. Just east of this short street you reach Interstate 5 (1980-1.3-15.1). Since hitchhiking on freeways is legal in Oregon, you can hitchhike up it 9 miles to the Mt. Ashland exit. Alternately, you can continue on Highway 66, then go south up Highway 273 to that exit, about a 12-mile route. This route is described in the opposite direction at the end of this chapter.

*   *   *   *

If you decide against the supply route, then continue east down the forested trail. The PCT stays on or north of the crest, but after 0.7 mile it crosses to its south side and in ¼ mile crosses a jeep road that climbs northeast back to the nearby crest. Not until 1987 was the next stretch—through sections 23, 24 and 26—completed. Rights of way across private property held up PCT construction for more than a decade.

The PCT continues its eastern descent, first past grass and bracken ferns, and then mostly past brush. Soon the trail switchbacks and then quickly reaches the shady grounds of Mt. Ashland Inn, a bed-and-breakfast establish-

ment opened Christmas 1987. The rates are very reasonable, as such establishments go, but they are nevertheless far too high for the average long-distance hiker. However, the owners, Elaine and Jerry Shanafelt, do freely offer water to passing hikers.

A minute's walk below the inn we cross a saddle (5490-1.5), and then parallel Road 20 for a generally brushy traverse over to another saddle (5110-0.8). Next we make a similar traverse, this one to a saddle with 4 roads radiating from it (4990-0.8).

Eastbound, the PCT is confined between an old crest road and Road 20 for the first ⅓ mile, then it parallels the latter as both descend east around ridges and across gullies. Three closely spaced gullies near the end of this descent provide spring-fed water before they coalesce to flow into East Fork Cotton Creek.

Because we are on private land, we aren't allowed to deviate from the trail's tread and aren't allowed to camp. Anyway, thick brush prevents us from doing either. About 0.4 mile past our last spring-fed gully, we cross a road (4610-2.5) that descends steeply southeast to nearby Road 20, which here turns southeast to cross a broad saddle. Then, after a short, steep descent of our own, we cross a road (4470-0.1) that climbs gently west up to a union with the first road at paved Road 20. Both dirt roads are private—off limits—as is a third road that we parallel east, then momentarily turn south to cross (4360-0.1). Now we parallel this road, staying just above it, dip in and out of a gully with a sometimes flowing freshet, then soon curve away from the road as we glimpse busy, nearby Interstate 5. Our path ends (4250-0.8) at an abandoned segment of old Highway 99, which we take for 140 yards around a hollow to a fork. Here we go left and descend an old, closed road 150 yards to trail's end on Highway 99. This trailhead is 250 yards north of where Mt. Ashland Road 20 ends at Highway 99 (4240-0.3), and that junction in turn is immediately north of where Interstate 5 crosses over the highway. Here, at the junction of Road 20 and Highway 99, our section ends. The Mesozoic granitic rocks we've traversed across along the eastern crest of the Siskiyou Mountains are now overlaid by mid-Tertiary, thick, basaltic andesite flows; and the Shasta red firs and mountain hemlocks have yielded to Douglas-firs and orange-barked madrones.

If you've hiked the PCT through much or all of California, you may want to celebrate your

R9, R10

Ashland's Emigrant Lake, along alternate route

entry into Oregon by visiting Callahan's Restaurant. Go north on Highway 99 for ⅔ mile to Highway 273 and on it cross under Interstate 5 at its Mt. Ashland exit. The restaurant is just east of it. This ever-popular place, closed on Mondays, serves only dinners, and though Callahan's is expensive by backpackers' standards, it is one of the better dining places along or near the entire Pacific Crest Trail. If you've been starving these last few miles, you'll be glad to know that each of their dinners includes all the salad, soup and spaghetti you can eat.

To resupply for another stretch of the PCT in southern Oregon, you can hitchhike 9 miles down Interstate 5 to the Highway 66 interchange and take the highway west into downtown Ashland.

*   *   *   *

An old, temporary PCT route offers you another way down to Ashland. From Callahan's (3950-0.9 mile from end of Road 20), you can go down tree-lined Highway 273 to a junction with Highway 66 (2290-6.7). Just east of it is the shallow upper end of Emigrant Lake, a popular fishing area; the deeper parts are relegated to water skiers, boaters and swim-

mers. Northwest, Highway 66 leads you to the main entrance to the Emigrant Lake Recreation Area (2150-1.8). Here a paved road heads southeast 0.4 mile up to a lateral dam, then curves north 0.6 mile to a public campground. Past the recreation area's entrance you'll come to fairly expensive but well-equipped Glenyan KOA campground (2140-0.2) with showers and a store. It caters to backpackers as well as to car campers, and the larger your hiking group, the cheaper your per-person camp fee will be. Continuing northwest on Highway 66, you meet Dead Indian Road (1920-2.6) before your highway turns west and climbs to cross Interstate 5 (1980-0.7-12.9) at the outskirts of Ashland. Some backpackers prefer to celebrate in Ashland rather that at Callahan's, for there is quite a selection of good-to-excellent cafes and restaurants. In addition, more cultured backpackers take in one or more performances of Ashland's Oregon Shakespearean Festival, which runs most of the year. If the weather has been dreary or snow patches abundant, then perhaps a Shakespearean comedy will lift your spirits. Just north of the festival's grounds is the Ashland Hostel (150 N. Main), which welcomes PCT hikers and even has a PCT register.

R10

Recommended Reading and Source Books

Pacific Crest Trail

Clarke, Clinton C. 1945. *The Pacific Crest Trailway*. Pasadena: The Pacific Crest Trail System Conference, 126 p.

Gray, William R. 1975. *The Pacific Crest Trail*. Washington, D.C.: National Geographic Society, 200 p.

Green, David. 1979. *A Pacific Crest Odyssey*. Berkeley: Wilderness Press, 148 p.

Ryback, Eric. 1971. *The High Adventure of Eric Ryback*. San Francisco: Chronicle Books, 199 p.

Schaffer, Jeffrey P., and Andy Selters. 1986. *The Pacific Crest Trail, Volume 2: Oregon & Washington*. Berkeley: Wilderness Press, 322 p.

Sutton, Ann, and Myron Sutton. 1975. *The Pacific Crest Trail: Escape to the Wilderness*. Philadelphia: Lippincott, 239 p.

Backpacking and Mountaineering

Darvill, Fred T. 1985. *Mountaineering Medicine*. Berkeley: Wilderness Press, 68 p.

Fleming, June. 1982. *Staying Found; The Complete Map & Compass Handbook*. New York: Vintage Books (Random House), 159 p.

Fletcher, Colin. 1984. *The Complete Walker III*. New York: Knopf.

Ganci, Dave. 1983. *Desert Hiking*. Berkeley: Wilderness Press, 178 p.

Kals, W. S. 1983. *Land Navigation Handbook; The Sierra Club Guide to Map and Compass*. San Francisco: Sierra Club, 230 p.

LaChapelle, Ed. 1985. *The ABC of Avalanche Safety*. Seattle: The Mountaineers, 112 p.

Manning, Harvey. 1986. *Backpacking: One Step at a Time*. New York: Vintage Books (Random House), 478 p.

McHugh, Gretchen. 1987. *The Hungry Hiker's Book of Good Cooking*. New York: Knopf, 286 p.

Peters, Ed, ed. 1982. *Mountaineering: the Freedom of the Hills*. Seattle: The Mountaineers, 550 p.

Roper, Steve. 1976. *The Climber's Guide to the High Sierra*. San Francisco: Sierra Club, 380 p.

Reifsnyder, William E. 1980. *Weathering the Wilderness; the Sierra Club Guide to Practical Meteorology*. San Francisco: Sierra Club, 276 p.

Wilkerson, James A., ed., 1985. *Medicine for Mountaineering*. Seattle: The Mountaineers, 438 p.

Winnett, Thomas, with Melanie Findling. 1988. *Backpacking Basics*. Berkeley: Wilderness Press, 134 p.

History and General Natural History

Bailey, Harry P. 1966. *Weather of Southern California* (California Natural History Guide 17). Berkeley: University of California Press, 87 p.

Brewer, William H. 1930 (1966). *Up and Down California in 1860–1864*. Berkeley: University of California Press, 583 p.

Browning, Peter. 1986. *Place Names of the Sierra Nevada*. Berkeley: Wilderness Press, 253 p.

Farquhar, Francis P. 1965. *History of the Sierra Nevada*. Berkeley: University of California Press, 262 p.

Gunsky, Frederic R., ed. 1988. *South of Yosemite; Selected Writing of John Muir*. Berkeley: Wilderness Press, 220 p.

Jaeger, Edmond C. 1965. *The California Deserts*. Stanford: Stanford University Press, 208 p.

King, Clarence. 1872 (1970). *Mountaineering in the Sierra Nevada*. Lincoln: University of Nebraska Press, 292 p.

Reid, Robert L., ed. 1983. *A Treasury of the Sierra Nevada*. Berkeley: Wilderness Press, 363 p.

Geology

American Geological Institute. 1976. *Dictionary of Geological Terms.* Garden City: Dolphin Books, 472 p.

Bailey, Edgar H., ed. 1966. *Geology of Northern California* (California Division of Mines and Geology, Bulletin 190). Sacramento: California Division of Mines and Geology, 508 p.

Hill, Mary. 1984. *California Landscape: Origin and Evolution* (California Natural History Guide 48). Berkeley: University of California Press, 262 p.

Sharp, Robert P. 1976. *Geology: Field Guide to Southern California.* Dubuque: Kendall/Hunt, 208 p.

Shelton, John S. 1966. *Geology Illustrated.* San Francisco: W. H. Freeman, 434 p.

Biology

Basey, Harold E. 1976. *Discovering Sierra Reptiles and Amphibians.* Yosemite National Park: Yosemite (Natural History) Association, 50 p.

Crampton, Beecher. 1974. *Grasses in California* (California Natural History Guide 33). Berkeley: University of California Press, 178 p.

Dale, Nancy. 1986. *Flowering Plants: The Santa Monica Mountains, Coastal and Chaparral Regions of Southern California.* Santa Barbara: Capra Press, 239 p.

Gaines, David. 1988. *Birds of Yosemite and the East Slope.* Lee Vining: Artemisia Press, 352 p.

Grillos, Steve J. 1966. *Ferns and Fern Allies of California* (California Natural History Guide 16). Berkeley: University of California Press, 104 p.

Horn, Elizabeth L. 1976. *Wildflowers 3: The Sierra Nevada.* Beaverton, OR: Touchstone Press.

Ingles, Lloyd G. 1965. *Mammals of the Pacific States.* Stanford: Stanford University Press.

Jaeger, Edmond C. 1969. *Desert Wild Flowers.* Stanford: Stanford University Press, 322 p.

Jaeger, Edmond C. 1961. *Desert Wildlife.* Stanford: Stanford University Press, 308 p.

Jaeger, Edmond C., and Arthur C. Smith. 1966. *Introduction to the Natural History of Southern California* (California Natural History Guide 13). Berkeley: University of California Press.

Jameson, Everett W., Jr., and Hans J. Peeters. 1988. *California Mammals* (California Natural History Guide 52). Berkeley: University of California Press, 403 p.

Keator, Glenn. 1978. *Pacific Coast Berry Finder.* Berkeley: Nature Study Guild, 62 p.

Keator, Glenn. 1980. *Sierra Flower Finder.* Berkeley: Nature Study Guild, 126 p.

Larson, Peggy. 1977. *The Deserts of the Southwest; A Sierra Club Naturalist's Guide.* San Francisco: Sierra Club, 288 p.

Munz, Philip A., and David D. Keck. 1968. *A California Flora and Supplement.* Berkeley: University of California Press, 1681 and 224 p.

Niehaus, Theodore F., and Charles L. Ripper. 1976. *A Field Guide to Pacific States Wildflowers.* Boston: Houghton Mifflin, 432 p.

Peterson, P. Victor. 1966. *Native Trees of Southern California* (California Natural History Guide 14). Berkeley: University of California Press, 136 p.

Peterson, P. Victor, and P. Victor Peterson, Jr. 1975. *Native Trees of the Sierra Nevada* (California Natural History Guide 36). Berkeley: University of California Press, 147 p.

Peterson, Roger T. 1961. *A Field Guide to Western Birds.* Boston: Houghton Mifflin, 366 p.

Stebbins, Robert C. 1972. *Amphibians and Reptiles of California* (California Natural History Guide 31). Berkeley: University of California Press 152 p.

Storer, Tracy I., and Robert L. Usinger. 1963. *Sierra Nevada Natural History.* Berkeley: University of California Press, 374 p.

Sudworth, George B. 1908 (1967). *Forest Trees of the Pacific Slope.* New York: Dover, 455 p.

Watts, Tom. 1973. *Pacific Coast Tree Finder.* Berkeley: Nature Study Guild, 62 p.

Weeden, Norman. 1986. *A Sierra Nevada Flora.* Berkeley: Wilderness Press, 406 p.

Whitney, Stephen. 1979. *A Sierra Club Naturalist's Guide to the Sierra Nevada.* San Francisco: Sierra Club, 526 p.

Whitney, Stephen. 1985. *Western Forests* (The Audubon Society Nature Guides). New York: Knopf, 672 p.

INDEX

Creating a Trail Guidebook

Our two-volume guidebook to the Pacific Trail is, we believe, state of the art in trail guides. What went into this guide?

First, each author had to plan how he would cover his section of the trail. This involved not only the usual preparations for hiking trips, but also communications with the government people responsible for the PCT, to determine the status of their plans for completing the trail. We had to know where we would be hiking and describing temporary route segments and alternate segments, and where we would be on permanent PCT. Then a helper had to be found, to leave an author off at Point A and pick him/her up at Point B, so as to avoid retracing of steps.

While hiking, the author was taking lots of photos, marking the USGS topo map to show where the trail really went, checking elevations and recording what he/she saw, and pacing off distances. Over the life of four editions of each volume, each author has covered his/her sections several times, and total trail miles hiked exceed 8000.

Back at the desk, the author wrote letters seeking information about events that affected the trail, such as fires, road-building, creation of some campgrounds and demolition of others, efforts to obtain easements over private lands, and development of water sources. With answers in hand, and using his/her field notes, the author then wrote the trail description.

Meanwhile, a cartographer was busy transferring the author's trail line to the maps that would be used by the printer, ignoring the faulty trail line on the USGS topo maps. The cartographer in fact had to create a base map and as many as three mylar overlays, to show black, blue and screened blue (for lakes) on the printed page.In fact, one major part of creating the book was tracing all the blue lines for streams and for lake outlines onto a separate overlay, so that the water would show as blue on the maps in the book. This task took several thousand hours of cartographer time.

Earlier, the cartographer and the editor had made a master plan for all the maps, of which there are 393 total in the two volumes. Since no map could be larger than a book page, whereas the original USGS topos were much larger than that, each USGS topo had to be cut up into several maps page-size or smaller, full page size being the most common.

Then the words of the manuscript were set into type, and proofs of the type were carefully proofread. Now an editor sat down with all the type, the photos and the maps to make a dummy, or layout, that would show where every molecule of ink would go on the book pages. In doing this, he needed to place a photo as close as possible to the text that described the area in the photo, and the same for each map. In fact, there was an additional requirement for placing the maps: where two consecutive maps were in an east-west alignment, they needed to be placed side by side on facing pages, so that the reader could imagine the trail jumping across the spine of the book and continuing directly on the facing page. Now one more task faced each author: dutchread the words on each dummy page to see what maps covered those words, and put the map designations at the bottoms of all the pages.

Finally everything was ready for the printer. But the authors' and editors' work was not finished. They had to inspect all the printer's negatives to be sure everything printed in place. Most crucially, the overlays for each map had to fit one another like a glove—or even better.

NORTH

Use these four pages for hitchhiking.

SOUTH

EAST

WEST

Pacific Crest Trail, Volume 1
1990 Supplement

p. 3, next-to-last paragraph, last line 7 should be M.

p. 37, second paragraph Delete lines 9 and 10 and substitute:
declination to get the true bearing. For example, if your compass indicates that a prominent hill lies along a bearing of 75°, and if the section you're hiking in has a

p. 176, column 2, paragraph 4, line 9 13.3 should be 37.9.

p. 180, column 1, next-to-last line Crest just *west* above us.

p. 183, column 2, line 15 Make it read: Walker Pass Campground, signed *Walker Pass Trailhead*, at the south end of that curve.

p. 187, paragraph 4 No rope needed at South Fork of Kern River. There are bridges now.

p. 196 The caption should read: Canebrake Road below Lamont Peak.

p. 198, column 2, paragraph 3, line 2 Change year-round to seasonal.

p. 198, column 2, paragraph 5, line 6 Change all-year to seasonal.

p. 221, Map H1 The John Muir Trail now stays north of Whitney Creek as it passes Crabtree Ranger Station.

p. 403, col. 2, line 6 to end of paragraph Schaffer prefers taking Old County Road to Castella. Though it winds, dips and climbs, it is shady and only lightly driven. More importantly, it provides access to the Sacramento River. After about a 1.4-mile hike along it, you reach a short trail down along the lower end of a cascading creek that originates in the southeast corner of Section 23. You'll find a wonderful Sacramento River swimming hole just upriver from the trail's end. About 1/3 mile farther along Old County Road is the state park's riverside picnic area, which is also worth a visit.

If you don't take this alternate route, then from the end of the PCT tread (at point 2200-3.7), head northwest down Old County Road to nearby Soda Creek Road (2150-0.1). On it you stroll a few minutes over to the wide Sacramento River, then to the nearby Southern Pacific railroad tracks. Unfortunately, no road connects your road to Dunsmuir--a town that has just about everything, including boot repair. So if you need services there, you may have to hike north along these patrolled tracks. After about 1.2 miles, you can branch onto a spur road and then take 3 miles of roads to central Dunsmuir.

Just past the railroad tracks you curve over to Frontage Road (2125-0.4), then cross under adjacent Interstate 5, where Section O ends at a locked gate, the eastern boundary of the west half of Castle Crags State Park (2130-0.1).

p. 407, col. 2, 2nd paragraph From the start of this section's PCT, you go almost 0.4 mile south up to a fair viewpoint, then angle west for a 160-yard stroll to a junction. From here a winding, though fairly level route--composed of segments of trails and roads--starts southeast, eventually winding about 1 1/4 miles west over to the park's paved road that climbs north toward Kettlebelly Ridge. On it you can wind first 0.3

mile southward and then 0.3 mile westward over to the park's PCT campsite (no. 25). Note that as of February 1990 this route of new trail segments and old road segments was not yet official and therefore was neither maintained nor recommended.

p. 417, col. 1, line 16 The Parks Creek Road ends just before Interstate 5, at Stewart Springs Road, which reaches the interstate about 3 miles west of Weed.